REAL-WORLD
ELECTRONIC VOTING
DESIGN, ANALYSIS AND DEPLOYMENT

CRC Series in Security, Privacy and Trust

SERIES EDITORS

Jianying Zhou

Institute for Infocomm Research, Singapore

jyzhou@i2r.a-star.edu.sg

Pierangela Samarati

Universita' degli Studi di Milano, Italy

pierangela.samarati@unimi.it

AIMS AND SCOPE

This book series presents the advancements in research and technology development in the area of security, privacy, and trust in a systematic and comprehensive manner. The series will provide a reference for defining, reasoning and addressing the security and privacy risks and vulnerabilities in all the IT systems and applications, it will mainly include (but not limited to) aspects below:

- Applied Cryptography, Key Management/Recovery, Data and Application Security and Privacy;
- Biometrics, Authentication, Authorization, and Identity Management;
- Cloud Security, Distributed Systems Security, Smart Grid Security, CPS and IoT security;
- Data Security, Web Security, Network Security, Mobile and Wireless Security;
- Privacy Enhancing Technology, Privacy and Anonymity, Trusted and Trustworthy Computing;
- Risk Evaluation and Security Certification, Critical Infrastructure Protection;
- Security Protocols and Intelligence, Intrusion Detection and Prevention;
- Multimedia Security, Software Security, System Security, Trust Model and Management;
- Security, Privacy, and Trust in Cloud Environments, Mobile Systems, Social Networks, Peer-to-Peer Systems, Pervasive/Ubiquitous Computing, Data Outsourcing, and Crowdsourcing, etc..

PUBLISHED TITLES

Location Privacy in Wireless Sensor Networks
Ruben Rios, Javier Lopez, and Jorge Cuellar

Real-World Electronic Voting: Design, Analysis and Deployment
Feng Hao and Peter Y. A. Ryan

Touchless Fingerprint Biometrics
Ruggero Donida Labati, Vincenzo Piuri, and Fabio Scotti

CRC Series in Security, Privacy and Trust

REAL-WORLD
ELECTRONIC VOTING
DESIGN, ANALYSIS AND DEPLOYMENT

EDITED BY

FENG HAO AND PETER Y. A. RYAN

CRC Press
Taylor & Francis Group
Boca Raton London New York

CRC Press is an imprint of the
Taylor & Francis Group, an **informa** business

CRC Press
Taylor & Francis Group
6000 Broken Sound Parkway NW, Suite 300
Boca Raton, FL 33487-2742

First issued in paperback 2020

© 2017 by Taylor & Francis Group, LLC
CRC Press is an imprint of Taylor & Francis Group, an Informa business

No claim to original U.S. Government works

ISBN-13: 978-1-4987-1469-3 (hbk)
ISBN-13: 978-0-367-65821-2 (pbk)

Visit the Taylor & Francis Web site at
http://www.taylorandfrancis.com

and the CRC Press Web site at
http://www.crcpress.com

Contents

Foreword

Voting is a unique task with many distinctive challenges. Many modern voters shop online, bank online, communicate online and wonder why they can't vote online as well. But when bank customers make deposits they get receipts, they can check records of their balances and they have established processes for resolving disputes. Shoppers know whether or not the goods they've purchased have been received, and they can see what charges have been incurred. None of these tools are typically available to voters.

If a bank were to transpose deposits and withdrawals, customers would immediately notice and complain. If an online retailer were to mislabel its offerings and send red jackets to those who ordered blue ones and vice-versa, it would be inundated with returns from angry customers. But in an election, if the votes for two candidates or parties were switched, who would know? We hope that election officials and equipment vendors are honest and highly-competent and that they would not allow such errors to happen, but how can voters be sure? Even under the best of conditions, traditional election systems cannot provide voters with the kind of assurances they receive in their other endeavors.

One of the most difficult aspects of elections is their extraordinary trust and privacy requirements. Most security systems protect insiders from outsiders. When a credit card is transmitted to make an online purchase, the principal threats are from third-parties who might wish to compromise the privacy or the integrity of the transaction. In contrast, every participant in an election system is potentially malicious: individual voters may wish to see how others voted, to sell their own votes to others, to unduly alter the election tallies, or even to disrupt the election and keep it from concluding; dishonest election officials may seek to disenfranchise voters, to learn how individuals voted, or to report inaccurate tallies; and corrupt equipment vendors might want to perpetrate all forms of mischief. Perhaps worst of all, surprising collusions may compromise elections: voters and election officials may conspire to sell votes; a coercive employer may conspire with an equipment vendor to ensure that employees are voting according to instructions; or observers may conspire with election officials to alter or discard votes.

Election officials should not know how individuals voted, and voters should not be able to show others how they voted. Indeed, the exceptional privacy requirement that voters be unable to reveal their votes – even if they desire to do so – makes voting especially difficult.

In the mid nineteenth century, the "Australian ballot" was introduced as a means of deterring coercion; today we take for granted this process of voting privately within a public environment where observers can enforce privacy, but it was a great innovation in its time. As elections have moved from paper to punch cards to lever-machines to electronic consoles and back – with many intermediate stops – the challenges of maintaining privacy and integrity have grown.

In the early 1980s, cryptographers began to propose new election designs with new properties and integrity guarantees. Numerous systems that have come to be termed as "end-to-end verifiable" have been developed using a variety of techniques. These E2E-verifiable systems allow voters to check for themselves that their votes are properly counted and thereby achieve the same kinds of assurances they have when banking or shopping. However, until recently these systems failed to give adequate attention to the human element. If secret-ballot elections were conducted among entities with extensive intrinsic computing power, then current solutions would be ideal. But unaided humans cannot realistically be expected to encrypt data. This leaves two likely alternatives. If voters use their own trusted devices, then the devices could retain information that enables vote-selling and coercion; voters could even be casting their votes on devices given to them by coercers. Alternatively, if voters use devices provided by election officials or other parties, mechanisms must be provided to assure voters that these devices are acting according to their wishes.

More recent abstractions such as "software independence" and "evidence-based elections" have been developed to capture the integrity properties desired in elections. But systems have not been developed which achieve these properties together with all the other essential requirements of practical elections. For instance, many of the existing systems allow voters to determine whether or not their votes have been accurately counted, but few give voters who discover mishandling of their votes any evidence that can be used to demonstrate this error to third-parties. (The fundamental difficulty is to demonstrate that a vote has not been counted properly without revealing the contents of the vote.) Providing this kind of "dispute resolution" is a major challenge in the design of election systems.

Tremendous progress has been made in the past few decades. We can now build voter-friendly poll-site election systems that achieve full end-to-end verifiability and have properties far superior to what voters have come to expect. We have also made substantial progress towards the dream of secure, high-integrity online voting, but significant problems remain to be solved before we can responsibly suggest that voting from home is a viable option.

This book explores recent innovations in both poll-site and remote voting systems and their application throughout the world. The requirements of elections are analyzed, the available tools and technologies are described and a variety of modern systems are presented in detail together with discussions of deployments. This is an invaluable resource for election professionals, researchers and policy makers alike.

Josh Benaloh
Microsoft Research

Preface

Assuring the integrity of the outcome of an election and guaranteeing the secrecy of ballots forms the foundation of a healthy democracy. For conventional voting, using paper ballots and hand-counting, procedures have evolved over time that by and large are perceived to be trustworthy in providing these guarantees. However, with the dawn of the digital age there are increasing trends to move away from traditional ways of conducting elections to ones using digital technologies. The most extreme form of this is the conduct of elections over the Internet. Any such moves bring a host of new, unfamiliar and often severe threats. On the other hand, digital technology can bring significant benefits in terms of convenience, efficiency, etc. The challenge of ensuring that elections conducted electronically provide at least as much security as traditional ones, and ideally more, has been taken up in earnest by the cryptography and security communities over the past couple of decades or so.

In 2003, Springer published a book entitled *Secure Electronic Voting* (ed. Dimitris Gritzalis). The book features a collection of chapters authored by then active researchers in the field. It presented the latest trends, threats and the state-of-the-art technologies in electronic voting (e-voting) at the time of its publication.

A decade on, significant advances have been made both in theory and practice, and the landscape of the field has changed dramatically. On one hand, e-voting has been widely deployed in democratic countries around the world, e.g., USA, India, Brazil and Estonia. But on the other hand, e-voting has also become very controversial. Many deployed e-voting systems have been reported to contain serious security vulnerabilities. Consequently, their use has been discontinued in a number of countries, including the Netherlands, Ireland and Germany. One central concern with these (discontinued) e-voting systems is a lack of verifiability: namely, the lack of any means of verifying that votes have been correctly recorded and tallied. The need to address the verifiability problem has encouraged the development of several academic solutions to the problem of end-to-end (E2E) verifiable voting, and the resulting systems to move from theory to practice. The deployment of E2E voting systems in real-world elections is in fact considered one of the most significant developments in the field in the last decade.

This book aims to cover all the major developments in electronic voting, in particular, E2E voting systems, from 2003 (taking the story forward from the Gritzalis book) to present "real-world" settings. It covers three broad areas: new e-voting protocols, new attacks reported on e-voting and new developments in the real-world use of e-voting.

Both editors of this book are lead designers of two different E2E voting systems, called Prêt à Voter and DRE-i, both of which have been implemented and used in practical applications (detailed in Chapter 12 and 13, respectively). These two systems and others (Scantegrity, Helios and STAR-Vote, as detailed in Chapters 10, 11 and 14, respectively) are examples of the diversity in the field. While providing similar E2E verifiability properties, these various systems are designed using different techniques, have different trade-offs and are suitable for different election scenarios.

In the light of these many advances in both the theory and the practice of e-voting since 2003, we felt that the time was ripe to take stock of the state of the art and to identify the remaining challenges. We are delighted and honored to be joined in this task by many of the most prominent researchers in the field, with expertise ranging from the legal and regulatory aspects of e-voting to cryptography, computer science and engineering.

We should note that this book is not intended to argue in favor of or against e-voting, but to present a factual account of what is known about the e-voting capabilities and limitations, based on the authors' experience in designing, analyzing and deploying e-voting systems in real-world settings.

This book is divided into three parts. The first part looks at the general principles involved in designing a secure e-voting system and deploying it in practice. It consists of the following two chapters.

■ In Chapter 1, Ronald Rivest, a professor at MIT and Madars Virza, a researcher at MIT revisit the notion of "software independence." This notion was first proposed by Ronald Rivest and John Wack in 2006, and since then has proved to be an invaluable guiding principle for designing secure voting systems.

■ In Chapter 2, Ben Goldsmith, drawing on his over 20 years' work experience in the International Foundation for Electoral Systems (IFES), lays out detailed guidelines for trialling e-voting in national elections. Many failures in past e-voting trials were the result of a lack of careful planning and appropriate management; this chapter provides guidance as to how these pitfalls may be avoided in the future.

The second part looks at real-world implementations of e-voting, in particular in national elections. It consists of the following five chapters.

■ In Chapter 3, Carlos Vegas and Jordi Barrat, researchers from the eVoting Legal Lab, present an overview of the current state of e-voting implementations worldwide. This chapter focuses on legal and sociopolitical issues in e-voting, and highlights the importance of three pillars for a successful e-voting deployment, namely: technical background, legal framework and a proactive society. Any weak point in these pillars may lead to the failure of the e-voting project.

■ In Chapter 4, Siamak Shahandashti, an ERC research fellow at Newcastle University, reviews the electoral voting systems that have been used in real elections worldwide. While academic research on E2E verifiable voting often focuses on the simple first-past-the-post system, it is worth noting that there are a great variety of voting systems that are far more complex. Supporting all these systems in the electronic context with E2E verifiability presents significant challenges to researchers in the field.

■ In Chapter 5, Kristian Gjøsteen, a professor at the Norwegian University of Science and Technology, gives an account of the Norgwegian e-voting trials in 2009 and 2011. This account is based on the author's experience of participating in these trials as a member of the steering group and as a consulting cryptographer for both trials.

■ In Chapter 6, Dylan Clarke, an ERC research fellow at Newcastle University, and Tarvi Martens, the chief architect of the Estonian remote Internet voting system, describe the Estonian Internet voting system. Since the first pilot in 2005, Internet voting has been used for the whole country in three sets of local elections, two European Parliament elections and three parliamentary elections.

■ In Chapter 7, Alex Halderman, an associate professor at the University of Michigan, reviews practical attacks on real-world e-voting systems, from poll-site DRE to online voting. This chapter is largely based on the author's personal involvement, as an independent security expert, in several research projects that uncovered serious vulnerabilities in e-voting systems deployed in real-world elections.

The third part of this book looks at E2E voting systems and their use in real-world applications. It consists of 7 chapters.

■ In Chapter 8, Taha Ali and Judy Murray, researchers at Newcastle University, present a comprehensive overview of existing solutions to building end-to-end (E2E) verifiable voting systems for both polling-station-based and internet-based elections. This chapter also contains a discussion on the legal framework for e-voting, which should be considered when adopting any E2E voting system for national elections.

■ In Chapter 9, Peter Hyun-Jeen Lee and Siamak Shahandashti, researchers at Newcastle University, review various attacks against E2E verifiable voting systems in the literature. While E2E verifiability can provide a theoretical guarantee of the tallying integrity, imprecise details in the specification of the technical system or the voting procedure may expose the system to unexpected attacks.

■ In Chapter 10, researchers in the Scantegrity team, including Richard Carbak, David Chaum, Jeremy Clark, Aleksander Essex, Travis Mayberry, Stefan Popoveniuc, Ronald Rivest, Emily Shen, Alan Sherman, Poorvi Vora, John Wittrock, and Filip Zagórski, recount a decade-long research effort in designing an E2E verifiable system known as Scantegrity. The Scantegrity system was adopted in the municipal elections of Takoma Park, MD, USA, in 2009 and 2011.

■ In Chapter 11, Olivier Pereira, a professor at the Université catholique de Louvain, describes a web-based E2E voting system called Helios. Helios was initially designed by Ben Adida in 2008 and later improved by Ben Adida, Olivier De Marneffe, Olivier Pereira and Jean-Jacques Quisquater in 2009. In 2009, Helios was used in the university presidential election at the Université catholique de Louvain (UCL), and since 2010, has been regularly used for elections in universities (Princeton, UCL), associations (International Association for Cryptologic Research, ACM) and private companies.

■ In Chapter 12, Peter Ryan, a professor at the University of Luxembourg (and one of the editors of this book), and his colleagues in the Prêt à Voter research team, including Steve Schneider of University of Surrey and Vanessa Teague of University of Melbourne, describe the evolution of the Prêt à Voter E2E voting system. Since its inception in 2004, Prêt à Voter has gone through several improvements, culminating in 2014 with the system being adopted in the Victoria State election in Australia.

■ In Chapter 13, Feng Hao, a reader at Newcastle University (and one of the editors of this book), describes a 10-year research journey that led to the design of an E2E voting system known as DRE-i. Differing from other E2E voting systems, DRE-i does not involve tallying authorities, hence the system is termed "self-enforcing." Since 2013, a web-based implementation of DRE-i has been used in the campus of Newcastle University to provide verifiable classroom voting applications.

■ In Chapter 14, Dan Wallach, a professor at Rice University, and his colleagues in the STAR-vote team, including Susan Bell, Josh Benaloh, Michael Byrne, Dana DeBeauvoir, Bryce Eakin, Gail Fisher, Philip Kortum, Neal McBurnett, Julian Montoya, Michelle Parker, Olivier Pereira, Philip Stark and Michael Winn, introduce the STAR-vote, a Secure, Transparent Auditable, and Reliable Voting System. It is planned that STAR-vote will be used for the elections at Travis County, TX, USA, in 2018.

This book is part of the CRC Series in Security, Privacy and Trust. We thank Dr. Jianying Zhou, the series editor, and Mr. Ruijun He, the CRC editor for reviewing and approving our initial book proposal. We greatly appreciate Mr. Ruijun He for his kindly agreeing to our request to make the book open-access two years from the publication. This is a key reason that we were able to attract many prominent researchers in the field to contribute to this book project. We also thank Ms. Marsha Pronin, the project coordinator at CRC Press, for her assistance in helping us prepare for this book and her patience along the way.

Last but not least, we would like to express our sincere thanks to chapter authors who joined us in writing this book, for their invaluable contributions on not only writing their own chapters, but also peer-reviewing other chapters. We feel we have learned so much from them. As editors and authors, we enjoyed working on this book, and we hope the reader will find the book useful and enjoy reading it.

Feng Hao Peter Y. A. Ryan
Newcastle University   University of Luxembourg

SETTING THE SCENE

Chapter 1

Software Independence Revisited

Ronald L. Rivest
Computer Science and Artificial Intelligence Laboratory
Massachusetts Institute of Technology (MIT)
Cambridge, MA 02139
`rivest@mit.edu`

Madars Virza
Computer Science and Artificial Intelligence Laboratory
Massachusetts Institute of Technology (MIT)
Cambridge, MA 02139
`madars@mit.edu`

CONTENTS

1.1   Introduction

Democracy depends on elections, yet elections are complex but fragile processes involving voters, election officials, candidates, procedures and technology. Voting systems are evaluated in terms of their security, usability, efficiency, cost, accessibility and reliability. A good voting system design should be based on sound principles.

The principle of "software independence" was introduced by Rivest and Wack [488] and Rivest [486]:

> A voting system is *software independent* if an (undetected) change or error in its software cannot cause an undetectable change or error in an election outcome.

For example, optical scan and some cryptographically-based voting systems are software independent.

Software independence is one form of auditability, enabling detection and possible correction of election outcome errors caused by malicious software or software bugs.

This chapter begins with a review of the definition of software independence as given by Rivest and Wack [488] and Rivest [486]; starting with a review of the issue of software complexity (Section 1.2) and a re-presentation of the definition of software independence and its rationale (Section 1.3). The reader is encouraged to consult the original papers [488, 486] for further details, elaboration and clarification of the original definition.

Further sections discuss evidence-based elections (Section 1.6), end-to-end verifiable voting (Section 1.8) and verifiable computation (Section 1.10).

1.2   Problem: Software Complexity of Voting Systems

We start by describing the problem that software independence addresses: the difficulty of assuring oneself that voted ballots will be recorded accurately by complex and difficult-to-test software in all-electronic voting systems. We emphasize that the problem is providing such assurance: the software may well be correct, but convincing oneself (or others) that this is the case is effectively impossible.

Electronic voting systems are complex and continue to grow more so. The requirements for privacy for the voter, for security against attack or failure and for the accuracy of the final tally are in serious conflict with each other. It is common wisdom that complex and conflicting system requirements lead to burgeoning system complexity.

Voting system vendors express and capture this complexity via software in their voting systems.

As an example, consider a direct-recording electronic (DRE) voting system, which typically provides a touchscreen user interface for voters to make selections and cast ballots, and which stores the cast vote records in memory and on a removable memory card. A DRE may display an essentially infinite variety of different ballot layouts, and may include complex accessibility features for the sight-impaired (e.g., so that a voter could use headphones and be guided to make selections using an audio ballot).

An issue, then, is how to provide assurance, despite the complexity of the software, that the voting system will accurately record the voter's intentions. A pure DRE voting system produces only electronic cast ballot records, which are not directly observable or verifiable by the voter.

Consequently, no meaningful audit of the DRE's electronic records to determine their accuracy is possible; accuracy can only be estimated by a variety of other (imperfect) measures, such as comparing the accumulated tallies to pre-election canvassing results, performing software code reviews and testing the system accuracy before (or even during) the election.

1.2.1 The Difficulty of Evaluating Complex Software for Errors

It is a common maxim that complexity is the enemy of security and accuracy, thus it is very difficult to evaluate a complex system. A very small error, such as a transposed pair of characters or an omitted command to initialize a variable, in a large complex system may cause unexpected results at unpredictable times. Or, it may provide a vulnerability that can be exploited by an adversary for large benefits.

Finding all errors in a large system is generally held to be impossible in general or else highly demanding and extremely expensive. Our ability to develop complex software vastly exceeds our ability to prove its correctness or test it satisfactorily within reasonable fiscal constraints (extensive testing of a voting system's software would certainly be cost-prohibitive given how voting in general is funded). A voting system for which the integrity of the election results intrinsically depends on the correctness of its software will always be somewhat suspect.

As we shall see, the software-independent approach follows the maxim, "Verify the election results, not the voting system."

1.2.2 The Need for Software-Independent Approaches

With the DRE approach, one is forced to trust (or assume) that the software is correct. If questions arise later about the accuracy of the election results (or if a recount is demanded), there is again no recourse but to trust (or assume) that the voting system did indeed record the votes accurately. We feel that one should strongly prefer voting systems where the integrity of the election outcome is not dependent on trusting the correctness of complex software.

The notion of "software independence" captures exactly this desirable characteristic of providing election results that are verifiable, without having to depend on the assumption that the software is correct.

For users of software-independent voting systems, verification of the correctness of the election results is possible. There need be no lingering unanswerable concern that the election outcome was affected or actually determined by some software bug (or worse, e.g., by a malicious piece of code).

1.3 Definition and Rationale for Software Independence

We now repeat the definition of software independence, and explore its meaning.

> A voting system is *software independent* if an (undetected) change or error in its software cannot cause an undetectable change or error in an election outcome.

A voting system that is not software independent is said to be *software dependent*—it is, in some sense, vulnerable to undetected programming errors, malicious code, or software manipulation, thus the correctness of the election results is dependent on the correctness of the software.

The first use of "undetected" in the definition is to give emphasis to software faults that are *undetected* not being able to cause *undetectable* changes; it is in parentheses because already-known faults may be dealt with by other means.

The intent of the definition of software independence is to capture the notion that a voting system is unacceptable if a software error can cause a change in the election outcome, with *no evidence available that anything has gone wrong*. A "silent theft" of the election should not be possible with a software-independent system. (At least, not a theft due to software...)

To illustrate the rationale for software independence, let us run a "thought experiment." Put yourself in the place of an adversary and imagine that you have the power to secretly replace any of the existing software used by the voting systems by software of your own construction. (You may assume that you have the original source code for the existing software.)

With such an ability, can you (as the adversary) change an election outcome or "rig an election" without fear of detection?

If so, the system is *software dependent*—the software is an "Achilles heel" of the voting system. Corrupting the software gives an adversary the power to secretly and silently steal an election.

If not, the system is *software independent*—the voting system as a whole (including the non-software components) has sufficient redundancy and potential for cross-checking that misbehavior by the software can be detected. The detection might be by the voter, by an election official or technician, by a post-election auditor, by an observer or by some member of the public. (Indeed, anyone but the adversary.)

In such a "thought experiment," we are considering the adversary as some evil agent that could load fraudulent software into voting systems. More realistically, we may consider this adversary to be an abstraction of the limitations of the software development process and testing process. (As such, for the purposes of determining whether a system is software-independent, one should presume that the software errors were present when the software was written and were not caught by software development control processes or by the certification process.)

As we have stated, complex software is difficult to write and to test, and will therefore contain numerous unintentional "bugs" that occasionally can cause voting systems to report incorrect election results. It would be extremely difficult and expensive to determine with certainty that a piece of software is free of bugs that might change an election outcome. Given the relatively small amounts of funding allocated for developing and testing voting system software, we may safely consider it as *effectively impossible*. Thus, the software itself is not considered evidence of a change in the election outcome for the purposes of the definition of software independence. Such "evidence" is too hard to evaluate.

1.3.1 Refinements and Elaborations of Software Independence

There are a number of possible refinements and elaborations of the notion of software independence. We now motivate and introduce the distinction between *strong software independence* and *weak software independence*.

Security mechanisms are typically one of two forms: *prevention* or *detection*. Detection mechanisms may also be coupled with means for *recovery*. When identification of participants and accountability for actions is also present, then detection mechanisms are also the foundation for *deterrence*. Given the importance of recovery mechanisms in addition to detection mechanisms, we propose the following two refinements of the notion of software independence:

A voting system is *strongly software independent* if an (undetected) change or error in its software cannot cause an undetectable change or error in an election outcome, *and moreover, a detected change or error in an election outcome (due to change or error in the software) can be corrected without re-running the election.*

A voting system that is *weakly software independent* conforms to the basic definition of software independence but is not strongly software independent—that is, there is no recovery mechanism.

1.3.2 Examples of Software-Independent Approaches

Currently, there are two general categories of software-independent approaches.

Voter-verifiable paper record (VVPR) approaches constitute the first category, since the VVPR allows (via a recount) the possibility of detecting (and even correcting) errors due to software. Accordingly, these voting systems can be strongly software independent.

The most prominent example in this category is the optical scan voting system used by most U.S. voters since the 2006 elections. The paper ballot is voter verifiable because the voter completes the ballot and can attest to its accuracy before it is fed into the optical scanner; the paper ballot thus serves as an audit trail that can be used in post-election audits of the optical scanner's electronic results. An electronic ballot marking system (EBM) may also be used to record the voter's choices electronically with a touchscreen interface and then to print a high-quality voter verifiable paper ballot for feeding into the optical scanner.

Another example in this category is the voter-verified paper audit trail (VVPAT) voting system, similar to a DRE but with a printer and additional logic. It produces two records of the voter's choices, one on the touchscreen display and one on paper (a VVPR). The voter must verify that both records are correct before causing them to be saved.

Cryptographic voting systems constitute the second category of software-independent voting system approaches. They can provide detection mechanisms for errors caused by software changes or errors [43, 143, 150, 340, 418, 501, 503]). At one level, they can enable voters to detect when their votes have been improperly represented to them at the polling site, and a simple recovery mechanism (re-voting) is available. At another level, they can enable anyone to detect when their votes have been lost or changed, or when the official tally has been computed incorrectly. Recovery is again possible. Most of the recently proposed cryptographic voting systems are strongly software independent.

Receipt-based cryptographic voting systems involve a physical, e.g., paper, receipt that the voter can use to verify, during the process of voting, whether his or her ballot was captured correctly. The contents of the receipt, in general, employ cryptography in some form so that the voter is able to verify that the votes were recorded accurately; the receipt does not show how the voter voted.

Approaches to software independence other than pure use of VVPR or crypto-graphic voting systems are potentially possible, although beyond the scope of our chapter.

1.4 How Does One Test for Software Independence?

This brings up a more subtle point in the definition. What aspects of the voting system make it "software independent?" Is it just the hardware and software, or does it also include the surrounding procedures? For example, is a voting system still software independent if no post-election audits are performed?

The answer is that a voting system is software independent if, after consideration of its software and hardware, it enables use of any election procedures needed to determine whether the election outcome is accurate without having to trust that the voting system software is correct. The election procedures could include those carried out by voters in the course of casting ballots, or in the case of optical scan and VVPAT, they could include election official procedures such as post-election audits.

The detection of any software misbehavior does not need to be perfect; it only needs to happen with sufficiently high probability, in an assumed ideal environment with alert voters, pollworkers, etc.

As an example, consider the EBM which prints out a filled-in optical scan ballot. Some voters may not review the printed ballot at all. Yet the EBM is still software independent; there is a significant probability that software misbehavior by the EBM will be detected (this is similarly true of VVPAT). For the purposes of the definition of "software independence," we assume that (enough) voters are sufficiently observant to detect such misbehavior. (If this assumption were discovered to be false in practice, some increase in voter education might be necessary.) Although some forms of such detectable misbehavior may leave no tangible proof of misbehavior, the definition of software independence does not require that all misbehavior have tangible proof; it is sufficient that the relevant misbehavior be detectable and reportable.

Continuing with this example, we note that there is also software in the optical scanner used to scan the ballots that might produce incorrect output. But such misbehavior is detectable by a post-election audit procedure that hand-counts the paper ballots, thus the optical scan voting system is software independent. (Note that such audits are typically statistical in nature and are thus not perfect detectors of misbehavior. But a well-designed audit will catch such misbehavior with reasonable probability. See [66, 285].

To illustrate further, then, say that no post-election audit of an optical scan-based election is required if the apparent margin of victory is more than 10%. An optical scan system would still be considered software independent in such an election, since the original voter-verified paper ballots are available for review, and software misbehavior can still in principle be detected. (As a side note: we feel that such post-election audits are always a good idea and that "no audit" should not be an option. If an apparent margin of victory is large, a smaller audit is appropriate.)

As a final example, say that electronic pollbook systems are used in an optical scan-based election, but the electronic pollbooks do not create a contemporaneous paper record for each voter. Thus, their software must be trusted to show that the number of optical scan records (paper and electronic) accurately reflect the actual number of voters who used the scanners. Are these systems software independent? We would argue that the answer is no for the electronic pollbook, as the design of this system has prevented an audit to determine if the number of optical scan records is correct, i.e., its software must be trusted to be correct. A contemporaneous paper record would have made the electronic pollbook software independent.

1.5 Discussion

1.5.1 Implications for Testing and Certification

Given the exceptional difficulty of proving software to be correct, it is a reasonable proposal to disallow voting systems that are software dependent altogether.

If testing and certification of software-dependent voting systems are to be nonetheless contemplated, then one should expect the certification process should be very much more demanding and rigorous for a software-dependent voting system than for a software-independent voting system. The manufacturer should submit a formal proof of correctness, with perhaps an assurance level corresponding to EAL level 6 or 7 [1] and public disclosure of the source code. Moreover, the voting system must permit proof it is running the software it is supposed to.

1.5.2 Related Issues

There may be other aspects of software misbehavior that don't quite fit our proposed notion of software independence. For example, software may bias a voter's choices in subtle ways (say by displaying one candidate's name in slightly brighter characters on a touchscreen). These issues fall outside the scope of software independence, since the correct "election outcome" isn't well-defined until the voter indicates her choice. Software independence is focused on the correctness of the election results, and not on other aspects of the voting process.

Some voting systems, such as certain STV (single transferable vote) systems, determine an election outcome in a way that may be randomized (e.g., for breaking ties). A voting system whose software breaks ties in different ways would not be

---

[1] https://en.wikipedia.org/wiki/Common_Criteria,
https://en.wikipedia.org/wiki/Evaluation_Assurance_Level

considered to violate software independence, as long as any outcome so determined is a legally acceptable election outcome given the cast vote records.

It is worth emphasizing that the records produced of voters' choices should be of sufficient quality and durability to be usable in a post-election audit.

1.6   Evidence-Based Elections

Recently (2012), Stark and Wagner proposed [541] the notion of "evidence-based elections," a broad framework for understanding how confidence in election outcomes can be achieved, through a combination of auditability (achieved via strongly software-independent voting systems) and auditing (specifically, compiliance audits and risk-limiting audits).

In this framework, strongly software-independent voting systems generate the audit trail (typically, but not necessarily, consisting of voter-verified paper ballots), while the compliance checks that the audit trail has not been corrupted or compromised, and the risk-limiting audit ensures (by appropriate statistical sampling and analysis) that the audit trail is consistent with the stated election outcome.

It is the combination of auditability and actual auditing that provides the evidence for the correctness of the election outcome. As they put it,

$$\text{evidence} = \text{auditability} + \text{auditing}$$

In this framework, the voting system software is not part of the evidence being evaluated during the audit. Furthermore, as Stark and Wagner argue effectively, trust in the software is not necessary for developing confidence in election outcomes. Indeed, the need to have time-consuming and expensive voting system certifications may be hampering the development of voting systems that enable elections that provide the evidence necessary to have trustworthy outcomes.

We endorse the "evidence-based elections" framework described by Stark and Wagner. Software independence is a necessary component of such a framework.

1.7   The Use of a Public Ledger

The development of the internet has made possible the "democratization" of many capabilities previously reserved for the few. The diversity and quantity of information available for public review, compared to the situation only two decades ago, is quite astonishing.

Of interest here is the availability of *transactional* data generated by users with some information system. Usually such information is made available in the form of a per-application database, maintained by the transaction service provider. Sometimes the transaction data is available only to the user involved in the transaction (e.g., credit-card data); sometimes it is public (e.g., real-estate transactions).

So, one may reasonably ask whether election data can or should be made available online and even made available to the public in the form of a "public ledger" or "public bulletin board."

There is no reason not to do so, except when doing so might violate voter privacy. Making election information available online should not enable voters to sell their votes or be coerced into voting in a certain way.

Indeed, making the audit trail publicly available may engender greater trust in the election outcome, since the public may help with the verification that the audit trail is consistent with their knowledge as to how they voted and with the stated election outcome.

The Bitcoin [403] block chain exemplifies an extreme position with respect to democratization: not only is the transaction ledger totally public, but the ledger is maintained without trusted third parties by a clever peer-to-peer mechanism based on incentives for "miners" who extend the block-chain containing the ledger by solving cryptographic puzzles.

Yet, while proposals have been floated, and even tested, for block-chain based voting,[2] it is important to distinguish the questions "(1) What information is on the audit trails?" and "(2) Is that information public?" The use of a public ledger (as, for example, provided by block-chain based ledger) provides an affirmative answer to (2), it does nothing to answer (1)—other mechanisms, such as those based on digital signatures, provided evidence as to what information is authentically part of the audit trail.

Whether the audit trail is made public on a peer-to-peer based public ledger (as with bitcoin) or is made public on a website maintained by election officials is not the key question; the critical questions are whether the audit trail is readable by the public and whether there is reason to believe that it is complete and accurate (the sort of questions asked in a compliance audit).

The notion of having the audit trail totally public is a good one. It existed in the early days of our republic, but disappeared when secret ballots and voting machines became the norm. *It is time to again make election audit trails public.*

In the context of a public ledger containing the audit trail, a strongly software-independent voting system enables the reconstruction of the correct election outcome from the public audit trail.

---

[2]http://www.coindesk.com/bitcoin-foundation-blockchain-voting-system-controversy/

1.8 End-to-End Verifiable Voting Systems

"Cryptographic voting systems" were mentioned briefly in Section 1.3.2 as an example of (strongly) software-independent voting systems; here we elaborate a bit more on their properties, and their relationship to software independence and evidence-based elections.

This line of research has progressed significantly since our original paper on software independence was published (2006).

The common name for such systems has evolved to "*end-to-end auditable voting systems*" (or sometimes "*end-to-end verifiable voting systems*," to emphasize that the verification covers all the way from the voter's head (where her choices are selected) to the final outcome (reflecting all cast votes):

■ a voter may verify that her vote is *cast as intended*,

■ anyone may verify that a given vote is *collected as cast*, and

■ anyone may verify that the votes are *counted as collected*.

In these systems, the collected cast votes are placed in a public ledger; to protect voter privacy, the votes are encrypted before being cast (e.g., with the public key of an election authority).

Some protocol, such as Benaloh's "*ballot casting assurance*" protocol [85], is needed to assure voters that their votes are being properly encrypted. *Such a protocol is essential for making the design software independent*; without it the voting terminal could misrepresent the voter's intent by encrypting something other than the voter's choice.

For some designs, such as "Prêt à voter" [499], "Scratch and Vote" [49] and "Scantegrity" [386, 133, 146, 144], ballots are preprinted, containing both plaintext (human-readable) choices and corresponding ciphertexts. For such designs one should include a process (a "ballot audit") for allowing voters (and other auditors) to randomly select preprinted ballots, spoil them (remove them from the pool of ballots eligible to be cast), and challenge the system to demonstrate that the ciphertexts properly represent the corresponding plaintexts. Again, such a ballot-auditing process is essential for making the design software independent; without it the ballot-printing subsystem could effectively cause voters' selections to be represented incorrectly by the corresponding ciphertexts.

The "ThreeBallot" design of Rivest [487] was proposed primarily for pedagogic purposes to illustrate the principles of end-to-end verifiable voting system design *without using cryptography*. ThreeBallot was not intended as a practical proposal, since each voter must submit *three* ballots, which must have an enforced relationship to each other (vote exactly twice in favor of a candidate to support him, vote exactly once in favor of a candidate to oppose him). The voter retains a randomly chosen one of her three submitted ballots as a receipt so that she can check for its presence in the public ledger. The question as to whether ThreeBallot is software independent reduces to a consideration of the device that enforces the necessary relationship of the three submitted ballots. Clearly, the device should not know which of the three ballots was retained by the voter as her receipt.

However, a maliciously programmed device in ThreeBallot might allow a voter to submit *three* ballots in favor of a certain candidate, which should not be allowed. Is this a violation of software independence? It seems not, since it requires not only that the device software be changed, but also that some voters collude in submitting illegal triples of ballots. Perhaps a new definition is needed.

We may define a voting system to be *vote validating* if it checks that each cast vote is valid, and *publicly vote validating* if anyone may determine from the public ledger that each vote is valid.

We see that ThreeBallot is thus vote validating but not publicly vote validating.

Note that vote validation is not the same as providing ballot assurance; the former checks that the cast vote is one of the possible allowed votes, while the latter allows a voter to check that her cast vote correctly captures her intent.

Some end-to-end verifiable voting system designs, such as the homomorphic method proposed by Baudron et al. [76], achieve public vote validation by providing each vote with a zero-knowledge proof of its validity (the vote and corresponding zero-knowledge proof of validity are posted together on the public ledger).

It is worth noting that the inclusion of such zero-knowledge proofs may provide malicious software with a means to cause an election to fail to produce an output: what should happen when one (or many) of such zero-knowledge proofs of input validity fail to verify? This is outside the scope of the notion of software independence, since the activity of the malicious (or erroneous) software will of course be detected.

Some end-to-end verifiable voting designs, such as Scantegrity [386, 133, 146, 144] and STAR-Vote [77], are "paper/electronic hybrid" methods using a combination of paper-based and electronic methods, so that the paper ballot audit trail provides a backup mechanism for recovering the correct election outcome should the electronic or cryptographic methods completely fail somehow. This design also provides comfort to those who don't quite understand or trust the cryptographic techniques being used. Furthermore, the auditing process may include checks of both the paper audit trail and the electronic audit trail. (Should they disagree on the correct election outcome, the paper audit trail should probably take precedence, unless there is evidence that the paper audit trail was damaged or incomplete.)

Many proposed end-to-end verifiable voting system designs use mix-nets to provide voter privacy; the mix-net scrambles (permutes) the collection of cast votes while not adding or deleting votes, nor changing the content of any cast vote. To make a mix-net verifiable, the mix-net servers provide a zero-knowledge proof of these desired correctness properties; this zero-knowledge proof is also posted on the public ledger. In the absence of a paper audit trail, such zero-knowledge proof methods are essential for providing software independence.

The other major category of end-to-end verifiable voting system proposals are those that are based on encryption methods with homomorphic properties [49, 76, 77]. Such methods do not need zero-knowledge proofs of correct mix-net operation, since they do not use mix-nets; the homomorphic aggregation of votes provides the desired anonymity. However, achieving software independence requires some method (such as a zero-knowledge proof) that provides assurance that the decryption of the aggregated tally was correctly performed.

Recently we have seen increasing attention to the possibility of running elections remotely "over the internet." In particular, the question is asked as to whether end-to-end verifiable elections can be run over the internet.

While voting over the internet has been done in Estonia [563], Springall et al. [535] argue that the Estonian voting system is not end-to-end verifiable and that it has numerous security vulnerabilities.

The Helios voting system [44] is perhaps the most widely used internet-based end-to-end verifiable voting system. Like any remote voting system (such as vote-by-mail), there is no pretense of avoiding voter coercion; indeed, Helios makes the possibility of coercion explicit by providing a "Coerce-Me" button(!).

Küsters et al. [356] have demonstrated an interesting "clash" attack on some versions of Helios and on some other end-to-end voting systems, wherein voters who vote the same way may be given identical receipts (so when voters look them up on the public ledger everything seems OK, but the clash attack thereby provides the attacker with the freedom to add new ballots to the collection of cast votes). (The same authors also have an interesting definition of *accountability* applicable to voting systems [336].) Here the vulnerability lies with the random number generator; manipulating it can cause receipts to become identical. Systems with such a flaw are not software independent.

Remotegrity [586] is an interesting extension to the Scantegrity system, employing *both* paper and electronic communications to allow remote voters to detect whether their votes have been tampered with, and to prove that such tampering exists without having to reveal how they have voted. Although Remotegrity utilizes a complex protocol involving code voting and scratch-off cards mailed to the voters, it does appear to achieve software independence, among other properties.

1.9 Program Verification

As we discussed in Section 1.2.1, evaluating a software system for errors is generally held to be impossible. That said, approaches exist to verify that a software conforms to a given *specification*.

Given a specification S describing the input/output relationships, and a program P it is possible to write a formal proof π that interfaces of P satisfy the requirements outlined in S. Moreover such proofs π are verifiable. This is called *program verifi-*

cation and is an active research area. Thus, by spending a considerable and highly skilled effort it is, in principle, possible to produce a proof that software used in voting conforms to a specification.

However, for such proof to be relevant it must be possible to determine that the particular program is in fact being executed by the hardware, and that the hardware executes *nothing else* that could interfere with the said program. As demonstrated by Checkoway et al. [154] the latter is extremely hard and believed impossible in general.

1.10 Verifiable Computation and Zero-Knowledge Proofs

In early days of the field, program verification techniques comprised the only set of techniques to try proving output of a computation correct. A relatively recent approach, which circumvents the outlined impossibility outlined faced by program verification techniques, is based on zero-knowledge proofs. Here, an output of a program is augmented with a proof that the *output* conforms to the specification, and thus is correct for the given input.

This is consistent with the "evidence-based elections" theme described above (Section 1.6), following the mantra of "verify the outcome, not the equipment," and is the approach we examine further in this section.

Proofs for end-to-end voting systems, e.g., those that verify correct shuffling of a mixnet or that vote is well-formed, can be seen as tailored examples of such zero-knowledge proofs. In contrast, recent years have seen a spark of availability of efficient *general-purpose* zero-knowledge proof systems. Provided people trust and accept them, those could greatly expand the domain of cryptographically verified voting schemes.

In more detail, a zero-knowledge proof system, given a program P, input x and secret input w, produces the output $z := P(x, w)$ and a proof π attesting to the fact that $z = P(x, w)$. Anyone, given x, P, z and π, can be convinced that there exists w such that $z = P(x, w)$, however the proof reveals nothing about w other than its existence. A weaker variant called *verifiable computation* system, assumes that there is no secret input w.

Zero-knowledge proofs in voting. As we explain next, zero-knowledge proofs are very powerful cryptographic tools with immediate applicability to voting. Consider the scenario of counting encrypted votes. Here x could comprise encrypted votes, w be the decryption key held by the election officials, and P be the program that does the tallying. Any observer, given encrypted votes, final election result and the corresponding proof, can be convinced that votes were counted correctly. Moreover, the observer does *not* need to trust the hardware used to produce the proof, nor that P's computation was not interfered with, etc.

More generally, the beautiful line of zero-knowledge works [261, 347, 393, 251] have culminated in constructions that admit efficient practical prototypes [81, 454, 82]; we refer the reader to [258] for a survey. Most efficient constructions sport linear verification time and constant-sized proofs (in practice: verification in few milliseconds and proofs of a few hundreds of bytes, respectively). In particular, this efficiency means that most recent developments can greatly speed up existing voting primitives (e.g., verifiable mixnets) and support new ones (e.g., proofs of correct decryption for complex encryption schemes).

That said, from a cryptographic perspective, constructions of very efficient zero-knowledge proofs tend to be a bit "heavy-weight" — current proposals tend to require complex theoretical machinery or strong cryptographic assumptions.

Moreover, all non-interactive proof systems require a *trusted setup* phase which, if done improperly or maliciously, yields the proofs vacuous. This is in line with preparations for regular elections, where mistakes could potentially turn out to be fatal. However, there is recent theoretical work that tries to lessen the trust requirements of the setup phase, but the degree of practicality such a solution would provide remains to be evaluated.

1.11 Conclusions and Suggestions

The history of computing systems is that, given improvements and breakthroughs in technology and speed, software is able to do more and thus its complexity increases. The ability to prove the correctness of software diminishes rapidly as the software becomes more complex. It would effectively be impossible to adequately test future (and current) software-dependent voting systems for flaws and introduced fraud, and thus these systems would always remain suspect in their ability to provide secure and accurate elections.

A *software-independent* approach to voting systems assures voters that errors or fraud in election results can be reliably detected. Since the correctness of the election results does not ultimately depend on the correctness of the software, one can reduce the effort and expense to test and certify voting system software.

Chapter 2

Guidelines for Trialling E-Voting in National Elections

Ben Goldsmith

International Foundation for Electoral Systems

CONTENTS

2.1 Terminology

The current discourse on electronic voting and counting technologies is scattered with various terms and phrases — electronic voting machines, e-voting, e-enabled elections, remote voting, precinct count optical scanning, etc. This array of terminology generally relates to slightly different technological solutions. The field of election technologies related to voting and counting is a rapidly changing field and the conceptual framework for consideration is still emerging. Therefore, it is easy to find the same terminology being used in different ways in different countries or regions, adding to the confusion caused by this proliferation of terms.

When people tend to discuss electronic voting, they are generally referring to two separate but sometimes related technologies — electronic voting and electronic counting. The traditional paper-based voting system consists of a voter manually marking the paper ballot and the ballot being counted by hand by election officials.

In elections using electronic voting or counting technologies one or both of these processes are automated using an electronic device.

In electronic voting an electronic device records the voting preference of the voter. This voting device may be located at the polling station or a remote location; for example, a personal computer is used to cast a ballot over the internet or a mobile phone is used to cast a ballot via text message or SMS. In electronic counting an electronic device is used to count the ballots cast, whether paper or electronic.

Any combination of manual/electronic voting/counting is possible. A full electronic solution involves an electronic voting machine, remote or otherwise, directly recording the preference of the voter through a ballot interface (e.g., a touchscreen), electronically counting the votes received at the end of polling and providing these results to election officials. Partial electronic solutions are also available whereby paper ballots are marked manually but counted by machine (e.g., optical scan solutions) or an electronic device is used to create a printed vote which is placed in the ballot box and counted by hand or electronically.

The various technological solutions offered by electronic voting and counting technologies mean there are many options available for election administrators while considering the introduction of such technologies. Electronic voting and counting technology vendors offer different ways of implementing each specific technical solution. The variety of technologies offered might be one factor which has led to very different experiences in countries which have used and attempted to use electronic voting and counting technologies.

This chapter discusses the guidelines for trialling electronic voting solutions, but the procedures are equally applicable to electronic counting solutions.

2.2   Context for E-Voting

In many areas of modern life today, technology dominates. It is believed that technology is progress; progress is good and should, therefore, be embraced. An initial look at the field of elections may lead to a similar conclusion, with some countries embracing the adoption of technology in the field of elections. Others have taken steps away from using technology in the electoral process, the best example being the Netherlands which used electronic voting machines for many years before withdrawing their use on security grounds. In many countries the use and possible use of voting technologies elicits fierce debate between advocates and opponents of these technologies.

How are we to reconcile these very different approaches to the suitability of electronic voting technologies? For a country considering electronic voting technologies, which is the right approach and when is it advisable to proceed using these technologies? The answer is, of course, that there is no one answer. The factors which may push one nation towards an electronic voting technology may not be present for another nation, or may indicate a different solution.

Furthermore, elections take place in a highly complex environment, at the meeting point of legal, cultural, political, logistical and environmental considerations. Even small changes can significantly affect the electoral process. In highly charged political environments like this there will always be those who see changes as suspicious, and wonder to whose advantage and to whose disadvantage the change will be.

In many ways election administrators have two major challenges when running elections. They need to deliver an election with integrity, which reflects the will of the voters, and also to deliver an election which the stakeholders believe has integrity. These are two very different challenges, and meeting one of these challenges does not guarantee meeting the other.

Any decision on whether to adopt voting technology has the possibility to affect either or both the integrity of the electoral process or the perception of this integrity, and therefore needs to be very carefully considered by decision makers. What is proposed in this chapter is a methodology for taking this decision. It is based on many years of experience in the electoral field across various election technology projects, and on the comments of other respected experts in the field.

At the core of this methodology is the application of a comprehensive feasibility study process, adapted to the electoral process and environment. It is important to note that feasibility studies take time to conduct. Countries wishing to consider the use of electronic voting technologies should expect the process to take years rather than months, and this is entirely appropriate given the complexity of the electoral process and the need to adequately assess and consult on these technologies. Any attempt to short cut the deliberation process may result in adopting a technology that does not suit the electoral context in question or in taking a decision without the support of key stakeholders.

The feasibility study methodology proposed here has four stages. Initially there is a largely desk-based study about the suitability of the voting technology from the perspective of the technical feasibility — the advantages likely to be achieved, the financial feasibility and the likely reaction from the stakeholders. If this recommends further investigation into the use of voting technologies then the next stage is to set the parameters for the conduct of a pilot project to trial the technology. Once these parameters are in place the pilot project can be conducted, and fully assessed afterwards. Then a final decision on the adoption, or non-adoption, of the technology can be taken. These four stages will be fully outlined later in the chapter, after a brief summary of international electoral standards that apply to electronic voting.

2.3   International Electoral Standards

When considering a change in any sort of system, especially an important one such as a voting system, it is vital that the underlying standards by which different systems can be judged are kept in mind. There are a number of different approaches to the challenge of judging electoral processes. In recent years, opinion appears to have coalesced around the concept of international electoral standards as defined by public international law [266].

Public international law based electoral standards are well elaborated in documents issued by the United Nations [241], the European Commission [167], the Organization for Security and Cooperation in Europe [243] and the Venice Commission [165]. The way these electoral standards are categorized by the different institutions is not exactly the same, but it does illustrate a common understanding of the content of international electoral standards. Drawing directly from the wording of Article 25 of the International Covenant on Civil and Political Rights (ICCPR), the core of these international electoral standards can be defined as the following:

■ **Fair Elections (without any distinctions)** – Elections should be conducted so as to ensure equal conditions for participation in the electoral process for all eligible candidates and voters, irrespective of gender, religion, ethnicity, political affiliation, language, literacy or disability.

■ **Genuine Elections** – Elections must be held for institutions which have authority, must be conducted in a credible manner, must present voters with real choices between candidates for election, with the results of elections representing the will of the people.

■ **Periodic Elections** – Elections must be held frequently enough to ensure that governmental authority continues to reflect the will of the people and that there is regular opportunity for the voters to change government.

■ **Universal Suffrage** – Legal and operational limitations on access to candidacy or the right to vote must be minimized and must not be discriminatory in nature, except where such limitations are reasonable or necessary.

■ **Equal Suffrage** – Voters should each be provided the same number of votes in each election being conducted and electoral districts should be reasonably equal in size so that each vote cast has a similar weight.

■ **Secret Ballot** – In order that voters be able to freely express their electoral preferences in the absence of intimidation, the ballot should be completed in private and it must not be possible to link a voter to a voting preference.

■ **Free Elections** – The electoral environment must be such that information on electoral contestants can be made available to voters, informed discussion about electoral options can take place and voters are able to make electoral choices without intimidation.

These political/electoral rights and standards do not operate in a vacuum. In fact political rights work in parallel with other human rights and a healthy electoral environment relies on the realization of these broader human rights. Human rights relevant to the conduct of elections include the rights to freedom of expression, freedom of information, freedom of assembly, freedom of association, freedom of movement, to non-discrimination and to self-determination (ICCPR).

Transparency is also an essential component for a credible electoral process. The requirement for transparency is derived in part from some of the human and political rights standards outlined above, such as the right to information and that elections are credible and conducted in a free and fair manner. It is also based on other international standards, such as anti-corruption standards, which require public affairs to be conducted in a transparent manner [561].

The international electoral standards outlined above are equally relevant for the use of technologies to assist the processes of voting and counting, as clearly stated in the Council of Europe's 2004 Recommendation on Legal, Operational and Technical Standards for E-voting, which states:

> "e-voting shall respect all the principles of democratic elections and referendums" [428].

Increasingly, the use of new technologies for voting is fundamentally changing the way these components of the electoral process are conducted. As a result, the use of technologies for voting is also challenging this body of international electoral standards.

Some of these standards are no longer adequate to deal with electronic voting technologies. Other technology-related operations are not covered at all by the existing set of standards. For example, it is clear that the use of electronic voting technologies will have little or no impact on the right to freedom of movement or freedom of association. However, other standards such as the secrecy of the vote or the fairness of the electoral process may be significantly impacted by the use of such technologies.

As a result, there have been initiatives in recent years to evolve these international electoral standards in order to cope with the challenges of using voting and counting technologies. The Council of Europe's 2004 Recommendation on Legal, Operational and Technical Standards for E-voting [428] did much to set the agenda for this adaptation of existing standards for electronic voting technologies. The Council of Europe has followed up this recommendation with the publication of an e-voting handbook [128] presenting guidelines for implementing e-enabled elections and guidelines on certification and transparency for e-enabled elections [430]; [431]. In 2006 the European Commission also published a report titled Methodological Guide to Electoral Assistance, which covers support for the introduction of election technologies, including electronic voting technologies and the standards that might be applicable in their use [166].

The OSCE's Office for Democratic Institutions and Human Rights [242]; [244]; [240], the Organization of American States [432], The Carter Center [137] and the National Democratic Institute for International Affairs [470] have also approached the issue of standards for electronic voting technologies from the perspective of observing elections in which these technologies are used. Elections using electronic voting technologies are inherently less transparent than paper-based elections, as electronic events take place which cannot be observed with the naked eye [244]. This makes it more difficult to determine the credibility of the electoral process and whether any fraud or mistakes have taken place in their conduct. In fact leading experts in the field of e-voting argue that the lack of transparency with electronic voting systems is the greatest challenge facing the implementation of such technologies [354].

As a result, the use of electronic voting technologies has presented particular problems for organizations attempting to observe and evaluate the conduct of elections. Publications by these leading election observation organizations are consequently highly relevant to the debate on emerging standards for the use of electronic voting and counting technologies.

In analyzing these important publications it is clear that some trends are emerging in the recommendations being made by all of these organizations about the conduct of elections using electronic voting technologies. Common themes can be seen in the following areas:

■ **Transparency** – Transparency is related to many of the more specific emerging standards below, but is important enough to merit discussion separately. Transparency is a general electoral standard, but one which is particularly challenged by the use of electronic voting technologies. Special focus needs to be placed on the realization of transparency while using these technologies. This means that as much as possible of the operation of the process using electronic voting technologies is transparent or observable [428]; [432]. However, access should be provided for observers in a manner that does not obstruct the electoral process [470].

■ **Public Confidence** – Closely related to and relying heavily upon transparency, is the requirement that voters understand and have confidence in the electronic voting technology being used [428]. Public confidence requires that stakeholders are involved in the introduction of electronic voting technologies [137], are provided information so they understand the technologies being used [428]; [432], simulations of the systems take place [470] and voters are informed well in advance about the introduction and what is required to participate [428]; [244].

■ **Usability** – Electronic voting technologies must be easy to understand and use for as many voters as possible [428]; [244]; [432]. Users (voters) should be involved in the design of electronic voting technologies [428] and in public testing [244]. Furthermore, these electronic voting technologies must try to maximize the accessibility of the voting system for persons with disabilities [428]; [244]; [432]; [470] and afford voters the possibility to stop and cancel their vote before confirmation of their choice [428]; [244].

- **System Certification** – Electronic voting technologies must be certified by an independent body before use and periodically thereafter. This ensures the system continues to meet the requirements of the electoral jurisdiction as well as the technical specifications for the system. Furthermore, the certification process should be conducted in a transparent manner providing electoral stakeholders access to information on the process [428]; [244]; [470]; [137].

- **System Testing** – Any electronic voting system should be subjected to a comprehensive range of testing before it is approved for use by an EMB [428]; [244]; [432]; [137]. This testing should take place transparently and with access for political actors [432]; [470].

- **System Security** – The opportunities for systematic manipulation of the results mean that system security needs to be taken extremely seriously. Security measures need to be taken to ensure that data cannot be lost in the event of breakdown, only authorized voters can use an electronic voting or counting system, system configuration and results generated can be authenticated and only authorized persons are allowed to access electronic voting, counting and results management functionality [428]; [137]; [432]. Attempts to hack into electronic voting machines or the election management system into which results are received, need to be detected, reported and protected against [244].

- **Audit and Recount** – Electronic voting technologies must be auditable [428]; [244]; [432] so it is possible to determine whether they operated correctly. It must be possible to use an electronic voting system to conduct a recount [428]; [244]. Such recounts must involve meaningful manual recounts of ballots cast electronically [244] and not merely a repetition of the electronic result already provided [470].

- **Voter Verified Audit Trail** – In addition to the above requirements for auditability in any electronic voting system, it must also be possible to assure voters that their votes are being counted as cast [137] while also ensuring that the secrecy of the vote is not compromised [244]. This requires that electronic voting systems create an audit trail which is verifiable. It should provide the voter with a token/code with which to perform the verification externally and not show the way in which the vote was cast. The most common solution to this for in-person electronic voting machines is through the production of a VVPAT, and this solution is emerging as a standard in this regard [244]; [470]. It should be noted that this VVPAT solution is not appropriate for remote electronic voting which uses electronic voting machines (e.g., internet voting, text message voting, etc.) as there would be nothing to stop a voter from removing the paper record of the vote, making vote buying and voter coercion possible.

- **Mandatory Audit of Results** – The existence of an audit trail for electronic voting systems achieves little if it is not used to verify that the electronic results and the audit trail deliver the same result. Doing so also serves to build public confidence in the operation of the electronic voting technologies. A mandatory audit of the results generated by electronic voting technologies should be required by law and take place for a statistically significant random sample of ballots [429]; [244]; [470].

■ **Secrecy of the Ballot** – The secrecy requirement is not a new standard but it is one that is made more difficult by electronic voting technologies. This is especially the case for remote electronic voting systems where voters have to first identify themselves and vote electronically using the same interface. The use of electronic voting technologies must comply with the need for secrecy of the ballot [428]; [244]; [137]; [432].

■ **Incremental Implementation** – Whenever electronic voting technologies are introduced they should be deployed in an incremental manner and should start with less important elections. This will allow public understanding and trust to develop in the new system, and provide time to deal with problems and resistance [244]; [137].

It is far too early at this stage to say that international standards have completed their evolution in order to adapt to the challenges posed by electronic voting technologies. Nevertheless, the trends that can be seen in these emerging electoral standards for the use of electronic voting technologies should be carefully considered as any new technology is assessed.

2.4 Decision in Principle

The "decision in principle" is the first stage in the feasibility study process. This critical stage aims to identify the objectives that are sought through the introduction of new technology before measuring available technologies against these objectives. Establishing this foundation, the agenda for change, first and foremost will do much to ensure that a well-considered decision is initially taken as to whether electronic voting technologies can meet the requirements of the elections in question. The issue of cost will also be addressed in this stage. This issue determines whether the technology is feasible from a financial perspective and whether the benefits to be obtained from the technology are sufficient to justify additional costs.

All the components identified in this stage are seen as important in reaching a decision in principle on the feasibility of electronic voting technologies. Other issues, specific to the electoral context, may be included for consideration. There is logic to the order in which these components are listed. The suggestion is that this order be roughly maintained while implementing this stage of the feasibility study. Components later in this stage are more productive if preceded by the earlier ones. However, the components of the decision in principle may need to be adapted to the specific electoral requirements being considered.

2.4.1 Decision in Principle Foundations

There are a number of building blocks to a well-constructed feasibility study process that should be clearly established at the start of the process.

2.4.1.1 Feasibility Study Mandate

It is critical at the outset of the feasibility study that the mandate of the study is clearly defined by the authority which initiated the feasibility study. This mandate should clearly outline the purpose of the study, the organization of the project, the timeline for the study, and the outputs of the study.

- **Purpose** – The objectives the study intends to meet need to be clearly identified, specifically the kinds of technologies that it is meant to address. A clear definition of the technologies to be addressed will have significant impact on the conduct of the feasibility study.

- **Feasibility Study Project Organization** – Management of the feasibility study will need to be entrusted to an organizational unit which plans and oversees the process. Often a Feasibility Study Committee will be established for this purpose.

  Including multiple stakeholders in the Feasibility Study Committee is an advantage because these voting technologies straddle the boundaries between legal, technical, social and political considerations. The Election Management Body (EMB) will need to be part of the Feasibility Study Committee since they will have a unique perspective on the possibility of implementing voting technologies. Information technology, government stakeholders, political party representatives, election-related civil society organizations (e.g., domestic observer organizations), organizations providing election technical assistance to the EMB, technology institutes and parliamentarians might all be considered for membership of the Feasibility Committee.

  A balance will need to be found between including stakeholders in the Feasibility Study Committee process and the effectiveness of the Committee.

- **Timeline** – An indication should be provided to the Feasibility Study Committee as to how long it should be before they report back to the mandating authority on their findings. A suitable amount of time should be provided for the study. A minimum of six months is required for a suitably comprehensive decision in principle to be reached. The later stages of the feasibility study could take years to complete as electronic voting technology specifications are developed, pilot machines procured and tested, legislation amended, procedures developed, training and voter education delivered, post-pilot consultations conducted and follow-on pilot projects implemented.

■ **Format of Report and Recommendations** – The mandate of the feasibility study should also indicate the recipient and the format of the report from the Committee on the decision in principle. The report may be required to provide recommendations on whether to proceed with piloting electronic technologies, on the most appropriate technology, specifications for the technologies recommended, a plan and timeline for proceeding with pilot testing, the budget for piloting and full adoption of the recommended technology, etc.

2.4.1.2 Vendor Relations

A dialogue with vendors is an essential part of any feasibility study. Information is required from the vendors about the technologies in order to understand the products which are currently available on the market. The information initially provided by vendors may leave many questions unanswered. This will require further clarification from the vendors. Through the course of the feasibility study the requirements which these technologies are being measured against may evolve, necessitating follow-on requests to vendors to see if they can still meet these changing requirements.

Many countries have clear regulations defining the way in which public institutions can communicate with companies which are, or may be, likely to submit tender proposals. The Feasibility Study Committee needs to ensure it understands any procurement and vendor relations regulations before it determines its communication strategy with vendors. It is suggested that one point of contact be established for the Committee's contacts with vendors. This point of contact (POC) should, to the extent possible, ensure that the same information is provided to all vendors. The POC may consider having the Committee approve all communications with vendors.

2.4.2 Feasibility Study Committee Working Groups

A comprehensive feasibility study needs to investigate the use of electronic voting technologies from a range of perspectives and deal with complex technical issues requiring the input of specialized personnel (e.g., lawyers, IT experts and communications specialists). Therefore, it may make sense to divide the work of the Feasibility Study Committee into several working groups where specialized personnel can be called.

The list of issues below represents the minimum key issues that should be addressed by the Feasibility Study Committee. Separate working groups need not be created to deal with each of these issues. It may be possible for one working group to cover several issues.

2.4.2.1 Issue 1 – Assessment of the Current System of Voting and Counting

A key component of any feasibility study on the use of electronic voting technologies will be to determine what the objectives are in changing the current system. Only by fully defining this will it be possible to determine if the available solutions can meet these requirements and whether it is feasible to implement them for the elections in question.

Answers to a number of questions need to be fully understood at the outset, including: What are the strengths and weaknesses of the current system? Can some weaknesses be addressed through reform of the current system, and what would be required to do so? What improvements are not possible to achieve through reform of the current system?

Answers to these questions are fundamental to the entire feasibility study, as they identify the challenges in the current system and the objectives for any change. The other issue topics build upon these findings.

2.4.2.2 Issue 2 – Assessment of the Advantages and Disadvantages Offered by Voting Technologies

Even if a significant agenda for change is identified, using electronic voting technologies may not be the solution. It is also important to recognize that using such technology presents new challenges to the conduct of elections.

Consideration of this issue will consist of two aspects, a general assessment in principle of what technology has to offer in terms of electronic voting technologies and an assessment of the solutions currently offered by a range of vendors. In order to do this, electronic voting technology vendors will need to be contacted and asked to provide information on their current products.

Consideration of this issue will need to address questions such as: What advantages and disadvantages does electronic voting offer compared to the current balloting systems? Are there external infrastructure requirements (such as power, communications, etc.) and resource requirements within the EMB that would be essential in implementing electronic voting, and do these currently exist? If not, what is required to provide the necessary infrastructure and resources? What would be the requirements a new electronic voting system would need to fulfill in order to meet the objectives for change identified? What specific challenges would the EMB face in implementing electronic voting?

Consideration of these questions forms a critical component of any feasibility study. It is essential that sufficient thought is given to these issues as failure to do so could fundamentally affect the success or failure of any technology project. Of particular importance is the development of a set of requirements that electronic voting would be required to meet. If this is not properly defined then the solution recommended by the feasibility study may not be appropriate for the electoral process.

2.4.2.3 Issue 3 – Review of IT Security Aspects

System security is an incredibly important feature of electronic voting technologies. These technologies are inherently less transparent than the use of paper ballots, where all steps in voting and counting are observable. If an electronic voting or counting system is to be properly trusted by electoral stakeholders it is important that the security challenges presented by the use of the technology are understood. Mechanisms should be in place to mitigate these security challenges and any security breaches should be easily identified.

There are a number of questions that need to be considered by the working group on this issue: Will the source code for the electronic voting or counting technology be open source or not? How will the source code be tested and certified? How will it be verified that the source code used for the conduct of elections is the same as the one tested and certified? What mechanisms are in place to ensure that the new system is protected against tampering? If results are electronically transmitted from electronic voting machines to a regional or central tabulation facility, how will the results be encrypted to ensure there is no unauthorized access or modification to the results?

The working group addressing these technical issues will need to make sure that it is able to clearly articulate the results of the discussions around these issues to the Feasibility Study Committee. This will be very important in order to provide technical requirements to the working group dealing with issue 2 above. It will also help define the technical components of any later procurement process and ensure any legal amendments properly address the technical issues discussed and agreed upon.

2.4.2.4   Issue 4 – Determining Technical Feasibility

Once a set of requirements for a possible electronic voting solution has been defined it will need to be determined whether products exist, or could be developed, which meet these requirements. A full consideration of this issue obviously requires information on current products. This information should be provided by vendors of electronic voting technologies. In order to avoid any bias in terms of which vendors are contacted, clear criteria for contacting vendors should be drawn up and all vendors which meet these criteria should be included in the process.

Once information has been received from a suitable number of vendors, each recommended product should be measured to see the degree of compliance with the set of requirements. This analysis of electronic voting technology products against the requirements will determine whether the use of these technologies for the elections in question is technically feasible or not.

If the result of this analysis is that no electronic voting technology products are found which meet the set of requirements, and therefore the needs of the elections in question, then a number of options are available.

Firstly, the requirements might be reconsidered to see if they were too demanding, and if a less demanding set of requirements might still suffice. Secondly, additional suppliers might be contacted to see if they have voting solutions which meet the requirements. Finally, suppliers could be approached to see if they could develop a new product that meets the requirements.

It may be that all these options fail to provide electronic voting technology products which meet the requirements identified in the feasibility study. In this case, the Feasibility Study Committee would conclude that electronic voting technologies on the market do not meet the needs of the electoral situation.

Finding that using electronic voting technologies for elections is not feasible is not a failure for the study. In fact, if the previous steps in the study are conducted comprehensively then the study will lead to a well-defined set of requirements for an appropriate electronic voting technology solution. This set of requirements will remain valid and can be used to reassess, on a periodic basis, any newly developed products.

2.4.2.5   Issue 5 – Cost Benefit Analysis

Should an electronic voting solution, or solutions, be found which meet the requirements then a further assessment will need to be made as to whether the implementation of these solutions would, on balance, be beneficial and cost effective.

There are two components to this analysis. Before the analysis can be conducted a limited number of electronic voting solutions will need to be selected for cost benefit analysis purposes, as the process is quite complex to conduct. The best electronic voting solution and the cheapest solution, which still meets the requirements, should be selected. Another electronic voting solution which is mid range in terms of cost and in terms of meeting the requirements could also be selected.

The first step is to identify the benefits that each solution provides compared to the current system of balloting. Similarly a list of disadvantages/challenges associated with each solution should be identified. The comparison of these two lists of advantages and disadvantages of the different electronic voting solutions will show the overall benefits of using each solution.

There is no predefined formula involved in this assessment of beneficiality. It could be that there are many disadvantages involved in using an electronic voting solution and only one benefit. However, that benefit could be of such critical importance that it would still support the introduction of electronic voting technologies. In addition, the importance attached to each advantage and disadvantage will be determined by the particular electoral circumstance. Therefore this analysis of advantages versus disadvantages is something that can be done in a committee format, but is probably something that should be consulted on very widely among internal and external electoral stakeholders to ensure there is consensus on the recommendations resulting from this assessment.

The second stage of this cost benefit analysis requires a comprehensive cost analysis of the technology and a comparison of costs associated with using this technology vis-à-vis the existing system of balloting and counting — likely paper-based voting.

A key component of this cost analysis is to recognize that the costs associated with using electronic voting technologies should not be considered solely on the basis of the initial investment but over the life cycle of the voting machines and systems. This means that the first election using electronic voting might be extremely expensive, but later ones much less so as the technology is reused.

It is also vitally important that all of the costs associated with the current system and any proposed electronic voting system be understood and factored into the comparative cost calculation. This means not only the cost of purchasing the electronic voting technology, but also its maintenance, storage, transportation, etc. Likewise, all of the costs associated with paper balloting need to be considered, not just the printing of ballots, but their transportation and storage, replacing ballot boxes and voting booths, destruction of ballots at the end of the process, etc.

A proper cost comparison of the current system versus an electronic voting system will need to calculate all of the associated costs of elections over the life cycle of the voting technology (likely somewhere between 10 and 20 years). The cost implications over this period will then need to be considered alongside the assessment of the advantages/disadvantages of each system.

It is likely that the "balance sheet" will be very mixed. There may be a significant additional cost involved in using electronic voting technologies but some important benefits resulting as well as some potential problems. It will be up to the Feasibility Study Committee to decide whether the benefits to be realized by using electronic voting technologies are sufficient to justify any additional expenditure and make its recommendation accordingly.

2.4.2.6   Issue 6 – Institutional Capacity

A critically important issue for the working groups to consider is whether the institutional capacity exists to implement electronic voting technologies. This issue does not only relate to the EMB, but also to other bodies which would support the conduct of elections using these technologies.

A number of key areas should be considered in order to reach this assessment:

■ The EMB will need to be organizationally strong enough to effectively manage the complex technical, IT and logistic challenges presented by implementing electronic voting.

■ The EMB's training division will need to be strong enough to communicate the procedural changes necessitated by using electronic voting machines to all staff who will implement them.

■ Staff working in polling or counting centers will have to be sufficiently IT literate to operate voting machines.

■ Strong voter education mechanisms will need to exist to educate voters on how to use the electronic voting system.

■ The independent certification of electronic voting and counting technologies is a very important aspect of building trust in the new technologies, and there should be independent capacity to conduct this testing and certification.

It may be that in assessing institutional capacities required for successful electronic voting projects, some or all of the assessments may state that the capacity does not exist. This will need to be added into the overall consideration of the decision in principle. However, a negative assessment of the capacity on any of these aspects of institutional capacity need not be an insurmountable obstacle. It may be that the capacity does not currently exist, but could be developed by certain strategies. Where this is the case any insight into possible strategies to develop the required capacity will represent important additional recommendations from the working group.

2.4.2.7   Issue 7 – Legal Reform Issues

The final issue for consideration concerns the possibility for using electronic voting technologies under the existing electoral legal framework. It may well be that the existing electoral legal framework makes reference to physical ballot boxes and ballot box seals, to actual ballot papers and the ways in which ballots are counted and adjudicated. Obviously processes do not occur in the same way with an electronic voting machine. The working group needs to assess whether it would still be in compliance with existing law.

The working group dealing with this issue may wish, and may be advised, to take a more comprehensive look at the legislation governing elections and how it would relate to the implementation of an electronic voting technology. Merely adapting the existing legislation so it does not preclude the use of voting technologies is not sufficient to properly regulate the use of these technologies.

Proper legislation and regulations governing the use of electronic voting will need to cover issues such as certification requirements, system and ballot security, transparency and audit mechanisms, dealing with audit discrepancies, challenges and disputes, and recounts.

The process of legal amendments may be a lengthy one, therefore, if legal changes are required in order to use electronic voting or counting technologies then it is prudent to start the process as early as possible, based on the findings of the working group.

2.4.3   Study Trips

The Feasibility Study Committee may consider the possibility of conducting one or more study trips to see other countries which have used or are using electronic voting technologies. It would make sense to visit countries which are implementing technologies of interest to the Feasibility Study Committee.

Any study trip should meet with a range of stakeholders, including the EMB, the technology provider, political party representatives, civil society representatives, voting activists and domestic election observation organizations. The study trip should seek to address the following issues:

- Types of technologies that have been or are being used.

- Process followed in taking a decision to adopt the technology.

- Stakeholder opinions on the advantages and disadvantages of these technologies.

- Challenges presented by using the technologies, and the ways in which these challenges had been met.

- Country specific factors which led to the success or failure of using these technologies.

The study trip should result in a formal report outlining the findings on all of the above issues.

2.4.4   *Vendor Demonstration*

There is only so much that can be revealed about a system by reading technical specifications and marketing materials about electronic voting solutions. A fuller understanding can only be achieved by seeing electronic voting technologies in action, initially through a demonstration. The demonstration environment allows for a detailed discussion between the Feasibility Study Committee and the vendors about the ways in which their products work, or could be adapted to work. Again it is important that a wide range of vendors are invited to present their products at the demonstration so any perception of favoritism in the process is countered.

It is recommended that participation in any vendor demonstration be widened to include representatives from political parties and civil society. These are important stakeholders in the electoral process; providing them access to the vendor demonstration will help their understanding of recommendations made by the Feasibility Study Committee. It also means that consultations held with these stakeholders can take place from a more informed starting point.

The timing of the vendor demonstration in the process of the feasibility study is important. If held too early in the process, the Feasibility Study Committee will not be sufficiently informed about the relevant issues.

2.4.5 Stakeholder Consultation

As identified earlier, it is essential that stakeholders participate in the feasibility study process so they can understand the work of the Feasibility Study Committee. Their participation also ensures they have the opportunity to present their opinions and concerns about the possible use of electronic voting technologies. This inclusion and openness is more likely to lead to acceptance of the resulting recommendation by the Feasibility Study Committee and should ensure that those recommendations take into consideration a wide range of perspectives in the use of electronic voting technologies.

At a minimum, consultation should be conducted with political party and civil society representatives, especially domestic observer organizations. However, this consultation could also be extended to key media representatives, political science institutes, government stakeholders, international election observers and technology industry leaders.

2.4.6 Decision in Principle

The decision in principle will be a result of considering all the issues outlined above — technical feasibility, beneficiality, financial feasibility and stakeholder acceptance. These various findings will have to be balanced against each other in order to reach the decision in principle.

If electronic voting technologies are found to be technically feasible and supported by stakeholders then the decision in principle may be that there should be no further steps to implement if the benefits to be achieved are not sufficiently greater than the disadvantages or the cost is too excessive or does not justify the expected benefits.

Even if the technologies are technically feasible, provide significant benefits over the existing system and are not excessively expensive, the decision may still be taken to not proceed if there is significant stakeholder concern or resistance to the introduction of these technologies. While it is not impossible to implement such technologies without the support of key stakeholders, to do so would be a risky strategy potentially leading to a wasted investment in electronic voting technology.

The Feasibility Study Committee will need to assess other less tangible costs and benefits, such as public and political perception. The Committee may need to consider both change management and risk management strategies in order to address issues identified during such an assessment.

Ultimately the decision in principle is a very difficult one to determine and a range of factors need to be considered by the Feasibility Study Committee. It should be recognized that to take an affirmative initial decision in principle does not commit the EMB to anything at this stage. The next stages in the feasibility study process are experimental. Therefore, a decision to proceed to these next stages does not mean that a decision has been made to fully implement the technology.

Whatever decision is reached at this stage of the feasibility study it will be important to ensure that the reasoning behind the decision is clearly elaborated by the Feasibility Study Committee, including any assumptions. This ensures that even if the decision in principle is to not proceed with investigating the use of electronic voting technologies, the work invested in the feasibility study can be used in the future as a starting point for reconsideration if requirements, financial considerations or electronic voting products change.

Should the Feasibility Study Committee decide there is sufficient reason to continue its consideration of using electronic voting technologies, then it will need to recommend that a pilot project be conducted and clearly define the mandate and parameters for this pilot. There are, however, a number of prerequisites that need to be in place before the actual pilot can be initiated.

2.5   Pilot Project Prerequisites

It is important to recognize there are certain issues that need to be addressed before any pilot project can be initiated. Other prerequisites are essential if the pilot is to be as effective as possible. These issues are fundamental to the way in which the pilot project is planned and conducted and should be established before this pilot process starts.

2.5.1   Pilot Project Mandate

Any pilot project conducted needs to be provided a clear mandate. There are a number of issues that will need to be defined to provide this clear mandate — the type of pilot project to be conducted, pilot locations, technological solutions that should be piloted (single solution or multiple solutions) and the issues that need to be explored in detail through the pilot.

2.5.1.1   Type of Pilot

The type of pilot can vary in a number of different ways and situations. Options in this regard are as follows:

- **Mock Pilot** – Electronic voting technology solutions could be piloted in an entirely different electoral situation, a mock electoral situation outside of the normal electoral process.

- **Parallel Pilot** – Electronic voting technologies could be piloted alongside an existing voting process such that all voters cast their ballots as normal using the existing system and then have the chance to cast a mock ballot.

- **Optional Pilot** – Electronic voting technologies could be piloted alongside the existing voting process, with voters having the option to either use the existing system or the electronic voting system.

- **Compulsory Pilot** – This type of pilot exclusively uses electronic voting technologies for selected members of the electorate. These voters would have to cast their ballots using the technology and these votes would provide part of the overall result.

The kinds of people who would participate in the pilot would vary with the different types of pilot, and it is important that whichever option is selected will ensure that a good cross section of voters participate in the pilot.

Clearly the best option for obtaining a definitive assessment of how the general electorate responds to using electronic voting technologies is where a section of the electorate is required to use the technology being piloted and is not able to opt out. This kind of pilot ensures that real electoral conditions occur. However, this is also risky. If the electronic voting solution being piloted is defective in some way or is seen to favor some of the electorate over others, then its compulsory use could be challenged in the courts at a later date. A successful challenge could call into question the validity of the election result in which the pilot was conducted and possibly require a repeat election to remedy the situation — for example, an electronic voting pilot in Finland was challenged and had to be re-run (Council of Europe 2010, 20 [429]).

2.5.1.2   Pilot Locations

The mandate will need to define the scale of the pilot to be conducted, in terms of number of locations that it will be held in, and some parameters as to where these locations might be.

It is advisable that electronic voting technologies be piloted in multiple locations, so that a cross section of the electorate can test the use of the selected technologies. This will require that consideration be given to the different kinds of voters that should be provided the opportunity to test the use of the electronic voting technologies. For example, only testing electronic voting technologies in urban locations would not be advisable as rural voters may have a very different reaction to using these technologies.

It may well also be that there is a range of environmental factors in which electronic voting technologies need to be tested, and therefore pilot locations will need to be selected accordingly. Initial pilots may also be chosen for constituencies/areas which are not contentious politically so as to avoid politically charged scenarios and allow trust to build in the pilot technologies. If the situation permits, a pilot could be conducted first in a single location to primarily test the EMB's ability to cope with the new process, procedures, training, voter education and logistical requirements. Subsequent pilots could be conducted at a number of locations representing a broader variety of the electorate.

Piloting remote electronic voting solutions, such as internet voting, may require a different approach to selecting pilot participants. The selection of participants for a remote electronic voting pilot may be limited by voter identification mechanisms that the remote voting system would utilize. Or the remote voting solution may be targeted at a specific section of the electorate, such as voters abroad, indicating that this entire group should take part in the pilot project.

2.5.1.3   Solutions Being Piloted

The decision in principle may indicate that one electronic voting solution best meets the needs of the electoral process. This does not mean that it has to be the only solution piloted. Likewise, if a specific type of technology is being piloted, then this does not mean that several other solutions cannot be tested as part of the pilot.

The mandate may indicate which specific technology is to be piloted and if a range of solutions or a single solution is to be piloted. It is recommended that more than one electronic voting solution be piloted. This is important if this is the first time these technologies are being investigated, allowing for greater understanding of the various systems. Where the solutions to be piloted have not been made clear in the mandate, this needs to be determined at an early stage of the pilot project management process.

2.5.2   Legislation

The process of taking the decision in principle should have identified if the existing electoral legal framework permits the use of electronic voting technologies, or whether changes are required to allow their use. If existing legislation does not allow the use of electronic voting technologies then the types of pilot identified above (optional or compulsory) will not be possible until legislation is changed to allow these technologies to be used.

Where legislative changes are required, they can be temporary in nature for a specific election or permit the piloting of new technologies on an ongoing basis. The latter approach provides maximum flexibility for the pilot process and means new legislation does not need to be passed for each election in which a pilot takes place. However, changing electoral legislation so that pilots can be conducted at any time could be seen as an invitation to use electronic voting technologies at the discretion of the EMB, and this may not be desirable.

In addition to legislative changes required to allow the use of electronic technologies, it is almost certain that electoral regulations will need to be changed. In most electoral jurisdictions these regulations are passed by the EMB, so changing them is less problematic than changing electoral legislation. It is still essential that the regulations be amended to facilitate the use of electronic voting technologies.

2.5.3 Electronic Voting Technology Specification

The steps conducted during the decision in principle process will help the Feasibility Study Committee, and the EMB, to ensure that any electronic voting technology pilot process is driven by the actual needs of the electoral process. The requirements, previously defined, will be central to drafting a comprehensive request for proposal for the electronic voting technology procurement process. The request for proposal will need to identify the technical specifications which a solution must comply with for it to be considered and also request information on other product and support related issues relevant to the bid selection process.

The technical specification will need to provide the following parameters for vendors to comply with:

■ Type of electronic voting solution for which quotes are being requested (e.g., electronic voting, electronic counting, remote voting solutions, etc.).

■ Scale of the pilot, including number of locations, number of voting machines required, scope of any remote voting pilot and number of registered voters the pilot will need to accommodate.

■ Details of any audit and integrity mechanisms required.

■ The electoral systems that need to be accommodated by the electronic voting technology.

■ Requirements for coping with multiple languages and scripts.

■ Details of any environmental conditions the electronic voting hardware would have to be able to deal with, including independent power requirements and extremes of heat, cold, humidity and dust.

■ Security requirements for the electronic voting technology.

■ Services that will be required from the vendor during the conduct of the pilot project in addition to delivery of the electronic voting solution (e.g., project management services, configuration, training and service support during the voting period in the pilot).

■ Anticipated delivery times for all services and goods to be provided.

■ Project management arrangements that would be put in place by the vendor to coordinate pilot project implementation issues.

Additional information will also be required for the selection process such as information not directly covered by the requirements for change. This information may relate to basic functionality of the electronic voting system, or functionality that all systems will have but will likely be implemented differently on each machine. This information includes issues such as intellectual property rights, election management systems, safety and security features, audit and integrity mechanisms, results transmission mechanisms, maintenance requirements and life expectancy of hardware.

In addition to the information sought in this request for proposal, vendors who submit proposals should be required to commit to implementing their solutions during the pilot in accordance with good practice for the conduct of elections.

2.5.4   Pilot Project Funding

The conduct of a pilot project will entail a number of costs, the least of which may be the procurement of any electronic voting equipment itself. A budget will need to be developed for the conduct of the pilot project. The budget will depend a lot on the scale of the pilot being recommended, and can draw heavily on the costs identified by the working group looking at the financial aspects of using these technologies.

It may be that the budget for the pilot project will be drafted at the same time that the decision in principle to proceed with a pilot is taken. It should almost go without saying that the process of implementing a pilot project cannot start before the budget required to conduct the pilot has been secured.

2.6   Pilot Project

Piloting electronic voting technologies is a way of testing many of the assumptions and conclusions reached during the process of reaching a decision in principle. This includes a practical assessment of actual benefits and disadvantages in using the piloted electronic technologies, the actual costs involved in implementing these technologies and the suitability of the list of requirements developed for electronic technologies. The pilot will also allow the Feasibility Study Committee to assess issues which could only be guessed at during the decision in principle stage of the process, including the ability of voters to properly use the new technology.

A good pilot will need to take into consideration the following issues.

2.6.1   Managing the Pilot Project

Implementation of an electronic voting technology pilot project is an incredibly complex task. It requires a good project management structure to ensure that it is planned effectively and that timelines and objectives are continuously monitored and amended as required. The implementation of the pilot will require a lot of components of the EMB to work effectively together, calling for significant commitment from the EMB to deliver on the various aspects of the project.

Successful management of the pilot will require a Pilot Project Committee, with representatives of all the major EMB functions and possibly also representatives from outside of the EMB. It will also require a dedicated project manager to work full time on the day-to-day management of the project. As well as an operational plan and implementation timeline, the Pilot Project Committee will need to establish a comprehensive risk management plan, especially if the voting technology is to be piloted in a live election.

2.6.2   *Procuring Electronic Voting Technologies*

The process of procuring electronic voting technologies can take some time and needs to be conducted in an open and transparent manner. The EMB needs to ensure it is in control of this procurement process in terms of defining the requirements for the technologies to be piloted. The process must not be vendor driven, with vendors telling the EMB what it is that they require.

Sufficient time will need to be provided during the procurement process for vendors to properly respond to the many facets of the request for proposals. A reasonable timeframe for such a request for proposals would be in the region of four to six weeks. Vendors should be allowed to seek clarifications on aspects of the request for proposals at a predefined date part way through the procurement process.

The procurement process itself should be open and impartial. Request for proposals should be widely published through the media and on the sponsoring institution's website; decisions should be taken according to pre-established evaluation criteria.

It is clear that the specification and resulting proposals will be complex and detailed documents. A Proposal Review Committee, possibly the entire Pilot Project Committee (depending on the size of this Committee), should review the proposals received and agree on the ranking against different evaluation criteria. On the basis of this, a recommendation will be made on which electronic voting solution, or solutions, will be procured for the pilot project.

2.6.3   *Testing and Certification*

Once delivered, it is essential that an EMB ensure that an electronic voting system not only meet the specifications developed for the system, but also meet the requirements of the electoral environment. There are many different types of testing and certification. The Council of Europe identifies the following in its E-Voting Handbook: acceptance testing; performance testing; stress testing; security testing; usability testing, and; review of the source code [429]. Conducting all these tests takes time and it is important that time for full testing is made available in the project timeline.

In addition to comprehensive testing of electronic voting technologies prior to use, it is increasingly seen as good practice to have these systems certified prior to use [428]. The purpose of certification is similar to testing, in that it determines whether the electronic voting technology operates correctly, but it is conducted by an independent body. There are no standards yet to cover how the testing and certification process should be conducted and each country conducting these processes has utilized its own solution to this challenge.

2.6.4   Polling and Counting Procedures

Many aspects of electronic technologies will likely be different from the existing system of balloting, especially if the existing system is a paper balloting system. The procedures for storage of the electronic voting machines, pre-polling preparations, transportation, security, placement in the polling station, demonstrating an empty ballot box, initiating polling, activation of the electronic voting machines for the voter and reporting of results will be different.

These changes in procedure will need to be carefully considered by a competent and experienced group of election management officials, in consultation with other stakeholders.

2.6.5   Voter Education

Educating voters on the use of new electronic voting technologies is essential [428], and must start before they are confronted with the new system on election day. A change in balloting system, especially if moving from paper balloting to an electronic voting solution, will be confusing for voters. This confusion, and problems in using electronic voting technologies, can be mitigated to a large extent by effective voter education in advance of the pilot project.

This voter education will need to communicate the existence of the pilot project and the type of pilot being conducted. Voter messages will need to be conducted in a targeted manner as the pilot will only be in a limited geographic area.

2.6.6   Training

Just as the education of voters in the use of piloted electronic voting technologies is essential to the success of the pilot, so is proper training of staff who will use the technologies. As already discussed, the procedures for many, if not most, aspects of polling and counting may be changed by the introduction of these technologies. Not only must new procedures be developed, but training on these new procedures needs to be effectively delivered.

This training will be required not only by polling staff, but also the staff required to prepare the electronic voting hardware at centralized facilities and staff who receive the results provided by the electronic voting technology. Procedures need to be drafted and tested and training materials for these procedures developed. These procedures need to cover the configuration of the hardware, setup of any machines in the polling station, conduct of polling, close of polls, production of results, transfer of results for tabulation and receipt of results for tabulation.

2.6.7   Stakeholder Outreach

Getting the support of key stakeholders will be important to the perceived and actual success of any pilot for electronic voting technologies. Providing access to the technology prior to elections will be one way of reaching out to key stakeholders. However, additional efforts to inform stakeholders should also be pursued.

Local candidates, party representatives, domestic observers, media and community representatives should be briefed by the EMB on the pilot project at the beginning of the planning process. They will need to be informed about the technology being piloted, the reasons why it is being piloted and the benefits that it is expected to bring to the process.

If stakeholders can be won over to the pilot process, they can be strong supporters of the process, acting as a channel for key voter education information and providing vital mechanisms for feedback on the success, or otherwise, of the pilot project.

2.6.8   Election Day Support

The piloting of an electronic voting system will likely involve many significant changes in the process of administering elections. Regardless of how good the training and documentation that is provided to electoral officials, there will inevitably be some problems in applying the procedures and training when electoral officials come to use electronic voting systems on election day.

A dedicated, centralized help desk is a good way of dealing with the many questions likely to be raised when implementing the kinds of changes to voting procedures that occur with the introduction of an electronic voting system. The help desk should be available from at least a few days before the conduct of elections to deal with questions that polling officials may have as they are issued electronic voting equipment.

The help desk operators must be thoroughly trained in all aspects of the electronic voting system, they must have a detailed help desk manual available and a shared log of issues raised and solved. They must have a set methods for dealing with issues not covered in manuals and training, which could include a direct hotline to one or more senior election officials authorized to make decisions as required.

2.6.9   Observation of the Pilot Project

The same rights to observe the electoral process should be applicable to an electronic voting technology pilot project [428]. The EMB may have to take additional measures to facilitate and encourage this observation for a number of reasons.

The conduct of elections using an electronic voting technology will be very different and will require special training for observers, media and political party and candidate agents that wish to observe the pilot. This training will be needed to ensure that these groups understand how the new system works, but also that they understand how they can and should observe the conduct of electronic voting technologies.

Furthermore, as observers, media and political representatives are key stakeholders in the process. Their trust in the system being piloted will be essential and, therefore, they should be actively encouraged to observe. This will build their understanding of the system being piloted and allow them to provide feedback to the Pilot Project Committee during the pilot project evaluation stage.

2.6.10   Mandatory Audit

As discussed earlier, the ability to verify the operation and audit the results of an electronic voting system is an emerging standard with respect to electronic voting technologies [428]. The way in which this auditability is provided for will vary depending on the type of electronic voting solution in question (e.g., it will be different for electronic voting systems, electronic counting systems and especially for remote electronic voting systems).

The audit of electronic voting pilots is necessary to ensure that the accuracy of pilot project results, both for the EMB but also in order to build the confidence of stakeholders. Therefore, for an electronic voting pilot the audits of the results should be mandatory. The (generally paper) audit trail should be manually counted and the results compared to the electronic results generated. Ideally this audit will take place in every location where the technology was piloted. This may not be possible for a larger pilot project. If only a sample of pilot locations is being audited it will be important to randomly select this sample and only make the selection known after the close of polling and counting. The audit should be fully observable by election observers, the media and political party and candidate agents.

2.6.11   Pilot Project Evaluation

A comprehensive post-pilot assessment of the pilot project is essential. It would not be enough to conclude that polling seemed to go smoothly, if it did. The post-pilot assessment needs to be conducted from the perspective of every key stakeholder in the process. Perceptions of these stakeholders about the use of the electronic voting technologies will be critical to any future adoption of the technology.

This pilot project evaluation needs to collect opinions, at a minimum, from the following stakeholders:

■ Voters who used the electronic voting technology

■ Voters who did not use the electronic voting technology

■ EMB staff involved in preparing the electronic voting technology for use

■ Polling staff using the electronic voting technology

■ Election management staff involved in the receipt and tabulation of results

■ Observers (domestic and international)

■ Candidates, and candidate and party agents

■ Representatives of other key stakeholders with a specific interest (e.g., people with disabilities if special voting mechanisms are being implemented for such voters)

The results of the pilot project will need to be assessed using many different methods, from statistical data collected about the use of the electronic voting technology to qualitative analysis of the process from the perspectives of key stakeholders.

In terms of statistical measures used to analyze the effects of using electronic voting technologies, the following will need to be considered: turnout; speed of voting; speed of results; complaints received; number of blank votes; help desk statistics; results of the audit; and election-related violence incidents. These statistics will need to be contextualized; for example a rise in turnout might be a result of a tight local electoral race and not the use of electronic voting.

These quantitative measures can only provide so much information about the pilot, they need to be supplemented by qualitative assessments of the following kinds of issues and questions: voters' experience with using the voting technology; whether the use of electronic voting resulted in voters not participating; polling station setup and operation; the process of polling; the process of closing the polls and generating results; audit procedures; the logistics of configuration, delivery, security, retrieval and storage of the voting machines; voting machine and system security; observation of the process; and comparison with the existing system of balloting. This qualitative data can be collected through a number of mechanisms, including interviews with different stakeholders, focus groups and surveys.

The evaluation of the pilot should be written up into a Pilot Project Report covering the process of conducting the pilot project, the conclusions and recommended next steps with respect to implementing electronic voting technologies.

2.7   The Decision on Adoption

The Pilot Project Report will need to be carefully reviewed by the Feasibility Study Committee, if it is different from the Pilot Project Committee. The Feasibility Study Committee may decide to accept, reject or amend the conclusions and recommendations of the Pilot Project Report.

A number of general conclusions and next steps may be reached as a result of the pilot project:

- **Not Proceed with Electronic Voting Technologies** – It may be decided that electronic voting technologies either do not meet the needs of the elections in question, or they do meet the needs but the benefits to be gained do not justify the resources and effort required to implement them or the disruption caused by implementing them. In either case it will be important to clearly identify the reasons why the recommendation is made to not proceed. This will be important in the future. If cost, functionality or ease of implementing the technologies changes, then this recommendation can be easily revisited.

- **Additional Piloting** – For a number of reasons it may be decided that a recommendation cannot be made to proceed with the implementation of electronic voting technologies, but also that investigation into their use should not be ended.

  It may be that the original specification developed for the electronic voting technologies was defective or insufficient, that solutions with different functionality or features would be better suited to the electoral environment. It may be that in the final analysis the electronic voting solutions provided did not properly meet the specification. The pilot project report may conclude that voter education was insufficient or the procedures used during the pilot were not adequate. Any of these conclusions would indicate that the piloting of electronic voting technologies should continue, as long as the anticipated benefits were still justified by the previous pilot findings.

  The initial pilot may also have been on a very small scale. Even if the results were very positive it may be decided that before a recommendation is made to move towards full implementation the pilot needs to be repeated, with an expanded scale and scope in order to better test the electronic voting solution. In fact, it makes sense to pilot electronic voting technologies on multiple occasions before moving ahead with a full-scale implementation.

- **Adoption of Electronic Voting Technologies** – If the pilot project was successful, demonstrating that electronic voting technologies worked effectively and delivered significant benefits to the electoral process, then the recommendation may be to proceed with the full-scale implementation of the technology. As indicated above, such a recommendation should not be based on a single, small-scale pilot, but on the successful conduct of a series of pilots or a single large-scale pilot.

Should the adoption of electronic voting technologies be recommended, it is still important to recognize that there may be important lessons to learn from the pilot project. Time must be provided so that lessons from the pilot can be properly adapted before the full adoption of electronic voting technologies. This may require technical specifications, polling and counting procedures, training plans and voter education schemes to be reconsidered and redrafted. The procurement process will most likely have to start anew; given the potential changes and the larger size of the contract for electronic voting products. Failure to learn from the pilot, however, could have serious implications for the success of the larger-scale adoption of electronic voting technologies.

Even where the recommendation is to move towards the full adoption of electronic voting technologies, the recommendation may be to move towards this adoption in a staggered manner, as other countries have done (such as India, which took 18 years to move from the first pilot to full national implementation). Such staggered adoption of electronic voting technologies may make a great deal of sense as it allows for the financial burden to be spread over several budget cycles. However, such staggered implementation may also be problematic as it entails fundamental differences in the way in which voting rights are applied for different voters.

At this stage of the process these recommendations should only be considered as preliminary. In the interests of openness and transparency it is important that these preliminary recommendations be subject to consultation with key stakeholders. The consultation process should be used to explain the details of the pilot project to stakeholders, the conclusions reached and the recommendations being made with respect to the adoption of electronic voting technologies.

It is to be hoped that this consultation process will complement feedback previously received by stakeholders throughout the process, but this may not be the case. Should the opinions of stakeholders be consistently opposed to the recommendations of the Feasibility Study Committee, then the causes and consequences of such disagreement will need to be carefully considered. It would be a brave, possibly foolhardy, EMB that proceeded with adopting an electronic voting solution against the opposition of all or most of the key stakeholders in the process.

Once the Feasibility Study Report has been finalized, after this consultative process, the full report should be made public and the main recommendations issued through a press release by the Feasibility Study Committee.

Acknowledgment

This chapter is largely based on a book written for the International Foundation for Electoral Systems [259], with many sections summarized and updated from that publication.

REAL-WORLD
E-VOTING IN
NATIONAL
ELECTIONS

Chapter 3

Overview of Current State of E-Voting Worldwide

Carlos Vegas

eVoting Legal Lab
`carlos.vegas@europe.com`

Jordi Barrat

eVoting Legal Lab
`jordi.barrat@urv.cat`

CONTENTS

3.1 Introduction

Several countries are currently using e-voting for elections and referendums and many others are conducting (or have conducted) feasibility studies. This chapter provides a general overview of e-voting implementation worldwide.

An appropriate classification and taxonomy is the very first step for overviews that refer to realities that vary a lot. And e-voting may encompass a wide range of e-enabled tools. As for this chapter, e-voting will include the casting and counting of votes. It is the definition used both by the Office for Democratic Institutions and Human Rights (ODIHR) and by the International Institute for Democracy and Electoral Assistance (IDEA). The term includes "the use of electronic voting systems, ballot scanners and Internet voting" (see p. 4-5 in [245]).

In 2015, the IDEA conducted a survey that intended to know the use of electoral Information and Communication Technologies worldwide (www.idea.int/elections/ict). Regarding e-voting, 19 countries confirmed its use "in politically-binding national elections (elections for public office or direct democracy initiatives),"[1] 16 countries "in politically-binding sub-national elections (e.g. elections for regional legislature or executive office etc.),"[2] four countries "in other elections with EMB participation (e.g., election of trade union leaders, non-binding referendums)"[3] and finally eight countries had abandoned e-voting.[4] Ninety-eight up to 249 countries did not reply to the survey.

This chapter does not intend to cover all cases or provide detailed lists. It will rather focus on some countries that, beyond their size, enable us to highlight particular features. All countries undertake similar and common steps, but each one also has to face legal and sociopolitical contexts that may lead to specific solutions. And such a comparison will provide a complete picture of the challenges that e-voting is facing nowadays worldwide.

The chapter chooses some cases that could be considered international references for either good or bad reasons. We will find good practices, but also negative approaches. At the end, the final outcome aims at being a more nuanced picture of the current challenges of any ongoing e-voting project. Particular features will be used as drivers for completing the whole comparison: the public nature of elections, the civic activism, the interaction between business and elections, the technical obsolescence, the political context and the voter's perception.

Given the table of contents of this book, where most chapters are authored by IT experts, this chapter compensates such an approach by stressing the importance of legal and sociopolitical issues. Any successful e-voting implementation needs a

---

[1]Armenia, Belgium, Bhutan, Brazil, Ecuador, Estonia, France, India, Mongolia, Namibia, New Zealand, Panama, Peru, Philippines, Russian Federation, Switzerland, UAE, USA and Venezuela

[2]Argentina, Australia, Bangladesh, Belgium, Bhutan, Bulgaria, Canada, India, Japan, Mexico, Mongolia, Peru, Philippines, Russian Federation, Switzerland and USA.

[3]Bolivia, South Korea, Panama and Switzerland.

[4]Netherlands, Kazakhstan, Germany, Finland, Norway, Paraguay, Romania, Ireland. The database also mentions the United Kingdom where e-voting has been piloted.

sound technical background, but it also requires an appropriate legal framework and a proactive society. These three pillars are interdependent and one weak point likely leads to the failure of the e-voting project.

3.2 The Public Nature of Elections

E-voting, actually any sort of e-enabled electoral tool, entails obscurity for a layman and addressing such a barrier has become a challenge for a definitive consolidation of electoral technologies. If compared with paper-based tools, evidence provided by e-enabled ones may be meaningless for a layman, due to their inherent technical complexity. While a paper recount can be understood and monitored by anybody, a computerized recount may provide correct final figures, but the procedure can only be understood by technical experts. Such inherent opacity of e-enabled tools somehow contradicts basic pillars of elections, which always rely on transparency and citizen oversight. And that is why using new technologies for electoral purposes will likely have to address particular concerns that are not present in other areas.

A decision of the German Constitutional Court in 2009 is considered a milestone. It had a direct impact on subsequent legal developments and e-voting implementations, like the Norwegian, the Estonian and the Swiss ones, that intend to provide better tools for election verifiability.

In March 2009 the German Constitutional Court banned voting machines that were in use for federal elections. They were machines supplied by Nedap, a Dutch vendor whose devices have also been implemented in the Netherlands and in France. Beyond other previous lawsuits that had had different outcomes (see p. 186 in [568]), this process was initiated by Ulrich Wiesner and his father regarding the 2005 federal elections. Despite the fact that there had been no major problems during the actual implementation of voting machines, the lawsuit intended to challenge the e-voting procedure as such. Once rejected by the Lower Chamber (Bundestag) as "obvious causeless" (see p. 186 in [568]), the suit ended with an outstanding decision of the German Constitutional Court based on the public nature of elections.

The Court highlighted that voting machines had an inherent shortcoming that was not linked with their actual performance. Even a successful implementation from a technical perspective would not be legally acceptable due to the fact that such devices do not comply with main democratic principles, namely the one that foresees the oversight of electoral procedures by different stakeholders, with no specialized knowledge being required. That is what the German Court called the public nature of elections: "every citizen should have the capacity to reliably monitor and understand, without specific technical knowledge, the central stages of an election" (§109; see also §119, 148 and 149). IT experts normally assume such important tasks as delegates, but the Court did not accept indirect confidence procedures.

The Court (BVerfGe, 2 BvC 3/07, March 3rd 2009) did not reject e-voting means as such. It only examined the Nedap's model and concluded that it did not comply with German constitutional principles, but e-voting remains feasible and legally acceptable in Germany provided the relevant solution takes into account the requirements and conditions set up by the Court.

Anyway, it is worth recalling that such machines did not include a paper trail, which is a component that might meet the Court's requirements. The decision was only based on a given e-voting model and thus future paper-trail implementations might be envisaged provided a previous assessment confirms their compliance with the Court's conditions. Actually the Court implicitly accepts that there could be acceptable measures taken to compensate the lack of publicity and direct citizen involvement (see §123).

Finally, the Court establishes an interesting comparison between e-voting and postal voting. It accepts the latter provided its benefits for the overall electoral system are sound enough, but the Court also assumes that postal voting will likely lessen some guarantees (e.g., the ballot will be handled without the direct supervision of electoral authorities, risk of impersonation). Therefore postal voting is admitted even though it does not comply with normal requirements. It is admitted "with the goal of ... achieving the highest turnout and therefore taking into account the principle of the universal suffrage" (§126).

The Court thinks that Nedap's machines do not provide similar benefits, but there might be other options like, for instance, internet voting (i.e., remote voting from unsupervised environments). Such a system and postal voting pursue the same goal and thus internet voting could benefit from the exceptional rules that the Court applies for voting by mail.

Legally speaking, it is worth recalling that the German Court has an important influence on other jurisdictions worldwide. Its case law is carefully analyzed. Taking into account such premises, other countries, like Norway, Estonia or Switzerland started using e-voting tools with a different approach, which aimed at complying with the public nature of elections.

All of them use internet voting and actually none is able to fully comply with the Court's requirements, since their systems still need specialized knowledge to be monitored, but different innovations enhance transparency and thus a greater independent and external oversight. Such countries are exploring how to provide enough citizen confidence though still requiring the active involvement of computer experts. Moreover, individual verifiability, whose use does not require special knowledge, also started being accepted in some cases.

Norway trialled internet voting in 2011 and 2013, at local and general elections. Voters could cast their ballots on the internet from uncontrolled environments during the advanced voting period. On election day only paper-based voting was possible.

The Norwegian government decided that openness would feature the project and it adopted some decisions that went far away from the normal procedure in other countries: a procurement based on a competitive dialogue, an open-source license and the so-called return codes.

The supplier (Scytl) was chosen after a competitive dialogue scheme among different companies and the documentation was available online. First, such a procedure "enables the EMB to have a dialogue and gather crucial information from the vendors before the official tendering process starts" (see p. 34 in [580]). Therefore, a competitive dialogue normally leads to a better final decision and it also enables an improved in-house expertise, which still remains a weak point in many countries.

Second, this case of competitive dialogue also improved citizen awareness. The documentation was published and thus anybody could supervise the decision-making process. Moreover, the government and the supplier agreed on a customized open-source license. It read as follows:

"The ... Ministry ... and [the Vendor] hereby grant to you ... the right to copy, modify, inspect, compile, debug and run the software for the sole purpose of testing, reviewing or evaluating the code or the system solely for non-commercial purposes" (see p. 9, excerpt, in [580]).

Such a situation differs a lot from what could be found in other countries and what is still being used nowadays. In 2007, for instance, the Kazakh EMB refused to publish the report issued by the certifying authority, which is something usual (for France and Belgium, see Barrat, [71] and [72]), but surprisingly the criteria with which the compliance should be assessed were not published either (see p. 87 in [331]).

Granting access to such data intends to enhance public confidence on electoral procedures, but it has never been easy to achieve on the grounds that disclosing selected documentation could be detrimental to "le secret industriel et commercial ... [et] compromettre le bon déroulement des élections."[5] That is, for instance, the reasoning provided by the French CADA (Commission d'Accès aux Documents Administratifs). CADA is an advisory body whose mission consists precisely on deciding, in the light of the regulations on the access to public information, which documents can be actually disclosed.

However, as the Norwegian case proves, advanced disclosure policies are being adopted, thereby addressing the problems highlighted by the German Constitutional Court in connection with the public nature of elections.

Finally, regarding Norwegian return codes, a confirmation message (return code) is sent to a second device and its content could be matched with the list of codes that the citizen should have already received before election day. Such a list links each candidature to a given code and the citizen will be able to confirm that the code received afterwards coincides with his/her choice. Therefore, individual verifiability

---

[5]"the commercial and industrial secrecy ... [and] endanger the correct electoral management." Available at: www.ordinateurs-de-vote.org/IMG/jpg/cada.jpg [November 20th 2015]

is improved. The voter confirms that his/her ballot was cast as intended and recorded as cast.[6]

The Norwegian system had some weak points [543] and return codes did not cover the whole process (i.e., casting, recording, tallying), but the system still remains a fair example of transparency and individual verifiability,[7] which are basic requirements concerning the public nature of elections. Last but not least, it is worth mentioning the positive attitude of the Norwegian government, who always understood that proactivity and openness were minimum preconditions for a successful e-voting project.

Estonia was also aware of e-voting new trends. The Election Act has been amended and, among other changes, it created "the EVC [Electronic Voting Commission] to organize the Internet voting and verify the electronic voting results. The establishment of the EVC formalized the Internet voting management structure and increased accountability and transparency" (see p. 4 in [449]). Moreover, return codes were also included: "verification is done using a separate smart device (mobile phone or tablet), which reads a code displayed on the voter's computer screen upon completion of voting. The mobile device then temporarily displays the voter's choice, enabling the voter to confirm that his/her vote was recorded as cast" (see p. 5-6 in [449]). Despite such innovative measures, some weaknesses were highlighted regarding, for instance, external audits and access to relevant documentation (see p. 6-7 in [449]; see also other pre-election reports, [535]).

Finally, in 2014 Switzerland approved a new regulatory framework that intends to consolidate a so-called second generation of e-voting systems, that is to say, projects that admit full universal and individual verifiability: "Eligible voters will receive codes with their voter identification card that will allow them to check that their ballot is recorded correctly and corresponds to their intention. From 2016, the Federal Chancellery also intends to provide universal verifiability, whereby any person or group can use mathematical means of verification" (see p. 6-7 in [450]).

Unlike in Germany, internet voting is used instead of voting machines by the above mentioned countries and therefore they differ on how to address the public nature of elections. With voting from uncontrolled environments it is not possible to implement some measures that are available for voting machines (paper-trail being the most obvious one). Return codes intend to simulate what a paper trail provides in a controlled environment, but return codes cannot achieve the same degree of universal and individual verifiability.

A Voter Verifiable Paper Audit Trail (VVPAT) entails different legal and managerial problems, namely based on the legal notion of what a vote is, either physical or virtual, and to which extent recounting mechanisms should be applied, but

---

[6]However, in 2011, a vote was not correctly recorded due to timeframe restrictions [75] and in 2013 a crypto mistake was discovered once the advanced internet-voting period had already started (see p. 8 in [448]).

[7]Universal verifiability is addressed by other means (e.g., disclosure of the source code, zero-knowledge proofs).

VVPAT directly addresses the challenge related to the public nature of elections too. If VVPAT is accepted, specific technical knowledge will not be needed anymore for supervising some key electoral steps. Paper trail machines are used in many countries (e.g., USA [283], Venezuela, Belgium).

In Venezuela, voting machines deliver a VVPAT that the voter has to insert in a traditional ballot box. At the beginning, management issues raised some concerns. Hausmann and Rigobón conducted a statistical analysis on fraud probabilities and concluded that the final outcome "is compatible with the hypothesis that the sample for the audit was randomly chosen *only* among those polling stations whose results had not been tampered with" (emphasis added; see p. 2, translated from Spanish, in [297]).

Despite being statistical (not proven) forecasts, the criticism highlighted a weak point and thus the electoral authorities improved the paper recount of a given percentage of machines. The sorting of polling stations will not be centralized anymore. At the end of election day, each precinct, where there may be several polling stations, will decide which machines will be submitted to a paper recount (see p. 39 in [138]). The solution addresses a potential manipulation, where only pre-selected and thus not tampered machines would be submitted to a paper recount. Random biases are still feasible with the new method, but their implementation is much more difficult.

The percentage of machines being audited increased a lot: 45% in 2005 and 59.32% in 2006. Such a strategy makes no sense from a statistical point of view, but "to extend the audit of closing to all electronic voting centers produced a positive result in the sense of improving the electorate's confidence, as well as that of the political class, in the transparency of the electronic vote and in the correct operation of the voting machines" (see p. 22-23 in [560]). However, there was still room for improvement. For instance, formal guidelines in case of discrepancies did not exist (see p. 42 in [138]).

Regarding Venezuelan e-voting case law, two lawsuits reached the Supreme Court. Both decisions tackled one of VVPAT's weak points, that is to say, the legal notion of what a vote is. A paper recount intends to enhance the overall verifiability, but discrepancies may appear and clear legal provisions should foresee which result prevails: the electronic one, the paper-based one or none (see p. 272 in [381]).

In Belgium, there had been *ticketing* experiences (see p. 8 in [201]) and recent petitions advocating for the reintroduction of VVPAT led to a new system that provides multi-purpose devices, which are able to be electronically counted and manually inspected: "the ... ballot [contains] two parts, a human-readable part and a machine-readable part ... like that, the voter has the opportunity to verify if the vote has been correctly registered; the voting paper would also serve as a VVPAT in the case of a necessary recount" (see p. 205-206 in [566]).

VVPAT introduction in other countries has created interesting disputes. India and Brazil may be used as references. Once a technical report [578] revealed that Indian EVMs were not tamper-proof, a Public Interest Petition was filed at the Delhi Court

advocating for the introduction of VVPAT. Despite its withdrawal by the local jurisdiction and the initial opposition of electoral authorities, the decision was appealed
and the Supreme Court, "in its judgement dated October 8, 2013, ... held that the 'paper trail' is an indispensable requirement of free and fair elections and that the confidence of voters in the system could only be achieved through transparency which
necessitated the need to introduce an accurate and verifiable system of voting" (see
p. 99-100 in [68]). Eight Indian states used VVPAT in 2014.

On the other hand, VVPAT is not allowed in Brazil due to a Supreme Court
ruling on November 6, 2013. For the time being, it is the final step of a long history
where VVPAT has been subjected to pendulous modifications. Two parliamentary
acts have been approved requiring VVPAT, in 2002 and 2009, but the former was
modified only one year later and the latter was rejected by the Supreme Court in
2013. In addition, the opposition to VVPAT mainly comes from electoral authorities
themselves ([118]).[8]

Finally, it is worth mentioning the *Association for Computing Machinery* (ACM)
statement on e-voting systems, where VVPAT is clearly recommended: "voting systems should enable each voter to inspect a physical ... record to verify that his or her
vote has been accurately cast ... Making those records permanent ... provides a means
by which an accurate recount may be conducted" ([41], excerpt).

Concluding, VVPAT, a physical guarantee, appears as a key measure to overcome
criticisms based on the public nature of elections. Its introduction makes sense if
we take into account the discussions that have taken place in many countries, but
such a conclusion also puts aside other potential strategies for enhancing electoral
trustworthiness.

For instance, if the ACM statement is compared with the decision of the German Constitutional Court, it is to note that the former does not include the nuances
underlined by the German Court, namely the paragraphs that foresee a potential reintroduction of e-voting solutions provided they protect other constitutional goods as
important as the public nature of elections. The ACM is much more restrictive and
one may wonder whether its statement is valid for democratic countries where not
fully verifiable voting channels are accepted (e.g., postal voting).

It is also worth recalling that VVPAT has inherent constraints. It is helpful to
compare the final results, but it provides no supplementary guarantees if other factors,
as important as the results, are to be considered. VVPAT cannot guarantee ballots'
randomization, an appropriate e-ballot layout nor a full deactivation of the voting machine after each voting session. Therefore, paper trail is helpful only to address some
issues, but, beyond technical safeguards, a correct protection of the public nature of
elections still needs further measures. A deeper and more nuanced understanding of
what citizen electoral supervision exactly means is required (see [73] and p. 81 in
[446]).

---

[8]https://www.youtube.com/watch?v=VKcJoMZHUmo [November 21st 2015]

3.3 Civic Activism

Civic activism is somehow "the other side of the coin" of the public nature of elections, whose details have been addressed above. The public nature of elections only makes sense if there are citizens, both individually and collectively, who care about what elections should be and monitor EMB's attitudes and decisions.

Moreover, civic activism has had great importance for e-voting development worldwide. While suppliers and EMBs have sometimes constituted limited partnerships that excluded civil society, specific NGOs initiated active protests that led to the reconsideration of some projects. The German and Dutch withdrawals, and other similar decisions, had likely not taken place without previous civic pressures. This section will present some significant cases: France, the Netherlands and Ireland. Shorter references will be made to Belgium and India as well.

The French association *Ordinateurs-de-vote*, whose motto is *Citoyens et informaticiens pour un vote vérifié par l'électeur* (Citizens and IT experts for a citizen verifiable ballot), is an NGO that started fighting against e-voting implementation when the French government took the decision, in 2003, to introduce e-enabled voting machines on the basis of an old article of the electoral code that allowed voting devices.

France is currently using both voting machines and Internet voting. Voting machines started being used in 2003 and right now there are three suppliers (i.e., indra, Nedap and ES&S) that are certified, although their actual use depends on each municipality. Internet voting is also used for overseas voters.

Despite the pressures of *Ordinateurs-de-vote*, the French electoral authorities have not accepted major changes. After the 2007 presidential and parliamentarian elections, when voting machines reached their largest use, civic and political criticism led to a moratorium (see p. 17 in [51]), but in 2015 the e-voting channel is still available and, what is more important, with no significant changes in terms of legal regulation or managerial improvements.

Moreover, after a controversial first stage (see p. 46-49 [51]), in 2012 a new Internet voting project was launched for overseas citizens. The Pirate Party is very actively filing complaints, but the courts have been rejecting them, the last one in July 2015, when the *Conseil d'État*, the highest judicial body for administrative matters, did not accept an appeal against data protection regulations (*Conseil d'État*, 10ème / 9ème SSR, decision 27th July 2015).

The Netherlands was a European e-voting pioneer. Voting machines that were supplied by Nedap and another local company, spread nationwide, except for the important exception of Amsterdam. Moreover, the Netherlands also used internet voting. But civic pressures reversed this path and the Netherlands came back to paper-based procedures.

As in France, in 1965 Dutch legislation foresaw specific paperless devices[9] for casting a ballot (article J32 Electoral Code; valid until 2010). The next two articles established some minimum requirements and delegated to the Executive further legal developments: one in 1989,[10] related to the overall electoral procedure, and another one in 1997, devoted to voting machines. (*stemmachines*).[11]

First trials took place in 1982 (see p. 330 in [416]), although massive implementations only occurred during the 1990s. Some pitfalls arose during this period and the system was fine-tuned accordingly. For instance, in 1998, the government was concerned with some aspects that would become crucial afterwards, both in the Netherlands and abroad. The government underlined "the need to narrow the risks arising from the total dependency on the companies who deliver the hardware and software" or "the need for more detailed regulations on the use of the software used to calculate the results" (see p. 330 in [416]). In 2002, new reports and updates addressed other doubts on the software that was used for the distribution of the parliamentary seats.

Despite all these incidents, Niemoller recalls that "the introduction and use of electronic voting machines in the Netherlands was rather uneventful, since all relevant actors agreed on the advantages of such a system (Nedap or other brands)" (see p. 331 in [416]).[12] It was thus a peaceful, long-lasting and settled e-voting system.

That is why, in 2004, the government decided to launch an internet voting program. The Rijnland Internet Election System (RIES) was used first for the internal elections of some water management boards, but in 2006 it was admitted as a voting means for overseas electors. Moreover, it is worth mentioning that the internet voting system included cutting-edge innovations that aimed at providing full verifiability though questioning the secrecy of the vote (see §III [328] and p. 15 in [427]). This pioneer experience was developed and improved by other countries later on, namely by Norway in 2011 [543].

When voting machines were ready to be adopted by Amsterdam, Rop Gonggrijp (b), in conjunction with the NGO Wij vertrouwen stemcomputers niet, managed to buy a Nedap voting machine and proved certain flaws that had been repeatedly denied by the electoral authorities [262].

Gonggrijp proved that the machines could be used for voting and for other purposes as well. They could easily become chess boards, for instance. Regrettably, both Nedap and the electoral authorities had stressed that the machines were limited to only one function. On the other side, the electromagnetic radiation enabled any citizen, with an appropriate device, to know the content of a given ballot.[13]

---

[9]Thanks to the right of access to public information, data on these first mechanical voting devices available at: wijvertrouwenstemcomputersniet.nl/Wob-8_buit [November 21st 2015]

[10]https://www.kiesraad.nl/sites/default/files/Elections_Decree_0.pdf [August 28th 2015]

[11]wijvertrouwenstemcomputersniet.nl/images/f/fa/Regeling.pdf [August 28th 2015].

[12]Jacobs and Pieters also think that the voting machines were "uncontroversial" (see p. 3 in [320]) and only "isolated incidents and accusations" (see p. 10 in [320]) might be highlighted. They mention, for instance, the complaints filed by Hans Janmaat in 1998 or that voting machines might benefit the 31st candidate.

[13]www.youtube.com/watch?v=B05wPomCjEY [November 21st 2015]

An official assessment of the overall e-voting project was conducted and, after the report was published in 2007, [14] the Netherlands came back to a paper-based voting procedure. Voting machines as well as the internet voting project were forbidden. Right now, the Netherlands are discussing again how to use e-enabled tools for voting and counting procedures [69].

The Irish case is similar to the Dutch one. The e-voting project also failed due to the criticisms raised by Irish Citizens for Trustworthy E-voting (ICTE), a local NGO, but it differs from the Netherlands because the program was stopped at a very early stage.

Counting procedures face important problems in Ireland. The Single Transferable Vote (STV) increases voters' capacity, but it also entails a complex counting. It is a proportional system where ranked votes are used in multiple candidate constituencies. Once the quota is determined, the surplus of votes is reallocated taking into account the second choices of the voter. The time elapsed until the publication of the results as well as potential mistakes due to manual counts are challenges that have to be taken into account.

Having in mind that e-voting might ease STV counting and tabulation procedures, the government bought a number of Nedap machines, but, once the machines received and warehoused, e-voting could never be fully implemented. The machines were piloted in 2001 (see p. 4 [388]) and 2002 (see p. 13 in [163]), but in 2004 the system was finally withdrawn just when a massive implementation was foreseen.

ICTE was founded in May 2003 (see p. 13 in [163]). It opposed using voting machines by means of academic reports or parliamentary hearings. Such initiatives aimed at highlighting machines' vulnerabilities, with special emphasis on the absence of a paper trail. This successful strategy deliberately focused on "not ever getting distracted by side-issues. By refusing to engage in meaningless arguments over money wasted, various reports and so on, simply constantly re-iterating the need for VVAT proved very successful" (see p. 21 in [163]).

Thanks to the right of access to public information, security reports were delivered to ICTE. Despite not having further details on the audit process, nor the full source code, which actually the government did not have either, ICTE discovered some flaws that were accepted by Zerflow, one of the suppliers: potential interferences on the voting interface and doubts on the management of the keys that gave access to the voting machine (see p. 8-9 in [389] and p. 22-23 in [316]).

Some issues were fixed, but the campaign had already influenced relevant stakeholders and unexpected decisions were taken. After the first parliamentary hearings, the commission "asks Minister to suspend roll-out and all spending, but a week later reverses this decision" and the day after, the government buys seven thousand voting machines, a number that is increased a month later (see p. 17 in [163]).

---

[14] *Voting with Confidence*, The Hague: Adviescommissie inrichting verkiezingsproces, 2007. *wijvertrouwenstemcomputersniet.nl/images/0/0c/Votingwithconfidence.pdf* [August 28th 2015]

Civic protests arose and finally an independent commission was created. Its report, whose preliminary draft was published in April 2004, did not recommend e-voting implementation for the immediate European elections, to be held in June 2004. The final report, which was published two years later, made a distinction between hardware and software: "the Commission concludes that it can recommend the voting and counting equipment for use at elections in Ireland, subject to further work it has also recommended, but that it is unable to recommend the election management software for such use" (see p. 194 in [442]).

It is worth noting that the government had not launched a previous participatory process, a democratic tool which is normally aimed at gathering different opinions from the citizenry and the relevant IT groups. Actually the official attitude was not very proactive: that "researchers have had to repeatedly use Freedom of Information legislation and expend enormous amounts of time and money obtaining information on what should be the most public and accountable of processes is indicative of an attitude and mind-set which does not lead to well-rounded well-specified design requirements" (see p. 18 in [316]). Although such a strategy has been overcome by other countries later on, namely by Norway, low official openness still subsists in many countries and it represents a menace for e-voting projects.

The proactive socialization of e-voting initiatives, including their more technical components, is an efficient vaccine that may prevent what happened in Ireland. The project was quickly stopped few weeks before the European elections and there already were some irreversible consequences, like the Irish ownership of thousands of devices that would never be used. In 2012 voting machines were finally sold for recycling [392] and there have not been other e-voting initiatives in Ireland so far.

Beyond these three references to civic activism (France, Netherlands and Ireland), other initiatives could also be mentioned, like the Belgian PourEVA (www.poureva.be) or the Indian VeTA (www.indianevm.com).

Finally, academia and IOs (international organizations) could be included in this section devoted to stakeholders that aim to influence electoral management. The Council of Europe's Recommendation 2004(11), on legal, operational and technical standards for e-voting remains as the unique international official document so far. There also are other important guidelines, but either they are white papers or handbooks (e.g., OSCE/ODIHR, IDEA) or they are approved by private foundations (e.g., The Carter Center, NDI, IFES). Academia has also played a key role in e-voting evolution with active groups advocating for a better electoral framework.

3.4   Business as Usual

Different activities can be identified along the electoral cycle, but voters always are the most important players. The whole process is conceived to guarantee their free political expression. EMBs, IOs, NGOs, academia, judges, media or political parties shape a complex picture with mutual interactions and finally private companies are also involved in a market that differs a lot from other business areas. That is why understanding the correct role of suppliers is a precondition for any e-voting project. Moreover, it is worth recalling that e-enabled elections will likely need much more support from private companies than other traditional electoral tools. Software development, IT maintenance and similar issues need highly specialized companies and therefore nowadays EMBs are much more dependent than a couple of decades ago.

If salesmen do not understand the specificities of the electoral market or if EMBs' in-house expertise remains weak, the outcome will likely be an unbalanced and unfair dialogue between a public institution and a private company. And such a situation normally leads to contracts that do not take into account the whole range of interests that should be considered. Private interests will be carefully protected whereas public values, that is to say, those linked to democracy and human rights, will be underestimated.

Three perspectives, with three different case-studies, will help us understand these problems. First of all, post HAVA period will show us how easy money becomes a bad ally. Second, the Peruvian EMB represents a good example of an e-voting strategy having in mind the importance of in-house expertise. Finally, Non-Disclosure Agreements (NDAs) reveal complex trade-offs between suppliers and EMBs. The Finnish case will be very instructive.

The Help America Vote Act (HAVA), approved in 2002, aimed at modernizing US electoral organization, but voting machines had a long history behind them. HAVA only intended to improve something that was already in use. For instance, lever devices had been adopted "by the 1930s, essentially [by] all of the nation's larger urban centers" [327], punch cards as well as scanners were incorporated in the 1970s and finally Direct Recording Electronic (DRE) voting machines shyly appeared in the 1970s [327].

E-voting pitfalls had already appeared, but the US 2000 presidential elections, where the Florida recount faced several problems,[15] made evident that a structural improvement effort was really needed. After this scandal, US authorities decided that the updating of the electoral management was the only way to avoid similar problems and HAVA was approved with such a goal.

HAVA created the Election Assistance Commission (EAC), which is a federal body that enhances coordination among state and federal EMBs. Approving guidelines, sharing good practices or conducting research activities provides a better knowledge of US electoral management and thus a better starting point for its improvement.

HAVA also foresaw federal funds with the aim of modernizing election management nationwide and obviously e-enabled tools appeared as the most appropriate so-

---

[15]After being appealed, the Supreme Court [*Bush v. Gore* 531 U.S. 98 (2000)] did not authorize a new recount and validated the results. Punch cards were highly criticized. The so-called *butterfly ballot* had a specific layout where the columns, with the names of the candidates, and the relevant holes overlapped. Democrats should punch the third hole despite having the second candidature on the left column. As a result, some electors presumably misvoted for Buchanan.

lutions. Many counties started a quick IT updating, but civic and academic awareness also increased. Avi Rubin led one of the most significant stages when he had access to Diebold machines' source code [493]. Rubin concluded that Diebold machines had a number of vulnerabilities that threatened electoral integrity. Such criticisms were not welcomed by the company, but the overall perception had already shifted. It seemed that voting machines did not include appropriate security measures and that some companies only aimed at taking advantage of HAVA's economic benefits. Among other factors, weak in-house expertise as well as limited financial autonomy also prevented EMBs from having reasonable forecasts (see p. 8 in [109]).

The activities of the Election Assistance Commission (EAC), new voluntary federal guidelines and an improved awareness of all stakeholders managed to address some problems. However, the discussion remains open in the US, partially due to initial errors [329].

The US experience shows that advanced in-house expertise is the only way to counterbalance the role of suppliers. Should the relevant EMB develop internal know-how on e-voting issues, with new staff hired and appropriate training activities, the suppliers would immediately adapt their sales protocol. They would quickly realize that superficial and non-nuanced arguments would no longer make sense. But it is not an easy task. Financial autonomy, reasonable timelines and a clear institutional commitment are needed to achieve EMB's advanced expertise.

The Peruvian experience is limited when talking about public office elections, but paradoxically the local EMB has an extensive background in the assessment and implementation of different e-voting solutions.

Binding experiences began in 2011, in a single municipality (Cañete), slowly continued in 2013, including a Lima district, and widened in 2014, when e-voting was used by various districts of Lima and Cañete provinces as well as by Callao (see p. 12 in [180]).

But trials had begun in 1996 (see p. 28-31 in [444]), with a first binding implementation for a school board (see p. 66-67 in [443]). The Peruvian EMB started using e-voting for a wide range of non-public office elections, either binding or not, for training purposes and for social familiarization. It is worth mentioning that voting machines had also been used by political parties, for their internal elections, which is an excellent means of socialization and eases future implementations. If political parties pioneer such new technologies, with a satisfactory outcome, they will likely accept them in other cases.

Almost two decades later, institutional maturity and awareness increased a lot and that is why the Peruvian case is important. The Oficina Nacional de Procesos Electorales (ONPE) constantly pursued greater in-house expertise and many outputs can be mentioned.

In terms of e-voting management, it is worth noting the evolving nature of the technical solutions used by the ONPE. It combined agreements with international suppliers with in-house technical solutions and partnerships with local academia. Institutional autonomy has not been lost. Moreover, research, a key parameter to assess institutional capacity, always accompanied practical issues, as the series of working-papers shows (for instance, [443] and [444]). *Elecciones*, an academic journal, also included a number of contributions with e-voting analysis. The eighth issue appeared a long time before the first binding implementation and the last issue reviews what has been done in recent years.

The Observatorio del Voto Electrónico en Latinoamérica (OVELAT) represents another initiative worth mentioning. Launched in 2011 and funded by the United Nations Development Programme (UNDP), it aims at being the Latin American meeting point for e-voting stakeholders. Finally, the ONPE also held two international conferences, in 2008 and 2013, the latter with the support of the Organization of American States (OAS).

Concluding, ONPE's strategy enhances a full e-voting package that includes the implementation itself as well as other initiatives. They have very different profiles, even modest ones, but all of them pursue the same goal: an informed public opinion and an advanced in-house expertise on e-voting issues.

Right now, Peruvian electoral authorities still envisage a future nationwide deployment (see p. 28 in [180]), but no new steps have been adopted. There is a positive citizen perception, but threats have also been identified, like the digital gap and an overall political distrust. Therefore ONPE aims at conducting new research and being aware of experiences worldwide (see p. 27-28 in [180]).

Finally, one should pay attention to Non-Disclosure Agreements (NDAs) and Finland is a good example for assessing transparency and the access to public information by independent experts. Upon agreement with the government, the Mathematical Department of the University of Turku conducted an audit whose report was published before the elections, but both Electronic Frontier Finland (EFFI) and an IT expert "refused to participate as they were not willing to sign the non-disclosure agreement required by the IT suppliers" (see p. 175 in [38]).

NDA's assessments are extremely illustrative since they are evidence of actual trade-offs between public and private interests. NDAs reveal the battle underlying any voting project that is managed by a private company [74] [284]. When citizens and electoral authorities focus on how to disclose and understand e-voting features, suppliers may be reluctant in order to protect their investments. In relation to the Finnish case, EFFI recalls that "TietoEnator, a Finnish company acting as a system integrator, required non-disclosure agreements that would have severely constrained the auditors' possibilities to publish their findings. The Ministry of Justice tried to arbitrate a better non-disclosure agreement, but were unsuccessful" (see p. 4 in [562]). In addition, in 2008 the Ministry of Justice had denied EFFI's petition founded on the right of access to public information. The Ministry argued that it was impossible to reveal data related to the "implementation of the security arrangements of information and communications systems... unless it is clear that the target of the security arrangements would not be compromised by their release." Likewise, "official documents that should be kept secret include documents containing information on a [sic] private trade or professional secrets as well as documents containing other comparable private business information" (see p. 3-4 in [562]).

E-voting praxis also evolves and transparency became a precondition for some significant cases afterwards [580]. Some suppliers also adapted their internal rules once acknowledging that elections are a specific market and need special rules. As already stated, Norway, for instance, was a good reference. Its government granted access to all relevant data [543].

Right now (October 2016), Finland is reconsidering whether to use e-enabled tools. In 2013, a working group was created and its final report, which was published in April 2015, recommends "an experiment with internet voting... in connection with the advance voting in consultative municipal referenda during a fixed-term of four years" (see p. 180 in [38]). Further uses, namely for parliamentary elections, are postponed.

3.5   Outdated Technologies

E-voting technologies have been in use for the last two decades at least and, given the evolving nature of this field, it is worth wondering how software and hardware will be adapted to new IT and legal standards. Moreover, the term e-voting encompasses a wide range of technologies so future adaptations will likely not be taken in a homogeneous way. Each model will face different needs. Updating could even be impossible for certain hypotheses, due to technical obsolescence.

Significantly, the US Report and Recommendations of the Presidential Commission on Election Administration,[16] published in January 2014, acknowledged the importance and challenges of outdated e-voting technologies: "a large share of the voting machines currently in operation were purchased ... as part of HAVA's provisions ... Those machines are now reaching the end of their natural life cycle" (see p. 63 in [164]). This section will analyze how some countries address such a challenge. Beyond the USA, already mentioned, in 2012 Belgium substituted its old e-voting computers and in the 1990s Venezuela also managed to replace scanners by DRE. Finally, legal frameworks have some particular features regarding technical updating.

In Belgium, e-voting was trialled in 1991, in two areas (see p. 6 [200]), but a real implementation only began in 1994 and reached up to 44% of the electorate. Such a figure depends on the municipalities, which have the final decision on whether to use voting machines. Two models were certified by the federal government: Digivote, that covered about 85% of the market, and Jites, used by the rest of the municipalities (see p. 13 in [200]). It is worth noting that the introduction of voting machines cancelled paper-based ballots. The voter had only one option.

Problems appeared (e.g., Schaerbeek) and criticisms arose mainly due to civic

---

[16]https://www.supportthevoter.gov/files/2014/01/Amer-Voting-Exper-final-draft-01-09-14-508.pdf [September 22nd 2015]

activism led by Pour une Étique du Vote Automatisé (PourEVA). And improved guarantees were introduced such as the creation of the Collège d'Experts, which is a significant innovation because similar entities hardly exist in other countries. The Collège is an independent body whose members are nominated by the parliamentary assemblies. The Collège issues a non-binding report that is delivered to the relevant assembly after each election. Such reports represent excellent starting points for the analysis of the Belgian case.

Despite such a problematic history, Belgium managed to not only maintain the system, but substitute an outdated solution by a new one that fits much better contemporary standards. The old machines have been in use since the 1990s and thus there were increasing managerial burdens. Each election required new software, but the hardware remained unchanged. It was warehoused by each municipality.

In May 2014, an important incident occurred and somehow confirmed the necessity of an updating that had begun a couple of years before. Several Jites's mistakes prevented counting all the ballots. As the Collège recalls, "this control mission has been by far the most difficult one" (see p. 6 in [202]; translated from French) and it stresses that "the bad quality of the source code entails de facto problems for its maintenance. Moreover, such a source code needs to be updated every election ... The '2014 elections bug' is partly due to Jites's gaps that had already been highlighted" (see p. 57 in [202]; translated from French).

In 2012, Smartmatic had already replaced some e-voting systems. Maintaining the asymmetric geographical distribution that existed before, new voting machines were accepted by Flemish municipalities and two areas within the Brussels region, but they were not deployed in Wallonia.

A massive substitution is not an easy task, at least from a legal perspective and for training capacities. Legally speaking, e-voting entails complex regulations and, taking into account that there are many different e-voting platforms, either the higher legislation keeps a generic approach, with only basic principles that hardly frame further decisions, or a given e-voting solution is depicted in detail, which might make more difficult upgradings or substitutions.

A highly detailed procurement was used in Belgium. A university consortium had been asked by the government to conduct an e-voting comparison worldwide, to assess the weakest points of the Belgian system and to propose new methods. The so-called BeVoting Report suggested up to five new solutions and the government chose one, on which the procurement was based. The government also asked the Council of Europe to conduct an assessment on the compliance of the five suggested methods with international technical, legal and operational standards.

As a result of this analytical approach, the distinction between voting machine and e-ballot box was maintained. Such a separated system is closer to the traditional paper-based one since there still are both voting booths and ballot boxes. Moreover, the voter can use different voting machines to check whether his/her token contains the correct value. As stated above, the new system includes a twofold token that combines a human-readable paper trail with a computer-based code.

Training may also become a barrier when e-voting replacements take place. Well-trained officials are crucial in any electoral process, whether e-enabled or not, and obviously new e-voting systems will likely need a certain time to achieve the degree of familiarization that the previous system already had.

Three years later, Belgium is still using e-voting and the new Smartmatic solution seems consolidated. However, the incident with the other machines in 2014 increased the overall criticisms and the petitions to reintroduce paper-based procedures. The asymmetric deployment of voting machines does not facilitate a systematic picture of Belgian evolution, but what is not doubtful is that the replacement took place successfully, which is the only feature that this section intended to highlight.

Venezuela is another interesting example of substitution of voting technologies. From 1999 to 2003 scanners were used nationwide as a first e-enabled tool for electoral procedures. However, in 2003 Venezuela decided to shift from e-counting to e-voting.

Finally, recent generations of e-voting platforms include new features and shaped new scenarios that have to be legally framed. Verifiability (e.g., return codes), transparency (e.g., source code disclosure, better NDAs), sharing institutional tasks (e.g., independent commissions) or fair procurements (e.g., competitive dialogue) need a specific legal approach. Also, regulations become obsolete and need regular updates.

3.6   The Political Context

The electoral management cycle as such is a technical concept that could remain protected from political influences, but the subject itself, that is to say, running elections and thus deciding who will hold the parliamentary majority and/or the cabinet, is closely related to political inputs. Any e-voting implementation should be aware of such a mutual interaction and adopt the relevant measures to avoid improper influences.

The interaction between the political context and election management may follow different patterns. We will highlight three cases. The assessment of the sociopolitical framework should be the starting point for any e-voting deployment. Given that electoral technologies always need to rely upon a trustworthy background, social cohesion and the political context may either strengthen or weaken such a precondition. Second, politics have priorities that may not match what e-voting actually needs. Honesty, transparency, non mass media-driven decisions or long-term programs ease e-voting implementations, but sometimes politics does not adhere to such parameters. Third, it is worth recalling that the final decision always belongs to representative institutions. Second-rate projects may remain in use provided a political consensus subsists and excellent e-voting programs may be hindered by political pitfalls.

Regarding the overall political context, Venezuela and Switzerland both provide paradigmatic case studies. Venezuela is an excellent example of how voting machines continue being used despite Venezuela's extremely political polarization. On the other hand, Swiss political and social cohesion, which is strengthened by a leading civic culture, has a clear impact on the development of the internet voting project.

The first modern Venezuelan technical electoral update took place in 1999 and was based on Indra's scanning machines (see p. 262-263 in [381]). Paper continued in use, but scanners led to an adaptation of ballots' size and, what is more important, a training program. Voters learned how to properly mark the ballots and thus avoid further problems with the scan (see p. 263 in [381]).

Just four years later, in 2003, Venezuela shifted its strategy and began using DREs, which were bought from a local company, Smartmatic. First pilots were accompanied by complaints about the secrecy of the vote and deliberate tampering.

In relation to the secrecy of the votes, concerns had two origins. First, voting machines had been deployed in conjunction with fingerprint devices. In 2006, for instance, voters were identified with biometric machines and, once their fingerprints had been recorded, voters could go to the relevant polling station. However, fingerprint machines were not connected to voting procedures and actually voters were identified again at the polling station by traditional means (i.e., ID card). Thus, the right to vote did not depend on the biometric control, but such an arrangement raised suspicions.

Second, personal data management became suspicious due to the so-called "Tascón list", that is to say, the citizens who had supported a recall referendum in 2004, but, in electoral terms, there was no link between the list and voting procedures.

Paper trail and software also raised some concerns and, as stated above, measures were taken for enhancing citizen confidence. As a result, further disagreements rather focused on strictly political issues and not on e-voting as such. Anyway, adding new parameters, like mixing biometric identification with voting procedures, entails new concerns and such innovations will have to prove to be mature enough and win social acceptance.

Switzerland is a very different case. First of all, only internet voting from uncontrolled environments is admitted and, despite being a pioneer, there are legal constraints that prevent quick deployments. Only three projects (Geneva, Neuchâtel and Zurich) have been authorized so far and the extension to other cantons has always been based on one of those authorized programs. Right now, as already stated, Switzerland launches the so-called second e-voting generation, which intends to improve verifiability.

However, this section is devoted to assessing how the sociopolitical context may impact e-voting projects and, regarding the Swiss case, it is worth highlighting that the use of internet voting is closely related to the previous acceptance of postal voting. It is used by an average of 69% of voters (90% in some cantons; see p. 177 in

[372]), which is an exceptional rate. Moreover, postal voting is very easy to use. Once the electoral materials have been delivered to the voter, s/he only has to drop the relevant envelope in any postbox. It is to note that there is a specific social background behind such a procedure. Only countries with a large and solid social consensus can use such voting channels without major complaints afterwards.

Internet voting was adopted taking into account such a positive context. A strong civic culture has been supporting this innovation. Some concerns arose and civic activists highlighted potential weaknesses, even before the court [308], but political influence remained one step behind technical aspects, which is a correct approach.

On the other hand, the next case will show how an improper political approach may have a negative impact.

In 2010 Barcelona held a local referendum focused on the urban reform of Diagonal Avenue, which is a strategic axis along which public transportation, namely tramway, is problematic. Several social and political discrepancies arose.

Although Spanish law is very restrictive in relation to local referendums, Barcelona enjoys a specific framework that, taking into account the needs of big cities, nuances the normal distribution of competences between central, regional and local authorities. This Carta Municipal entitles the City Council to "gather citizen opinions by means of popular consultations" (art. 35 Law 22/1998, de la Barcelona Municipal Act; translated from Spanish). The main advantage consists in excluding a previous authorization of the central government. Detailed rules (Normes Reguladores de la Participació Ciutadana) were approved on November 22, 2002, and finally, as a first implementation, the City Council called for a referendum to be held from May 10 to May 16, 2010 (see p. 1 in [191]). Specific legal guidelines (Document de Bases) were also adopted for this referendum.

Internet voting was available from controlled and uncontrolled environments. Such a flexible organization intended to achieve a high turnout, which is a key political parameter when there are sharp discrepancies, as was the case.

An independent commission was created as well. Among other competences, it monitored the proper implementation of the legal framework and validated final results (see p. 15 in [191]). The commission was composed by external experts coming from different bodies (e.g., Parliament, Catalan Technical University).

It is worth noting that the project was managed by Scytl and Indra conjointly. Both companies are Spanish and competitors in the electoral market worldwide. Therefore they do not usually launch initiatives together. Anyway, on this occasion, the City Council "finally offered the contract to Indra Sistemas, who subcontracts Scytl's e-voting platform" (see p. 21 in [191]; translated from Catalan).

Bitter political disputes accompanied the referendum and several complaints arose (e.g., ballot layout), but the next paragraphs will focus on two specific issues: ID management and the protocol for addressing negative events.

Regarding ID management, safeguards against impersonation proved to be too weak. Voters requested a password online and they had to provide a cellular phone number and personal such as birthdate or similar information. As such data are somehow available on the Internet, a journalist impersonated a politician, a member of the City Council (see p. 51 in [191]). When he tried to cast a ballot, he was informed that he was supposed to have already voted the day before and therefore he could not cast a ballot again. Given the scandal, operators removed the first vote, which is also a controversial measure, and allowed a second ballot from the same ID (see p. 62 in [191]). The impersonator was identified, brought before the court and declared innocent due to the lack of conclusive evidence [472].

Concluding, the City Council intended to raise turnout, which was politically reasonable, but critical procedural steps, like the ID management, were weakened.

This case also provides other elements that, going beyond the anecdote, represent important lessons for further e-voting projects. That is the case of the comic incident that happened when the mayor tried to vote (see video in [52]) and unfortunately the system did not work (see p. 31 in [191]). Once in front of the computer, the mayor detected some problems, asked a technical adviser for help and they agreed to dissimulate. They would say to the media that the mayor had properly cast his ballot. Actually it was not true and the lie was discovered just a few hours later when, reading the lips, one could realize that the adviser was telling to the mayor that it would be worth not fixing the problem at that time and lying to the media. Despite the scandal, the City Council did not change its information for two days, but finally the mayor was forced to admit his mistake. He informed that he had cast his ballot the same first day in the afternoon, but he had been refusing this explanation during two days. Once again, (bad) politics seemed more important than technical issues and good management. Politics may cause the failure of e-voting projects.

Finally, when talking about the interaction between politics and technical management, it is worth recalling that politicians, that is to say, representative institutions always (have to) retain the final decision. Democracy also matters.

Norway is a very good example. It started using internet voting in September 2011, for local elections, but it was the final step of a long implementation during which the EMB proved to be aware of common e-voting challenges. As stated above, procurement procedures based on a competitive dialogue, transparency of the overall project or in-house expertise are hardly difficult to find in other countries. However, the Norwegian parliament had always expressed great concern. Secrecy, for instance, was a big issue for politicians [534]. The composition of the parliament guaranteed political support to the use of internet voting, but, after the 2013 parliamentary elections, the new government decided not to maintain the program.

Similar outcomes may be found when a country adopts EMB's transformations. Ongoing e-voting projects can be discontinued due to a new institutional framework, new intergovernmental relationships and new legal responsibilities. That happened in Mexico after expanding the powers of the federal EMB and thus lessening local leaderships. Despite being a federal state, Mexico had launched different local e-voting initiatives. Coahuila, which was the pioneer, Jalisco or the capital itself had used voting machines and even internet voting for citizens living abroad. Each case faced particular problems, but the new centralized federal EMB, created in 2014, makes more difficult such a variety of initiatives. In June 2015 theăInstituto Nacional Electoral (INE) trialled its own voting machines, with non-binding effects [421], but only a single e-voting project is foreseen nationwide.

3.7 Voters Matter

E-voting platforms should comply with a number of specifications that normally range from IT requirements to legal and even social preconditions, but any e-voting solution should always have only one main target, which is the voter. If the elector fails to cast his/her ballot, any other potential e-voting advantages will become meaningless. And that has happened in some countries.

Usability and accessibility are important components therefore. Traditional paper ballots also face some constraints that may prevent them from being user-focused and fully accessible. Beyond the legal framework that imposes some layouts, "the ballot paper form and content needs to be easily understandable. Simplicity aids speed of voter flow, and assists all voters — not only those less literate — to vote with confidence that they have not made a mistake."[17] The Brennan Center for Justice compiled up to 13 bad practices, like splitting candidates for the same office onto different pages or columns, placing response options on both sides of candidate names, not writing short, simple instructions or placing instructions far from related actions [419]. For instance, the so-called butterfly ballot, already mentioned, did not comply with basic usability standards.

Regarding e-voting, Brazil and India represent countries that accepted such a technology provided a very easy way to operate with the computer was implemented. Venezuela also accepted DRE machines with the same premise. Second, some failures have a direct link with usability issues. The Finnish project was quite small, actually only three municipalities, but it illustrates fairly well what usability weaknesses may entail. Finally, accessibility is a key parameter for e-voting development. Voting technologies open new opportunities for those citizens who cannot use ordinary electoral procedures.

As for the first group of countries, Brazil started using e-counting machines in 1982, just after the dictatorship, but the final outcome was not satisfactory. A parallel counting proved that the official results were inconsistent (see p. 69 in [118]). It was the so-called Proconsult case, in relation to the company that managed the system.

---

[17]ACE Project / Ballot Paper Design: http://aceproject.org/ace-en/topics/vo/voc/voc02/voc02a

Such a bad precedent has somehow impacted the subsequent implementation of e-voting technologies in Brazil.

Later on, in 1996 the first voting machines started being deployed on a gradual basis. Initially, only towns over 200,000 inhabitants were entitled to introduce voting machines, but they spread very quickly and in 2000, with only two in-between elections, voting machines were used nationwide.

Having identified the weaknesses of the traditional Brazilian electoral system, e-voting machines were supposed to face local *caciques*, that is to say, leaders that used to tamper with electoral results. E-enabled tools would prevent such manipulations and therefore improve the integrity of the process. But Brazilian authorities were also aware that digital illiteracy might become an important barrier for an efficient implementation of voting machines. The final decision intended to address both problems (*caciques* and illiteracy) with user-friendly voting machines.

Such devices simulate a traditional telephone. There is a numerical keyboard and the voter only types his/her national ID code and the number of his/her political choice. Each candidature has a given number that is intensively advertised during the electoral campaign. Afterwards, the screen displays the chosen option and the voter only has to press a button confirming it. The vote is already cast. Obviously, the system could be improved, but it is worth highlighting its simplicity.

As a positive feature, simulating a traditional telephone eases the cultural change entailed in the lack of a physical paper ballot. Such a transition should always draw the attention of e-voting experts due to its important consequences. The principle of equality, a legal cornerstone, may be damaged if the e-voting systems do not take into account those citizens who are less familiar with new technologies [391]. And that is especially important when the paper based procedure totally disappears, as in Brazil.

Other countries also adopt similar strategies in order to address such a digital gap. India, for instance, is using voting machines that are far away from cutting-edge computers. Again, there is a voting board, where the candidatures are displayed, and the voter only has to press one physical button, check the screen and confirm his/her option by pressing another button. Venezuela is another interesting case because it acknowledged the digital gap problem and intended to face it with a sensitive board that replicates the previous paper-based ballot. Again, voters interoperate with a user-friendly device, in this case fairly similar to what they used before, and confirm later the option that is displayed on the screen, which is a supplementary device.

On the other hand, in Finland, usability pitfalls led to interrupting the internet voting project. In 2008, Finland trialled internet voting from controlled environments thanks to a temporary authorization included in Law 880/2006. Scytl, a Catalan company, and TietoEnator, a local partner, were in charge. The project was initially limited to local elections and internet voting was only used in three municipalities — Karkkila, Kauniainen and Vihti. Moreover, voters could choose between two voting channels, the internet one and the traditional.

If a citizen wanted to use the internet voting channel, a smart card was given to him/her and, once the preferred option was selected, "the voter had to confirm her choice by pressing the visible OK button on the screen ... the system gave a message that the voting had successfully been finished and asked the voter to remove the voting card from the card reader and to return it to the election official" (see p. 174 in [38]). Finally, the system transmitted the relevant data to a central server.

After election day, some inconsistencies were discovered. In some polling stations, the total number of citizens who had been identified as actual voters was higher than the total number of votes that had been recorded and transmitted by the relevant computers. It was established that some voters had left the polling station before confirming their option by pressing the final voting button. The computer did not save their options as actual votes therefore. TietoEnator identified a "total of 232 cases ... it seemed that in these cases the voter, for one reason or another, had removed the voting card from the card reader before confirming the choice by pressing the OK button" (see p. 175 in [38]; 232 cases or up to 12,234 of internet votes, that is to say, 1.89%).

The first appeal filed against this system was refused by a local court, but the Supreme Administrative Court accepted the complaint and required by-elections in those three municipalities. The Finnish internet voting project stopped here.

Usability performance as well as the information provided to the voter raised as key factors for understanding what had happened. A deficient interface layout did not indicate that the voting session was not yet ended. Such a weakness had been detected during previous tests, but it was not fixed (see p. 178 in [38]). Written (not graphics) information also included other mistakes since it explained that the single action of choosing, without pressing the confirmation button, was enough.

Undervoting cases are a common concern when using voting machines. The Sarasota one, for instance, during a Florida congressional district race in 2006, was very similar. It "violates many of the basic usability principles ... The instructions are not clear and simple; they use the passive rather than the active voice; single instructions sprawl over many lines, while two different instructions share the same line; and the instructions are center-aligned rather than left-aligned on the page" (see p. 56 in [419]).

Finally, citizens also need accessible voting means. We use accessibility as "a set of measurable characteristics that indicate the degree to which a system is available to, and usable by, individuals with disabilities" (see p. 7 in [417]). The targeted group is therefore the key difference between usability and accessibility.

Traditional paper-based electoral procedures include several accessibility drawbacks that could be overcome with e-enabled tools. Internet voting, for instance, may help people with reduced mobility. And voting machines in general may include multilanguage support, which is especially appreciated in some countries, or advanced accessibility measures for impaired people. However, new technologies also raise new concerns. Remote electronic voting, for instance, may inherit, "all the accessibility and usability issues ... [and] it adds new issues related to the technologies that enable remote electronic voting. accessibility and usability of remote electronic voting systems present complex challenges that must be resolved to ensure voter efficiency, effectiveness, satisfaction, privacy and independence when voting remotely" (see p. 38 in [417] NIST).

3.8 Conclusions

Through examination of several case studies concerning various facets of e-voting technology and implementation, we have shown that e-voting is much more complex than what could be initially expected.

Proper computer design and maintenance is obviously needed, but there are other factors that cannot be neglected, as often happens unfortunately. Moreover, such factors use different perspectives and thus an interdisciplinary approach, which would be based on a permanent dialogue between technical, legal and social practitioners, is highly desirable.

Among other elements, legal aspects will highlight that the public nature of elections prevents implementing certain technical solutions. Democratic awareness will also recall that elections pursue public interests and thus private companies have to adapt their role to such a specific market. Civic activism as well as an advanced in-house expertise will facilitate a correct management approach and finally usability issues will underline that the voter has to be recognized as the key electoral player.

E-voting is being used, or at least considered, almost worldwide. And right now there are already good and bad experiences. The chapter aims at giving certain clues that have influenced e-voting implementations so far.

Acknowledgment

Barrat is supported by the Public Administration School of Catalonia (R+D Projects 2014) and the Spanish R+D Ministry (DER2015-68706-P).

Chapter 4

Electoral Systems Used around the World

Siamak F. Shahandashti

Newcastle University, UK

CONTENTS

4.1 Introduction

An *electoral system*, or simply a *voting method*, defines the rules by which the choices or preferences of voters are collected, tallied, aggregated and collectively interpreted to obtain the results of an election [249, 489].

There are many electoral systems. A voter may be allowed to vote for one or multiple candidates, one or multiple predefined lists of candidates, or state their preference among candidates or predefined lists of candidates. Accordingly, tallying may involve a simple count of the number of votes for each candidate or list, or a relatively more complex procedure of multiple rounds of counting and transferring ballots between candidates or lists. Eventually, the outcome of the tallying and aggregation procedures is interpreted to determine which candidate wins which seat.

Designing end-to-end verifiable e-voting schemes is challenging. Indeed, most such schemes are initially designed to support relatively unsophisticated voting methods in which ballot structure and tallying rules are straightforward. However, extending such a scheme to support more complex voting methods may not be trivial. Issues such as efficiently encoding preferential ballots with a large number of candidates and preserving voter privacy when transferring ballots during multiple rounds of counting can introduce considerable design challenges. Such challenges are evidenced for instance by the compromises made in the design of the state-of-the-art vVote system used for recent Victorian elections [184]. There have been a few works attempting to address these challenges (see, e.g., [581] and the references within), nevertheless achieving practical end-to-end verifiable schemes supporting complex voting methods remains an area of research with many open questions. A good understanding of how different voting methods work is a prerequisite for tackling such open questions. In this chapter we aim to provide an introduction to the diverse voting methods used around the world.

Mathematically, an electoral system can be seen as a *function* that takes as input the choices or preferences of the voters and produces as output the results of the election. Voting theory, and more broadly *social choice theory*, provides a formal framework for the study of different electoral systems, and in general social choice functions. A social choice function in this framework is a function that takes as input a set of individual orderings of a set of alternatives and produces a social ordering of the alternatives. This formalization was first put forth by Arrow [65], a pioneer of modern voting theory.

In practice however, there is much more to an election than just the electoral system, and these other issues are equally (if not more) important as the choice of the electoral system in ensuring fair and free elections and establishing public trust. Among these issues are (pre-election) voter registration, observer missions during the election, and post-election audits. From a legal point of view, the electoral system is only one part of the much wider electoral laws and regulations which govern the rules and procedures involved in calling, running and finalizing an election from the start to the end. These rules and procedures include those of voter eligibility, candidate nomination, party campaigning, election administration, and announcement of results. In this chapter however, we mainly focus on electoral systems.

Electoral systems can be categorized in multiple different ways. Two common criteria for categorization are whether the system is designed to produce one winner or multiple winners, and whether the system is designed to produce results that are roughly proportional to the vote share of each party or the system is based on the "winner takes all" approach. In the remainder of this chapter however we have chosen not to be bound to such categorizations. Instead, we follow the ideas underlying different electoral systems and work our way from the more immediate design ideas to the more elaborate ones.

4.2 Some Solutions to Electing a Single Winner

Perhaps the most natural solution to elect a single winner is to elect the candidate with the most votes. This idea is the basis of the so-called first-past-the-post electoral system.

In a **first-past-the-post (FPTP)** system, each voter can vote for one candidate and the single candidate with the highest number of votes wins. The winner might achieve an absolute majority of votes (i.e., more than a half), or merely a plurality of votes (i.e., most votes relatively). The system is also known as **single-member plurality (SMP)** or **simple plurality**. In the case of a race with only two candidates such a system is also called a **simple majority** system.

First-past-the-post is used, among other places, in USA presidential elections (48 states) [111], UK lower house elections [394], Canada [382], India [298] and Malaysia [276].

There are variants of the first-past-the-post system that require the winning candidate to achieve a *quota*, i.e., a threshold of votes, which is higher than the natural quota. For instance, in a two-candidate election, the winning candidate might be required to receive a quota which is greater than half of the votes: in the United States upper house, a so-called filibuster preventing legislation may be stopped only if the legislation receives three-fifth of the votes [239]. These systems are sometimes called **quota** systems, and in the case of a two-candidate election a **super-majority** system.

Note that in the first-past-the-post system, each voter is restricted to vote for only one candidate. If this restriction is lifted, the resulting system is called approval voting.

In an **approval voting** system, each voter may vote for (i.e., approve of) any number of candidates and the single candidate with the highest number of votes (i.e., approvals) wins.

Approval voting is used among other places by the Mathematical Association of America [21], the Institute for Operations Research and the Management Sciences [17] and the American Statistical Association [2].

Although first-past-the-post provides a simple solution to elect a single winner, it does not guarantee an absolute majority if there are more than two candidates. One way to make sure that the winner receives an absolute majority is to choose the two candidates with the most votes for a second round of voting.

In a **two-round system (TRS)**, each voter votes for one candidate. If a candidate receives more than half of the votes, they are declared the winner. Otherwise, the two candidates with the highest number of votes are chosen as the only candidates for a second round of voting, and the rest of the candidates are eliminated. In the second round, each voter can vote for one of the two remaining candidates, and the candidate with the highest number of votes wins. The system is sometimes abbreviated as **2RS** and is also known as **run-off voting** and **double-ballot**.

The two-round system is used in many countries to elect members of the parliament and directly-elected presidents, e.g., in both presidential elections and lower house elections in France [214].

There are other variations of TRS in which all candidates receiving a certain quota become eligible for the second round, or a candidate can be declared a winner in the first round if they meet certain conditions, e.g., achieve a certain quota and have a certain lead over the second candidate.

To avoid the cost of a second round of voting, an idea is to ask voters for their preferences between the candidates on the ballot.

In the **contingent vote** system, voters rank the candidates in order of preference. The ballots are then distributed between the candidates based on their first preference votes. If a candidate receives more than half of the ballots (i.e., the first preference votes), they are declared the winner. Otherwise, the two candidates with the highest number of first preference votes are chosen as the only candidates for a second round of counting, and the rest of the candidates are eliminated. In the second round of counting, the ballots stating an eliminated candidate as the first preference are redistributed (or transferred) to one of the two remaining candidates based on which candidate is ranked above the other. Eventually, the candidate with the highest number of votes is declared the winner.

A variant of the contingent vote where the voters are restricted to express only their top two preferences is used to elect the directly elected mayors in England, including the Mayor of London [31]. Another variant where the voters are restricted to express only their top three preferences is used in the Sri Lankan presidential elections [480, p. 135]. Note that these variants do not guarantee an absolute majority for the winner.

An alternative to ensure an absolute majority for the winner is to carry out multiple rounds of voting and in each round only eliminate the candidate with the lowest number of votes.

In the **exhaustive ballot** system, the voter may vote for one candidate of their choice in each round of voting. If a candidate receives an absolute majority of the votes, they are declared the winner. Otherwise, the candidate with the lowest number of votes is eliminated and the next round of voting is carried out between the remaining candidates. These steps are repeated until a candidate receives an absolute majority.

The exhaustive ballot system is used among other places to elect the members of the Swiss Federal Council [553], the President of the European Parliament [3], the speakers of the Canadian House of Commons [13], the British House of Commons [14], and the Scottish Parliament [554], the host city of the Olympic Games, and the host of the FIFA World Cup.

To avoid multiple rounds of voting, the voters can be asked to state their preferences on the ballots. This is the basis for the following system.

In the **instant run-off voting (IRV)** system, the voters rank the candidates in order of preference. The ballots are then distributed between the candidates based on their first preference votes. If a candidate receives more than half of the ballots (i.e., the first preference votes), they are declared the winner. Otherwise, the candidate with the lowest number of allocated ballots is eliminated and their allocated ballots are redistributed (or transferred) to the next ranked candidate on each ballot who is not yet eliminated. These steps are repeated until a candidate is allocated an absolute majority of the ballots and is declared the winner. The system is also known as the **alternative vote (AV)**.

The instant run-off electoral system is used among other places in the Australian lower house elections [229] and the Irish presidential elections [197].

Partial ranking of the candidates might be allowed. In this case, all the candidates ranked on a ballot might get eliminated before the final round. Such ballots are called *exhausted* ballots. The system guarantees an absolute majority only among the ballots that are neither spoiled nor exhausted by the last round of counting. On the other hand, voters might be asked to submit a full ranking of all the candidates on the ballot so as to minimize exhausted and hence "wasted" ballots. However, in practice this usually leads to an increase in the number of invalid votes.

As an example of IRV, consider the results shown in Table 4.1 for the election of mayor in Derwent Valley council from the 2014 Tasmanian local government elections [9]. There were a total of 3878 valid ballots, which means the initial quota for absolute majority was $\lfloor 3878/2 \rfloor + 1 = 1940$, where $\lfloor \cdot \rfloor$ denote the floor function. The first five columns show the progressive total ballots for the five candidates. As seen in the table, in the first count no candidate achieves absolute majority, and hence the candidate with the lowest number of votes, PBi, is eliminated. PBi's 333 ballots are examined and transferred to their respective second preferences: in this case, 73 to PBe, 86 to MEv, 60 to CLe, and 62 to FPe. Fifty-two ballots do not have a second preference stated, and hence are exhausted. This means that in the next round the quota for absolute majority is reduced to 1914. No candidate achieves majority in the second and third rounds of voting and further two candidates are eliminated and

Table 4.1: An example of instant run-off voting (IRV): The 2014 mayoral election results in Derwent Valley council, Tasmania, Australia

Candidates							
PBe	PBi	MEv	CLe	FPe	Exhausted	Majority	Remark
870	333	1632	423	620	0	1940	Count 1
+73	-333	+86	+60	+62	+52		PBi excluded
943	0	1718	483	682	52	1914	Count 2
+154		+147	-483	+135	+47		CLe excluded
1097		1865	0	817	99	1890	Count 3
+386		+307		-817	+124		FPe excluded
1483		2172		0	223	1828	Count 4
							MEv elected

their ballots transferred. In the final round, MEv has 2172 ballots which is above the absolute majority quota of 1828 and hence MEv is elected.

The IRV method discussed above is the single-winner version of an electoral system known as the single transferable vote (STV) which we will discuss later in this chapter. These methods were proposed by Thomas Hare [295], and hence are sometimes collectively known simply as the Hare system.

While Hare's method eliminates the candidate with the lowest first-preference votes in each round, a variant called **Coombs' method** [169] eliminates the candidate with the highest last-preference votes in each round. In other words, in each round Hare excludes the least liked candidate, whereas Coombs excludes the most disliked candidate.

4.3 Some Solutions to Electing Multiple Winners

To elect multiple winners, one could of course simply extend the first-past-the-post system and elect multiple candidates with the highest number of votes. Let us assume the desired number of winners (or seats) is n.

In a **block-vote (BV)** system, a voter votes for up to n candidates. The candidates are then ordered based on the number of votes they have received and the first n candidates are declared winners. The system is also known as **plurality-at-large voting** and **multiple non-transferable vote (MNTV)**.

The system is used among other places in elections in Lebanon [509].

The **single non-transferable vote (SNTV)** system can be seen as a block-vote system in which the voters are restricted to vote for only one candidate. This system is used among other places in the Japanese upper house elections [175].

A block-vote system in which the voters can vote for more than one but fewer than n candidates is known as **limited vote (LV)**. The Spanish upper house elections use this system, in which the voters may vote for up to three candidates whereas four winners are elected [312].

Another variant of the block-vote, sometimes called the **party block-vote (PBV)**, requires voters to vote for a party (or in general a predetermined list of candidates) instead of voting directly for candidates. After the count, the party with the highest number of votes is allocated all the n seats. This variant can be thought of a first-past-the-post election between parties. It is used among other places in Cameroon [480, Annex A] and Singapore [480, Annex A].

The party block-vote system, like many other systems based on the "winner takes all" paradigm, may produce results that are significantly skewed towards one or more popular parties. The underlying idea of the so-called **Proportional Representation (PR)** electoral systems is to ensure that the number of elected candidates from each party (or coalition of parties) is to some extent proportional to their respective share of the votes.

In the **list voting** or more specifically **party-list PR** system, each party presents a list of candidates and seats are allocated to each party in proportion to the number of votes the party receives.

In what is known as the **closed-list** variant, the voters vote for a list, and after the number of seats allocated to each party is determined, that number of candidates on top of the party list are elected. Hence, the order in which candidates get elected from each list is pre-determined merely by the party and the voters do not get to choose it. The closed-list system is used among other places in national parliamentary elections in Argentina [480, Annex A], Portugal [174], Spain [312] and South Africa [267]. The system is also used in the European parliament elections in many countries including Germany, France, United Kingdom (excluding Northern Ireland) and Spain [548, Part 5].

On the other hand, in the **open-list** variant, the voters vote for candidates, and the number of votes each candidate receives influences the order in which candidates are chosen from a party list at the end of the election. Since voter preferences can influence the order of the elected candidates, such systems are also known as **preferential** list voting. There are multiple different deployments of this variant which give the voter varying amounts of influence. Hence, some scholars suggest using the term "open list" exclusively for the systems in which the order of elected candidates is solely determined by voter preferences, and refer to the systems in which the order of elected candidates is determined by a combination of party list orders and voter preferences as **flexible** list voting (see, e.g., [529, 249]). Open-list voting is used widely around the world including in the Brazilian [414], Dutch [58], Czech [352] and Swedish [514] lower house elections. The system is also used in the European parliament elections in many countries including Italy, Poland and the Netherlands [548, Part 5]. The open-list systems used in Luxembourg and Switzer-

Table 4.2: An example of the d'Hondt method of Proportional Representation voting: 2011 election results in the Częstochowa constituency, Poland

Party	vote	vote/2	vote/3	vote/4	seats
PO	34.97	17.49	11.66	8.74	3
PiS	27.36	13.68	9.12	6.84	2
RP	13.39	6.70	4.46	3.35	1
SLD	10.49	5.25	3.50	2.62	1
PSL	8.77	4.39	2.92	2.19	0
PJN	2.14	1.07	0.71	0.54	0
NP	2.06	1.03	0.69	0.52	0
PPP	0.84	0.42	0.28	0.21	0

land parliamentary elections are unique in that they allow for *panachage*, i.e., voters are allowed to split their preferences between multiple parties [565, 375].

A two-round variant of the closed-list system is in use in French regional elections [375]. Any party with at least a predetermined threshold of the votes may contest the second round. In the second round, the seats are allocated to the parties proportionally to their shares of the votes.

There are various methods for seat allocation based on each party's share of the votes. The two most common categories are the highest average and the largest remainder methods.

In the **highest-average (HA)** methods, the number of votes for each party is successively divided by a set of *divisors*, resulting in a series of quotients called *averages*. Eventually, n of the top values among the averages of all parties are determined and the number of averages selected for each party gives their share of the final n seats.

One of the most widely used highest-average methods is the **d'Hondt** method in which the divisors are $(1, 2, 3, 4, \ldots)$. The method is used among many other places in the Polish lower house elections [400]. Table 4.2 shows the results for the lower house constituency of Częstochowa in the 2011 Polish parliamentary elections according to the Polish national electoral commission [25]. The constituency has seven seats. The first two columns show the parties with their (rounded) percentage of valid votes. The third, fourth, and fifth columns show the votes for each party divided by the divisors 2, 3, and 4, respectively. The seven highest averages in the table, shown underlined, determine the number of seats allocated to each party. For instance, since the PiS party has 2 of the highest 7 averages, it wins 2 of the 7 seats. The idea here is that any change in the allocated number of seats would put a party in disadvantage in terms of average number of votes per seat. For example, PO's 3 seats means they have a seat on average for every 11.66% of votes, whereas if PO's third seat were allocated to PSL instead, it would mean that PSL would get a seat on average for every 8.77% of the votes.

The **Sainte-Laguë** method is similar to the d'Hondt method, but uses the divisors $(1,3,5,7,\ldots)$ instead. Other highest average methods also follow the same principle, but utilize different divisors. Among these are the **modified Sainte-Laguë** method with divisors $(1.4,3,5,7,\ldots)$, the **Imperiali** method with divisors $(2,3,4,5,\ldots)$, and the **Danish** method with divisors $(1,4,7,10,\ldots)$.

In the **largest remainder (LR)** methods, first a *quota* is calculated, representing the number of votes required for a seat. Then the number of votes for each party is divided by the quota to obtain a quotient consisting of an integer and a fractional part. The fractional part is called a *remainder*. Each party is allocated a number of initial seats equal to the integer part of their quotient. This will amount to a total of n_i initial seats. The remaining $n - n_i$ seats are distributed between the $n - n_i$ parties with the largest remainders, giving each such party an extra seat.

The **Hare** quota and the **Droop** quota are two widely used quotas in LR systems. The Hare quota is calculated by dividing the total number of (valid) votes to the number of seats. The Droop quota is calculated by dividing the total number of (valid) votes to the number of seats plus one, and then adding 1 to the result. Fractions are usually disregarded in calculating quotas. In other words, we have:

$$\text{Hare quota} = \left\lfloor \frac{\text{no. of votes}}{\text{no. of seats}} \right\rfloor \quad \text{and} \quad \text{Droop quota} = 1 + \left\lfloor \frac{\text{no. of votes}}{1 + \text{no. of seats}} \right\rfloor .$$

Other quotas that are used include the **Hagenbach-Bischoff** quota which is one less than the Droop quota, and the **Imperiali** quota which is calculated by dividing the number of votes into the number of seats plus two.

The Droop quota is used in the national and provincial elections in South Africa [267]. Table 4.3 shows the Gauteng Provincial Legislature results in the 2014 South African National and Provincial Elections [15]. The table only shows the first eight parties. The first two columns show the parties and their respective number of votes. There are 73 seats to be allocated. The total number of valid votes is 4,382,163. The Droop quota hence is calculated as $\lfloor 4,382,163/(73+1) \rfloor + 1 = 59,219$. Dividing the votes for each party by the quota gives the quotient, the number of initial seats (the integer part of the quotient), and the remainder (the fractional part of the quotient). The total number of initial seats is 68 which leaves 5 extra seats to be allocated to the 5 parties with the largest remainders, shown underlined in the table.

The South African system is an example of a PR system without a *threshold*. However, most PR systems require a threshold to be achieved for the party to be eligible for any seats. The lower the threshold is, the more proportional the results will be.

Some argue that in many of the systems discussed so far, especially if the number of seats is relatively low, there is a potential for many votes to be so-called "wasted." For example, in Table 4.2, votes for the last four parties, although counting for more than 10% of the votes, do not count toward electing any candidate and are arguably wasted. The single transferable vote (STV) system, which can be seen as a generalization of the instant run-off (IRV) to elect multiple winners aims to minimize votes

Table 4.3: An example of the largest remainder method of Proportional Representation using the Droop quota: 2011 Gauteng Provincial Legislature election results, South Africa

Party	votes	quotient	initial seats	remainder	extra seats	total seats
ANC	2,348,564	39.66	39	0.66	1	40
DA	1,349,001	22.78	22	0.78	1	23
EFF	451,318	7.62	7	0.62	1	8
VF+	52,436	0.89	0	0.89	1	1
IFP	34,240	0.58	0	0.58	1	1
ACDP	27,196	0.46	0	0.46	0	0
COPE	21,652	0.37	0	0.37	0	0
NFP	20,733	0.35	0	0.35	0	0

being wasted by asking voters to declare their preferences. This way, if a preferred candidate does not receive enough support to be elected, the vote is transferred to the next preferred candidate and finally counts towards electing one of the candidates on the voter's list. STV was first proposed in the 1850s by Thomas Hare [295].

In the **single transferable vote (STV)** system, the voters indicate their preferences between the candidates by ranking them on the ballot. In each round of counting if a candidate achieves a certain *quota*, he or she is elected. Otherwise, the candidate with the lowest number of votes is eliminated from the race. Then either the elected candidate's *surplus* votes or all of the eliminated candidate's votes are transferred to the next candidate appearing on the preference list who is neither already elected nor already eliminated. The process continues until either all seats are allocated or the number of candidates remaining in the race is reduced to the number of remaining available seats.

STV is used in parliamentary elections in Ireland [248] and the upper house elections in Australia at the national level [229], and in the Scottish local council elections [94] and Tasmanian lower house elections [231] at the subnational level. The system is also used in the European parliament elections in Ireland, Northern Ireland and Malta [548, Part 5].

The quota normally used with STV is the Droop quota. Transferring ballots for the eliminated candidates is similar to that of IRV. However, in case a candidate achieves higher votes than the quota, their ballots above the quota are called a surplus and may be transferred. One may think of this process as transferring a portion of the elected candidate's ballots that are not needed for them to be elected. Hence, all the transferable ballots are examined, and the share of each next preference from the surplus votes is determined. This usually results in fractional ballot transfers between the candidates. The rules governing when and how exactly the surplus transfers should be carried out are different between elections in different countries.

Table 4.4: An example of single transferable vote (STV) using the Droop quota: 2009 Aboriginal Land Council of Tasmania (South) election results, Australia

Candidates						
K	M	N	S	Exhausted	Quota	Remark
7	13	18	33	0	24	Count 1
+1.63	+4.09	+3.27	-9			S elected
8.63	17.09	21.27	24	0	24	Count 2
-7	+4	+3				K excluded
1.63	21.09	24.27	24	0	24	Count 3
						N elected

Determining STV election winners can be complex and often consists of tens of rounds of counting. Here however we consider a less complex example. Table 4.4 shows the results of the 2009 Aboriginal Land Council of Tasmania elections in the South Region [27]. The total number of votes is 71, and two candidates are to be chosen. Hence, the initial Droop quota is $\lfloor 71/3 \rfloor + 1 = 24$. As the table shows, in the first round, candidate S's first preference votes are more than enough to get him elected. Thus, S is declared elected in the first round. However, since S only needs 24 votes to get elected, S's surplus votes, 9 votes in this case, are transferred to his corresponding second preferences. To do this fairly, all the 33 votes are examined. In this case, 6 of S's ballots list K as the second preference, 15 list M and 12 list N. That is, $6/33$ of any transferring ballot should go to K, $15/33$ to M and $12/33$ to N. Now that 9 ballots are transferring, $9(6/33) \approx 1.63$ ballots go to K, $9(15/33) \approx 4.09$ to M and $9(12/33) \approx 3.27$ to N. The totals in the second round do not push any candidate above the quota, hence the candidate with the least votes, K, is eliminated and K's 7 votes are distributed, in this case, 4 to M and 3 to N. This gives N enough votes to be declared the second winner.

The above example was a rather straightforward case of determining STV winners. However, note that in many cases for instance if there are multiple winners in any round, or if there are exhausted ballots and hence the quota changes, there could be different methods for how and when to transfer votes. Although the difference between such different methods might seem insignificant, they may lead to different outcomes in the election. The transfer rules are usually agreed on and published in detail before the election, and as mentioned before, they vary considerably between different jurisdictions.

4.4 Blending Systems Together

Elections with single-member districts are praised for clearly tying a representative to a constituency and hence fostering a higher degree of accountability for elected representatives. On the other hand, elections with multi-member districts using Proportional Representation (PR) systems such as party-list are designed to produce results in which the number of seats each party wins is to a great extent proportional to the party's share of popular vote. To combine the positive aspects of these two types of systems, many jurisdictions run two systems alongside each other.

In a **Mixed Member Proportional (MMP)** system, one voting method is used for electing individual representatives for each constituency, and besides this first method, a second PR method is used to compensate for any disproportionality produced by the constituency results. In some MMP systems, the voter is able to vote in each method separately. In other systems however, the voter votes for the constituency representative only, and the party vote is calculated by aggregating the candidate votes in all of the constituencies in a larger PR district. There may be a single national PR district or several subnational ones.

The MMP system is used among other places in parliamentary elections in Germany [507], Hungary [95], Mexico [204] and New Zealand [571], which use combinations of first-past-the-post and list-PR.

In a **two-tier** system, two parallel and independent methods are used: one voting method is used for electing individual representatives for each constituency, and a PR method is used to elect members proportional to party vote shares independently of how many seats the parties win at constituency level. The PR method districts are larger than the constituencies, usually several subnational districts or a single national district. Two-tier systems are also known simply as **parallel** systems.

The two-tier system is used in parliamentary elections among other places in South Korea [484], Japan [479] and Thailand [307], which use first-past-the-post alongside list-PR, and in Lithuania [400], which uses the two-round system alongside list-PR.

4.5 Other Solutions

In this section, we review some of the other systems that are less widely used in national and subnational elections.

In the **Borda count**, each voter ranks the candidates on the ballot. The candidates each get a number of points based on their rank, according to a point allocation scheme which is decreasing with respect to rank. For instance, if there are k candidates on the ballot, the i-th ranked candidate is allocated $k - i$ points, i.e., $k - 1, k - 2, \ldots, 0$ points respectively for candidates in the order of preference. The points each candidate receives in all ballots are summed up and the candidate with the highest sum of points is declared the winner.

This system is used in a few political elections around the world including Nauru [481] and Kiribati [481], and other places such as the Eurovision Song Contest [36]. In Slovenia, the Borda count, which is used to elect the representatives for the Hungarian and Italian-speaking ethnic minorities, allocates $k + 1 - i$ points to the i-th ranked candidate, i.e., $k, k - 1, \ldots, 1$ points respectively for candidates in the order of preference. In parliamentary elections in Nauru, the i-th ranked candidate is allocated $1/i$ points, i.e., $1, \frac{1}{2}, \ldots, \frac{1}{k}$ points, respectively, for candidates in the order of preference.

In the **cumulative voting** system, each voter has a fixed number of points to share between a number of candidates, and the single or multiple candidates receiving the highest total points are declared winners.

Cumulative voting is used among other places in Norfolk Island Legislative Assembly elections where each voter gets nine votes to share between the candidates with the restriction that no more than two votes can be given to any single candidate [93]. Besides, the system is used in some local elections in the United States (see, e.g., [5, 7]), and also in board elections in corporate governance (see, e.g., [112, p. 270]), where typically each shareholder is given a number of votes proportional to their share.

In a **range voting** system, the voter rates the candidates on the ballot, i.e., gives each a score, and the candidate with the highest sum of scores is declared the winner. Approval voting can be seen as an instance of range voting in which only binary scores, i.e., approve or disapprove, are allowed. A variant called **majority judgement** calculates the winner based on the median score for each candidate.

Range voting is used in scoring some sports competitions such as figure skating [20] and gymnastics [193] where a truncated mean of the scores from multiple judges determines the final results. It is also used in web-based scoring and recommendation systems such as the Internet Movie Database (IMDb) where a weighted mean of the individual scores determines the final scores [16].

In **Condorcet methods**, the voter usually ranks the candidates, and Condorcet winner is the candidate, if any, which is pair-wise preferred to all other candidates by the majority of voters. The Condorcet winner is not guaranteed to exist. Any method that elects the Condorcet winner, if any, is generally known as a Condorcet method. A Condorcet method for n candidates can be thought of as running $\frac{1}{2}n(n - 1)$ simple majority elections between all possible pairs of candidates, and finding if there is a candidate that beats all others in their corresponding head-to-head election.

There are various methods to calculate the Condorcet winner if any, and otherwise produce a plausible replacement winner. For instance, in the method known as **Smith/IRV**, the counting produces a so-called *Smith set*, defined as the smallest non-empty set of candidates such that every candidate in the set defeats every candidate outside the set in a pair-wise election. The Condorcet winner is guaranteed to be in the Smith set. Hence, if the Smith set includes only one candidate, that candidate is declared the Condorcet winner. If the Condorcet winner does not exist, then the IRV method is used to elect a winner between the candidates in the Smith set.

In the system known as **Black's method** if the Condorcet winner exists, they are declared the winner, and otherwise the Borda count is used to calculate the winner.

Another Condorcet method known as the **Schulze method** [519] involves finding preference paths between candidates and comparing them based on the so-called "strength" of the paths. The method outputs a complete ordering of the candidate and hence can be used to elect multiple candidates.

Condorcet methods, and specifically the Schulze method, are fairly popular within the free software and free culture communities, and for instance are used in the internal elections of the several national Pirate Parties [491, p. 213], the Debian project [8], Ubuntu [29], KDE [24] and the Free Software Foundation Europe [6].

4.6 Which Systems Are Good?

Every one of us might have already had a favorite electoral system before reading this chapter, or might have set our mind on one while reading the chapter. We might think that our favorite system is obviously superior to the others we know of and have our reasons supporting our argument. However, social choice theorists on the one hand and electoral assistance experts on the other hand would be able to provide a variety of counter arguments pointing towards the weaknesses of our favorite system compared to other systems. In this section we aim to go through some of the better known comparative strengths and weaknesses of the electoral systems we have discussed, from both the theoretical and practical points of view.

4.6.1 A Theorist's Point of View

Social choice theory provides a variety of results on the merits of different electoral systems. Some of these results are naturally expected, while some utterly unexpected. Nonetheless, the results are interesting on both sides, either providing a solid theoretical foundation to build upon in the former case, or challenging our common understanding of such systems and compelling us to rethink and design better systems in the latter case.

4.6.1.1 Majority Rules

Let us first limit our attention to elections with only two candidates. Perhaps one of the expected, and yet illuminating early results in this case is May's theorem, which pretty much settles the question of which system is the best choice in elections with two candidates. To define a notion of a good system, let us start by defining the following criteria:

■ a system is called *egalitarian*[1] if it treats all voters equally;

---

[1]This criterion is often called *anonymity* in modern social choice theory. We use May's original term to avoid confusion with anonymity from the security viewpoint.

- a system is called *neutral* (with respect to candidates) if it treats all candidates equally;

- a system is called *monotone* if the candidate who wins an election would still win if one or more voters change their vote in favor of the winning candidate and everyone else votes the same way; in other words, it is impossible for a winning candidate to become a losing candidate by gaining votes; and

- a system is called *nearly decisive* if the only way a tie can occur is when the two candidates receive exactly the same number of votes.

The above criteria seem quite natural to expect from a good electoral system. In fact, May has shown that the simple majority system is the only system that can satisfy all four criteria [384].

Theorem 4.1 May's theorem

In an election with two candidates, the only electoral system that is egalitarian, neutral, monotone, and nearly decisive is the simple majority method.

May's theorem is definitive in that the simple majority system is the only system that could satisfy the above reasonable requirements. In fact, even if we do not care about the electoral system being decisive, an extension of May's theorem states that the only two-candidate electoral systems that are egalitarian, neutral, and monotone are the following ones: simple majority, super-majority and a third nonsensical system which results in a tie regardless of the number of votes for the two candidates [489, p. 20]. On the other hand, if we define a (strictly) decisive system to be one that always produces a winner (i.e., never ends in a tie), then it is not hard to see that the three properties of equality, neutrality and decisiveness are inherently contradictory; that is, there is no electoral system for two candidates that is egalitarian, neutral, and decisive. This statement is true even when elections with more than two candidates are considered. This leads us to believe that (strict) decisiveness might be too strong a requirement to expect from an electoral system.

4.6.1.2 Bad News Begins

Now consider elections with more than two candidates and a single winner. Equality and neutrality can still be defined similarly. Equality can be formalized by requiring that the outcome of the election stays the same if any two voters exchange their ballots. Similarly, neutrality can be formalized by requiring that if candidate A is replaced with candidate B on all ballots, and vice versa, i.e., candidate B is also replaced with candidate A on all ballots, then the same replacements are replicated in the outcome of the election.

Formalizing monotonicity in the case of more than two candidates needs to be elaborated on to define a precise sense of the voters changing their votes *in favor of* the winning candidate. In the case of only two candidates, it is clear that this means changing a vote for the losing candidate to a vote for the winning candidate. For an election with more than two candidates, let us consider the rather general case where voters rank the candidates on the ballots. We can now specify what is meant by changing a vote in favor of the winning candidate as changing the rank of the winning candidate on a ballot with the rank of a losing candidate which is ranked higher than the winning candidate, and vice versa.

Let us now define more criteria to assess our electoral system against. All of these are criteria that we would naturally want a good system to satisfy.

- a system satisfies the *majority* criterion if whenever a candidate receives a majority of the first preferences, the system elects B as the winner;

- a system satisfies the *Condorcet* criterion if it elects the Condorcet winner whenever such a winner exists;

- a system satisfies the *Pareto* criterion (also called *unanimity*) if whenever every voter prefers candidate A to candidate B, the system does not elect B as the winner; and

- a system satisfies the *independence of irrelevant alternatives (IIA)* criterion if the following holds: consider an election in which A is elected the winner, and a second election in which all voters rank A above or below B the same way they have done in the first election, but may change their preferences of other candidates; the system must not choose B as the winner in the second election; in other words, IIA requires that the electoral system's preference between any two candidates depends only on the individual voters' preferences between those two candidates.

Note that if a candidate receives a majority of first preferences, the candidate beats all other candidates in head-to-head contests, and hence is the Condorcet winner. Thus, the Condorcet criterion is a stronger criterion than the majority criterion, i.e., the Condorcet criterion implies the majority criterion. In fact, the Condorcet and IIA criteria are incompatible as stated by the following theorem [489, p. 55].

Theorem 4.2

There is no electoral system for an election with more than two candidates that satisfies both the Condorcet and the independence of irrelevant alternatives (IIA) criteria.

The above theorem is one of several impossibility results in social choice theory. Each of these results shows the impossibility of electoral systems satisfying a set of criteria simultaneously. Such results can be seen as a contributing reason why the debate over the merits of different electoral systems is far from settled. A fundamental issue with distilling a social preference from a set of individual preferences which eventually is responsible for many such results is the following observation.

The **Condorcet paradox** is the observation that majority preferences can be "ir-rational" (specifically, intransitive), even when individual preferences are "rational" (specifically, transitive).

To see an example of this paradox, consider an election with three candidates A, B, and C. Assume we have three voters whose preferences are as follows. The first voter prefers A to B, and B to C, and since we are assuming rational voters, also A to C; or in shorthand $A \succ B \succ C$. The second voter's preferences are $B \succ C \succ A$ and the third voter's $C \succ A \succ B$. Now the majority of voters prefer A to B, B to C and C to A. This means that although the individual preferences are transitive, the majority preference is intransitive.

4.6.1.3 Arrow's Impossibility Theorem

A well-known impossibility result which has been described as "the single most im-portant result in the history of voting theory" [310] is Arrow's impossibility theorem. Arrow considers electoral systems that provide a full ranking of the candidates as out-come. He defines the following criteria in addition to the ones we have discussed so far:

- a system satisfies the *unrestricted domain* criterion (or universality, the term originally used by Arrow) if it does not place any restriction other than transi-tivity on how voters can rank the candidates;

- a system satisfies the *non-imposition* criterion (or citizen sovereignty, the term originally used by Arrow) if its outcome is not restricted (i.e., not imposed) in any way other than being transitive; in other words, every transitive outcome is possible in the election depending on individual orderings; and

- a system satisfies the *non-dictatorship* criterion if there is no single voter (i.e., a dictator) whose vote determines the outcome of the election regardless of how others vote.

Note that non-dictatorship is a weaker criterion than equality, i.e., equality implies non-dictatorship.

Arrow's impossibility theorem basically says that the only unrestricted-domain electoral systems which are monotone and independent of irrelevant alternatives are either imposed or dictatorial [64].

Theorem 4.3 Arrow's impossibility theorem

There is no electoral system for an election with more than two candidates that satisfies the unrestricted domain, monotonicity and independence of irrelevant alter-natives (IIA) criteria and is neither imposed nor dictatorial.

Arrow's impossibility theorem is pretty strong in ruling out the possibility of existence of any fair electoral system that satisfies three reasonable criteria that one may expect from a good system. It can be even stated in a stronger form since monotonicity, IIA and non-imposition together imply the Pareto criterion. In its stronger form, the theorem basically says unrestricted domain, Pareto and IIA properties are incompatible [310].

Theorem 4.4 Arrow's impossibility theorem (strong form)

There is no electoral system for an election with more than two candidates that satisfies the unrestricted domain, Pareto and independence of irrelevant alternatives (IIA) criteria and is not dictatorial.

Although Arrow's impossibility theorem states that certain desirable criteria are incompatible with each other, what it does not say is that there are no reasonable systems around. The question of choosing the right system hence becomes that of the choices we make between the desirable criteria to achieve a compromise.

One possible compromise would be to consider systems in which the voter's ranking of candidates is restricted in some way, and hence the system does not support an unrestricted domain. Of course this should be done in a way that neutrality is still kept intact. An example of such a system is the approval electoral system in which candidate rankings on the ballots are restricted to either approval or lack thereof. By compromising on the unrestricted domain criterion, approval voting is able to achieve monotonicity, Pareto and IIA. Note that the Condorcet paradox is absent in the setting of approval voting since collective preference, as defined by comparing the number of approvals for each candidate, is transitive.

When faced with a choice between Pareto and IIA, the more accepted view seems to support a compromise on IIA. IRV and Borda are both examples of systems which do not restrict voter's rankings of candidates in any way and at the same time achieve Pareto and provide some guarantees comparatively weaker than IIA.

4.6.1.4 Gibbard–Satterthwaite Impossibility Theorem

Consider a single-winner election with three candidates A, B and C using the Borda count. Assume A and B are the only main contenders with a realistic chance of winning. Consider a voter, Alice, whose preferences are as follows: 1st A, then B and C last. If Alice reflects her preferences as they are on the ballot box, i.e., she puts $A \succ B \succ C$ on the ballot, it is said that she votes *sincerely*. However, knowing that the realistic race is only between A and B, it would make sense for Alice to mark $A \succ C \succ B$ on her ballot to give her first preference a better chance of winning. This would be a case of so-called *strategic* or *tactical* voting in which considering contextual information the voter misrepresents her preferences on the ballot to favor a candidate over a relatively less preferred candidate.

It is often argued that an electoral system should ideally ensure that, no matter the contextual circumstances, the best voting strategy for a voter always is voting sincerely, i.e., reflecting their actual preferences. However, a significant theoretical result known as the Gibbard–Satterthwaite theorem rules out the existence of such ideal electoral systems altogether under some natural conditions. In the following we briefly discuss this theorem.

Let us for the moment limit our attention to single-winner systems only. A basic fairness criterion is to require that every candidate should be able to win. In the following the definition of this criterion is listed along with that of strategy-proofness.

- a system is said to have an *unrestricted range* if its winner can be any candidate; and

- a system is said to be *strategy-proof* (or non-manipulable) if there are circumstances under which strategic voting by a voter leads to a winner which is actually preferred by the voter to a candidate that will win if the voter votes sincerely.

Mathematically, an unrestricted range is equivalent to the voting function being surjective or onto. Having an unrestricted range can be seen as a form of the non-imposition criterion for single-winner systems. Note that neutrality implies an unrestricted range, so having an unrestricted range can be thought of as a relaxation of neutrality. Yet Gibbard and Satterthwaite have independently shown that even under such a relaxed version of neutrality there is no strategy-proof electoral system other than dictatorship [253, 515].

Theorem 4.5 Gibbard–Satterthwaite theorem

There is no unrestricted range electoral system for an election with more than two candidates that is strategy-proof and is not dictatorial.

The results of Gibbard and Satterthwaite further demonstrate a one-to-one correspondence between strategy-proof systems and systems satisfying Arrow's criteria. Duggan and Schwartz have proved a generalized version of the theorem not restricted to single-winner systems [208].

In light of such impossibility results, and with completely strategy-proof systems out of the question, electoral systems may be examined based on the specific manipulation strategies to which they are prone. The choice of a system can then be made based on the occurring probability and severity of such possible manipulation strategies in the contextual circumstances of a specific election.

Table 4.5: Selected electoral system and criteria they satisfy

System	Equ.	Neu.	Maj.	Con.	Mon.	Par.	IIA
FPTP	✓	✓	✓	✗	✓	✓	✗
Approval	✓	✓	✗	✗	✓	✓	✓
TRS	✓	✓	✓	✗	✗	✓	✗
Contingent	✓	✓	✓	✗	✗	✓	✗
Exhaustive	✓	✓	✓	✗	✗	✓	✗
IRV	✓	✓	✓	✗	✗	✓	✗
Borda	✓	✓	✗	✗	✓	✓	✗
Cumulative	✓	✓	✗	✗	✓	✓	✗
Schulze	✓	✓	✓	✓	✓	✓	✗

4.6.1.5 Systems with Respect to Criteria

Table 4.5 lists selected electoral systems and criteria they do and do not satisfy. A tick (✓) indicates that the system on that row always satisfies the criterion on that column, whereas a cross (✗) indicates that the system does not necessarily satisfy the criterion. The criteria discussed in this chapter and presented in the table are a selective set of those discussed in social choice theory.

Note that, assuming that voters do not change their minds between multiple rounds of an election, the TRS and contingent votes can be thought of as the same system in theory, and hence the two systems have the same properties in Table 4.5. The same statement is also true about the exhaustive vote and IRV systems.

In some cases, it is easy to see why a system satisfies a specific criterion; e.g., a candidate that achieves a majority obviously achieves a plurality as well, and hence FPTP satisfies the majority criterion. In other cases, the reason for a tick or a cross might be less obvious. We leave the task of justifying the ticks to the reader, but give some counter-examples to explain some of the crosses in the following. Figure 4.1 contains the counter-examples we are going to use to this end. Each counter-example is a profile of an election which specifies the number of voters that have a specific candidate preference. For instance, the profile indicated as "Election 1" basically says 4 voters have the preference $A \succ B \succ C$, 2 the preference $B \succ C \succ A$ and 3 the preference $C \succ B \succ A$.

Consider Election 1 in Figure 4.1. A FPTP election would record 4 votes for A, 2 for B and 3 for C, and hence the FPTP winner would be A. However, in one-on-one elections, B would beat both A and C, 5–4 and 6–3, respectively, and hence B is the Condorcet winner. In fact even C beats A 5–4 in a head-to-head election, which means FPTP might even elect a *Condorcet loser*, i.e., a candidate that loses against all other candidates in head-to-head elections. Also note that if the third group change their preference from $C \succ B \succ A$ to $B \succ C \succ A$, the winner of FPTP will change to B, despite the fact that the voters who have changed their mind still rank A the same

Election 1		
4	2	3
A	B	C
B	C	B
C	A	A

Election 2			
6	5	4	2
A	C	B	B
B	A	C	A
C	B	A	C

Election 3					
30	1	29	10	10	1
A	A	B	B	C	C
B	C	A	C	A	B
C	B	C	A	B	A

Figure 4.1: Counter-examples of election profiles

way with respect to B and C, i.e., they still think $C \succ A$ and $B \succ A$. Thus FPTP does not satisfy the Condorcet and IIA criteria.

Consider Election 2 in Figure 4.1 from [451]. With either two-round system (TRS) or instant run-off voting (IRV), C is eliminated in the first round, and in the second round between A and B, C's votes go to A and hence A wins the TRS or IRV elections. Now consider the case where A is able to gain the support of the last group of 2 voters and change their preference to $A \succ B \succ C$. In that case, B gets eliminated in the first round, and in the second round C beats A 9–8. Thus, A loses the second election despite gaining votes. This shows that TRS and IRV (and hence the contingent and exhaustive vote systems) are not monotone.

If any of the four systems above, i.e., TRS, IRV, contingent or exhaustive, is used to elect the winner in Election 1 in Figure 4.1, the Condorcet winner B will be eliminated in the first round and C will be the eventual winner. Hence, these systems do not necessarily elect the Condorcet winner.

Consider Election 3 in Figure 4.1 from Condorcet [192]. It is not hard to see that A is the Condorcet winner but using the standard Borda count, i.e., allocating 2, 1 and 0 points for the 1st, 2nd and 3rd preferences, respectively, elects B as the winner. In fact, even in a generalized Borda count where p_i points are allocated for the i-th preference, A receives $31p_1 + 39p_2 + 11p_3$ points and B $39p_1 + 31p_2 + 11p_3$ points. Since p_1 needs to be greater than p_2 for the system to make sense, this example shows that no generalized Borda count can guarantee electing the Condorcet winner.

Approval voting is a bit trickier in that the outcome of the election not only depends on voter preferences, but also on the number of candidates each voter approves. This means, unlike some other systems such as FPTP, TRS and Borda, in an approval voting election for each election profile there might be multiple possible outcomes based on voters' behavior. For instance, in Election 1 in Figure 4.1, if all voters only approve their top candidate, A would win the election, whereas if all voters approve their top two candidates, B would win, and at the same time, if the first and third groups of voters approve one candidate and the second group approves two, then C would win. A similar situation may happen even if a candidate has a majority. Thus, approval voting without any restriction on how many candidates may be approved by voters does not satisfy the majority and Condorcet criteria.

All counter-examples used for FPTP and Borda may be also used for cumulative voting since both FPTP and Borda can be seen as instances of cumulative voting.

4.6.2 A Practitioner's Point of View

In practice, electoral systems are usually broadly categorized as *majoritarian, proportional*, and *mixed* systems. Majoritarian systems are based on the general principle that a single candidate with a plurality of votes is elected to represent and pursue the demands of a specific (usually geographic) constituency. FPTP, TRS, IRV and other similar systems hence fall in this category. Proportional systems on the other hand, are based on the general principle that the elected body of candidates proportionally reflects the diverse range of views in a heterogeneous society. This category includes multiple list voting systems and STV, although STV is sometimes referred to as semi-proportional. Mixed systems aim to attain the best of both worlds by incorporating elements from the above two types of systems. MMP and two-tier systems are examples of mixed systems. This categorization is a general guide and some systems, most notably SNTV, do not seem to fit in any of the categories.

The underlying principles of the majoritarian and proportional systems correspond to two different conceptions of "representation": *principal–agent* and *microcosm*, as put forth by McLean [390]. The principal–agent conception defines representation as an agent acting on behalf of a principal, whereas the microcosmic conception defines representation as statistically typifying the group being represented. McLean argues that the two conceptions are each entirely reasonable but inconsistent with each other.

Rae distinguished three main components of an electoral system: *district magnitude, electoral formula* and *ballot structure* [476]. District magnitude refers to the number of candidates elected in each electoral district; electoral formula is the algorithm used to calculate the winner(s); and ballot structure refers to the information collected from the voter on a ballot. Rae further argues that classification of electoral systems often deals with only one component, namely the electoral formula, and leaves the other two out, whereas district magnitude and ballot structure have significant effects on how an electoral system performs. Based on district magnitude, systems can be classified into single-member and multi-member district systems. Different ballot structures on the other hand lead to categorizing systems based on three aspects: first, the number of votes allowed: either one, more than one but less than the number of seats or equal to the number of candidates or seats; second, the type of information the voter is asked to provide: either nominal, ordinal or cardinal; and third, for whom the voter votes: either for individuals or for groups of individuals (e.g., parties) [104]. Systems using nominal ballots (i.e., voting for one option) include FPTP, TRS and closed-list PR; systems using ordinal ballots (i.e., ranking the options) include IRV, STV and Borda count; and systems using cardinal ballots (i.e., rating the options) include approval and range voting.

Majoritarian systems are praised for their ability to produce a clear tie between an elected candidate and a constituency, which in turn implies a clear responsibility and accountability of the elected candidate towards the constituency. Besides, most majoritarian systems (with, e.g., IRV being an exception) are simple to understand and do not require complex mathematics to calculate the results, and hence they are considered to encourage transparency. However, such systems tend to favor large parties and do not usually produce results that reflect the shares of votes received by different parties. Thus, minority groups and smaller parties may not be able to win any seat and are encouraged to integrate into the larger parties. In some contexts, e.g., when there are two dominant parties, this can be seen as a positive feature since it produces a clear winner and hence a strong and stable government as well as a strong opposition and government alternative.

Proportional systems on the other hand emphasize accurately representing the make-up of diverse electorates. The greater the number of candidates to be elected from an electoral district, the more proportional the results tend to be. Such systems should result in governing coalitions that represent a wide range of views in the political scene, although in some contexts, negotiations to build a coalition may take a long time. Proportional systems tend to facilitate fragmentation of the party system. Besides, since multi-member districts are required to guarantee any degree of proportionality, proportional systems usually lack the clear link between a specific candidate and the constituency. In contrast with proportionality, the greater the number of candidates to be elected from an electoral district, the weaker such links tend to be.

While the principal–agent and microcosmic conceptions describe an elected body's collective role in representing the electors, an elected candidate's individual representative role may be defined as that of either a *delegate* or a *trustee*. A delegate in this characterization is expected to listen to and reflect the views of the electors, whereas a trustee is thought to be entrusted by the electors to use his or her own judgment and decide on behalf of the electors. Farrell argues that in "party-based" electoral systems there is a greater tendency for elected representatives to act as trustees, whereas comparatively in "candidate-based" systems there is more incentive for elected representatives to act as delegates [230].

Majoritarian systems are considered more susceptible to strategic voting compared to proportional systems. In a FPTP system for example, a voter might vote for a candidate that they do not prefer but think has a better chance to win. Proportional systems, on the other hand, are considered to encourage voters to declare their actual preferences.

Majoritarian systems, especially those using single-member districts, are prone to district boundary irregularities, known as *malapportionment* and *gerrymandering*, that might arise as a result of the process of district delimitation [230, pp. 202–205]. Malapportionment refers to the situations in which there are imbalances between the populations of different electoral districts that favor one party over others. Gerrymandering refers to the practice of (re)drawing electoral boundaries in shapes that are expected to disproportionately boost the number of seats won by a specific party. Some proportional systems, especially those using smaller multi-member districts, are susceptible to such irregularities as well. Generally speaking, the greater the number of candidates to be elected in districts, the less they have the potential to suffer from malapportionment and gerrymandering [310, Ch. 10]. These issues however may be resolved by putting a neutral body in charge of district delimitation.

A widely accepted characterization is that of Duverger who argues that the single-ballot plurality systems favor party dualism, whereas two-round majority systems and proportional systems favor multipartism [210]. He further argues that majoritarian systems may encourage "personality parties," i.e., those based on a leader's popularity, and geographic minority parties, whereas proportional systems generally encourage "permanent minority parties," such as ethnic or religious ones, but discourage "personality parties." The effects of mixed systems are less understood as these systems only relatively recently have been adopted by a considerable number of countries.

Proportional systems tend to be more accommodating in adjusting representation towards historically under-represented groups and minorities. In established democracies, systems based on multi-member districts have shown a strong increase in women's representation, whereas this trend is much weaker in systems based on single-member districts [383].

Votes that do not count towards the election of any candidate are usually referred to as *wasted* votes. Systems such as FPTP tend to leave a larger number of wasted votes, whereas proportional systems with low thresholds, IRV and STV aim to reduce the number of wasted vote. A related issue is *vote splitting*, and it happens when similar candidates compete in an election and their potential supporters' votes tend to be split between them, which possibly allows a candidate representing a less popular overall viewpoint to win. FPTP particularly suffers from this issue, whereas TRS is considered less susceptible, and proportional systems with low thresholds, IRV and STV are considered relatively immune to vote splitting.

The two-round system is unique among the discussed systems in that it possibly requires the electoral administration to run a second election in a short period, hence significantly increasing the election cost. On the other hand, this unique property enables voters to change their minds from the first round to the second and accelerate consensus building between parties to coalesce behind the candidates in the second round.

Among the multiple highest average (HA) seat allocation methods for list electoral systems, the Danish method is considered to comparatively favor smaller parties; the Sainte-Laguë method is considered neutral; the modified Sainte-Laguë and Imperiali methods are considered to favor larger parties; and the d'Hondt method is considered to favor larger parties the most. Among the largest remainder (LR) methods, smaller quotas are more favorable to larger parties. Considering all proportional systems, it has been shown that they can be generally ordered from the most to the least favorable to the larger parties as follows [247]: LR using Imperiali quota, d'Hondt, STV, LR using Droop quota, modified Sainte-Laguë, LR using Hare quota and Sainte-Laguë, and finally the Danish method.

Mixed systems tend to produce election results that, in terms of proportionality, fall between majoritarian and proportional systems. However, some criticize such systems for effectively creating two classes of elected candidates with different mandates and hence undermining the cohesiveness of the elected body of representatives.

Among the systems that do not fall in the three categories mentioned above, SNTV is considered to be easy to understand, to accommodate the representation of minority parties better compared to majoritarian systems, and to fragment the party system less compared to proportional systems. However, SNTV tends to result in many wasted votes, and parties need to consider complex strategic decisions as to how many candidates to put forth as the system suffers from issues similar to vote splitting.

Acknowledgment

The author is supported by the ERC Starting Grant No. 306994.

Chapter 5

E-Voting in Norway

Kristian Gjøsteen

Department of Mathematical Sciences
Norwegian University of Science and Technology
Trondheim, Norway
`kristian.gjosteen@math.ntnu.no`

CONTENTS

5.1 Introduction

In 2008 the Norwegian parliament authorized trials of electronic voting in Norway. This lead to trials of electronic voting from home during the 2011 local elections and 2013 parliamentary elections.

The author participated in these trials from 2009 as a member of the steering group for the 2011 trials and as a consulting cryptographer for both trials.

The following is an account of the two trials from a cryptographer's point of view. The account touches on more than cryptography, since the author was involved in much more than just the cryptography.

To understand certain choices made during these trials, it is necessary to understand the Norwegian electoral system and what Norwegians consider important about elections. These topics are discussed in Sections 5.2 and 5.3.

The Norwegian government wanted to buy a suitable electronic voting system. This process is discussed in Section 5.4. Eventually, a vendor was chosen, but we were not entirely happy with the vendor's electronic voting system. Section 5.5 discusses why we were unhappy and what remedy we chose.

Eventually, the electronic voting system was deployed. The results are discussed in Section 5.6.

5.2 Elections in Norway

Norway has four different elections: municipal, county and parliamentary, as well as elections to Sametinget, a representative body for the Sami.[1] While the elections share certain common features, there are important differences.

Before an election, each participating political party nominates a *list* of candidates. The voter chooses one of these party lists to submit as his ballot. Before submission, the voter may modify the ballot.

- In municipal elections, the voter may modify the list by marking specific candidates (so-called personal votes) or writing in candidates from other party lists. (Note that arbitrary write-ins are not allowed.)

- In county elections, the voter may modify the list by marking specific candidates (so-called personal votes), but may not write in candidates from other party lists.

- In parliamentary elections and elections to Sametinget, voters may modify the list by reordering or deleting candidates.

For all the elections, the political parties are essentially awarded seats in proportion to the number of ballots they receive. (For parliamentary elections, multiple representatives are elected for each district.) The elections differ in how list candidates are ranked after the election.

For municipal elections, candidates are ranked by the number of times they are marked by their party's voters or written in by other parties' voters. Ballots with

---

[1] The Sami are Norway's indigenous people.

write-in candidates are split between the party the list belongs to and the parties of the written-in candidates. (Note that while write-in candidates typically influence which candidates are selected, they may also change the number of seats awarded to each party.)

For county elections, the political parties are awarded seats in proportion to the number of ballots they receive. Candidates are ranked by the number of times they are marked by their party's voters. (Note that there are no write-ins in county elections.)

For parliamentary elections, ballot modifications to a candidate's order (or striking) will be discarded unless more than half of all voters have made the same change for that candidate. Ballot modifications never change the candidate ordering for parliamentary elections.

The Electoral Roll

The Norwegian electoral roll is derived from a national registry run by the Norwegian tax administration some three months before the election.

After the election, the list of who voted is considered confidential, but election researchers may be given access to it.

The Ballot

Logically, a Norwegian ballot consists of a sequence of values. For each election, the first of these values describes the party (possibly no party, as implied by a blank ballot).

- For municipal elections, the remaining values describe candidates and are chosen from a large (up to a few thousand) set of possible values. Their order does not matter.

- For county elections, the remaining values describe candidates nominated by the party and are chosen from a small (less than one hundred) set of possible values. Their order does not matter.

- For elections to parliament and Sametinget, the remaining values describe re-ordering or striking, and come from a small (less than sixty) set of possible values. Their order matters.

The entire sequence of values is required to count the ballot correctly. That is, none of these elections is equivalent to a series of (simpler) independent races.

Ballot Casting

Voters may vote in advance for roughly one month before election day. About 30% of all voters voted in advance in the 2013 parliamentary elections.

Advance voting inside Norway is usually done in polling stations (typically in the city hall or a local public library), although temporary polling stations may be organized, e.g., at universities or nursing homes. Mobile voting booths are available for those with special needs.

Voters abroad may only vote in advance at Norwegian embassies or consulates, or they may send their ballots by mail. They may not vote on election day.

On election day, voters vote at regular polling stations.

While almost all voters use official paper ballots, almost any piece of paper may serve as a ballot. In this case, the voter expresses his intended ballot simply by writing it on the piece of paper. This is mostly relevant for advance voting abroad, where voters may not have thought to acquire official paper ballots before deciding to vote.

Voters with special needs (e.g., blind voters) need help to prepare their ballot. (The paper ballots are stored in containers marked with braille writing, so that blind voters can choose the correct paper list. But blind voters cannot reliably modify their ballot.) At any time, during advance voting or on election day, voters may ask for assistance from poll workers in preparing their ballot.

Counting

After the polling stations close, the paper ballots are counted, mostly by machines. Preliminary results usually arrive within a few hours, and accurate results are ready by next morning.

A long time ago, there were strict formal requirements for ballots. This caused many ballots to be discarded, and voters were reluctant to modify their ballots, since any mistake might invalidate the ballot. Today, the principle is that as long as the intention of the ballot is sufficiently clear, the ballot should be counted as intended.

The counted ballots are stored until after the next election. The ballots can be made available to election researchers, but they are otherwise considered confidential and the general public will not be allowed to inspect the ballots.

Benefits of Electronic Voting

Using electronic voting machines in polling stations would have the following benefits for Norwegian elections:

■ Counting time for a fully electronic election could be significantly reduced.

■ Voters with special needs could modify their ballots unassisted.

For any election with a significant fraction of paper votes, counting time would not be significantly reduced. Since Norway's ballots are reasonably easy to count using optical scanners, there is little to be gained in accuracy.

Using electronic voting from home would have the following benefits for Norwegian elections:

- General access would be improved. While most people in Norway live reasonably close to a polling station, many people do not.

- Voters with special needs could modify their ballots unassisted.

- Voters abroad could vote more easily.

5.3   Requirements

Any voting scheme is subject to a number of requirements, often shaped by long tradition, only some of which are relevant for security.

No Influence on Outcome

The voting scheme should as far as possible not influence the election outcome. For instance, if it is hard to modify a ballot, fewer voters will modify their ballot, which will change the outcome of Norwegian elections.

Another example of functionality that would be suspect in an electronic voting system is allowing the voter to search for candidate names in order to write their name on the ballot. This could increase the number of write-in candidates relative to the existing paper voting scheme, which could change the outcome.

Correctness

Correctness is perhaps the most important requirement for Norwegian elections. The final count should correctly reflect the ballots cast, and moreover, the intention behind the ballots cast. There is no requirement that official ballots should be used. A blank ballot (or indeed any piece of paper) with a legible party name written on it will be counted as a vote for that party.

Secrecy

Secrecy is important in Norwegian elections, and this is reflected in voting procedures. Secrecy of the ballot is in a sense mandatory. You are allowed to tell anyone what you voted, obviously, but you should not be able to prove that you are telling the truth. Modern technology makes this difficult to enforce, but the intention is clearly encoded in rules and regulations.

To prepare the ballot in a polling station on election day, the voter must enter an enclosure alone. There, the voter will select and possibly modify the ballot. The voter folds the paper ballot to hide its contents before leaving the enclosure and placing the ballot in the ballot box.

One common mistake is to fold the ballot the wrong way so that its contents are visible. Polling station attendants will send any voter making this mistake back into the enclosure with instructions to come out with a correctly folded ballot.

Coercion Resistance

Coercion prevents the free exercise of the right to vote, which is essential for democracy. Any system that makes coercion easier will be suspect in Norway.

Without secrecy, preventing coercion is impossible. This is one more reason for caring about secrecy.

Since the Norwegian ballot is so complicated, so-called Italian attacks would be possible. The number of possible ballot modifications is so large, that a random choice of modifications is likely unique. Random modification choices will tend to cancel out. Keeping the counted ballots secret is a countermeasure against this kind of attack.

While poll workers do observe straightforward attempts at coercion during ordinary paper voting, they also observe less obvious coercion. Often this takes the form of trying to help other voters, and there is no explicit coercion. If challenged, the coerced voter may not even agree that he was coerced, even though he would have voted otherwise without the coercion.

This has important implications for mechanisms that provide resistance to coercion. For instance, the mechanism must not require that the voter actively tries to prevent coercion (à la kill codes) or recover from coercion (cancelling a coerced ballot submission).

Verifiability

Norwegians expect the government to make mistakes. But we do not expect the government to deliberately try to cheat us. This level of trust means that there is no demand for verifiability in Norway. This does not mean that verifiability is undesirable, only that any verifiability must be achieved without compromising more important properties.

5.4 Buying a Voting System

The municipalities are responsible for running elections in Norway. By 2008, municipalities had acquired many different election administration and paper ballot scanning systems, of widely differing quality and capability. The central government wanted to improve on this rather inefficient state of affairs, and decided to have an election administration system developed which it could later offer to municipalities free of charge.

The Norwegian parliament had already decided to try electronic voting. The government felt that the best approach was limited trials of remote internet voting.

The two projects, election administration and internet voting, were combined into one acquisition process. Since it later turned out that no single company could assemble a good bid for both parts of the project, it seems reasonable to ask if this was a wise decision.

The Acquisition Process

The acquisition process was organized as a "competitive dialogue," a somewhat obscure process where over a number of rounds the participating vendors would get to influence the final specification. (Eventually, many of the proposals were not submitted by individual companies, but by consortiums. The word "vendor" in the following will also refer to these consortiums.)

One curious feature of the process was that every tender would be completely transparent, from the proposed solution down to contract details such as financials. There were two slightly different reasons for this transparency.

Politically the spirit of the open source movement was important, where openness was important in and of itself. This meant among other things that the final source code license was an item of discussion.

The project organization considered transparency a vital strategy for ensuring both security and belief in security. One of the main goals of an election system is to convince the losers that they really lost. This implies that security is a necessary property for an election system, but it is not sufficient. We also need a widespread belief in the security.

Some vendors did use the competitive dialogue process to object to this transparency, even claiming that transparency was bad for security. Such arguments were rejected and the requirement was retained.

The main unsolved security problem identified by the Norwegian government prior to the competitive dialogue was that the voter's computer could be compromised. Any proposal must give the voter tools to preserve ballot integrity.

So-called return codes à la Chaum's SureVote [141] and the British CESG study [34] were a plausible solution to the integrity problem that was known to the Norwegian government, but alternative solutions were still sought. In the event, no convincing alternative was proposed.

While preserving confidentiality against a compromised computer was obviously desirable, this was not a requirement since it would most likely be very difficult without compromising usability. However, any proposal that included even a partial solution would have a significant advantage over other proposals. In the event, no plausible solutions to preserving confidentiality against a compromised computer were proposed during the competitive dialogue.

One property much desired of any solution was understandability. Cryptography, especially the kind of cryptography usually employed in common academic voting protocols, is very hard to understand for non-experts. The Norwegian government believed that it would be easier for the public to understand and accept simpler systems. In the event, no non-cryptographic solution was proposed.

The Proposals

The fourth round of the competitive dialogue was supposed to see preliminary submissions with sufficient detail for independent security analysis. Five proposals were submitted. One vendor submitted a detailed cryptographic proposal for part of the voting system along with sensible and correct analysis. One submission contained a partial description that allowed some analysis to be done. Several submissions were sorely lacking in details, preventing any realistic analysis.

The Norwegian government requested the assistance of the security and cryptography groups at the Norwegian universities, as well as from other groups.

Where analysis was possible, multiple issues were found, some of them serious. Where no or partial analysis was possible, some possible issues were identified, but largely these submissions were ignored by the external analysis teams. All issues identified were reported to the vendors.

The fifth and final round required complete proposals. Three complete proposals were submitted. Every proposal used return codes to protect the integrity of the ballot from a compromised voter's computer, though they used very different underlying cryptographic solutions.

The same groups that participated in analysis after the fourth round now did one more round of analysis. After minor clarifications and corrections, it was clear that two of the proposals could plausibly be fixed to provide secure solutions. One proposal could not be fixed.

One plausible proposal was significantly cheaper than the other two proposals, which made the job of choosing the winning proposal easy. (At this point it should be repeated that the government was buying both an internet voting system and an election administration system. Internet voting was a fairly small part of the total contract.)

The Winning Bid

The winning bid was submitted by a consortium consisting of the Norwegian company Ergo, which had previously delivered voting systems to Norwegian municipalities, and the Spanish company Scytl, an electronic voting specialist.

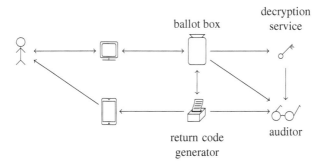

Figure 5.1: The voter uses his computer and his phone to communicate with an infrastructure consisting of four players. The decryption service and the auditor are only active during counting.

Scytl's proposed solution (similar to a later published version [54]) was based on Scytl's existing products. A brief overview of the different players and how they communicate is given in Figure 5.1.

The *voter* instructs the *voter's computer* which ballot to submit. The computer encrypts the ballot, signs it on behalf of the voter and then submits it to a *ballot box*.

A voter is allowed to submit multiple electronic ballots and a single paper ballot. If the voter submitted a paper ballot, that ballot is counted, otherwise the final electronic ballot will be counted.

When counting begins, any electronic ballot that should not be counted is removed from the ballot box. The remaining encrypted ballots are given to a *decryption service* where they are shuffled and rerandomized using a Scytl-developed protocol, somewhat similar to randomized partial checking. Finally, the shuffled ballots are verifiably decrypted.

To implement return codes, the voter's computer adds a special "encryption" of the ballot which is sent to the ballot box. The ballot box does some extra work on the special "ciphertext" to produce a new ciphertext that is sent to a *return code generator*. The return code generator decrypts the new ciphertext with a special key and applies a pseudorandom function to the result to derive the return code. The return code is sent to the voter's mobile phone.

As originally described, the voter had to enter a special secret number (printed on his poll card) into the voting client to get return codes, and this step was optional. Strictly speaking, this was neither usable nor secure, but the solution could obviously be modified to be both usable and secure.

5.5 Cryptographic Protocol

While we believed that Scytl's proposed cryptographic protocol could be made sufficiently secure, we were not entirely happy with it. In particular, we had found numerous minor problems with it during analysis, and we were not entirely sure that we had found every flaw.

Some time after it was clear that Ergo and Scytl had submitted the winning tender, the author realized that it was possible to improve upon Scytl's proposed protocol, and that it would be possible to prove positive statements about the security of the modified protocol. The modified protocol was also significantly more efficient.

In order to understand why Scytl's protocol was modified and what the modifications were, we must first look at Scytl's proposal.

5.5.1 Scytl's Proposal

We can divide the execution of Scytl's proposed voting protocol into three phases: setup, ballot submission and counting.

In a system based on return codes, the main challenge is for the voting infrastructure to deduce the correct return codes to send the voter, without looking at the voter's ballot.

Scytl's solution is to construct the random-looking return code function rc in such a way that the voter's computer can create encryptions of the ballot and the return code that can be related by reasonably efficient non-interactive zero knowledge (NIZK) proofs such that it is hard to create ciphertexts with inconsistent ballot and return code.

Scytl [54] describes a variant of the proposed protocol. We briefly sketch a slightly modified version of this variant's ballot submission protocol, which is sufficiently similar to Scytl's proposal for our purposes. Recall that in the Norwegian elections, a ballot consists of a party list and a sequence of zero or more list modifications.

The protocol relies on a group G with a generator g. There is an encoding function f that maps lists and list modifications to group elements. We also have a hash function H and two pseudorandom functions PRF_1 and PRF_2.

Setup

The setup phase must produce one election public key y_1 satisfying $y_1 = g^{a_1}$, where a_1 is secret-shared among the electoral commission. A second public key y_3 satisfying $y_3 = g^{a_3}$ is produced, where the a_3 is known only by the return code generator. (Note that y_2 and a_2 will appear later.)

For return codes, two symmetric keys k_2 and k_3 are generated for the ballot box and the return code generator, respectively. Also a secret s is generated for each voter.

For a per-voter secret s, we define the function rc taking a list or list modification v to a return code as follows:

$$\hat{rc}(v) = f(v)y_1^{H(j\|s)},$$
$$\check{rc}(v) = \hat{rc}(v)y_1^{PRF_1(k_2,H(s))}, \tag{5.1}$$
$$rc(v) = PRF_2(k_3, \check{rc}(v)).$$

The voter receives the function rc in the form of a table listing every list and list modification v along with the corresponding value $rc(v)$. This table is printed on the voter's poll card.

Ballot Submission

Ballot submission begins when the voter authenticates himself to the voting system through his computer.

When the voter has authenticated himself, his computer receives the per-voter secret s, the election public key y_1 and the return code generator public key y_3.

The computer first sends a hash of the per-voter secret $H(s)$ to the ballot box, which then computes $PRF_1(k_2, H(s))$ and sends the result back to the computer.

The voter enters his ballot into the computer. Recall that the ballot consists of a party list and a sequence of zero or more list modifications. The sequence of length l is padded with blank values to reach a given, fixed length n. Then each of these values is encrypted independently.

To encrypt the ith value v_i, the computer chooses a random number r_i and computes a ciphertext

$$(x_i, w_i) = (g^{r_i}, y_1^{r_i} f(v_i)). \tag{5.2}$$

The computer then computes an encryption of the return code under the return code generators public key

$$\hat{w}_i = y_3^{r_i} y_1^{H(v_i\|s)} f(v_i),$$
$$\check{w}_i = \hat{w}_i y_1^{PRF_1(k_2,H(s))}. \tag{5.3}$$

Note that $\hat{w}_i x_i^{-a_3} = \hat{rc}(v_i)$ and $\check{w}_i x_i^{-a_3} = \check{rc}(v_i)$.

Finally, the computer generates NIZK proofs that show that the computer knows the decryption of the ciphertext, that the ciphertext decrypts to a valid vote, and that the partial ciphertext is consistent with (x_i, w_i) in the above sense. To simplify the NIZK proofs, a number of secondary values are computed as well.

The computer then submits the ciphertexts $(x_1, w_1), \ldots, (x_n, w_n)$, the partial ciphertext $\check{w}$, the NIZK proofs, a number of secondary values and a signature on everything to the ballot box.

The ballot box verifies the signature and the NIZK proofs. It then passes everything to the return code generator.

The return code generator also verifies the signature and the NIZK proofs. Then it computes the ith return code as $PRF_2(k_3, \widecheck{w}_i x_i^{-a_3}) = rc(v_i)$. (The return code generator must know the result of $\widecheck{w}_i x_i^{a_3}$ for the padding value, so that it can determine the real ballot length l.) It sends some of the values $rc(v_1), \ldots, rc(v_l)$ to the voter's mobile phone, signs a hash of the ciphertexts $(x_1, w_1), \ldots, (x_n, w_n)$ and sends the signature to the ballot box.

Upon receipt of the signature, the ballot box stores the voter's ciphertext and sends the signature to the voter's computer.

The voter's computer reports success. When the text message with the return codes arrives, the voter consults his table to verify that he received the correct return codes.

Counting

At the start of the counting phase, the ballot box selects the ballots that should be counted. If a voter submitted a paper ballot, all their electronic ballots are discarded. Otherwise, all but the last electronic ballot are discarded.

Before the encrypted ballots to be counted are passed to the decryption service, they are "compressed." An encrypted ballot consisting of n encryptions $(x_1, w_1), (x_2, w_2), \ldots, (x_n, w_n)$ of the values $v_1, v_2, \ldots, v_n$ is compressed to the ciphertext $c = (x, w)$, where

$$x = \prod_{i=1}^{n} x_i \qquad \text{and} \qquad w = \prod_{i=1}^{n} w_i.$$

When the decryption service decrypts this ciphertext, it decrypts to the product

$$\prod_{i=1}^{n} f(v_i).$$

The group G lies inside a prime field, and the function f encodes values v_i to field elements corresponding to small primes. By factoring the product, the values $v_1, v_2, \ldots, v_n$ can be recovered up to order.

In the event that order matters, we can use the equations

$$x = \prod_{i=1}^{n} x_i^i \qquad \text{and} \qquad w = \prod_{i=1}^{n} w_i^i.$$

which will produce the decryption

$$\prod_{i=1}^{n} f(v_i)^i.$$

Since values cannot repeat, this allows us to recover all the values in the correct order.

The decryption service first shuffles the compressed ballots using a Scytl-designed verifiable shuffle [53], then it verifiably decrypts the ballots.

The verifiable shuffle depends on the underlying cryptosystem being homomorphic: the decryption of the product of two ciphertexts is the product of the decryptions of the two ciphertexts.

We describe the shuffle only for a square number n^2 of ciphertexts.

The process begins when the shuffler receives the ciphertexts $c_1^{(0)}, c_2^{(0)}, \ldots, c_{n^2}^{(0)}$ to be counted from the ballot box. It rerandomizes and shuffles the ciphertexts several times, creating $c_1^{(1)}, \ldots, c_{n^2}^{(1)}, c_1^{(2)}, \ldots, c_{n^2}^{(2)}$, etc.

The verifier chooses a partition P_0 of the ciphertexts $\{c_i^{(0)}\}$ into n subsets each containing n ciphertexts and sends this partition to the shuffler. The shuffler reveals the corresponding partition P_0' of the ciphertexts $\{c_i^{(1)}\}$, and proves that for each subset $S \in P_0$ and corresponding subset $S' \in P_0'$, the product of the ciphertexts in S and S' have the same decryption.

Next, the verifier chooses a partition P_1 of the ciphertexts $\{c_i^{(1)}\}$ into n subsets each containing n ciphertexts, such that for any $S \in P_0'$ and $S' \in P_1$, the intersection of S and S' contain exactly one ciphertext. The shuffler reveals the corresponding partition P_1' of the ciphertexts $\{c_i^{(2)}\}$, and proves that for each subset $S \in P_1$ and corresponding subset $S' \in P_1'$, the product of the ciphertexts in S and the product of the ciphertexts in S' have the same decryption.

If the decryption service simply modifies or replaces some ballots, it is extremely unlikely that it will be able to provide the correct proofs for corresponding subsets. The decryption service could try to make modifications that cancel out, but since he is unlikely to be able to predict the partition chosen by the verifier, this will also most likely fail.

The verifier, on the other hand, will be unable to trace ciphertexts through the subsequent shuffles. This means that even though he knows both who submitted each input ciphertext and the decryption of each output ciphertext, he cannot correlate the two.

Challenges

As is well known, understanding and analyzing cryptographic protocols is a very hard problem, and a lot of work is involved in establishing confidence in a protocol's correctness. The cryptographic discipline of provable security has been developed to make it easier to establish this confidence.

Careful analysis of the proposed protocol shows that the voter's computer does not actually prove that the ballot and the return code are consistent. While it is not difficult for the voter's computer to create an encryption of a random return code, this is not sufficient to actually break the system, since the voter should notice the incorrect return code. We were not able to find unfixable attacks against the system during our brief analysis.

We tried to prove various properties for Scytl's proposed protocol or minor variations of it, but we were unsuccessful. Obviously, we cannot claim that it is impossible to prove interesting properties about this protocol, but it would seem to be difficult.

The conclusion was that, after various minor changes, we were unable to break Scytl's proposed protocol, but we were also unable to argue convincingly for its correctness. While the protocol was considered acceptable, it did not inspire great confidence.

5.5.2　Modifications

We were least happy with the ballot submission phase of Scytl's proposed protocol. A short time after it was clear that Ergo and Scytl would win the tender, the author realized that there was an alternative to Scytl's proposed way of computing and encrypting return codes. The essential insight was that we were already using a homomorphic cryptosystem, namely ElGamal, which allows us via ciphertext operations to apply certain functions to the contents of ciphertext. What if the return code function was one of those functions?

Originally, all of the modifications to Scytl's protocol were conceived at the same time, but for ease of understanding, we introduce them as two separate modifications. The first modification is about how we compute the return codes. The second modification reduces the amount of work the voter's computer has to do, and simplifies handling the per-voter secret.

Computing Return Codes

The author had earlier proven that the exponentiation map $\zeta \mapsto \zeta^s$ [254] could be considered a pseudorandom map when the elements v were restricted to carefully chosen subsets of the group elements.

Again, we begin by defining the return code function rc. For a per-voter secret s, we define the function rc taking a list or list modification v to a return code as follows:

$$\check{r}c(v) = f(v)^s,$$
$$rc(v) = PRF_2(k_3, \check{r}c(v)). \tag{5.1'}$$

Observe now that given the encryption (x, w) of $f(v)$ from (5.2), (x^s, w^s) is an encryption of $\check{r}c(v)$.

This suggests the following approach. To encrypt the ith value v_i, the computer chooses a random number r_i and computes (x_i, w_i) as in (5.2). It also computes the ciphertexts

$$(\bar{x}_i, \bar{w}_i) = (x_i^s, w_i^s)$$
$$(\check{x}_i, \check{w}_i) = (\bar{x}_i, y_3^{r_i s} f(v_i)^s). \tag{5.3'}$$

Note that $w_i x_i^{-a_1} = f(v_i)$ and $\bar{w}_i \bar{x}_i^{-a_1} = \check{r} c(v_i) = \check{w}_i \check{x}_i^{-a_3}$.

The computer creates three NIZK proofs. The first proves that it knows the decryption of $(x_1, w_1), \ldots, (x_n, w_n)$. The second proves that the ciphertext $(\bar{x}_i, \bar{w}_i)$ has been created by raising (x_i, w_i) to the correct power. The third proves that the two ciphertexts $(\bar{x}_i, \bar{w}_i)$ and $(\check{x}_i, \check{w}_i)$ decrypt to the same value. All of these NIZK proofs are completely standard and quite efficient.

One of the significant computational improvements relative to Scytl's proposed protocol is that there is no longer any need for a computationally expensive proof that the ciphertext contains a valid ballot. (This proof is needed in Scytl's proposed protocol to prevent an attack that destroys a ballot. After our modifications, invalid ballots will almost always result in incorrect return codes, which the voter should notice.)

Two problems remain. First of all, the protocol is computationally heavy for the voter's computer. Second, handling the per-voter secret s is complicated. (The original Scytl proposal envisaged the user typing it into the computer, which does not work very well. Presumably, a new infrastructure player could be introduced to handle these secrets.)

Øberg [426] analyzed essentially this protocol and proved a number of strong security properties. In fact, this protocol is slightly more secure than the protocol used in the trials. But handling the per-voter secret would have been a significant problem for deployment.

The Ballot Box Takes Over

The goal of the next set of modifications is to reduce the computational work at the voter's computer and remove the need for distributing the per-voter secret s. The changes required for this do not come for free. The computational workload for the infrastructure increases slightly and the security properties of the protocol change.

There are two stages to this solution. The first is that only the ballot box should know the per-voter secrets, and it should create the ciphertexts $(\bar{x}_i, \bar{w}_i)$ and $(\check{x}_i, \check{w}_i)$. Intuitively, this seems unsafe, but careful analysis actually shows that this is actually safe.

Shifting the computational burden like this introduces a new problem. Unlike the client, the ballot box does not (and must not) know the voter's ballot, so $(\check{x}_i, \check{w}_i)$ cannot be computed as in (5.3'). Thus the second stage of our solution was to tamper with the election keys, which allows the ballot box to turn a ciphertext encrypted under the election public key into a ciphertext encrypted under the return code generator's public key.

The setup phase must now be changed as follows. First, the per-voter secret s

should still be generated, but all of them should be given to the ballot box. Next, a third public key y_2 satisfying $y_2 = g^{a_2} = y_3 y_1^{-1}$ is produced, where a_2 is known only by the ballot box. Note that the three decryption keys now satisfy $a_2 = a_3 - a_1$ modulo the group order.

The return code function rc remains as defined in (5.1').

To encrypt the ith value v_i, the voter's computer chooses a random number r_i and computes (x_i, w_i) as in (5.2). It also creates a single NIZK proof, proving that it knows the decryption of $(x_1, w_1), \ldots, (x_n, w_n)$. The computer then signs the ciphertext and the NIZK proof on behalf of the voter and passes it on to the ballot box.

The ballot box verifies the signature and the NIZK proof of knowledge. The ballot box knows the voter's secret s and for each ciphertext (x_i, w_i) computes two ciphertexts

$$\begin{aligned} (\bar{x}_i, \bar{w}_i) &= (x_i^s, w_i^s), \\ (\check{x}_i, \check{w}_i) &= (\bar{x}_i, \bar{w}_i \bar{x}_i^{a_2}). \end{aligned} \tag{5.3''}$$

Note that $\bar{w}_i \bar{x}_i^{-a_1} = \hat{rc}(v_i) = \check{w}_i \check{x}_i^{-a_3}$, since

$$\check{w}_i \check{x}_i^{-a_3} = \bar{w}_i \bar{x}_i^{a_2} \bar{x}_i^{-a_3} = \hat{rc}(v_i) \bar{x}_i^{a_1} \bar{x}_i^{a_2 - a_3} = \hat{rc}(v_i) \bar{x}_i^{a_1 + a_2 - a_3} = \hat{rc}(v_i).$$

The ballot box also produces two NIZK proofs showing that it did its computations correctly. These NIZK proofs are completely standard and quite efficient.

5.5.3 The Modified Protocol

We now give a brief summary of the modified protocol [255].

Setup

The setup phase must produce one election public key y_1 satisfying $y_1 = g^{a_1}$, a ballot box public key y_2 satisfying $y_2 = g^{a_2}$ and a return code generator key y_3 satisfying $y_3 = g^{a_3}$. The three public keys satisfy $y_3 = y_1 y_2$. The election decryption key a_1 is secret shared among the electoral commission, while a_2 is given to the ballot box and a_3 is given to the return code generator.

For each voter, a secret number s is generated and given to the ballot box. Also, for each voter, a random injective function h from $\{f(v)^s\}$ (where v ranges over all the lists and list modifications) to the set of return codes is chosen. These functions are given to the return code generator.

For a per-voter secret s and random injective function h, we define the function rc taking a list or list modification v to a return code as follows:

$$\begin{aligned} \check{rc}(v) &= f(v)^s, \\ rc(v) &= h(\check{rc}(v)). \end{aligned} \tag{5.1'''}$$

The voter receives the function rc in the form of a table listing every list and list modification j along with the corresponding value $rc(v)$.

Ballot Submission

Ballot submission begins when the voter authenticates himself to the voting system through his computer.

When the voter has authenticated himself, his computer receives the election public key y_1.

The voter enters his ballot into the computer. Recall that the ballot consists of a party list and a sequence of zero or more list modifications. The sequence is padded with blank values to reach a given, fixed length. Then each of these values is encrypted independently.

To encrypt the ith value v_i, the computer chooses a random number r_i and computes a ciphertext

$$(x_i, w_i) = (g^{r_i}, y_1^{r_i} f(v_i)). \tag{5.2'''}$$

The computer generates a non-interactive zero knowledge proof of knowledge that shows that the computer knows the decryption of the independently encrypted ciphertexts.

The computer then submits the ciphertexts, the NIZK proof and a signature on everything to the ballot box.

The ballot box verifies the signature and the NIZK proof. For each ciphertext (x_i, w_i), it then computes a ciphertext and a partial ciphertext:

$$\begin{aligned} (\bar{x}_i, \bar{w}_i) &= (x_i^s, w_i^s), \\ \check{w}_i &= \bar{w}_i \bar{x}_i^{-a_2}. \end{aligned} \tag{5.3'''}$$

It also creates two NIZK proofs showing that the ballot box has computed these values correctly.

The ballot box then sends everything it received, the ciphertexts and partial ciphertexts and the NIZK proofs to the return code generator.

The return code generator verifies all the NIZK proofs and the voter's signature, then for each ciphertext $(\bar{x}_i, \check{w}_i)$ computes the return codes using the formula

$$h(\check{w}_i \bar{x}_i^{-a_3}).$$

If any of these computations fail (which can only happen if $\check{w}_i \bar{x}_i^{-a_3}$ is not in the domain of h), the return code generator knows that the original ballot is invalid and informs the ballot box of this fact. In this case, the ballot box will reject the ballot and inform the voter's computer that the ballot was rejected.

Otherwise, a subset of the return codes is sent to the voter's phone. The return code generator then signs a hash of the encrypted ballot (which consists of n ciphertexts $(x_1, w_1), \ldots, (x_n, w_n)$ and a NIZK proof of knowledge π)

$$H(\text{voter identity}, (x_1, w_1), \ldots, (x_n, w_n), \pi) \qquad (5.4)$$

and sends this signature to the ballot box, which verifies it and sends it on to the voter's computer.

When the voter's computer receives a valid signature on the encrypted ballot it submitted, it informs the voter that the ballot has been correctly submitted.

When the voter's phone receives the return codes, the voter uses the function rc to verify that the return codes match the submitted ballot. When the voter's computer says that the ballot has been correctly submitted, the voter accepts the ballot as cast.

Counting

Counting proceeds exactly as in Scytl's original protocol. The only minor difference is that the role of the auditor was clarified.

The auditor receives the entire contents of the ballot box. It also receives a list of every ballot seen by the return code generator, in order. The auditor verifies that the two parties agree on which ballots were submitted.

Next, the auditor receives a list of ballots that the decryption service received from the ballot box. Based on the contents of the ballot box, the auditor recomputes which ballots should be counted and compares this list with the list received by the decryption service.

Finally, the auditor participates in the decryption service's verifiable shuffle and also verifies the final decryption.

Verifiability

The protocol can be modified to provide limited verifiability. The voter's computer presents the hash of the submitted ballot (5.4) and the return code generator's signature to the voter. The ballot box publishes a signed list of hashes of accepted ballots. Finally, the auditor verifies the ballot box's list.

The voter can now download the ballot box's list of hashes and verify that the hash displayed by the computer is present in the list. In the event that the hash is not present, the return code generator's signature allows the voter to complain convincingly.

What Was Achieved?

The main achievement is that it is possible to prove clearly stated security claims about this protocol relative to reasonable cryptographic assumptions. (Though there remains a technical problem related to the proof of knowledge [256].) A secondary achievement was that the computational load was significantly reduced.

Provided that at most one of the infrastructure players is corrupt and the voter follows the protocol correctly, we can prove that:

■ If the auditor accepts the result, at most one ballot per voter was counted.

■ If the voter accepts the ballot as cast as intended, and does not later revote or complain about a forgery, the ballot is counted as intended up to certain changes to the list modifications.

■ If the voter's computer and the return code generator are both honest and the voter does not complain about forgeries, the content of the voter's ballot remains private.

■ A corrupt return code generator learns the number of list modifications in each ballot submission, and if a voter submits multiple ballots, learns where these ballots differ.

We developed attacks against the protocol to prove that the above claims cannot be significantly strengthened.

The proof is a mix of classical protocol analysis techniques and standard mathematical analysis relying on variants of the Decision Diffie–Hellman problem.

The Decision Diffie–Hellman variants are used to show that no single infrastructure player can see the ballots encrypted by honest computers. A crucial ingredient is the computer's proof of knowledge which prevents a corrupt ballot box from using the return code generator as a decryption oracle.

During ballot submission, the voter's computer will not accept a ballot unless both the ballot box and the return code generator has seen the ballot. This ensures that the auditor can detect any cheating by either the ballot box or the return code generator. Furthermore, the auditor can ensure that the decryption service receives the correct encrypted ballots.

The proofs produced by the decryption service ensures both that the decryption service cannot cheat and that the auditor cannot learn anything about particular encrypted ballots.

If we accept the basic premise underlying the security proof (that at most one infrastructure player is compromised), the cryptographic protocol ensures correctness and secrecy, and it makes a decent attempt at providing coercion resistance. Even though verifiability is not important, it can be modified to provide limited verifiability. The cryptographic protocol was therefore a good match for Norwegian elections.

Further Improvements

After the 2011 election, the author developed a second version of the protocol [256] (incorporating ideas worked out by Lund [373]) that significantly reduced the computational effort required. There are two main ideas behind this improvement.

First, instead of encrypting every ballot value separately, all the values were included in a single encryption. Technically, the encryption key now consists of n values $y_{11}, y_{12}, \ldots, y_{1n}$, and given a (padded) ballot $v_1, v_2, \ldots, v_n$, the computer chooses a single random number r and computes

$$(x, w_1, w_2, \ldots, w_n) = (g^r, y_{11}^r f(v_1), y_{12}^r f(v_2), \ldots, y_{1n}^r f(v_n)). \tag{5.2''''}$$

The ballot box key a_2 must now be split into n parts $a_{21}, a_{22}, \ldots, a_{2n}$, and the ballot box now computes two ciphertexts

$$\begin{aligned}
(\bar{x}, \bar{w}_1, \bar{w}_2, \ldots, \bar{w}_n) &= (x^s, w_1^s, w_2^s, \ldots, w_n^s), \\
(\check{w}_1, \check{w}_2, \ldots, \check{w}_n) &= (\bar{w}_1 \bar{x}^{a_{21}}, \bar{w}_2 \bar{x}^{a_{22}}, \ldots, \bar{w}_n \bar{x}^{a_{2n}}).
\end{aligned} \tag{5.3''''}$$

The return code generator's key a_3 is also split into n parts $a_{31}, a_{32}, \ldots, a_{3n}$, and the return code generator computes the ith return code as

$$h\left(\check{w}_i \bar{x}^{-a_{3i}}\right).$$

Second, the NIZK proofs were replaced by batch variants. This amounts to a significant performance improvement.

The security proof was also significantly improved, and we were able to improve our security claims through better modelling of certain underlying infrastructures.

5.6 Deployment

As 2010 progressed it became clear that remote internet voting was politically controversial. The main objection was coercion, and the politicians were not convinced by the countermeasures planned (i.e., revoting). Most opposition parties declared loudly that they would vote against remote internet voting. As the debate unfolded, it turned out that the largest (by far) of three governing parties was also essentially opposed to remote internet voting.

Curiously, even though there was a clear majority in parliament essentially opposed to remote internet voting, the three government parties (which commanded a majority in parliament) voted to go through with trials during the 2011 local elections.

Due to political controversy, the decision to hold a new trial in 2013 was not made immediately after the 2011 trial. Until the second half of 2012, little work was done on preparing a new trial. When the government eventually did decide to hold a new trial, there was limited time for new developments.

5.6.1 The 2011 Election

A small number of municipalities were selected for the 2011 trial, with approximately 160,000 voters in total. Two government organizations were selected to run the ballot box and the return code generator, while the responsible government department would run the decryption service. A professional election observer was hired to run the auditor.

Scytl produced the implementation of the software. The software that would run on the voter's computer was delivered via a web browser. The user interface was a fairly standard web application, but when the voter pressed the button to submit his ballot, that ballot was sent to a Java applet running in the browser, which would then run the voting protocol and deal with all the cryptography. The Java applet did not have a user interface and was, provided the voter's web browser was correctly configured, hidden from the voter.

The trial was largely uneventful. Most of the mishaps were in the election administration system. There was one very interesting problem with the internet voting system, however. Because of problems at the printer service responsible for printing poll cards, incorrect return codes were printed on some poll cards. This mainly affected one of the larger municipalities participating in the trials.

Though there exists no exact data on the number of errors, the best available estimate is that about 1% of the poll cards in the affected municipality were printed with incorrect return codes. Out of the nearly 50,000 eligible e-voters in that municipality, about 8,500 voters chose to cast an electronic vote.

It seems reasonable to assume that opting for electronic voting and receiving a misprinted poll card are independent events. In other words, if our assumptions hold, we would expect that about 85 voters both voted electronically and received a misprinted poll card. During voting, misprinted poll cards caused 74 voters to call the election help desk to report incorrect return codes. That 74 out of an estimated 85 voters noticed the incorrect return codes is a remarkably high number. (Coincidentally, during earlier pre-election pilots there was a self-reported 90% verification rate, which is remarkably consistent with the above numbers.)

Unfortunately, the estimate on the number of misprinted poll cards is too uncertain to say anything about how efficient return codes are as a security mechanism for detecting certain attacks. The best we can say is probably that if a corrupt computer just tampers with the ballot, the probability of discovery may very well be large.

During the local elections, 28,001 voters voted electronically. A total of 55,785 electronic ballots were cast in the two available contests (municipal elections and county elections). Of these, 2428 ballots were cancelled by re-voting, of which 653 by a paper vote. This makes up 4.35% of the votes.

While this does indicate that many voters were aware that they could re-vote, it does not indicate that voters in general could use this countermeasure against coercion.

5.6.2 The 2013 Election

The principal problem with the 2011 trial was the Java applet used to do the cryptography in the voter's computer. A significant number of voters found it hard to establish and maintain a working Java web browser installation. Java in the browser was also a significant general security liability.

While the desirability of Java had decreased significantly since 2010, the effective (and recognized) capabilities of JavaScript with respect to cryptography had increased significantly over the same time period. Therefore it was decided to develop a JavaScript implementation of the cryptography for the voter's computer.

It was also decided to use the further improvements to the cryptographic protocol described at the end of Section 5.5.3. Since the part that ran on the voter's computer had to be completely redone anyway, the effort involved in modifying the other parts of the system was modest. The performance improvements would significantly benefit a JavaScript implementation.

While verifiability was never important for the politicians or the general public, it was still felt that improving verifiability would be worthwhile. This was implemented more or less as described in Section 5.5.3.

Another area for improvement was the verifiable shuffle used during decryption. It was felt that a proper non-interactive proof of shuffle would be an improvement, and some work was done to identify a suitable shuffle to implement or buy an implementation of. Unfortunately, this turned out to be impractical and was not done before the 2013 trial.

A Bug with Consequences

About half-way through advance voting, a "statistical anomaly" was discovered with some test data. After a brief investigation, a serious bug was found in Scytl's implementation.

For a long time, cryptography in JavaScript was difficult since there was no standard source for randomness. Eventually, this was solved by entropy gathering code and documented interfaces in modern browsers providing pseudorandomness suitable for cryptography.

Scytl's JavaScript cryptography relied on a deterministic pseudorandom bit generator seeded with randomness extracted by entropy gathering code and delivered by whatever randomness sources were available in the browser. While one could imagine simpler constructions, this is a reasonable architecture.

Unfortunately, Scytl's generator implementation replaced its state with a fixed, public state after every invocation. The implication is that the first time Scytl's cryptography used the generator, it would provide proper randomness. But for any subsequent use, the generator would provide the exact same response,[2] and this response was completely predictable by anyone.

Looking at the equations in Section 5.5.3, we see that a single random number r appears in (5.2''''). Since the first use of the generator returns proper randomness, one could hope that the encryption would be properly done.

However, due to the way the random number was sampled, the generator was often used more than once, and the result would be a fixed random number. The consequence was that about 60% of all ballots submitted before the bug was fixed were encrypted with the same, known random number. Anyone observing any such ciphertext could trivially decrypt it.

Unfortunately, the remaining ballots were not secure. The voter's computer also generates a proof of its knowledge of the ballot encrypted. It turns out that when this proof is generated with predictable randomness, it reveals the randomness r, which in turns reveals the ballot. (A Schnorr proof is used to prove knowledge of the random number r used for encryption, but when you know the randomness used in the Schnorr proof, you can easily compute r.) The consequence was that anyone observing any such ciphertext could easily decrypt it.

While all of this was bad, it was not yet a disaster. The system was designed so that the cryptography protected against the compromise of the ballot box, the return code generator and the auditor. But when these players were not compromised, the cryptography was no longer a single point of failure. For example, the encrypted ballot was sent from the voter's computer to the ballot box through an encrypted channel (TLS), so no eavesdropper would see the ciphertexts.

The ballot box and the return code generator were well-protected systems and very few people (none of which were Scytl employees) had access to them. After the bug was discovered, the number of people who had access was reduced even further and security was tightened even further. A subsequent audit of all logs concluded that the encrypted ballots had not leaked. During counting and auditing, great care was taken to ensure that encrypted ballots did not leak.

The conclusion was that this had been a cryptologic disaster, since the cryptology completely failed to protect the confidentiality of the ballots. However, fortunately it was only an electoral near-disaster, since other security measures allowed us to conclude that no ballots leaked.

Not All Bad Things Must Come to Pass

During the response phase, we recalled that the cryptologic specification [256] specified that the return code generator should compute the hash to be signed as in (5.4). When the computer's random numbers are replaced by fixed values, this hash depends only on the voter's identity and his ballot, nothing else.

---

[2]The generator was periodically reseeded, but this seems not to have saved the day.

This would not be an extra problem for the system as originally designed [256]. But after the design, the system had been modified to provide limited verifiability as described in Section 5.5.3. And as part of these modifications, the hashes computed by the return code generator had been published on the internet.

Based on the available evidence, it did at first look as if several thousand voter-ballot pairs had been published on the internet, essentially in clear text.

Fortunately, it quickly transpired that Scytl's implementation deviated (a perfectly harmless and accepted deviation) from the specification by also including an authentication token in the hash. This authentication token contained sufficient randomness to erase any connection between the ballot and the hash. There was no electoral disaster.

In passing, it is interesting to note that publishing the hashes actually breaks the security proof. Adding some randomness before hashing (like Scytl's implementation did) makes the proof work again.

Why Did the Bug Go Undiscovered?

Any manual testing of Scytl's generator (e.g., by invoking the generator repeatedly from the JavaScript console) would have revealed the bug. A thorough code review should also have revealed the bug. A visual inspection of any one of the numerous test datasets generated during testing would also have revealed the bug. (In fact, the bug was discovered essentially by visual inspection of test data, but far too late.)

It is clear that this bug should have been discovered, but it was not discovered. Why?

Clearly, such a vital piece of cryptographic code should have been carefully written, but it was not. Scytl's internal code reviews failed to spot the bug.

The Norwegian government hired contractors to do an independent code review of critical cryptographic code. Unfortunately, due to time limitations, the code that would run on the voter's computer was excluded from the review. To the author, it seems likely that the contractors would have found the bug if they had looked at the code.

Before the 2011 elections, numerous test datasets were generated and a large number of statistical tests were applied to the ciphertexts. Due to the limited time available, these tests were not repeated ahead of the 2013 elections. It is certain that the statistical tests used in 2011 would have discovered the bug.

Obviously, the bug should never have been in the code. But it seems clear that if the decision to do trials in 2013 had been made in a more timely fashion, this bug would have been discovered.

5.7   Concluding Remarks

Politicians Worry about Coercion

Before the two trials, the politicians' main worry was coercion. There is no solid evidence that coercion would be a problem for a nationwide election, but the two trials and their evaluation did not provide any evidence to the contrary, namely that coercion would not be a problem.

Norwegian voters abroad are allowed to vote by mail, a form of voting highly susceptible to coercion. It is the author's opinion that if coercion is a real problem, Norwegian voters abroad will be better served by internet voting than by the current system.

The then government lost its parliamentary majority in the 2013 elections, and the new majority installed a minority government. The new government has decided not to have any further trials of this electronic voting system. In fact, there seems to be a complete lack of enthusiasm for electronic voting in general, and there are currently no plans for electronic voting of any kind.

The World Has Changed

Since the system was designed, the world has also moved on. The system relies absolutely on the independence of the voter's computer and his phone, and in particular, that if the voter's computer is compromised, the voter's phone will not be compromised. This was a reasonable assumption in 2009–10. What about today?

Many modern phones will now happily forward text messages to their owner's computer, and this forwarding is relatively easy to turn on. If a compromised computer can prevent the return code generator's text message from reaching the voter, the compromised computer will be able to vote without the user noticing.

Furthermore, modern phones have begun to cooperate more closely with computers. This means that if the voter's computer is compromised, it is much more likely that the voter's phone could also be compromised.

Finally, it turns out that many people now use modern phones instead of computers. Forcing these people to use a computer to vote will be quite unnatural (which was an issue during the 2013 election), but allowing them to vote from their phone compromises the protocol's security properties.

Since the underlying assumptions may no longer be valid, it seems reasonable to doubt the security of the system. On that basis, it seems perfectly reasonable not to do any further trials.

Nobody Cares about Bugs

Curiously, nobody cared about the near-disaster caused by the bug in the random number generator. The closest the bug came to being discussed in the press was a complaint about the title of the government's press release. It is clear that people in general and politicians in particular do not care about the same things as security experts and cryptographers.

Chapter 6

E-Voting in Estonia

Dylan Clarke

Newcastle University, UK

Tarvi Martens

Estonian Electronic Voting Committee

CONTENTS

Estonia has one of the most established e-voting systems in the world. Internet voting — remote e-voting using the voter's own equipment — was piloted in 2005 [377] (with the first real elections using e-voting being conducted the same year) and has been in use ever since. So far, the Estonian internet voting system has been used for the whole country in three sets of local elections, two European Parliament elections and three parliamentary elections [19].

This chapter begins by exploring the voting system in Estonia; we consider the organization of the electoral system in the three main kinds of election (municipal, parliamentary and European Parliament), the traditional ways of voting and the methods used to tally votes and elect candidates. Next we investigate the Estonian national ID card, an identity document that plays a key part in enabling internet voting to be possible in Estonia.

After considering these prerequisites, we describe the current internet voting system, including how it has evolved over time and the relatively new verification mechanisms that are available to voters. Next we discuss the assumptions and choices that have been made in the design of this system and the challenges and criticism that it has received. Finally, we conclude by discussing how the system has performed over the 10 years it has been in use, and the impact it appears to have had on voter turnout and satisfaction.

6.1 Voting in Estonia

The current Estonian system of governments started in 1991 when the country declared independence from the Soviet Union. The Riigikogu (Parliament of Estonia) consists of 101 members who are elected for a period of four years [240]. The electoral seats are divided among 12 districts (shown for 2011 in Table 6.1). Candidates stand for a particular district and each voter casts one vote for his favorite candidate among those standing in the district in which he lives. This vote can also have an indirect effect on other districts due to the way in which electoral seats are allocated. Seat allocation occurs in the following manner [23]:

Every party with candidates standing in more than one district must submit an ordered listing of their candidates. This list indicates their preference for the order in which seats awarded to the party as a whole will be allocated (if there are seats left for which no individual candidate has won outright). The allocation of seats takes place in three rounds, with each round only proceeding if there remain unallocated seats after the previous round.

The first round takes place on a district level and is based on a simple quota. This simple quota is calculated by dividing the number of votes cast in the district by the number of seats in the district. Any candidate who has received votes equal to or greater than the simple quota is elected.

The second round also takes place on a district level and is based on the number of votes allocated to each party in the district. The candidates for each party are ordered by the number of votes they received and the total number of votes for the party in this district are calculated. If the total number of votes for the party is less than 5% of the votes cast then the party is awarded no further seats. Otherwise, the total number of votes for the party is then divided by the simple quota, and the number of candidates from the party who were elected in the first round is deducted. This gives the number of candidates to be elected for each party in round two, and the actual candidates to be elected are determined using the list of candidates ordered by number of votes.

The third round takes place on a national level and is again based on the number of votes allocated to each party in Estonia as a whole. A modified version of the d'Hondt method is used to allocate the remaining seats between parties, and the ordered list that each party submitted before the election is used to decide which candidates are elected for each party.

The modified d'Hondt method works as follows: Each remaining seat is considered in turn and a quotient is calculated for each party, with the party with the highest quotient winning the seat. The quotient is calculated by dividing the total number of votes for the party by a function of the number of seats awarded to the party so far (in the Estonian election the function of the number of seats is $f(n) = (1+n)^{0.9}$). As with the second round, parties that have received less than 5% of the total votes cast are not allocated any seats, even if they have the highest quotient at some point.

Estonia elects six candidates to the European Parliament for a period of five years. Each voter casts one vote for his favorite candidate as with Riigikogu elections, but all candidates are elected nationally rather than on a district basis. Each party submits an ordered list of candidates, with independent candidates being treated as if they were part of a candidate list with one candidate. European Parliament seats are allocated in the same way as for round three of Riigikogu elections, except that the function of the number of seats already allocated used in the d'Hondt method is $f(n) = 1+n$.

Each city or rural municipality elects councillors every four years. The number of councillors elected depends on the size of the municipality and the methods used for allocating seats are as follows: For all municipalities with one electoral district, seats are first allocated in the same way as for round one in the Riigikogu elections, and remaining seats are allocated in the same way as for the European Parliament elections. For municipalities with more than one electoral district, a similar method is used to that in Riigikogu elections. Rounds one and two are performed within districts and round three, if required, is performed within the municipality as a whole. The d'Hondt method used in round three uses the function $f(n) = 1+n$ rather than the function used in Riigikogu elections.

We note that, while the allocation of seats in these elections is relatively complex, the actual voting is very simple. Each voter has only to chose her favorite candidate and cast one vote for that candidate.

Voters are allowed to vote in a variety of ways, with the primary methods being voting in person at polling stations, and internet voting which we address in future sections. Voters who choose to vote in person have the choice of either voting on election day or casting an advance vote during an earlier period (initially three days but extended to seven days from 2009 onwards) [240]. This advance vote can either be cast in their own voting district, or in any other district at a designated place for outside-district voting. Provision is also made in parliamentary and European Parliament elections for voters who are overseas to cast votes during the advance period.

Table 6.1: Electoral districts for Riigikogu elections (2011)

District Number	Area	Seats
1	Tallinn (Haabersti, Põhja-Tallinn and Kristiine districts)	9
2	Tallinn (Kesklinn, Lasnamäe and Pirita districts)	11
3	Tallinn (Mustamäe and Nõmme districts)	8
4	Harjumaa (exluding Tallinn) and Raplamaa	14
5	Hiiumaa, Läänemaa and Saaremaa	6
6	Lääne-Virumaa	5
7	Ida-Virumaa	8
8	Järvamaa and Viljandimaa	8
9	Jõgevamaa and Tartumaa (excluding Tartu)	7
10	Tartu	8
11	Võrumaa, Valgamaa and Põlvamaa	9
12	Pärnumaa	8

Advance voting takes place differently depending on whether the vote is cast inside-district or outside-district. In both cases, the voter enters a private booth and fills out a ballot paper. When voting inside-district, the voter then folds the ballot paper, allows an official to attach a seal to it and deposits it in the ballot box. When voting outside-district the voter places the ballot paper into an envelope, and then places the envelope into a second envelope with their name, address and personal identification number written on it. This outer envelope is then placed in a ballot box for outside-district voters, to later be delivered to the district in which the voter is registered.

There is some opportunity for those who have used internet or advance voting to cancel out a vote with one that has higher precedence. Internet votes can be cancelled by casting any type of physical advance vote, and advance votes cast outside of the voter's district can be cancelled by casting an advance vote inside the district.

It is not possible to cancel out an internet or advance vote by casting a vote on election day, as polling stations will not allow those who have used one of these mechanisms to cast a ballot.

Voters who are unable to make use of other voting methods due to ill health or unexpected circumstances are allowed to apply to cast a home vote on election day. This vote is cast in person when two election officials visit their home to receive the ballot [30, 23].

6.2 Estonian National ID Cards

The Estonian national ID card was first introduced in 2002 [380]. It is a mandatory identity document for all Estonian citizens and permanent residents over the age of

15. The document has the card holder's full name, gender, national identification number, date of birth, citizenship status, card number, card expiration date and photo printed on it, and can be used as a primary travel document with the European Union. The card has also been used in the past as a ticket for public transportation in major cities such as Tallinn [10]; when a ticket was purchased the cardholder's national identification number was stored in a central database and ticket inspectors could then read the card with a handheld terminal and query the database when they encountered the card holder.

More importantly from our point of view, the ID card contains a chip with digital versions of the printed data, two 2048-bit RSA key pairs and certificates for these key pairs. The first key pair is used for authentication and the certificate binds the citizen's public key to their name, national identification number and a government issued e-mail address. The second key pair is used for digital signing and the certificate binds the citizen's public key to their name and national identification number.

The chip is also capable of answering authentication challenges using the first key pair, and generating digital signatures using the second key pair, removing any need for the private keys to be communicated outside of the chip. Interaction with the chip takes place using a personal computer with a card reader and custom software.

The citizen is issued three PINs with the card which are used as follows: PIN1 is required by the card before answering each authentication challenge and PIN2 is required by the card before generating each digital signature. If PIN1 or PIN2 is entered incorrectly three times then the card is locked until the third longer PIN PUK is entered.

The national ID card is valid for 5 years, and after this point the certificates expire. The certificates are also revoked if the owner reports the card stolen or compromised.

Estonian citizens and permanent residents are also allowed to request two other forms of digital identification: Digi-ID and Mobiil-ID. Digi-ID is a card similar to the national ID card that is designed only for online use. The Digi-ID card does not have a printed photo of the citizen, and contains less personal data than the national ID card, while still providing the authentication and digital signature functionality [32].

As of December 2014, Digi-ID has also become available to people who are not citizens or permanent residents of Estonia. Possession of a Digi-ID card allows a non-resident to make use of the Estonian authentication and digital signature mechanisms online, without conferring any additional rights with regard to Estonia. If the Digi-ID card becomes popular outside Estonia then this has the potential to increase the investment in the Estonian ID card system and the scrutiny to which it is subject, a situation that can only be positive for an e-voting system relying on the security of the ID card system.

Mobiil-ID provides similar functionality to Digi-ID, but is built into a mobile phone SIM card rather than a chip and PIN card. This enables the citizen to perform digital authentication and signing using their mobile phone with no extra hardware.

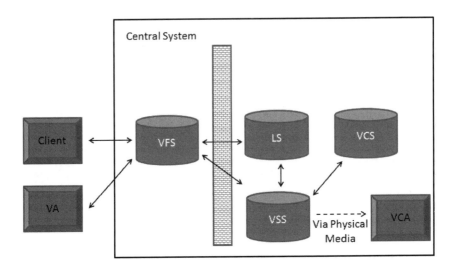

Figure 6.1: System components

6.3   The Internet Voting System

The Estonian internet voting system is built around the simple and well-studied concept of public key cryptography [12]. Voters encrypt their ballots with the public key of the election system, and then digitally sign them with their own private key. This private key is the signing key on the voter's national ID card, which guarantees that every voter will have a private key and a means of using it, and that the election authority can reliably associate each voter with their correct public key.

Simplicity is a concept that is heavily emphasized in the system design. Rather than try to provide absolute end-to-end verifiability and provable anonymity and privacy, the designers instead attempted to produce a system that can provide as much security as a paper-based system, while using simple components and well-understood technologies.

The system does not make use of a technology such as mix-nets to protect voter privacy. Instead, a simple separation of functions is used, where no one piece of hardware or user ever holds both the server's private key and a ballot with the digital signature attached. Vote integrity is protected both by this separation of functions and by the use of auditable logs produced by each component.

We begin by detailing the seven main components of the system (shown in Figure 6.1); we then provide further details of the interplay between the components, and finally we describe how the audit logs and the verification application can be used to check certain properties of the system.

6.3.1   System Components

1. **The voting application (client):** The client is downloaded to the voter's PC and allows the voter to communicate with the vote forwarding server and cast a ballot. The client is available for Windows, Mac OS and Linux.

2. **The verification application (VA):** The VA is an application for smart phones and tablets that enables the voter to verify that their ballot is held by the VSS. It is designed as a smart phone and tablet application so that the voter will use two independent devices during voting: a PC to cast the ballot and a smart phone or tablet to verify that it is stored correctly. The verification protocol used is explained in Section 6.3.3.

3. **The vote forwarding server (VFS):** The VFS authenticates voters and forwards requests between the client and other server-side components. The VFS is the only server-side component that is publicly accessible. It produces web server and application logs, but does not produce logs of voting activity. The VFS also holds lists of all eligible voters and candidates.

4. **The log server (LS):** The log server is accessible by the VFS and VSS. It stores log entries from these two servers.

5. **The vote storage server (VSS):** The VSS receives votes from the VFS and stores them if they are correctly signed. It is responsible for communicating with the VCS to check signature validity, the VFS to provide receipts to the client and providing a list of anonymized ballots to the VCA. The VFS also handles the deletion of any ballots belonging to voters who voted at a polling station and the logging of all actions performed.

6. **The validity confirmation server (VCS):** The validity confirmation server has the ability to check that signing certificates used to create digital signatures are valid and to provide signed confirmation attesting to this fact. The VCS is an external component, and is used by all service providers making use of Estonian national ID cards for authentication and/or digital signing.

7. **The vote counting application (VCA):** The vote counting application is air-gapped from the rest of the internet voting system and is only used after the voting period has concluded. It is responsible for decrypting all of the valid votes and tallying them by constituency. The VCA connects to an HSM that holds the private key corresponding to the election public key. It also has the capability to store its own logs, separate from those in the LS.

6.3.2   Normal System Operation

Normal system operation involves the following steps:

1. The voter downloads the voting client.

2. The voter uses his national ID card (or Digi-ID card) and card reader to authenticate to the VFS. This requires the voter to enter PIN1 into the card reader in the same way that he would authenticate for any other service with the ID card.

3. The client requests the list of candidates for the voter from the VFS.

4. The VFS checks the voter list and determines the voter's voting region.

5. The VFS checks the candidate list and produces a list of all candidates in the voter's voting region.

6. The VFS forwards the regional candidate list to the client.

7. The voter chooses a candidate to vote for.

8. The client generates an encrypted ballot for that candidate. The encrypted ballot consists of the chosen candidate, encrypted with the election public key. A random number generated by the client is also used in the encryption.

9. The client prompts the voter to sign the encrypted ballot.

10. The client uses his ID card to sign the encrypted ballot. This requires the voter to enter PIN2 into the card reader.

11. The client sends the signed encrypted ballot to the VFS.

12. The VFS receives the signed encrypted ballot and forwards it to the VSS.

13. The VSS receives a signed encrypted ballot from the VFS, and contacts the VCS to query whether the certificate used for signing is valid.

14. The VCS checks the certificate and informs the VSS. If the certificate is valid then it provides signed validity confirmation.

15. If the certificate or signature is invalid then the VSS rejects the ballot and informs the VFS which in turn informs the client. The protocol then stops at this point.

16. If the digital signature and the signing certificate are valid then the VSS stores the encrypted ballot and also stores the voter's identification number and a hash of the ballot in the log file LOG1

17. The VSS checks if the voter has already voted.

18. If the voter has already voted then the VSS stores a hash of the previous ballot, the voter's identification number and the revocation reason in LOG2 and deletes the previous ballot.

19. The VSS sends a receipt to the VFS to be forwarded to the client. At this point the voter can choose to follow the verification procedure detailed in Section 6.3.3.

20. When the voting period has ended, a list of e-voters is printed from the VSS, for each polling station. Each list is sent to the corresponding polling station and checked against the list of people who have voted. If the voter has voted at the polling station then a request for cancelling the e-vote is sent from the polling station. Any ballots from these voters are deleted, with the voter's identification number, a hash of the ballot and the reason for revocation being stored in LOG2.

21. The VSS sorts all ballots by constituency and removes their digital signatures, storing these digital signatures as a proof of who has voted. It then stores the hash of each vote in LOG3 (which is titled "votes which go for counting").

22. The encrypted ballots without signatures are then exported onto physical media and transferred to the VCA.

23. The VCA accepts, via physical media, the list of encrypted ballots sorted by constituency.

24. A threshold number of election officials insert cryptosticks with USB interfaces into the VCA.

25. This HSM decrypts all of the encrypted ballots.

26. The VCA then processes the decrypted ballots for each constituency in turn. For each ballot, the VCA checks if the candidate chosen is a valid candidate for the voter's constituency.

27. If the candidate is not valid then the vote is not counted and the hash of the ballot is recorded in LOG4.

28. If the candidate is valid then the tally for that candidate is increased by one and the hash of the ballot is stored in LOG5.

6.3.3 Auditing and Verification Capabilities

Immediately upon completion of tallying it is possible to audit the consistency of the system by checking that the entries in LOG1 are the same as the combined entries in LOG2 and LOG3 (i.e., that the ballots accepted by the VFS are the same as the combination of the ballots revoked by the VFS and the ballots sent for counting to the VCA) and that the entries in LOG3 are equal to the combination of the entries in LOG4 and LOG5 (i.e., that the ballots sent to the VCA are the same as the combination of the invalid ballots and valid ballots). This auditing is likely to detect system faults, but will not necessarily detect malicious intruders as they may have the capability to determine what is logged.

The verification application allows the voter to verify that the vote they submitted is held on the vote storage server. This verification proves the content of the vote to the voter, which may provide some risk of coercion. However, this verification can only be performed for up to 30 minutes after the vote has been cast, can only be performed three times, and does not leave the voter with a proof of vote. Remote voting systems generally have a vulnerability to coercion as a coercer could simply decide to present when the vote was cast; this verification mechanism merely gives the coercer an extra 30-minute window in which to be present. The voter also still has the option to re-vote. The verification protocol is as follows:

1. When the voter casts a vote, the voting application generates a random number that is used in the encryption of the ballot.

2. When the encrypted vote is received, the vote forwarding server gives the voting application a session code referring to this encrypted vote.

3. The voting application generates a QR code containing the random number and the session code.

4. The voter uses the verification application on a separate device to scan this QR code.

5. The verification application contacts the vote forwarding server and requests the encrypted vote corresponding to the session code.

   (a) If more than 30 minutes have elapsed from the vote being cast then the vote forwarding server refuses to send the encrypted vote and the protocol ends here.

6. The verification application receives the encrypted vote and the list of candidates in the voter's district.

7. The verification application uses the random number to generate an encryption for each valid candidate until it finds an encryption that matches the encrypted vote.

8. The verification application outputs the name of the matching candidate.

We note that the requirement for the verification application to use a brute force approach to discover the correct candidate prevents the application from discovering which candidate the voter expects to be contained in the encrypted vote. This prevents an attacker from building a malicious verification application that simply returns the candidate that the voter inputs. However, this does not prevent more sophisticated attacks where a malicious verification application communicates with a malicious voting application via some side channel to discover which candidate it should claim is encrypted. The verification application also does not address the situation where a malicious vote storage server provides a different encrypted vote to the verification application from the one that is stored.

However, as interesting as these theoretical attacks may be, in practice they are unlikely to be possible without detection. If malicious verification and voting applications are delivered widely to voters there is a high chance of detection either due to a comparison between the malicious application and the genuine application, or a malfunction caused due to interoperability problems between malicious and genuine applications. Similarly, attempts to modify the vote forwarding server or vote storage server would have to circumvent many checks and security systems.

6.4 Internet Voting Assumptions and Reception

The Estonian National Electoral Committee produced a comprehensive security and risk analysis for the internet voting system in 2003 and updated it in 2010 to include further concerns and developments [11]. This analysis showed that the system had been considered both as an electronic voting system and as a distributed application, with the relevant security concerns for both highlighted. Many of the issues discussed and conclusions reached were standard in these fields, but we highlight some of the less usual assumptions.

"Universal verifiability" was listed as a theoretical requirement as it was considered contradictory to the requirement of non-coercion in remote voting scenarios where it is assumed a coercer can see and influence any votes cast by the voter. Verifiability in the style of "recorded-as-intended" was introduced later (in 2011) when the prevalence of smartphones allowed the introduction of the verification application.

The guarantee that votes will never become public (translated as absolute [failsafe] of votes in the English version of the document) is also treated as theoretical given that unforeseen advances in cryptanalysis and computing power in general might lead to adversaries being able to break the cryptography used for the encryption of votes. Therefore further attention is paid to procedural controls like the handling and destruction of e-votes.

The Estonian internet voting system has received considerable criticism in the academic literature. This criticism covers both theoretical and practical security concerns. The lack of traditional end-to-end verifiability causes voters to have to rely on secure hardware and carefully crafted security procedures to ensure the integrity of the vote.

A relatively early criticism of the system was that using card readers without their own display and keypad was a risk to the integrity of the vote [518]. This risk arises from the fact that interaction with the ID card takes place through the same home computer used for voting. If the computer is compromised then the attacker can control both what is sent to the server and what is sent to the ID card, with the voter having no other means to monitor the process.

This threat may be partially mitigated by the more recent introduction of the verification application, allowing the vote to be confirmed on a second piece of hardware, and the increase in the number of voters using card readers that feature an independent keypad.

The use of log files as a significant part of the system audit has also been criticized [518]. Log file discrepancies are a good method for discovering system faults, but a malicious attacker with control of one or more components may be able to control what is logged in such a way that their modification of votes is undetectable.

More recently, the security of the system as used at the 2013 local elections was criticized by Springall et al. [535]. These criticisms were divided into four main areas: inadequate procedural controls, lax operational security, insufficient transparency and vulnerabilities in published code. The paper then went on to detail client and server side attacks that the authors were able to mount against their own reproduction of the Estonian internet voting system.

The Estonian National Electoral Commission responded to the initial reports of these criticisms with a statement in which they claimed that all of the attack vectors discussed had already been accounted for, it was not feasible to effectively conduct any of the attacks to alter the results of the voting and that numerous safeguards were in place to detect attacks and prevent tampering [4]. This statement also claimed that the website containing the criticisms had numerous factual and detail errors, and did not sufficiently detail the attacks. These alledged errors were not listed, so it is unclear as to whether this claim also applies to the paper, or just the website at that time.

Springall et al. responded in turn and disputed all of the claims in the Estonian National Electoral Commission's statement [22].

The internet voting system has received considerably more approval from the general public and the political parties of Estonia. The 2011 OCSE/ODIHR Election Assessment Mission Report [240] claimed that "Election stakeholders expressed confidence in the overall process, including the Internet voting." It did however also note that a legal challenge was made alleging a lack of reliability, secrecy and security of the internet voting system. This complaint was dismissed as unfounded and a challenge of this decision by the Center Party was dismissed by the Supreme Court as it was not filed in time. A further complaint was made alleging that some client names were hidden under certain display settings in the voting application, but this complaint was also dismissed as being without evidentiary basis.

6.5   System Performance

The Estonian internet voting system has been used in eight major elections over ten years; three Riigikogu elections, two European Parliament elections and three local elections. The percentage of voters using the internet voting system has grown over time for each of these three types of elections [28].

The first local election, which was also the first election in which internet voting was used, had only 1.9% of voters using internet voting. This increased to 15.8% for the second local election and to 21.2% for the third local election.

The first Riigikogu election had 5.5% of voters using internet voting, and this increased to 24.3% for the second Riigikogu election and 30.5% for the third Riigikogu election. Simiarly, the first European Parliament election had 14.7% of the voters using internet voting, while the second had 31.3% of voters using internet voting.

These figures show both that internet voting is used by a significant percentage of voters in Estonia and that the system is capable of handling large volumes of voters. The 24.3% of voters in the 2011 Riigikogu election equated to 140,846 people casting at least one internet vote each.

This large-scale usage of the internet voting systems has not highlighted any observable major failures. The OCSE/ODIHR EAM for the 2011 Riigikogu elections did detail one minor fault; a single vote was found to have been cast for an invalid candidate, something which should not have been possible due to the design of the voting application [240].

Chapter 7

Practical Attacks on Real-World E-Voting

J. Alex Halderman

University of Michigan

CONTENTS

7.1 Introduction

Many democracies rely on e-voting systems for binding elections, whether for in-person voting at poll sites or for remote voting over the Internet. (See Ch. 3 for an overview of the current state of e-voting worldwide.) Yet in practically every case where a fielded e-voting system has been publicly scrutinized by capable independent security experts, it has turned out to have serious vulnerabilities with the potential to disrupt elections, compromise results, or expose voters' secret ballots. This chapter highlights some of the most significant results from these studies and attempts to explain why real-world e-voting security failures are so widespread. It focuses on two classes of systems: poll-site DREs (Section 7.2) and online voting (Section 7.3).

E-voting faces a wide variety of potential attackers beyond those considered in traditional elections. These include insider attacks from system administrators, cybercriminals working for dishonest candidates, "hacktivists" seeking to disrupt elections as a form of political protest, and even sophisticated nation-states applying offensive cyberwarfare capabilities. We can roughly divide these attackers' goals into three categories: (1) *Tampering with the election outcome*, e.g., to favor particular candidates; (2) *Discovering how people voted*, e.g., to retaliate against those who voted against the attacker's preferred candidates, as a means of enforcing vote buying or coercion; and (3) *Disrupting or discrediting the election process*, e.g., through denial of service, conspicuous tampering, or the false appearance of such problems.

Defending against all these potential attacks simultaneously is difficult, for several reasons. First, some of the central security properties that an e-voting system needs to provide are in tension. Countermeasures against vote tampering—such as backups, logs, and receipts—tend to make it harder to strongly protect ballot secrecy. Likewise, mechanisms for protecting ballot secrecy—such as encrypting voted ballots and avoiding incremental backups—make detecting and responding to compromise more difficult. Second, election software tends to be more complex than one might naively assume, creating large numbers of opportunities for bugs and vulnerabilities to occur. Third, even if the code that's supposed to be running an election system is perfect, there is no way to guarantee that it is the actual code (and the *only* code) that is running on election day.

Elections are not just an ordinary application that has to be kept safe. Given the money and political power in play during a high-stakes election for public office, the incentive to cheat is enormous, and the consequences of a fraudulent outcome could threaten social order and national sovereignty. Election systems are critical infrastructure, as important to defend as the power grid or financial system. Yet most deployed e-voting systems have been built to the same level of quality as typical commercial IT projects, far below the appropriate level for critical infrastructure.

These challenges have been compounded because many e-voting system vendors and election officials have shied away from rigorous public security scrutiny. They've used electoral laws, intellectual property claims, computer intrusion statutes, and non-disclosure agreements to create impediments for concerned citizens and security researchers. As a result, the hardest part of finding security problems with fielded e-voting systems has often been to legally gain access to the systems for study. (Of course, actual criminals intent on rigging an election are unlikely to be deterred by the need to break the law.) It's unfortunate that officials and skeptical researchers are sometimes at odds, since ultimately both groups are working to see elections conducted well, and since, as this chapter shows, voters have good reason to be worried about the current state of e-voting security.

Figure 7.1: The Diebold AccuVote-TS was the most common DRE in the U.S. [233].

7.2 Touchscreen DREs

Direct recording electronic (DRE) voting machines are essentially general-purpose computers running specialized election software. Computer scientists have long been skeptical that voting systems of this type can be made secure. Experience with computer systems of all kinds shows that it is exceedingly difficult to ensure the reliability and security of complex software or to detect and diagnose problems when they do occur. Yet DREs rely fundamentally on the correct and secure operation of complex software programs.

7.2.1 Diebold

In the United States, the first touchscreen DRE to receive significant public scrutiny was the Diebold AccuVote-TS, shown in Figure 7.1. The AccuVote-TS and its newer relative the AccuVote-TSx were, in the mid-2000s, the most widely deployed electronic voting platform in the U.S. In the November 2006 general election, they were used in 385 counties representing over 10% of registered voters [211]. More than 33,000 of the TS machines were in service nationwide [205].

In most respects, the AccuVote-TS was a prototypical DRE. It interacted with the user via an integrated touchscreen LCD display. To authenticate voters and election officials, it used a motorized smartcard reader. On the side of the machine, behind a locked metal door, was a memory card slot that poll workers used to load ballot definitions and retrieve election results. The machine was also equipped with a small printer that recorded the final vote totals. Internally, the hardware resembled that of a laptop PC or a personal digital assistant. It included a RISC processor, 32 MB of RAM and 16 MB of flash storage. When the machine was first switched on, it loaded a boot-loader from the on-board flash. The boot-loader loaded the operating system, Windows CE 3.0, and Windows launched an application called BallotStation that conducted the election.

The first major study of these machines was carried out in 2003 by Kohno, Stubblefield, Rubin and Wallach, who studied a leaked version of the BallotStation source code and found many design errors and vulnerabilities [351]. (Diebold employees had stored a copy of the code on a company FTP site that was accessible to the public, where it was discovered by Bev Harris of BlackBoxVoting [330].) Diebold responded that the findings were "unrealistic" and pointed out that the researchers did not test with a real voting machine or a production version of the software [206].

Public concern in light of Kohno's study led the state of Maryland to authorize two security studies. The first, by SAIC, reported that the system was "at high risk of compromise" [521]. The second, conducted by RABA, a security consulting firm, confirmed many of Kohno's findings and suggested design changes to the Diebold system [475]. A further security assessment was commissioned by the Ohio Secretary of State and carried out by Compuware [168]. It examined several DRE systems including the AccuVote-TS and identified a number of high-risk security problems. Although these commercial studies reached similar conclusions, none of them offered the public a detailed technical description of the security issues they found.

Independent researchers finally had an opportunity to study the AccuVote hardware in 2006. Harri Hursti examined the hardware and compiled boot-loader firmware of AccuVote-TS and TSx systems [315]. He discovered problems with a software update mechanism that could allow malicious parties to replace the programs that operated the machines.

The same year, Feldman, Halderman and Felten at Princeton obtained an AccuVote-TS from a private party and reverse engineered its hardware and software [233]. They confirmed the results of the earlier studies by building working demonstrations of several reported attacks, and they also discovered a variety of serious new vulnerabilities. Their main findings were:

1. They confirmed Hursti's discovery that anyone who had physical access to the machine—or to a memory card that would later be inserted into a machine— could install malicious software. This could be achieved by opening the machine and replacing a socketed ROM chip inside, or, more easily, by exploiting back-door features in Diebold's boot-loader firmware. When the machine booted, it checked the removable memory card to see whether certain spe-

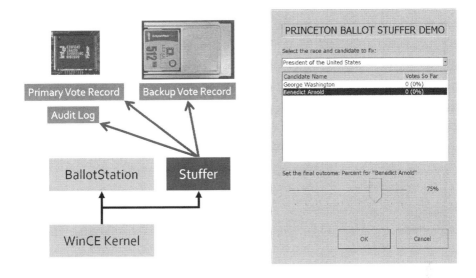

Figure 7.2: The Princeton Diebold study demonstrated vote-stealing malware that could spread from machine to machine while changing all records of the vote [233].

cial files existed. If a file named `explorer.glb` was present, the machine would launch Windows Explorer in place of Diebold's BallotStation election software, allowing an attacker to manipulate the software and files on the machine. Alternatively, if the memory card contained a file named `fboot.nb0` or `nk.bin`, the machine would replace the boot-loader code or operating system partition in its on-board flash memory with the file's contents. This was apparently intended as a software update mechanism, but there were no cryptographic integrity checks or on-screen confirmation prompts.

2. The Princeton team went on to create demonstration vote-stealing malware that modified all of the vote records, audit logs, and protective counters stored by the machine, so that even careful forensic examination of the files would find nothing amiss. All of these records were under the control of user-space software running on the machine. The demonstration malware, illustrated in Figure 7.2, was a Windows CE application that ran invisibly in the background alongside the BallotStation application. It included a user interface that allowed the attacker to interactively control which candidate would receive what fraction of votes. The malware parsed each new ballot as it was cast and then switched the minimum number of votes necessary to ensure that the favored candidate always had at least the desired percentage of the total.

3. The researchers developed a voting machine virus that could spread the vote-stealing code automatically and silently from machine to machine during normal pre- and post-election activities. The virus propagated via the removable memory cards by exploiting the software update mechanism to replace the ex-

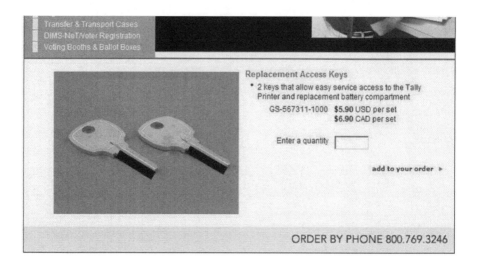

Figure 7.3: Voting machine keys for sale on Diebold's website [277]. The key cuts (blacked out by this author) were shown clearly enough to produce working replicas.

isting boot-loader in the machine's on-board flash. Once installed, the virus copied itself to every memory card inserted into the infected machine. If those cards were inserted into other machines, they too would become infected. As a result, an attacker could infect a large population of machines while only having temporary physical access to a single machine or memory card. Once the virus infected a machine, removing it would require factory service, since the malicious boot-loader disabled in-field software updates.

Although the unauthenticated update mechanism made it easy to tamper with the machine's software given access to the memory card, an attacker might still have to bypass one physical security feature: the lock on the memory card door (Figure 7.1, bottom right). Yet even in this respect, the AccuVote-TS gave attackers a variety of weaknesses to choose from:

1. The lock was of poor quality and could be picked using only paperclips.

2. All AccuVote-TS machines shared the same key cuts, so stealing the key to any one of them would allow an attacker to open them all.

3. The exact same key is commonly used in office furniture, jukeboxes, and hotel minibars, and is for sale at many online retailers. The Princeton team purchased copies of the key from several sources, and all could open the machine [234].

4. Diebold itself sold replacement keys, although they could only be purchased by municipalities that already owned the machines. However, the company's online catalog included a photograph of the key (Figure 7.3) that was detailed enough to allow anyone to create a working copy by filing a key blank [277].

A poll worker, technician, or other person who had private access to a machine for as little as one minute could use these methods with little risk of detection. Poll workers often do have such access; in a widespread practice called "sleepovers," machines are sent home with poll workers the night before the election.

While some of these problems could be eliminated by improving Diebold's software—such as by changing the firmware to properly authenticate software updates—others reflect deeper architectural problems with DREs. Since all records of the vote are under software control, if that software is malicious or malfunctioning, the integrity of the election results is lost.

7.2.2 Top to Bottom

Following these Diebold-focused studies, two states commissioned comprehensive security reviews of their election technology that encompassed products from several major e-voting vendors. In 2007, California Secretary of State State Debra Bowen organized a study, the California Top-to-Bottom Review (TTBR) [130], that examined systems manufactured by Hart InterCivic, Sequoia Voting Systems, and Diebold Election Systems (which changed its name to Premier Election Solutions during the study). David Wagner of the University of California, Berkeley, led a 40-person team that performed documentation review, source code analysis, red team testing, and accessibility review. The scope of testing included not only the voting machines but also their back-end election management software, making the TTBR the most comprehensive real-world e-voting security evaluation to date.

One subset of the TTBR team analyzed the Diebold AccuVote-TSx DRE (a newer model than the AccuVote-TS studied previously), AccuVote-OS optical scanner and GEMS election management system [129]. They discovered software flaws, including buffer-overflow vulnerabilities, that attackers could exploit to install malicious software on the voting machines and on the election management back-end systems. These flaws could be used to spread a vote-stealing virus that would propagate even more efficiently and be more difficult to detect than the virus developed by the Princeton team. Furthermore, the AccuVote DRE failed to protect ballot secrecy, since the digital ballot records were retained in the order in which they were cast and contained a time stamp for each vote. This would allow election workers who observed the order in which individuals cast their ballots to discover how those individuals voted. The team concluded that because "the vulnerabilities in the Diebold system result from deep architectural flaws, fixing individual defects piecemeal without addressing their underlying causes is unlikely to render the system secure" [129].

Other TTBR review teams analyzed voting systems from Sequoia Voting Systems and Hart InterCivic and reached similar conclusions. The Sequoia team uncovered "numerous programming, logic, and architectural errors" as a result of poor design and software engineering practices. These included buffer-overflow vulnerabilities and weak or ineffective cryptography, largely based on hard-coded cryptographic keys [105]. Once again, these problems could allow vote-stealing code to spread virally and compromise both the integrity of the election result and the secrecy of voters' ballots. The Hart review team discovered that the machines—which were connected via a local-area network inside the polling place—failed to properly secure their network interfaces, allowing voters or poll workers to connect to unsecured network links and cast votes, eavesdrop on voted ballots and even modify the software [317].

In light of the TTBR's findings, Secretary Bowen decertified DRE voting machines from all three vendors and then recertified them for limited use subject to stringent security and post-election auditing requirements [130]. In particular, California would only permit the Diebold and Sequoia DREs to be used for early voting and to operate a single machine at each poll site for accessibility purposes.

Later in 2007, Ohio Secretary of State Jennifer Brunner initiated a similar statewide voting technology review, known as Project EVEREST [434]. The study examined systems from Elections Systems and Software (ES&S), Hart InterCivic and Premier Election Solutions, under the leadership of Patrick McDaniel from Penn State [387]. Remarkably, although the EVEREST team studied the same Diebold and Sequoia systems as California, they found yet more vulnerabilities that had been overlooked in the earlier security reviews.

In the wake of these studies, most U.S. states moved away from DRE voting. By the 2014 general election, 70% of American voters were casting ballots on paper [92].

7.2.3 The Test of Time

An e-voting system must withstand not only the attacks known when it is designed but also those invented during its intended service lifetime. Because the development, certification and procurement cycle for voting machines is unusually slow, the service lifetime can be 20 or 30 years. It is unrealistic to assume that any design, however good, will remain secure for so long.

Checkoway et al. [154] illustrated this in a study of the Sequoia AVC Advantage, a DRE designed in the early 1980s that was still in use in 2009 in New Jersey Louisiana and various other states. Appel et al. had performed a security review and found that the AVC Advantage could be tampered with by replacing the socketed ROM chips where their software was stored [60], but the question remained whether the machines could be manipulated without physical access.

The AVC Advantage was designed with a form of data-execution prevention (DEP) as a defense against buffer-overflow attacks. A circuit on the motherboard prevents the machine from executing any instruction fetched from its RAM, as opposed to the separate ROM chips containing the election software. This protection seemed strong in the 1980s, but two decades of advances in attack techniques have rendered it less effective. Checkoway et al. showed that they could bypass the defense using return-oriented programming, an exploitation technique introduced in

2007 [523] that allows an attacker to combine short instruction sequences already present in the ROM into a Turing-complete set of "gadgets," from which any desired behavior can be synthesized. The team demonstrated that they could use this method to inject vote-stealing code from the machine's removable ballot cartridges [154].

Another question surrounding the life-cycle of DRE voting machines is whether they can be safely discarded when they are taken out of service. This author discovered in 2010 that government-surplus Diebold DREs he had purchased still contained vote records from real elections [279]. As the California TTBR showed, the AccuVote machines store ballots in a predictable order, which allows an attacker to reconstruct the order in which votes were cast. By combining data left in machines' internal flash memory with records from polling places, it might be possible to determine how individuals voted. Flash memory is tricky to completely erase [573], and more work is needed to establish adequate procedures for sanitizing the internal storage of surplus DREs before they are sent for disposal.

It would be a shame if obsolete or insecure DREs ended up in landfills, since they are often rugged PCs that could be repurposed for a range of useful purposes. Halderman and Feldman demonstrated one such application in 2010 [281]. They started with a Sequoia AVC Edge DRE that had recently been retired from elections in Virginia and reprogrammed it as a fully functional PAC-MAN machine (see Figure 7.4).

7.2.4 Around the World

Elections around the world are remarkably diverse in terms of local laws and technical requirements, and many countries prefer that election equipment is manufactured domestically, as a matter of national sovereignty. Despite this diversity, in every country where DRE voting security has been rigorously assessed, researchers have found serious vulnerabilities.

The Netherlands

In 2006, Gonggrijp and Hengeveld examined the Nedap ES3B, a DRE used by about 90% of Dutch voters [263]. The researchers were affiliated with *Wij vertrouwen stemcomputers niet* ("We do not trust voting computers"), a concerned-citizens' group founded by Gonggrijp. After obtaining Nedap machines from two municipalities, they reverse engineered the hardware and software and discovered a variety of problems. They concluded that the system's basic security design was lax—for example, a privileged maintenance mode was accessible using a hard-coded password ("GEHEIM," the Dutch word for "SECRET"). Moreover, they showed that an attacker with temporary physical access to the machine could quickly replace the socketed EPROM chips containing its software. To demonstrate the risks, they developed vote-stealing malware called Nedap PowerFraud that could surreptitiously change votes while the election was underway. They also reprogrammed one of the machines to play chess (see Figure 7.5), in response to a dare from Nedap's founder.

Figure 7.4: Voting researchers converted a surplus Sequoia AVC Edge DRE into a working PAC-MAN machine to show how easily its software could be modified [281].

Gonggrijp and Hengeveld also discovered a serious threat to voter privacy that had not been considered in previous research. They discovered unintended radio emanations from the ES3B that could be picked up on an inexpensive radio scanner or short-wave receiver from several meters away. The signal was different depending on whether or not the machine's display was showing text with an accented character. The display would show the name and party of the selected candidate, and since only one major political party in the Netherlands had an accent in its name, this side-channel could leak substantial information about the voter's choice [263].

Subsequent to these findings, The Netherlands abandoned DRE voting and returned to manually counted paper ballots [545]. In Germany, where Nedap DREs had also been widely adopted, the findings influenced a legal challenge to the use of electronic voting. In 2009, the German Federal Constitutional Court ruled that paperless DREs were unconstitutional and that e-voting was only permissible if "the essential steps of the voting and of the determination of the result can be examined by the citizen reliably and without any specialist knowledge" [122] (see Ch. 3).

Figure 7.5: Dutch researchers showed that they could quickly replace the firmware ROMs in the Nedap ES3B DRE to tamper with votes ... or make it play chess [263].

Brazil

Brazil has used DRE voting machines nationally since 2000. Although the legislature briefly adopted a VVPAT requirement in 2002, it was eliminated the following year [483]. The electoral authorities have long maintained that the machines are completely secure, but they refused until recently to allow any meaningful independent review of the hardware and software. In 2009, they inaugurated a series of periodic public security tests, and outside experts first had some limited access to the voting machines' source code in 2012, during the second round of this public testing.

A team of researchers from the University of Brasília, led by Diego Aranha, took part in the 2012 tests [62]. They uncovered serious weaknesses, including mishandling of encryption keys and insecure software engineering practices. Most significantly, they discovered a major flaw in the machines' privacy protections.

Brazil's DREs (see Figure 7.6) store a digital record of each vote, but, to safeguard the secret ballot, the records are kept in a shuffled order produced using a pseudorandom number generator (PRNG). When examining the source code, the researchers found that, rather than using a cryptographically secure PRNG, the Brazilian machines were programmed to use the C `rand()` and `srand()` functions (a notoriously insecure PRNG). Moreover, the PRNG was seeded using the time (in

Figure 7.6: Brazil's DRE voting machines failed to properly shuffle electronic vote records, potentially allowing malicious insiders to deanonymize them.

seconds) when the machine was initialized. As the researchers pointed out, this time is also recorded on the printed "zero tape" and in the system's logs that accompany the vote database. As a result, a malicious insider or external attacker who gains access to the data recorded by the DRE could completely reverse the shuffling process and associate every voter in sequence with their ballot choices, fully compromising the secret ballot [62].

Although the electoral authorities downplayed these findings (the judges in the public test awarded the researchers' team a score of 0.03 points out of a possible 400!), DRE security issues received widespread public attention following the close outcome of the 2014 presidential race. A legal challenge and security audit conducted by the losing political party concluded that the paperless DREs were not possible to audit [474]. In response, the national legislature overrode a presidential veto to pass a law reintroducing a VVPAT requirement [61].

Argentina

Some municipalities in Argentina use an unusual e-voting system called Vot.ar, which relies on paper ballots with embedded RFID chips [570]. Voters use a touch-screen ballot marker that prints their selections while simultaneously storing them in the RFID chip. The ballots are collected in a ballot box and then counted using an

RFID reader. The totals from each polling place are transmitted electronically to a central counting server to produce the election results.

During elections in Buenos Aires in July 2015, various independent researchers uncovered problems with Vot.ar. Joaquín Sorianello found that the private keys used to transfer the polling place results were publicly available on the Internet [106], potentially allowing an attacker to monitor or manipulate the returns. An anonymous leaker published the Vot.ar source code [471], and it was analyzed by a group of researchers who discovered a major flaw in the vote counting logic [56]. As a result of this flaw, an attacker could manipulate the data stored in the RFID chip so that a ballot would be counted as multiple votes.

Rather than responsibly addressing these concerns, authorities in Argentina attempted to suppress them. The Buenos Aires Metropolitan Police raided Sorianello's home and seized his computers, and a judge ordered Argentinian ISPs to block some of the websites where information about the system's security was being shared [106].

India

India, the world's largest democracy, is also the world's largest user of DRE voting. In the 2014 parliamentary election, more than 550 million voters cast their ballots on 1.4 million machines [575]. India's DREs look very different from those used in the U.S. and Europe. A marvel of engineering minimalism, they are simple, battery-powered embedded systems, consisting of a ballot unit used by voters and a control unit used by poll workers (see Figure 7.7). They lack upgradable software and interfaces for digitally loading ballot designs or offloading results. Instead, workers press buttons to reset the machines and set the number of candidates on the ballot. After the election, the control unit shows the vote total for each candidate on an LED display.

The Election Commission of India has never permitted a rigorous independent security review of the machines, known in India as EVMs, and has kept many details of their design secret, but it has maintained that they are "fully tamper-proof." This claim was challenged in 2010 by a team led by a self-taught engineer and business owner from Hyderabad named Hari K. Prasad. He collaborated with this author, Rop Gonggrijp and several others to perform a detailed security study of a machine provided by an anonymous government whistle-blower [578].

The researchers demonstrated two attacks that involve physically tampering with the machines' hardware. The DREs are stored between elections in low-security facilities that typically contain thousands of machines, so large-scale unauthorized access is a credible threat. The first attack was to replace the LED display in the control unit with a look-alike, shown in Figure 7.8, that would substitute fraudulent totals when showing the election results [578]. The dishonest display contained a hidden Bluetooth radio that the attacker would use to select the winning candidate on a smartphone app.

Figure 7.7: Halderman, Prasad, and Gonggrijp studied an Indian DRE provided by an anonymous whistle-blower [578]. The simple embedded system design consists of a ballot unit used by voters (*left*) and a control unit used by poll workers (*right*).

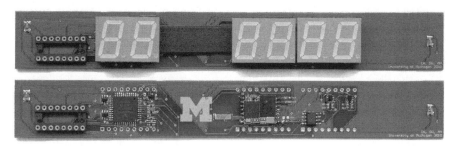

Figure 7.8: Researchers demonstrated how attackers could replace the display in the Indian DRE with a dishonest look-alike. They added parts (*bottom*), hidden under the LEDs, that substitute fraudulent vote totals when showing election results [578].

The second attack was a digital form of ballot box stuffing—which had been a widely reported problem in India prior to the introduction of e-voting [574]. The researchers constructed an inexpensive hand-held device that could be attached to the DREs' memory chips to quickly modify the vote records [578]. This attack could be performed by criminals who took over a poll site or by insiders during the interval between voting and counting, which may be several weeks in India.

Both attacks were made far easier and cheaper by the machines' minimalist design. (Among other simplifications, the EVMs do not use even basic cryptography to protect vote data.) They illustrate how DREs' vulnerabilities stem not only from complexity, as exhibited by systems in the U.S. and Europe, but more fundamentally from the need to protect against tampering for the entire life-cycle of the equipment.

A few months after Prasad and his coauthors published their study, he was arrested by authorities demanding to know who provided the machine [278]. Although Prasad was detained for more than a month, he refused to name his source [559]. The arrest drew national and international attention and led the leaders of India's major political parties to ask the Election Commission to implement a paper trail and other security measures [313]. The Election Commission subsequently began trials of a VVPAT printer attachment [555]. In 2013, the Supreme Court of India ruled that such a paper trail was "an indispensable requirement of free and fair elections" [549] and directed the government to fully implement the VVPAT, though as of 2015 the printers had only been introduced in some constituencies [413].

7.3 Internet Voting

Conducting elections for public office over the Internet raises severe security risks, beyond even those facing poll-site systems. Election servers must be accessible from the public Internet, exposing them to the potential for remote compromise and denial of service. Voters interact with these servers from their own devices, which are frequently infected with malware. Several researchers have cataloged threats to internet voting (e.g., [322, 492]), even as others have proposed systems and protocols that may be steps to solutions someday (see Section III of this book). Although a number of states and countries have charged ahead with systems for collecting votes online (see Chapters 5 and 6), every such system that has received rigorous independent security scrutiny has been shown to have significant vulnerabilities.

Among the practical challenges to secure internet voting are:

The Poor State of Software Security

Real-world internet voting systems tend to be built on top of commercial-off-the-shelf (COTS) software, which, despite the use of the term "commercial," includes most everyday open-source software. Unfortunately, the dominant security practice for COTS developers is still "penetrate and patch." While this approach is suitable for the economic and risk environment of typical home and business users, it is not appropriate for critical security systems, such as voting applications, due to the severe consequences of failure.

Architectural Brittleness in Web Applications

Getting web security right is complicated, and small mistakes in the implementation and configuration of web applications can result in total compromise. In this sense, the web is a brittle platform for secure application development. This is illustrated by the vulnerabilities in the Washington, D.C., and New South Wales web-based Internet voting systems, described below. In both cases, vulnerabilities resulting from small oversights—which could have been prevented by changing single lines of code—jeopardized the integrity of election results. Mistakes like these are common in web applications, and they are hard to eradicate because of the multitude of places in the software that they can exist, any one of which might be overlooked.

Exposure to Internet-Based Threats

Unlike poll-site voting, online voting systems necessarily have servers that are accessible from the public Internet. Consequently, they expose what might otherwise be a regional election to attackers from around the globe. Over the past decade, attackers have become increasingly sophisticated, and critical systems such as elections now face potential attacks from advanced cybercriminals and even state-sponsored attacks. In addition to compromising the central voting server, attackers could launch denial-of-service attacks aimed at disrupting the election, they could try to redirect voters to fake voting sites, and they could conduct widespread attacks on voters' client machines, perhaps using pre-existing botnet infections. These threats correspond to some of the most difficult unsolved problems in Internet security and are unlikely to be overcome soon.

While Internet-based financial applications, such as online banking, share some of the threats faced by Internet voting, there is a fundamental difference in ability to deal with compromises after they have occurred. In the case of online banking, transaction records, statements and multiple logs allow customers to detect specific fraudulent transactions—and, in many cases, allow the bank to reverse them. Internet voting systems cannot keep such fine-grained transaction logs without violating ballot secrecy for voters. Even with these protections in place, banks and merchants suffer billions of dollars of online fraud every year but write it off as part of the cost of doing business [364]. Fraudulent election results are more difficult to tolerate.

7.3.1   The Washington, D.C., Internet Voting System

In 2010, the District of Columbia developed an Internet voting pilot project that was intended to allow military and overseas absentee voters to cast their ballots using a website [542]. Prior to deploying the system in the general election, the District held a unique public trial: they conducted a mock election during which anyone was invited to test the system or attempt to compromise its security [190].

A team from the University of Michigan, led by this author, participated in the trial. Within 36 hours of the system going live, the Michigan team had gained nearly complete control of the election server. They successfully changed every vote and revealed almost every secret ballot. Election officials did not detect their intrusion for nearly two days—and might have remained unaware for far longer had the intruders not deliberately left a prominent clue. This case study was the first to analyze the

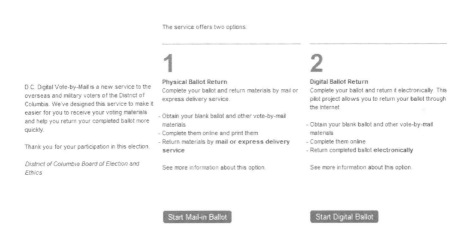

Figure 7.9: Washington, D.C., built an Internet voting system to allow overseas military voters and other expats to return votes via a website [579].

security of a government Internet voting system from the perspective of an attacker in a realistic pre-election deployment. The story, which the Michigan team recounted in a blog post [280] and a later research paper [579], dramatically illustrates the dangers and challenges that face Internet voting in practice.

The D.C. system was created by the Washington, D.C., Board of Elections and Ethics (BOEE) and was officially known as the D.C. Digital Vote-by-Mail Service. It was developed as an open-source project in partnership with the nonprofit Open Source Digital Voting Foundation's TrustTheVote project [447]. The software was written using the popular Ruby-on-Rails framework and the COTS Apache web server and MySQL database. To protect the servers, D.C. used a range of standard security mechanisms, including HTTPS, firewalls, and an intrusion detection system.

Months prior to the election, each eligible voter received a letter by postal mail containing a sixteen-character PIN and instructions for using the system. After visiting the election website (Figure 7.9) and logging in with their PINs, voters would download their ballots as PDF files, fill them in using a PDF reader, and upload them back to the server. To safeguard ballot secrecy, the server immediately encrypted each uploaded ballot using a public key. When the voting period had ended, officials would transfer the encrypted ballots to an airgapped computer, decrypt them using a private key and print them for counting alongside mail-in absentee ballots.

D.C. opened the election server for the mock election on September 28, 2010. (This trial was scheduled to conclude only three days before the system would be made available for use by real voters.) After a few hours of examining the source code, the Michigan team found a devastating vulnerability.

The problem had to do with the code that processed uploaded ballots. Whenever a voter uploaded a ballot, the server would store it on disk using a temporary filename and encrypt it by executing a command called `gpg` with the name of this temporary file as a parameter, for example: "`gpg "/tmp/ballot12345.pdf"`". The Michigan team realized that although the server replaced the filename with an automatically generated name ("`ballot12345`" in this example), it kept whatever file *extension* the voter provided. Instead of a file ending in ".`pdf`," an attacker could upload a file with a name that ended in almost any string, and this string would become part of the constructed command.

This would not have been a problem, except that the voting system developers mistakenly wrapped the filename in double quotes rather than single quotes. The server processed the command using the Bash shell, and in Bash, filenames in double quotes can contain special characters that cause the computer to run other commands. For example, the filename "`ballot12345.$(sleep 10)`" would cause the server to pause for ten seconds before responding (executing the command "`sleep 10`"). Consequently, by uploading ballots with carefully crafted filenames, an attacker could execute arbitrary code on the election server.

On the second day of the mock election, unbeknownst to the voting officials, the Michigan team started exploiting the vulnerability against the D.C. server. They carried out several attacks that illustrate the devastating effects that criminals could have during a real election if they gained a similar level of access:

1. *Stealing secrets.* As soon as they had breached the server, they began collecting crucial secret data, including the database username and password, the public key used to encrypt the ballots, and log, history and configuration files. This information would aid the attackers in compromising the system again if their infiltration was discovered and cut off.

2. *Changing past votes.* Next, they modified all the votes that had already been cast, replacing them with ballots marked with write-in votes for other candidates (see Figure 7.10). Although the system encrypted voted ballots, the attackers simply discarded the encrypted files and replaced them with forged ballots that they encrypted using the public key they had stolen.

3. *Changing future votes.* The attackers modified the code for the server software to rig the system so that future votes would be replaced in the same manner. This was possible because the server had been improperly configured such that the election software had sufficient privileges to modify itself.

Official Ballot
District of Columbia Mock Election
PRECINCT 22
September 17, 2010

INSTRUCTIONS TO VOTER

1. TO VOTE YOU MUST DARKEN THE OVAL TO THE LEFT OF YOUR CHOICE COMPLETELY. An oval darkened to the left of the name of any candidate indicates a vote for that candidate.
2. Use only a pencil or blue or black medium ball point pen.
3. If you make a mistake DO NOT ERASE. Ask for a new ballot.
4. For a Write-in candidate, write the name of the person on the line and darken the oval.

DELEGATE TO THE U.S. HOUSE OF REPRESENTATIVES	AT-LARGE MEMBER OF THE COUNCIL	UNITED STATES REPRESENTATIVE
Vote for not more than (1)	Vote for not more than (1)	Vote for not more than (1)
[ ] **Alice Example** Democratic	[ ] **Joan Example** Statehood Green	[ ] **Latoya Example** Republican
[ ] **Bob Example** Republican	[ ] **Kimberley Example** Democratic	[ ] **Marcus Example** Statehood Green
[ ] **Carol Example** Statehood Green	[ ] **Liam Example** Republican	[ ] **Newton Example** Democratic
(■) or write-in	(■) or write-in	(■) or write-in
Skynet	Johnny 5	Colossus
MAYOR OF THE DISTRICT OF COLUMBIA	**MEMBER OF THE COUNCIL WARD ONE**	**MEMBER OF ADVISORY NEIGHBORHOOD COMMISSION 1B DISTRICT FOUR**
Vote for not more than (1)	Vote for not more than (1)	Vote for not more than (1)
[ ] **Duane Example**	[ ] **Mary Example**	[ ] **Orlando Example**

Figure 7.10: A team from the University of Michigan hacked into the D.C. Internet voting system during a mock election and replaced every ballot with a set of write-in votes for evil robots and artificial intelligence systems from science fiction [579].

4. *Compromising the secret ballot.* The attackers installed a backdoor that let them view any ballots that voters cast after the attack. This modification recorded the votes, in unencrypted form, together with the names of the voters who cast them, violating ballot secrecy.

5. *Stealth... and a "calling card."* To test how well election officials could detect and recover from such an attack, the Michigan team did not immediately announce what they had done. Like a real attacker, they attempted to alter the server's logs and other files to remove evidence of the intrusion. However, they also left a deliberate clue: they modified the website so that after a user voted, their browser would begin playing "The Victors," the University of Michigan fight song. Nevertheless, the attack remained active for two days before other testers pointed out the fight song and D.C. officials took the server offline.

Recovery from such attacks is difficult; there is little hope for protecting future ballots from this level of compromise, since the code that processes the ballots is itself suspect. Using backups to ensure that compromises are not able to affect ballots cast prior to the compromise may conflict with ballot secrecy in the event that the backup itself is compromised.

Figure 7.11: D.C. invited the public to try to compromise their Internet voting systems. A team from the University of Michigan hacked in and changed all the votes in a mock election. They also accessed webcams in the data center, shown here [579].

The Michigan attackers found a variety of additional vulnerabilities during the tests, including routers and other network equipment with easily guessed passwords. They also found video cameras in the server data center that had no passwords at all, allowing attackers to identify individuals with access to the facility and learn the schedule of security patrols (see Figure 7.11). Interestingly, although the D.C. system included a network intrusion detection system (IDS) device, it was not configured to intercept and monitor the contents of the encrypted HTTPS connections that carried the attack. This resulted in a large "blind spot" for the system administrators.

The final problem discovered by the Michigan team—and perhaps the most devastating, from an operational perspective—was that one of the election administrators had uploaded a file to the mock election server that contained the login credentials for all of the real voters who were eligible to vote online. An attacker who stole these credentials from the known-insecure test server could have used them to cast votes in the real D.C. election, which was set to begin only days later. Since these credentials had to be delivered by postal mail, there was no time to send replacements.

Based on these results, the D.C. Board of Elections and Ethics decided not to allow online ballot return during the real election. Voters were still able to download and print ballots to return by postal mail, which reduced the round-trip delivery time by about half with far less security risk.

The D.C. trial illustrated that, due to the brittleness of the web platform, small mistakes—like using double quotes in place of single quotes in one line of a complex program—can be enough to compromise all the votes in an online election. Although the specific vulnerabilities that the Michigan team exploited would be simple to fix in retrospect, it is far more difficult to guarantee that no such mistakes exist.

7.3.2 Estonia's Internet Voting System

Several countries have experimented with casting votes over the Internet, but none uses Internet voting for binding political elections to a larger extent than Estonia [329]. When Estonia introduced its online voting system in 2005, it became the first country to offer Internet voting nationally, and, in recent national elections, more than 30% of ballots were cast online [223]. Many Estonians view Internet voting as a source of national pride, but one major political party has repeatedly called for it to be abandoned [225]. Although Estonia's Internet Voting Committee maintains that the system "is as reliable and secure as voting [the] traditional way" [224], its security has been questioned by critics from Estonia (e.g., [368, 436]) and abroad (e.g., [531, 535]). See Chapter 6 for a perspective on the system by one of its creators.

Most Internet voting schemes proposed in the research literature use cryptographic techniques to achieve a property called end-to-end (E2E) verifiability (see Chapter 8). This means that anyone can confirm that the ballots have been counted accurately without having to trust that the computers or officials are behaving honestly. In contrast, Estonia's system is not E2E-verifiable. It uses a conceptually simpler design at the cost of having to trust the integrity of voters' computers, server components, and the election staff. Rather than proving integrity through technical means, Estonia relies on a complicated set of procedural controls.

Security researchers have questioned whether these controls are adequate to secure modern elections [535, 531], pointing out that the threats facing national elections have shifted significantly since the Estonian system was designed. Cyberwarfare, once a largely hypothetical threat, has become a well-documented reality [513, 379, 557, 556], and attacks by foreign states are now a credible threat to a national online voting system. As recently as May 2014, attackers linked to Russia targeted election infrastructure in Ukraine and briefly delayed vote counting [160]. Given that Estonia is an EU and NATO member that borders Russia, multiple states with significant offensive cyber capabilities might be motivated to interfere in its elections.

Despite these concerns, the system was not subjected to a detailed independent security analysis until 2014, when a team of international researchers published a paper pointing out a variety of weaknesses [535]. The team observed operations during the October 2013 local elections, conducted interviews with the system developers and election officials, assessed the software through source code inspection and reverse engineering, and performed tests on a laboratory reproduction of the system.

Although Estonia uses a number of safeguards—including encrypted websites, security chips in national ID cards, and a smartphone-based vote confirmation system, shown in Figure 7.12—the researchers showed that they all can be bypassed by a realistic state-level attacker [535]. They demonstrated client-side malware that steals the voter's credentials and then silently replaces the cast vote. Such malware could be delivered by pre-existing botnet infestations or by infecting the voting client

Figure 7.12: Voters in the Estonian Internet voting system can confirm their votes by scanning a barcode with a smartphone app [535]. Researchers showed that this mechanism could be bypassed by malware on voters' computers or election servers.

before it is delivered to voters. They also demonstrated server-side attacks that target the centralized vote counting server. Estonia lacks any mechanism to allow voters or election officials to verify the correct operation of the counting server. By introducing malware into the server—say, through a supply-chain attack [337]—a foreign power or dishonest insider could arbitrarily change the reported results.

The researchers also observed serious lapses in the operational security practices of Estonian election officials [535]. These include administrators downloading security-critical software over unsecured Internet connections, typing secret passwords and PINs on camera in videos published to YouTube during the election, and preparing the voting software for public distribution on insecure personal laptops (see Figure 7.13), among other examples. While practices like these might be considered acceptable risks or understandable accidents in a low-security system, a critical system such as a national election platform calls for much stricter procedural controls.

The 2014 study concluded that there are multiple ways that state-level attackers, sophisticated online criminals or dishonest insiders could successfully attack the Estonian Internet voting system, and that such an attacker could plausibly change votes, compromise the secret ballot, disrupt elections or cast doubt on the integrity of results. Since these problems stem from basic architectural choices and fundamental limitations on the security and transparency that can be provided by procedural controls, the researchers recommended that Estonia suspend the use of the system [535].

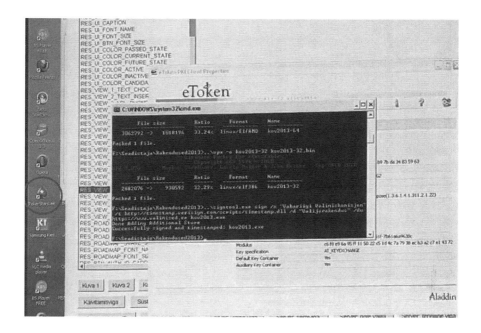

Figure 7.13: Researchers noted dangerous lapses in operational security during Estonia's 2013 election. Here, officials digitally sign the Internet voting client for distribution to the public using a laptop that has online gambling software installed [535].

Unfortunately, Estonian public discourse concerning election technology has become dominated by partisanship, and the national leadership has opted to continue online voting for now in spite of the known security risks.

7.3.3 The New South Wales iVote System

The world's largest deployment of online voting to-date was during the March 2015 state election in New South Wales, Australia. In this election, absentee voters had the option to use a web-based online voting system called iVote, which was developed by e-voting vendor Scytl in partnership with the New South Wales Electoral Commission. Over 280,000 votes were returned through iVote (about 5% of the total), exceeding the 70,090 Norwegian online votes in 2013 [522] and the 176,491 in the 2015 Estonian election [223].

Voters registered and cast their votes using websites managed by the electoral commission. Upon online registration, they were given an iVote ID number and asked to choose a six-digit PIN. These allowed them to log in to an online voting application written in JavaScript and HTML. After casting their votes, they received twelve-digit receipt numbers. Optionally, voters could call a telephone verification service and enter their receipt numbers to hear an automated system read back their votes.

The system's design is further described in reports published by the electoral commission [423, 115]. However, no source code was made available to the public, and the published descriptions lack sufficient detail for independent experts to completely assess the system's security. Prior to the election, the commission performed its own security studies (e.g., [425, 424]), and officials declared that the vote was "... completely secret. It's fully encrypted and safeguarded, it can't be tampered with" [39].

While online voting in the March 2015 election was underway, Vanessa Teague of the University of Melbourne and this author performed an independent, uninvited security analysis of public portions of the iVote system [282]. They discovered critical security flaws that had been overlooked by the commission's analyses and testing.

The central flaw that Halderman and Teague found had to do with iVote's use of HTTPS. The system relied on HTTPS to deliver the voting web application to users' browsers without tampering. Unfortunately, configuring a web server to use HTTPS correctly is nontrivial—operators must provision a browser-trusted certificate, select appropriately strong cryptographic ciphersuites and ensure that older, insecure versions of TLS and SSL are disabled, among other details [401].

The researchers tested the main iVote server, `cvs.ivote.nsw.gov.au`, and found that it used a safe HTTPS configuration. However, iVote also included third-party JavaScript from an external server, `ivote.piwikpro.com`, as shown in Figure 7.14. (Piwik is an analytics tool used to track site visitors.) The PiwikPro server turned out to have poor HTTPS security and was vulnerable to several attacks.

One of these vulnerabilities was the FREAK attack [102, 209], short for Factoring RSA Export Keys. FREAK is a TLS vulnerability that was publicly disclosed on March 3, 2015, less than two weeks before the iVote system opened. Halderman and Teague showed that a network-based man-in-the-middle could exploit FREAK to impersonate the Piwik server and inject malicious JavaScript into the iVote web application. Many popular browsers were susceptible to FREAK, including Internet Explorer, Safari, and Chrome for Mac OS and Android [209]. Although patches were released for most browsers about a week before iVote opened, it is likely that many users had not yet applied the updates.

The Piwik server was also vulnerable to an even more powerful TLS attack that affected *all* popular browsers: the Logjam attack [50], which was publicly disclosed two months after the election. The researchers were aware of this flaw at the time because Halderman was part of the team that discovered it, but they could not talk about it publicly since responsible disclosure was still underway. In other words, the voting security researchers had a zero-day TLS vulnerability that would have allowed them to attack any voter's iVote session.

Halderman and Teague showed that these flaws would allow an attacker to violate ballot privacy or steal votes. To do this, the attacker would intercept connections from

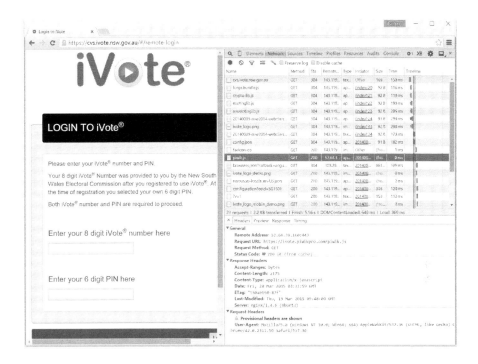

Figure 7.14: The New South Wales Internet voting website imported JavaScript from a third-party server that suffered from several TLS vulnerabilities [282].

the voter's browser to the Piwik server and use FREAK or Logjam to replace the real Piwik code with malicious JavaScript, as shown in Figure 7.15. This code would execute in the context of the user's iVote session, where it could arbitrarily change the operation of the iVote web application. The researchers demonstrated malware that would steal the voter's PIN and the content of their secret ballot, then substitute a different vote of the attacker's choosing.

Although these attacks require becoming a man-in-the-middle, criminal attackers have many well-documented ways to achieve this, including compromising insecure WiFi access points, poisoning ISP DNS caches, attacking vulnerable routers, and hijacking BGP prefixes. (Such attacks are one of the main threats that HTTPS is intended to guard against.) These attacks are especially practical in the context of a large election, since the attacker can opportunistically target any insecure hosts or infrastructure in the region where voting is taking place.

Such an attack might be caught by iVote's optional telephone-based verification system, but Halderman and Teague pointed out several ways that an attacker could circumvent this mechanism, including a variety of tricks to reduce the probability that a given voter would notice a problem. For instance, they could misdirect the voter to a fake verification phone number that reads back the voter's intended choices.

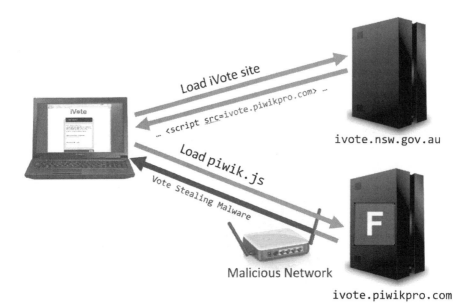

Figure 7.15: Researchers showed that a man-in-the-middle attacker could exploit the vulnerabilities in the Australian iVote system to inject vote-stealing code [282].

Even more simply, the attacker could delay submitting the real vote and displaying a receipt number for a few seconds, in hopes that the voter does not intend to verify and leaves the website. If the voter navigates away without seeing a receipt number, there is no chance to verify, and the attacker can substitute a fraudulent vote.

Another way to circumvent verification would be to mount a variant of the "clash" attack [357]. The attacker would intercept a voter's online registration session and assign him or her the iVote ID and PIN of a like-minded person who had already voted, preferably one who cast a simple vote likely to be repeated. Later, if the victim's choices match those of the first voter, all of the verification will look right to both voters. The attacker can safely reuse the target voter's registration credentials to get a new iVote ID and PIN and cast an arbitrary vote. While the registration server itself was protected by HTTPS, the main iVote gateway from which voters reached it ran plain HTTP. This gave a man-in-the-middle attacker the opportunity to misdirect registration attempts to a fake site of the attacker's choosing.

Of course, the verification design also compromises privacy and exposes voters to coercion, since it makes it easy to prove how you voted to anyone just by handing over your credentials and receipt number. Furthermore, the design does not provide strong evidence to support or disprove voter complaints, so it is difficult to distinguish an attack from the baseline level of complaints due to voter error.

After confirming that the attack was possible, Halderman and Teague notified the authorities of the vulnerability by contacting the Australian CERT [282]. The electoral commission responded the next day by modifying the iVote server configuration to disable Piwik. After the vulnerabilities were removed, the researchers made their findings public [551, 550] and later published a formal paper [282].

By the time the vulnerability was fixed, online voting had been taking place for five days, and 66,000 votes had already been cast. The closest seat in the parliamentary results was eventually decided by a margin of 3,177 votes, less than 5% of this number [422]. While we may never know whether anyone exploited the opportunity for electoral fraud, we know the opportunity was there—and if Internet voting continues to be deployed on such large scales, it will not be the last opportunity.

7.4 Conclusion

Democracy relies on voters having well-founded trust in the processes used to collect and count their votes. Unfortunately, when it comes to real-world e-voting systems, the case studies in this chapter provide abundant grounds for skepticism.

In light of such results, restoring trust will require shifting the burden of proof from the skeptics to system designers and operators. E-voting systems need to be designed to produce sufficient evidence to convince rationally skeptical observers that the outcome is correct. This could take the form of observable physical records (such as paper ballots) or cryptographic proofs, so long as they can be publicly audited to the necessary levels of assurance.

Yet evidence in support of the outcome is not sufficient. It is preferable to prevent problems with the outcome, rather than merely detecting them. And many other problems discussed in this chapter would not be caught by auditing such evidence—for example, attempts to disrupt the election or to violate voter privacy. To safeguard against these, e-voting systems need to be engineered to a level of security quality far greater than that of typical information technology systems, on par with other kinds of critical infrastructure. Elections should provide convincing evidence that this level of quality has been achieved, by being transparent about their security measures and engineering processes, and by making source code available for public review.

As we have seen, typical real-world e-voting systems are not designed to provide these kinds of evidence—of the integrity of the outcome or of the quality of their engineering. In most cases, they rely fundamentally on the correct and secure operation of secret software that is tasked with collecting and counting votes in secret.

One promising way forward is to hasten the transition of end-to-end verification (Chapter 8) from research to practice. Most of the fielded systems described in this chapter look quite different from the e-voting systems proposed by researchers that will be discussed later in this book. On one hand, real-world e-voting systems tend to be less sophisticated—sometimes their functionality amounts to little more than counting button presses. On the other hand, unlike research prototypes, they have to cope with practical consideration ranging from price competition to the necessity of being usable enough for non-technical voters and poll workers. We need more research—and closer collaboration between researchers and election officials—to develop verifiable e-voting systems that are suitable for real-world use.

E2E VOTING SYSTEM AND REAL-WORLD APPLICATIONS

Chapter 8

An Overview of End-to-End Verifiable Voting Systems

Syed Taha Ali

School of Computing Science
Newcastle University, UK
taha.ali@newcastle.ac.uk

Judy Murray

School of Geography, Politics and Sociology
Newcastle University, UK
judy.murray@newcastle.ac.uk

CONTENTS

8.1 Introduction

The use of cryptography to secure elections was first suggested by Chaum in 1981 in a highly influential paper on anonymous communications [153]. Chaum described new cryptographic primitives, or building blocks, and proposed various applications for these, including the possibility of conducting remote electronic elections. This idea proved popular in the academic research community, and, over the next two decades, a multitude of voting systems appeared in the literature, a handful of which resulted in actual prototype solutions [179] [306]. However, research in this domain was, for the most part, confined to academia and progressed independently of developments in real-world election technology.

In the last 15 years however the situation has dramatically altered. Research in securing elections has received a significant boost for two main reasons: First, the gridlock in the US presidential election of 2000 between George W. Bush and Al

Gore cast a spotlight on the deficiencies of the US voting infrastructure where voters faced considerable difficulties in casting votes due to confusing ballot designs and punch card voting machines [363]. This flurry of national attention led to passage of the Help America Vote Act (HAVA) in 2002 which, among other provisions, allocated generous funding for research to improve voting technology [162].

Second, multiple investigations in recent years have highlighted glaring reliability and security issues in electronic voting machines which render them vulnerable to hackers and compromise the integrity of elections [351] [232] [578] [535]. Indeed, there have been numerous documented instances of voting machines inexplicably malfunctioning during live elections, flipping candidate votes, or randomly adding and subtracting candidate votes. Since then, academic research interest in securing elections has soared, and prompted the formation of dedicated conferences and journals and research organizations [1] [18].

This renewed focus has led to the development of a new type of voting system with **end-to-end verifiable (E2E) security** properties. This highly promising advance, due to individual efforts by Chaum [143] and Neff [418] in 2004, harmonizes theoretical research innovation with the ground realities of election administration to provide strong guarantees on the integrity of elections. We describe next a typical usage scenario which encapsulates the spirit of E2E voting systems.

On election day, our voter, Alice goes to the polling station to cast her vote. She identifies herself to polling staff as a legitimate voter and is guided to a private booth with a voting machine, where she chooses her candidate on the touchscreen. The machine issues her a *receipt*, which is essentially a cryptographically masked copy of her vote. In the booth, Alice can also verify, either visually, or by challenging the machine, that her vote was **cast as intended**, i.e., the cryptographic obfuscation does indeed represent her chosen candidate and not another. After polls close, the system posts copies of all receipts on a public bulletin board or website where Alice confirms that her vote has been **recorded as cast**, i.e., her receipt is included in the lot and it matches the physical copy she has in her hand. In the final step, all receipts on the website are processed in a series of cryptographic computations to yield the election result. The algorithms and parameters for these operations are specified on the website, and any technically-minded person, including Alice herself, can therefore verify that her own vote was **tallied as recorded** and that the tally is indeed correct.

This scenario is starkly different from the current state of real-world elections where Alice has to implicitly trust the voting system and its administrators for the credibility of the election. Dishonest polling staff have been known to manipulate election results. Furthermore, the internal operations of voting machines are opaque to Alice and she has no assurance that the machine is actually doing what it is supposed to.[1] E2E voting systems, on the other hand, preclude trust in personnel and machines and make the voter herself an active participant in auditing the election at

---

[1]This realization was fundamental to the decision of the Federal Constitutional Court of Germany in 2009 declaring electronic voting as "unconstitutional" and thereby marking Germany's return to paper-based voting [37].

every step and certifying its result. If a voting machine loses Alice's vote or switches it to another candidate, her receipt on the website will reflect this change and Alice can file a complaint, using her own physical copy as evidence. If polling staff tamper with the final tally, any third party running the tallying or verification algorithm on their own computers will pick up on it. Furthermore, since Alice's receipt is an obfuscation of her choice, she cannot use it to convince a third party of how she voted, thereby thwarting vote-selling and coercion.

We provide here a comprehensive high-level introduction to the field of E2E voting. The writing is aimed at the layman with little knowledge of cryptography and attempts to communicate a clear and intuitive appreciation of E2E voting systems. This chapter is organized as follows: we introduce security properties of voting systems in Section 8.2. In Sections 8.3–8.4, we summarize the workings of some twenty of the most influential E2E voting systems, classified into four distinct categories, as per their reliance on cryptography (cryptographic and non-cryptographic systems), ballot format (physical and electronic ballots) and mode of voting (precinct-based and remote voting). This is followed by a discussion of open challenges to mainstream deployment of E2E voting systems in Section 8.5. We conclude in Section 8.6.

8.2   Security Properties of Voting Systems

Here we describe key security properties characterizing E2E voting systems. Many of these properties are intimately related whereas others are in direct conflict. The merits of a system are typically assessed on the basis of what properties it provides and how successfully their inherent conflicts are harmonized within the system.

8.2.1   Vote Privacy

The privacy of the vote is widely recognized as a fundamental human right and is enshrined in Article 21 of the Universal Declaration of Human Rights [67]. The rationale behind this, dating back to ancient Greece and Rome [286], is that if outside parties become privy to a voter's choice, it opens the door to bribery and intimidation, ultimately corrupting the electoral process. Vote-buying was not uncommon in the Western world up until the last century [547] and still persists in some developing countries [323] [265]. Likewise, voters may be intimidated by criminals, local politicians, or even family members, to vote a certain way. These fears directly motivated the notion of the *secret ballot*, which is typically implemented nowadays by providing the voter a private voting booth at the polling station. Her ballot bears no distinguishing marks and her vote is cast in the ballot box where it mixes with all the other votes, making it very difficult, if not impossible, to ascertain her choice.

In contrast, voting systems in the early research literature (such as [161] [91] [83] [140]) explicitly maintained the voter-ballot linkage by issuing the voter a receipt enabling her to track her vote on a public bulletin board. In 1994, Benaloh and Tuinstra [89] (and independently, Niemi and Renvall [415]) pointed out that this strategy allowed the voter to prove her vote to a third party after the election, thereby facilitating vote-buying and coercion. The authors introduced the notion of *receipt-freeness* which proved influential and several voting systems that followed (such as [89] [415] [508] [437] [438] [309]) dispensed with receipts entirely, focussing instead on ensuring transparency and integrity of the tallying operations. However, in 2004, Chaum [143] reintroduced the use of receipts, with the important distinction that the contents of the receipt are cryptographically masked, thereby maintaining the voter's privacy.

Juels, Catalano and Jakobsson [335] in 2005 argued that a coercer may yet influence a voter's choice without explicit knowledge of her vote, and described three such modes of coercion: the coercer may prevent the voter from voting, he may appropriate her voting credentials, or force her to vote for a candidate at random. The exact difference between receipt-freeness and coercion resistance is a subtle one [194]: in receipt-freeness, the coercer is assumed to be restricted to observing the election and using evidence provided by a cooperating voter. In the case of coercion resistance, the coercer is more powerful, and may craft specific votes for the voter to cast or even interact with her in some way while she is voting. Juels et al. proposed a solution to defend against these threats which we describe in Section 8.3.3.2.

Researchers have therefore progressively refined notions of vote privacy over the years into the following key properties:

■ **Ballot Secrecy**: the voting system must not reveal who the voter voted for.

■ **Receipt-Freeness**: the voting system should not give the voter any evidence to prove to a third party how she voted.

■ **Coercion-Resistance**: the voter should be able to cast a vote for her intended choice even while appearing to cooperate with a coercer.

Intuitively, we see that each property encapsulates the previous one: coercion-resistance implies receipt-freeness which in turn implies ballot secrecy.

8.2.2 Vote Verifiability

In real-world elections, the voter has to implicitly trust voting machines and polling staff for the integrity of the elections. Typically there are ancillary processes in place to improve voter confidence in results, such as exit polls, random audits, and opening the tallying process to the public. On the other hand, voting systems in the research literature attempt to minimize the voter's dependence on personnel and machines, and use cryptography to provide ironclad guarantees on election integrity. Sako and Kilian [508] distinguished between two forms of verifiability:

- **Individual verifiability**: a voter can verify that her vote is included in the set of all cast votes.

- **Universal verifiability**: an observer can verify that the tally has been correctly computed from the set of all cast votes.

E2E voting systems recast the notion of verifiability in terms of three core steps:

- **Cast-as-intended**: the voter can verify the voting system correctly marked her candidate choice on the ballot.

- **Recorded-as-cast**: the voter can verify that her vote was correctly recorded by the voting system.

- **Tallied-as-recorded**: the voter can verify that her vote was counted as recorded.

This translates as follows: the voter first confirms the system has correctly encrypted her vote. She then tracks her vote on the bulletin board using her receipt and confirms that it is correctly recorded. Integrity of the result is ensured by rigorously auditing the tallying process and requiring the system to publish cryptographic proofs of correct operation. This three-step verification therefore covers the entire life cycle of the vote, and the voter can be confident that if there is any tampering or breakdown in the system it will be discovered in one of the checks.

These two conceptions of verifiability are also linked: in most E2E voting systems, cast-as-intended and recorded-as-cast checks are verified by the voter, i.e., together they provide individual verifiability, whereas the tallied-as-recorded step may be undertaken by voters and observers alike, i.e., it provides universal verifiability.

8.2.3 Other Properties

We list here certain additional properties also vitally important in voting systems:

- **Eligibility verifiability**: an observer can verify that each vote in the set of all cast votes was cast by an eligible voter.

- **Accountability**: in case vote verification fails at some stage, possibly due to error or fraud, the voter should be able to conclusively prove that it failed to the relevant authorities, without compromising the secrecy of her ballot.

- **Robustness**: the system should be robust to a certain degree of malfunction or corruption and still deliver correct results. A small number of misbehaving voters or system failures should not disrupt the election.

- **Usability**: the system should enable voters to cast their votes easily and effectively.

- **Accessability**: the system provides equal opportunity for access and participation (including guarantees on vote privacy and verifiability) to voters with disabilities.

8.2.4 Conflicts and Challenges

Several of the key properties described thus far conflict with each other in subtle ways, resulting in a variety of technical and legal challenges. For instance, as noted in the discussion on receipt-freeness, vote privacy clashes with vote verifiability. If a voter can successfully prove her vote to a third party outside the polling station, she could easily sell her vote or be coerced into voting for a certain candidate. A detailed treatment of this tension between verifiability and privacy in voting systems may be found in [334] and [407].

Similarly, there is a tension between vote verifiability and usability. Requiring voters to verify their vote negatively impacts usability by adding extra steps to the process, which may prove confusing for the voter [339] [40] [402]. Furthermore, experimental trials have noted that only a very small percentage of voters actually verify their vote [133] [395], which may critically undermine the security guarantees of these voting systems. We discuss these issues in greater detail in Section 8.5.2.

Accessibility also conflicts with vote privacy. Adapting voting systems to provide audio/visual aids or human assistance for voters with disabilities may create situations where the voter's candidate choice is revealed to a third party. Likewise, deploying voting systems for remote scenarios, such as postal or Internet voting, while significantly more convenient compared to in-person voting at polling stations, results in a marked deterioration in vote privacy [485]. In her home the voter is not guaranteed privacy and is also vulnerable to coercion.

Faced with such situations, designers of voting systems typically incorporate technological remedies or procedural safeguards into the system, prioritize certain security requirements over others or perhaps even focus on satisfying certain properties in a weaker form. We encounter several such examples in the following sections.

8.3 Cryptographic E2E Voting Systems

In this section, we describe notable E2E voting systems which rely on cryptography to guarantee E2E verifiability. These systems are further categorized depending on the ballot format they support: *physical ballots* (i.e., paper ballots) as opposed to *electronic ballots*, and their mode of deployment, for *precinct-based voting* (i.e., in-person voting at polling stations) versus *remote voting*.

There is considerable cross-fertilization across categories. Many systems incorporate common cryptographic primitives and procedural innovations. Furthermore, several systems share a common lineage and design philosophy which we have attempted to highlight in our presentation. We have also included certain systems which provide only a subset of E2E security properties, i.e., they are not strictly E2E verifiable, but nevertheless make an important contribution to the field.

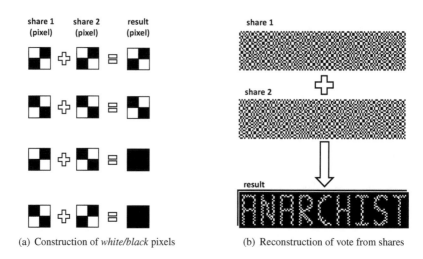

(a) Construction of *white/black* pixels   (b) Reconstruction of vote from shares

Figure 8.1: Generating a Votegrity receipt (with a vote for *Anarchist*).

8.3.1 Precinct-Based Voting with Physical Ballots

This category comprises precinct-based systems in which the tally is computed from receipts of paper ballots which voters mark by hand or using a machine. These systems are directly descended from Votegrity, and prominent examples include Scantegrity and Prêt à Voter, which have been deployed in politically binding elections.

8.3.1.1 Votegrity

Votegrity [143] was invented by Chaum in 2004 and is one of the very first and most influential E2E voting systems.[2] Votegrity uses visual cryptography to render the verification process more intelligible to the layman.

In **visual cryptography** [405], an image is split into multiple shares, such that individual shares do not yield any meaningful information about the original image and appear to contain random information. However, when the shares are overlaid the original image is reconstructed. As depicted in Figure 8.1(a) for the case of two shares, each pixel symbol is subdivided into four sub-pixels. When the shares are superimposed, identical pixels on both layers result in a semi-transparent or *white* pixel, whereas, if the two pixels are different, the resulting pixel will be opaque or *black*. Individual pixels on a layer reveal no information about the final result.

Vote processing in Votegrity is undertaken by a group of election trustees.[3]

---

[2] Several systems in the literature predating Votegrity offer what are arguably E2E security properties but these are primarily theoretical protocols based on abstract and idealized assumptions. Votegrity is the first E2E verifiable voting system to address the human complexities and practical realities of elections.

[3] The term *election trustee* in this chapter is taken to refer specifically to election personnel who handle cryptographic keys used in the voting systems.

Public-key cryptography is employed to maintain voter privacy and integrity of the tally. In this paradigm, each trustee possesses two keys, a *public* key he uses for data encryption and which is publicly posted, for example, on the election website or in a directory, and a *private* key used for decryption, which he keeps strictly private. These two keys are mutually related such that any entity can use the trustee's public key to encrypt data but only the trustee himself can decrypt it since he alone owns the corresponding private key. Many security protocols, including voting systems, specify multiple trustees to diffuse responsibility and trust. In this case, a system's security, may only be compromised if all trustees secretly collude. Trustees are therefore typically chosen such that they are mutually distrusting, i.e., they may belong to competing political parties and include activists and members of citizen groups.

On election day, Alice casts her vote at her local polling station. She enters her candidate choice on a voting machine, and presses a button, and a printer attached to the machine prints patterns on two strips of paper using visual cryptography. These strips are presented superimposed under a custom viewfinder, and the voter's choice is clearly visible. The example in Figure 8.1(b) depicts a vote for *Anarchist*.

Pixels on both strips are generated using a pseudorandom function, i.e., the patterns on the individual images appear random to an observer but are actually generated in a deterministic manner.[4] The voting machine also imprints a serial number and some validating information on both strips. Alice randomly chooses one of the strips as a receipt to take home. The machine shreds the other strip, issues the chosen strip to Alice, and saves a digital image of it to memory.

After polls close, the system publishes all saved voter receipts on a public bulletin board or website. Alice can locate her receipt using the serial number and verify that the digital image and validating information matches with her physical receipt. If there is any discrepancy, i.e., if the online receipt is missing or if the two versions do not match, she can initiate an inquiry with election authorities.

Votegrity's key breakthrough is this new role of the receipt. The printed information includes character strings which appear random to an observer but are actually a digital encoding of data which enables election trustees to fully reconstruct both original strips, and thereby the vote itself. When the voting machine generates the strips, it encrypts a digital copy of the visual patterns on both using the trustees' public keys, and this encryption, or *ciphertext*, is then printed on the receipt. The encryption may be understood with the analogy of an onion, where the vote is successively encapsulated in multiple skins or layers of encryption, each corresponding to a particular trustee. In the public-key paradigm only trustees can decrypt a vote by applying their private keys individually to remove corresponding layers of encryption.

The system decrypts cast votes in a privacy-preserving and verifiable manner using **decryption mixes**. A mix, invented by Chaum [153], is essentially a *permutation box* which accepts multiple data items, removes a layer of encryption, shuffles the items, and outputs them. A **mixnet** consists of multiple such mixes connected to-

---

[4]Details on construction of the patterns can be found in [143] and [152].

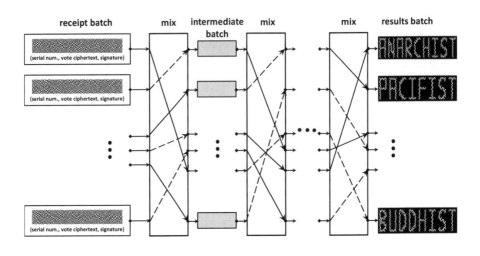

Figure 8.2: Votegrity decryption, mixing and audit process.

gether in cascading order such that the outputs of one feed into the next, as depicted in Figure 8.2. A mixnet effectively obscures the link between an input and an output and is a key ingredient in various anonymous communications protocols. Each mix is operated by an individual election trustee.

All receipts on the bulletin board are fed into the mixnet. The first mix strips the serial numbers from the receipts in addition to decryption and shuffling. Each mix removes a layer of encryption from the ciphertexts, figuratively peeling the onion, using the private key of the trustee operating the mix. The final result is a set of fully decrypted, or *plaintext*, votes stripped of any identifying information regarding the voter. These votes are then tallied in a straightforward manner.

Each mix processes its batch privately. Alice can be assured her vote is secret as revealing it would require that all the trustees collude to track her vote across each mix. However, there is still the issue of integrity: Alice cannot be sure the mixes are correctly processing the receipts and not altering them in transit. Chaum suggests election authorities publicly audit the mixes using a technique known as **randomized partial checking** [321]. The key idea is very simple: after tallying is concluded, each mix is forced to reveal a randomly chosen selection of half its inputs and outputs. These are posted on the bulletin board so that any observer can verify that the mix decrypted and mixed the items correctly. If a mix tampers with a single vote, there is a 50% chance it will get caught in a random check. The odds of being detected increase with every additional vote the mix manipulates, and would be close to 100% if a mix manipulates enough votes to influence a large-scale election.

However, while it is essential that mixes be subjected to this check, it is also vital that no receipt on the bulletin board be traced through the mixes to a plaintext vote. This is accomplished by selecting input-output links in an exclusory manner such that no *end-to-end* path across the mixnet is revealed. For example, considering the first two mixes in Figure 8.2, using dashed lines to denote unmasked links, we see that paths revealed in one mix are kept strictly private in the adjacent mix.

Now that the entire system has been described, we discuss the security properties it offers: when Alice casts her vote, she can visually verify that the printer correctly printed her candidate choice. Furthermore, each strip is digitally signed by the voting machine. **Digital signatures** are cryptographic equivalents of real signatures and have legal standing in several countries. In this case, the voting machine itself has a public/private key pair and their role is reversed: the machine's private key is used to mathematically compute a "signature" on the information on the receipt. This is a string of data which any observer can easily verify using the voting machine's public key (available via the bulletin board or in a public directory). Successful verification is undeniable proof of origin, as only the machine possesses the private key responsible for the signature. In case of a dispute, a digital signature is thus non-repudiable proof that the receipt was issued by a legitimate voting machine.

By digitally signing each strip, the machine may therefore be considered to have *committed* itself to both strips. Alice then chooses one layer at random to take home. If the machine were to cheat and put fraudulent information on single strips for a significant number of voters, it would be detected with very high probability.

Outside the polling station, Alice can verify, using the public keys of the trustees, that the ciphertext on the receipt is indeed a correct encryption of the visual pattern on her receipt. This gives her high assurance that her vote was cast as she intended. She can ensure the system correctly recorded her vote by verifying her physical receipt on the bulletin board. When mixing and tallying are undertaken, the inputs and outputs of every mix are publicly posted on the bulletin board. Any observer, including Alice, can monitor the random checks on the mixnets and confirm the results. Randomized partial checking is well-suited to audit elections as it does not rely on complex cryptography and is therefore efficient and relatively easier for the voter to appreciate. Any observer can verify the final tally for themselves by adding up all the decrypted votes. Furthermore, none of the information on the receipt or the bulletin board leaks any knowledge of the contents of Alice's vote which a third party may exploit to bribe or intimidate her. The visual image on her receipt is incomprehensible without the second strip which the voting machine shredded during the vote-casting phase, and theoretically it could represent a vote for *any* candidate.

In short, Alice can now audit the election at every key stage herself and need not trust election authorities for election integrity. Furthermore, election verifiability is independent of underlying infrastructure such as voting machines or vendor software. Technically-minded voters can create (and distribute) software to perform the necessary verifications using the information on their receipts and the bulletin board.

Votegrity has proved immensely influential and inaugurated new directions for research in secure elections. Several systems that followed borrow the basic receipt-and-mixnet template and improve on practical aspects. We consider these next.

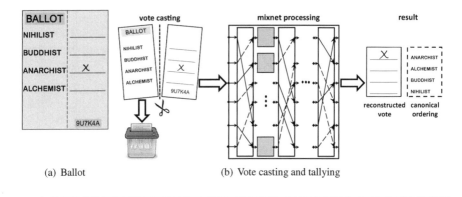

(a) Ballot　　　　　　　　　(b) Vote casting and tallying

Figure 8.3: Voting with Prêt à Voter(casting a vote for *Anarchist*).

8.3.1.2　Prêt à Voter

Prêt à Voter [499], initially proposed by Ryan in 2004 as a variant of Votegrity [500], was later developed into an independent system by Chaum, Ryan and Schneider [151]. Prêt à Voter is described in detail in Chapter 12. We provide a brief overview.

Prêt à Voter replaces Votegrity's visual cryptography element with a paper ballot and randomized candidate ordering. The ballot, depicted in Figure 8.3(a), is detachable into two halves along the perforated line in the middle. The left half lists candidates in randomized order. The right half has corresponding marking spaces and a random-looking string of alphanumeric characters, referred to as the *onion*, printed at the bottom. The onion encodes the permutation of candidate names on the specific ballot relative to a standard *canonical* ordering, encased in multiple layers of encryption using the public keys of the election trustees, as in Votegrity.

The workings of the system are presented in Figure 8.3(b). To vote, Alice marks her candidate choice on the ballot, detaches the two halves and shreds the left side with the candidate ordering. She then scans the right-hand side and takes it home as her receipt. After polls close, all scanned receipts are posted on the bulletin board where Alice can verify her vote is correctly recorded. However, she cannot prove her choice to a third party with just the right half of the ballot since her mark could potentially correspond to any candidate.

Vote processing is analogous to Votegrity. All receipts on the bulletin board are passed through a series of mixes operated by election trustees who use their private keys to successively peel the onion, thereby reconstructing the voter's choice as per the canonical candidate ordering. The mixing process is audited using randomized partial checking. The reconstructed votes are tallied in a straightforward manner.

Verification needs to be performed on another front as well: voters need assurance that ballots are well-formed, i.e., the onions in the lower right half of the ballot correctly encrypt the randomization of candidates on the ballots. Prêt à Voter includes a step allowing Alice to audit her ballot in the polling booth by requesting the system

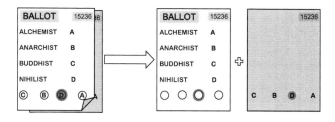

Figure 8.4: The Punchscan ballot (with a vote for *Nihilist*).

to decrypt the onions and prove that they correspond to the candidate ordering. Audited ballots do not count towards the tally and are discarded and Alice may audit as many ballots as she likes until she is satisfied the system is not cheating and then cast her actual vote. The authors also recommend that election authorities publicly audit a set of ballots prior to the election to create public confidence. A sufficiently sized random sampling of ballots should be picked, making it very hard for a malicious party to distribute large numbers of malformed ballots without detection. After polls close, any leftover ballots should be similarly audited for greater confidence.

Prêt à Voter is one of the most prominent E2E voting systems and extensive work has been done in maintaining and extending it. Notable contributions include adapting Prêt à Voter for different electoral systems [299] [581] and voting scenarios [467], enhancing its usability [374] [498] [182] and implementing the system [103].

A variant of Prêt à Voter was used in binding state elections in the Australian state of Victoria in 2014 [125] [183].

8.3.1.3 Punchscan

Punchscan [238], invented by Chaum in 2006, is especially suited for elections where rules mandate a uniform candidate ordering on ballots. Punchscan takes inspiration from Votegrity's notion of layers and from Prêt à Voter's randomization of voter choices on the ballot. The system is described in detail in Chapter 10.

The Punchscan ballot, shown in Figure 8.4, consists of two layers. The top layer has the candidate names ordered using numbers or letters (*a, b, c, d*, etc.) and a set of holes at the bottom. The lower layer contains a random ordering of the same letters. When the layers are overlaid, the letters are visible through the holes. In the polling booth, Alice marks her choice, using a marker to daub the appropriate hole, thereby marking both layers at the same time. The layers are then separated. When considered individually, the top layer only indicates which hole she chose, whereas the lower indicates the letter she selected, and both layers are needed by a viewer to discern her candidate choice. Alice randomly picks one layer to cast and shreds the other. She retains a copy of the cast layer as her receipt.

Vote processing is similar to the systems described earlier. When polls close, Alice can check the bulletin board to verify that her vote was recorded as cast. The ballot serial number, printed in the top right corner on both layers of the ballot, encodes encrypted information which enables election trustees to determine the voter's choice. Punchscan replaces the back-end decryption mixnet of earlier systems with an anonymizing database referred to as the *Punchboard*.

The Punchboard consists of three interlinked tables. The first one lists all markable options on all created ballots, whereas the last lists the candidate corresponding to each option. For instance, for Figure 8.4, the first table will list an entry for the third option which corresponds to a vote for *Nihilist* in the last table. However, the direct links between entries on these these two tables are shuffled via an intermediate table and the shuffling pattern is masked using encryption. This is conceptually similar to how a mix randomizes its inputs but is far more efficient as votes do not have to be encrypted and decrypted multiple times. Instead the system transmits the marks on each receipt over the set of secret paths directly to the appropriate candidates, incrementing their vote count accordingly.

The Punchboard and ballots are generated by election trustees prior to the election and their configuration is kept strictly secret. A preliminary audit is conducted in which half the ballots are randomly picked and publicly revealed along with the corresponding paths in the Punchboard. Any party can verify that votes cast on these ballots would most certainly have been routed to the right candidates and thereby derive confidence in the system. Audited ballots are then destroyed and the remaining half used in the polls. After tallying concludes, the Punchboard is again audited using randomized partial checking, i.e., each path is partially decrypted to prove the system is operating correctly without revealing any end-to-end paths in the process.

Some attacks have been discovered against Punchscan [341] and corresponding procedural safeguards have been recommended (described in greater detail in Chapter 9). Other notable research contributions include adapting Punchscan for remote scenarios [467], reducing opportunities for privacy violation [136], and merging Prêt à Voter and Punchscan for stronger privacy [564].

Punchscan source code was released under an open-source license and the system was trialled in elections of the University of Ottawa's Graduate Students' Association in 2007 [216]. Punchscan was later merged into the Scantegrity voting system.

8.3.1.4 Scantegrity

Scantegrity [146], developed in 2008 by a team of researchers including David Chaum and Ron Rivest, enhances existing real-world voting systems with E2E verifiability. The advantage of this approach is that infrastructure, such as optical scan technology, is already widely deployed and voters are familiar with its usage.

The Scantegrity ballot, depicted in Figure 8.5, lists the candidates with randomly picked code letters assigned to each. A ballot serial number is printed in the top right-hand corner, expressed both in human-readable and barcode format. In the polling

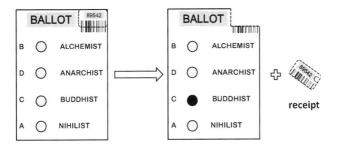

Figure 8.5: The Scantegrity ballot (with a vote for *Buddhist*).

booth, Alice marks the candidate of her choice and scans the ballot into an optical scanner as she would using a regular optical scan voting system. She then detaches the perforated corner of the ballot and notes down on it the code letter for her candidate. This small stub is her Scantegrity receipt.

After polls close, election authorities tally the results of the optical scan system. Scantegrity vote processing runs independently of this count. Election authorities post all ballot serial numbers and the corresponding code letters onto the bulletin board, where voters can verify that their code letters have been correctly recorded by the system. The code letter by itself does not reveal the voter's choice of candidate to a third party as the letters are randomly assigned on ballots. Similar to Punchscan, every code letter on every ballot translates to a vote for a specific candidate in an anonymizing database, in this case referred to as the *switchboard*. Votes are routed accordingly over encrypted paths in a privacy-preserving and auditable manner.

This system suffers a few disadvantages: a coercer may force a voter to mark a certain code letter regardless of which candidate it is assigned to, thereby effectively randomizing her vote. Furthermore, there is no guarantee the voter correctly records the same code on her receipt that she marks on the ballot, and dispute resolution entails a complicated mechanism which involves producing the physical ballot.

Scantegrity II [146] resolves these issues by printing candidate codes on the ballot using invisible ink which are revealed only when the voter marks her candidate choice using a special pen. These codes are randomly assigned and are of sufficient length that they cannot simply be deduced by guesswork. If a voter therefore lodges a complaint citing a valid code, her complaint is very likely genuine. The process is depicted in Figure 8.6 with a vote for *Buddhist*. The voter retains the candidate code *ODX* and ballot serial number *1679-253* as a receipt.

Scantegrity II was trialled in a binding governmental election for the offices of mayor and city council members in Takoma Park, Maryland [526]. The system and the resulting deployment are described in greater detail in Chapter 10. The experience led to further modifications to the system to incorporate features requested by voters and election officials, resulting in Scantegrity III [527].

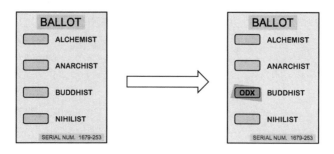

Figure 8.6: The Scantegrity II ballot (with a vote for *Buddhist*).

8.3.1.5 Scratch & Vote

In a paper in 2006, Adida and Rivest [49] noted that mixnets entail complicated mix-ing and auditing protocols, and require the voter to have faith that election trustees will not collude to subvert the election. To address these shortcomings, they invented Scratch & Vote (S&V), which combines the user-friendly voting experience of Prêt à Voter with the backend simplicity of homomorphic encryption.

Ballots are encrypted using **homomorphic encryption**, a cryptographic primi-tive which enables them to be tabulated while still in encrypted form. The result of a homomorphic addition on a set of ciphertexts is equivalent to an addition operation performed on the set of plaintexts. Only the result of the addition operation is de-crypted, thereby preserving the individual voter's privacy. Homomorphic encryption was first applied to electronic voting in 1985 by Josh Benaloh in his landmark work [161] [91] and is a key ingredient in several voting systems that follow.

To provide voters with further security assurances, S&V distributes the corre-sponding decryption key among multiple election trustees using threshold cryptog-raphy, thereby minimizing risk of abuse of cryptographic credentials. **Threshold cryptography** [457] is conceptually similar to visual cryptography (discussed earlier in Section 8.3.1.1) in that a decryption key is mathematically split into several shares which are distributed among mutually distrusting trustees. The decryption therefore requires the explicit cooperation of a threshold amount of these trustees, and at no time does any party possess the complete key.

Furthermore, vote encryption is also **probabilistic**. In public-key cryptosystems, we recall that the public key used for encryption is not secret, it is accessible to every-one. If Alice's vote were therefore encrypted in a deterministic manner, an attacker could easily mount a **brute-force attack** to deduce it, i.e., he could use the trustees' public keys to encrypt every possible voting option on Alice's ballot and compare the ciphertexts thus generated with those printed on Alice's receipt or on the bul-letin board. Probabilistic encryption techniques insert random numbers into the en-cryption algorithm so that every encryption operation on the same plaintext yields

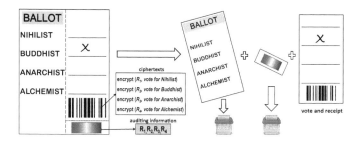

Figure 8.7: The S&V ballot and vote casting process (with a vote for *Buddhist*).

different ciphertexts. These random numbers are large enough that they cannot be simply guessed and they are kept strictly secret. Probabilistic encryption is important in several security protocols and is used in all the voting systems described in this chapter relying on encryption, including the ones described earlier. The reason for highlighting its use here is that, in S&V, the probabilistic nature of the encryption plays a vital role in the vote verification process.

The S&V ballot, depicted in Figure 8.7, detaches into three parts. The left half lists candidate names in randomized order. The right side bears corresponding markable spaces and a barcode. This barcode encodes multiple encrypted data, each ciphertext corresponding to a *vote* for a particular candidate on the ballot. In the lower right corner, a detachable scratch surface conceals the random numbers used to encrypt the barcode data. Any party can therefore scratch off this surface to reveal the random numbers, use them to independently encrypt the candidate choices, and compare it with the barcode data, thereby confirming that the ballot is correctly formed.

At the polling station, every voter is handed two ballots, one to audit and one to cast. Alice randomly selects one, removes the scratch surface and verifies that the candidate ordering corresponds to the barcode data. The authors note that voters generally do not possess the technical expertise to perform this check and suggest that trusted helper organizations may assist them at the polls by providing equipment and guidance. Removing the scratch surface also invalidates the ballot and it can no longer be used. Alice then proceeds to cast her vote with the second ballot, as depicted in Figure 8.7. In a manner similar to Prêt à Voter, she marks her chosen candidate, removes and discards the left side, and hands the ballot to a member of polling staff. He ensures the scratch surface on the ballot is intact, and detaches and destroys it without revealing the underlying content. This step is vital as knowledge of the random numbers would allow a coercer to reconstruct Alice's vote from her receipt. The ballot, now consisting only of the voter mark and the barcode, is cast. Alice is issued a scanned copy as a receipt.

After polls close, Alice can verify on the bulletin board that her vote is correctly recorded. To tabulate results, election staff examine each cast ballot and extract the particular ciphertext from the barcode corresponding to the voter's mark. This ci-

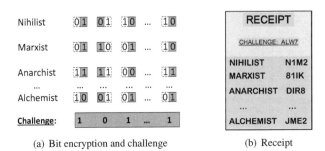

(a) Bit encryption and challenge   (b) Receipt

Figure 8.8: Vote verification and receipts for MarkPledge (with a vote for *Anarchist*).

phertext is essentially an encrypted electronic ballot where the underlying plaintext assigns a "1" to the candidate of the voter's choice and "0" for all others. An addition operation is performed over all extracted ciphertexts such that the ones and zeros assigned to candidates in the individual votes are directly summed up. Election trustees then engage in a protocol to decrypt the result using their individual shares of the decryption key, and post cryptographic proofs of correct decryption on the bulletin board. Any observer can easily download the contents of the bulletin board and run his own checks to verify that votes have been correctly summed and decrypted. Individual votes are never decrypted, thereby maintaining voter privacy.

Adida and Rivest also present extensions to this basic scheme, including steps to adapt S&V to a Punchscan ballot, facilitate multiple races and include larger numbers of candidates. They discuss procedural missteps and attacks which weaken the security of S&V and note that these are common to systems like Prêt à Voter and Punchscan, where ballots are filled out by hand.

8.3.2 Precinct-Based Voting with Electronic Ballots

This category consists of systems where electronic votes are cast and tallied in a precinct-based setting. Systems in this category are characterized by inventive combinations of various cryptographic primitives and include influential systems such as MarkPledge and the notion of Voter Initiated Auditing.

8.3.2.1 MarkPledge

MarkPledge [418], invented by Neff in 2004, is, alongside Chaum's Votegrity, one of the earliest E2E voting systems. The key innovation of this system is a novel front-end protocol allowing voters to directly challenge voting machines in the polling booth to prove that they are encrypting votes correctly.

On the MarkPledge ballot, each candidate is assigned a row of *indexes* denoted by pairs of bits, as shown in Figure 8.8(a). A *No* vote is denoted by dissimilar combinations such as (0,1) and (1,0), and a *Yes* vote is denoted by a pairs of similar bits, (1,1) or (0,0). When Alice chooses a candidate, the voting machine will assign her chosen candidate a *Yes* vote and *No* votes to all the rest. The machine then individually encrypts every bit in each index on the ballot and displays on-screen a *commitment* for the chosen candidate. This commitment is essentially a bitstring, a series of bits where each individual bit corresponds to the *Yes/No* content of each index, i.e., *both* ciphertext bits for the chosen candidate. For example, the commitment 1,1,0,...,1 for *Anarchist* (encoded in an alphanumeric format as *DIR8*) implies that the bits, as depicted, are (1,1), (1,1), (0,0),....,(1,1) which are all *Yes* combinations whereas all other candidates are assigned *No* combinations.

As in Scratch & Vote, a probabilistic encryption technique is used to encrypt votes. Once the machine has encrypted her vote, Alice can challenge it by making it reveal the randomness used in encrypting either the right or the left bit of indexes (but not both) for all candidates. This process is depicted in Figure 8.8(a). Alice's challenge consists of a bitstring, where a 0 denotes bits on the left-hand side and 1 denotes bits on the right-hand side. Alice can thus confirm that each revealed bit matches with the commitment displayed earlier by the machine. The machine cannot predict beforehand which bits Alice will choose, and if it has tampered with her vote (by encrypting *No* bit combinations for her candidate of choice), there is a very high probability that the deception will be revealed in the bits that Alice forces the machine to unmask. This mechanism assures Alice that the machine has encrypted her vote correctly and that her vote is cast as intended.

Once the challenge is concluded, the machine then generates *No* votes for all other candidates on the ballot with the important innovation that it populates Alice's chosen right/left bit positions to make it appear that they are *Yes* votes. All this information, including encrypted indexes, the machine's commitment, Alice's challenge, and the random elements are printed on Alice's receipt in the form of short strings of alphanumeric characters, as depicted in Figure 8.8(b). After polls close, all receipts are posted on the bulletin board and voters can confirm that their votes are correctly recorded. Votes are decrypted and tallied using mixnets in an auditable process similar to schemes described earlier in Section 8.3.1.

Alice only needs to ensure that the commitment string the machine originally displayed is printed next to the candidate of her choice (i.e., *DIR8* for *Anarchist* in this case) and she has to retain this string in memory for a short period while challenging the machine. A coercer, examining her receipt at a later time, will only see *Yes* votes for every candidate, and will be unable to deduce her actual vote. Alice alone can differentiate her original *Yes* vote from a fake Yes vote, due to the challenge interaction in the privacy of the polling booth, but is unable to prove it to a third party. This is also the reason that the machine only decrypts the right or left bit position, and not both, during a challenge: if Alice were to record the randomness used to encrypt both bits of an index, she could easily prove her vote to a third party.

MarkPledge is analyzed in greater detail by Adida and Neff [47] who propose that *helper organizations*, consisting of political party members or activist groups, assist the voter with more detailed verification checks. Joaquim and Ribeiro suggest a mechanism to make the Markpledge cast-as-intended verification process faster and more efficient [325]. This front-end verification technique has also inspired other systems: Joaquim et al. propose two remote E2E voting systems, VeryVote [326] and EVIV (an End-to-end Verifiable Internet voting system) [324] which combine this technique with code voting (described later in Section 8.3.3) and mixnets.

8.3.2.2 Bingo Voting

Bohli, Müller-Quade and Röhrich invented Bingo Voting [108] in 2007, inspired by the concept of a bingo machine as a source of randomness to protect voter privacy.

In the election setup phase, election trustees generate strings of random numbers, such that there is one random number per voter for each candidate on the ballot (i.e., for m voters and n candidates, $m \times n$ random numbers are generated, grouped such that each candidate is assigned one set of n numbers). These numbers, referred to as *dummy votes*, are kept secret, but the trustees publicly commit to them on the bulletin board before elections using a commitment scheme.

A **commitment scheme** is a cryptographic primitive which enables a party to publicly commit to a chosen secret without revealing it until a later time. This may be intuitively visualized with the analogy of a locked box which a *prover* publicly entrusts to a *verifier*. At a later time, the prover uses his secret key to unlock the box and reveal its secret contents. No one else can open the box. Commitment schemes are also *binding* in the sense that the prover cannot alter the contents of the box without being detected by the verifier. In our case, election trustees cannot change the dummy votes once the commitment has been published. Commitment schemes are employed in various security protocols, and applications include timestamping data and trusted computation.

Alice chooses her candidate on a voting machine in the polling booth. The booth also contains a mechanical device, similar to a bingo machine, which Alice uses to generate a fresh random number. The device displays this number and transmits it to the voting machine which assigns it to Alice's candidate choice. The other candidates are assigned numbers chosen from the pool of pre-generated dummy votes. This particular configuration of candidate names and random numbers constitutes Alice's vote and the voting machine issues her a receipt. Alice simply has to confirm that the random number she has generated herself in the booth is assigned to the candidate of her choice on the screen of the voting machine and on her receipt. After polls close, all issued receipts are published on the bulletin board.

Tallying is straightforward. Every time a vote is cast for a certain candidate, all other candidates are assigned dummy votes. In this way, a dummy vote initially allocated to the chosen candidate in the pool of dummy votes is not used. Therefore, the final tally can be computed by examining this pool and the candidate with the largest number of unused dummy votes is the winner of the election.

However, election trustees need to prove that voting machines correctly allocated the dummy votes to candidates. Moreover, this needs to be accomplished without publicly differentiating between dummy votes and voter-generated random numbers on receipts, else voter privacy would be compromised. First, election trustees publish the list of unused dummy votes on the bulletin board alongside their respective commitments and the corresponding reveal information. Next, the trustees publish cryptographic proofs testifying to the integrity of the receipts, i.e., each receipt contains exactly one voter-generated random number, each dummy vote used in the elections was correctly allocated by the machines, and it was used only once. These proofs can be verified by any observer and do not reveal any information which may enable him to identify dummy votes and voter-generated random numbers.

Alice verifies her vote was cast as intended by ensuring the random number she generates in the voting booth is assigned to the candidate of her choice on her receipt. She ensures her vote is recorded correctly by verifying her receipt on the bulletin board. Her privacy is preserved and she is protected from coercion as the newly generated random number assigned to her candidate is indistinguishable from the dummy votes assigned to the other candidates on the receipt. She checks the revealed commitments and the cryptographic proofs to verify that every random number used in the election is strictly accounted for and that the tally has been correctly computed.

Bingo Voting was deployed in student parliament elections in Karlsruhe University, Germany, in 2008 as described in [70]. Another study examines the ramifications of corrupted voting machines on Bingo Voting and prescribes solutions which may be generalized for other voting systems [107]. Liu et al. [369] note that reliance on a random number generator is a potential security vulnerability and devise an alternative solution. Henrich [303] analyzes the feasibility of deploying Bingo Voting for recent real-world elections in the United States, Germany, and India.

8.3.2.3 Voter Initiated Auditing

In most of the systems described thus far, random checks are integral to the security guarantees of the systems. When Alice casts her vote, she has no explicit guarantee that the machine has encrypted her vote correctly. For certain systems like Punchscan or Scantegrity which use physical ballots, she has no direct assurance that the candidate randomization or marking options on her ballot are correctly encoded. Her confidence, instead, derives from the random audits conducted on the system at every key juncture and the knowledge that these audits are overseen by multiple trustees. With these checks, Alice may be certain that any significant malfeasance will be detected.

In contrast to this approach, in 2006, Josh Benaloh introduced the notion of **voter initiated auditing** [84] [85] [86] to give the voter immediate confidence that her vote has been correctly cast. In this paradigm, when Alice chooses her candidate, the voting machine prints an encryption of the vote on her receipt but does not dispense it. Instead, the machine asks Alice whether she wishes to *cast* the vote or *challenge* it. If she trusts the machine, she selects the *cast* option and the printer issues her the receipt. If Alice is uncertain that the machine has encrypted her vote correctly, she can challenge it to prove it is honest (this step is often referred to as a "Benaloh" challenge). The machine then prints on the receipt, alongside the encrypted vote, the contents of Alice's ballot and the randomness used to generate the encryption. This data allows Alice, or any other party, to replicate the encryption step independently using the election public key, as described earlier in Section 8.3.1.5.

The novelty here is that the machine essentially *commits* to the vote encryption by printing it on the receipt before Alice chooses whether to cast or challenge. If Alice initiates a challenge, she can check if the machine performed the encryption correctly. She is welcome to challenge the machine as many times as she likes until she is confident that the machine is honest before finally casting her vote. If the machine has cheated by encrypting a vote for a different candidate, the odds that it will get caught increase with every challenge.

Voter Initiated Auditing was originally proposed by Benaloh, not as a new system, but as a vote-casting technique to augment existing real-world voting systems with E2E security guarantees, a goal it shared with Scantegrity. It has since then directly inspired other well-known systems such as Helios, VoteBox, and STAR-Vote.

8.3.2.4 VoteBox

VoteBox [510], proposed by Sandler, Derr and Wallach in 2008, attempts to resolve myriad practical issues encountered in building secure and usable voting systems.

VoteBox follows the template set by Voter Initiated Auditing. The system uses homomorphic encryption and the decryption key is predistributed among multiple election trustees using threshold cryptography. On election day, Alice makes her candidate selection on a voting machine, which encrypts her vote and then offers her the option to challenge or cast it. If challenged, the machine prints extra encryption and randomness information on her receipt. Alice takes this to a special terminal in the polling station dedicated to assisting voters to verify challenged votes. Alice may mount as many challenges as she likes before casting her vote.

All receipts are posted on the bulletin board where Alice can verify her vote is correctly recorded. Tallying consists of straightforward homomorphic addition after which election trustees engage in a protocol to decrypt the final result and provide cryptographic proofs attesting to correct decryption. Voters and observers alike may download the contents of the bulletin board and verify the computations.

Apart from its E2E security qualifications, a key contribution of VoteBox is how it brings together various innovations in the research literature to address a range of security and reliability issues regarding the practical side of electronic voting. We list a few highlights: the authors go to considerable lengths to minimize and partition the amount of trusted code running on voting machines. Distinct functions of the voting machine are modularized in hardware and clearly partitioned, thereby enabling administrators to efficiently audit hardware faults. The voting experience is standardized across all voting machines by specifying a graphical user interface

(GUI) consisting of pre-rendered bitmap images which correspond to the actions of voters using the machine [584].

Voting machines log all *machine events* (system messages, the complete record of encrypted votes, and voter challenges and machine responses) using secure logging techniques [511]. All machines broadcast and record event logs over a local network, so that, were a voting machine to fail on election day, all its data up to the point of failure may be retrieved from the storage of other machines. This also makes things considerably more difficult for an attacker who now has to compromise all machines in the precinct to tamper with votes undetected. Furthermore, the local network is connected to the Internet using a data diode [332] which enforces strict one-way data flow, i.e., logs of voting machines in the precinct are publicly broadcast over the Internet, yet remote attackers are not able to hack into the machines.

VoteBox has inspired some enhancements: RemoteBox [512] extends VoteBox to secure elections in remote voting facilities such as overseas embassies and consulates. VoteBox Nano [439] reimagines the VoteBox design using only low-cost hardware components, such as field programmable gate arrays. This approach obviates the need for an operating system or software on voting machine, which an attacker may potentially corrupt. Furthermore, any tampering with hardware may be visually detected by polling staff very easily on election day.

8.3.2.5 Wombat

Wombat [80], invented by Ben-Nun et al. in 2011, combines the frontend of Voter Initiated Auditing with Prêt à Voter-style mixnet processing in the backend.

On election day, Alice makes her candidate choice on a voting machine, which prints a *dual* ballot as shown in Figure 8.9(a). Her candidate choice is printed in plaintext followed by a detachable portion bearing her electronic vote, i.e., a barcode representing her encrypted vote. Before dispensing the ballot, the machine offers Alice the choice to challenge or cast her vote. If challenged, the machine prints a barcode with randomness information at the bottom of the ballot, as shown in Figure 8.9(b), which Alice can use to verify her vote. She can mount as many challenges as she likes before casting her vote.

If Alice chooses to cast her ballot, the machine prints "For Casting" on her ballot as in Figure 8.9(c) and dispenses it. Alice folds the ballot as shown, using the adhesive strip to conceal the plaintext. She then exits the voting booth and hands her ballot to a poll worker. He scans the encrypted vote and uploads it to the election website. He next stamps both halves of the ballot and detaches them. The folded plaintext vote is cast in a ballot box, and the barcode is issued to Alice as her receipt. Alice can later verify that her receipt is correctly recorded on the bulletin board. Mixnets are used to shuffle and decrypt the votes which are then tallied. The mixnet protocols also provide proofs of correct operation. All decrypted votes and mixnet proofs are published on the bulletin board where they may be verified by voters and observers.

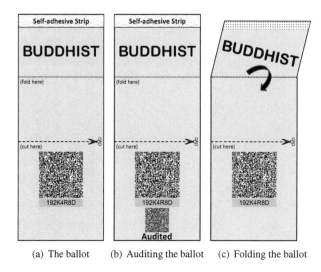

   (a) The ballot   (b) Auditing the ballot   (c) Folding the ballot

Figure 8.9: Verifying and casting a Wombat ballot (with a vote for *Buddhist*).

Like Scantegrity, Voter Initiated Auditing, and STAR-Vote (described next), Wombat produces both an electronic voting record and a parallel paper trail. This **dual voting** approach has considerable advantages: it is familiar to voters who may be more used to paper-based voting systems. The electronic system may fail, for instance, due to network outages or trustees may misplace cryptographic credentials, in which case the paper votes are a handy backup. Paper trails are also a good tool to audit the elections, and make an attacker's job much harder. To subvert an election, he would need to successfully compromise both the electronic and the paper record.

The team behind Wombat has placed considerable emphasis on practical aspects of the system. Guidelines to implement Wombat securely are detailed in [273]. At an early phase they discovered that giving voters the challenge-or-cast option proves confusing and is unnecessary as only 2-3% of voters need exercise the challenge option to assure election integrity. This inspired the design decision to hide the challenge option, so that voters intending to audit the machine issue the challenge themselves by tapping the screen while the machine is printing the ballot.

Wombat uses Verificatum [577], a free and open-source mixnet solution which has also been used in the 2013 Norwegian Parliamentary elections. The system is supplemented by an open-source Android app for vote verification. Alice can take a picture of the ciphertext and audit information on her ballot using her smartphone and the app verifies that the vote is correctly encrypted and signed. The app also confirms that cast votes are correctly posted on the election website.

Wombat has been deployed in binding elections [80]. In 2011, it was used for student body elections at the Interdisciplinary Center in Israel, involving multiple races and more than two thousand voters. In 2012, the Israeli political party Merez, used Wombat for intra-party elections, involving approximately 830 voters.

8.3.2.6 STAR-Vote

In 2011, election administrators from Travis County in Texas, seeking to overhaul their election system, reached out directly to the academic research community to assist in building a secure and low-cost voting system. The result is STAR-Vote (STAR stands for Secure, Transparent, Auditable and Reliable) [77]. Like Wombat, STAR-Vote brings together the convenience and usability of electronic voter machines with end-to-end cryptographic verifiability and a paper trail audit mechanism. The system is described in detail in Chapter 14. We provide a brief overview.

At the polling station, Alice is issued a paper slip with her "voting credentials" which identifies the appropriate ballot for her. She inputs the credentials in a voting machine and makes her candidate choice. The machine electronically encrypts and records Alice's vote and issues her a receipt consisting of an encrypted commitment to her vote and related information (such as the ID of the voting machine, the time of voting, etc.). The system also generates a paper trail: the machine additionally prints out a physical copy of the marked ballot. Alice visually confirms her choice is correctly marked and then casts it by hand into a nearby ballot box. The election result is tallied from the electronic vote record. In parallel to E2E verification checks, audits are conducted on the paper ballots to further validate the results.

After casting her vote, Alice may challenge the machine to prove it correctly encrypted the vote. In this case, she informs a poll worker who assists her in verifying that the encrypted commitment on her receipt is indeed correct. Alice may repeat this process until she is satisfied and then cast a final vote. This check is in the spirit of Voter Initiated Auditing but with the key difference that here the challenge and verification steps occur *after* vote casting, not before, and are initiated by voters. This is in the interests of system usability: for voters not interested in challenging the machine, the voting process is fairly similar to that of existing real-world systems.

After polls close, all encrypted votes are posted on the bulletin board where voters can compare against their receipts. Tallying consists of homomorphic addition of the cast ballots. The decryption key is pre-shared among multiple trustees who cooperate to decrypt the result in a verifiable manner. Challenged votes are posted as well, along with verifiable decryptions, and these are excluded from the final tally.

After the elections, **risk-limiting audits** [367] are conducted on the paper ballots. A random selection of ballots is checked on two counts: first, verifying if data on the paper ballots corresponds to the electronic record. The second check determines if the tally of the random sample approximates the electronic results within an acceptable margin. This "belt and suspenders approach" [362] of incorporating multiple safeguards aims at giving voters and observers strong confidence in the system.

The STAR-Vote system architecture inherits several engineering innovations from VoteBox including strict partitioning of program modules, a GUI consisting of pre-rendered graphics, and secure auditable logging of machine events.

STAR-Vote is slated for deployment in elections in Travis County in 2017 [365].

8.3.2.7 DRE-i

Hao, Randell and Clarke noted that voting systems are vulnerable due to their reliance on *tallying authorities*, i.e., trustees tasked with tallying election results who need to be implicitly trusted not to misuse their privileges [290]. Furthermore, as demonstrated in a real-world trial of the Helios system [46], trustees may lack the technical expertise to manage cryptographic credentials securely. To address these concerns, Hao et al. proposed DRE-i (Direct Recording Electronic with Integrity) [288], an E2E voting system which dispenses with tallying authorities entirely. DRE-i is described in detail in Chapter 13.

The DRE-i ballot consists of pairwise strings of encrypted data, or *cryptograms*, assigned to each candidate, depicting *Yes* and *No* votes. When Alice makes her candidate choice on a voting machine, a *Yes* cryptogram is assigned to her candidate and *No* cryptograms to all the others. The machine issues her a receipt listing the candidates with the assigned cryptograms. Individually the *Yes/No* cryptograms do not reveal any information about Alice's choice and resemble strings of random data. Before casting her vote, Alice has the option of challenging the voting machine to prove it is not cheating. If challenged, the machine reveals both *Yes/No* cryptograms for each candidate on the ballot. Any party can now differentiate between *Yes* and *No* votes, and confirm that they are correctly assigned.

All receipts are published onto the bulletin board where they may be verified by voters, alongside proofs that the vote is **well-formed**. This is a privacy-preserving cryptographic proof, used in several of the voting systems described in this chapter, which allows any observer to verify that the ciphertext on the bulletin board contains a vote for only one candidate, without revealing the voter's identity or candidate choice. The votes are then combined in a homomorphic operation to yield the final tally. There is no decryption step. Any observer can therefore download the contents of the bulletin board and replicate the addition to confirm the results.

Self-tallying voting systems have been proposed earlier in the literature, for small-scale scenarios such as boardroom elections [270] [344] [291], but Hao et al. differentiate these from DRE-i which enables self-tallying within the broader framework of E2E verifiable voting, a paradigm they refer to as *self-enforcing electronic voting* [290]. A verifiable classroom voting system based on DRE-i has been implemented and used [287].

8.3.3 Remote Voting with Electronic Ballots

This category comprises systems which enable voters to cast their votes over the Internet and includes prominent systems JCJ/Civitas and Helios. As we noted earlier in Section 8.2.4, remote voting poses unique challenges which restrict the use of some of these systems in politically binding elections.

8.3.3.1 Adder

Adder [343] invented by Kiayias, Korman and Walluck in 2006, is a fully-functional open-source online voting system. Adder is suited to both small and large-scale elections, as well as surveys and data collection applications.

Adder includes a preliminary setup phase in which multiple election trustees engage in a cryptographic protocol to create a public key for the election which is then published on the election website. The corresponding decryption key is distributed among the trustees using threshold cryptography.

To vote, Alice navigates her web browser to the election website, logs in using voting credentials which identify her as an eligible voter, and downloads the election public key. Alice makes her candidate choice and her web browser then generates and encrypts her vote using the election public key and computes and appends a proof of well-formedness. All encrypted votes received by the system are posted on an online bulletin board, where voters can verify they have been correctly recorded.

After polls close, an addition operation is performed over all the encrypted votes on the bulletin board. Election trustees then publicly provide partial decryption information using their individual shares of the decryption key, which enable the server to decrypt the tally. All intermediate computations are posted on the bulletin board.

Adder's security properties are fairly intuitive: the voter encrypts and transmits her own vote and can later verify it is correctly recorded on the bulletin board. Privacy is ensured because individual votes cannot be decrypted unless a threshold amount of these election trustees collude. Voters and observers alike can audit the tallying and decryption process by accessing the bulletin board and verifying each step.

However, Adder is vulnerable to critical security issues common to Internet voting systems. The first is the **untrusted terminal problem**: it is trivially easy for malicious software on Alice's computer to leak knowledge of her vote or switch her vote to another candidate without her knowledge, and she cannot detect this by examining the ciphertext. Second, physical privacy cannot be guaranteed. Someone may be standing at Alice's shoulder while she votes. Furthermore, a coercer, such as a political activist or a family member, may force her to vote a particular way. This threat is also common in other remote voting scenarios, such as postal voting [544].

8.3.3.2 JCJ and Civitas

The system designed by Juels, Catalano and Jakobsson in 2005, commonly referred to as JCJ [335], is notable in that it is the first online voting scheme to offer a high level of coercion-resistance. JCJ combines various cryptographic primitives in a novel protocol that has proved very influential in the research literature.

JCJ assumes that prior to elections, there is an in-person voter registration phase, conducted in a trusted and private environment, where Alice receives a voting credential from the election registrar. This credential is her proof of eligibility and can be used to vote in several different elections. After the registration phase concludes, the registrar publishes an encrypted list of all voting credentials on the bulletin board. Alice then uses a public algorithm to generate any number of *fake* credentials which are indistinguishable from her real one to a third party. She can use these to cast votes under coercion or even freely yield these to coercers to vote on her behalf. Votes cast using fake credentials will show up on the bulletin board as legitimate cast votes but will ultimately be rejected by the system prior to tallying. It is assumed the coercer is not monitoring Alice for the entire duration of the election and she gets some private moments to vote using her real credential.

Votes are cast online. Alice's vote includes her candidate choice and her voting credential and is encrypted with the public key of the election trustees. Also attached is a cryptographic proof enabling any observer to verify that the vote is well-formed and includes a usable credential (real or fake). After polls close, all vote ciphertexts received by the system are published onto the bulletin board where Alice can verify that hers was correctly recorded.

Election trustees then process votes on the bulletin board. Vote proofs are examined and malformed votes or those with unusable credentials are discarded. A **plaintext equivalence test** is used to check if multiple votes have been cast using the same credential. This cryptographic test compares encrypted votes in a pair-wise manner and simply identifies, without decryption, any ciphertexts which include a common credential. No direct information about the credentials or votes themselves is revealed in this test, i.e., voter identities and candidate choices are still secret. If multiple votes using the same credential are identified, they may be processed according to some *revoting* policy such that only one vote per credential is actually counted. For instance, only the most recent vote could be retained and all others using the same credential could be eliminated.

However, this batch still contains votes cast using fake credentials which have to be identified and discarded. All votes are passed through a **re-encryption mixnet**. As opposed to decryption mixes (described earlier in Section 8.3.1.1) which peel off layers of encryption from the vote, re-encryption mixes instead simply inject fresh randomness into the ciphertext. This *re-randomization* generates a batch of completely new ciphertexts which are still encryptions of the original plaintext data, i.e., votes and credentials. These new ciphertexts are then shuffled and output.

The plaintext equivalence test is then again run, this time to compare the encrypted credential in each new ciphertext with the encrypted list of valid voting credentials published by the election authority prior to the election. All votes with fake credentials can then be identified and discarded by the system without revealing the credentials themselves. Leftover votes are then decrypted and tallied in a straightforward manner to yield the election result.

The equivalence tests and the mixing and tallying processes are conducted in a publicly verifiable manner, and all intermediate results are posted on the bulletin board where observers can audit them for correctness. This mix-and-compare process is what gives JCJ the property of coercion-resistance. The re-encryption mixnet effectively breaks the association between cast votes and counted votes such that a coercer has no way of determining if the credential he holds is real or fake and if the vote he cast was included in the final tally or not.

However JCJ has a key disadvantage: the processing time and computation costs of this scheme are very high because compute-intensive plaintext equivalence tests need to be performed for every vote. There have been several suggestions in the literature to optimize this process, including [63], [536], and [275].

Civitas [159], proposed by Clarkson, Chong and Myers, is the first concrete implementation of JCJ along with important modifications, most notably a secure protocol for voter registration. In the original JCJ protocol, a corrupt registrar could simply issue a fake credential to Alice without her being able to detect the deception. However, in Civitas, the registrar functionality is distributed across multiple mutually distrusting trustees. Alice individually contacts these to receive portions of her credential which she then combines into a final credential. The implicit assumption is that some trustees are honest, thereby allowing her to construct the right credential.

Distributing registration functionality for JCJ has also been discussed in [355]. Koenig et al. [350] suggest enhancements, including protection against a potential denial-of-service attack whereby attackers flood the bulletin board with votes with fake credentials, thereby creating severe processing delays. Other proposals include formalizing the voting-process in Civitas, a user interface inspired in part by Helios (described next), and credential management using smartcards [411] [408].

The core JCJ architecture has inspired other E2E voting systems which improve upon its various usability aspects. For instance, Selections [158] provides an easier way for voters to register and manage credentials by incorporating the use of *panic passwords*, i.e., voting credentials that the voter may create on the fly. Trivitas [123] adapts Civitas to further simplify the non-intuitive and complex verifiability process for the layman voter by introducing the notion of *trial votes*. These are cast alongside regular votes, and are processed in much the same way, except that trial votes are decrypted and revealed at different stages, enabling the voter to derive strong confidence that her actual vote is being correctly handled. Caveat Coercitor [269] extends JCJ's coercion-resistance property for more general scenarios including leakage of voting credentials by malware, corrupt registrars and impersonation attacks.

8.3.3.3 Helios

Helios [44], invented by Adida in 2008, is an online voting system intended for scenarios where privacy and integrity concerns are paramount but the risk of coercion is low, i.e., in settings such as student body elections, clubs and online communities. Helios does not introduce any novel features as such, but successfully brings together different innovations in the literature to build an efficient and highly usable voting system. Helios is described in detail in Chapter 11. We present a brief overview:

To vote, Alice uses her web browser to navigate to the election website and marks her choice on an online ballot form. Her vote is encrypted locally on her computer, a digital receipt is printed on the screen. In the spirit of Voter Initiated Auditing, Alice is then offered the opportunity to cast or challenge her vote. She can challenge the system multiple times until she is convinced it is encrypting her choice correctly. When she is ready to cast her vote, she authenticates herself to the system as an eligible voter and uploads the ciphertext. The system posts it on an online bulletin board where she can verify it at a later time against the receipt she received earlier.

After polls close, encrypted votes on the bulletin board are processed using re-encryption mixes to effectively break the association between voter identity and cast votes after which votes are decrypted and tallied. The initial version of Helios employed the Sako–Kilian mixnet protocol [508] which published cryptographic proofs allowing third parties to confirm that the mixnet processed the data correctly. In 2009, Helios was updated to Helios 2.0 which improved efficiency and voter privacy by replacing the mixnets with a homomorphic encryption scheme and distributing the election decryption key among multiple election trustees.

Helios provides E2E guarantees but, as noted earlier, is not suited for political elections where the risk of coercion is high. Adida acknowledges this as a general limitation of remote voting systems and suggests that Helios might in fact educate voters on this threat. For this reason, the initial version of Helios included a "Coerce Me!" button, which Alice could press when casting her ballot, thereby emailing a coercer complete details of how she voted. Adida also notes that a corrupted version of Helios may impersonate absent voters and cast ballots on their behalf, making it all the more important that voters engage in the verification process.

Helios has proved very influential and is actively being maintained. The source code is available under an open-source license. Helios has been the subject of multiple usability studies [572] [338] [40]. A number of vulnerabilities have been discovered in the implementation of Helios [222] [302] [99]. Examples include cases where attackers may copy and re-cast previously cast votes [173], and a corrupted system may dispense identical receipts to different voters while modifying their actual votes undetected [357]. Many of these issues have been fixed in later versions of Helios. Improvements have also been suggested: Helios has been modified to enable new properties such as self-tallying [207] and stronger privacy guarantees [97] [196].

Helios has been used in several binding elections: the Université Catholique de Louvain used Helios in 2009 to elect the University President in an election with

Candidate	Vote Code	Acknowledgment Code
ALCHEMIST	5962	218931
ANARCHIST	2168	854269
BUDDHIST	3756	129853
MARXIST	1247	875391
NIHILIST	9881	039852

ID: 4896327

Figure 8.10: Sample code sheet.

about 5000 registered voters [46]. Helios has also been deployed for student elections at Princeton [399] and internal elections of the International Association for Cryptologic Research (IACR) [26] and the Association for Computing Machinery (ACM) [42]. Helios has also been adapted to accommodate different voting schemes such as single transferable vote (STV) and ranked voting schemes. Examples include Zeus, built by Louridas et al. [371], and another variant developed by Bulens et al. [121]. Both of these systems have been deployed in dozens of university-level elections.

8.3.3.4 Pretty Good Democracy

Pretty Good Democracy [506] is an online voting system developed by Ryan and Teague in 2013. Pretty Good Democracy relies on threshold cryptography and code voting to provide a subset of E2E verifiability properties.

Code voting was first suggested by Chaum as a solution to the untrusted terminal problem [142] and now serves as a key component in several online E2E voting systems [326] [358] [586] [324] [459]. The key idea is simple: codes are used to set up a private authenticated channel between voters and election trustees. Prior to polls, the trustees send each voter a physical *code sheet* in the mail which assigns unique, randomly picked *vote codes* and *acknowledgment codes* to each candidate on the ballot as depicted in Figure 8.10. These codes are alphanumeric strings of a length that resists simple guessing attacks. Each code sheet bears a unique ballot ID.

To vote, Alice logs onto the system, and inputs the ID on her code sheet, followed by the vote code for the candidate of her choice. For example, she would type in *2168* to vote for *Anarchist*. The system responds with the corresponding acknowledgment code, in this case, *854269*. Since the codes are randomly assigned and known only to Alice and the trustees, a malware on her computer or an attacker eavesdropping on network traffic cannot deduce her vote nor alter it in any meaningful way without being detected. Furthermore, Alice's vote code assures the trustees that they are communicating with Alice herself, since it should be difficult for an attacker to procure her code sheet. Likewise, if Alice receives the correct acknowledgment code, she can be certain her vote was correctly received by the trustees and not an attacker masquerading as a trustee. If either party enters a wrong code, the protocol fails.

After polls close, ballot IDs for all votes received by the system are published on the bulletin board and Alice can check that hers is included in the list. Decryption mixnets are then used to anonymize votes prior to tallying, similar to Votegrity and Prêt à Voter, and the process is likewise audited using randomized partial checking.

The bulletin board does not display vote receipts otherwise it would be trivially easy for Alice to prove her vote to a third party using her code sheet. However, displaying only ballot IDs of cast votes opens up the possibility that a corrupt tallying authority may alter votes undetected. To address this vulnerability, Ryan and Teague employ threshold cryptography to distribute system functionality among the election trustees. When the system receives Alice's vote code, it engages in a cooperative protocol with a threshold number of trustees to generate the appropriate acknowledgment code and record Alice's vote in the system. It is therefore not possible to alter votes unless a large number of these trustees are corrupt, which should reassure Alice to a degree that her vote has been correctly recorded by the system.

However, Pretty Good Democracy only partially addresses the problems associated with remote voting. There is still the threat that someone may be standing at Alice's shoulder when she votes and may even coerce her to vote for a certain candidate. Alice may sell her vote by giving her code sheet to someone else. An online attacker may pose as a fake election server and her vote may be lost. Similar attacks have been observed in remote voting scenarios such as postal voting. The authors, therefore, explicitly recommend that Pretty Good Democracy only be used for low-risk elections such as for student bodies and professional societies and not for politically binding elections.

Pretty Good Democracy has inspired other systems: Pretty Understandable Democracy [120] simplifies the way votes are processed. Virtually Perfect Democracy [78] introduces personalized voter smartcards into the protocol to increase trust in the system and provide an element of coercion resistance. Pretty Good Democracy has also been adapted for ranking-based voting schemes such as single transferable vote (STV) and instant-runoff voting (IRV) [301].

8.3.3.5 Remotegrity

Remotegrity [586] is an online E2E voting protocol, proposed by Zagorski et al. in 2013. Remotegrity is not a full-fledged system but an extension to precinct-based systems like Scantegrity and Prêt à Voter, specifically aimed at absentee voters, and uses an innovative combination of code voting and scratch surfaces to ensure votes are securely recorded.

As an absentee voter, Alice receives via post a Scantegrity ballot (described in Section 8.3.1.4) and a Remotegrity authorization card, as depicted in Figure 8.11. The authorization card contains an authentication serial number, and three types of codes: multiple authentication codes, a lock-in code, and an acknowledgment code.

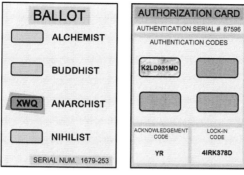

(a) Scantegrity II ballot

(b) Remotegrity authorization card

Figure 8.11: Voting with Remotegrity (casting a vote for *Anarchist*).

To vote, Alice logs on to the system and enters her ballot serial number and the authentication serial number on her authorization card. This allows the system to check that she has not already cast a vote. Alice next obtains the vote code on the ballot for the candidate of her choice (*XWQ* for *Anarchist*). From the authorization card, she scratches off an authentication code at random. These two codes are sent to the system as a single message and are posted on the bulletin board. The election trustees verify that the authentication code is valid. They then append an acknowledgment code to it, digitally sign the whole message, thereby certifying it as genuine, and update the entry on the bulletin board. At a later time, Alice checks the bulletin board and verifies that her vote has not been maliciously altered and confirms the acknowledgment code and the trustees' signature. She then approves the updated entry by scratching off and submitting the lock-in code on her authorization card. The system again updates the bulletin board entry to include the lock-in code.

When polls close, the trustees check all entries to verify the lock-in codes are correct. They then input the ballot serial numbers and the corresponding vote codes for each entry into the Scantegrity tallying system. These votes are then tallied alongside precinct-cast votes using the Scantegrity Switchboard in a publicly verifiable manner (as described in Section 8.3.1.4 and Chapter 10).

The use of codes effectively defeats malware and hackers who may tamper with Alice's computer. The scratch surfaces act as tamper-evident seals. If the election trustees were to cast a vote on Alice's behalf, Alice could produce her authorization card with the authentication code scratch surfaces still intact as proof of malfeasance. If they were to change her vote after she submitted it, she could refuse to commit to it with her lock-in code. If the trustees were to append the lock-in code themselves, her authorization card, with the lock-in scratch surface still intact, would prove that she did not authorize that vote. The trustees may issue authorization cards with invalid codes, but this may be detected by conducting public audits in which randomly chosen authorization cards are examined for integrity. The protocol therefore en-

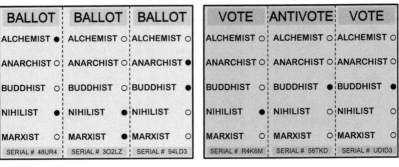

(a) The ThreeBallot ballot   (b) The VAV ballot

Figure 8.12: Voting with ThreeBallot and VAV (with votes for *Nihilist*).

sures that Alice's vote is cast and recorded by the system as she intended. Regarding the verifiability of the tally, Remotegrity inherits Scantegrity's security guarantees. However, Remotegrity does not protect against vote coercion or vote buying.

Remotegrity was successfully trialled in municipal elections in Takoma Park, Maryland, in 2008 [586]. The system is described in detail in Chapter 10.

8.4 Non-Cryptographic E2E Voting Systems

These systems represent an interesting experiment in the overall research on E2E voting. Systems such as ThreeBallot, Twin and Aperio emulate E2E verifiability properties in a wholly precinct-based paper-ballot format without resorting to any cryptography. This approach has only produced a handful of workable systems thus far, but it has generated valuable new insights about E2E voting in general. Additionally, due to their exclusion of complex cryptography, these systems aid in communicating fundamental principles of E2E verifiability to the layman.

8.4.1 ThreeBallot, VAV and Twin

ThreeBallot [487], introduced by Rivest and Smith in 2007, derives its name from its unique ballot design, consisting of three detachable ballots, as depicted in Figure 8.12(a). Each ballot is assigned a unique serial number printed at the bottom. In the polling booth, Alice marks the ballots such that each candidate is marked once whereas the candidate of her choice is marked *twice* Figure 8.12(a) represents a vote for *Nihilist*. Alice's vote can therefore be understood as a composite of the three ballots. The ballots are then detached. Alice randomly chooses one as a receipt and scans a copy to take home. She then casts all three ballots into the ballot box.

After polls close, all cast ballots are published on the bulletin board, and Alice uses her receipt to verify the corresponding ballot is correctly recorded. The tally is computed by simply adding up all ballots on the bulletin board. Since each candidate receives one vote by default, the result is inflated by the number of voters, which is accordingly subtracted from the tally. Any observer can replicate and verify the tally.

An important distinction to be made here is that Alice's receipt is not an encryption of her vote. Instead, the receipt testifies to a key component of the vote which has been delinked from the other components. Alice's privacy is maintained as the receipt reveals nothing about her actual vote unless examined in conjunction with the two other ballots she cast, and these could be any on the bulletin board. Furthermore, if any party tampers with her ballots, Alice has a one in three chance of detecting it on the bulletin board. For large-scale tampering, the odds are much higher.

ThreeBallot's non-intuitive ballot marking scheme may impact usability: in a mock election, a large number of voters experienced difficulty using ThreeBallot and more than 30% of initial cast votes proved invalid [333]. There are also security issues: a coercer may force Alice to mark her ballots in certain unique patterns which he can later identify on the bulletin board. These issues and potential solutions are documented in [487] [59] [304] [155] [341] and are also discussed in Chapter 9.

Rivest and Smith also presented two systems that are variations on ThreeBallot, VAV (Vote/AntiVote/Vote) and Twin [333]. The VAV ballot suite, depicted in Figure 8.12(b), consists of two *Vote* ballots, and one *AntiVote* ballot. The marking process differs from ThreeBallot in that only one candidate is marked on each ballot. The *AntiVote* ballot essentially *cancels* out one *Vote* ballot, and both have to be marked identically. The leftover *Vote* determines Alice's actual choice. Figure 8.12(b) depicts a vote for *Nihilist*. Alice scans one of the three ballots at random to use as a receipt. Tallying and verification processes for VAV are very similar to ThreeBallot.

Twin is based on traditional voting systems in that the voter casts only one ballot, but with the innovation that Alice does not take home her own receipt but that of another voter. In this scenario, a big bin in the polling station is periodically filled with valid receipts. After casting her vote, Alice makes her way to the bin, draws out a receipt at random, and takes a copy home, which she later verifies on the bulletin board. These receipts are therefore referred to as *floating receipts*. This system is very easy to use, and though individual vote verifiability is sacrificed, voters can still verify the election tally and coercion resistance is ensured.

8.4.2 *Randell & Ryan's Scratch Card Voting System*

In 2006, Randell and Ryan proposed a voting system [478] that augments the Prêt à Voter ballot with scratch surfaces and dispenses with cryptography and mixnets.

The ballot, depicted in Figure 8.13, is detachable in two halves along the middle. Candidate names are listed in randomized order on the left side with corresponding markable spaces on the right. The Vote Identification Number (VIN), functioning as

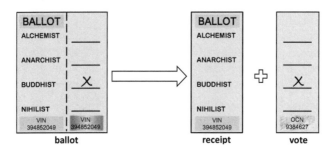

Figure 8.13: The Randell & Ryan Scratch Card Voting ballot.

a unique serial number for the ballot, is duplicated on both halves, except on the right it is printed atop a scratch surface. The scratch surface conceals an encoding of the candidate ordering on the ballot, referred to as the Order of Candidate Names (OCN).

On election day, Alice marks her candidate choice on the ballot, detaches the right side and casts it in the ballot box. The left side serves as her receipt. Election staff will accept her vote only if the scratch surface is still intact. After polls close, VINs of all cast votes are published on a bulletin board and Alice can ensure the system received her ballot. To process votes, election officials first remove the scratch surface of each cast vote. This reveals the OCNs, enabling them to reconstruct the original candidate ordering on the ballots, and thereby deduce the voters' choices and compute the tally. More importantly, removing the scratch surface also destroys the VIN on top, protecting voter privacy. Once the VIN is removed, Alice's vote can no longer be differentiated from other cast votes.

The OCNs are simple codes, each of which maps to a different candidate ordering. Prior to casting her vote, Alice can audit her ballot by simply removing the scratch surface, decoding the OCN and verifying if it matches the candidate ordering on the ballot. However, removing the scratch surface invalidates the ballot, and she will need a new one to cast her vote. Alice can audit as many ballots as she likes until she is convinced the ballots are correctly formed, and then cast her vote.

This system provides a subset of E2E properties. Only received VINs are published on the bulletin board, providing Alice assurance that her vote has been received, but not that it has been recorded and tallied exactly as she cast it. Cast ballots are not published as it would make it trivially easy for any party to deduce voters' choices from their receipts. Furthermore, removing the scratch surface irretrievably destroys the link between cast votes and counted votes, and Alice has no means of verifying that election officials correctly included her vote in the tally and did not replace it with a fake one. To increase transparency, Randell and Ryan suggest instituting random audits, and incorporating paper trails into the system.

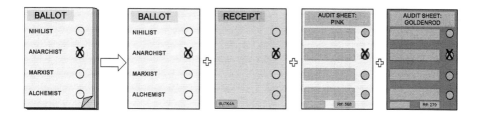

Figure 8.14: The Aperio ballot assembly with a vote for *Anarchist*.

8.4.3 *Aperio*

Aperio[215], developed by Essex Clark and Adams in 2010, is intended for low-tech minimal environments, such as elections in developing countries. Aperio derives inspiration from Punchscan in its use of ballots with stacked sheets which enable audit trails to defend against ballot box stuffing and ballot tampering.

The Aperio ballot suite, depicted in Figure 8.14, consists of a ballot with randomized candidate names, a receipt layer and multiple distinctly colored audit layers (we assume two audit layers in this example, colored pink and goldenrod). The sheets are backed with carbon paper so that marks made on the ballot are copied onto the lower layers. Receipt and audit sheets each bear a unique reference number, the receipt serial number and the audit reference number, respectively.

In the election setup phase, election trustees assemble the ballot suites by superimposing the individual sheets and binding them together. They also generate two lists for each individual audit layer: a *receipt commitment list* linking each receipt serial number to an audit reference number, and a *ballot commitment list* linking the audit reference number to ballot candidate ordering. Figure 8.15 includes sample entries for these lists for the ballot suite in Figure 8.14. These commitment lists are secured in separate tamper-evident envelopes and placed in safe custody prior to polls.

To cast her vote, Alice marks her candidate choice on the ballot suite and hands it to a member of the polling staff who ensures that the counterfoil is still intact. If not, the vote is rejected. If intact, the staff member then separates the four sheets. The ballot is cast in the ballot box, the receipt is issued to Alice to take home, and the audit sheets are cast in corresponding pink and goldenrod-colored audit boxes. After polls close, results are tallied by simply counting the votes in the ballot box.

To audit the election, the trustees retrieve the receipt and ballot commitment lists. They check the envelope to ensure there has been no tampering. A coin is publicly tossed, and, depending on the result, one of the two colored audit boxes is used to generate a *receipt audit trail* and the other to generate a *ballot audit trail*. For example, if the pink box is chosen to audit receipts, the envelopes containing the pink receipt commitment list and the goldenrod ballot commitment list are opened.

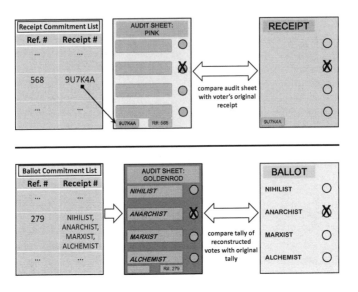

Figure 8.15: Auditing receipts and ballots in Aperio.

The envelopes containing the pink ballot commitment list and the goldenrod receipt commitment list are destroyed.

The commitment lists and audit sheets enable individual reconstruction of the vote and the receipt, as depicted in Figure 8.15. The pink audit sheet already bears the mark for Alice's candidate choice. Election staff search for the sheet's audit reference number (*568* in our example) in the receipt commitment list and note the corresponding receipt serial number (*9U7K4A*) by hand on the sheet. This step effectively reconstructs Alice's receipt. Reconstructed receipts are posted on the bulletin board where voters can verify them against the receipts issued to them earlier.

Likewise, the reference number on the goldenrod audit sheet (*279* in this case) identifies a specific candidate ordering in the ballot commitment list. Trustees write this ordering on the sheet, thereby reconstructing the vote. These votes are then counted independently and results are compared with the official tally.

Aperio's key novelty is that receipts and ballots are audited separately. The act of destroying the unused commitment lists effectively decouples the ballots from the receipts, thereby preserving voter privacy. Alice can verify her vote was correctly recorded by comparing her receipt against the reconstructed receipts. Election trustees and observers ensure the votes have been correctly counted if the tally of the reconstructed votes matches the original results. However, as in the case of paper-based E2E systems, certain coercion attacks, such as randomized voting, still apply.

Aperio has inspired an electronic counterpart, Eperio [218], which employs cryptographic primitives to similarly verify votes against commitment lists. Another system, Hash-Only Verification (*Hover*) [219], uses this verification approach in conjunction with the Scantegrity optical-scan system to reduce reliance on election trustees and make the voting system intelligible to non-technical voters.

8.5   The Way Forward for E2E Voting Systems

As described thus far, considerable work has been done on developing E2E voting systems and reconciling theoretical notions with practical realities. However, to fully transition these systems into the real world, a host of pressing technical issues, usability concerns and legal dilemmas still need to be resolved. In this section, we briefly overview progress and outstanding challenges in these domains.

8.5.1   Technical Issues

As often happens when prototyping theoretical systems, the implementation itself may introduce security flaws. Karlof et al. [340] analyzed two systems, Votegrity and MarkPledge, and described several scenarios where voter privacy and election integrity may be compromised by exploiting flaws in how the systems were built. For instance, malicious software on voting machines could encrypt votes in a manner that surreptitiously leaks information regarding the voter's candidate choice. Malicious voting machines may sabotage an election by issuing large numbers of forged or invalid receipts. Large-scale attacks would be detected but may negatively impact public confidence in the system. Human factors also need to be considered. For instance, voters who do not intend to verify their votes may discard their receipts on polling premises where a poll worker could collect them and later manipulate the corresponding votes without fear of detection. Various such attacks and proposed solutions are described in Chapters 7 and 9.

Researchers have presented various practical guidelines to implementing voting systems: Karlof et al. advocate a **systems approach** [340] which essentially states that security analyses of such systems should not examine system components in isolation but consider the entire system and how the individual parts interact with each other. Bruck et al. strongly caution against "all-at-once" approaches [117] to building voting equipment where diverse functionality is bundled together into the same hardware components. They propose a highly **modular architecture**, dubbed *Frog voting*, which clearly partitions processes such as voter registration, vote recording, casting, tallying, and auditing, thereby reducing complexity, simplifying certification, and encouraging incremental innovation. Rivest and Wack have proposed the principle of **software independence** [486] (detailed in Chapter 1) urging that the integrity of election results should not be dependent on the software used by the system. Popoveniuc et al. [466] also detail a series of security checks which ensure E2E verifiability properties of a voting system.

A second major direction of research has been to improve individual components of voting systems. There is a significant body of work on **securing electronic voting machines**. For instance, researchers have proposed the use of trusted hardware, i.e., specialized tamper-proof chips which protect cryptographic credentials and guarantee that voting machines run trusted software [456] [237] [532]. Researchers have also identified critical security properties that voting machines must ensure, and proposed corresponding solutions [396] [101]. Another key component in E2E voting systems is the **public bulletin board** and various solutions have been put forward to implement it [300] [185] and make it robust against attacks [350] [274].

Online voting has also received considerable attention. Proposed methods to defeat hackers and malware include the use of visual cryptography techniques [455], CAPTCHAs [468], voice recognition [464] and deploying assistive handheld devices [582]. However, voter privacy and coercion concerns still persist.

Unfortunately, most of these solutions have been proposed piecemeal and it is unclear if and how they will fit together. There have been very few attempts, like VoteBox (described earlier in Section 8.3.2.4), to harmonize these various innovations in the context of a complete E2E voting system. Substantial work is still needed in this domain before E2E voting systems are deployed for mainstream use.

8.5.2   Usability

The importance of usability for a voting system cannot be emphasized enough and usability oftentimes conflicts with security properties. Ensuring system usability is also complicated by the fact that elections occur only rarely and voters must be able to vote with near 100% success while having little or no experience or training on that voting system. This problem also extends to poll workers and election officials who may have limited technical expertise and experience regarding certain systems. For these reasons, the National Institute of Standards and Technology (NIST) has advocated a broad all-encompassing perspective to study usability within the context of the complete voting system, including the physical environment, the voting product, the ballot, the voter and all personnel involved in the process [360].

At this particular stage in the development of E2E voting systems, the central usability concerns are whether voters can successfully cast their votes using these systems, and more importantly, whether or not they are able to undertake the verification process. Regarding vote casting, evidence suggests that certain design features of these systems are problematic. In one study, the ballot design of Prêt à Voter, requiring voters to shred half of their ballot to ensure vote privacy, caused confusion [516]. Another study involving Helios, Prêt à Voter and Scantegrity II found that a significant number of voters failed to cast a vote with each system [40]. Troublingly, many of those voters thought they had in fact successfully cast a vote. It also took almost twice as long to cast a ballot as with a traditional paper-based system.[5]

Individual vote verification is a new and novel concept for voters and adds a layer of complexity. Critically, voters are active participants in auditing the election and certifying its results, and if, for whatever reason they are unable to verify their votes, the system's security guarantees become moot and the system is not auditable. Recent testing and "live" applications of E2E systems have resulted not just in consistently low rates of voter verification but even lower rates for those who actually report discrepancies [195] [395]. This is likely due to two reasons.

First, voters do not see the need to verify their vote. One possible explanation for this is that **trust-transference** from election authorities to voter does not happen. As Olembo et al. [440] discovered, voters may initially verify their vote out of curiosity, but after continued use of the system, they establish trust in the system and verification is deemed unnecessary. In line with this conclusion, recent usability testing involving Helios and a Galois-designed prototype based on STAR-Vote, found that participants had a tacit level of trust in any voting system provided it was officially branded, e.g., *Jurisdiction X Official Election Website* [402]. The participants considered verification unnecessary if a voting system met this basic criterion.

The second concern is complexity. The verification process of Helios has repeatedly been found to be difficult [339] [402]. The reasons may be technical or even that the voters may not understand what to do since the verification language is not related to prior voting experience on their part. Research suggests that terms like "audit," "verifiability" or "ballot fingerprint" lack clarity for voters, cause confusion and do not engender trust in the voting system [441]. This is critical as voters need to understand the necessity of verification to be motivated to invest the extra effort in verifying their vote. The intuition behind verification also needs to be effectively communicated. As Schneider et al. discovered in their study concerning Prêt à Voter, simply confirming that an encrypted vote on a bulletin board corresponded to a receipt did not provide sufficient security guarantees for voters themselves [516].

Several technical solutions have been proposed in the literature, including simplifying security elements or enhancing voting systems to facilitate individual vote verification [404] [498], bundling multiple receipts to enable mass verification [107], or involving third parties in the process, such as activist groups or helper organizations [49] [47], but these require further study from a usability perspective.

Overall, research in the usability of E2E voting systems is still in an early stage and significant work is needed to demonstrate that these systems are accessible to non-expert users while simultaneously maintaining the desired security properties.

---

[5]However, we would note here that the Scantegrity team has critiqued the implementation of the Scantegrity system used in this study [386].

8.5.3 Legal Framework

It is a common perception that numerous attempts to introduce new voting technology, for example in Britain, Finland, Ireland and Quebec, have failed in large part due to the absence of a comprehensive supporting legal framework [55]. Indeed, many of the issues regarding new voting technologies are not due to the technology itself, but rather the lack of ancillary processes that establish trust in the voting system. A new paradigm, like E2E voting, requires legislators to craft an appropriate legal framework that embeds election norms and details administrative procedures to address risks, problems and threats. This includes aspects such as testing requirements, implementation instructions and processes for problem resolution.

A useful guiding principle in constructing a legal framework is that of **functional equivalence**. Any new legal framework must essentially function in an equivalent way to the legal framework for existing voting systems, i.e., the new framework must be at least as good, if not better, than the old one. Towards this end, legislators need to identify the distinct purposes served by existing voting systems and ensure that new rules also address the same needs. Applying this criterion to E2E voting systems requires consideration that current electoral values and community expectations are preserved, while making specific legislative changes to ensure that voting experiences using E2E voting systems are as good as or better than existing procedures.

Another overarching concept is that of **nondiscrimination** [370]. A new legal framework should not have the unintended consequence of discriminating against any voter. For instance, in the United States, any electronic technology, including voting equipment, needs to be Section 508 compliant [433], i.e., it must attempt to fully accommodate disability groups. If E2E voting systems cannot successfully cater to certain voter groups, legislation must set out clear alternatives to avoid discriminatory legal challenges. A good example is the case of absentee voting, where eligibility requirements are defined, permitting certain groups to cast their votes remotely. Furthermore, legislation should not unduly limit technological choices to certain vendors or technology in cases where a better technology or solution exists. Excessive detail in legislation can inhibit innovation and create legal *technology locks* [55].

An additional function of a legal framework is to **minimize and mediate error and risk**. No electoral mechanism, be it electronic or paper, is ever absolutely secure from every possible error or risk, and the greater question is whether the regulatory framework provides voters and political stakeholders confidence that risk is minimized and contingencies are in place to cover the range of possible circumstances.

Regarding specific properties to be included in legislation, Schwartz and Grice detail the following **normative values** addressing electronic voting systems [520]:

■ Accessibility and facilitate reasonable accommodation
■ Voter anonymity
■ Fairness
■ Accurate and prompt results

- Comprehensible and transparent processes
- System security and risk assessment
- Detection of problems and remedial contingencies
- Legislative certainty and finality
- Effective and independent oversight
- Cost justification and efficiency

Many of these values could be embedded into a legal framework in the form of technological choices within the specifications of an E2E voting system. For instance, to deter coercion, voters may be permitted to change or update their vote once it has been cast, as is the case of elections in Estonia [376]. Similarly, if multiple modes of voting are available, legislation may specify that an electronic vote can be revoked if the voter casts a paper ballot. Other technological specifications that may be considered election norms include the capability to detect undervotes and overvotes on marked ballots prior to casting and the ability to cast a blank ballot as a protest vote without it being considered technically invalid.

It should be recognized that constructing a legal framework involves trade-offs between competing norms. An illustrative example is the case of Dutch voters and the Rijnland Internet Election System (RIES) [246], an online voting system used for the Rijnland District Water Board Elections in 2004. In the interest of transparency, most of the RIES technology was made open-source. RIES provides a degree of verifiability but weak privacy. Upon voting, the system generated a technical code, enabling voters to verify their vote was included in the tally. However, if a voter disclosed her code, any third party could determine her actual vote. In terms of norms, therefore, transparency trumped voter privacy. Whereas this particular example may not directly apply to most E2E voting systems, where cryptography obfuscates the contents of the voter receipt, it is indicative of the conflicts legislators will have to wrestle with in preparing a legal framework for these new systems.

8.5.4 Uptake of E2E Voting Systems

Broadly speaking, uptake of a new voting system depends on how successfully it incorporates existing election norms, and equally importantly, how effectively this perception is communicated to voters. Research on Internet voting lists four factors which may serve as a good starting point to discuss the uptake of E2E voting systems [445]. These are security, privacy, accountability and economic feasibility.

Regarding security and privacy, in Section 8.2 we have already motivated the fundamental requirement for voting systems to ensure vote privacy and election integrity. However, security also needs to be considered in terms of **reliability**, i.e., how a system isolates and reacts to failure. While a comprehensive legal framework will considerably ameliorate failure reaction, a voting system should be designed so that there is no single point of failure. As a risk assessment of large-scale events notes [311]: "If failure in one part of an information system can cause failure in other interconnected parts, then the system is susceptible to cascade failure." Furthermore, in the words of Pieters and Becker [461]: "It is not only important that a system is reliable, it is also important that people believe that the system is reliable."

Fostering a common understanding of the risks associated with a voting system may actually advance acceptance. Risk exists even in paper-based elections but these are generally known, accepted and tolerated risks. Transparency and accountability are key to minimizing risk, and risk perception, by detailing and perhaps even publicly demonstrating potential risks and corresponding remedies. The legal framework should require the electoral authority to establish a set of procedures and tests to be completed before the voting system goes live. Additionally, procedures should be legislated that provide solutions for potential risks and these should be updated before each election to ensure protection against new threats or vulnerabilities.

Moreover, comprehensive and high-quality voter instruction is critical to uptake of a new system and typically falls under the auspices of the legal framework ensuring equal access. Voter education is particularly important for a new paradigm like E2E voting. These systems are radically different from existing systems that voters are accustomed to, the intuition behind certain procedural steps may not be immediately clear, and they have been known to confuse voters [516] [40] [402]. Furthermore, these systems task voters with the extra responsibility of vote verification, the necessity of which needs to be adequately explained and motivated. Dissemination of this instruction can take many forms, including programs to educate the general public about E2E voting systems via various media, supplying user-friendly instructions, public demonstrations of the technology and maintaining phone help-lines to walk voters through the voting and verification processes.

8.6 Conclusion

In this chapter we have undertaken a comprehensive introduction to the burgeoning field of end-to-end verifiable voting. We have traced the development of privacy and verifiability properties in the literature and described the workings of current state-of-the-art E2E voting systems. In our classification, we have attempted to track the intellectual evolution of these systems and highlight the key cryptographic and procedural techniques employed by their designers to harmonize security and usability concerns. We have also discussed current challenges to the deployment of these systems, consisting of outstanding technical, legal and usability issues.

Advances in E2E verifiable voting have the potential to restore trust in elections and improve democratic processes in society and, for that reason, we believe that the importance of these developments must not be underestimated. Our intention, in writing this chapter, has been to make the important innovations in this field accessible to a wider audience. We hope our work serves as a useful resource in this regard and assists in the future development of E2E voting.

Acknowledgments

The authors wish to thank Peter Hyun-Jeen Lee and Feng Hao for constructive discussions and Siamak F. Shahandashti, Jeremy Clark and Peter Ryan for helpful comments on the manuscript. This work is supported by ERC Starting Grant No. 306994.

Chapter 9

Theoretical Attacks on E2E Voting Systems

Peter Hyun-Jeen Lee

Newcastle University, UK

Siamak F. Shahandashti

Newcastle University, UK

CONTENTS

9.1 Introduction

An election, whether it is paper-based (as in traditional elections) or computer-based (e.g., e-voting), has always been open to threats due to the high stakes for the winner. A survey shows there have been hundreds of election frauds over the last decade in the US alone.[1] Common attacks included vote buying, double voting, stealing absentee ballots and so on which can influence the election outcome. A natural question that arises is then, "how do we ensure the election outcome is correct and if not, detect it?".

In traditional paper-based elections, voters must rely on the trusted party to count the votes. Thus, the verifiability is largely dependent on the trusted party to perform the tallying process correctly and there is no convenient way for voters to independently verify the result. E2E verifiable voting systems, on the other hand, try to minimize such dependency and provide every voter means to verify the correctness of the election outcome (i.e., integrity of the election).

E2E verifiable voting systems achieve the verifiability of elections via cast-as-intended (CAI), recorded-as-cast (RAC) and tallied-as-recorded (TAR) [334]. CAI ensures the voter can verify that his choice is correctly marked on his ballot, RAC ensures the voting system stores the ballot correctly and TAR ensures all the cast votes are correctly included in the final tally. Thus, if malicious voters (or even corrupted election officials) attempt to alter the election result, such attempts will leave evidence which honest voters can use to verify that the integrity of the election is lost.

Privacy is another important property for E2E verifiable voting systems. In the absence of privacy, the relation between the votes and the voters will be visible to others. Such a relation then can be used to coerce voters, leading the voters to vote for the choice of the coercer instead of their own. Although such votes will syntactically remain valid, they should be treated as being semantically invalid since they do not reflect the true intentions of the voters. However, it seems almost impossible (if not impossible) to determine a voter's true intention from a cast ballot. It is thus best to prevent coercions by ensuring the votes remain secret.

A common approach to realizing E2E verifiability is by introducing receipts in the system. These receipts have two main requirements. One is to ensure E2E verifiability of the system by serving as voter verifiable evidence. Another is to do so without revealing any information about how voters have voted. These seemingly contradicting requirements contribute towards making E2E verifiable voting systems complex.

[1] http://www.rnla.org/survey.asp

The aim of this chapter is to aid the readers to become aware of various pitfalls while designing an E2E verifiable voting system. In the following, we will review the existing attacks against E2E voting systems in the academic literature. The attacks are divided into three categories — integrity, privacy and coercion, depending on the specific property each attack aims to compromise.

9.2 Integrity

Integrity ensures the correctness of the election outcome and hence perhaps is the most important property an E2E voting system should possess. This section discusses various attacks against well-known E2E verifiable voting systems which aim at compromising the integrity of an election.

9.2.1 Misprinted Ballots Attack

In a voting environment, it is generally expected that there are trusted parties (e.g., election officials) who handle critical operations such as verifying identity of a voter, counting the tally and so on. When such trusted parties behave maliciously, one can no longer have confidence in the outcome of an election. Kelsey et al. [341] introduced an attack where the election official intentionally misprints a portion of ballots to alter the election outcome, hence the attack is named misprinted ballots attack. Prior to demonstrating the attack, we start by briefly describing Punchscan in order to familiarize the readers with the system.

Punchscan is an E2E verifiable voting system which makes use of optical scanning of marked ballots. In Punchscan, a ballot consists of two sheets. The front sheet has a list of candidates with associated letters, a serial number and a hole for each candidate. The back sheet has the letters associated with the candidates printed such that when two sheets are overlayed, the letters appear under the holes. A voter casts his vote by marking the letter corresponding to the candidate of his choice with a bingo dauber. He then must choose which sheet (front or back) to keep as a receipt and discards the other one. The receipt can later be checked against the public bulletin board (PBB) released by the election authority.

The attack involves an interaction between a voter and the corrupted election official (the attacker). To begin with, the attacker replaces a portion of ballots with tampered ballots. Then, whenever a voter chooses the front sheet as his receipt, the attacker gives a tampered ballot to the voter. A tampered ballot has two sheets, a tampered back sheet and an untampered front sheet. The back sheet is tampered such that the ordering of letters is swapped. Thus, a voter who intends to cast a vote for the candidate of his choice will instead end up casting a vote for a swapped candidate. An example of misprinted ballots attack is shown in Figure 9.1. A voter who intends to vote for Jake sees the tampered ballot and marks the second hole then scans the front

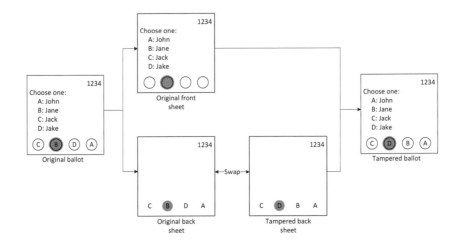

Figure 9.1: Misprinted ballots attack against Punchscan: Tampered ballot cast by a voter gets linked to the original ballot which results in a vote swap.

sheet. The system however, correlates this scanned copy to the original ballot and the vote goes to Jane instead. The back sheet which is the only evidence of tampering gets destroyed as a part of the legitimate voting process.

A proposed remedy for this attack is to have the election official commit to a ballot *before* asking the voter to choose a receipt sheet. This way, the election official has a chance of being caught as he no longer has a priori knowledge of whether the voter will keep the front sheet as the receipt or not. For example, if the election official picks a tampered ballot but the voter decides to choose the back sheet as his receipt, then this will allow the voter to later find out that the election official misbehaved.

9.2.2 Trash Attack

One of the important assumptions in many E2E verifiable voting systems is that the voters should check their receipts. Some voters however choose to discard their receipts to the bin which can be an indication that they will not check their receipts against the PBB. An attacker (e.g., election officials) can exploit this voter behavior to manipulate the votes corresponding to the discarded receipts with a high confidence of not being caught. This attack is called trash attack [88].

A suggested countermeasure in [88] is to use a hash chain. That is, in order to generate a receipt for a voter, the system creates a hash which is dependent on the current vote as well as the previous vote. However, this approach raises two concerns which do not seem to have been documented in the literature. One concern is user privacy issue. Because each vote is now dependent on another vote, there is an inherent ordering that is present in the receipts. Thus, a receipt can act as publicly verifiable evidence that shows a voter was present at the voting booth for a given period of time. This may discourage privacy-keen voters to participate in elections.

Another concern is the performance issue. Helios, for example, is a distributed online voting system where multiple voters can simultaneously cast their votes in real time. However, hash chaining being a linear process prohibits concurrent processing of ballots; thus a voter may have to wait a considerable amount of time until his vote gets processed.

9.2.3 Clash Attack

Clash attack [356] is another example of exploiting the weakness in the receipt management of E2E verifiable voting systems. In a sense, clash attack can be viewed as a stronger attack as it works even when the voters verify their receipts against the PBB. The main idea behind clash attack is that the attacker has the power to issue *duplicate* receipts to multiple voters as if they were legitimate receipts. This can be done either by the corrupted authority or by an external attacker who takes control of the voting machine and the PBB. Then, for each duplicated receipt one vote can be safely manipulated. Certain implementations of several well-known systems such as Wombat [33], ThreeBallot [487] and Helios [44] were shown to be vulnerable to clash attack. The following sequence of events describes the attack procedure for a variant of Helios.

1. The browser and the PBB are compromised.

2. The browser always uses the same sequence of random numbers $(r_i)_{i=1}^n$ to generate i-th ciphertext $C_i = Enc_{pk}(c, r_i)$ where c is the candidate chosen by the voter and n is the maximum number of audits.

3. All the voters who have voted for the same candidate and audited the same number of times receive the same receipt.

4. The attacker keeps one receipt for verification purposes and replaces all the remaining cast ballots then publishes the corresponding receipts on the PBB.

5. Each voter verifies that his receipt appears on the PBB and believes his vote was cast correctly.

Clash attack works because the system can be manipulated to produce duplicate receipts without voters detecting it. Thus, even a careful victim who checks his receipt against the PBB will not be able to detect the attack as his receipt will appear on the PBB. This attack can be mitigated if an additional requirement is added to ensure every receipt is unique. One suggested approach is to use the voter-contributed randomness in addition to the machine-chosen randomness during encryption. Then,

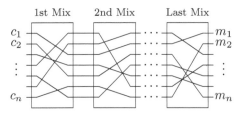

Figure 9.2: A Chaumian mix-net.

assuming the entropy of the voter-chosen randomness is high enough (i.e., the randomness chosen by a voter is highly likely to be different from the randomness chosen by another voter), the resulting receipt will be unique.

9.2.4 Flawed Mix-Net

Prior to describing the attacks on mix-nets, a brief introduction to the concept is presented for the readers who are not familiar with mix-nets. Mix-nets were originally proposed by Chaum in 1981 [153]. A mix-net is a series of servers (also known as mixes), each taking a tuple as input and producing a tuple of the same size as output, where each server obfuscates the relation between its input and output by mixing (i.e., applying a random permutation). The aim is to shuffle a tuple securely, that is, the correspondence between the input values to the first mix and the output values of the last mix remains secret even if some mixes are corrupted by an adversary. Figure 9.2 shows an example of a mix-net.

There are two main types of mix-nets: Chaumian mix-nets [153] and homomorphic mix-nets [453]. In both mix-nets, the input to the first mix-net is a tuple of ciphertexts. In Chaumian mix-nets, each input ciphertext is calculated by encrypting the plaintext consecutively under the keys of the mixes starting with that of the last mix. During the mixing operation, each mix "peels off" a layer of encryption by decrypting its input values with the last mix peeling off the last layer and outputting the original plaintexts. Figure 9.2 shows a Chaumian mix-net. In homomorphic mix-nets, each input ciphertext is a homomorphic encryption of the plaintext. During the mixing operation, each mix simply re-randomizes each encryption, resulting in a new ciphertext corresponding to the same plaintext. Eventually, the output tuple of the last mix needs to be decrypted to retrieve the original plaintexts. A homomorphic mix-net may be represented similarly to Figure 9.2 with the only difference that the output of the last mix will be re-encrypted ciphertexts rather than plaintexts.

In order to guarantee the correctness of the mixing, random partial checking (RPC) is proposed [321]. RPC is a well-known technique which works by each mix revealing the relation between the randomly chosen half of its input and output. In Chaumian mix-nets, this relation is revealed by providing the randomness necessary to encrypt a given output to a given input. In homomorphic mix-nets, it is revealed by exposing the randomness used by the mix-server to re-encrypt. Revealing half of the relations ensures cheating mixes are caught with a high probability, while at the same time the end-to-end input and output relationship remains secret with a high probability thus protecting the sender privacy. To achieve this, mixes are grouped in pairs of consecutive servers, then within each pair, the output ciphertexts of the first mix (which are the same as the input ciphertexts to the second mix) are randomly divided into two sets, and each mix is challenged to reveal the relations for one of the sets.

However, it was shown that the original description of RPC has weaknesses which enable attackers to break the sender privacy and the correctness of shuffling [342]. The attacks work on both Chaumian and homomorphic mix-nets. These attacks are then extended to the RPC implementations of systems such as Civitas [159] and Scantegrity [146].

Khazaei and Wikström [342] observed that in the existing implementations of mix-nets at the time, two crucial well-formedness checks were often missing: checking for duplicate ciphertexts and checking for permutation consistency.

Assume that there are duplicate ciphertexts in the input of a mix in a Chaumian mix-net. They should result in duplicate plaintexts. However, a corrupted mix can replace one of the duplicate outputs with an arbitrary value, while keeping the other one unchanged. If the cheating mix is challenged on any of the duplicate input ciphertexts, it will be able to successfully claim that the input ciphertext corresponds to the unchanged output. The mix is not caught unless it is asked to show the relation for the injected output.

Khazaei and Wikström further observed that in the RPC implementations after a mix was challenged on revealing the relations for some input or output ciphertexts, the only verification test which was carried out was to check if each relation is valid. They argue that this leaves the mix free to claim relations with collisions, e.g., two or more output ciphertexts corresponding to the same input. Lack of such permutation consistency checks enables mixes to get away with incorrect shuffling.

As an example, the attack which breaks the integrity of the election is described below. The rest of the attacks which break the privacy of the election are described in Section 9.3.

Rigging an Election without Detection

This attack exploits the lack of permutation consistency checks in RPC. It applies to all homomorphic mix-nets, and to those Chaumian mix-nets that do not implement duplicate ciphertext removal. Duplicate ciphertext removal refers to the practice of inspecting the inputs to a mix and removing any duplicate ciphertexts. Suppose an attacker takes full control of the first mix. Then, he can set multiple output ciphertexts to ciphertexts corresponding to the same input. This will amplify the vote corresponding to the repeated ciphertext and compromise the integrity of the election. An extreme case of this attack where the first mix replaces all the outputs with ci-

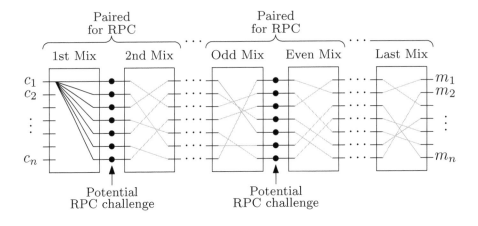

Figure 9.3: Rigging an election.

phertexts corresponding to the first input is shown in Figure 9.3. Note that in RPC the first mix is challenged to reveal relations for half of its *output* only since the first mix is paired with the second mix. Hence the first mix will be able to provide a valid relation for any challenged output and if the relations are not checked for permutation consistency the attack will not be caught. Note that the first mix is not able to provide a valid relation for most of its input ciphertexts, but these are not challenged in RPC. Also note that in general any mix with an odd index can carry out this attack by repeating its input ciphertexts.

The countermeasure proposed by Khazaei and Wikström is to verify permutation consistency in RPC, i.e., to check that all the revealed input-output relations have distinct positions. As they also mention though, this check was missed in the Civitas and Scantegrity implementations of RPC.

9.3 Privacy

It is important that an E2E verifiable voting system hides how a voter has voted from other voters (ideally even from the system itself) thereby providing privacy. While privacy is important in its own right, compromise of privacy can lead to coercion attacks which then can lead to the loss of integrity. In this section, attacks which aim to compromise privacy are discussed.

9.3.1 Replay Attack

Suppose a small mock election of three voters is run. Two voters Alice and Bob cast their votes legitimately. Then, Charlie duplicates Alice's vote. If both Alice and Bob voted for the same candidate then obviously there is no privacy (i.e., the tally will reveal the winner whom both Alice and Bob have voted for). Had they voted for different candidates, the candidate that Alice voted for will win the election with two votes, hence revealing her vote which in turn will reveal Bob's also. This demonstrates that simply *replaying* another voter's vote can result in a breach of privacy. This replay attack was shown to be applicable to Helios 2.0 [173].

Apparently, the aforementioned scenario is somewhat artificial and does not reflect real-world elections. It was however, shown that replay attack can be applied to real-world elections through a French election case study [173]. The case study was conducted based on a statistical model which reasonably resembles an actual election indicating that the attack does pose a threat in the real world.

As a simple remedy for replay attack, ballot weeding is proposed [173]. Ballot weeding involves checking for duplicate ballots in the system under the assumption the signature of knowledge, which acts as a proof that the cast ballot is well formed, is not malleable (i.e., cannot be altered in such a way that verification still succeeds).

Replay attack can be extended to ballot-blinding attack where each copy of a vote made can be distinct. The technique requires a basic understanding of a well-known encryption algorithm called ElGamal encryption. Let $p = bq + 1$ be a large prime where q is also a prime and $b \geq 2$. A generator $g \in \mathbb{Z}_p^*$ with order q is chosen. Further, the secret key $x \in \mathbb{Z}_q$ is chosen and the corresponding public key $X = g^x \pmod{p}$ is computed. Encryption requires choosing $r \in \mathbb{Z}_q$ and computing the ciphertext $(R, S) = (g^r, mX^r)$. (R, S) for a given message $m < p$. (R, S) can be decrypted by computing $m = R^{-x}S$.

Algorithm 1 Blind a ballot (R, S) with a public key X

1: **procedure** BLIND($(R, S), X$))
2:     Pick a random $z \in \mathbb{Z}_q$
3:     Compute $(R', S') = (g^z R, X^z S) = (g^{z+r}, X^{z+r}m)$
4:     **return** (R', S')
5: **end procedure**

Ballot-blinding attack is similar to the replay attack in that it exploits malleability of the ciphertext to tamper the ciphertext while keeping the vote *unchanged*. The corresponding proof, which is a non-interactive zero knowledge proof for proving wellformedness of the ciphertext, can also be blinded in cooperation with the original voter (i.e., the original voter *consents* to another voter copying his vote *without* revealing his vote to the copier). Thus, allowing the copier to create an undetectable copy of the original vote. As shown in Algorithm 1, the attack requires a randomness z chosen at the time of blinding with the public information, the ciphertext and the public key. Blinding the accompanied proof is more technically involved and interested readers are referred to [198] for details.

Desmedt and Chaidos [198] note that this attack works for online voting but not for the polling station-based voting due to the cooperation requirement. The main difference between the two types of voting systems is that it is relatively easier to enforce procedural requirements during the election in polling station-based voting than in online voting.

9.3.2 Kleptographic Attack

Algorithm 2 Embed a secret message c into the randomness part of an ElGamal signature (r, s)

1: **procedure** EMBED(c)
2:     $p = qm + 1$ ▷ m is smooth and $\mathbb{F}_p^*$ is a subgroup of order q generated by g^m
3:     $k' \in_R \mathbb{Z}_q$
4:     $k = c + k'm \pmod{p-1}$
5:     **return** $r = g^k \pmod{p}$
6: **end procedure**

Algorithm 3 Retrieve the secret message c given an ElGamal signature (r, s)

1: **procedure** RETRIEVE(r)
2:     find z such that $(g^q)^z = r^q \pmod{p}$ ▷ i.e., $z = \log_{g^q} r^q$
3:     $c = z \pmod{m}$
4:     **return** c
5: **end procedure**

E-voting schemes which make use of *randomness* are potentially vulnerable to kleptographic attack. For example, Helios [46] uses ElGamal encryption as the encryption method which is a randomized algorithm. A randomized algorithm takes a stream of random bits in addition to the input (e.g., vote) to produce an output. Thus, each encryption of the same vote will look distinct which helps to achieve voter privacy in elections.

Kleptographic attack works by constructing a subliminal channel in the random bits used in encryptions. The presence of a subliminal channel does not change the protocol nor can it be detected without reverse engineering the software. This makes a subliminal channel an attractive choice for leaking confidential information to a third party.

The attack was initially motivated by the question whether there exists a signature scheme with a broadband covert channel without revealing the sender's private key. This was shown to be true using ElGamal signature as an example [57]. Algorithms 2 and 3 show how an attacker can embed a secret message and retrieve it, respectively. Note that step 2 in Algorithm 3 is computable because the group order is smooth (e.g., let B be the smoothness bound, that is for a prime $p = qm + 1$, B is the largest prime in m, it is computable in time $O(\sqrt{B})$ using Pohlig–Hellman [435] and Pollard's rho [463]).

A typical high level structure of ElGamal signature can be viewed as a tuple (r, s) where s is the signature on a message and r is the randomness used in creating s. The similar structure is used for ElGamal encryption and hence the attack is immediately applicable. The authors further show how to convert their covert broadcast channel into narrowcast by pre-sharing secrets among the communicating parties.

It was later shown that such a channel also exists in DSA-like schemes [585]. Gogolewski et al. [257] demonstrated the kleptographic attacks against a number of e-voting schemes [349, 143, 418, 151]. Kleptographic attack poses a real threat to e-voting schemes using randomness as it is hard to detect. It should be noted however that kleptographic attack is tailored to exposing secrets. Thus, provided that the publicized data remain unmodifiable (e.g., encrypted ballots stored on append-only PBB), the integrity of the election result may still be retained.

Gogolewski et al. [257] suggest a potential approach to solving this problem by pre-generating all the randomness and use these as random-tapes. Then, zero knowledge proofs can be used to show that the generated ballots indeed used the randomness from the random-tapes. However, the authors note that zero knowledge proof itself makes use of randomness which again can be a source for a kleptographic channel therefore this does not completely solve the problem.

9.3.3 Pfitzmann's Attack

Pfitzmann's attack [460] can be adopted to compromise the sender privacy in a homomorphic mix-net with RPC. Suppose the first mix is corrupted. The attacker targets an input ciphertext c sent by a sender S to the first mix. The attacker then chooses a random δ and, while keeping c, replaces another output of the first mix with $c^* = c^\delta$. Finally, the attacker searches for a pair of plaintexts m and m^* output by the last mix such that $m^* = m^\delta$. This indicates to the attacker that with all but negligible probability, m and m^*, respectively, correspond to c and c^*. This leads to the conclusion that m was sent by S, thus breaking sender privacy for S. RPC will detect this attack with a probability of $\frac{1}{2}$ since only half of the input-output relations for the first mix are challenged.

Pftitzmann's attack can be generalized to compromise the privacy of s senders while keeping the probability of detection at $\frac{1}{2}$ [342]. Now the attacker targets ciphertexts $c_1, ..., c_s$ and chooses $\delta_1, ..., \delta_s$. Then, the first mix replaces one of its outputs with $c^* = \prod_{i=1}^{s} c_i^{\delta_i}$. By observing the outputs of the last mix, the attacker can identify $s + 1$ messages $m_1, ..., m_s, m^*$, respectively, resulting from $s + 1$ ciphertexts $c_1, ..., c_s, c^*$ if $m^* = \prod_{i=1}^{s} m_i^{\delta_i}$ satisfies. If so, the attacker concludes that c_i is an encryption of m_i for every i, breaking sender privacy for s senders. The probability that the attack is discovered by RPC is still $\frac{1}{2}$ since only one of the outputs of the first mix is replaced.

9.3.4 Duplicate Ciphertext Attack

Duplicate ciphertext attack as its name suggests works by injecting multiple sets of duplicate ciphertexts into the mix-net [342]. Then, a special relation imposed among the ciphertexts enables the attacker to determine the corresponding plaintexts. The attack is applicable to the Chaumian mix-net with RPC. Together with the assumption that the attacker corrupts $s(s+1)/2$ senders and the first and last mixes, the attack works as follows:

1. The attacker targets the first s ciphertexts input to the first mix: c_i for $1 \leq i \leq s$.

2. The attacker obtains c_i' by decrypting the outer-most encryption layer of the s ciphertexts with the secret key of the first mix.

3. The attacker makes i independent encryptions of c_i' (i.e., 1 encryption for c_1', 2 encryptions for c_2', and so on) using the public key of the first server.

4. The previous step generates $1 + 2 + ... + s = s(s+1)/2$ ciphertexts and the attacker sends each of these to a corrupted sender to submit.

5. For an ith targeted ciphertext there are i duplicates. Thus, the attacker can identify the correspondence between the targeted ciphertexts and the input ciphertexts to the last mix based on the number of duplicates that exists in the input list of the last mix. Hence, the attacker breaks the privacy of the s targeted ciphertexts.

The attack works because there is no check for duplicates at every mix. Note that RPC only applies duplicate removal at the input of the first mix and this attack is able to bypass that. A simple remedy for this attack therefore is to mandate the check for duplicates at every mix. This attack can compromise the privacy of $\mathcal{O}(\sqrt{N})$ senders as $s + s(s+1)/2$ cannot be greater than the maximum number of senders N.

9.3.5 Breaking Privacy without Detection

This attack, proposed in [342], takes advantage of lack of permutation consistency checks in RPC to compromise the privacy of the votes. Here, the adversary needs to corrupt two input ciphertexts to the system and the first two mix servers. The attack works only for homomorphic mix-nets.

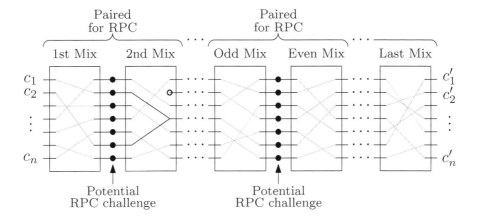

Figure 9.4: Breaking privacy without detection.

Assume the adversary can control the first two ciphertexts c_1 and c_2. We describe how the attack works based on Figure 9.4. The adversary chooses c_1 and c_2 to be re-encryptions of the same ciphertext. The first mix shuffles honestly, but it keeps records of the positions of c_1 and c_2 in its output and the randomization factors used for those two. The second mix is now able to assign both of these input ciphertexts to one output ciphertext since all the randomization factors between the two are known. This enables the second mix to have one of its output locations (second location in Figure 9.4) free to be set as desired. The adversary sets this ciphertext similar to the generalized Pfitzmann's attack equal to a ciphertext calculated from a set of s targeted input ciphertexts. This way the attacker will be able to find the correspondence between the input and output ciphertexts for the s chosen input ciphertexts and hence break the privacy of the voters who cast the votes embedded in the targeted ciphertexts. The proposed countermeasure to this attack is to implement permutation consistency checks in RPC.

9.4 Coercion

If an e-voting system leaves evidence of how voters have voted (e.g., receipt with a pattern which can be used to deduce the vote cast with a high probability), the system becomes vulnerable to coercion attacks. The vulnerability may be inherent in the system due to design flaw or could have been introduced by external means (e.g., scratch-off cards). This section describes how such coercion attacks can influence the election outcome and how they can be mitigated.

9.4.1   Forged Ballot

In Punchscan and Prêt à Voter, a ballot splits into two halves. While combined halves allow humans to read the vote, each half does not reveal the vote and acts as a receipt which voters can take home. Therefore, Punchscan and Prêt à Voter both require that voters destroy the halves of their ballots. If a voter secretly brings a forged ballot to the polling station, then he can destroy the forged ballot instead of the actual ballot after his vote [341]. This allows the voter to retain the complete proof of his vote leaving the system vulnerable to coercion attacks. A possible solution to this problem is to force the election officials to check the IDs of the two halves. Then, the voter has a risk of getting caught if he is unable to guess in advance the ID of the ballot that he will be given at the polling station.

9.4.2   Vote against a Candidate

Another attack that works against Punchscan causes votes to be randomly distributed among the candidates [341]. Suppose the attacker wants Jake who is a strong candidate to lose the election in Figure 9.1. The attacker will offer: (1) $10 for any front sheet receipt showing "D: Jake" with the first hole marked; (2) $5 for any back receipt marked for "D." If there are n number of vote sellers, each of them will return the front sheet receipt showing "D: Jake" with the first hole (or any single fixed hole would work too) marked if he gets such a ballot. This randomizes the votes away from Jake assuming the letters "A-D" have an even chance of occurring at each hole because "D" will appear on the first hole with a probability of $\frac{1}{4}$ only.[2] Returning a back receipt marked for "D" then indicates that the voter did not vote for Jake since he would have been better off with marking the first hole if he indeed had a ballot showing "D: Jake." More concretely, let $\mathcal{E}_1$ be the event that a voter gets a ballot with "D: Jake" and $\mathcal{E}_2$ be the event that "D" appears in the first hole. Then, this will result in about $\frac{1}{n^2}$ (since $\Pr(\mathcal{E}_1) \approx \frac{1}{n}$ and $\Pr(\mathcal{E}_2) \approx \frac{1}{n}$) of voters voting for Jake. Now, the remaining $\frac{n^2-1}{n^2}$ votes will be distributed evenly among $(n-1)$ candidates giving each candidate $\frac{n^2-1}{n^2}/(n-1) = \frac{n+1}{n^2}$ votes.

9.4.3   Scratch-Off Card Attack

The key idea behind this attack is that *possession of one receipt and knowledge of the other (destroyed) sheet is sufficient to determine the voter's selection* [341]. It is possible to force non-interactive (i.e., does not require vote buyer-seller interaction) challenge and response at the time of voting by using scratch-off cards.

---

[2]Indeed, if Jake were to be a weak candidate (e.g., supported by less than 25% of the voters) then this attack will have the opposite effect. However, in such a case Jake would not be a favorable target to an adversary.

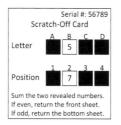
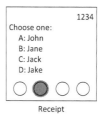

Figure 9.5: An example of scratch-off card attack.

Suppose voters who have pledged to vote for Jane are given scratch-off cards with two rows of pads. As shown in Figure 9.5, the first row has a pad for each letter that can be associated with Jane and the second row has a pad for each possible position. If a voter honestly scratches the two pads, then he would scratch the pad below the letter B for Jane and the pad below position 2 as the letter B appears on the second hole, which will reveal 5 and 7, respectively. The *challenge* to the voter is the sum of these two numbers and the voter's *response* is to choose which sheet (either front or back) as the receipt. If the sum is even, then the voter should return the front sheet, otherwise the back sheet.

A suggested countermeasure is to force the voter to choose a receipt sheet before seeing the ballot [341]. Then, the voter has the risk of being caught as he cannot foretell whether the sum will be even or odd, putting the attacker at an advantage. The attacker's power can be weakened if the voter is allowed to spoil his vote, thus allowing him to recast his vote until he obtains a ballot which satisfies the scratch-off card.

9.4.4   Spoiling Ballots

This attack extends the scratch-off card attack by requiring the voters to commit the serial numbers which appear on their ballots in addition to forcing the voters to commit to their choices. As shown in Figure 9.6, the scratch-off card now has an additional row of pads. After the voters commit their choices, each voter must compute the sum of the three numbers and if the sum is congruent to $1 \pmod{10}$, he must spoil the ballot. The strength of this attack is that the voter no longer has to depend on the commitment he makes prior to seeing his ballot. He can return any sheet (front or back) as long as the condition to spoil the ballot does not hold although it may have lower probability of catching the voter's deception. For example, assuming the sum of three numbers is evenly distributed the deception by voters will be caught with a probability of $\frac{1}{10}$.

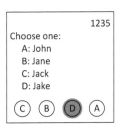

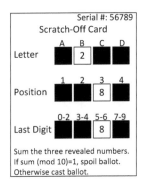

Figure 9.6: Punchscan: Spoiling ballot.

9.4.5 Pay-per-Mark and Pay-for-Receipt

The following two attacks show how the presence of patterns in receipts can leave the system open to coercion attacks. These attacks work because the machine randomly marks opscan bubbles which satisfy voters' choices. If voters are given the full control of how to mark opscan bubbles, then the attack can be mitigated.

Pay-per-Mark. Recall that in ThreeBallot, a voter marks exactly two opscan bubbles for the candidate he votes for and exactly one for the candidates he does not wish to vote for. Suppose a vote buyer offers some cash reward per mark for a particular political party. Then, a voter who does not vote for the party will end up with a receipt with $\frac{n}{3}$ marks for the party on average where n is the total number of questions. A voter who votes for the party on the other hand will end up with a receipt with $\frac{2n}{3}$ marks on average.

Pay-for-Receipt. This attack requires that a voter gives his receipt to the attacker after he has voted. The attacker then checks the receipt to see whether it matches one of the expected ballots. Suppose a voter is directed to vote for John but not for Jane as shown in the ThreeBallot in Figure 9.7. If the voter votes as directed by the attacker then the voter is guaranteed to obtain a valid receipt. If instead the voter votes for Jane then the voter will obtain a valid receipt with a probability of $\frac{1}{3}$. If the voter votes for neither of them, then he will obtain a valid receipt with a probability of $\frac{2}{3}$.

BALLOT	BALLOT	BALLOT
John ●	John ●	John ○
Jane ○	Jane ○	Jane ●
Jack ●	Jack ○	Jack ○
Jake ○	Jake ●	Jake ○
/*u2#35x9p%!	@4yu2m<8xw7=	i)82;tn&m,2z

Figure 9.7: Pay-for-Receipt

9.5 Conclusion

We have reviewed various attacks against E2E verifiable voting systems in the literature. The attacks exploited vulnerabilities both in the procedural aspect (e.g., not requiring users to check for duplicate receipts) and the technical aspect (e.g., exploiting homomorphic property of underlying encryption). This suggests that in order to build an E2E verifiable voting system, relying on procedural enforcement or technology alone may be insufficient — one must consider the both.

We have also witnessed the attacks which focus on coercion by offering incentives to corrupted voters and other attacks which are aimed at influencing the election result more aggressively by actively tampering votes in cooperation with the corrupted authority. Many of the attacks came with the remedies, which unfortunately however, do not always completely resolve the problems. Thus, providing the complete solutions for these known attacks will be the first step towards convincing the general public to accept the new voting technology as an improvement to the paper-based voting.

Acknowledgments

The authors would like to thank Syed Taha Ali, Feng Hao and Shahram Khazaei for reviewing an earlier version of this chapter. This work is supported by ERC Starting Grant No. 306994.

Chapter 10

The Scantegrity Voting System and Its Use in the Takoma Park Elections

Richard T. Carback
Draper Labs

David Chaum
Voting Systems Institute

Jeremy Clark
Concordia University

Aleksander Essex
Western University

Travis Mayberry
US Naval Academy

Stefan Popoveniuc
The George Washington University

Ronald L. Rivest
MIT

Emily Shen

MIT

Alan T. Sherman

UMBC

Poorvi L. Vora

The George Washington University

John Wittrock

AppNexus

Filip Zagórski

Wrocław University of Technology

CONTENTS

10.1   Introduction

The Scantegrity project began with a simple question: is it possible to design a voting system offering the strong security properties of cryptographic end-to-end (E2E) election verification with the intuitive look and feel of a paper optical-scan ballot? This chapter recounts a decade-long research effort toward answering this question, from the design of Scantegrity's precursor Punchscan, all the way to the first governmental election run by an E2E voting system.

The main focus of this chapter is on the Scantegrity II voting system (hereafter referred to as simply *Scantegrity*) and its use in the municipal elections of Takoma Park, Maryland, in 2009 and 2011. To our knowledge, the Takoma Park election of 2009 was the first use of an E2E-verifiable voting system in an in-person secret-ballot governmental election anywhere in the world, as well as being the first governmental election held in the United States to run on open-source software.

We also describe the *Punchscan* voting system and its use in the 2007 election of the University of Ottawa Graduate Students Association/Association Étudiant(e)s Diplômé(e)s (GSAÉD), which, to our knowledge, is the first time an E2E voting system was used in a binding election.[1] Additionally, this chapter describes the remote voting system *Remotegrity* and accessible Scantegrity variant *Audiotegrity*, and their use in the 2011 Takoma Park election. We also briefly recount a number of smaller, non-binding elections run during the course of this project.[2]

---

[1] A binding election is one whose outcome is binding on a constituency, though it need not be a political election. It could be, e.g., a primary, party, union, stockholder or student government election. Whereas a non-binding election is effectively an opinion poll.

[2] These elections are documented on `punchscan.org` and `scantegrity.org`.

10.1.1 Key Properties

End-to-End Verifiable

Loosely speaking, a cryptographically end-to-end verifiable (E2E) voting system is designed to provide the following security properties:

(a) A voter has the means to check that her ballot was included unmodified in the set of cast ballots, and receives evidence that convinces her if it is not.

(b) Anyone has the means to check that the set of cast ballots were counted correctly, and receives convincing evidence if they were not.

(c) The preceding checks are performed in a way that upholds the secrecy of every voter's ballot.

Additionally, Scantegrity provides an additional security property:

(d) If a voter's ballot was recorded incorrectly, she can prove this fact to others without revealing her vote. Similarly, if her vote was recorded correctly, but the voter makes a spurious claim, the election officials can prove this fact to others.

We refer to this last property as *dispute resolution*. This particular property is important in an E2E setting because it allows the electorate as a whole to attribute fault to the actual at-fault party: the elections officials or the voter. It is also special in the sense that not all E2E systems provide it.

Most of the assumptions made by the Scantegrity voting system and its variants are standard to E2E voting systems: a threshold of election trustees is required to be honest for privacy, cryptographic primitives used are assumed secure and an append-only, public bulletin board with authenticated write-access is assumed to exist. In addition, Scantegrity's privacy and dispute resolution properties require that symbols printed in invisible ink or beneath scratch-off are not visible.

Practical Aspects

From a practical perspective, a major design goal of Scantegrity is to provide voters with an intuitive interface. We focused on paper optical-scan ballots for a variety of reasons: it is a predominant mode of ballot casting, and is legally mandated in a number of jurisdictions, such as the United States; it provides a degree of recoverability in the event of an electronic failure; used in a precinct-scan configuration, it does not require electricity at the polling place. Scantegrity itself offers a number of advantages over other optical-scan based E2E systems:

(a) The verifiability elements are constructed as an overlay on the optical scan ballot, making them compatible with pre-existing layouts.

(b) Participation in the verification process is opt-in; voters can (in principle) ignore the Scantegrity-related components and vote as they would otherwise on a plain paper optical-scan ballot.

10.1.2 Outline

In this chapter, we trace through a couple of iterations of deploying, redesigning, and redeploying an E2E system. We begin by describing the Punchscan system and its use in an election in 2007. We then describe the lessons learned from that election, which led to the development of Scantegrity and an early variant, *Scantegrity I*. The former improved on the dispute resolution properties of the latter, and was used by Takoma Park in 2009 and 2011. We recount some of the modifications we made to the original Scantegrity proposal for the election, and how feedback from a preliminary mock election further refined the system, as well as the results of the election itself.

Scantegrity was deployed again in the municipal election of Takoma Park in 2011. For this election, we developed and deployed the remote voting system Remotegrity and the accessibility-enhanced Scantegrity variant Audiotegrity. Both of these systems were tested in an open test before the 2011 election, and we document the feedback and how it contributed to changes to the systems finally fielded in 2011.

We end this chapter with a description of the results of usability tests that demonstrate high levels of confidence in Scantegrity, and high levels of support for the verification receipt, even when voters indicated they did not understand the underlying cryptographic mechanisms. While E2E system usability is an understudied subject, the data we collected after the Takoma Park mock and municipal elections currently represents the largest dataset of voter and poll worker reactions from an E2E system.

Following the two Takoma Park elections, there has been considerable activity towards the development of E2E voting systems intended for larger government elections. The state of Victoria, Australia, used vVote for elections in November 2014 (see Chapter 12, this volume), and Travis County, Texas, is considering STAR-Vote as a potential future voting system (see Chapter 14, this volume). There has also been an interest in the use of remote E2E systems.

10.1.3 Organization of This Chapter

This chapter is organized as follows. Section 10.2 describes the Punchscan voting system and the first binding E2E election. Section 10.3 describes the Scantegrity voting system and Section 10.4 its use in the Takoma Park election of 2009. Section 10.5 describes the Remotegrity system, and Section 10.6 describes the Audiotegrity variant of Scantegrity. Section 10.7 describes the use of all three systems in the Takoma Park election of 2011. Section 10.8 summarizes the results of our voter and poll worker surveys in both Takoma Park elections. Section 10.10 concludes.

10.2   The Punchscan Voting System

The Punchscan voting system represented an early attempt to combine E2E verifiability with a paper optical-scan ballot. In this section we describe the Punchscan voting system and our experience fielding it in the 2007 election of the University of Ottawa Graduate Students Association/Association Étudiant(e)s Diplômé(e)s (GSAÉD). We discuss our experiences in this election, and how they went on to motivate the design of the Scantegrity.

10.2.1   Voter Experience

A Punchscan ballot consists of two sheets of paper (see Figure 10.1). The upper sheet consists of a serial number and list of candidate choices. Beside each candidate is an independent and pseudorandomly assigned letter/symbol. Toward the bottom of the ballot, a number of holes are punched in the paper. A second sheet of paper contains letters that are printed such that they show through the holes on the top page. These letters are the same as those found on the top page, but in an independent pseudorandom order.

A bingo dauber is employed as the marking implement, and the voter selects one of the punched holes to daub. The holes are sized such that daubing will distribute ink to both pages. The voter marks her ballot as follows: she (1) chooses her preferred candidate, (2) observes the letter beside her preferred candidate, (3) marks the punched hole showing the corresponding letter, (4) selects one of the sheets (either top or bottom) and shreds it (e.g., using a paper shredder supplied in the voting booth). At this point she exits the polling booth and provides the remaining sheet to the polling staff to be scanned. The voter retains a copy of this sheet as a receipt. Notice that the receipt alone is not sufficient to recover voting intent:

1. If the voter retains the top sheet it shows which letters are associated with which candidates, and the punched hole the voter marked, but not the underlying letter,

2. If the voter retains the bottom sheet it shows which letter was marked, but not which candidate that letter corresponds to.

After the election, receipts are posted on an election website. If a voter's receipt is absent from the website or is incorrectly displayed, she is able to file a complaint, and can provide her receipt as evidence. The receipts are tallied in a verifiable manner, as described in [465].

10.2.2   Election Set-Up

Prior to the election, election administrators determine a set of officials and a minimum threshold of officials required to conduct the election tasks. In order to protect

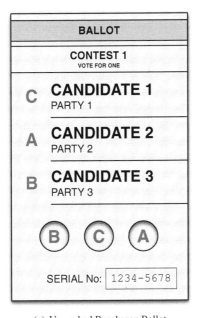

(a) Unmarked Punchscan Ballot

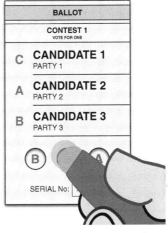

(c) Marking the ballot (with bingo dauber)

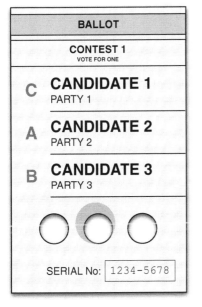

(b) Marked top sheet

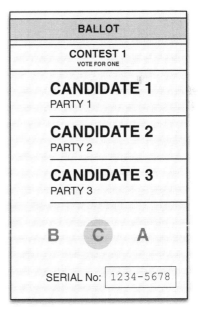

(d) Marked bottom sheet

Figure 10.1: Punchscan ballot depicting a vote for Candidate 1. The voter retains either the marked top or bottom sheet as a receipt (the other is shredded).

ballot secrecy it is required that any valid subset of election officials contains *at least one* honest party. If all *t* officials collude, i.e., not even one of them is honest, they can link ballot receipts to the candidate voted for (the integrity of the tally is, however, invariant even with full collusion).

The officials first generate and threshold-share a secret value. This value seeds a pseudorandom number generator (PRNG) from which all the election data can be deterministically produced and reproduced. For each task, the election officials convene and use a trusted computing platform with no persistent memory to generate the seed from their secret shares and to generate the election data. The computer is trusted for privacy: that is, it is trusted to not leak election secrets. Aside from the public output produced during each session, no state is saved in any form. Every session regenerates the state from the shared secret. If the computer performs incorrect computations so as to change the election outcome, this will be detected during an election audit. That is, our trust model does not require that the computer be trusted for election integrity.

In the first meeting, a threshold number of officials input their shares along with the number of candidates, and the number of ballots to generate. Since voters may spoil ballots as part of the audit process, more ballots than voters need to be produced (by some predetermined factor). Cryptographic commitments to the verifiable shuffle and decryption are generated and publicly posted. All intermediate values, internal state and secret values are purged upon powering down the system.

In the second meeting, a threshold number of officials regenerate the shared secret seed which is then used to regenerate the election data. A cut-and-choose proof that the commitments are correctly formed is provided on the bulletin board. The challenges are generated randomly and non-interactively using stock market data and random extraction techniques described by Clark and Essex [156, 157].

10.2.3 Ballot Printing and Voter Privacy

As a pre-election audit, half the (unvoted) ballots, and associated proof-of-shuffle are publicly disclosed. The remaining ballots are printed using a private XML file containing the necessary information. In that sense the entity responsible for ballot printing must be trusted to maintain voter privacy. This *trusted printer problem* is a difficulty with any paper-based E2E election system. Toward addressing the trusted printer problem, Essex et al. [217, 220] proposed a system for *oblivious printing* by combining visual cryptography with invisible ink, and developed a number of secure multiparty protocols for generating and distributing ballot images under encryption. In subsequent work Essex et al. [221, 219] show how oblivious printing could be integrated into a Scantegrity-like voting system with fully distributed trust.

10.2.4 The First Binding E2E Election

In 2007 the University of Ottawa Graduate Students Association/Association Étudiant(e)s Diplômé(e)s (GSAÉD) deployed Punchscan to elect executive positions within the association and to conduct a referendum on a bylaw.[3] The election consisted of five polling stations and was held over two days. There were approximately 1000 eligible voters, of which 154 voted. The election consisted of six contests, each of which had two candidates/options. While Punchscan offers support for a distributed election authority, GSAÉD opted to have the chief returning officer (CRO) act as the sole trustee.

To prevent the loss of votes in the event of a power outage, hard drive failure or other unpredictable event, we made a paper record of information on the scanned receipt. While this record does not contain information sufficient for a hand count, it could be used with the underlying cryptographic information to reconstruct the tally.

Ballot Printing. Under the supervision of the CRO we printed batches of ballots using five inkjet printers. We experienced difficulty with the top sheets jamming due to the holes. Printing took about 1 hour and upon completion, the ballots were placed into boxes, sealed and signed along the seal by the CRO.

Vote Casting. Voters were given their double-layer paper ballot on a clipboard, and the clipboard contained a plunger lock that fastened the ballot to the clipboard through aligned holes in one corner (such that removing the ballot would tear it). Voters filled out the ballot in a private voting booth. Upon returning from the booth, the voter was instructed to choose either the top or bottom sheet for shredding. This sheet was ripped out of the locked assembly and shredded in view of the poll workers. The assembly with the remaining sheet still locked in was returned to the poll worker. The poll worker unlocked the clipboard and removed the sheet. The sheet was scanned with an optical scanner and the software's interpretations of the marks were displayed on a computer screen. The voter approved the marks and cast the ballot electronically. The sheet was then placed in the printer, which printed symbols on the sheet according to the scanning software's interpretation of the marks (e.g., overlaying an X on unmarked positions and an O on marked positions), printed a digital signature of the marks, and printed an additional record of the marks in the corner of the ballot. The corner was cut off by the poll worker and retained as a paper backup, while the sheet itself was given to the voter as a receipt.

Vote Tallying. After the polling stations were closed, the Punchscan team, the CRO, and a scrutineer gathered to generate the results. The ballot receipts were uploaded to the Punchscan server and posted. The CRO then entered her passphrase to deterministically regenerate the election data that was committed to prior to the election. Once generated, the tally was computed using this information and the receipt infor-

---

[3] Authors Clark and Essex were members of GSAÉD at the time.

mation. The tally and a commitment to its proper computation were also posted on the Punchscan server. Through a web-interface, voters could check that their receipts match the posted information. Our server logs showed that the image files of 83 of the ballots were requested.

As with the pre-election audit, the following day, the tallying procedure was audited using stock market data and a cut-and-choose protocol. This audit is also based on an open specification and is software independent.

10.2.5   Lessons Learned

Over the course of the election the poll workers experienced some technical failures: at times the polling place software became unresponsive, the printers jammed or lost wireless connectivity needed to maintain the electronic pollbook. In these instances, the poll workers manually recorded the serial number and mark positions made by the voters. These were electronically input later on, and any transcription errors would be subject to detection through the online receipt verification check. The ink from bingo daubers also caused problems in the scanners if they were fed in before they were completely dry.

We confirmed that the security mechanisms of Punchscan were not well understood by the voters. In particular, voters did not understand the security benefits of the indirection of Punchscan. Many voters indicated that the voting process was burdensome. We observed voters who appeared to not realize that they were to receive a receipt and wanted to leave immediately after marking their ballots. Furthermore, when it was explained to them that they would receive a receipt, some voters refused it. Further, approximately 85% of the voters chose to shred the top sheet and keep the bottom page as their receipt, indicating that the choice of which sheet is kept is not uniformly random.

Toward Scantegrity. Overwhelmingly the biggest criticism of Punchscan centered around the ballot marking procedure. The voter is required to follow a strategy of indirection: mark the hole containing the letter appearing beside the desired candidate. While at some level this is not more complicated than many administrative tasks the average person encounters in day-to-day life, what eventually became clear to us from this exercise was that we needed to improve the usability of the ballot.

Following the GSAÉD election we formulated a new research question: is it possible to design an E2E-enabled ballot that (1) still allows the voter to simply produce a privacy-preserving receipt of their choice while (2) not requiring any special ballot marking strategy beyond that of conventional optical-scan. This question ultimately led us to develop Scantegrity.

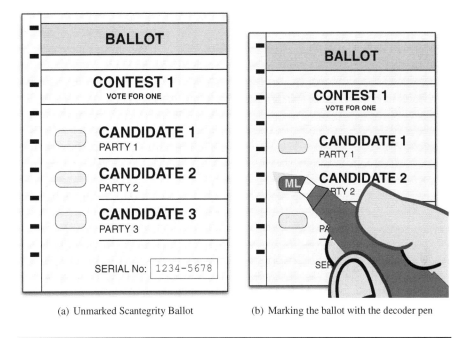

(a) Unmarked Scantegrity Ballot   (b) Marking the ballot with the decoder pen

Figure 10.2: Scantegrity ballot depicting a vote for Candidate 2. The voter would retain confirmation code `ML` and serial number as a receipt.

10.3   The Scantegrity II Voting System

In this section, we consider Scantegrity, the successor to Punchscan, which is quite different in many regards from Punchscan and other E2E systems. Relative to Punchscan, Scantegrity is designed to improve upon practically, which makes itself apparent in a few ways. First, it uses a single-sheet paper ballot and a simple-to-perform obfuscation technique: code substitution. Next, Scantegrity is not designed as a replacement to existing voting systems but rather an augmentation. It can be added as a cryptographic layer to any optical scan system without interfering with the two existing methods for counting optical scan ballots: electronically from the scanned images and manually with the paper ballots. Finally, it has essentially no impact on the voter who does not wish to participate in the verification process.

10.3.1   Ballot Features

The Scantegrity ballot is shown in Figure 10.2. It consists of two parts: a ballot and a detachable receipt. Like an optical scan ballot, the main body of a Scantegrity ballot contains, for each contest, a list of valid selections printed in a canonical order predetermined by polling place procedures (e.g., alphabetical, rotated across precincts, etc.). Next to each selection is a markable region, oval in shape, called a bubble. In the bubbles associated with each selection, a short alphanumeric code is printed in invisible ink that is not human readable until marked by the voter. We refer to these codes as confirmation codes. In an election with n ballots and m candidates, there are $m \cdot n$ confirmation codes. Each confirmation code is pseudorandomly drawn from a suitable space: in the example, a confirmation code consists of two alphanumeric characters. The voter records their confirmation code(s) on the receipt and will use this information to conduct an important component of the audit.

Each Scantegrity ballot ensemble also contains three serial numbers. These are used to identify the ballot and to provide the voter with the ability to report the failure of aspects of the audit under certain scenarios. The ballot contains one of these numbers in the form of a machine-readable barcode that is not easily read or memorized by a human. Since many optical scanners use marksense technology, which only records whether a region is marked or unmarked, a suitable encoding of this number must be used (e.g., a data matrix for marksense scanners). For the ith ballot, we refer to this serial number as α_i. The receipt portion contains two additional serial numbers, β_i and γ_i, which are printed in invisible ink and are individually detachable from the receipt.

10.3.2 The Scantegrity Back-End

The Scantegrity backend performs the verifiable tally of the voted confirmation codes. Intuitively, it treats each bubble as a distinct unit. Three values associated with each bubble—its confirmation code, whether it was voted or not, and its candidate—are stored across separate tables:

■ Table **P** is not published but is used to print the ballots and to generate the other tables. It contains a row for each ballot and a column for the ballot ID, the confirmation codes for each candidate and two receipt IDs.

■ Table **Q** is the same as **P** except the confirmation codes in each row have been independently shuffled. From **Q** alone, it cannot be established which candidate was voted for if a certain confirmation code is revealed. Each cell in **Q** is individually committed to.

■ Table **S** contains a placeholder for each bubble in the election, ordered under each candidate. At the end of the election, a bubble may be marked, unmarked or selected for a print audit.

■ Table **R** contains a row for every bubble in the election in random order. Each row in **R** connects to a unique confirmation code in **Q** and to a unique placeholder in **S**. Each **Q**-pointer and **S**-pointer is individually committed to.

All codes, serials, permutations, and commitment random factors are generated pseudorandomly. The combination of confirmation code and receipt ID is unique across the election. See Figure 10.3 for an example. Note that while this description is simpler and appears somewhat different from that in [145], the two descriptions are equivalent.

Ballot ID (α)	Adams	Burr	Jefferson	Pinckney	Receipt ID (β)	Receipt ID (γ)
01	EN	PL	JG	VE	8860	3478
02	IV	QU	SA	WC	3813	2448
03	AY	EY	XW	SI	2381	3492
04	BV	SY	ZK	HJ	1337	4592
05	SH	SR	OF	XJ	3492	3472

(a) **P**

α	κ_0	κ_1	κ_2	κ_3	β	γ
01	JG	EN	PL	VE	8860	3478
02	QU	IV	WC	SA	3813	2448
03	AY	EY	SI	XW	2381	3492
04	HJ	ZK	SY	BV	1337	4592
05	SR	XJ	SH	OF	3492	3472

(b) **Q**

	Adams	Burr	Jefferson	Pinckney
0				
1				
2				
3				
4				

(c) **S**

Q-Pointer	Marks	S-Pointer
$(05, \kappa_1)$		$(2, \text{Pinckney})$
$(03, \kappa_3)$		$(4, \text{Jefferson})$
$(02, \kappa_1)$		$(4, \text{Adams})$
$(01, \kappa_3)$		$(3, \text{Pinckney})$
$(01, \kappa_2)$		$(4, \text{Burr})$
$(05, \kappa_3)$		$(3, \text{Jefferson})$
$(04, \kappa_2)$		$(3, \text{Burr})$
$(04, \kappa_0)$		$(4, \text{Pinckney})$
$(03, \kappa_0)$		$(0, \text{Adams})$
$(04, \kappa_3)$		$(3, \text{Adams})$
$(02, \kappa_3)$		$(1, \text{Jefferson})$
$(03, \kappa_1)$		$(2, \text{Burr})$
$(05, \kappa_0)$		$(1, \text{Burr})$
$(01, \kappa_1)$		$(2, \text{Adams})$
$(02, \kappa_2)$		$(0, \text{Pinckney})$
$(04, \kappa_1)$		$(0, \text{Jefferson})$
$(03, \kappa_2)$		$(1, \text{Pinckney})$
$(05, \kappa_2)$		$(1, \text{Adams})$
$(01, \kappa_0)$		$(2, \text{Jefferson})$
$(02, \kappa_0)$		$(0, \text{Burr})$

(d) **R**

Figure 10.3: Tables P, Q, R and S as generated by the election officials before election day. Table P is kept private. The publicly published versions of tables Q, R and S contain commitments to the information shown above. For example, a vote for Jefferson on ballot 04 would reveal the confirmation code ZK. The corresponding row of table R points to position $(04, \kappa_1)$ in table Q (containing ZK) and the position $(0, \text{Jefferson})$ in table S, which will be marked if the voter selects Jefferson on ballot 04.

10.3.3 Election Day

The voter marks the ballot as she would any optical scan ballot, using a pen with special ink provided in the booth. As the ink in the pen reacts with the ink printed on the ballot, the background of the bubble immediately turns dark, leaving a confirmation code visible in the foreground (see Figure 10.2). The relative darkness of any marked bubbles to unmarked ones will allow an optical scanner, employing dark mark logic, to register the bubble as marked. The foreground of the marked bubble is human-readable and a voter interested in participating in the election audit may record the code on the receipt portion of the ballot. Uninterested voters may disregard the codes.

When the voter has satisfactorily marked her ballot, it is returned to the poll worker. The poll worker places the main body of the ballot into the scanner, which records the ballot serial number and the marked choices. After a successful scan, the two serial numbers on the receipt, β and γ, are developed by the poll worker and the voter may leave with the receipt. It is expected that public interest groups will make available the possibility of creating a copy of receipts to alleviate the need for concerned but time-constrained voters to personally participate in auditing the election.

Voters may also opt to check that the ballots are printed correctly. In order to do this, the voter requests a ballot to be print audited, reveals all the confirmation codes on the ballot, and chooses one of the receipt serial numbers, β or γ, to retain with the codes. The election authority can keep the other code as a record of both: the ballot that was audited and the code which was kept by the voter.

If the voter makes an error in marking her ballot or wishes to register a protest vote through spoiling their ballot, the ballot is returned to the poll worker. Without seeing the contents of the ballot, the poll worker detaches the right side of the receipt, γ, from the ballot. The main body and left receipt, α and β, are shredded in view of the voter. The right receipt is retained by the poll worker and used in balancing the number of ballots issued with the number of ballots tallied, print audited or spoiled.

10.3.4 *Posting and Tallying*

After the close of polls, the election officials publish a list of all the voters who voted and the tally given by the underlying optical scan system. The electronic ballot images from the scanner, the list of audited ballots and list of spoiled ballots are entered into the trusted workstation by the trustees. Tables **Q**, **R** and **S** are regenerated and used to translate the votes into the corresponding confirmation codes (these codes were revealed by the voter but not recorded by the scanner, which only records voted bubbles). The commitments in table **Q** to the confirmation codes and serial numbers that were revealed during the election are opened; this demonstrates that the confirmation code was indeed one of those on the ballot. Corresponding marks are posted in **R** and **S** (exemplified in Figure 10.4). Anyone can now compute the tally from **S**. This tally is checked against the one reported by the optical scanners or manual recount. Opening such commitments preserves ballot secrecy: for each confirmation code opened in **Q**, it cannot be determined which candidate that code corresponds to.

Once the results are posted, a voter who has made a receipt of her confirmation codes can go to the election website and look up her voted ballot by either receipt serial number. She checks that, in the row of **Q** corresponding to her ballot, all and only her confirmation codes appear. Anyone can check that the opened commitments match the confirmation codes on the election website. If any of the confirmation codes from the voter's receipt do not appear posted in **Q**, the voter should file a dispute.

Q-Pointer	Marks	S-Pointer
$(03, \kappa_3)$	A	(4, Jefferson)
	✓	
$(03, \kappa_0)$	A	(0, Adams)
	✓	
$(03, \kappa_1)$	A	(2, Burr)
	✓	
$(03, \kappa_2)$	A	(1, Pinckney)
	✓	

(a) R

α	κ_0	κ_1	κ_2	κ_3	β	γ
01			PL		8860	3478
02				SA	3813	2448
03	AY	EY	SI	XW		3492
04		ZK			1337	4592
05			SH		3492	3472

(b) Q

	Adams	Burr	Jefferson	Pinckney
0	A		✓	
1	✓		✓	A
2		A		
3				
4	✓		A	

(c) S

Figure 10.4: Tables Q, R and S as published after the close of the election. For each revealed confirmation code in table Q, the row corresponding to that code in table R and the element corresponding to that code in table S have been flagged. For each row of table R, either the commitment to the Q-pointer or the commitment to the S-pointer has been opened and published. Note that the revealed confirmation codes in table Q (other than those for ballot 03, which is a ballot chosen for a print audit), the rows flagged in table R and the flags in table S are in one-to-one correspondence.

10.3.5 Auditing the Results

For those ballots that were chosen for a print audit, election officials open the commitments to all the information associated with the ballot (i.e., the confirmation codes in **Q** and the **Q**- and **S**-pointers in **R**) *except* the value of β or γ that the voter did not take with her after the audit. Anyone with access to the printed ballot with exposed confirmation codes can check that the revealed values are consistent with the committed and printed values.

To verify that the marks were added correctly to tables **R** and **S**, the election officials will be challenged to open either the **Q**-pointer or the **S**-pointer in table **R**; i.e., the first or third column (exemplified in Figure 10.5). If a mark was recorded for the wrong candidate, then either (i) the mark is not consistent with the corresponding mark in **R**, (ii) the marks in **R** and **S** match but the status of the corresponding confirmation code (revealed or unrevealed) in **Q** is inconsistent or (iii) the tables are consistent but the revealed code in **Q** does not match the receipt. The receipt check

Q-Pointer	Marks	S-Pointer	Q-Pointer	Marks	S-Pointer
$(05, \kappa_1)$					$(2, \text{Pinckney})$
$(03, \kappa_3)$	A	$(4, \text{Jefferson})$	$(03, \kappa_3)$	A	$(4, \text{Jefferson})$
$(02, \kappa_1)$					$(4, \text{Adams})$
$(01, \kappa_3)$					$(3, \text{Pinckney})$
$(01, \kappa_2)$	✓			✓	$(4, \text{Burr})$
$(05, \kappa_3)$					$(3, \text{Jefferson})$
$(04, \kappa_2)$					$(3, \text{Burr})$
$(04, \kappa_0)$					$(4, \text{Pinckney})$
$(03, \kappa_0)$	A	$(0, \text{Adams})$	$(03, \kappa_0)$	A	$(0, \text{Adams})$
$(04, \kappa_3)$					$(3, \text{Adams})$
$(02, \kappa_3)$	✓			✓	$(1, \text{Jefferson})$
$(03, \kappa_1)$	A	$(2, \text{Burr})$	$(03, \kappa_1)$	A	$(2, \text{Burr})$
$(05, \kappa_0)$					$(1, \text{Burr})$
$(01, \kappa_1)$					$(2, \text{Adams})$
$(02, \kappa_2)$					$(0, \text{Pinckney})$
$(04, \kappa_1)$	✓			✓	$(0, \text{Jefferson})$
$(03, \kappa_2)$	A	$(1, \text{Pinckney})$	$(03, \kappa_2)$	A	$(1, \text{Pinckney})$
$(05, \kappa_2)$	✓			✓	$(1, \text{Adams})$
$(01, \kappa_0)$					$(2, \text{Jefferson})$
$(02, \kappa_0)$					$(0, \text{Burr})$
(a) Heads			(b) Tails		

Figure 10.5: Table R as published after the close of the post-election. According to a coin-flip, either the entire correspondence between Q and R is revealed, or the entire correspondence between R and S. In an actual election, many independently permuted copies of R will be generated and can be audited in this fashion.

probabilistically detects (iii), while the present challenge will detect either (i) or (ii). The challenge is generated with a publicly verifiable random number [157].

Any interested party can check that the commitments are correct: that each revealed **Q**-pointer in table **R** either connects a revealed code in table **Q** to a marked element in table **R** or connects a hidden code to an unmarked element, and that each revealed **S**-pointer in table **R** either connects a marked element in table **R** to a marked element in table **S** or connects an unmarked element to an unmarked element. Essentially, the audit checks that marks are mapped unchanged from table **Q** through table **R** to table **S**.

Currently the soundness of each check is only $\frac{1}{2}$. However by generating and using k independent **R** tables throughout the election, each with a unique pseudorandom mapping from **Q** to **S**, the soundness increases to $1 - \frac{1}{2^k}$ through auditing each independently.

10.3.6 Dispute Resolution

Dispute resolution—between a voter or observer claiming the evidence points to election fraud, and election officials and/or the voting system claiming otherwise—

is one of the key features of Scantegrity. If a dispute cannot be resolved, then a default position must be taken, which will generally either allow a corrupt election authority to get away with fraud or allow a malicious party to prompt a reelection (or at least cast doubt on the result) by filing spurious disputes.

To file a dispute, the voter must be on the registration list as being eligible to vote or as having cast a ballot, and only one dispute may be filed per voter. (If the voter wishes to allow a third party organization to check her receipt, she might sign over the right to her dispute.) Disputes are filed within a period of time. After the period closes, the trustees open Q completely, revealing all the confirmation codes and receipt numbers on all ballots (except spoiled ballots), and use this information to address the disputes.

The most likely dispute is that a voter's confirmation code does not match the one appearing on the website. In this case, the voter provides the ballot ID and a claim of what the correct confirmation code(s) should be. Disputes of this type could be (i) the result of the voter making a transcription error, (ii) a mischievous voter attempting to call into question the legitimacy of the election, (iii) an error by the scanner or (iv) evidence of fraudulent behavior.

With a transcription error, the claimant's code is likely close to the revealed code. Once Q is opened, the voter can verify that none of the other codes that appeared on the ballot match her code exactly. Since voters do not see the confirmation codes of the unrevealed candidates on the ballot when they file, the probability that a code that a voter claims to have received is actually one of the other codes committed to for her ballot is very small if the voter made a transcription error or is merely guessing. The election officials eliminate from consideration any disputes for which none of the opened codes match the claimed code. We consider the remaining disputes to be plausible discrepancies.

Plausible discrepancies could still be the product of cases (i) or (ii); however, the probability is small (and can be made smaller by increasing the length of the confirmation codes). They are more likely (iii) or (iv). The election officials should set up a statistical trigger, based on various election parameters, such that when a given number of plausible discrepancies is reached, the ballots are rescanned to rule out (iii) and then the election is considered to have strong evidence of fraud.[4]

Another type of dispute that a voter may have is that her ballot is improperly designated as voted, print audited or spoiled. A voter who cast her ballot knows both receipt serial numbers $\{\beta_i, \gamma_i\}$. If a ballot is represented as print audited or spoiled, either one or neither of these codes will be open in Q. Similarly the voter retains evidence that a ballot was print audited by knowing all the confirmation codes on the ballot. If a ballot is represented as voted or spoiled, either one or none of the confirmation codes will be open in Q. If the voter's claimed receipt code(s) or full

---

[4]If this were to happen, it would hopefully trigger litigation (as well as a criminal investigation). In Canada, any elector or candidate may apply for a contested election proceeding and if heard, the judge reserves the power to invalidate the election result (upon appeal to the Supreme Court of Canada).

set of confirmation codes match their committed values, the dispute is designated as a plausible discrepancy.

10.4   The 2009 Takoma Park Election

On November 3, 2009, we deployed Scantegrity in its first binding election. This marked the first time an E2E system was used for in-person voting in a governmental election.[5] The election was run by the city of Takoma Park, Maryland, USA to elect city councilors and a mayor.

The system deployed in the Takoma Park elections is very similar to that described in Section 10.3, except that the cryptographic backend is a modified version of the Punchscan backend [465]. This backend was written in Java 1.5 using the BouncyCastle cryptography library.[6] We opted to utilize the Punchscan backend because it was already implemented and tested in previous elections as described in Section 10.2.

10.4.1   Requirements

Voters voted for one of six wards, at a single polling station. The mayor race was common to all wards and the councillor race was specific to the ward. Voters were issued one of six ballot styles based on their ward. The city has approximately 17,000 residents and 10,934 voters were registered. The turnout was 1,728 voters.

Ballot. The ballot was required to be worded in both English and Spanish. A bilingual ballot was used instead of different sets of ballots for each language. For each ward, the ballot consisted of two contests. The joint mayor contest contained two named candidates and a write-in candidate. The ward councilor races varied between one and two named candidates and a write-in candidate for each. The Scantegrity system treats the option "write-in candidate" as a single candidate, with a corresponding confirmation code. Hence all write-in votes are grouped together in the initial tally. If the number of write-ins could be relevant to determining the winner (either of the election or the round in a multi-round scoring protocol), the actual candidates voted for are then examined. In this election, write-ins were not a factor in any of the contests.

Instant Runoff Voting (IRV). Takoma Park has used IRV in municipal city elections since 2006. IRV is a ranked-choice system where each voter assigns each candidate a rank according to her preference. Prior to using Scantegrity, Takoma Park's IRV bal-

---

[5]The Rijnland Internet Election System (RIES) deployed in the Netherlands in 2004 and 2006 [272, 314, 264] took a significant step toward the first real-world E2E election.

[6]http://www.bouncycastle.org

lots were arranged with a matrix for each contest, with candidates on the rows and preference order on the columns. We adapted this style and put confirmation codes in each cell.

Absentee Ballots. Takoma Park offers the option of casting a ballot by mail. It was too expensive to include a decoder pen with each absentee ballot, so we used Scantegrity ballots without the confirmation codes. This means absentee voters cannot verify the codes (although they can verify that their ballot was received, because a confirmation code would be posted on the website). 70 absentee ballots were cast.

Voter Registration. Registration was handled by the city of Takoma Park. Scantegrity did offer the option of provisional ballots, which would allow voters to vote but the ballots would be escrowed until the voter's eligibility was confirmed. If confirmed, the ballots are added to the tally (this itself may break the secrecy of the ballot if the set of approved ballots is small, however this is a known issue in any election system providing provisional voting).

Disclosed Source Code. All the software used in the election—for ballot authoring, printing, scanning and tally—was published well in advance of the election as commented, buildable source code, which may be a first in its own right. Moreover, commercial off-the-shelf scanners were adapted to receive ballots in privacy sleeves from voters, making the overall system relatively inexpensive.

Election Authority. It was decided that the election would have four trustees (the chair, vice chair and a member of the Board of Elections, and the city clerk) and any two were required to regenerate the election data.

10.4.2 Mock Election

In April 2009, we held a mock election to test and demonstrate feasibility of the Scantegrity system, as well as train the poll workers. The mock election was held during Takoma Park's annual Arbor Day celebration at the city hall. Volunteer voters, recruited from people attending the celebrations, voted on a mock ballot with questions relating to trees. Turnout was 95 voters. The election system used in the mock election was very close to the system described in Section 10.3. We uncovered several minor issues and one main issue: the average time-to-vote was unacceptably high at 8 minutes.

We identified two main impedances to voter flow. The first was filling out the ballot. The mock ballot had two IRV questions with four and five candidates, and two single-response questions. A fully marked ballot would consist of marking 11 bubbles and recording 11 confirmation codes. We reasoned that the election ballot would be quicker to fill out because the ballot was much shorter (at most 6 bubbles/codes) and voters would likely have a preconceived notion of who to vote for.

The second impedance was the scanning station. During the mock election, voters would have their ballots scanned, be shown a representation on a monitor screen of what was scanned, and manually click to accept the interpretation and electronically cast the ballot. Then the receipt would be detached and the receipt codes would be revealed by the poll worker. Finally, the ballot was deposited in the ballot box. In the real election, we eliminated the verification step. Ballots were deposited into a slot, which resulted in the ballot being scanned and deposited into the ballot box. We removed the receipt from the ballot itself and instead provided separate verification cards. Voters who wanted to verify their ballot could copy the ballot serial number and confirmation codes onto the card.[7] Additionally, we eliminated the receipt codes from the ballots. Instead of using them to provide dispute resolution, we relied on the assumption that the poll book would correctly maintain the number of cast, audited and spoiled ballots, as well as the original copies of any spoiled or audited ballots (for audited ballots, a photocopier was provided, and the voter and an election official signed the copies). Finally, we decided to use a second scanning station in the actual election. Through these modifications, the average time-to-vote in the actual election was reduced to under 3 minutes.

In the mock election, we used locks to prevent chain voting like we did in the Punchscan election however these were unpopular with the poll workers and eliminated. Last, we changed the confirmation codes from two letters (from a reduced set eliminating easily confused characters) to three decimal digits. In retrospect, we should have eliminated 0 and 8 from the set of digits.

10.4.3   The Election

The preparation of the election followed essentially the same steps as the Punchscan election, so we eliminate some details. The ballots were designed to closely resemble the ballots used in Takoma Park's previous municipal election. Each ballot contained some instructions for marking an IRV ballot and for marking and verifying a Scantegrity ballot.

Ballot Printing. We had the invisible ink, developing ink and decoder pens specially manufactured for our use. The ballots were printed on off-the-shelf CMYK inkjet printers. We kept the black ink in the CMYK printer cartridge and replaced the other 3 inks with the invisible ink, a dummy ink, and a fluorescent ink. The invisible ink is actually visible as a light yellow but turns dark gray when developed with the pen (see Figure 10.6). The dummy ink is the same yellow color but does not develop. We print it around the invisible ink to make the inks indistinguishable. Finally, we print

---

[7]This also makes it difficult to determine if a voter intends to verify their ballot or not. Recall in the Punchscan election, we had the difficulty of uninterested voters refusing their ballot-specific receipts or discarding them at the polling place.

Figure 10.6: Photograph of our invisible ink implementation showing marked oval, confirmation code and decoder pen (foreground).

a random scatter pattern over each bubble with the fluorescent ink to further obfuscate attempts at reading the undeveloped codes. Over many months, the invisible and dummy inks oxidize differently and the codes can become visible but this is not an issue if the ballots are printed shortly before the election.

Voter Education. Articles in the city newspaper before the election introduced the verification mechanisms provided by Scantegrity and explained how voters could check their confirmation codes online. This also appeared on the city's election website. During the election, a local radio station covered the election and the use of Scantegrity, prompting many curious voters to attend the polling place. Finally, the ballot itself contained some instruction. Voter education was identified as a main area to improve in future elections.

Election Day Set-Up. The scanning station was the only Scantegrity-specific equipment. It consisted of a netbook, located in a lockbox, to control the scanner. Upon booting, the scanning software ran automatically off an attested, read-only SD card in the netbook. The election data was written onto USB sticks. Scantegrity is software-independent and auditors will detect if the scanner misbehaves in a way that affects the tally, however we strove to prevent this to avoid having to rerun aspects of the election. The scanner itself was embedded into the form factor of the scanning station. An uninterruptible power supply was also used in the case of a power failure.[8]

Voting. Polls were open from 7 am to 8 pm. Ballots in privacy sleeves were issued to registered voters. Voters would mark their ballots in the voting booth, optionally fill out a verification card, and be directed to the scanning station. At the scanner, voters simply dropped the privacy sleeve (with the ballot in it) into a slot. A rivet

---

[8]If use of the scanner was somehow lost, the Scantegrity election could still proceed without a problem. Ballots would be collected and scanned centrally later. The confirmation codes provide a cryptographic chain-of-custody over the ballots.

in the privacy sleeve prevented it from reaching the scanner, while the ballot itself slipped out and into the scanner's intake. The bottom of the scanner was inside the ballot "box" (which was actually a large bin on wheels making the scanner at waist height). The privacy sleeve could be removed from the slot and returned to the ballot issuing station by the poll workers.

Print Audits. During the day, an independent auditor from Electronic Privacy Information Center (EPIC), Lillie Coney, would visit the polling place at an unannounced time and select a random set of ballots. All the codes on these ballots were revealed and the auditor retained a copy of them for conducting a print audit against the cryptographic information.

Tallying. The trustees used the Scantegrity software to generate the tally at 10 pm. The Chair of the Board of Elections (and one of the trustees) announced the results to those present at the polling place at the time (including candidates, their representatives, voters, etc.); this was also televised live by the local TV station. Confirmation codes and the election day tally were posted on the Scantegrity website. The tally was updated the next day with votes from approved provisional ballots, which did not change the outcome.

Hand Count and Certification. Members of the Scantegrity team and the trustees conducted a hand count of the ballots and certified the results. The hand count and the Scantegrity count differed slightly because officials were able to better determine voter intent during the hand count. For example, in the mayoral race, the scanner count determined that 646 votes were cast for candidate Schlegel, 972 for Williams, 15 for various write-in candidates, and 90 were not cast. The certified hand count totals were 664 votes for Schlegel, 1000 for Williams and 17 for write-in candidates. Thus 48 of a total of 1681 votes in this race would not have been counted by a scanner count alone. The discrepancy was caused by voters marking ballots outside of the designated marking areas. Such marks, while not read by the scanner by definition, are considered valid votes by Takoma Park law. Similarly, 8 of a total of 447 votes for Ward 1 council member, 8 of 251 for Ward 2, 16 of 431 for Ward 3, 10 of 210 for Ward 4, 2 of 81 for Ward 5 and 11 of 199 for Ward 6 were added to scanner vote totals after hand counting.

Dispute Resolution. On November 6, the dispute resolution period ended. Scantegrity received a single complaint by a voter who had trouble deciphering a digit in the code and noted it as "0," while the Scantegrity website presented it as "8." The opening of commitments demonstrated that the digit was, indeed, "8." The voter requested that codes be printed more clearly in the future. He also stated that if he were not a trusting individual, he would believe that he had proof that his vote was altered.

Post-Election Audit. On November 6, trustees used the Scantegrity software to conduct the cut-and-choose audit (with a public challenge computed from stock market data). By November 9, two independent auditors retained by Takoma Park[9] had verified the results with auditing scripts they independently wrote and published based on the Scantegrity protocol. The auditor from EPIC later verified that all the ballots she collected were printed correctly.

Receipt Check. The Scantegrity website recorded 81 unique ballot ID verifications, of which about 66 (almost 4% of the total votes) were performed before the dispute resolution deadline. We also were informed that at least a few voters had checked their codes through one of the independent auditor's websites, both of which had made the confirmation codes available. The number of voters who checked their ballots, while not large, was sufficient to have detected (with high probability) any errors or fraud large enough to have changed the election outcome.[10]

10.5   The Remotegrity Voting System

Following the 2009 election, Takoma Park requested the use of Scantegrity in the 2011 election. Note that absentee voters were not able to participate in election verification in 2009, and voters unable to independently mark paper ballots had done so with assistance. For the 2011 election, we provided functionality for remote E2E voting, as well as for E2E voting with an audio interface. In this section we describe Remotegrity, the remote E2E system used in 2011. In Section 10.6 we describe the audio voting system Audiotegrity.

Consider the remote voting problem for an election that uses Scantegrity in the polling place. One could mail Scantegrity ballots with the special pens to absentee voters, who could mark the ballots and mail them back, later checking online for their Scantegrity codes as an in-person voter would. Using this approach, however, the absentee voter would not have the in-person voter's ability to prove cheating. If an absentee voter claimed her vote was absent from the bulletin board, and cited a valid combination of code and ballot serial number, an independent observer would not know whether she was lying and had not mailed in her ballot, or the election administrator had dropped her vote. Thus, while we may use Scantegrity ballots for remote voting, we need additional steps that allow an independent observer to determine if a voter's vote had been correctly included in the tally or not. As it would be very cumbersome to conduct a voting protocol with multiple steps over postal mail,

---

[9]Ben Adida and Filip Zagórski—both cryptographic voting researchers; while Zagórski later drove the design, development and use of Remotegrity in the 2011 election, he was not part of the Scantegrity team for the 2009 election.

[10]We omit detailed calculations, noting these calculations become quite complex due to the use of IRV. Also, these calculations make certain assumptions (e.g., independence) that may or may not hold in practice.

we propose a system that is hybrid: the ballot and authentication credentials are delivered over postal mail and all consequent protocol steps are carried out over the Internet.

Remotegrity is a hybrid mail/internet extension to the Scantegrity in-person voting system, enabling secure, electronic return of vote-by-mail ballots [586]. It provides voters with the ability to detect unauthorized modifications to their cast ballots made by either malicious client software, or a corrupt election authority—two threats not studied in combination prior to Remotegrity. Not only can the voter detect such changes, they can prove it to a third party without giving up ballot secrecy; that is, Remotegrity possesses the dispute resolution property. Nothing about Remotegrity requires that it be used with Scantegrity. It can be used with any coded vote system.

10.5.1 Voter Experience

The remote voter receives an envelope containing a Scantegrity ballot and an authentication card. The authentication card bears a visible serial number and acknowledgment code. It also bears several authentication codes and one lock-in code under scratch-off surfaces, such as those used for lottery tickets (see Figure 10.7). At the appropriate step in the protocol, the voter scratches off the required surface to determine the code underneath and enters it online. In the event that the code is used in the protocol but the corresponding surface is not scratched off, one may assume that someone impersonating the voter entered the code.

In order to vote, the voter uses a computer to access the election website and enters her ballot serial number and authentication card serial number to ensure that neither has been used. If either has already been used, she is in possession of unused cards and hence this provides evidence of a problem.

If neither card has been used, she marks the Scantegrity ballot, revealing a confirmation code. She also scratches off an authentication code and enters both codes with both serial numbers at the election website.

A few hours later she accesses the election website again and checks if the election authority has responded with the acknowledgment code, indicating that the election authority has received a valid confirmation code for her ballot. The probability that the computer she voted from unilaterally changed her vote, by correctly guessing another valid confirmation code on her ballot, is small. Hence the election authority has, with high probability, received the correct confirmation code.

The voter now scratches off her lock-in code and enters it in, signalling to all observers, voters and the election authority that she is satisfied that her confirmation code is correctly recorded. The voting system signs the final record, indicating that the lock-in code is valid.

At the end of the election, all valid locked-in confirmation codes entered using Remotegrity are combined with all Scantegrity codes voted in person and the election outcome is tallied as with Scantegrity.

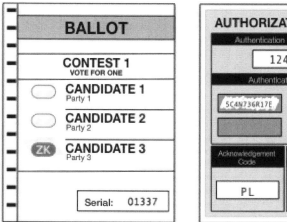 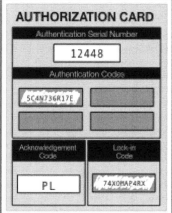

Figure 10.7: A Remotegrity package showing the ballot with one marked position and serial number (left) and the authentication card with one authentication code and the lock-in code scratched off. This figure represents a hypothetical final state of the cards after the voter has completed all steps [586].

10.5.2 Security Properties

In this section we provide informal arguments for the security properties of Remotegrity.

Privacy. The voter does not directly enter her vote into the computer she votes from. Hence her vote is private. As with mail-in voting, however, it is possible for a coercer to be present while she votes and to ensure she votes as instructed. Additionally, it is possible for the voter to produce her marked ballot and confirmation code to prove how she voted to a coercer who is not present while she votes.

Integrity: Impersonation. If someone has already voted using the voter's ballot or authentication card, she detects it before she votes on the Scantegrity ballot or scratches-off any fields on the authentication card. She can hence produce the unused cards to prove that there is a problem. There should be mechanisms in place to allow her to vote, with another ballot and/or credentials if necessary.

Integrity: Malware on Voting Terminal—Vote Deletion or Unilateral Replacement. If the computer the voter votes from does not convey her confirmation number at all, the election authority will not respond with the acknowledgment code. If the computer attempts to unilaterally change her vote, it would need to change the code to another one valid for her ballot. The probability of this is small. Hence, in this case too, the election authority will not receive a valid confirmation code for the ballot, and will not respond with the acknowledgment code. In both cases, the probability that the computer will be able to correctly guess the acknowledgment code and show it to the voter is very small. Hence, with high probability, the voter will know that her confirmation code has not been recorded and she can try to vote again from another computer.

If the voter does not see the acknowledgment code after several attempts, she has experienced a distributed denial of service attack either from all the computers she has attempted to vote from, or the election authority. In either case, she has in her possession her authentication card with an unscratched lock-in field. This proves that she has not completed the voting protocol and should be allowed to vote through another means, such as in person.

Integrity: Vote Replacement. If the election authority colludes with the terminal, it knows valid confirmation codes from the voter's ballot and can post an incorrect but valid confirmation code on the website, and return the valid acknowledgment code. The voter can respond by neither scratching off nor entering her lock-in code. If the election authority does lock in the incorrect confirmation code by entering her lock-in code, the voter can show her unscratched lock-in field to prove cheating and should be allowed to vote through another means, such as in person. If the election authority does not lock in the incorrect confirmation code, the voter cannot prove cheating, but her unscratched lock in field does prove that she has not completed the protocol and she should be allowed to vote through another means.

Summary. Thus, in the worst case, the voter experiences (a) a denial of service: either from all the computers she has access to or from the election authority which either does not respond with the acknowledgment code or enters an incorrect confirmation code or (b) an attempt to change her vote by the entry of an incorrect but valid confirmation code that is locked in. In (a) the voter can demonstrate that she has not completed the voting process and can vote in person, but cannot prove a denial of service. In (b) the voter can prove cheating and the changed vote is deleted and she is allowed to vote.

10.6 Audiotegrity

Audiotegrity is a voting system which enables voters with differing physical abilities to cast votes in the Scantegrity model, while preserving Scantegrity's dispute resolution and verification properties. It does so through the use of an audio interface provided by a computer, which reads options to a voter and records their votes without the intervention of a voting official. Votes are recorded on a ballot that is designed to look exactly like a marked Scantegrity ballot. Audiotegrity provides nearly all of the dispute resolution and verification properties of Scantegrity while making it possible for a large subset of the population who previously could not independently cast a secret ballot to do so. Audiotegrity was used along with Scantegrity in the 2011 election in Takoma Park.

10.6.1 The Voting Process with Audiotegrity

Audiotegrity can be thought of as an extension to Scantegrity, and it shares many properties with the original system. Audiotegrity consists of a computer with monitor and large-format keypad with Braille stickers on the keys, a set of headphones with an attached microphone, and a printer. The interface supports multiple race formats, inclusive of all formats with which Scantegrity has been used.

The Audiotegrity voting station is slightly separated from the main voting floor by a privacy screen, as selections are displayed on a screen in large print for the benefit of those with visual disabilities who can read large type. Selections are made on a large format keypad in a process similar to that used with a touch-tone telephone menu. The printer is next to the voting station, and will later print both ballot and confirmation card, which are of different sizes so as to be distinguishable by touch. "Speak-in" votes are also allowed by the system, facilitated by a microphone on the voting headset. The voter can speak their desired vote for any race in the election, and their voice will be interpreted later by election officials, as with handwritten votes. These votes are identifiable by a pseudorandom number which is printed on the ballot in the space for the write-in candidate.

The system produces a marked Scantegrity ballot and confirmation card face down. The voter can choose whether to cast or audit their ballot before looking at the printed ballot (this prevents a coercion attack described in [341]). The voter can then check that the machine has marked their ballot correctly, and either cast it, or make a copy to take home for later ballot audit steps (which are identical to those for Scantegrity).

10.6.2 Dispute Resolution Properties

The main attack vector that Audiotegrity needs to protect against is sabotage of the computer (in this case used as an assistive marking system), partially described in [116]. A voter who does not examine the printed ballot (such as, for example, a voter with visual disabilities) cannot know if the computer has marked their ballot correctly. If, however, all voters use the same voting system, a computer marking the ballot incorrectly will be caught by voters who do examine the ballot. The voter cannot prove that the system marked the ballot incorrectly, so voters are allowed to spoil a ballot and vote again as many times as they desire. The number of spoiled ballots for a given voter is not made public, which eliminates a particular coercion threat. If we assume that the system cannot know if a voter will examine her ballot or not, and if all voters who do examine it have correctly printed ballots, then those who do not check can be confident that, with high probability, their ballots were printed correctly.

Once the ballot is printed, and if it is printed correctly, it now functions as a Scantegrity ballot, with all of the Scantegrity dispute resolution and verification properties. If the system provides incorrect confirmation numbers for the voter's choice of candidate, it is caught during a Scantegrity print audit. The voter can prove that the system provided the wrong confirmation numbers because their vote is marked on the ballot, and Scantegrity has previously committed to the confirmation numbers for the serial number of that ballot. If the voting system posts a confirmation number to the bulletin board which is incorrect, this can also be resolved with Scantegrity.

Audiotegrity's dispute resolution properties are superior to those of fully electronic systems, and are only slightly weaker than those of Scantegrity. In particular, the Scantegrity voting system allows for a voter to be able to prove all attempts to cheat. Using Audiotegrity, a voter is able to prove all attempts to cheat except when the assisstive device prints an incorrect vote.

10.7 Takoma Park Election, 2011

In late 2010 we were approached by the Takoma Park Board of Election regarding the possiblity of becoming involved in their upcoming municipal election of 2011. We provided demonstrations of prototypes of Remotegrity and Audiotegrity in a couple of election board meetings in the first half of 2011. The city of Takoma Park held an open test of Audiotegrity and Remotegrity on June 8, 2011, in the Takoma Park Community Center. The test was publicized in the local news media and election officials sent announcements to various special-interest listservs. The test was not restricted to Takoma Park residents, and all who were interested were allowed to test the system. About 25–30 individuals tested the system and 17 individuals filled out a survey. The purpose of the survey was not usability research, but to obtain feedback on the systems in an informal manner, and to make potential users of the systems aware that Takoma Park might choose to use them in the election. Because we collected the data informally and interacted considerably with participants while they were testing the system, and the number of participants was very small, we do not present the data from our surveys. To obtain a qualitative, independent, albeit brief, assessment of the test, the reader may refer to a blog article [348].

We presented the results of the surveys to the Board of Elections (BOE) (many of whom had participated in the test) in the June meeting. The BOE outlined a number of concerns, centered around the usability and security of Remotegrity (because of the protocol's use of the Internet, and the problems Washington, DC, had had with an Internet voting trial—see Chapter 7, this volume). In the July meeting, the Board members communicated to us that they had confidence in the technology, but they were concerned about the procedures, which appeared ad hoc, about potential security mishaps, and that the system had not been peer-reviewed. In this meeting, they communicated that they were leaning towards not using Remotegrity, but would go ahead with a mail-in Scantegrity ballot.

In the August Board meeting, we proposed (and they agreed) that the city provide voters with the option to use Remotegrity in addition to mailing back marked ballots. Only marked ballots would be counted, but voters using Remotegrity could test/audit the system, and, if they chose to lock in their vote, could communicate that the system was accurately recording their vote. Instructions for voting and auditing would be sent in separate envelopes in the same package, with appropriate marking, so as not to overwhelm voters not interested in the audit. Thus the system we finally used had some major differences with the protocol described in Section 10.5. Voters were not required to lock in (this means that, in practice, an election authority colluding with the voting terminal to change the vote could not be distinguished from the voter by a third party). Second, the Remotegrity system included ballots with visible codes (these ballots correspond to Scantegrity I [146]). This avoids the requirement of mailing invisible ink development pens. Third, voters needed to submit marked paper ballots by mail for votes to be counted; this eliminated any dependence on the Internet, but made it possible for the EA to ignore a mailed-in ballot. However, the Scantegrity codes of the votes were posted on the election website and voters could check if their votes made it in the count.

We made some changes to Audiotegrity as well, based on the criticisms and concerns of some participants: we provided variable speed and volume for the audio and obtained a professional recording for the real election. We also changed the instructions to make them more understandable. The Audiotegrity protocol used in Takoma Park was different from that described in Section 10.6 in a few aspects. No public declaration was required to cast or audit, and the ability to audit the ballot was not publicized widely. This was to simplify the process for the first use of the system. We chose to give audio confirmation codes to the voter before the printing began. Again, this was a consequence of the fact that we were not planning on many voter audits in this election and we wanted to provide voters with visual disability some of the information that sighted voters got. A better way to do this would be to provide digital media with confirmation codes on it.

Both systems were deployed on November 8, 2011.

The Remotegrity bulletin board contains 123 entries which correspond to 119 voters. Only 5 ballots were submitted online, and two of these were not counted as the corresponding paper ballots were not mailed in. While the number of voters who used the online system was small, full preparation and a complete implementation were required to deploy the system. Additionally, even voters who did not use the online system to enter or lock in their votes could check their confirmation codes online.

Audiotegrity was used to cast a few votes including by poll workers and auditors. Audits were made on the system by the election auditor, Neal McBurnett. This election marked one of the first times (if not the first) where the voting system design did not prevent a voter with visual disability from independently casting an E2E ballot in a secret ballot precinct-based public election.

We are not able to provide information on how Audiotegrity votes were audited. We intentionally do not keep information on Audiotegrity ballot IDs after the election, in order to reduce the ability to distinguish between Audiotegrity and Scantegrity ballots.

Votes from both systems were combined with the Scantegrity votes cast in person, and a combined verifiable Scantegrity tally with the details of a tally audit was provided.

At the election certification meeting, Audiotegrity was called out as a valuable contribution by the chair of the board of elections and a council member.

10.8   Usability Studies

We surveyed voters and election judges during the 2009 and 2011 Takoma Park Municipal elections. These survey studies [135, 134] provide insight into the election experience with Scantegrity. They are among a handful that study voters using E2E voting systems, and are unique in being conducted for a binding election. While binding elections constrain research methodologies, these observational studies survey real voters under actual conditions that yield observations of the true voter and election judge experiences.

In the first election, we hypothesized that voters would have increased confidence but otherwise have no significant effect over traditional optical scan systems due to the cryptographic protocol. In the second election, we expected voters to show increased comfort with Scantegrity.

As hypothesized, we did not find evidence that the cryptographic protocol negatively affected voter perception in either election. The majority of voter reactions to Scantegrity were positive and we saw no consistent strong demographic effects between the two elections. Negative reactions correlated highly with problems in the voting experience, which pointed to problems with implementation (voting process issues, trouble reading the confirmation numbers, difficulty with filling out the ballot for instant runoff, cumbersome receipt process, etc.).

In this section we briefly summarize related work, our methodology and the highlights of these results. Readers interested in deeper analysis of the data should refer to the data reports available online [135, 134].

10.8.1   Related Studies

Sherman et al. [526, 525] report on focus groups and a survey similar to ours conducted at a preparatory mock election. In the mock election, Scantegrity team members worked side-by-side with election officials to demonstrate capabilities of the system, and the surveys from voters during this election were positive. Carback et al. [133] focus primarily on the technical and administrative aspects of the deployment of Scantegrity at Takoma Park, including lessons learned and briefly touching on survey findings.

There are few user studies on E2E systems. Most studies are preliminary usability studies such as the student projects at UMBC (on Punchscan), MIT (on 3Ballot) [333], and the University of Surrey, England (on Prêt à Voter). These studies focus on user interface. We are not aware of other studies which focus on public acceptance, public reaction, and administrative challenges.

Acemyan et al. [40] attempted a comparative study of Scantegrity with Helios and Prêt à Voter and did not find fault with Scantegrity's verification mechanism, although they did point to problems with voter completion rates attributable to a poor optical scan implementation. Their system differs in critical ways to the one deployed in the municipal elections, requiring voters to scan the ballot and then separately drop it into a ballot box as well as providing mismatched voting instructions which likely confused subjects in their study. A detailed criticism of their study is provided by McBurnett et al. [386].

Using expert review, laboratory studies, and a field experiment with 1540 participants, Herrnson et al. [305] found that voting system interface and ballot styles had an impact on voter satisfaction, the need for help and voter's abilities to cast their ballots as intended. He also found that verification technologies typically had a negative impact on voter experience. Results of this experiment varied by voter demographics and voting experience.

Examining social issues, Newkirk [412] found that public opinion remained remarkably stable between 2004 and 2008. During that time, Direct recording electronic (DRE) systems were the top-rated systems for voter trust, followed closely by precinct count optical scan (pcos) systems. Voters rated vote-by-mail, central count optical scan and Internet voting less trustworthy.

Norris [420] describes a telephone survey of registered voters in Maryland in which voters provide strongly positive opinions about the usability and accuracy of touchscreen voting. Voters were also positive about the reliability, trustworthiness and count-accuracy of touchscreen machines, while admitting that the systems could be corrupted by malware.

10.8.2 Methodology

Our research protocols and questionnaires were approved by UMBC's Institutional Review Board, as required for experiments with human subjects. The study participants comprised election judges who administered the election and voters who voted in the election. Election judges operated the system, but select members of our research team filled vendor roles, working separately from the survey and observation teams.

Our survey team surveyed voters in the exit polling area. In the first election, every voter was asked to fill out a survey. In the second, every 3rd voter was asked to minimize the effect of selection bias. After the election, judges were handed a questionnaire to fill out and return by mail.

Observers were stationed in each polling room. For each observation they filled out a standard form to indicate how long the voter took to vote and any incidents (e.g., problems with scanner, asking for help, etc.). Observers and surveyors were separated and did not switch roles throughout the day.

In 2011, our team was allowed to observe election day events, but we were not permitted to serve as election judges nor to interfere with the elections process. Additionally, only two representatives were permitted in each of the two voting areas at once. Observers were treated separately, and interacted minimally with our team throughout the day. Similarly, our surveyors stayed outside the polling place and did not interact with voters outside of when they exited the polling place.

Two members of our team acted as technical support when needed, fulfilling the role that a vendor would during election day.[11] Before the election the technical support team was directed to set up the scanning stations under supervision by an election judge. After the election they were asked to disconnect the scanning stations and to collate the memory sticks for tabulation by the election night tabulation software. The technical support team members did not interact with participants in the survey.

10.8.3 Known Limitations

Outside of avoiding selection bias in the second election, both studies share the same limitations. Our data cannot be construed as fully representative, but should be considered informative and indicative of how E2E verifiable audit mechanisms will be received in other jurisdictions at the municipal level.

Takoma Park does not have a history of election fraud, "dirty politics," or similar concerns that would make its residents distrustful of the election process there. There was voter turnout even in uncontested wards, indicating a strong sense of civic duty in at least the subset of the population that showed up to vote. While the population of Takoma Park is very diverse, the exit survey data indicates that many of the people who came out to vote were highly educated and frequent computer users. Also, Takoma Park uses Instant Runoff Voting, which is not used in many jurisdictions in the United States.

The small number of questions on each ballot worked in the system's favor. Increasing the number of questions on the ballot would likely decrease impressions of

---

[11] In Maryland, technical support representatives from the election vendor are available to election judges at each polling site on election day.

usability, although this is, to varying degrees, the case for any system. It is unknown if a ballot as long as the typical Maryland state ballot could achieve this level of satisfaction from voters, and it would be difficult to change the Scantegrity system to support such a ballot.

Because these studies are observational, we are unable to address the question of the effects of the confirmation number receipts as well as we would have liked. Respondents to the questionnaire reported that the presence of a receipt increased their confidence in the results, but how many would have high confidence in the results if they had also used a system without a receipt? A comparative study which looks closely at this issue would be needed to address this question.

There were several miscellaneous technical problems throughout the voting day during both elections. A respondent who was the victim of, or witnessed, any of these issues was likely to have a negative response, and it is impossible to control for these types of issues in a real-world environment. Lastly, our survey sampled few voters with disabilities.

10.8.4   Voter Response

The primary feature of our surveys were Likert questions designed to capture voter satisfaction. Both surveys skewed toward positive voter satisfaction, although the 2009 survey had 2 low-response rate questions with poor wording. Results of selected comparable Likert questions are combined in Figure 10.8.

To understand if voter demographics affect voter experience we used ordinary least squares (OLS) regression of the combined dependent voter satisfaction variable against the demographics factors we collected. The cronbach's α of the satisfaction variable was .97 ($N = 142$) in 2009 and .84 ($N = 435$) in 2011.

The resulting dependent satisfaction variables had means of 5.69 (StdDev = 1.7, $N = 271$) and 5.84 (StdDev = 1.04, $N = 463$), respectively. Because the data was negatively skewed (-1.94 and -2.08) and had high kurtosis (5.92 and 8.9) we analyzed the cubes (x^3) of the values (skew = -.86 and -.44, kurtosis = 2.69 and 2.93).

The regression analysis did not agree on statistically significant effects between 2009 and 2011. Table 10.1 shows the statistically significant effects and their magnitudes each year.[12] Refer to the individual publications for the full tables and additional discussion.

10.8.5   Observational Results

In the 2011 Takoma Park election our passive observers tracked 314 voters as they carried out the voting process. One voter did not complete the voting process. Twenty-six voters appeared confused, but did not ask for help.[13]

---

[12] Please note the regression models are slightly different between 2009 and 2011.

[13] We did not have the resources in the 2009 election to collect this observational data.

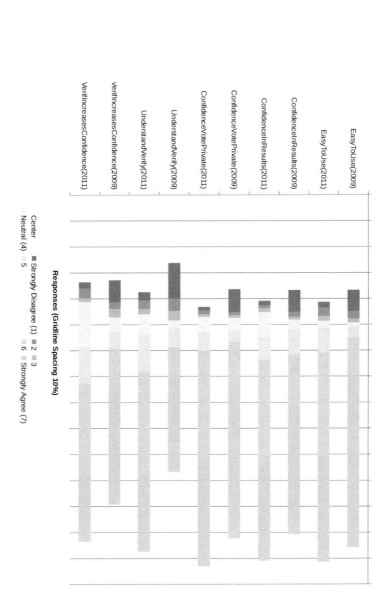

Figure 10.8: Voters were more positive towards Scantegrity in 2011 compared to 2009. This figure is a horizontal bar chart showing distributions around the neutral position of the Likert questions. The width of each bar represents the total number of respondents for that question, and each bar is divided into subsections whose width represents the respondents in that category.

Table 10.1: Significant factors affecting voter satisfaction with Scantegrity in 2009 and 2011. Entries are OLS coefficients, standard errors, t-values and probabilities. All entries are one-tailed. No factors showed as significant between both 2009 and 2011, and 2011 data featured significant factors dominated by voter experiences (e.g., problems voting, voting in 2009, etc.).

-	2009				2011			
Category	Est	StdErr	t	P> $|t|$	Est	StdErr	t	P> $|t|$
Female	33.53	15.76	2.13	.02	11.81	8.06	1.47	.14
Income	-6.89	5.10	-1.35	.09	4.27	4.30	0.99	.32
T. Screen	-47.52	25.96	-1.83	.03	-1.78	14.52	-0.12	.90
P. Card	48.32	18.43	2.62	.01	8.31	8.19	1.014	.31
No-Eng.	-39.99	33.04	-1.21	0.11	86.60	40.64	2.13	.03
Eyesight	NA	NA	NA	NA	-33.58	18.70	-1.80	.07
Op. Scan	NA	NA	NA	NA	21.23	8.64	2.46	.02
Und. Ver.	NA	NA	NA	NA	49.99	10.43	4.79	.00
Vote 09	NA	NA	NA	NA	-19.98	9.74	-2.05	.04
Ver. 09	NA	NA	NA	NA	23.41	13.74	1.70	.09
New Vot.	NA	NA	NA	NA	77.84	41.01	1.90	.06
Prob. Vot.	NA	NA	NA	NA	-68.97	14.02	-4.92	.00

Voting times ranged from 43 seconds to 19 minutes and 36 seconds (the second longest time was 9 minutes and 54 seconds, the skew was highly positive at 2.81 for timing data), with a mean of 3 minutes 27 seconds, a median of 3 minutes, and a standard deviation of 1 minute 56 seconds. Most of the time was spent marking the ballot. The average time to vote was slightly longer than during the November 2009 election, when the median voting time was 2 minutes 30 seconds. None of the voters performed a print audit.

The number of times a voter spoiled a ballot, asked for help or a judge intervened during the voting process is shown in Table 10.2. Note that, per process, the judge is supposed to intervene to explain the voting process. This happened in most but not all cases.

The verification website recorded 81 unique IP addresses in 2009 and 119 in 2011. Most addresses submitted multiple requests to the submission form, but our system did not record if different ballot confirmation numbers were checked between submissions. If each address only checked 1 ballot, this represents verification rates of 4.7% (1723 voters) and 6.1% (1951 voters), respectively.

Table 10.2: Frequency of different events observed in the polling place by four different observers (O1 to O4) across 314 observations at random time intervals during the election.

Event	O1	O2	O3	O4
Voter spoiled a ballot	4	0	0	0
Voter asked for assistance	30	8	1	0
Judge intervened with voter	156	136	16	2

10.8.6 Election Judge Response

In both elections, the judges identified as their main challenge the need to provide more instructions to voters, in comparison with non-Scantegrity elections. Specifically, voters needed more instructions on how to fill out the ballot and how to use the verification card. Many voters also needed instructions on how to mark the ballot using IRV.

Overall, election judges felt that the revised and increased educational efforts concerning verification paid off. By contrast, many voters in 2009 did not understand that they could verify their votes and that, to do so, they needed to write down the exposed code numbers. The judges noted that some people who voted in 2009 already knew how to verify from that election. The process worked more smoothly than in 2009.

Election judge recommendations focused on improving instructional materials, separating voter types to better serve their needs (e.g., special attention for voters with disabilities), and improvements to the voting equipment (e.g., automated receipts, improved scanners, etc.). Judges appeared to see the value of the verification option and agreed with voters that it improved confidence in election results.

10.8.7 Study Findings

Scantegrity is not too complex to use and administer in the context of the elections at Takoma Park. The verification system's existence does not appear to impact voter experience negatively. Voter's experience showed high levels of confidence in Scantegrity. While it is non-trivial to address if certain voting populations will be disadvantaged by this system, we do not have evidence that there are disadvantaged groups over a traditional optical scan system.

Voters appeared to accept the system even if they did not understand it. This study shows high levels of support for the verification receipt, even when voters indicated they did not understand the cryptographic mechanisms behind it. While voters appreciated the extra security as the presence of the verification increased their confidence, this contrasts with the number of people who reported intent to verify and more so with the 3–5% of voters who actually checked their ballot data. It appears that, even though voters appreciated the technology, they did not necessarily care to use it.

In both elections, there were no negative comments about the verification option itself. We also had enough verifiers to ensure election security. Many voters expressed deep gratitude for the system and judges reported less confusion about verification in the second election.

The general process of creating a receipt remains a problem absent automation, and it does impact voter experience. This election experience inspired us to develop an automatic receipt printer [527]. Judges and observers noted increased time to vote due to the verification mechanism. Many voters expressed frustration with a number of practical problems (codes being hard to read, not writing down all necessary information, problems understanding how to use the pen, etc.), but note, however, that the overwhelming majority of surveyed respondents agreed that the system was easy to use. Most of these issues can be fixed or streamlined with better equipment. For example, individuals with vision disabilities reported problems despite our efforts to improve code legibility.

We paid attention to the ostensibly small details. Instructions for IRV and how to record a receipt were checked carefully for clarity. Takoma Park used an official staff member to create translations of these instructions. The scanner recognized ballots being placed into the system with a beep. More work can still be done to modify the voting process and technology to improve the voter and election judge experiences.

We believe that the development of practical, easy-to-use and well-accepted E2E verifiable audit technology will greatly improve election results assurance, voter confidence, election transparency, and independent election verifiability, and provide solutions to chain of custody issues. Takoma Park's diverse voting population offers insight into the acceptance of such systems.

The findings of this study increase the knowledge and understanding of how to successfully implement E2E verifiable post-election audit technology and allows other jurisdictions to use our report and project data to implement similar systems in their districts. It indicates that voters are positive about the system, that they value the security provided, that the extra work of optionally noting down confirmation codes does not significantly impact the voter experience negatively and that they accept it in spite of not understanding its inner workings completely. Election judge responses indicated that the system was not too hard to administer, and we did not observe significant relationships between demographic data and responses while voters were highly satisfied with the system.

Most voters and judges were positive about the system, and very few people expressed any doubts about the post-election audit mechanism. Even voters who did not plan to verify had few negative reactions, and most either did not trust computers at all or did not understand the audit system.

For future work, a clear measure of the confidence increase (or decrease) the receipt provides is necessary. A comparison study between Scantegrity and a commercial optical scanning system is an obvious next step. Another area to explore is whether enough voters will use the receipts.

More work needs to be done for voter education. Despite significant efforts, educating voters before the election turns out to be a significant challenge, and we believe that most voters learned about it through the video while waiting in line or when interacting with the election judges. Education ahead of the election requires getting voters' attention on a matter that they think they already understand ("I show up and check a box"). It is likely that there will continue to be a need for informing voters close to the moment of voting (waiting in line, as they are handed their ballot and verification card). For populations that need more time to assimilate information, such as senior citizens and non-native English speakers, what can we do to educate them ahead of time so that when it comes time to vote, they can make an informed decision rather than simply skipping it because it just seems too confusing?

If vote verification becomes an expected part of voting systems, it will be important to ensure that all voters who want to verify their vote have the means to do so. For voters who don't have access to a computer and want to verify their vote later on, is there a way to help them get access to the means to verify their vote?

These conclusions should of course be considered in view of the setting: a municipality without a history of election fraud, civil contests rather than vitriolic or heavily partisan contests, a voter turnout comprised primarily of people who are highly educated and comfortable with computers. Responses might have been different in a situation that had more voters who were distrustful of their election process, less comfortable with computers or lacking computer access, or voting in a hotly contested and/or highly charged election.

10.9   Current Status of the Project

As an academic project, our main interest was in proving the feasibility of running E2E elections in the real world. The logistics and expenses of continuing to run elections, however, became difficult as all of the students on the project eventually graduated and began working in new areas in industry and academia. We decided to suspend active development on the Scantegrity project after the 2011 election at Takoma Park, leaving on good terms with the city.

10.10   Conclusions

In 2005, just after the introduction of the first human verifiable E2E voting systems, a list of recommendations were proposed by Karlof, Sastry and Wagner [340] for realizing the full deployment potential of cryptographic voting techniques. To summarize, they recommended the following:

- **Certification**: a new framework for evaluating E2E systems and criteria for their certification by an independent body,
- **Usability evaluation**: review of the systems by usability experts and running trials with questionnaires,
- **Recoverability**: the ability to fall back to a reliable underlying system, such as hand-countable paper ballots
- **Transparency**: full disclosure of source code and documentation of the systems.

As of 2005, these were all open problems. Through our work, and the work of others in the community, progress has been made on all four.

Certification

In the United States, the Election Assistance Commission (EAC), with guidance from the National Institute of Standards and Technology (NIST), provides vote system guidelines (VVSG). These guidelines now include E2E voting systems. In 2010, NIST held a workshop on E2E voting systems and we reported our experiences with the mock election at Takoma Park (the workshop preceded the actual election).

Usability

While independent usability evaluation of all E2E systems is significantly deficient from the literature, the data we collected after the Takoma Park mock and municipal elections currently represents the largest dataset of voter and poll worker reactions from an E2E system.

Recoverability

The introduction of Scantegrity, which simply added E2E verification to an otherwise normal optical scan system, represents a major step forward for recoverable E2E systems. Most paper-based E2E systems are like Punchscan, without a recoverable paper audit trail. This has benefits from a privacy perspective—the E2E system is the only interface to the real tally (even the scanner does not know how you voted). But it also creates a concentrated point of failure. We believe systems like Scantegrity are a first step toward verifiability, and increased voter privacy should follow after time.

Transparency

Both Punchscan and Scantegrity are fully open-source projects (although they license patented technology; see disclosure below). In fact, to our knowledge, the Takoma Park election also has the distinction of being the first open-source government election held in the United States.

The successful E2E voting pilot at Takoma Park demonstrates that voters and election officials can use advanced cryptographic techniques within an election, and, with reference to our polling data, be satisfied with its usability. We believe the Scantegrity system and the 2009 and 2011 elections demonstrate a significant advancement in the technical maturity of E2E voting. We can now say it is ready for real binding governmental elections. The remaining hurdle for the acceptance of cryptography in elections is when voters stop asking why we are using it, and start demanding why we are not using it.[14]

Acknowledgments

Ben Adida and Filip Zagórski performed pre- and post-election audits for the 2009 election. Lillie Coney audited paper ballots. Robert Araujo and Neil McBurnett performed pre- and post-election audits for the 2011 election. Neil McBurnett did in-person ballot-print audits and also audited the Audiotegrity audio interface. Noel Runyan provided expertise for the design of Audiotegrity. The Board of Elections of the City of Takoma Park and the City Clerk displayed infinite patience and shared with us their considerable experience with elections.

We were not compensated by the City of Takoma Park for either election. Clark was/is supported by NSERC. Vora was/is supported in part by NSF awards 0505510, 0831149, 0937267, 1137973 and 1421373, and a grant from the NSA. Zagórski is partially supported by Polish National Science Centre contract number DEC-2013/09/D/ST6/03927.

Sherman was supported in part by the Department of Defense under IASP grants H98230- 09-1-0404 and H98230-10-1-0359 and by the National Science Foundation under SFS grant 1241576. Survey work at the 2011 Takoma Park election was supported in part by the U.S. Election Assistance Commission under grant EAC110150I.

---

[14]Adapted from Stu Feldman's roadmap for technical maturity (as quoted in [250]): (i) You have a good idea. (ii) You can make your idea work. (iii) You can convince a gullible friend to try it. (iv) People stop asking why you are doing it. (v) Other people are asked why they are not doing it.

Chapter 11

Internet Voting with Helios

Olivier Pereira
Université catholique de Louvain
ICTEAM – Crypto Group
Louvain-la-Neuve, Belgium

CONTENTS

11.1   Introduction

Helios is a voting system designed to enable practical open-audit, end-to-end verifiable elections with only the support of a web browser. Since 2009, Helios has been used by several hundreds of thousands of voters from various institutions: universities (including Université catholique de Louvain [46, 121] and Princeton University [212]), associations (including the International Association for Cryptologic Research [90] and the Association for Computing Machinery, [42]) and a number of private companies.

The choice of making it possible to create, run and tally an election with only the support of web browsers has several implications. The first is to bring end-to-end verifiable elections to anyone who can access the Internet. Using Helios does not require using any dedicated hardware, installing any specific software or having a physical mail address. This is also true for the whole election audit process: all audit operations can be performed from a basic laptop. Any voter can verify that his vote is included, unaltered, in the tally, and anyone can verify that the tally is correct. These audit operations do not require any privileged access to some data or infrastructure: they only require the manipulation of public data. Furthermore, and contrary to traditional paper voting, the audit operations do not require any kind of continuous watch: there is no chain of custody that needs to be maintained in order to perform a meaningful audit. As a result, an independent audit of the tally can be performed by anyone and at any time after the end of an election, something that would be infeasible in any large-scale traditional paper election. We will elaborate on these various operations and guarantees later in this chapter.

Helios guarantees the confidentiality of the votes by using distributed encryption (since version 2.0): votes are encrypted directly on the voter's computer and, only then, are sent to the Helios server which does not ever see any decryption key, unless the election organizers decide otherwise. Decryption keys are independently generated by trustees and are never combined: no partial decryption key should ever leave the trustee's computer. As a result, corruption of *all* the trustees of an election would be needed to perform any illicit decryption.

Still, Helios inherits the important limitations that seem to be inherent to pure Internet elections – while mitigating them to some extent. First, Helios provides very limited security guarantees to voters who would rely on a compromised computer for submitting their vote. If a malware controls the computer of a voter, and if this computer is the only interface that the voter uses for the election, the computer can display anything the voter wants to see while doing something completely different in the background (e.g., submit a vote for a different candidate or relay the vote in the clear to a third party). But, contrary to non-verifiable systems, Helios offers several audit possibilities that make it possible for a voter to detect vote alterations that would be performed by a malicious computer, provided that the voter can access an honest computer at some point, a computer that does not even need to be connected to the Internet. These observations also apply to the Helios server which, if corrupted, would be forced to leave evidence of any alteration of the votes it would perform, enabling detection as long as an honest device can be used.

Second, Helios does very little to protect voters from coercion – even though some forms of coercion resistance can be obtained through external measures, e.g., by forcing voters to use Helios in the privacy of a voting booth and in the absence of cameras. But, if the election organizers let the whole interaction between the voter and the system happen in an unsupervised context (no voting booth, no in-person registration process . . .), a coercer could effectively dictate his behavior to a voter, from the beginning to the end of an election, and verify the compliance of the voter to his instructions. Still, even in this case, Helios offers a limited form of protection: voters are allowed to submit as many ballots as they want, and only the last one is tallied. This feature, besides its huge advantages for dealing with voters using an unreliable Internet connection or uncomfortable with a browser interface, enables voters who would feel pushed to vote in an undesired way at a specific moment (being "trapped" in a voting party with colleagues for instance) to submit another ballot at a later time, in a safe context.

It is of course most important to keep these limitations in mind, and to decide whether they are relevant in a specific context, before deciding to make any use of Helios in an election.

11.1.1 Helios History

The initial version of Helios, designed by Adida and presented in 2008 [44], was a web-based variant of a *simple verifiable* voting scheme by Benaloh [84], which was itself inspired from a protocol by Sako and Kilian [508]. In this version, the Helios server acted as a single trustee for the confidentiality of the votes, while guaranteeing open-audit properties. The Helios server generated a pair of keys for a public key encryption scheme; the public key was used by all voters to encrypt and submit their vote from their browser; the Helios server performed a (single) verifiable shuffle of the received ballots in order to cut them from the identity of the voters, and eventually decrypted all shuffled ballots individually. The security model for Helios 1.0 was summarized as: "Trust no one for integrity, trust Helios for privacy."

In the summer of 2008, the design of Helios 2.0 by Adida, de Marneffe, Pereira and Quisquater [46] started, resulting in the Helios protocol that is still in use today, and in the first use of an end-to-end verifiable voting system in a legally binding, multi-thousand voters election, in March 2009. A first major modification of Helios 2.0 was to abandon the shuffle-based approach and to move to a simpler and much more efficient solution based on the homomorphic aggregation of votes, inspired by a protocol by Cramer, Gennaro and Schoenmakers [178]. In this approach, and by relying on an appropriate encryption scheme, all encrypted votes are aggregated (and possibly weighted) into an encryption of the election outcome, which is eventually decrypted. A second major decision was to strengthen the vote privacy model by moving to the use of a distributed encryption scheme, in such a way that no single entity or device would, at any time, be in touch with enough keying material to decrypt individual ballots. In particular, this removed the need to have any decryption key being manipulated by the Helios server at any time, therefore considerably limiting the consequences of a server compromise. The web architecture was also considerably modified, making the various components (administration, ballot preparation, bulletin board) more independent. Eventually, various features, like the possibility to publish voter aliases instead of public voter IDs on the board, were also introduced there. The details of the Helios protocol are described in Section 11.3.

Since 2009, the functionalities offered by the Helios web application were further refined, offering new authentication modes, audit features, improved interfaces, and taking advantage of the advances in the design of web browsers to maximize compatibility. These aspects are described in Section 11.2 and some are further discussed in Section 11.4. We conclude in Section 11.5 by describing several Helios variants and extensions that have been designed and sometimes actually deployed.

11.2 Election Walkthrough

We start by describing, from a functional point of view, the process of voting in, managing and auditing a Helios election.

11.2.1 Voting in a Helios Election

11.2.1.1 Invitation to Vote

The first contact of a voter with a Helios election usually happens through an email inviting to vote. This email contains a description of the election, a link to the voting booth, and a voter ID and password that need to be used in order to submit a ballot. An election fingerprint, provided as a tracking number, is also provided, and identifies the election in a unique way (we explain how it is computed in Section 11.2.2.1).

Several variants of this process are possible:

- Helios can make use of external authentication services, like those provided by Google or Facebook (of course, these external credentials are never accessible to the Helios server) or, in some cases, custom authentication services like a university SSO or LDAP service. In this case, a vote invitation will not contain credentials.

- Helios can add a voter alias in the invitation to vote. While using an explicit voter ID is a way to improve the democratic control of who submitted a ballot in an election (a notion sometimes called eligibility verifiability [353]), many organizations consider that their list of members is private, and do not want an election to be an occasion to indirectly publish a member list. In some other cases, even if the member list can be made available to the voters, the act of voting is considered to be private, due to coercion concerns. In these situations, the Helios server makes it possible to keep the voter ID private, and only publishes anonymous aliases: this is enough for a voter to track his own ballot, but not to verify who submitted the others ballots included in the tally. This approach is also sometimes adopted as a line of defense in the case of a catastrophic failure that would result in the decryption of individual ballots, or simply of the natural evolution of computing power that would make it possible to break encryption: having ballots associated with anonymous aliases and not with real identifiers may prevent a malicious party to determine who's ballot was decrypted. Other solutions to these concerns, that do not hurt eligibility verifiability, are discussed in Section 11.5.3.

11.2.1.2 Submitting a Ballot

Using the link to the voting booth, voters can submit a ballot to the election server. Helios has an open API, which means that anyone (voter, candidate, activist …) could program a ballot preparation system (BPS) that can be used to submit ballots in any election – this has been proposed as a programming class project in some universities. However, most voters actually use the BPS provided by the Helios website, even if using a different BPS might have some advantages in terms of trust – a voter might feel more confident that his vote will be properly prepared if he uses a ballot preparation system provided by a candidate he supports.

The Helios BPS is served as a single web page: as soon as the voting booth is loaded in a (recent) browser, a voter can go offline, make his choices, have them encrypted, have all the cleartext choices and randomness erased, and only come back online in order to submit the encrypted ballot. Voting using the Helios BPS is a 3-step process.

1. The voter selects his answers to the different questions that are displayed, in a form that is similar to the sample ballot from Figure 11.1. A ballot can contain any number of questions, each of these questions offering the possibility to be answered by making a number of choices determined by the election rules, e.g., one single choice, any number of choices (for approval voting), or a number within a specific range, e.g., from 0 to the number of seats available in the election. For the moment, Helios does not support write-ins or ranked voting, which would require using very different cryptographic techniques. Some Helios extensions have been used however, that can accommodate arbitrary ballot formats – see Section 11.5.1.

2. When the voter has completed his choices, he is invited to review them and to make any changes that he may desire – see Figure 11.2. In the meantime, the ballot has been encrypted, and a ballot tracker is made available to the voter. This tracker uniquely identifies the encrypted ballot while preserving the secrecy of the vote, and makes it possible for the voter to challenge the BPS and, later, to verify that his encrypted ballot has been properly recorded by the voting server and included in the tally. The voter is invited to record or print this tracker immediately.

3. The voter can then decide to submit his ballot to the Helios voting server, which will prompt him to provide his credentials and send his ballot. Requiring voter authentication at the very end of the voting process has serious advantages. It makes it possible for anyone to review the ballot style and the ballot preparation process, possibly in collaboration with other persons in case of doubts, without any fear of having their credentials stolen. It also makes it harder for a corrupted Helios server to serve a tampered version of the BPS as a function of the voter credentials (possibly targeting a specific voter population with malicious software), since the identity of the voter is unknown when the BPS is served.

It can be observed on Figures 11.1 and 11.2 that the election fingerprint, which was part of the invitation to vote, is displayed at the bottom of each screen of the BPS, for verification by the voter. This fingerprint is not simply served from the Helios server, but actually recomputed by the BPS as a function of all election parameters: election URL, ballot encryption keys, questions, answer rules ... This feature provides a safety measure for the voter and could also help detect a malicious Helios server or vote invitation when an independent BPS is used.

It can eventually be observed in Figure 11.2 that two different options are presented to the voter: either simply submit the ballot to the Helios server, or verify that

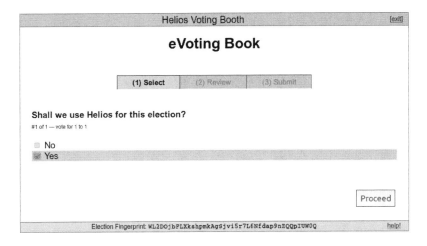

Figure 11.1: Selection of an answer in the Helios Ballot Preparation System.

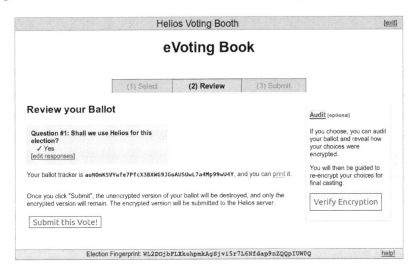

Figure 11.2: Ballot review in the Helios BPS, and choice to submit or verify its content.

the ballot has been encrypted correctly (see the frame on the right of the ballot). We will come back to this feature in Section 11.2.3.

Any voter can repeat the whole ballot preparation and submission procedure any number of times: only the last received ballot will be taken into account, and voters can check this thanks to their ballot tracker.

11.2.2   Election Management

A public Helios instance is hosted on `https://vote.heliosvoting.org/`, from which anyone can create and manage elections. This page also contains a link to the Helios code repository, currently hosted on Github, which makes it possible for anyone to host a personal Helios server. The code is released under Apache 2.0 license.

11.2.2.1   Election Creation

When creating a new election, the election administrator first defines the election name, as well as several general features: whether the election is intended to run with a closed or open list of voters, whether voter aliases are to be used (see discussion in Section 11.2.1.1), and what contact address should be offered to the voters for support. As an interesting feature, Helios also offers the possibility to have the lists of answers randomized every time they are displayed by the BPS. This feature makes it possible to remove inequalities that may result from the position of some candidates on a ballot (e.g., top of the list), when this is considered to be useful.

In a second step, the election administrator is invited to define three lists.

Questions An arbitrary list of questions can be included in a single election. For each of the questions, a list of proposed answers is defined, together with the minimum and maximum number of answers that the voter is allowed to pick. The computational complexity of ballot preparation caused the size of these lists to be a common bottleneck when Helios 2.0 was released, but this limitation largely disappeared thanks to the evolution of the browsers, which made it possible to considerably improve the efficiency of the ballot preparation process.

Voters The list of voters who are allowed to submit a ballot in an election, when it is defined in advance, can be uploaded to the Helios server as a comma-separated value (CSV) file, including the voter ID, email address and full name to be used in the email vote invitation.

Trustees The trustees are the parties that are trusted to maintain the confidentiality of the votes, and to take part in the tally decryption process. By default, the Helios server is configured to serve as a trustee, but it can be revoked, and any number of new trustees can be added. Trustees have a very sensitive role. Each of them needs to generate a pair of keys, made of a public and a secret component (further technical explanations are available in Section 11.3.2.) The public key needs to be uploaded to the Helios server, while the secret key must be kept safe and ... secret. At tallying time, all trustees are required to take part in the decryption of the election results, by making use of their secret key. As a corollary of this tallying procedure, if any trustee is missing, there will be no way to obtain the election result, and it is likely that the election will need to be restarted. More robust procedures have been proposed in the literature, in order to be able to tolerate a limited number of failing trustees [457, 252], but they are considerably more difficult to use, requiring multiple rounds of interactions between the trustees, which is why Helios relies on this single-pass procedure that maximizes confidentiality – see also Section 11.5.4.

Practically, trustees are registered through the management interface, in a way that is similar to the voter registration process. They receive an email with a URL, from which they reach a web page that enables them to generate their key pair, upload the public component, save the secret one, and test whether the whole process succeeded.

When the questions and voters have been defined, and when the trustees have returned their public key, the election can be frozen. From that moment, no change can be made in any of the election parameters, and the election fingerprint is computed as a hash of all election parameters. This election fingerprint should be broadcast through various channels: depending on the elections, it has been printed in institutional newspapers, displayed on the election pages of the institution and/or included in the invitation to vote.

When the election is frozen, the voters can be invited to vote, and Helios offers a mailing mechanism that includes various templates and supports the distribution of the election credentials and optional aliases. Voters can then submit their ballots, as explained in Section 11.2.1. Every time a ballot is received, the Helios server checks its validity and keeps it for inclusion in the tally. When a voter submits more than one ballot, only the last one is used in the tally (which can be verified using the recorded-as-cast verification procedure explained in Section 11.2.3.2) while the others are archived.

11.2.2.2 Election Tally

Once the voting time is over, the Helios server computes an encryption of the election tally, by aggregating the last valid ballot received from each voter, using the homomorphic property of the encryption scheme that is used to protect the votes, as described in Section 11.3.2. This is a public operation, which anyone can perform as easily as the Helios server.

Then the trustees are invited to decrypt this tally. By connecting to the Helios trustee interface through their browsers, the trustees can download the encrypted tally, see its fingerprint, load their private key in their browser (it will never leave the browser), perform their partial decryption of the tally, and upload the result of this decryption to the Helios server. Just as for the ballot preparation, there is no need to use the Helios web interface for this purpose: another software, managed independently, could perform the same operations and submit the partial tally decryption.

No information about the tally can be obtained as long as one of the trustees did not submit its partial tally decryption. But as soon as all the trustees completed their duty, the Helios server combines the partial decryptions into the full election tally and makes that tally available. Again, this combination of the partial decryptions is a public operation.

When the tally is complete, all the information that is needed for verifying the election becomes available from the Helios server. Besides, the secret keys stored by the trustees can be destroyed: they are of no use for the audit, and this destruction decreases the risks of a key compromise in the future.

11.2.3 Election Audit

The audit of a Helios election includes three types of verifications.

1. The *cast-as-intended* verification enables any voter to obtain the assurance that the ballot he submits captures his vote intent.

2. The *recorded-as-cast* verification enables any voter to obtain the assurance that his ballot has been properly recorded on the Helios server.

3. The *tallied-as-recorded* verification enables anyone to verify that all the valid recorded votes are included in the tally. This verification is sometimes separated into the notions of universal verifiability and eligibility verifiability [353].

Together, these verification steps provide what is often called *end-to-end verifiability*.

11.2.3.1 Cast-as-Intended Verification

The ballot tracker displayed to the voter before the submission of the ballot (see Figure 11.2) is expected to be a faithful fingerprint of the encrypted voter intent. A voter can however legitimately question this, and be willing to find out whether this ballot really captures his intent.

Helios offers the possibility to challenge the ballot preparation system through a process that is often referred to as a *Benaloh challenge*. The key ingredient of this challenge lies in the moment at which the ballot tracker is displayed to the voter, that is, after the completion of all ballot preparation tasks (the full ballot information is in there), but before the voter authenticates to submit his ballot. This means that, when the BPS displays the ballot tracker, it does not know whether this ballot is intended to be posted to the Helios server, or if this ballot preparation is just part of an audit. The Benaloh challenge proceeds by offering the voter two options: either to authenticate and submit the ballot as described in Section 11.2.1.2, or to require a ballot audit and verify the encryption by clicking on the button in the frame in Figure 11.2.

If the second option is chosen, the BPS is required to provide all the data it has used to prepare the ballot, including all the randomness that has been used for encryption. Based on these data, the voter can now use a single ballot verification software to verify that the ballot matches its vote intent, is valid, and matches the committed ballot tracker. Since the BPS had to display the ballot tracker before the voter marked its intent to audit the ballot, it cannot adapt its behavior when the audit is requested: the data that is provided must match that ballot tracker.

Helios provides a single ballot verifier, accessible as a single web page but, as usual, there is no need to use software included in Helios for that task. Another possibility that the Helios web interface offers is to post the audited ballot on a public ballot tracking center. There, the ballot will be verified by the Helios server and by anyone volunteering to do so. This may simplify the task of the voter who then does not need to run any verification software by himself, but only to check on the ballot tracking center whether his ballot has been declared valid for the correct vote intent and ballot tracker.

In any case, a ballot that is audited cannot be submitted anymore, since the access to the audit data could violate the privacy of the vote. The goal is to verify whether the BPS behaves honestly on a specific device, and not to verify whether the specific ballot that a voter wants to submit has been correctly prepared.

We may then wonder how effective can this inherently probabilistic procedure be. The high-level response is as follows: suppose that a malicious party manages to corrupt the BPS and wants to influence the election outcome by flipping 1% of the votes (or any proportion p). Then, as soon as around 100 (or around $1/p$) ballot audits are triggered randomly during the election (by voters, activists …), we can expect that the corrupted BPS will be detected at least once, which can in turn trigger more audits and investigations. Interestingly, the bound we mention above does not depend on the number of voters, which makes this process particularly efficient in a large-scale election. However, the effectiveness of the audit procedure really depends on the corruption model that is considered and on how the verification of the audited ballot is performed.

Corrupted ballot preparation system. The use of a corrupted ballot preparation system, originating from any source, is the typical situation in which the Benaloh challenge works: any vote manipulation by the BPS will be discovered by any honest single ballot verifier.

Corrupted Helios server. A malicious Helios server could go a bit further than corrupting the BPS, in some cases: if a voter uses the Helios BPS and the Helios single ballot verifier, then collusion can happen, and the verifier could be able to falsely convince the voter that his vote has been properly encoded. The same thing could happen if the voter decides to post his ballot on the ballot tracking center, and if nobody but the Helios server attempts to verify the ballot. This stresses the importance of using independent auditing tools when running a Helios election (see also Section 11.5.7).

Corrupted voting client. If the device that the voter uses is under control of the adversary, then the Benaloh challenge can only be effective if the voter is able to access an uncorrupted device at some point. If this is not the case, then the corrupted device will be able to display everything that the voter expects to see, whatever happens in the background. For instance, the corrupted client can prepare a ballot for candidate *A*, even if the voter wants to vote for *B*, display the ballot tracker for the *A* ballot and, if asked for an audit, alter the output of any ballot verifier running on the same device to make it claim that the ballot encodes a vote for *B*. This scenario, already described in [46], has been practically illustrated by Estehghari and Desmedt [222] for instance. In this demonstration, a malicious PDF document is forged, and is distributed as the program of a candidate. If the PDF file is opened with a specific version of Adobe Reader, a vulnerability of Adobe Reader is exploited in order to install a malicious plugin in Firefox, before making Firefox crash. Once the voter restarts Firefox, the malicious plugin becomes active and monitors the web connections of the users and performs the modifications described above to alter any vote that would be prepared in this browser in a way that would apparently pass all the verification steps as long as the voter keeps using this corrupted Firefox instance. Taking the audit data into another browser or device that would not be corrupted would be enough to detect the manipulation, but this definitely reduces the usability of the process, and is one of the reasons why we do not advise using Helios (and any other pure Internet voting system that we are aware of) in a setting where corrupted voting clients are a plausible scenario.

Corrupted TLS/PKI The access to a single ballot verifier or to the ballot tracking center will most likely depend on the availability of an authentic Internet connection. An attacker who manages to subvert TLS or a certification authority is likely to be able to provide a voter with a modified BPS and ballot verification tool, or with a modified view of the ballot tracking center, which would bypass the verification process. Similar issues can happen for the other verification procedures described below.[1]

One last difficulty may arise from this cast-as-intended verification process: the lack of evidence. If a voter claims that a ballot audit failed, there is no way for a third party to decide whether a system component is corrupted or if the voter made a mistake, either a honest one, or with the intent of raising unjustified suspicions about the system. Furthermore, even with an honest and careful voter, it might be really hard to determine whether a failed audit results from a corrupted voter device or from a malicious third party (e.g., the Helios server.) A voter could possibly try to record on camera his interactions with the voting system and his audit, but no third party would still be able to determine whether the voter device is corrupted (maybe by the voter himself) or if a third party is corrupted. So, in all cases, it will not be possible to draw conclusions from voter complaints, but such complaints will certainly be a useful alert calling for further investigations in order to collect evidence.

---

[1] We discuss the impact of a TLS/PKI failure here because these are elements on which Helios relies. Of course, errors in the Helios cryptographic protocols can have a similar impact. These will be discussed in the sections below.

Despite having never raised any actual difficulty in practice, this lack of an effective dispute resolution procedure creates a risk of denial of service attacks on elections, and finding practical solutions to this potential difficulty is one of the important open challenges in the area of verifiable voting technologies.

11.2.3.2 Recorded-as-Cast Verification

Once a voter is convinced that the ballot tracker displayed by the BPS correctly captures his vote intent, this ballot tracker can serve as a basis to verify the proper recording of the ballot. A voter can do that by connecting to the Helios Ballot Tracking Center web page, which displays the ballot trackers of all the votes intended to be used in the tally, and by verifying whether his ballot is actually displayed there, with the right tracking number.

Just as the access to the ballot preparation system, the access to the ballot tracking center does not require any authentication. This makes it harder for a corrupted Helios server to adapt the list of ballots depending on the voter accessing the tracking center. It also makes it easy to delegate this verification: a voter can send his tracking number to activists, or even broadcast it on social networks for verification by others. Still, the verification of the ballot presence at a given time during the election does not guarantee that the ballot will still be there, unmodified, and used as part of the tally. Therefore, it is useful that voters inspect the ballot tracking center when there is a public agreement on the ballots that will be used in the tally, that is, when the hash of the encrypted tally is made available to the trustees before decryption.

In some elections [46], an audit day has been organized before the tally: the election organizers published a digitally signed version of the ballot tracking center content, and a full day was left to the voters for verifying that their ballot was listed there. Of course, it would be still possible for malicious election organizers to sign different versions of the ballot tracking center and to target the distribution channels properly, but they would need to take the risk that someone would discover the existence of two different signed lists of ballots, which would be immediate evidence of corruption. Designs for a more robust and distributed ballot tracking center have also been proposed, including by Culnane and Schneider [185].

As for the cast-as-intended property, dispute resolution difficulties may arise if a voter complains that his ballot was not properly recorded: it may be impossible to decide whether a component of the system failed, or if the voter is trying to mislead the election organizers and participants. Solutions to this problem have been explored, either as procedures external to the normal system usage (see [46] for instance) or as internal extensions, e.g., by Culnane et al. [181] for the Prêt-à-Voter system.

Also, a voter might be subverted into connecting to a corrupted ballot tracking center, in which case verification would clearly offer no guarantee. This could happen in various ways. For instance, an attacker could modify vote invitations, making the voters believe that their ballot needs to be submitted and verified from the wrong place (note that this would also require to be able to modify the election fingerprint or to corrupt the BPS in order to avoid detection.) Alternatively, if TLS or the PKI on which a voter relies fails, a voter might have his ballot erased or replaced, and be displayed an alternate ballot tracking center despite using the correct URL.

11.2.3.3 Tallied-as-Recorded Verification

The two verification processes that we just described are largely individual: a voter checks what happens with his vote, independently of anyone else's vote.

The tallied-as-recorded verification is universal in the sense that anyone will care not only about whether his own vote was properly included in the tally, but also whether all the other votes that were included in the tally were valid votes submitted by valid voters.

The starting point for the tallied-as-recorded verification process is the ballot tracking center: from there, anyone can collect the list of people who submitted ballots and the corresponding tracking numbers. Unless the election administrators decide to obfuscate the voter names using aliases, this list provides the information that is needed to verify that the ballots were submitted by real voters. In case of doubts (voter credentials could have been stolen, or there might be ballot stuffing performed on a corrupted Helios server), it is also possible to contact voters in person, possibly at random, and to ask them to confirm their ballot tracker.

Once the list of tracking numbers is confirmed, the second step of the verification process consists in downloading the full list of ballots from the Helios server, and checking whether all these ballots match the expected tracking numbers. Based on these ballots, the validity of all the votes can be verified by inspecting the proofs that they contain. When the validity of all the ballots is verified, the encrypted votes can be aggregated into an encryption of the tally. Eventually, the correctness of the decryption of the tally can also be checked, by verifying the decryption proofs provided by the trustees. All these steps heavily rely on cryptographic techniques, which are detailed in the next section, and are detailed in the online Helios documentation, making it possible for any programmer to implement a verification system, which many programmers did.

This tallied-as-recorded verification process is considerably more demanding than the other verification steps: it certainly requires considerably more computational power, more than is typically available in a browser for any election of reasonable size. However, this verification step is also the one that can most naturally be delegated to third parties (activists, candidates), as it focuses on a global property of the election.

11.3   The Use of Cryptography in Helios

Helios makes heavy use of cryptography in order to enable the verification of an election without degrading the privacy of the votes. This section outlines the cryptographic protocols used in Helios, and discusses the various assumptions on which they rely. These cryptographic techniques are fairly close to an original proposal by Cramer, Gennaro and Schoenmakers [178]. A more detailed exposition of these techniques is available in the tutorial of Bernhard and Warinschi [100].

11.3.1   *Arithmetic and Computational Assumption*

The protocols implemented in Helios make use of a multiplicative cyclic group $\mathbb{G}$ of prime order q, in which the Decisional Diffie–Hellman (DDH) problem [110] is believed to be hard. This means that, given a generator g of $\mathbb{G}$ and a triple g^a, g^b, g^c where a and b are chosen at random in $\mathbb{Z}_q$, it is believed to be hard to decide whether c has also been chosen at random in $\mathbb{Z}_q$, just as a and b, or whether $c = ab$.

Among the various possible choices for $\mathbb{G}$, we opted for a subgroup of 256 bit prime order q of $\mathbb{Z}_p^*$, the multiplicative group of integers modulo a 2048 bits prime p. This choice provides us with a reasonable compromise between simplicity (no need to implement elliptic curve arithmetic), efficiency (exponentiation with a 256 bit q is approximately 8 times faster than if we choose $q = (p-1)/2$) and security (the resulting security level approximately corresponds to a medium-term protection as described in the ECRYPT report [35]).

11.3.2   *Encryption*

ElGamal [213] is the simplest public key encryption scheme whose security relies on the hardness of the DDH problem. It works as follows.

- ■ The secret decryption key is a random value x chosen in $\mathbb{Z}_q$, from which the public encryption key is computed as $y = g^x$.

- ■ A message $m \in \mathbb{G}$ is encrypted by picking a random r in $\mathbb{Z}_q$, and computing a ciphertext as $(c_1, c_2) = (g^r, my^r)$.

- ■ A ciphertext (c_1, c_2) can then be decrypted as $m = c_2/c_1^x$, using the decryption key x.

This encryption scheme guarantees indistinguishability of ciphertexts [260] if the DDH problem is hard in $\mathbb{G}$: anyone who would be able to derive any single bit of information about the plaintext corresponding to a given ciphertext would also be able to solve the DDH problem in $\mathbb{G}$. This encryption scheme is used in Helios to protect the votes, and indistinguishability of ciphertext implies, in particular, that no one will be able to even recognize if two ciphertexts encrypt the same vote or not.

When presented a ballot with a list of candidates, a voter expresses his choices by encrypting "0" or "1" for each candidate, depending on whether he wants to support that candidate or not. This "0" or "1" are actually encoded as g^0 and g^1, which are two elements of $\mathbb{G}$, as needed for ElGamal encryption. This encoding, resulting in a scheme that is often called "exponential ElGamal," brings an extra benefit: it makes ciphertexts additively homomorphic. Indeed the product of an encryption of g^a and an encryption of g^b is an encryption of g^{a+b}. This feature is most useful for counting the votes: given a series of ciphertexts encrypting all the voters' choices regarding one candidate, we can simply multiply all those ciphertexts together, which provides an encryption of the number of voters who supported that candidate. This last ciphertext is the only one that is decrypted, which guarantees the confidentiality of the individual votes.

We however do not want to trust a single entity to not decrypt any individual vote. To this purpose, we distribute the key generation and distribution procedure among a set of trustees $T_1, \ldots, T_n$. This is performed as follows.

■ For key generation, each trustee T_i generates an ElGamal key pair $(x_i, y_i = g^{x_i})$ and keeps x_i secret. The election public key is then computed as $g^x = \prod g^{x_i}$. At no point does any single party learn x.

■ For the decryption of a ciphertext (c_1, c_2), each trustee T_i computes and publishes a decryption factor $d_i = c_1^{x_i}$. The plaintext is eventually computed as $c_2 / \prod d_i$.

This procedure is a simplified version of the threshold protocol proposed by Pedersen [458]. While it does not provide robustness against failing trustees, it is considerably simpler to use, as it proceeds in a single asynchronous round and does not require any private channel between pairs of trustees for key generation. In practice, some robustness can be obtained by pairing trustees in order to have at least two copies of each secret x_i.

The use of the exponential variant of ElGamal has one potential downside, though: the ElGamal decryption process actually provides the exponential encoding g^m of the message m that we want to recover, and not m. This means that an extra step is actually needed in order to complete decryption: the extraction of the discrete logarithm of g^m in base g. Given that m is typically upper bounded by the total number of voters, this extraction is hardly a problem in practice: our simple implementation of Shanks' baby-step giant-step algorithm [524] can extract a 40-bit discrete logarithm in a matter of seconds on a standard laptop [46].

If decryption efficiency had been a problem, Paillier encryption [452] would have offered a considerably more efficient solution. However, generating a Paillier key pair in a distributed way [188] is considerably more challenging, due to the need of building an RSA modulus with unknown factorization.

11.3.3 Zero-Knowledge Proofs

The verifiability of the election and confidentiality of the votes heavily rely on the use of zero-knowledge proofs, used to prove three types of statements:

1. Trustees are required to prove that they know the private key that matches the public key they are publishing;

2. Trustees are required to prove that they honestly contribute to the tally of the elections;

3. Voters are required to prove the validity of the ballot they submit.

11.3.3.1 Sigma Protocols

Helios makes use of sigma protocols to prove all these statements. We only outline these protocols here, and invite the interested reader to consult Damgård [187] for further details.

A sigma protocol defines a three-pass interaction between a prover P and a verifier V, as depicted in Figure 11.3. In the first message, called the *commitment*, P submits a list of random values a, typically made of elements of $\mathbb{G}$, to the verifier. This commitment will be used to blind the secret values about which P wants to make a statement. The second message, called the *challenge*, contains a random integer e, chosen by V. It is crucial for the soundness of the proof that P does not know e when he commits through a. Eventually, P sends the *response* f to V, which is typically made of elements of $\mathbb{Z}_q$. V eventually makes use of the proof statement, a, e and f to decide whether he accepts the proof.

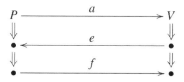

Figure 11.3: A three-pass sigma protocol.

We of course do not want to rely on interactive proofs in an election: the provers should be able to submit proofs of their statements once and for all and make these proofs available to anyone for future verification. This is where the strong Fiat–Shamir transformation comes into play [236, 99]. This transformation modifies the second step of the protocol, by computing the challenge e as a hash of the commitment a and of the statement to be proven, instead of having the challenge selected by V. The resulting proofs are computationally sound and non-interactive zero-knowledge in the random-oracle model [79]. Having described the common pattern of all proofs used in Helios, we turn to the actual proof descriptions.

11.3.3.2 Proving Honest Key Generation

The first context in which Helios requires proofs is during key generation by the trustees. It is clear from the key generation described above that, if all trustees collude or have their secret key stolen, then no privacy is guaranteed. We however want to make sure that, as long as one trustee behaves honestly, the privacy of the votes is protected.

Observing the key generation process described in Section 11.3.2, and assuming that we have n trustees, a malicious T_n could subvert the process to his advantage as follows. T_n would first wait until all other trustees have submitted their own public key $y_i = g^{x_i}$. Then, he would generate a key pair $(x, y = g^x)$ of his own, and publish a public key $y_n = y/\prod_{i=1}^{n-1} y_i$. As a result, the election public key would be computed as $y = \prod_{i=1}^{n} y_i$, and T_n would be able to decrypt all individual votes by himself, using the secret key x he choose.

The key element that makes this attack possible is that T_n is not required to prove to anyone that he knows x_n. And it is easy to verify that any algorithm that would be able to produce both x_n and x in such a setting would also be able to solve the discrete logarithm problem in $\mathbb{G}$ (which is harder than solving the DDH problem in that same group).

This problem is then solved by requiring all the trustees to prove that they know the decryption key matching the public key they submit. This can be done using a protocol due to Schnorr, which is depicted in Figure 11.4 (a). The commitment of this protocol is computed as g^s for a random $s \in \mathbb{Z}_q$, the challenge is made of an element of $\mathbb{Z}_q$, and the computation of the response is performed in $\mathbb{Z}_q$ as well. At the end of the protocol, V accepts the proof only if $g^f = ay^e$.

The soundness of this proof follows from two observations:

1. If, after having submitted a commitment a, the prover P is able to provide a response f that passes the proof acceptance test performed by V, then P is most likely able to do so for more than one single value of the challenge e. Indeed, if e were the only value for which P knows the correct f, then the probability of P to complete a proof successfully would be $1/q$, which would be an event that is infeasible to observe.

2. As soon as we trust that P would be able to submit two responses f_1 and f_2 to two distinct challenges e_1 and e_2, based on a single commitment a, we also trust that P knows x. Indeed, we can verify that $x = \frac{f_1 - f_2}{e_1 - e_2}$.

The intuition behind the zero-knowledge property of this protocol is the following one: V does not learn anything from this interaction (except for the knowledge of x by P) because V is able to produce an interaction that follows the exact same distribution, just by himself: V would pick e and f at random from $\mathbb{Z}_q$, then compute $a = g^f/y^e$. This zero-knowledge property is usually called *honest verifier*, because the simulation of the interaction is based on the assumption that, in a real protocol execution, V actually picks e at random, and not as a function of a for instance. This is not a problem, since we only use the non-interactive version of this protocol and model the hash function as a random oracle

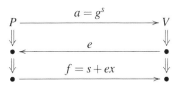

(a) The Schnorr protocol proves the knowledge of the x matching a public key $y = g^x$.

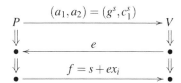

(b) The Chaum–Pedersen protocol proves that d_i is the decryption factor computed with the x_i matching public key y_i and the ciphertext component c_1.

Figure 11.4: Two sigma protocols used in Helios.

11.3.3.3 Proving Correct Decryption

Honest key generation is crucial for privacy. It does not guarantee, however, that the decryption of the tally is performed correctly. A single trustee could indeed try to manipulate the outcome of an election by cheating when computing his decryption factor. Consider for instance a trustee T_i who, instead of computing his decryption factor for a ciphertext (c_1, c_2) as $d_i = c_1^{x_i}$, computes and submits a factor $d_i' = d_i/g^v$. As a result, the plaintext will be computed as the discrete logarithm of $c_2 / \left(\frac{\prod d_i}{g^v} \right)$ in base g, which adds v to the correct decryption of (c_1, c_2) and v votes to a candidate. Of course, a malicious trustee will not manipulate a single ciphertext, which would increase the total number of votes and provide evidence of malfeasance (except in the case of approval voting), but will add a number of votes to one candidate, and remove that same number of votes from other candidates, keeping the total correct.

This problem can be avoided by making use of a sigma protocol due to Chaum and Pedersen [149], depicted in Figure 11.4 (b). This protocol is a kind of parallel version of the Schnorr protocol, and is used to prove that the discrete logarithm of y_i in base g is equal to the discrete logarithm of d_i in base c_1. Compared to the Schnorr protocol, the commitment is now made of two group elements, computed from a single random $s \in \mathbb{Z}_q$ selected by the prover P. Furthermore, the verifier V only accepts the proof if both $g^f = a_1 y_i^e$ and $c_1^f = a_2 d_i^e$ are satisfied. The soundness and zero-knowledge properties of this protocol follow from the same arguments used for the Schnorr protocol.

11.3.3.4 Proving Ballot Validity

A Helios ballot contains a series of questions, each with a number of possible answers. For each question, the voter is allowed to pick a number of answers, defined by the election rules: this can be just one answer, any number of answers (for approval voting) or a number within a fixed range.

For each of these answers, the ballot preparation system encrypts a "0" or a "1," depending on the choice of the voter, which makes it easy to multiply ciphertexts in order to obtain an encryption of the tally. However, once the voter choices have been encrypted, it is not possible anymore to determine what was encrypted: this is crucial for privacy. Furthermore, thanks to the homomorphic tallying technique, individual ballots are never decrypted. This very effective technique may open a new line of abuse, though: a malicious voter could try to encrypt values that are very different from 0 and 1 – say 1000 for one candidate and -999 for another. As a result, a voter might be able to add or remove an arbitrary number of votes from any candidate.

In order to avoid this potential problem, voters are required to use sigma protocols to prove the validity of their ballot. More precisely, the voters are required to prove that each of the ciphertexts they submit is either an encryption of 0 or an encryption of 1, and that the product of all these ciphertexts is an encryption of an integer lying in the prescribed range, indicating that a valid number of answers have been selected by the voter. (Of course, for approval voting, we can avoid that last proof since the number of selected answers is arbitrary.)

The sigma protocols that are used are disjunctive variants of the Chaum–Pedersen protocol, as proposed by Cramer, Damgård and Schoenmakers [176]. The Chaum–Pedersen protocol can indeed be used by a voter to prove that a ciphertext is an encryption of a fixed value v: compared to Figure 11.4 (b), y will take the place of c_1, c_2/g^v will take the place of d_i, and r, the randomness used to compute the ciphertext, will take the place of x_i.

As such, this protocol is not sufficient for our purpose: a voter needs to prove that a ciphertext encrypts either 0 or 1, without revealing which one: we actually need a *disjunctive* version of Chaum–Pedersen. To this purpose, we first observe that it is easy to generate a Chaum–Pedersen proof transcript that passes the verification procedure, even without knowing any secret, and even for a false statement: as before, we can choose arbitrary random values for e and f, then compute a_1 and a_2 in such a way that the verification equations are satisfied. This of course does not contradict the soundness of the proof: the *simulated* proof that we just produced has been computed by selecting e before a_1 and a_2, which will never happen in a real execution of the protocol. But we can exploit this strategy to produce a proof that one statement out of two is correct: the idea is to combine the computation of two proofs: one that proves that a ciphertext encrypts 0, and one that proves that same ciphertext encrypts 1. Of course, only one of the two statements can be true. Therefore, we will produce a simulated proof for the false statement, that we combine with an honest proof of the true statement.

More precisely, the prover will produce a simulated proof transcript $((a_1^{sim}, a_2^{sim}),$ $e^{sim}, f^{sim})$ for the statement that is false, then generate commitments (a_1^{real}, a_2^{real}) to be used for proving the statement that is true. After submitting the real and simulated commitments to the verifier, the prover obtains a challenge e. From this global challenge, he derives the challenge for the real proof, computed as $e^{real} = e - e^{sim}$, and complete that proof by computing the response f^{real}. Eventually, the real and simulated challenges and responses are submitted to the verifier, who checks both proofs individually, and also checks that the sum of the challenges matches the global challenge e. Since both proofs check, and since the proof generation process is entirely symmetric from an observer's point of view, there is no way for any observer to decide which of the two proofs is the simulated one. So, by using this technique, a prover can demonstrate to anyone that he only encrypted 0s and 1s, and in a quantity that satisfies the election rules. This process can easily be generalized to prove that a ciphertexts encrypts a value that lies within an arbitrary range: simulated proofs can be produced for all the incorrect values from the range, with a real proof being produced for the correct value only.

So, while the honest key generation proof was crucial to privacy, the last two proofs that we discussed guarantee the correctness of the result: all tallied ballots are valid, and they are tallied correctly.

11.3.4   Protocol Analysis

The protocol implemented in Helios has been analyzed in a growing body of literature.

The security properties expected from Helios were outlined in the original papers: Helios is expected to offer end-to-end verifiability. The privacy of the votes relies on the honesty of at least one trustee. Moreover, the security of the voting client is also crucial for privacy: a malware recording all actions of the voters would easily violate privacy. Internally, a malicious BPS could transmit votes in the clear, in parallel with the normal ballot preparation. Coercion resistance is only offered in a very weak form, as usual for unsupervised voting systems: voters have the possibility to revote if they felt coerced to vote at some moment, but the coercer will be able to observe on the ballot tracking center that a new ballot has been submitted.

Several of these properties have been elaborated in more detail using requirement engineering techniques, including by Langer, Schmidt, Buchmann and Volkamer [359]. Volkamer and Grimm [569] also used Helios as an example in their analysis of the resilience of Internet voting systems, identifying the number of parties to be corrupted in order to make Helios fail, in different settings.

11.3.4.1   Works on Verifiability

Shortly after the release of Helios 2.0, Kremer, Ryan and Smyth [353] analyzed the verifiability of Helios, based on a symbolic model expressed in the applied pi calculus. Their analysis highlights the importance of eligibility verifiability, and stresses how the use of voter aliases changes the security model.

Küsters, Truderung and Vogt [356] also highlighted the difficulties arising from the use of voter aliases, through an attack pattern that they called *clash attacks*. For instance, they consider a malicious election administrator who would know that several voters will vote in the same way. To those voters, the administrator will distribute a unique voter alias, hoping that this will remain unnoticed. Furthermore, assuming that the person controlling the distribution of the BPS can guess when these voters intend to load their BPS, the administrator feeds these voters a modified BPS that uses fixed randomness. In this way, all these voters who share a single alias will prepare the exact same ballots, with the same ballot tracker. These ballots will pass cast-as-intended validity tests, since they are correctly built. Then, when the voters submit these ballots, they will appear on the ballot tracking center, but all under a single alias – hence the clash. Voters will not notice this, unless one of those ballots is posted online for audit, which may make duplication visible, or if they observe that a ballot already appears on the ballot tracking center for their alias before they vote. Eventually, if the attack works, the election administrator can create for himself as many fresh voter aliases as there are clashing ballots, and use them to vote freely in order to obtain the expected number of ballots displayed on the ballot tracking center. Such a scenario does not work if explicit voter ids are used, since these voter ids would prevent clashes from happening. The same paper also discusses the accountability of Helios, a strong form of verifiability that requires the possibility to identify which system component failed: it was pointed out that Helios does offer very little accountability, because most Helios operations are not authenticated by the party realizing them.

The works that we just described all assumed that the cryptographic primitives used in Helios presented the expected properties. Bernhard, Pereira and Warinschi [99], while investigating the ballot privacy in Helios, explored the lower-level cryptographic properties of the protocols used in Helios, and of the non-interactive zero-knowledge proofs in particular. As explained before, these proofs are made from sigma protocols made non-interactive thanks to the Fiat–Shamir transformation. This transformation however comes in various flavors in the literature: in the weak variant, only the proof commitment is hashed; while in a strong variant, the proof statement is hashed as well. The weak variant was used in Helios and Bernhard et al. show that, given the specific way in which these proofs are used in Helios, i.e., given that parties would be able to choose their proof statement as a function of the proof challenge, this can actually break the soundness property. Several attack scenarios are demonstrated from there. In the most important one, a coalition of a voter with all the trustees would make it possible to build a single ballot encrypting an arbitrarily chosen number of votes, in such a way that this ballot would pass all the verification procedures and even be indistinguishable from a regular ballot. In order to prevent this, the strong Fiat–Shamir transform should be adopted in Helios.

11.3.4.2 Works on Ballot Privacy

Cortier and Smyth [173], in parallel with Wikström, investigated privacy properties of Helios and observed that Helios did not do anything to prevent a voter from taking someone else's ballot (from the ballot tracking center, for instance) and resubmitting it as his own. While this is a serious privacy threat in mix-net-based elections, as demonstrated by Pfitzmann and Pfitzmann [460], the privacy impact of this possibility is much more limited in a scheme based on homomorphic tallying like Helios. Nevertheless, situations like the following one could happen: in an election with three voters, one voter could decide to copy someone else's encrypted vote, and then deduce the content of this vote from the election result. Of course, the voter who copies the ballot needs to forfeit his own vote in order to learn the vote of another party. Ballot copying can be prevented in Helios by using a non-malleable (NM-CPA) encryption scheme in order to prevent the submission or rerandomized versions of previous ballots, and by rejecting identical ciphertexts from the ballots to be included in the tally [99, 97]. In other works, ballot copying has also been identified as a useful feature of a voting system (despite its potential impact on privacy), e.g., for liquid democracy, and variants of Helios exploiting this feature have also been proposed (see Section 11.5.5).

In further works, it was shown that a large subset of the Helios protocol, using non-malleable encryption and rejection of duplicate ballot, would offer ballot privacy and independence in the sense of a simple ideal functionality [98, 96].

11.3.4.3 Miscellaneous Works

In an early work, Groth [271] analyzes the CGS protocol [178], which was a precursor of the protocol implemented in Helios. This analysis is performed in the UC framework, and shows that the CGS protocol implements an ideal voting functionality under reasonable assumptions. This analysis provides an increased confidence in the general protocol approach that is used in Helios, but the analyzed protocol also differs from the one in Helios in many sensible ways: the ballot preparation process includes the voter id, voters can submit only one ballot, the Benaloh challenge was not part of the protocol ... An interesting feature of the use of the UC framework lies in the very natural way in which the intended properties of the voting system are captured, i.e., by showing that running a protocol is as good as interacting with an ideal voting functionality that receives votes, possibly intercepted by an adversary, and computes the corresponding tally.

11.4 Web Application Perspective

Offering strong verifiability properties does not reduce the need of a high-quality software. From a security point of view, verifiability only makes it possible to detect errors, while it is of course most desirable that no error happens. The privacy of the vote also depends on the software, and is mostly orthogonal to end-to-end verifiability. Besides, the usability of a voting system is crucial, and is also often seen as a security feature.

Helios, since version 2.0, is a Django application and makes heavy use of JavaScript for most of the sensitive parts of the system. In particular, the ballot preparation system is a pure JavaScript application. The code of Helios is available on Github.[2]

A Helios server can be accessed from a browser and offers three main components: it serves the election administration interface, the voting booth, and the ballot tracking center. A single ballot verifier is also available as a separate component. Besides, a Helios server offers a public API, which can be used to access all election data (public keys, list of voters, ballots, ...) as JSON strings. This API is the main interface used by external audit tools.

11.4.1   The Browser Interface

The use of Helios confronts voters, trustees and election administrators with a number of uncommon features: the availability of a ballot tracker and tracking center, a key management process for trustees, the requirement for voters to authenticate at the end of the voting process, etc.

The Helios interface was refined on various occasions since the initial Helios design, based on user feedback and on independent studies that have been performed (see also Section 11.5.6). Being able to run several elections within a single large organization with a dedicated helpdesk was a source of particularly valuable information. In particular, it showed that many of the original features of Helios become part of voter habits very quickly.

Cultural factors also mattered in many cases: different countries use different ballot and form presentation styles in their official communications, and voters tend to express preferences for the presentation styles with which they are the most familiar. Other aspects of Helios do not have common counterparts in the life of the voters and provide a "clean slate" in terms of presentation. For instance, while it was feared that asking voters to perform extra verification steps (e.g., look for their ballot on the ballot tracking center) would be a major obstacle, we observed that voters get used to it fairly quickly, and even complain about a lack of security if they are later invited to vote with a voting system that does not offer these audit possibilities.

Still, some security features keep presenting usability obstacles. For instance, the cast-as-intended verification procedure is arguably challenging to perform. The length of the tracking numbers can also be perceived as fairly demanding when a voter needs to perform a verification. Here, the difficulty lies in the need to have digests that are reasonably efficient to compute but also guarantee collision resistance.

---

[2]https://github.com/benadida/helios-server/

While base64-encoded SHA-256 hashes are used for the moment, other representations and hash function choices might be beneficial. The secret key management process can also be fairly challenging. In order to simplify the key generation process as much as possible, Helios uses a distributed key generation mechanism that does not tolerate the failure of any trustee. These key generation and decryption processes are often performed by persons selected for their standing in the election and not for their computer expertise, which is consistent with their role but often turns out to be practically challenging, especially when the manipulation of secret data is involved. It would be a very useful step forward to design procedures that would further simplify this process and make it possible to tolerate a limited number of failures.

11.4.2 Cryptography in the Browser

Running in a browser the relatively sophisticated cryptographic operations that are needed for the preparation of a ballot proved to be a challenging task.

The early versions of Helios made use of LiveConnect to access the Java Virtual Machine (JVM) from JavaScript. The JVM provided secure randomness and offered support for expensive computational operations like modular exponentiations. This was however a major source of voter complaints, due to the unavailability of the JVM, or due to the lack or difference of support of the JVM in various browsers.

The performance of the JavaScript interpreters included in the browsers however considerably increased during the early years of Helios: between 2009 and 2011, the speed of a JavaScript modular exponentiation increased by a factor of 10 to 20, making it possible to perform the necessary computation directly inside the browser, without relying on a JVM [45]. In 2011, the SJCL library [539] was integrated into Helios, with the support of Emily Stark, Mike Hamburg, Tom Wu and Dan Boneh, which made it possible to prepare a full ballot directly in JavaScript. Workers are also used to performing most of the computation in the background, while the voters make their choices: most of the computational work that is needed to prepare a ballot is indeed independent of the voter choices.[3]

Secure randomness remained an issue for a fair amount of time. At first, entropy was collected from various sources like the movements of the mouse, and then expanded, using a mechanism inspired from the Fortuna design [235]. As an extra measure, randomness was also provided by the Helios server together with the voting booth. While this last source of entropy does not offer any protection from the server, it can provide a safeguard from the rest of the world in case of failure of the local entropy sources. More recently, the JavaScript Web Cryto API was extended to provide a source of secure randomness, which is typically collected from the system.

As of today, the Helios BPS uses JavaScript cryptography and workers for the ballot preparation, which runs quite well in the recent browsers. When an old browser

---

[3]For instance, when computing an ElGamal ciphertext (g^r, my^r), the two exponentiations are independent of m and represent at least 99% of the computational effort.

that does not support these features is used, the ballot preparation is delegated to the Helios server. This does not change the situation regarding the verifiability: the cast-as-intended verification just verifies a slightly different BPS. In terms of privacy, a corrupted Helios server could violate the privacy of these voters by recording their votes but, as discussed above, a corrupted Helios server could also serve a malicious BPS that would leak the voter choices anyway. This strategy then seems to provide an important usability improvement with a limited security impact.

11.4.3 Application Security

The structure of the Helios protocol considerably reduces the operational security requirements of a voting server. Regarding privacy in particular, the Helios server only needs to store public information: election descriptions, public keys, encrypted votes, and audit data. The secret keys of the trustees never reach the Helios server and, with the exception discussed above of old browsers using the Helios BPS, no cleartext vote ever reaches the server either (and no cleartext vote is ever stored there). These features makes it easy to deploy standard database replication tools for robustness, and to closely monitor the server content during an election, without fear of privacy loss. Still, active corruption or bugs on the Helios server might have very damaging effects, including data losses and the corruption of the BPS.

In a similar way, bugs in the Helios voting clients might cause corruption or loss of privacy. Several independent reviews of the Helios code have been performed and documented. Heiderich, Frosch, Niemitz and Schwenk [302] reviewed the Helios code, identified several potential attack sources (XSS, . . .), and proposed fixes that have been integrated. Pouillard [469], together with a team of researchers in Denmark, spotted that the ballot verification procedure implemented on the Helios server would accept some invalid votes: when voters are allowed to pick a number of candidates within a prescribed range, the Helios server would check the range proof, but not verify that the range for which the validity of the vote is proven matches the election definition (the proof would be valid, but for a wrong statement). This would enable a malicious voter to pick a number of candidates outside of the prescribed range, while being accepted by the Helios server – even though this fraud could be detected by any independent election verification tool.

11.5   Helios Variants and Related Systems

A number of variants of Helios have been proposed during the last few years, and some of them have also been implemented and used in elections. Several tools were also designed, that provide support for the audit of elections and for specific tasks like key generation.

11.5.1 Mix-net-Based Variants

A mix-net-based election, in its simplest form, works as follows: voters encrypt their votes submit them to a server. The votes then pass through a network of mixers who verifiably shuffle them (sequentially) in order to anonymize them (this could be seen as shaking the urn), before the distributed decryption of the anonymized votes happens.

This approach has some serious advantages. Most importantly, it can conveniently and efficiently accommodate arbitrary ballot formats, including ranked voting or write-ins, since there is no need to prove the validity of a ballot in the encrypted domain: validity can be checked after decryption. This advantage was the primary motivation for the development of mix-net-based variants of Helios.

Another potential advantage is that, from an educational point of view, the voting and tallying process of a mix-net-based election mimics more closely traditional paper elections – at least, when ignoring the technical details, which can actually be more cumbersome than in a homomorphic election process. The tallying procedure of a mix-net-based election is indeed considerably more complex: mixing ballots is a computationally demanding task, and the trustee decryption procedure now requires to decrypt at least one ciphertext per voter, instead of one ciphertext per question in the homomorphic approach. These constraints strongly support the homomorphic approach implemented in Helios when it can be used. Besides, the algorithms involved in a verifiable mix-net are quite sophisticated, making their implementation a fairly challenging task.

Two mix-net-based variants of Helios implementations have been described:

■ Bulens, Giry and Pereira [121] made an efficient implementation based on the HTDH2 encryption scheme, which they designed as a variant of the TDH2 scheme by Shoup and Gennaro [528], and on a proof of shuffle by Terelius and Wikström [576, 552]. This variant has been used in dozens of elections, in universities and private institutions.

■ Tsoukalas, Papadimitriou, Louridas and Tsanakas [558] later made another implementation, with a verifiable shuffle based on the Sako–Kilian [508] scheme (following Helios 1.0) which, while being considerably less efficient, is also considerably simpler. Zeus has been used in dozens of elections in Greece, including some in a highly emotional context, providing an interesting experience.

11.5.2 Variants Aiming at Countering Ballot-Stuffing

The ballots displayed on the tracking center do not contain any secure personal information: the tracking center only has public voter names (or aliases) and encrypted votes, whose preparation only requires public knowledge. As a result, a corrupted

Helios server could add, remove or modify ballots quite easily. It would of course take the risks of being detected, especially when aliases are not used: any ballot to be included in the tally needs to be associated to a voter name, which opens the risk of complaints being introduced by any of the prejudiced voters. Limiting the impact of a corrupted Helios server is still desirable.

Helios-C is a Helios variant designed by Cortier, Galindo, Glondu and Izabachène [172] that aims at reducing the possibilities of ballot stuffing by relying on a separate registration authority, which is expected to not collude with the party recording the ballots. That authority distributes voter credentials, which are then used to digitally sign ballots. This prevents ballot stuffing as long as no collusion happens (and credentials are not stolen).

An alternate solution was proposed by Srinivasan, Culnane, Heather, Schneider and Xia [537]. Here, while still relying on a separate authority, the voting process is simplified for the voters, who now only need to store a token instead of a full cryptographic key.

11.5.3 Variants Aiming at Perfectly Private Audit Data

The Helios audit data used for the tallied-as-cast verification contain encrypted votes. But any encryption scheme comes with decryption keys and it may be the case that, due to some manipulation error or some hacking, a malicious party would be able to collect enough decryption keys to recover ballots. Besides, since the security of encryption relies on computational assumptions (the hardness of the DDH problem in this case), it is definitely possible that, in the future, someone will be able to decrypt encrypted votes, either because of the availability of more powerful computers, or because of some algorithmic breakthrough that would provide more efficient methods for breaking encryption.

In order to counter these potential issues, it has been proposed to use Helios variants that would offer perfectly private audit data, or everlasting privacy towards the public. In these variants, all the data provided by the system, and the audit data in particular, are perfectly hiding in the sense of information theory. This means that, no matter what key is leaked, and no matter what computational power is available to the adversary, the privacy of the votes remains guaranteed. Still, voters need to submit information about their vote that, for a computationally unbounded adversary with intrusion or network control capabilities, may eventually make it possible to recover the votes. But this kind of attack would require a significantly higher level of preparation.

■ Demirel, van de Graaf and Samarone [196] proposed a solution based on the Paillier encryption scheme and Pedersen commitments in matching groups, following a proposal by Moran and Naor [398]. Proposals based on a distributed mix-net acting on secret shares have also been made [119], in the spirit of the secret-sharing based approach of Cramer et al. [177].

■ Cuvelier, Pereira and Peters proposed another solution, based on new encryption schemes called **PPATs** and **PPATc** [186]. This approach, being based on prime order groups instead of composite groups (like Paillier encryption), brings practical key generation procedures and is considerably more efficient from a computational point of view.

11.5.4   Variants Based on Full Threshold Encryption

Threshold key generation makes it possible to tolerate the failure of a limited number of trustees, which seems highly desirable for a high-stake election. Several teams implemented such a procedure:

■ Cortier, Galindo, Glondu and Izabachène [170] and Pieter Maene [378] implemented variants of the Pedersen procotol for threshold key generation [457]. The key generation is integrated in the web browser and becomes considerably more complex, requiring several rounds of interaction between the trustees, but better fault tolerance is also obtained.

■ Neumann, Kulyk and Volkamer [409] designed an Android Application that automates and considerably simplifies the key generation process: the trustees are required to run the App at the same time, to perform some simple verifications, and the key generation protocol executes in the background, based on peer-to-peer communication.

11.5.5   Variant Supporting Vote Delegation

The possibility to produce ballot copies, pointed to as a source of privacy issues in the work of Cortier and Smyth, has also been seen as a useful feature offered by Internet voting systems. An increasing number of elections indeed use *vote delegation*, making it possible for a voter to delegate his vote to someone else. Examples include liquid democracy, used in the German Pirate party.

Posting ballots on a bulletin board can provide an interesting way of implementing this delegation process, with the convenience that voters may not need to explicitly delegate their vote to others, but could simply submit a copy of someone else's ballot. This idea is explored by Desmedt and Chaidos [198], who propose a variant of Helios explicitly enabling ballot copies. In a first simple non-interactive variant, ballot copies can be noticed by an external observer. In another variant, the voters can produce ballot copies that are indistinguishable from any other ballot, at the cost of interacting with their delegate.

11.5.6   Alternate Helios Frontends

Karayumak, Kauer, Olembo, Volk and Volkamer [338, 339] ran a usability analysis of Helios, based on a cognitive walkthrough, from which they designed alternate Helios interfaces. These alternate interfaces were also investigated through a user study. The proposed modifications include several changes in the voting and audit process, alternate phrasing, as well as improved consistency in the voting booth design.

Further changes in the individual verification processes were proposed by Neumann, Olembo, Renaud and Volkamer [410], who discuss the possibility to delegate the recorded-as-cast verification to third parties using an Android App and a QR-code to simplify the access to the ballot tracking center.

Various other groups designed alternate Helios frontends, modifying various visual aspects (see [378] for instance), or translating it into various languages.

11.5.7   Audit Tools

Independent Helios election audit tools are definitely highly desirable: they provide more resistance to corruption, they can help detect bugs, either directly in the Helios code or in the underlying libraries, and they can even serve as a backup for election data.

- de Marneffe designed the Helios election monitor [48]. This Web2Py application, when given the URL of an election on a Helios server, polls the Helios server every few minutes to download newly submitted ballots. It provides a full bulletin board, verifies the validity of each ballot, warns about revotes, provides graphs of the voting rates, and completes the tallied-as-recorded verification when the election results are available. The Helios election monitor also provides a single ballot verifier. All the verification procedures in this monitor are based on external cryptographic libraries, improving the code independence with Helios.

- Roeder designed Aethon and Pyrios [490]. Aethon is a tool providing a web interface from which a full tallied-as-cast verification can be performed: the auditor browser picks all audit data from the Helios server, and pushes them back to the Aethon server, which performs the verifications and displays the results. Pyrios is a more recent Go library, and offers similar functionalities, except that all the verifications now run locally on the computer of the auditor.

11.6   Conclusion

Seven years after the first use of Helios in a large-scale legally binding election in 2009, Helios and its various forks are routinely used by associations and private companies to run end-to-end verifiable Internet elections, and several hundreds of thousands of votes have been verifiably tallied.

Before running this first election, we had a lot of concerns about running an end-to-end verifiable election. What would be the reaction of the voters to the verification steps that we propose? Would these verification features be dismissed or embraced? How would we be able to handle auditors raising concerns about the election, especially when knowing how little accountability Helios offers? Most of these concerns faded now. The verifiability features of Helios do not appear to prevent anyone from voting, and we found that a surprisingly large number of voters do look for their vote on the ballot tracking center. Furthermore, many voters start feeling that checking a ballot tracking center should be a natural part of any remote voting system: how could they possibly know that their vote was correctly recorded otherwise? We also faced very few auditor complaints and, in all cases, it has been possible to dismiss these complaints quite easily: the public nature of the Helios server content makes it possible to collect detailed logs without creating any risk for the privacy of the votes, and these logs showed to be very helpful for clarifying situations. Furthermore, various simple conflict resolution procedures can also be organized, taking advantage of the fact that Helios always keeps the link between voters and their encrypted vote.

Our assessment of the effectiveness of verifiability features also was nuanced. While the invitation to consult the ballot tracking center was very well received by the voters overall, we found that most organizations refuse to display a ballot tracking center containing voter names and to publish lists of voters. This makes ballot stuffing fairly hard to detect by any auditor who would not have privileged access to election data. Except for this aspect, the tallied-as-recorded aspect of the audit appears to be largely effective, with several independent tools having been built. Cast-as-intended verification remains an important challenge, however: as of today, there is no independent and stable ballot verifier available online, and voters are simply invited to use the verifier offered by the Helios server, which is an important limitation if a corrupted Helios server is part of the threat model. Besides, if a corrupted voting client is part of the threat model, the verification process requires the possibility for the voter to access a honest device at a later time, which is definitely demanding.

Similar concerns appear about the privacy of the votes: the Helios ballot preparation system remains the only convenient and largely available way of preparing a ballot, and voters therefore essentially have to trust the Helios code regarding the privacy of their vote (or read the code that they received, which is an option for very few people only). Again, this situation could be improved if some trusted organizations or candidates were offering an independent ballot preparation system.

On a positive side, we found that the requirement to provide election audit data in real time and at all steps of an election is a very effective constraint placed on election organizers: even if they suspect that some aspects of the election will not be verified, they can never be sure, and audit data need to be committed anyway. A malicious Helios server trying to stuff extra ballots knows that these ballots need to be associated to a voter, and that this is evidence of a malicious behavior if an investigation is started. In a similar way, serving a malicious ballot preparation system always leaves evidence that can possibly be collected and investigated, even more since the BPS is a human-readable script that is distributed without access control. Overall, we feel that this requirement for the organizers to commit on audit data is, in itself, already a very strong motivation for adopting an end-to-end verifiable system.

Acknowledgments

We would like to thank Vanessa Teague for her insightful comments and suggestions about this text, as well as other anonymous reviewers. This chapter also largely benefited from numerous fruitful discussions and collaborations: with Ben Adida, of course, but also with many others, including Josh Benaloh, David Bernhard, Philippe Bulens, Véronique Cortier, Damien Giry, Steve Kremer, Olivier de Marneffe, Ron Rivest, Mark Ryan, Ben Smyth, Dan Wallach, Bogdan Warinschi and Douglas Wikström.

Chapter 12

Prêt à Voter — The Evolution of the Species

Peter Y. A. Ryan

Department of Computing Science and Communications
University of Luxembourg, Luxembourg
`peter.ryan@uni.lu`

Steve Schneider

Department of Computer Science
University of Surrey, UK
`s.schneider@surrey.ac.uk`

Vanessa Teague

Department of Computing and Information Systems
University of Melbourne, Australia
`vjteague@unimelb.edu.au`

CONTENTS

12.1 Introduction

Prêt à Voter provides a practical and highly usable approach to end-to-end verifiable elections with a simple, familiar voter-experience. It assures a high degree of transparency while preserving secrecy of the ballot. Assurance arises from the auditability of an evidence trail created by the execution of the election, rather than the need to place trust in the system components. The original idea has undergone numerous enhancements since its inception in 2004, driven by the identification of threats, the availability of improved cryptographic primitives and the desire to make the scheme as flexible as possible. This evolution culminated in the development and deployment of the system for use in the State of Victoria in Australia for the state election in November 2014. This chapter presents the key elements of the approach and describes the evolution of the design up to that deployment. We also describe the voter experience, and the security properties that the schemes provide.

The main advantage of Prêt à Voter compared to other end-to-end verifiable voting systems is that the auditing necessary for cast-as-intended verification can be performed before the voter has expressed any preference. Hence voters can be helped to verify without any impact on the privacy of the vote and without the possibility of any dispute arising as to what selection the voter made.

In the next section we give an outline of the notion of *end-to-end verifiability*. This is followed by a high-level outline of the Prêt à Voter approach to E2E V. Section 12.3 describes the logic and structure of verification audits. Section 12.4 gives an overview of the underlying cryptographic protocols, with explanations of how they developed, a description of options for different voting schemes and pointers to more detailed descriptions in prior publications. This concludes the theoretical description of Prêt à Voter. In Section 12.5 we describe pollsite procedures for encouraging voters to act according to those assumptions, including making ballot audits an automatic side-effect of ballot casting.

In Section 12.6 we describe some complementary methods of verification that can be used to improve the overall robustness of the process, because they depend on different assumptions from those of the cryptographic protocol. Section 12.7 introduces the notions of accountability and dispute resolution, i.e., the importance of being able to distinguish genuine verification failures from false claims of failure. Section 12.8 is a general discussion of potential attacks on the basic version of Prêt à Voter and possible countermeasures. The final section is an overview of the deployment of Prêt à Voter in a state election in Victoria, Australia, the first time an end-to-end verifiable voting system has run in a state election anywhere in the world (Section 12.9). Open problems and research directions are included in the conclusion.

12.1.1 End-to-End Verifiability

The purpose of end-to-end verifiability (E2E V) is to provide a high level of assurance to all parties that the announced outcome is correct in terms of the legitimately cast votes. This assurance should not depend on the correct behavior of the various components, but rather should stem from immutable evidence generated from the execution of the election. In particular, E2E V seeks to provide each voter with the means to confirm that her vote is correctly included in the tally. However, this has to be done with great care to ensure that it does not provide any way for the voter to demonstrate to a third party how she voted. In practice, this goal is achieved by providing voters, when they cast their vote, with a receipt that holds their vote in encrypted form. They can later use this receipt to confirm that their vote is correctly included in the tally. Once we have the votes collected together in encrypted form we can use standard cryptographic techniques to anonymize and decrypt the votes in a way that can be checked independently, providing universal verifiability of the processing of the votes.

The primary innovation of Prêt à Voter is the way that this encrypted vote is created: voters receive a pre-printed ballot form listing the candidates in a randomized order along with an encryption of this order. This serves as a reference against which they express their choices or preferences. The plaintext version of the candidate list is then destroyed leaving the receipt which carries the voter's selection in encrypted form. A number of important benefits flow from this approach that we detail in Section 12.2.3.

Prêt à Voter is designed to provide the three key ingredients required for E2E verifiability:

Cast-as-intended verification Each voter gets evidence that their vote is cast as they intended;

Recorded-as-cast verification Each voter gets evidence that their vote is included unaltered in the tally;

Universally verifiable tallying Everyone can check that the list of (encrypted) recorded votes produces the announced election outcome.

Eligibility verifiability can also be incorporated by simply attaching a verifiable identity to the public encrypted vote. This is discussed more below.

This chapter outlines the evolution of Prêt à Voter, drawing on the earlier literature on Prêt à Voter and incorporates lessons from the recent deployment in a binding government election in the Australian state of Victoria [184].

Candidates	Your vote
Obelix	
Panoramix	
Asterix	
Idefix	
	7rJ94K
Destroy	Retain

Figure 12.1: Prêt à Voter ballot form.

12.2 Outline of Prêt à Voter

Here we outline the main ingredients of the Prêt à Voter scheme [494, 151, 504]. The key innovation of the Prêt à Voter approach is the way votes are encoded in a randomized frame of reference, i.e., a randomized candidate list. An important observation about this way of encoding the vote is that, in contrast to previous schemes, there is no need for the voter to communicate her vote to an encryption device. What is encrypted is the information that defines the frame of reference for any given ballot form, and this can be computed in advance. We will return to the significance of this observation later when we discuss the threat model. Incidentally, this encoding has another advantage: the randomization of the candidate list results in fairness as a fixed ordering tends to favor candidates near the top of the list. However, it precludes preprinted cards or fixed instructions telling voters how to vote, because the instructions must vary according to the permutation. Depending on the electoral practice in force, this may or may not be an issue.

In the next section we present the basic voter experience when using Prêt à Voter, leaving aside at this stage the various auditing options available to the voter.

12.2.1 The Voting Ceremony

At the polling station, our voter Anne pre-registers and chooses at random a ballot form from a pile of forms individually sealed in envelopes. Example forms are shown in Figures 12.1 and 12.2. Note that the order of the candidates and the cryptographic values vary from form to form.

In the privacy of the booth, Anne removes the ballot from its envelope and makes her selection in the usual way by placing a cross in the right-hand column against the candidate of choice, or, in the case of a single transferable vote (STV) system for example, she marks her ranking against the candidates. Once the selection has been made, she detaches and discards the left-hand column that carries the candidate order. The remaining right-hand column now constitutes the (encrypted) receipt, as shown in Figure 12.3.

Candidates	Your vote
Asterix	
Idefix	
Panoramix	
Obelix	
	$N5077t3$
Destroy	Retain

Figure 12.2: Another Prêt à Voter ballot form.

Your Vote
X
$N5077t3$
Retain

Figure 12.3: Prêt à Voter ballot receipt encoding a vote for "Idefix."

Anne now exits the booth with this receipt, registers with an official and casts her receipt in the presence of the official: the ballot receipt is placed on an optical reader or similar device that records the cryptographic value at the bottom of the strip, that we will refer to henceforth as the ballot *cipher* and denote Θ, and an index value ι indicating the cell into which the X was marked.

In practice, the ballot *cipher* will actually be a unique serial number or pointer to a full ciphertext previously committed to the web bulletin board (WBB), an append-only, public broadcast channel with memory.

The digitized copies of the receipts are transmitted to a central tabulation server which posts them to the WBB. Only the tabulation server, and later the tabulation tellers, can write to this and, once written, anything posted will remain unchanged. Voters are encouraged to visit this WBB and confirm that their receipt appears correctly and, if their receipt does not appear, or appears incorrectly (i.e., with the X in the wrong position), they can appeal. Note that, as the voters hold physical, authenticated receipts, they have demonstrable grounds for complaint if their receipt fails to appear on the WBB.

It is also possible to have representatives of *helper organizations* [43] at hand at the polling stations. They could offer a service: helping audit ballots, checking digital signatures and possibly checking of posting of receipts to the WBB.

12.2.2 *Vote Counting*

The value printed on the bottom of the receipt, which we will refer to as the ballot *cipher*, is the key to extraction of the vote. Buried cryptographically in this value is the information needed to reconstruct the candidate order and so interpret the vote value encoded on the receipt. This information is encrypted under the secret keys shared using a threshold scheme among a number of tellers. Thus, only a threshold set of the tellers acting in concert are able to reconstruct the candidate order and so interpret the vote value encoded on the receipt. In practice, the value printed on the ballot form will be a pointer to the full ciphertext committed to the WBB during the setup phase.

The ciphertext associated with each ballot will have as its plaintext a value σ that encodes a permutation of the N candidates. Thus each ballot form may be thought of as a tuple:

$$(\pi, \Theta)$$

where π is the candidate order and the encrypted term $\Theta = \mathcal{E}(\sigma)$ is the ciphertext. The ballot is well-formed if and only if the plaintext candidate order printed on the ballot agrees with the order encoded in the σ value. A receipt has the form:

$$(\iota, \Theta)$$

where ι is an index value indicating where the voter placed her X or a vector recording her rankings, approvals, etc., depending on the voting method.

After a suitable period, once any disputes over recording and inclusion of receipts are suitably resolved, we can start the counting process. Here we will describe counting using *anonymizing mixes* to guarantee ballot secrecy, but other approaches are possible, for example, if Paillier encryption is used it would be feasible to use homomorphic tabulation [49].

We assume that the candidate list information has been encrypted in the ballot ciphertexts using a randomizing algorithm that supports re-encryption, e.g., ElGamal or Paillier. We also assume for the moment that the index value, indicating the position of the X for example, has been absorbed into the ciphertext to give a pure ElGamal or Paillier term. Details will be presented a little later. Tabulation proceeds in two phases: first a mixing phase to provide privacy (rather like shaking the ballot box) followed by a decryption phase (unsealing and unlocking the ballot box). The first phase will be performed by a set of *mix tellers*. The mix tellers do not need to know any secret keys in order to perform a re-encryption, only the public key under which the encryption was performed.

At the end of the mixing process, the batch of receipts will have undergone a number of re-encryptions and shuffles and are ready to be decrypted. Decryption will then be performed by a threshold set of decryption tellers who hold secret shares for the ballot decryption key.

Once all this is completed, the final, decrypted, anonymized votes appear in the final column of the WBB and these can be tallied in a conventional fashion and can be verified by anyone.

12.2.3 Advantages of Prêt à Voter

The main advantages of Prêt à Voter over earlier E2E schemes is that ballot auditing is independent of the vote and that it is readily adaptable to handling more complex voting methods such as STV.

Voters may challenge a preprinted ballot to check that its ciphertexts match the plaintext vote encoding (candidate order) shown on the ballot. When they have challenged enough ballots to feel confident that the ballots are all likely to be well-formed, they choose an unchallenged one to vote on. This means that ballot auditing is not privacy invasive and furthermore dispute resolution is clear cut: the ballot is either well-formed or it isn't and there is no question of having to rely on the voter's claim as to what vote they input. Wombat and STAR-Vote also print a plaintext representation of the vote beside the voter's ciphertext, which can be demonstrated not to match, however even if they do match the voter could still claim to have input something different.

Another advantage of the Prêt à Voter approach is that voters do not have to spend time inputting (dummy) selections before auditing. This is in contrast with schemes such as Helios and Benaloh's simple voter-verifiable elections, in which a voter has to go all the way through the process of inputting a vote selection before challenging. For simple ballots, it probably does not make much difference, but for complex voting schemes, the ease of verification before voting is a significant advantage.

Later systems, such as Punchscan and Scantegrity, that adopted the idea of pre-prepared ballot forms, inherit these features.

Another main difference between Prêt à Voter and many other schemes is that the secret information in the ballot is actually used for ballot printing, rather than for expressing the vote. This shifts the risk of privacy breach from a DRE (or equivalent, used for vote casting) to the processes that generate the ballot forms. Depending on the process details and the threat model, this may be an advantage or a disadvantage. Centralized printing might allow the machine to be better protected, but the paper itself then has to be carefully kept secret. Print-on-demand in a polling place means weaker assumptions on printout secrecy, but also many machines spread through polling places that must be protected. This is discussed further in Section 12.4.3.

Note also that clash attacks, in which the same receipt is provided against two votes that are the same, are harder in Prêt à Voter, because an attacker would have to guess how someone will vote before contriving a collision of receipts. In other E2E systems in which a device creates an encryption of the vote on demand, the device could simply record previous votes and when it encounters a repeat vote it simply copies the receipt it produced earlier. Such threats are typically countered by using a trustworthy source of entropy for the encryption, but even here we have to ensure that the device actually employs the entropy provided.

Backup with a plaintext paper record is an emerging theme of end-to-end verifiable voting systems. Scantegrity II [133], STAR-Vote [77] and Wombat [80] all provide this feature as a natural artefact of the voting process. This allows auditing or manual counting of the paper trail to provide evidence of election integrity independent of the end-to-end verifiability. Prêt à Voter does not automatically produce such a centralized paper trail, and its only deployment in a real election was in a case in which avoiding paper records was specifically requested (see Section 12.9). However, in general it improves robustness to combine end-to-end verifiability with a more traditional paper trail. This is explored in Section 12.6.

12.3   Auditing the Election

So far we have described the process under the assumption that all the steps are executed correctly. However, we do not want the integrity of the election to rely on the entities involved behaving correctly and so we now introduce the mechanisms to detect any malfunction or corruption.

12.3.1   Auditing the Ballot Generation Authority

The first place that things could go wrong is in the creation of the ballot forms. If a ballot form is incorrectly constructed, in the sense that the candidate list shown on the form does not correspond to the order given by the σ value buried in the ballot ciphertext, then the voter's choice will not be accurately encoded. Note that throughout this chapter we are assuming that the voter makes her mark or marks in the right place relative to the printed candidate list. We therefore need a mechanism to detect incorrectly constructed forms, without revealing encryption keys.

If, as we have done above, we assume that the ballot forms are created in advance, we can perform a random audit on a proportion of the forms. So, we require the ballot creation authority (or authorities) to create an excess number of forms, perhaps four or five times as many as actually required, and allow independent organizations to make random selections of an appropriate proportion. For these selected forms, the randomization factors are revealed, so allowing the auditors to recompute the Θ and π and confirm that they agree with those printed on the forms. Alternatively, zero-knowledge proofs of correct decryption could be provided, which avoids having to reveal the randomization.

A rather elegant way of revealing the audit information for selected forms while ensuring that it is kept secret for ballot forms that are used to cast votes, is the "Scratch and Vote" mechanism of Adida and Rivest [43]. Here, the audit information is printed on the ballot forms but concealed by a scratch strip. Revealing the information by removing the strip automatically invalidates the form for voting. In the '06 version of Prêt à Voter [504], this information was revealed by having the decryption tellers online to reveal the audit information. The Adida/Rivest approach avoids the need to have the tellers online and provides a procedural mechanism to enforce the mutual exclusion of casting and auditing.

The process of auditing a ballot form is accomplished by recomputing the values on the form from the cryptographic values. Thus the ciphertext is recomputed from the representation of the candidate order σ, the randomization and the teller public keys.

$$\Theta = \{\sigma\}_{PK_T}$$

If these agree with the values printed on the form, we may conclude that the form was correctly formed.

Voters should always have the opportunity to audit on demand. In addition, audits may be performed by appropriate authorities before, during and after the election.

12.3.2 Auditing Mixing and Decryption

Next, we need to confirm that the mix tellers perform all their actions correctly. In the case of decryption mixes the mixing and (partial) decryptions occur in parallel. We need to show that each teller correctly decrypts its layer of encryption for each ballot. The point is to ensure that the set of votes in the input is the same as the set of votes output.

The technique for auditing the mix tellers in the early versions of Prêt à Voter that used decryption mixes was based on *randomized partial checking* [321]. Half the links are randomly chosen to be revealed and verified. The choice of links, while essentially random, is carefully constrained in such a way as to ensure that no decrypted vote can be traced back to the original ballot receipt. We do not go into the details here as the approach has been superseded by the zero-knowledge proofs of shuffles for re-encryption mixes described below.

When we use re-encryption mixes, the mixing and decryption phases are separated out and we deal with these in the next two sections.

12.3.2.1 Auditing the Mixes

Numerous techniques have been proposed for proving correct mixing of encrypted values quite efficiently, for example the approach proposed by Neff [406]. For a comprehensive survey see [43] or [189].

12.3.2.2   Auditing the Decryption Tellers

Finally, once the ballots have been mixed, we also need to confirm that they are all correctly decrypted. Here we can be more direct and can separately audit every decryption as we do not need to worry about anonymity at this stage. Given that we are using randomizing encryptions here, the process of checking the correctness of the decryptions is not quite trivial: we cannot simply perform the encryption of the claimed plaintext and check the result agrees with the ciphertext, as would be possible for a deterministic algorithm. And of course we don't want to reveal the secret keys. There are efficient ways to prove correct distributed decryption in zero knowledge, for example using [178].

12.4   Cryptographic Components

Most of the published versions of Prêt à Voter use anonymizing mixes to eliminate any link between the receipts and their eventual decryption. In theory, homomorphic tabulation could also be used, given suitable encodings of the votes and encryption algorithms. In fact, the vVote implementation, described in detail in Section 12.9, uses a hybrid of techniques to compress and uncompress votes (a vector of preferences) in order to make their pass through the mix more efficient.

In this section we briefly describe the evolution of the mixed-based approaches.

12.4.1   Decryption Mixes

The original version of Prêt à Voter [151], employed Chaumian decryption mixes and RSA encryption. The ciphertexts defining the candidate permutations were constructed as layers of RSA encryption. The ith layer is encrypted under the public key of the ith mix server. Suppose that we have m layers. To mix a batch of such terms, the batch is passed to the mth server who strips off the outer layer of encryption, shuffles the resulting terms and outputs them to the $(m-1)$th server. The $(m-1)$th server then strips off the next layer, shuffles them and passes them on to the $(m-2)$th server and so on.

Decryption mixes had one very pleasing feature when used in Prêt à Voter: permutations can be encoded in the randomization at each layer of the encryption. The final permutation of the candidates printed on the ballot can thus be constructed as a product of the permutations defined at each layer, moving outwards from the inner layer. Consequently, during the tabulation mixes, the representation of the vote can be transformed as the ballots passed through the mixes by the inverse permutations, moving in reverse order from the outer layer inwards. Suppose that the vote is represented as a vector. For a simple choice of one candidate the vote will have a 1 on the position corresponding to the voter choice in the basis given by the original candidate ordering on the ballot, with 0s elsewhere. As the ballot moves through the tabulation mix, the vector representation is transformed according to the inverse of the permutations that was used to form the final permutation shown on the ballot form. In effect the transformations of the vectors that occur during the tabulations mixes undo the permutations applied in the construction of the ballot.

The result of this is that it is possible to arrange for all the ballots to emerge from the tabulation mixes with the voter's selection presented in the standard candidate ordering. Consequently, all information about the original ordering on the ballot is washed out, avoiding any danger of an attacker being able to partition the mix according to such information. Full details of these constructions can be found in [151].

However, decryption mixes have several downsides. Mix servers need decryption keys and hence have to be pre-determined. If auditing reveals that one of them has cheated there is no privacy-preserving way to redo the mixing and audit. A further drawback is that the size of the ciphertexts grows with the number of mixes used.

In re-encryption mixes, the servers do not need any secret keys, just knowledge of the public key. Consequently, any failing server is easily swapped out. Note also that re-encryption mixes can be independently repeated with different re-encryption factors, or even run in parallel. A number of techniques to prove in zero-knowledge the correctness of a shuffle are available for re-encryption mixes, whereas decryption mixes require partial random checking (RPC) techniques, [321, 342] that necessarily leak some information about the shuffles.

Such considerations prompted the investigation of the use of re-encryption mixes in place of decryption mixes. This has many advantages but also entails some drawbacks when applied to Prêt à Voter, as described below.

12.4.2   Re-encryption Mix-nets

12.4.2.1   Re-encryption Mixes with Cyclic Shifts

Re-encryption mixes for Prêt à Voter were first investigated in [504]. Here, the ciphertexts on the ballots defining the candidate order comprise a single layer encryption with a randomizing algorithm such as ElGamal. Now mixing involves each mix server taking the input batch of ciphertexts, re-encrypting each term, i.e., re-randomizing and outputting the resulting set in secret, shuffled order to the next server.

As mentioned earlier, there are a number of clear advantages in moving to re-encryption mixes, but there is also one major downside, at least when done in the most obvious way. With decryption mixes we have a natural way to transform the vector of voter choices as the ballot moves through the mixes in such a way as to ensure that the final vector aligns with the canonical order of the candidates. With re-encryption mixes there is no obvious analogue of this. We could simply send the receipts, $(\iota.\Theta)$ through the mix leaving the ι vector unchanged and finally decrypt the Θ to reveal the original ballot permutation. This would indeed allow correct tabulation, but it reveals the original candidate permutation and allows an attacker to partition the mix according to the various ι values.

A possible fix, which works at least for simple voting methods in which the voter just selects a single candidate, is to restrict the candidate permutations to cyclic shifts of the canonical order. We can then exploit the homomorphic nature of the encryption algorithm to absorb the index value into the Θ term. Suitably constructed, this now becomes an encryption of the index value translated to the canonical order. Thus we can now treat the Θ' terms as regular ElGamal ciphertexts and send them through the re-encryption mixes in the usual way. We omit the details here; full details can be found in [503].

This eliminates the partitioning problem, but still has a couple of problems: it will only work for simple "X marks the candidate" style voting, and it is arguably rather fragile. Suppose that an attacker is able somehow to undetectably shift the position of the Xs on some ballots. Suppose further that he knows that the majority of these votes will be for some candidate B while he favors candidate F five down in the list. Then he simply shifts a suitable number of the Xs to $X + 5 \pmod{N}$, where N is the number of candidates.

Of course, the auditing mechanisms should make this impossible, but nonetheless this possibility is a bit troubling, hence the next enhancement described in the next section.

12.4.2.2 *Re-encryption Mixes with Affine Transformations*

In order to counter the fragility issue described above, and to slightly broaden the scope of voting methods, the use of affine transformations of the candidate list instead of simple cyclic shifts is proposed in [505]. Now we have two ciphertexts, one concealing a shift factor and the other a scaling factor. The approach works best with a prime number of candidates. The result is less fragile: an attacker does not know how to manipulate the position of the X to produce a predictable switch of candidates.

The approach also accommodates voting where up to two candidates can be selected, but of course this is a rather modest improvement in flexibility. The real challenge is to handle full permutations, which we address in the next section.

12.4.2.3 *Re-encryption Mixes with Full Permutations*

For preferential voting the vote is a full vector of rankings. The cipher schemes used in re-encryption mixes (ElGamal and Paillier) do not provide a homomorphic way of composing permutations, and so it is not possible to combine the list of preferences with the encrypted candidate list to obtain the vote in encrypted form as a single ciphertext. It is an open problem as to whether this can be done in some other way.

Therefore the way we handle full permutations coupled with re-encryption mixes is simply to provide N ciphertexts, one for each candidate, in the permuted order. A vote is the rank ordered list of these ciphertexts, which can then be processed by the mix-net in the usual way, simply handling tuples (lists) rather than single ciphers. This approach first appears in [581] and is used in the vVote system that we describe in detail later.

12.4.3   Distributed Generation of Ballots

As already mentioned, one key feature of Prêt à Voter is the absence of any single machine that knows both the ciphertext and the corresponding plaintext vote. However, on closer examination this is not quite so clear cut: anyone who observes the printed ballot form with its attached ciphertexts and candidate list can easily infer the contents of the vote when it appears on the bulletin board. This also applies to a single machine that generates the preprinted ballot form. Such a machine could also use deliberately badly-chosen randomness to leak this information to a third party without explicitly communicating it (this is sometimes called a "subliminal attack" [530][1]). This has motivated many schemes for distributing the generation of ballot forms [477], for printing them on demand so that only the intended voter sees them [182], or altering the form that will appear on the bulletin board so that it is no longer recognizable by the entity that originally created it.

In summary, the overall aims of such constructions are:

■ To make sure the randomness is good,

■ To make sure no single (electronic) entity knows the ciphertext-plaintext link.

Overall, however, this remains an incompletely solved problem. The ballot forms must eventually be printed, and although there are some preliminary investigations into distributing the printing process itself [217], these do not yet seem practical.

12.4.4   The Bulletin Board

Prêt à Voter shares with most end-to-end verifiable voting schemes the assumption of a bulletin board, which is an authenticated broadcast channel with append-only memory. Although in theory a fairly simple object, the bulletin board turns out to be difficult to implement in practice. One important insight of the vVote project in Victoria was the advantage of splitting the two functions of the bulletin board. One part is a robust and secure database with redundancy, tolerance of failures, and a method of acknowledging receipts. This is the real-time repository of election data. The second part, which corresponds to the theoretical "bulletin board," is a static transcript of the day's transactions, including vote generation, auditing, casting and,

---

[1] In earlier versions of this work we referred to this as a *kleptographic attack*, which is not quite the right term.

on the final day, mixing and decryption. It contains all of the information that the system commits to before, during and after the election.

12.5 Facilitating Verification and Privacy

E2E V ensures that errors or corruption are detectable, but this is not enough: it is essential that audit steps are actually performed to ensure that problems are actually detected. Thus, electoral integrity depends on people actually performing the verification tasks, so it's important to make it easy to do so. In the case of voters, it is important that they understand the purpose and importance of the checks available to them and are thus motivated. Some procedures are optional for the voters, but some really need to be enforced, for example, receipt freeness follows from the *compulsory* shredding of the candidate list in the polling place.

Auditing the proper construction of the ballot is arguably the most important and least intuitive of Prêt à Voter audits. We describe below some possibilities for making it easier.

12.5.1 Encouraging Cast-as-Intended Verification (Ballot Auditing)

The separation of ballot auditing from actual voting in Prêt à Voter permits many methods of encouraging cast-as-intended verification without any appearance of authorities influencing people's votes. Anyone can help anyone else to audit a preprinted ballot. Electoral authorities or other parties could offer explicit encouragement or incentives to audit, or appoint independent ballot auditors who would challenge ballots in public in addition to voter-initiated auditing.

It is important to make auditing as effortless and automatic as possible. There are various ways this could be achieved. One proposal is the double-sided forms of [497], which has the advantage of automatically assigning two ballots to each voter and enforcing the mutual exclusion of voting and auditing of any ballot. Here, each side of a form carries an independent Prêt à Voter ballot form. The voter arbitrarily selects one side to vote and the other for audit. The forms actually have a third, blank column opposite the candidate list on the other side, as shown in Figures 12.4 and 12.5. These images of the two sides should be thought of as being related by a rotation about the vertical axis. Thus, detaching the candidate list on the voted side detaches the blank column of the flip side, so leaving an intact Prêt à Voter ballot for audit. The two sides of the resulting receipt where the voter has cast a vote for Idefix on the second side is shown in Figures 12.6 and 12.7.

Now the side selected for casting is scanned and posted to the WBB as usual, but also the flip side, with a complete Prêt à Voter ballot is scanned and posted for

Obelix		
Asterix		
Idefix		
Panoramix		
	$3Wa3Kc$	

Figure 12.4: Dual Prêt à Voter ballot form; side 1.

Asterix		
Idefix		
Obelix		
Panoramix		
	$Yu78gf$	

Figure 12.5: Dual Prêt à Voter ballot form; side 2.

public auditing. Note that this mechanism enforces the mutual separation of casting and auditing.

12.6 Enhancing Robustness Using Parallel Verification Mechanisms

This section describes several methods of providing evidence of a correct election outcome that are different from the main logic of end-to-end verification. The idea is to provide some redundant means of auditing or verifying the election outcome, relying on different assumptions that may remain true even if the assumptions of the end-to-end verification protocol are not. Examples include confirmation codes (Section 12.6.3), or retaining at the polling place either a plaintext human-readable vote (Section 12.6.2) or a copy of the encrypted receipt (Section 12.6.1).

Obelix	
Asterix	
Idefix	
Panoramix	
	$3Wa3Kc$

Figure 12.6: Dual Prêt à Voter ballot receipt; auditable side.

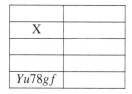

Figure 12.7: Dual Prêt à Voter receipt; vote carrying side.

Combining such methods requires careful thought because the assumptions are different, and may result in an inconsistent state. For example, the plain human-readable paper record may be corrupted even when the end-to-end verifiable voting data are correct. Resolving discrepancies between different evidence trails could be problematic.

12.6.1   Verified Encrypted Paper Audit Trails

A VEPAT (verified encrypted paper audit trail) mechanism was proposed in [495] as a way to counter the possible lack of diligence of voters in checking receipts against the WBB. The idea is to keep one or more complete copies of the cast votes locally at the polling site. These copies could then be made available to independent observers to perform checks against the WBB. Of course, great care has to be taken to ensure the integrity of such paper audit trails, as corruption of the trail could end up undermining the credibility of a valid electronic count. A possibility is to record the ballots on a till roll which is very hard to tamper with. Usually for VVPAT, i.e., with plaintext ballots, this is not possible because of the privacy concerns arising from preserving a record of the order in which votes are cast.

Note that this also serves to counter the so-called *trash* attacks in which voters throw away their receipts which normally would indicate to an attacker that these receipts will not be checked, and hence allow an insider attacker to manipulate or suppress publication of such votes.

12.6.2   Human Readable Paper Audit Trails

The idea of introducing a human readable paper audit trail (HRPAT) was introduced in [496] and later elaborated in [374]. This was prompted by the observation that many people seem uncomfortable with relying on cryptography and so having a more conventional plaintext record of cast votes as a fall-back could assuage such concerns and foster a higher level of trust in the system. Again there may be dangers in this in that manipulation of the audit trail could end up casting doubt on a valid electronic count.

We do not go into the details here, as they can be found in [374], but we just give an indication of the mechanism. Now the ballots have two layers: the lower layer is a regular Prêt à Voter ballot form, but without the usual cipher term. The upper part comprises another copy of just the receipt column, without the candidate list but with the usual cipher term, overlaid over the lower layer. The voter marks her selection on the upper layer in the usual fashion and a carbon paper or similar mechanism transfers the marks to the lower layer. The voter then detaches the upper layer that now forms the receipt in the usual way. The lower part still carries the candidate list and so the vote is represented in the clear. The lower layer is folded and dropped into a ballot box observed by the voting officials. This creates a plaintext paper audit trail and, inter alia, provides a mechanism to help ensure the voter relinquishes the candidate order.

Whether such a mechanism actually increases the assurance in a technical sense is debatable, if there is any possibility of manipulation of the paper audit trail this may actually weaken the overall assurance by undermining the credibility of the electronic count. Another concern is that voters might deliberately manipulate the ballot marking in such a way as to produce differently marked upper and lower ballots, leading to a discrepancy later. Possible countermeasures are proposed in [374] but as always, they are not infallible.

This relies on different assumptions, in particular that the voters verify their plaintext paper vote, and that the paper records are properly audited (or manually counted) afterwards.

12.6.3   Confirmation Codes and Signatures

There are various methods for confirming that a (threshold) number of authorities have recorded each ballot. Although this doesn't contribute to end-to-end verifiability (because all the trustees may be corrupt, and may subsequently drop or modify the ballot), it can give voters an immediate and easy way to check, in the polling place, that their vote has been received and recorded.

Several standard methods of acknowledging receipt by a threshold set of trustees are applicable to Prêt à Voter, including

- acknowledgment codes that need a threshold to decrypt/derive and return them to the voter,

- (threshold) digital signatures.

The first approach was proposed in [498] and introduced ideas and construction from Pretty Good Democracy, [506], into Prêt à Voter. A threshold set of trustees cooperate to register the vote and reveal a secret shared confirmation code.

The second was proposed for vVote in [181] and instead of revealing a confirmation code it provides a threshold signature. In both cases, the voter needs a way to check, in the polling place, that the returned code or signature is valid. Procedures need to be established to handle situations in which codes do not match or signatures prove not valid.

12.7 Accountability, Dispute Resolution and Resilience

The possibility for voters to verify parts of an election process introduces new attack vectors: to falsely claim that an attempted verification has failed in order to cast doubt on the accuracy of the election outcome. Of course, traditional voting is vulnerable to the same problem, although they typically provide little or no opportunity for voters to uncover errors or fraud. There are numerous examples of disappointed candidates who contest results alleging electoral fraud. Distinguishing truthful from false claims is essential for any election system.

In general, every possible defaming attack is matched to some genuine attack on electoral integrity—the point is that the claim of a failed verification is plausible because it corresponds to some possible attack that could alter the votes. The aim of design for accountability and dispute resolution is to distinguish between a true detection of the attack, and a false claim of detection.

Prêt à Voter provides evidence of most kinds of attack. However, depending on the exact polling place procedures and mechanisms of authenticating printouts and receipts, there are some ways of fabricating printouts or receipts that make it look as if they were received from the legitimate authority but are invalid.[2] Some ideas for attempting to defend against such attacks are described in Section 12.7.2.

12.7.1 Cast-as-Intended Verification

As discussed already, in Prêt à Voter cast-as-intended verification is equivalent to establishing the well-formedness of the ballots. This is achieved by challenging preprinted ballots, which means that this verification step automatically produces evidence when there is a failure. This is in contrast to most other E2E V systems that depend on the voter's declaration of how she asked the machine to vote. In Prêt à Voter, in order to fabricate a failed verification, an attacker would have to generate a ballot form that looked genuine but encoded inconsistent values and smuggle it into the system. Countermeasures to this of course exist: the usual anti-counterfeiting mechanisms such as special paper stock, digital signatures, chain of custody, etc. In the vVote setting for Victoria's state election (Section 12.9), printed ballots were dig-

---

[2]For example, a voter could make a good receipt/vote but not cast it, then complain later that it doesn't appear on the bulletin board. Depending on exact procedures, and how much work is put into authenticating receipts and ensuring that only authenticated receipts are left with voters, this sort of attack might succeed.

itally signed to prevent this attack. The techniques described below for guaranteeing the authenticity of receipts could be applied to preprinted ballots too.

12.7.2 Authenticity of Receipts (Included-as-Cast Verification)

When a voter complains that her receipt has been omitted from the bulletin board, there should be some process for establishing whether the problem lies in a misbehaving electoral system or a misbehaving accuser. A verified encrypted paper audit trail (Section 12.6.1) helps, but assumes that the paper audit trail is hard to manipulate. Such assumptions are routinely made for conventional voting systems, and indeed for a VEPAT mechanism with a till roll style the assumption is probably more justifiable. Nonetheless, it is important that the voter's receipt itself needs to include evidence that it is genuine, which can be tested by a third party.

There are several methods of providing evidence of the validity of a receipt, listed here in increasing order of difficulty of forgery. In each case, the crucial questions are

■ how difficult it is for an accuser to forge a valid-looking receipt, and

■ how difficult it is for a misbehaving poll-site to trick a voter into leaving with an invalid receipt.

Possible technologies include:

Anti-counterfeit paper: Receipts could be printed on paper that is distinctive and otherwise unavailable. Producing a fake one would be as hard as stealing some of the paper. Voters need to be able to recognize the paper in order to identify false receipts from a corrupted polling place.

Franked or stamped receipts: Receipts could be stamped, die-cut or signed (by hand) at the polling place. The security properties would be similar to traditional commercial receipts, and voters would need to know what sort of mark, stamp or die-cut to expect.

Digitally signed receipts: Voters receive a digital signature on all the data on their receipt. The voter must be able to check the signature in the polling station, before she leaves. Since obtaining the receipt happens in controlled conditions and the voter is under supervision through to doing the signature check, a claim of an incorrect signature at that point demonstrates that there has been an attack.

This is based on the assumption that a voter behaves honestly while in the polling station. (For example, we have to guard against smuggling in and switching in a fake receipt.) Once a voter leaves the polling station then she cannot later come back in with an incorrect signature.

This solution was used in the vVote project—see Section 12.9.

Confirmation codes This approach was originally proposed by Chaum for Scantegrity II. The idea is that when the voter casts her vote she gets a code specific to that ballot and vote. Such codes are fairly sparse and hence hard to guess. If we can ensure that the voter only sees the code for her vote, then knowledge of this code can provide evidence in the event of a challenge. Suppose that the voter checks the code posted to the WBB against her ballot and finds that it does not agree with the code revealed to her. When she challenges there is a procedure to verifiably open all the codes for that ballot. If it turns out that the code claimed by the voter is indeed a valid code and different to the one posted then this provides good support from the voter's challenge. If however, the code she claims does not correspond to any valid code for this ballot then this is a strong indication that the challenge is false. Of course, great care has to be taken to ensure the integrity and secrecy of these codes. Furthermore, the voter needs a way to confirm that she has been given the correct code at the time of casting.

12.7.3 Tally Verification

Disputes about the proper mixing and decryption of receipts on the bulletin board are the easiest to resolve, because multiple verifiers can be applied and examined until they agree. Thus, if a problem is detected with say the posted output of one of the mix servers, then it is clear which entity is responsible. Furthermore, for many such errors in the tabulation process we can recover quite easily, for example by swapping out a defective/corrupt mix server and re-running the mix.

12.8 Vulnerabilities and Countermeasures

This section describes known vulnerabilities in the basic version of Prêt à Voter. Some depend on the exact version of Prêt à Voter being used. Most have workarounds at the cost of some extra complexity in the procedures or protocol.

12.8.1 Ballot Stuffing

Prêt à Voter, like most E2E systems, does not by itself address ballot stuffing. The fact that the link from a voter's receipt to the voter's identity does not need to be kept secret permits some simple means of guaranteeing that only eligible voters can vote. One possibility is simply to list the voter's name against their receipt on the bulletin board. This allows for public eligibility verifiability, because everyone can check the entire list of included voters. It also protects privacy, though not everlastingly—in time the cryptographic algorithms may be broken and votes may be revealed [397].

To counter concerns about the long-term secrecy of votes, we could simply list the names of voters who cast votes in random order with respect to the list of receipts.

Another possibility, since Prêt à Voter is an attendance voting scheme, is to use existing procedures for roll markoff (however secure or insecure they are) and ensure that the number of votes legitimately cast at each location is correctly recorded and reconciled with the numbers on the bulletin board. This means that prevention of ballot stuffing depends on the security of polling-place procedures.

12.8.2 Information Leakage

The device that prints the ballot forms learns their candidate ordering. Depending on the exact version of Prêt à Voter being used, it can probably also recognize the corresponding receipt afterwards. If it leaks this information it violates vote privacy.

Although an honestly constructed receipt does not leak information about the vote except given the decryption key, a dishonestly constructed ballot form might produce a receipt that does leak the vote, in two conceptually different ways:

print channels: This involves embedding information in subtle features of the printed ballot form, and hence into the receipt. Possibilities include slightly modified layout, fonts or colors. Depending on the method of tabulation, such information may or may not be carried onto the bulletin board, but could certainly be used by someone with direct contact with the voter's printed receipt.

subliminal channels: This involves embedding information into the randomness used to generate the encrypted ballot form itself. (Public key encryption generally requires additional randomness to produce each ciphertext.) The randomness could be chosen in a way that was deliberately weak, or deliberately known in advance to a colluding attacker. This information would be immediately replicated on the bulletin board.

Methods for secure distributed generation of randomness exist and can be employed here, but they solve only the subliminal attacks, not the plain information leakage or the leakage via print channels. There is some work on distributed printing of secret information [217], but at the moment the production of ballot forms still has important trust assumptions for privacy.

12.8.3 Retention of the Candidate List

A voter who retains their randomized candidate list can use it to prove how they voted. It is challenging to devise a polling place procedure that forces the destruction of the list without revealing the list to observers. The HRPAT mechanism mentioned earlier could provide such a mechanism. An alternative, rather pleasing approach is to have a supply of alternative candidate strips in the voting booths. Now a coercer does not know if the voter retained the real strip or just picked up an alternative. Of course care needs to be taken to avoid the coercer being able to distinguish real from dummy by, for example, aligning perforations.

12.8.4 Forced/Coerced Randomization

Although a voter cannot produce evidence of having voted a particular way, and hence cannot be coerced to do so, a coercer can still insist on a receipt of a particular form, for example, one with a checkmark in the first location, or one in which preferences are in ascending order. This makes the voter cast a random vote. The effect is ameliorated if the voter can select from a variety of ballots, including for audit, without observation by the coercer. She may then be able to choose one that simultaneously keeps the coercer happy and expresses the vote she wants. This may not necessarily work for complex ballots such as preferential ones, however, because it may take a very large number of ballot forms to make the coercer's demand consistent with the voter's intention.

12.8.5 Chain Voting

In the chain voting attack, as it applies to conventional voting, a coercer smuggles a ballot out of a polling place, fills it out and gives it to a voter approaching the polling station with instructions to cast it and bring an unmarked ballot back out. The coercer uses the new ballot to repeat the attack with a new voter.

In Prêt à Voter, the chain voting attack is to smuggle out a printed ballot form, record the candidate order, then send a voter back into the polling place with instructions to vote in a particular way and return with both a receipt derived from that form and a new, unmarked, ballot form. Since the coercer has already recorded the voter's candidate order, the receipt reveals the vote. The new ballot form is used to repeat the attack with a new voter.

As in conventional paper-based voting, [296], a simple counter is to give the receipt a unique, detachable serial number and record this at the time the ballot is passed to the voter. When the voter returns to cast her vote, the official checks that it matches the one recorded and then detaches it from the ballot before it is cast. This ensures that the voter casts the same ballot she was provided when she registered. Another possibility is setting a limit for the time elapsed between receiving a ballot form and casting the vote—this doesn't completely solve the problem, but it reduces the window of opportunity for the attack.

A further idea [501], is to have a scratch strip over the ballot serial number, possibly overprinted with an ephemeral serial number. This is required to be intact until the point at which the receipt is scanned. Election officials check the ephemeral serial number is intact and corresponds to the number handed out to the voter. It is then removed to reveal the true serial number before scanning. This ensures that everyone votes on the form they received at registration time, without giving officials a way to link the final receipt with its candidate list.

12.8.6 Trash Attacks

The "trash attack" [88] is an attack on counted-as-cast verifiability. If the attacker controls the bulletin board or uploads his own data to the bulletin board, and happens to know that a particular voter will not check the inclusion of their receipt, then the encrypted vote can be safely substituted. The name "trash attack" refers to such an attacker noticing a certain receipt in the trash, and hence inferring that the voter won't be able to verify it later. There are simple mitigations for the classic form of this attack, for example a VEPAT (Section 12.6.1), or a photocopier in the polling place allowing voters to distribute their receipt to others.

In general without an independent copy, the more general class of attack, in which a cheating authority somehow learns that a certain voter will not verify the inclusion of their receipt, remains an important problem.

12.8.7 Clash Attacks

The "clash attack" [357] is a vote dropping technique that applies to many cryptographic voting schemes. An attacker (as a server or ballot generator) arranges to give several different voters identical receipts. All affected voters see their receipt appear on the public WBB, and yet only one vote has been counted.

The attack works only if the voters subsequently cast identical votes. The attack is in general harder for Prêt à Voter than for direct-encrypting schemes such as Helios and Wombat, because the attacker must commit to the identical ballot before learning the person's vote.

Overall this attack is no more effective, requires more conspirators and has a higher probability of detection than the simple misalignment of the candidate names on the ballot by a corrupt printer.

12.8.8 Psychological Attacks

Particularly for privacy, there is always the possibility for a coercer to claim that they can infer a person's vote when they actually can't. Successful coercion depends on the voter believing this claim, not on the claim being true. Since Prêt à Voter's public-key-based privacy mechanisms are probably too complicated for many voters to understand, and since there are indeed genuine opportunities for some information leakage by particular components, it is hard to defend against this attack. This problem is not specific to Prêt à Voter.

12.9   Prêt à Voter Goes Down-Under

This section describes a design based on Prêt à Voter for the Australian state of Victoria. More details are given in [184], of which this section is a summary. The system ran successfully in the state election in Victoria (Australia) in November 2014, taking a total of 1121 votes from supervised polling places inside Victoria and at the Australian High Commission in London.

The protocol itself is end-to-end verifiable, meaning that there are no human or electronic components which must be trusted for guaranteeing the integrity of the votes (although vision impaired voters must assume that at least one device reads accurately to them). There are probabilistic assumptions about the number of voters who audit Prêt à Voter ballots, the number of voters who check that their receipt printout matches their intended vote, and the number who check that their receipt appears on the Web Bulletin Board (WBB). It also provides voters with evidence of malfeasance, assuming that they check the signature on their receipt before they leave the polling station. Since this is a polling-station scheme, we do not address eligibility verifiability. Prevention of ballot stuffing is by existing procedural mechanisms.

12.9.1   *Significance of the VEC Election*

End-to-end verifiable election protocols are well studied in the academic literature, but (with the notable exception of the Scantegrity II project in Takoma Park, MD [133]) had not previously been deployed in binding government elections. This project demanded new protocols for addressing issues that arise in practice but had not been adequately considered in the literature, and provided new insights into the important difference between practical requirements and academic security goals. Our main contributions are:

1. A version of Prêt à Voter usable enough for real people, even for the very complex ballots used in Victoria, with some practical evidence about its use in a real election.

2. Scalable cryptographic protocols that are fast enough for long preferential ballots. Details are in [182].

3. A clear account of what is achieved by running an end-to-end verifiable system as part of an electoral process that also includes a traditional paper-based system for other votes. The paper elements mean that the whole electoral process is not end-to-end verifiable, but end-to-end verifiability of the subset improves the weakest links in the paper system and hence the security of the overall system. This is substantially better than substituting an unverifiable electronic system in the same place.

4. An informative account of the challenges of implementing and deploying a

verifiable system and lessons about the distinction between theory and practice.

This project does not achieve verifiability all the way to the announcement of the election result, because it runs alongside an existing paper-based system that relies on scrutineers to check that the cast votes are included unaltered in the final count. In summary, the vVote system provides:

■ cast-as-intended verification,

■ recorded-as-cast verification and

■ an output list of decrypted recorded votes, with a universally verifiable proof of proper mixing and decryption.

An important practical advantage of an end-to-end verifiable election scheme, compared to simpler methods of electronically assisted voting, is that it provides for electronic transfer of ballot information from distant supervised locations, supported by verifiable evidence of correctness. This is particularly important for distant polling places (e.g., overseas) and for allowing any voter to vote at any polling place. Since this project commenced, a problem in the transport of West Australian Senate ballots in the 2013 federal election has focused national attention on the security of processes for transporting paper ballots. A security problem and verification flaw in an Internet voting system in neighboring New South Wales [282] has emphasized the importance of genuinely verifiable electronic election outcomes.

12.9.2 Challenges of Combining End-to-End Verifiability with Traditional Victorian Paper Voting

A large part of the challenge arises from the special requirements of Victorian parliamentary elections. Voting is complex: for some ballots, voters typically choose from among about 30 candidates—they rank at least 5, and up to all candidates in their order of preference. Each polling place must accept votes for any race, thus serving residents of any district in the state.

The system provides privacy and receipt-freeness under reasonable assumptions about the correct randomized generation and careful deletion of secret data, and of course assuming a secure mix-net and that a threshold of decryption key sharers do not collude. It depends on both the electronic ballot marker and the printer protecting their secret data. It does not defend against ballot signature attacks [203] (often called "Italian Attacks") or other subtle coercion issues, but neither does the current paper-based system. It also reveals how many preferences a person cast. A precise statement about privacy, its assumptions and limitations, is in [184].

Another challenge is producing an accessible solution for voters who cannot fill out a paper ballot unassisted. This is a primary justification for the project, but producing a truly verifiable solution for such voters is extremely difficult, because many of them cannot perform the crucial check that the printout matches their intention (though see [148] for a verifiable and accessible protocol). We provide a way for them to use any other machine in the polling place to do the check, in which case the cast-as-intended property depends upon at least one of the machines in the polling station not colluding with the others to manipulate the vote.

12.9.3 Specific Design Choices

12.9.3.1 Computer-Assisted Voting

The main departure from standard Prêt à Voter is the use of a computer to assist the user in completing the ballot. This is referred to as an "electronic ballot marker" (EBM). This modification is necessary for usability for all voters, and especially for particular voter groups: as described above, one of the drivers for the vVote project was accessibility, with the requirement to provide the secret ballot to blind, partially sighted and motor-impaired voters, for whom electronic assistance is necessary.

A ballot form can consist of a permuted list of about 30 candidates. It seemed infeasible for a voter to fill in a Prêt à Voter ballot form correctly without assistance. Indeed, simply filling in an ordinary paper ballot with about 30 preferences is a difficult task.[3] Computerized assistance is an important benefit of the project, and trusting the device for privacy seemed an almost unavoidable result of that usability advantage. Hence vVote depends on stronger privacy assumptions than standard Prêt à Voter, because the machine used for voting learns the vote. The vVote implementation took steps to minimize this risk, including the deletion from the EBM of all information about the vote cast, and deleting all information about the ballot form from the printer device after it has been printed.

12.9.3.2 Unified Scanner and EBM

We have already described why completing the ballot needs to be assisted by a computer. Our original design [124] included separate steps for filling in the ballot and then scanning the printed receipt. This was designed to separate the information of how the person voted from the knowledge of what their receipt looked like: the EBM learned how the person voted, but could not subsequently recognize their ballot (and hence link it to the individual voter), while the scanner knew the receipt but did not know the corresponding plaintext. However, user studies determined that a three-step voting process was too cumbersome for use. Also the necessity of print-on-demand

---

[3]Since some people deliberately vote informally, it is difficult to say exactly what percentage of people accidentally disenfranchise themselves by incorrectly filling in their vote. About 2% of votes in the 2006 state election were ruled informal because of "numbering errors" [567] , but the overall informality rate is closer to 10%, especially when there are many candidates on the ballot. See, e.g., `https://www.vec.vic.gov.au/Results/stateby2012distributionMelbourneDistrict.html`

meant that there was already an Internet-connected machine in the polling place that was trusted for maintaining privacy of the information on the printed ballot, including which candidate ordering corresponded to which receipt. For these reasons, the Victoria Electoral Commission insisted that the protocol unify the job of the scanner and the EBM, though it retains a separate print-on-demand step. The voter first collects their ballot form, and has an opportunity to audit it, then goes to an EBM to fill in the ballot, then the EBM sends the receipt electronically and also prints a paper record of the receipt column for the voter to check. This now means there are two online machines in the polling place (the EBMs and the ballot printers) that are trusted for vote privacy.

Receipts are digitally signed by the WBB when printed by the EBM. We provided a signature checking mobile app on Google Play that voters could download. In principle this provided accountability and defense against defaming. In practice the process for allowing voters to check, before they leave the polling place, that they had received a valid signature, was too complex for most voters to bother with.

Other significant departures are print on demand (rather than ahead of time) and printing the two halves separately (rather than overprinting a ballot), and hence the need to commit to the ciphertexts on the bulletin board before they are printed.

12.9.4 Handling Complex Ballots and Printing Them on Demand

A key requirement of the vVote project was that every polling place should allow voting in any of the 88 races being conducted across the State of Victoria. For the numbers of ballots required, and the number of candidates on each ballot, it would be infeasible for ballot forms to be centrally generated and distributed, due to the computational load required for all of the cryptographic operations necessary. This led to the design of new protocols for the distributed generation and on-demand printing of complex ballots by the print servers in the polling place [182]. Although prior designs had existed in the literature, they were not computationally feasible for the number and complexity of Victorian ballots.

The novel idea is that the printer generates a permuted list of candidate ciphers using randomness values generated by a distributed set of peers. (A similar construction is also used in Wombat.) The printer undertakes the expensive crypto operations, but does not have any influence over the values used in those operations. This prevents the printer from mounting subliminal attacks which use the randomness to encode information, or otherwise having any influence over the ciphertexts.

12.9.5 The Web Bulletin Board

The design of Prêt à Voter, in common with other end-to-end verifiable voting systems, assumes the availability of a web bulletin board (WBB): a way of posting information publicly which cannot be removed or changed once it has been posted. Although conceptually straightforward, no previous implementation of a WBB was available with the key properties listed below required to support Prêt à Voter, and so a WBB design was developed to provide the required functionality. Details of the protocols and properties can be found in [185].

The key properties are as follows:

1. the WBB displays only items that have been posted to it;

2. the WBB needs to provide a receipt in real-time (in the order of seconds) for any post that it accepts, so that voters obtain the evidence of their vote being accepted naturally as part of the voting process;

3. the WBB needs to be able to decide in real time whether it will accept or reject a post (for example, it will not accept two votes associated with the same ballot form, and it will not accept both a vote and an audit request for the same ballot form);

4. any item for which a receipt is provided must appear on the WBB;

5. it must not be possible to undetectably alter previous posts.

Properties 2, 3 and 4 together mean that a mechanism such as a blockchain for receiving posts is not suitable here: blockchains are not designed to handle posts where immediate posting is critical; it typically takes tens of minutes for a new block of items to appear.

Receipts are signed by the WBB to counter the possibility of dishonest voters faking receipts to falsely claim that posted items have been removed (known as a *defamation attack*). Hence alteration of posted items could be detected and challenged by means of the signed receipts. A smart-phone app was developed to allow voters to check the signatures on the spot.

Furthermore, the WBB is required to be robust in order to support a live election, and in particular there should be no single point of failure. This necessitates a peered implementation, with several servers collecting the information and agreeing on which posts to accept and reject. A peered implementation requires the use of a threshold signature scheme so that the peers can collectively contribute to signing printed ballots and receipts, and where agreement of a sufficient number is required for agreement of the WBB as a whole.

These requirements were achieved by separating the function of the WBB into two elements: receiving items, and posting information publicly. Receipt of items needs to be done in real time because voters are waiting; and the system also needs to be able to handle many simultaneous posts. Hence a distributed protocol for the WBB peers was designed for which each peer had its own view of the state of the WBB, and could take local decisions on whether or not to accept a post and provide its signature share on a receipt. The global WBB is an aggregation of the local peers, and behaves in the required way: if a threshold of peers provides their share of a signature then the voter obtains a receipt, and the post is held by the majority of the peers.

On the other hand, publication of the posts does not need to be done immediately. If peers have different views of the collection of posts, then they need to run a conciliation protocol which brings them back into agreement, and they then jointly sign and publish the collection of posts. In the Victorian election this was carried out once per day: the record of that day's voting was published at the end of each day.

The threshold required is strictly greater than 2/3 of the number of peers. For example, if there are 7 peers then any collective signature requires a share from at least 5 of them. As long as a threshold of peers follows the protocol correctly for any particular post, a receipt will be given, and the post will appear on the collectively agreed bulletin board at the end of the day. Hence the WBB is robust against fewer than 1/3 of peers going down, requiring rebooting, being dishonest or being the subject of an attack, and will deliver on the key properties listed above as long as a threshold behaves properly. It is also important to note that in fact property 5 will hold no matter how many peers are dishonest, but that there will be no attempt to alter previous votes (even if detectable) as long as a threshold of peers is honest.

12.9.6 *vVote-Specific Vulnerabilities and Countermeasures*

vVote's departures from standard Prêt à Voter, described in Section 12.9.3, have security implications that are described there. vVote also requires specific, and in some cases novel, countermeasures against particular attacks as described here:

Chain voting: vVote includes some technical measures to defend against chain voting. Printed ballot forms expire after 5 minutes if they have not been used to start a session, and the private WBB refuses to allow the same ballot form to be used to start another voting session once it has been used to start one. This means someone who sneaks an unused printed ballot form out of the polling place has 5 minutes to send it in with another voter. If someone sneaks one out having used it to start a session (and the tablet sits there with session active), then attempting to sneak this back in will not work as the ballot cannot be used to start a fresh session and the abandoned session "locks."

Clash attacks: Serial numbers are jointly generated to guarantee their uniqueness, but this doesn't prevent a corrupt printer from printing off exactly the same ballot, with the same serial number, for many different voters. The attack is detectable by ballot printing audit: such an audit would identify that the ballot has already been voted on and thus expose the corrupt printer.

The printer would have to collude with a corrupt EBM that merely reused the WBB signature, without resubmitting multiple instances of the same vote to the WBB. If the second voter voted differently from the first, the EBM would be unable to produce a valid signature on the receipt, and unable to post it to the WBB.

subliminal attacks: The output of the printers is entirely determined by the randomness that is sent to them, and other publicly committed information. Hence they have no opportunity to provide any information which may be skewed in a particular way. Correct information posted therefore cannot leak information from the printer. Incorrect information will be detected with some non-negligible probability by the ballot-generation audit processes.

Although the whole group of randomness generation authorities can collude to mount a subliminal attack, a smaller collusion has insufficient information.

12.9.7 *Practical Experiences*

A University of Surrey survey of voters leaving the Australia Centre in London having cast their votes is most indicative of the system with the entire voter cohort. The VEC (Victoria Electoral Commission) ran an anonymous online questionnaire of the poll workers asked questions about equipment setup and voter support. Both surveys asked about verifiability, trust and security.

The overall results were that voters were generally satisfied with the usability of the system, but there was a wide variation in understanding the security assurances provided. For example, some voters answered that they thought that the receipt revealed their vote. Although most voters trusted the system implicitly they nonetheless took part in the verifiability steps and many said they would check receipts at home. No voters reported that the process took "too long" despite the added task of aligning and checking printed preferences in the receipt column against the candidate list.

The electoral commission also ran their own survey of poll workers. Their main findings were:

- System features for accessibility were well used.

- The system did not require much intervention in the voting session.

- The verifiability measures were well used. A quarter of respondents saw electors check their printed preferences against their candidate list. Only two respondents handled electors who believed that the result did not match their vote.

- Staff may have not fully understood verifiability.

- Although more than half of respondents stated the system was Too Difficult to Operate or Not Very Reliable, two thirds stated they would be happy to support it if more voters came to use it.

Unfortunately the importance of ballot printing audits was not well understood by the VEC, who decided not to advertise the option to voters. They did implement the necessary code, and train the poll workers to respond properly to a voter who requested an audit, but the only mention to voters was in an article on a University of Melbourne website, written by the authors. In principle the deterrent against ballot manipulation was still present, because a cheating printer that rearranged the candidate list would have had to consider the possibility of a ballot audit. However, the fact is that there were no such audits, and hence no quantifiable evidence to support the accuracy of the election result. If vVote is deployed in future elections, the ballot auditing step must be advertised to all voters, and they must be encouraged to perform it.

Another significant deviation from Prêt à Voter processes was a decision not to provide for voters to shred the candidate lists, but rather to keep them securely for shredding later. This decision followed from the security requirements of a traditional polling place, which of course vVote had to run alongside. Traditionally, paper ballots are carefully controlled and kept well away from shredders, for good reason. Future deployments of vVote will have to consider how to provide the crucial privacy process for Prêt à Voter, without compromising the integrity of the parallel paper-based process.

More detail about the practicalities of the deployment is given in [126].

12.10   Conclusions

The Prêt à Voter approach to verifiable voting has proven to be highly fruitful and adaptable, leading to many variants and enhancements and ultimately to a real deployment in a public, binding election. The Prêt à Voter approach has one great advantage:

■ a simple ballot auditing procedure that depends only on the well-formedness of the ballot and is thus wholly independent of the vote or voter. This ensures full accountability, avoids vote privacy issues and means that, in addition to voter initiated audits, audits can be performed by independent scrutineers.

The original concept has been refined in many ways over the years to make it more usable, more secure and more flexible, but much more remains to be done. For example, there is doubtless still scope to make the auditing steps simpler and more natural, ideally as a side effect of the main task: to cast the vote. The procedures need to be refined and elaborated to address resilience and recovery.

Further research is required into the socio-technical aspects of verifiable voting systems in general. Such systems are large complex, security critical systems comprising, aside from the cryptographic protocols at the core, physical components, humans, procedures, etc. To date most analysis has been of the cryptographic primitives and protocols, with little work understanding the environment in which these reside.

It is also important to better understand the behavior and attitude of the users to the security procedures they are asked to perform. It is essential that voters, and election officials, understand the principles of the system well enough to have confidence in the security guarantees it provides and be sufficiently motived to perform the checks. Verification protocols have to be simple enough for people to understand and use. It is desirable for voters and officials to understand the security measures well enough not to be deflected from the correct procedures by social engineering style attacks.

It is one thing to design and even implement a cryptographic protocol, and quite another to organize the polling place verification procedures that underpin the protocol's fundamental assumptions. In a real deployment the designers can recommend, but not dictate, the procedures deployed in the polling place. This increases the necessity of making those procedures simple and intuitive. End-to-end verifiability is a property of a system, but verification is hard work that someone actually has to do. If the system is verifiable but not verified then it may not produce the evidence trail that it was designed to build.

The practical advantage of the vVote deployment was to improve the flexibility and verifiability of distant pollsite voting, obviating the need for the VEC to return paper ballots by courier, while still providing evidence that the ballots were correct. Prêt à Voter is very adaptable, but it is well suited only to an environment where a reasonable number of voters actually perform the verification steps. The researchers' challenge is to streamline the verification steps so that they produce genuine evidence of a correct election outcome, while the whole system remains appealing enough to be selected by election officials for deployment.

Acknowledgments

Many people have contributed to Prêt à Voter, its design and implementation, over many years. These include Craig Burton, who was the overall vVote project lead for the Victorian Electoral Commission; Chris Culnane, who was the lead architect of the Surrey contribution to vVote; David Chaum, James Heather, Rui Joaquim, Thea Peacock, Sriramkrishnan Srinivasan, Zhe Xia, and many others. We should also like to thank Olivier Pereira for a careful reading of the chapter and many helpful comments and suggestions and the many other people with whom we have had fruitful discussions over the years, notably Ron Rivest. Ryan would like to thank the EPSRC for funding under the DIRC project and subsequently the FNR Luxembourg for support under the SeRTVS and STAST projects. Schneider is grateful to EPSRC for funding under grant EP/G025797/1.

Chapter 13

DRE-i and Self-Enforcing E-Voting

Feng Hao

School of Computing Science
Newcastle University, UK
feng.hao@ncl.ac.uk

CONTENTS

13.1 Introduction

In this chapter, I will describe a journey of exploring a verifiable e-voting system that can be deployed in practice. This journey started in 2005 when I was a second-year PhD student working under the supervision of Ross Anderson in the security group, Computer Laboratory, University of Cambridge. The liberal research environment in the Computer Lab encouraged PhD students to freely explore topics of their interest, not necessarily confined by their original PhD proposal. While working on "biometric encryption" (which was my original PhD topic), I became interested in cryptography and wanted to learn more in this field.

One particular cryptographic problem that caught my interest was the "Dining Cryptographers problem," which was first introduced by David Chaum in 1988 [139]. In 2005, Piotr Zieliński and I proposed an efficient solution, called Anonymous Veto network (AV-net). The AV-net protocol proves to be more efficient than other solutions in all three aspects: the number of rounds, the computational load and the message size. As it turns out, seemingly different problems in cryptography are often inherently related. We soon discovered that the fundamental technique involved in solving the Dining Cryptographers problem could be applied to tackle other cryptographic problems, one of which was electronic voting. With my collaborators, we extended the Anonymous Veto network protocol to small-scale boardroom voting [291] and then further adapted the boardroom voting protocol to a centralized setting to make it suitable for large-scale elections [288]. The result is an end-to-end (E2E) verifiable voting protocol called direct recording electronic with integrity (DRE-i). In contrast to other E2E voting systems that require tallying authorities (TAs), DRE-i does not involve any TAs.

The design of the DRE-i protocol shows that the involvement of TAs is not indispensable to achieve E2E verifiability. This leads to the creation of a new category of voting systems that are E2E verifiable and also TA-free. We name this new category "self-enforcing e-voting" (SEEV). In 2013, we received a €1.5m European Research Council (ERC) Starting Grant (in which I am the principal investigator) to further the investigation on SEEV. More details about the research results and the experience of trialling SEEV systems in real-world applications will be explained in this chapter.

Contrary to the custom of thanking people in the end of an article, I would like to express my sincere thanks to my collaborators here. This journey has been greatly helped by a few people, especially: Piotr Zieliński, Peter Ryan, Matthew Kreeger, Brian Randell, Dylan Clarke, Siamak Shahandashti and Peter Lee. Without their valuable inputs (which I will explain in more detail), the results would not have been attainable.

In the following sections, I will start the journey by first describing a well-known problem in cryptography, called the "Dining Cryptographers problem."

13.2 Dining Cryptographers Problem

David Chaum is well-known for making several seminal contributions to cryptography. In the e-voting field, two of his papers are especially influential. The first is a visual cryptographic voting scheme based on a touchscreen direct recording electronic (DRE) machine [143]. This work inspired a genre of subsequent voting schemes that are built on a similar concept but improve Chaum's original scheme in various aspects, e.g., Prêt à Voter, Punchscan, Scantegrity and Scantegrity II. The second paper is about a mixing technique, known as mix-net [153], which involves a chain of mixing servers to randomly permute the inputs such that the relationship between the inputs and outputs is unknown unless all servers are corrupted. This mix-net concept has been widely adopted in many e-voting systems to protect voter anonymity.

As compared to extensive studies on Chaum's above two papers, another paper of Chaum's has received much less attention from the voting community. That paper first introduces the "Dining Cryptographers problem" [139].

13.2.1 Description of the Problem

As described in the original 1988 paper [139], three cryptographers sit around a table in a restaurant for dinner. A waiter informs them that the dinner arrangements have already been paid for, but the identity of the payer is unknown. This leads to one of two possibilities: either National Security Agency (NSA) has paid for them or one of the cryptographers has paid without telling others. The three cryptographers respect each other's right to make an anonymous payment, but they want to find out if NSA has paid.

13.2.2   Chaum's Original Solution: DC-net

Essentially, the Dining Cryptographers problem requires a secure multi-party computation (MPC) protocol on a Boolean-OR function: given a binary input of '1' or '0' (which correspond to "I paid" or "I did not pay," respectively) from each participant, the protocol allows participants to compute the Boolean-OR of all input bits without revealing the value of each individual bit. If every participant sends '0', the Boolean-OR will be '0' which means none of the participants paid (so NSA must have paid). On the other hand, if one or more participants send '1', the Boolean-OR of inputs will be '1' which means NSA did not pay.

In the same paper [139], Chaum proposed a solution, called the Dining Cryptographers Network (or DC-net). The DC-net protocol works in two stages. In the first stage, each two cryptographers establish a 1-bit secret, say by tossing a coin behind a menu. In the second stage, every cryptographer publicly announces the exclusive-OR (XOR) of the two secret bits that he holds if he did not pay, or the opposite of the XOR if he did pay. After the second stage, every cryptographer computes the XOR of the three announced bits. If the result is '0', it means no one has paid (so NSA must have paid); otherwise, it indicates one of the cryptographers has paid, but the identity remains unknown to the other two. This protocol can be generalized to n participants where $n \geq 3$. All n participants form a fully connected graph with each person being a vertex and each shared secret key an edge. Figure 13.1 illustrates how DC-net works with an example of five participants.

The Dining Cryptographers problem is essentially the same as the "anonymous veto problem" in the MPC literature [113], except that in the latter an input bit of '1' is interpreted as "veto" and '0' as "not veto". Several anonymous veto schemes [270, 345, 113] proposed in past research can be applied to solve the Dining Cryptographers problem. However, those techniques are generally complex, lacking the simplicity and elegance of Chaum's original DC-net solution.

13.2.3   Limitations of DC-net

Although DC-net has been commonly regarded as a classic technique in cryptography, it has not been used in practical applications. Further analysis shows that this technique has several major drawbacks. First, the pairwise keys are complex to set up. Given n participants, the total number of pairwise keys has the complexity of $O(n^2)$. Second, message collision is problematic. If two participants, or in the general case any even number of participants, send the '1' message ("I paid") at the same time, their messages will cancel out each other (see Figure 13.1(d)). Chaum calls this a "collision" and suggests to resolve this problem by retransmission [139]. However, the exact retransmission mechanism is not specified. Third, the message can be easily jammed. The participant who chooses to announce his bit last can trivially suppress any messages sent by previous people. In the paper [139], Chaum acknowledges this

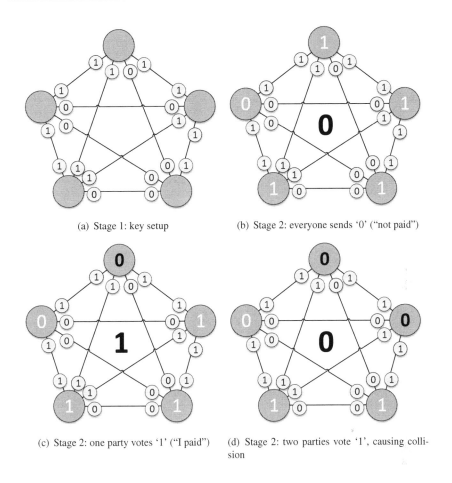

(a) Stage 1: key setup

(b) Stage 2: everyone sends '0' ("not paid")

(c) Stage 2: one party votes '1' ("I paid")

(d) Stage 2: two parties vote '1', causing collision

Figure 13.1: An illustration of the DC-net protocol for five participants. A collision occurs when an even number of participants send the '1' messages at the same time.

attack as a "disruption." He suggests catching the disrupter by setting up traps, but this can make the system rather complex.

13.2.4 First Attempt on a New Solution

I was motivated to find a solution to address the limitations of DC-net. After numerous failed attempts, I happened to find that by juggling random public keys in some particular order, it seemed to be able to perform secure multi-party computation on the Boolean-OR function. The result is a two-round cryptographic protocol that performs secure MPC on the Boolean-OR function. This initial protocol has never been published. As I will explain, what was published later [292] is a more efficient variant of this protocol. Nonetheless, I think the original solution is still interesting enough that I will take the opportunity to describe it here.

First, we need to define a finite cyclic group suitable for cryptography. For example, we can use the same group setting as DSA [546]. Let p and q be large primes such that $q \mid p - 1$, and g be a generator of the subgroup of Z_p^* of prime order q. Assume there are n participants in the network ($n \geq 3$). The task is to enable these participants to securely compute a Boolean-OR function while preserving the privacy of each individual input.

The protocol works in two rounds. Here, one "round" refers to a step in the protocol, in which operations from all participants can be performed simultaneously without depending on each other. In the protocol description below, all modular operations are performed with respect to modulus p, so unless stated otherwise, the explicit "mod p" notation is omitted for simplicity.

Round 1 *Every participant P_i selects two random values $x_i, y_i \in_R \mathbb{Z}_q$ and broadcasts g^{x_i} and g^{y_i}.*

Round 2 *Every participant P_i broadcasts $A_i = (\prod_i g^{x_i})^{a_i}$ and $B_i = (\prod_i g^{y_i})^{b_i}$ where $a_i = y_i$ and $b_i = x_i$ if the participant sends '0' or uses random values for a_i and b_i if the participant sends '1'.*

$$(a_i, b_i) = \begin{cases} (y_i, x_i) & \text{if } P_i \text{ sends '0',} \\ (r_i, s_i), \text{ where } r_i, s_i \in_R \mathbb{Z}_q & \text{if } P_i \text{ sends '1'.} \end{cases}$$

After the second round, each participant compares $\prod_i A_i$ and $\prod_i B_i$ (with respect to modulo p). If they are equal, it means all participants sent '0'; otherwise, it means one or more participants sent the message '1'. However, the identities of those participants who sent '1' remain unknown.

The correctness of the protocol is easy to verify. If all participants have sent '0', we have

$$\prod_i A_i = (\prod_i g^{x_i})^{\sum_i y_i} = g^{\sum_i x_i \cdot \sum_i y_i} \bmod p,$$

$$\prod_i B_i = (\prod_i g^{y_i})^{\sum_i x_i} = g^{\sum_i y_i \cdot \sum_i x_i} \bmod p.$$

Obviously, $\prod_i A_i = \prod_i B_i$ if everyone sends '0'. On the other hand, if one or more participants send '1', the newly added randomness will break the equality.

The essence of this protocol is very similar to the original DC-net design. Both work through the cancellation of random factors. In DC-net, if every cryptographer sends '0' (i.e., "I did not pay"), all random secrets used for encrypting the inputs bits will cancel each other out. This makes the final XOR result be '0' (i.e., no cryptographer has paid). Similarly, in the above two-round protocol, if every participant sends '0', the random secret factors, namely x_i and y_i, will cancel each other out. As a result, $\prod_i A_i / \prod_i B_i = g^0 = 1$.

One key difference between the two solutions is that DC-net does not use public key cryptography, while the new scheme is built on public key cryptography. The use of public key cryptography allows the application of well-established zero knowledge-proof (ZKP) primitives to enforce all participants to honestly follow the protocol specification, hence effectively addressing the "disruption" attack [139]. So far for the simplicity of description, I have omitted the ZKPs in the above protocol specification, but I will highlight their important role in the next section after presenting the final version of the protocol.

One distinctive advantage of the new scheme is that it requires only two rounds. This is more efficient than all other anonymous veto protocols [345, 270, 113] that use public key cryptography. In fact, it can be proved that the 2-round efficiency is the best achievable for the secure MPC on the Boolean-OR function [294].

13.2.5 *Improved Solution: AV-net*

I was keen to share this finding with colleagues in the security group and get their feedback. A few people became interested. In particular, Piotr Zieliński, another PhD student in the same group, was attracted to this problem. Zieliński was a mathematician by training. To my surprise, he quickly came up with a clever improvement.

Zieliński's improvement was to optimize the random-factor cancellation process. In my original solution, the cancelation works based on the following equation (when everyone sends '0'):

$$\left(\prod_i g^{x_i}\right)^{\sum_i y_i} / \left(\prod_i g^{y_i}\right)^{\sum_i x_i} = 1 \tag{13.1}$$

Zieliński quickly pointed out that it was sufficient to use just one variable to achieve the same cancellation effect. The key element in his proposal is the following proposition:

Proposition 13.1 Cancellation Formula

Given $x_i \in_R \mathbb{Z}_q$, $y_i = \sum_{j<i} x_j - \sum_{j>i} x_j \bmod q$ *for* $i = 1, \ldots, n$, $\sum_i x_i y_i = 0 \bmod q$.

The above proposition is called the "cancellation formula" [292, 291, 288]. As will become clear later, this simple-looking formula proves to be incredibly powerful. While a mathematical proof about this proposition can be found in [292], Table 13.1 gives an intuitive illustration on the correctness of this cancellation formula.

The protocol was subsequently revised based on using the new cancellation formula. This constitutes the final version of the protocol published at Security Protocols

Table 13.1: An illustration of the cancellation formula for five participants [292].

	x_1	x_2	x_3	x_4	x_5
x_1		$-$	$-$	$-$	$-$
x_2	$+$		$-$	$-$	$-$
x_3	$+$	$+$		$-$	$-$
x_4	$+$	$+$	$+$		$-$
x_5	$+$	$+$	$+$	$+$	

Note: The summation $\sum_{i=1}^{n} x_i y_i = \sum_{i=1}^{n} x_i (\sum_{j=1}^{i-1} x_j - \sum_{j=i+1}^{n} x_j)$ is the addition of all the cells, where $+, -$ represent the sign. They cancel each other out.

Workshop (SPW'06) [292]. A complete description of the final protocol, including the zero knowledge proofs, is given below (also see [292]).

Round 1 *Every participant P_i selects a random secret $x_i \in_R \mathbb{Z}_q$ and publishes g^{x_i} and a zero-knowledge proof for proving the knowledge of the exponent x_i.*

When this round finishes, each participant P_i computes

$$g^{y_i} = \prod_{j=1}^{i-1} g^{x_j} \Big/ \prod_{j=i+1}^{n} g^{x_j}$$

Round 2 *Every participant P_i publishes $A_i = (g^{y_i})^{c_i}$ and a zero-knowledge proof for proving the knowledge of c_i, where $c_i = x_i$ if P_i sends '0' or a random value otherwise.*

$$c_i = \begin{cases} x_i & \text{if } P_i \text{ sends '0'}, \\ r_i \in_R \mathbb{Z}_q & \text{if } P_i \text{ sends '1'}. \end{cases}$$

After the second round, each participant computes $\prod_i A_i$. If everyone sends '0', we have $\prod_i g^{c_i y_i} = \prod_i g^{x_i y_i} = 1$. On the other hand, if one or more participants send the message '1', we have $\prod_i g^{c_i y_i} \neq 1$. Under the Decision Diffie–Hellman assumption, the two messages, $g^{x_i y_i}$ and $g^{r_i y_i}$, are indistinguishable [291]. Thus, the Boolean-OR function is computed securely without revealing each individual input.

In the protocol, senders must demonstrate their knowledge of the discrete logarithms without revealing them: more specifically, the knowledge of x_i in Round 1 and the knowledge of c_i in Round 2. This can be realized by using the Schnorr non-interactive zero-knowledge proof [517, 147], a standard primitive in cryptography. The use of the ZKPs ensures that all participants honestly follow the specification, hence greatly restricting the freedom of an active attacker.

Zieliński's improvement is significant in two aspects. First, by using the new cancellation formula, every participant needs to generate just one ephemeral public key, instead of two. The computational load is reduced by half, as is the size of the transmitted data. Second, after the improvement, the protocol becomes "ultimately simple" — i.e., as simple as possible, but not simpler. The "simplicity" of a protocol is a powerful feature. It not only facilitates security analysis of the protocol, but also has a direct impact on efficiency. As detailed in [292], the improved protocol proves significantly more efficient than related techniques [113, 270, 345] in all three aspects: the number of rounds, the computation load and message sizes. In fact, this exceptional efficiency was not the design goal, but a natural outcome of our striving for "simplicity."

Apart from the efficiency aspects, the most critical consideration of a security protocol is whether it is secure. We tried our best to learn from the past why many protocols failed, so to make sure the same mistakes would not be repeated in our case. The understanding of previous attacks is helpful and necessary, but not sufficient to ensure a protocol secure against (undiscovered) attacks. The necessity of being able to mathematically "prove" the security of a protocol naturally arose as compelling.

In the end, we proved that the protocol was secure based on the assumption that certain number theoretical problems (particularly, discrete logarithm) were intractable. Essentially, the security of the protocol was reduced to solving the underlying number theoretical problems. In other words, breaking the protocol would imply immediate solutions to those problems, which elite mathematicians have been trying hard to solve for hundreds of years but to no avail. This reductionist proof greatly solidified our confidence in the security of the protocol.

When the design work was completed, we gave the protocol a name called "Anonymous Veto network" (AV-net) and tried to get it published.

13.2.6   Presentation at SPW 2006

We first submitted the paper to a major cryptographic conference. All reviewers seemed to like the protocol, but in the end they decided not to accept the paper as they found "no practical value" in solving the Dining Cryptographers problem.

We were disappointed, but found it difficult to disagree. In fact, I could not see any practical value either. Nonetheless, it was an interesting problem, which we enjoyed solving. That was perhaps what really mattered. Still, subconsciously I felt there should exist "practical value" somewhere, but I needed to investigate further.

We then submitted the paper to the Security Protocols Workshop (SPW'06), held locally at Cambridge. We were pleased that our paper was accepted. While presenting the paper in the workshop, I wanted to make the Boolean-OR computation problem sound more practically relevant, so I came up with the following puzzle.

A Crypto Puzzle

During an open meeting, the Galactic Security Council must decide whether to invade an enemy planet. One delegate wishes to veto the measure, but worries that such a move might jeopardize the relations with some other member states. How can he veto the proposal without revealing his identity?

The puzzle and our solution seemed to have attracted significant interest from the audience. Various aspects of the AV-net protocol were queried by experienced cryptographers present at the workshop, but after active probing, no weakness of the protocol was identified (see the transcript of discussion at [293]).

Near the end of the Q&A, Bruce Christianson, a professor from the University of Hertfordshire and one of the organizers of the workshop, raised an interesting question (see transcript [293]):

> **Bruce Christianson**: *"Suppose we're voting on whether to admit some-one to our club, and it requires two no votes to blackball, can we gener-alise this approach in that way?"*

The essence of the question concerns extending the AV-net protocol to perform a Boolean-tallying function. More formally, given a binary input of '1' or '0', the protocol should allow n participants to securely tally the number of '1's while preserving the privacy of each individual input. This is essentially a boardroom voting problem [344, 270]. One may interpret the input bit '1' or '0' as "Yes"/"No" in a single-candidate election.

13.3 Boardroom Electronic Voting

Christianson's question made us realize that the research project was unfinished. We were joined by Peter Ryan who became interested in this problem too. Three of us started to work together, trying to extend AV-net to a more general boardroom voting protocol.

13.3.1 Open Vote Protocol

While the question was clear, the solution had remained elusive for quite some time. As it turned out, the key to the solution is a 1-out-of-2 ZKP technique, due to Cramer, Damgård and Schoenmakers (also known as the CDS technique) [176]. With the understanding of the CDS technique, the answer to Christianson's question gradually became clear.

The result was a new protocol called "Open Vote." For simplicity, we first consider a single-candidate election. Each voter casts either "0" or "1" (which corresponds to "No" or "Yes"). The tally is represented by the count of the "Yes" votes. The protocol operates in the same group setting as AV-net. It runs in the same two rounds.

Round 1 *Every participant P_i selects a random value $x_i \in_R \mathbb{Z}_q$ and publishes g^{x_i} together with a zero knowledge proof for proving the knowledge of x_i.*

When this round finishes, each participant P_i computes

$$g^{y_i} = \prod_{j=1}^{i-1} g^{x_j} / \prod_{j=i+1}^{n} g^{x_j}$$

Round 2 *Every participant P_i publishes $A_i = g^{x_i y_i} g^{v_i}$ together with a zero knowledge proof showing that v_i is one of the two values $\{1, 0\}$.*

$$v_i = \begin{cases} 1 & \text{if } P_i \text{ votes "yes"} \\ 0 & \text{if } P_i \text{ votes "no"} \end{cases} \tag{13.2}$$

After the second round, everyone is able to tally votes. To tally the "yes" votes, each participant, or in fact anyone observing the protocol, can compute $\prod_i A_i = \prod_i g^{x_i y_i} g^{v_i} = g^{\sum_i v_i}$. The value $\sum_i v_i$ on the exponent is the tally of "yes" votes. The equality holds because of the same cancellation formula as is used in AV-net, namely $\sum_i x_i y_i = 0$ (see Proposition 13.1). Since $\sum_i v_i$ is normally a small number, it is not difficult to compute its value by using exhaustive search or Shanks' baby-step giant-step algorithm [361].

As in AV-net, senders must produce valid zero knowledge proofs to prove that they follow the protocol specification honestly. In the first round, each participant needs to demonstrate the knowledge of the exponent, which can be realized by using the same Schnorr's technique [517]. In the second round, each participant needs to demonstrate that the encrypted vote is one of the two values $\{1, 0\}$ without revealing which one. This can be realized by using the standard CDS technique [176].

13.3.2   Extension to Multi-Candidate Election

So far we have only considered a single-candidate election. Obviously, if there are only two candidates, then the same single-candidate protocol is still applicable — instead of selecting "Yes"/"No", the voter choose "Candidate A"/"Candidate B".

To support more than two candidates, there are a few methods proposed in the literature [76, 177]. A straightforward way is to run the single-candidate protocol in parallel for k candidates. Each voter casts a "Yes"/"No" vote to each of the candidates. The tallying for each candidate is done in parallel.

A second method, based on [177], assumes k independent generators, $g_1, g_2, \ldots, g_k$, one for each candidate respectively. The first round remains the same. In the second round, each participant sends $g^{x_i y_i} \cdot \rho_i$ with a 1-out-of-k zero knowledge proof showing that ρ_i is one of $\{g_1, g_2, \ldots, g_k\}$ (using the generalized CDS technique [176]). For tallying, one computes $\prod_i g^{x_i y_i} \cdot \rho_i = g_1^{c_1} \cdot g_2^{c_2} \cdots g_k^{c_k}$ where c_1 to c_k are the counts of votes for the k candidates correspondingly.

A third method is to adopt an encoding scheme defined in [177]. Assume there are n voters. Compute m so that m is the smallest integer to satisfy $2^m > n$. Now the encoded value is defined 2^0 for the first candidate, 2^m for the second candidate, 2^{2m} for the third candidate, and so on, up to $2^{(k-1) \cdot m}$ for the kth candidate. In other words, redefine Equation 13.2 as:

$$
v_i = \begin{cases}
2^0 & \text{if } P_i \text{ votes candidate 1} \\
2^m & \text{if } P_i \text{ votes candidate 2} \\
\ldots & \ldots \\
2^{(k-1)m} & \text{if } P_i \text{ votes candidate } k
\end{cases}
$$

The tabulation is basically the same as before: $\prod_i g^{x_i y_i} g^{v_i} = g^{\sum_i v_i}$. The superincreasing nature of the encoding ensures that the total $\sum_i v_i$ can unambiguously be resolved into the tallies for k candidates, respectively. In other words, we have $\sum_i v_i = 2^0 \cdot c_1 + 2^m \cdot c_2 + \ldots + 2^{(k-1)m} \cdot c_k$, where c_1 to c_k are the counts of votes for the k candidates correspondingly.

Among the three methods, the first one is the simplest, while the other two are more complex in terms of exhaustive search. Given n votes, k candidates and that each vote is cast to one of the k candidates, the maximum number of tries for the exhaustive search in the first method is $k \times n$. In comparison, for the other two methods, the maximum number of searches for determining the tallies is $\binom{n+k-1}{k-1} = O(n^{k-1})$ (see the Combinations with Repetitions problem [538]). This is less scalable than the previous $k \times n$, but exhaustive search may still be feasible when k is relatively small.

13.3.3 Presentation at WISSec 2009

When designing the boardroom voting protocol, we followed the same design principle as before: i.e., striving for "simplicity." Again, this leads to exceptional efficiency. The Open Vote protocol proves to be more efficient than other boardroom voting protocols [270, 344] in all three aspects: the number of rounds, computational load and message sizes [291]. The key in achieving such efficiency is attributed to the use of the "cancellation formula" (Proposition 13.1).

Besides efficiency, the protocol also enjoys two attractive theoretical features. The first is "self-tallying." There are no tallying authorities involved at all. The second is "maximum voter privacy." The privacy of the voter is protected at the maximum level – only a full-collusion attack that involves corrupting all other voters can compromise the voter's privacy. (We refer the reader to [291] for security proofs.) With the security proofs completed, we felt we had finally addressed Christianson's question with an affirmative answer.

The paper was accepted by the journal *IET Information Security* for publication. In the meantime, I was invited to present the paper at the 2009 Benelux Workshop on Information and System Security (WISSec'09). The workshop produced no proceedings, but provided a good opportunity for researchers to exchange ideas and share their findings. This workshop was held at the Université catholique de Louvain (UCL), Belgium, where the famous Helios election was conducted a year earlier to elect the university president. This made the workshop particularly relevant to e-voting research.

While presenting the paper at the workshop, I modified the crypto puzzle at SPW'06 to fit the new problem of secure computation of a Boolean-tallying function.

A Crypto Puzzle - Follow-up

In the Galactic Republic, the chancellor is seeking re-election in the Senate. Some delegates do not want to vote for him, but worry about the revenge. All communication is monitored. There is no secret talk between delegates. In addition, no trusted third parties exist. How to arrange a voting such that the voters' privacy will be preserved?

This new crypto puzzle generated quite some interest from the audience. However, the real inspiration of the workshop turned out to be a following presentation on Helios. The paper is titled "Electing a University President Using Open-Audit Voting: Analysis of Real-World Use of Helios" due to Ben Adida, Olivier de Marneffe, Olivier Pereira and Jean-Jacques Quisquater [46]. Helios is a verifiable remote voting system, which was adopted in 2008 in Université catholique de Louvain to elect the university president. It was a real-world application of e-voting and was commonly considered a milestone in the field. I was impressed by the Helios achievement and its impact on the field. While sitting in the audience to hear about the Helios work, I could not help asking myself a question.

> **Me**: *"Can we extend the Open Vote protocol to do a similar campus election as Helios?"*

This question made the journey move on to the next goal: a practical e-voting system that can be used in real-life applications.

13.4 Large-Scale Electronic Voting

The Open Vote protocol is designed only for *small-scale* boardroom elections; extending it to support *large-scale* elections presents a non-trivial challenge. Matthew Kreeger, a colleague at Thales E-Security, became interested in this problem. Two of us then started working together to explore a solution.

13.4.1 From Decentralized to Centralized

The Open Vote protocol is a decentralized voting system. There is no central election authority. The election is essentially run by the voters themselves. This naturally requires cooperative interactions between voters. In the best case, two rounds of interactions are needed, as the case of the Open Vote protocol.

However, a decentralized design has critical weaknesses, which make it unsuitable for any large-scale election, such as the one conducted by Helios [46]. First, the multi-round interactions between voters make the process vulnerable to disruptions (i.e., denial of service attacks). If some voters drop out between rounds, the election will be seriously disrupted and may have to be restarted. Second, in the decentralized setting, every voter independently manages a secret key and performs cryptographic operations. This assumes that voters have a high level of expertise (or have a commonly trusted application to do it for them). Third, exhaustive search is required to determined the tally. While this is feasible in a single-candidate election, the computation can become very expensive in a multi-candidate election especially when there are many candidates.

To extend the Open Vote protocol to support "large-scale" elections, it is essential to change its decentralized structure to a centralized one for better scalability and robustness. Of course, a change in a security system is never free, as it involves trade-offs.

13.4.2 Trade-off

The main trade-off concerns voter privacy. Instead of voting in a decentralized way, voters now cast votes through a centralized interface, e.g., a touchscreen DRE (Direct Recording Electronic) machine at a polling station. This implies that, "maximum voter privacy," a theoretically attractive property of the Open Vote protocol, will be lost. When a voter selects a choice on the touchscreen, the machine inevitably learns the voter's choice. (However, this does not necessarily mean the voter's privacy must be compromised, since her identity remains unknown to the machine if an anonymous voting procedure is followed.)

In the centralized setting, a critically important requirement of a voting system is to ensure the "integrity" of the election result. The standard method of assuring "integrity" is to allow voters to verify the result at two levels. At an individual level, every voter should be able to verify that her vote has been recorded correctly (through voter-initiated auditing) and has been included into the tallying process (through checking the receipt against a bulletin board). At a universal level, every voter should be able to verify the integrity of the tallying result (by cryptographically checking the data published on the bulletin board). Systems that satisfy both levels of verifiability are commonly known as being end-to-end (E2E) verifiable.

We observed that E2E voting systems proposed in the past generally involved a set of trustworthy tallying authorities (TAs) to administrate the tallying process. TAs are assumed to be selected from different parties with conflicting interests and are subject to a cryptographic threshold-control scheme, e.g., based on Shamir's secret sharing [546]. In addition, TAs are assumed to be able to "independently" manage their private keys and write their own "trusted" software to perform tallying tasks. However, as highlighted in the campus election using Helios, the practical implementation of TAs can be "a particularly difficult issue" [46].

We wondered if the involvement of TAs was really necessary. To prove it was not, we set out to design a voting protocol that is E2E verifiable and TA-free. The result was a new protocol called direct recording electronic with integrity (DRE-i). This protocol was designed based on adapting the previous Open Vote protocol from a decentralized setting to a centralized one, while preserving an important property: namely "self-tallying." I will describe the details of the DRE-i protocol in the next section (also see [288]).

13.4.3   Direct Recording Electronic with Integrity

The DRE-i protocol consists of three stages: setup, voting and tallying. The protocol itself is applicable to either local voting at a polling station or remote voting over the internet. Here I will focus on describing it in the context of the former using a touchscreen DRE machine as the voting interface and then explain how it can be adapted to remote voting.

13.4.3.1   Setup

The setup is done before the election. It involves 1) setting up the system's private signing key, 2) preparing the electronic ballots and 3) publishing commitment data on a public bulletin board. For simplicity, it is assumed that the system consists of one DRE machine, but it can be easily generalized to include more machines.

First, the DRE machine generates a private signing key, say using ECDSA [546]. The public key is published on the bulletin board (a publicly accessible website).

Subsequently, the DRE machine pre-computes n electronic ballots where n is the product of the maximum number of eligible voters and a safety factor (> 1). This safety factor is to allow the generation of extra ballots for auditing purposes, as I will explain later. Typically, a safety factor is a value between 5 and 10.

For each of the n ballots, the machine generates a random private key $x_i \in_R [1, q - 1]$ and computes its corresponding public key g^{x_i}. When this has been done for all n ballots, the machine computes:

$$g^{y_i} = \prod_{j<i} g^{x_j} / \prod_{j>i} g^{x_j} \qquad (i = 1, \ldots, n)$$

Here, the result g^{y_i} is called a restructured public key. It is computed by multiplying all the random public keys before i and dividing all the random public keys after i (as in the Open Vote protocol [291], but all keys are generated in a centralized process).

For a single candidate election, each ballot contains two values: "Yes" and "No". The ciphertext for the yes-vote is $g^{x_i y_i} \cdot g$, and for the no-vote is $g^{x_i y_i}$. In addition to the ciphertext, a zero-knowledge proof (ZKP) is needed to prove that the ciphertext is well-formed – i.e., the ciphertext is indeed in the form of $g^{x_i y_i} \cdot g^{v_i}$ where v_i is one of the two values $\{0, 1\}$. We can use the 1-out-of-2 ZKP [177] for this purpose.

Here, we define "cryptogram" as the combination of an encrypted vote and its associated ZKP. Hence, a yes-cryptogram refers to the combination of the yes-vote $g^{x_i y_i} \cdot g$ and the associated 1-out-of-2 ZKP. Similarly, a non-cryptogram refers to the combination of the no-vote $g^{x_i y_i}$ and the corresponding 1-out-of-2 ZKP.

Overall, the pre-computation generates a table (Table 13.2) that satisfies the following four properties.

1. *Well-formedness.* Given any cryptogram in the table, anyone is able to verify that it is an encryption of one of the two values: "Yes" and "No" (which correspond to adding "1" and "0" respectively in the tallying process);

2. *Concealing.* Given only one cryptogram in a selected row, it is not possible to distinguish whether it is "Yes" or "No";

3. *Revealing.* Given both cryptograms in a selected row, anyone is able to tell which one is "Yes" and which is "No";

4. *Self-tallying.* Given an arbitrary selection of a cryptogram from each row, anyone is able to tally how many "Yes" votes there are in the selection.

The protocol allows the flexible choice of pre-computation in the implementation. In the description above, all cryptograms are pre-computed before the election, which serves to minimize any latency in voting on election day. Alternatively, the cryptograms can be computed on-demand in real time during voting. If cryptograms are pre-computed, they will need to be kept confidential alongside the secret x_i values; in contrast, if cryptograms are computed on-demand, only the x_i values need to be kept secret.

Table 13.2: Setup phase.

Ballot No	Random public key	Restructured public key	Cryptogram of no-vote	Cryptogram of yes-vote
1	g^{x_1}	g^{y_1}	$g^{x_1 \cdot y_1}$, 1-of-2 ZKP	$g^{x_1 \cdot y_1} \cdot g$, 1-of-2 ZKP
2	g^{x_2}	g^{y_2}	$g^{x_2 \cdot y_2}$, 1-of-2 ZKP	$g^{x_2 \cdot y_2} \cdot g$, 1-of-2 ZKP
...	...	...	...	...
n	g^{x_n}	g^{y_n}	$g^{x_n \cdot y_n}$, 1-of-2 ZKP	$g^{x_n \cdot y_n} \cdot g$, 1-of-2 ZKP

Note: Data in the first three columns are published on a public bulletin board before the election as commitment so they cannot be retrospectively changed later. Data in the last two columns are kept secret; they are either computed on-demand during voting or pre-computed before the election.

13.4.3.2 Voting

On election day, voters enter the polling station with their ID documents for authentication. After being authenticated successfully, each voter randomly takes an authentication token, which may be a smart card or a one-time passcode. The voter then enters a private booth and uses the token to authenticate herself to the voting machine. The token allows the voter to cast one vote. The voter's real identity remains unknown to the machine.

On the touchscreen interface, the voter is promoted to select a choice for the single-candidate election: "Yes" or "No". To cast the vote, the voter follows two basic steps.

In the first step, she touches the screen to select a choice. The DRE machine prints the following data on the paper receipt: the ballot serial number i and the cryptogram of the selected choice (see Figure 13.2). The receipt is appended with a digital signature signed by the machine to prove the authenticity of the printed data.

In the second step, the voter is given the option to either confirm or cancel the previous selection (Figure 13.2). If the voter chooses "confirm," the machine continues to print "finish" on the same receipt, followed by a digital signature that covers the entire receipt. In this case, a valid ballot has been cast. If the voter selects "cancel," the machine prints the selected choice in plaintext (i.e., "Yes" or "No" in this single-candidate example), followed by the other (unused) cryptogram and a digital signature. In this case, a dummy vote has been cast. The voting interface is then returned to the initial Yes/No screen for the voter to start over with a different (unused) ballot. As will become clear later, a dummy vote does not add to the total tally. The voter is free to cast as many dummy votes as the system allows (up to the safety factor defined in the setup stage), but is restricted to cast only one confirmed vote.

The option of "cancel" is to allow user auditing. When the voter makes a choice, a single cryptogram is printed on the receipt. Based on the "concealing" property, a single cryptogram does not reveal any information about the user's choice. This is necessary for preventing coercion and vote selling. However, a dishonest DRE ma-

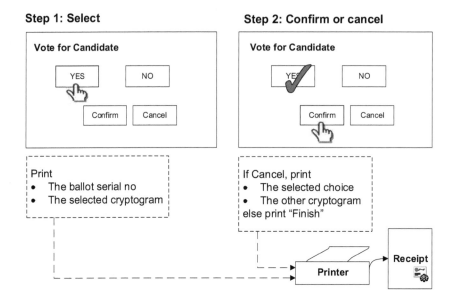

Figure 13.2: The voting procedure in the DRE-i protocol.

chine may cheat by swapping the cryptograms, so the cryptogram of the unselected choice is printed on the receipt. This swapping-attack will be detected once the voter chooses to cancel the vote based on the "revealing" property. At this point, the voter checks if the plain-text choice printed on the second part of the receipt matches her selection in the previous step. If not, she should raise a dispute immediately to the administrative staff in the polling station.

After voting, the voter leaves the private booth with a receipt for the confirmed ballot and possibly several receipts for cancelled (dummy) ballots. To ensure her vote has indeed been included in the tallying system, the voter checks that the same data on receipts (including dummy votes) are published on the bulletin board. This can be done with the assistance of voluntary helpers in the polling station. The data printed on the receipt is essentially public, so it can be shown to anyone. In a real election, this kind of verification is best performed on-site, say before exiting the polling station; then any irregularity can be identified and dealt with immediately.

When the election finishes, any unused ballots will be automatically cancelled by the system with the two cryptograms published on the bulletin board. These are effectively treated as dummy votes.

13.4.3.3 *Tallying*

When the election is finished, the DRE machine announces the tally of the "Yes" votes that it has counted internally, just like existing practice in a real-world DRE-

Table 13.3: Ballot tallying.

No	Random	Restructured	Published Votes	ZKPs
i	pub key g^{x_i}	pub key g^{y_i}	V_i	
1	g^{x_1}	g^{y_1}	Valid: $g^{x_1 \cdot y_1}$	a 1-of-2 ZKP
2	g^{x_2}	g^{y_2}	Valid: $g^{x_2 \cdot y_2} \cdot g$	a 1-of-2 ZKP
3	g^{x_3}	g^{y_3}	Dummy: $g^{x_3 \cdot y_3}$, $g^{x_3 \cdot y_3} \cdot g$	two 1-of-2 ZKPs
...	...	...	...	...
n	g^{x_n}	g^{y_n}	Dummy: $g^{x_n \cdot y_n}$, $g^{x_n \cdot y_n} \cdot g$	two 1-of-2 ZKPs

based election. However, in contrast to existing practice, the DRE machine must publish additional audit data, which includes making all receipts available on the bulletin board. The audit data allow the public to verify the integrity of the announced tally.

Public verification simply involves multiplying all the published votes V_i (see Table 13.3 for an example). For dummy ballots, only the no-votes are included in the multiplication. Thus, we have:

$$\prod_i V_i = \prod_i g^{x_i y_i} g^{v_i} = \prod_i g^{v_i} = g^{\sum_i v_i}$$

Because of the cancellation of all random factors (based on the "cancellation formula" in Proposition 13.1), the result of the multiplication is $g^{\sum_i v_i}$, where the exponent represents the tally. Although the exponent can be calculated by exhaustive search, there is actually no need to do so in DRE-i. Because the machine announces the tally, one merely needs to verify if the tally is correct. This is done by raising the base g to the power of the announced tally and comparing it against $g^{\sum_i v_i}$. This operation takes only one modular exponentiation. Similarly, in a multi-candidate election, exhaustive search for the tallying results is not necessary either. Verifying the tally is much easier than calculating it.

13.4.4 Publication of the DRE-i Paper

When the design of the DRE-i protocol was complete, we made the paper publicly available at IACR ePrint (No. 452, 2010) [289], and meanwhile tried to find it a good home for its publication.

However, the difficulty of getting the DRE-i paper published exceeded my expectation. What the DRE-i protocol shows is a new way of constructing an E2E verifiable voting system – it differs from previous E2E designs in that it realizes the E2E verifiability *without* involving any tallying authorities. But, publishing a new idea in academic research is never easy. The paper was repeatedly rejected by various conferences in the field. It was not until four years later that it was finally published by the *USENIX Journal of Election Technology and Systems* (Vol. 2, No. 3, 2014) [288].

Part of the reason for rejection is that the system was not implemented in any practical application, so its practical feasibility remained unclear to the reviewers. This gave me the motivation to build a DRE-i prototype and put theory to the practical test.

13.5 Trial Elections

In December 2010, after working in the security industry for three years, I joined the School of Computing Science, Newcastle University, as a lecturer. I was glad to become a full-time researcher again, and was able to find more time to pursue the DRE-i work further.

13.5.1 Prototyping DRE-i

Shortly after I joined the faculty, my research was jump-started by the support of an internal Research Initiative Fund (RIF) in the school. The funding allowed me to recruit a research assistant for six months to implement DRE-i and conduct trial elections. Although the funding only lasted for six months, the support was timely and encouraging, especially because the DRE-i paper was still going through the process of receiving rejections. As it happened, Dylan Clarke, a final year PhD student in the school, was looking for an assistant post. Clarke had several years professional software development experience before doing his PhD. He proved to be an ideal candidate for this project.

For the ease of conducting trials, we decided to have an Internet-based implementation of DRE-i, instead of a local touchscreen-based one. The protocol remains basically the same as described in Section 13.4.3. The pre-computation is the same as before. During voting, the voter follows the same two steps to cast or audit a vote. However, instead of using a touchscreen, the voter uses a web interface. The receipt is displayed on the web page, instead of being directly printed out on paper as in local voting. The tallying process is exactly the same as before.

While the underlying DRE-i protocol remains the same, using it for Internet-based voting instead of polling-station-based voting has security implications. First, since there is no physical private booth, a voter may now vote under the direct duress of a coercer. Second, as voting is remote, a voter may simply transfer (or sell) her voting credential to a third party. Third, if the voter finds any mismatch of data in the printed receipt, it is no longer possible to raise the dispute and have it be dealt with swiftly on the spot. For these reasons, Internet voting is commonly considered only suitable for elections with low coercion risks. This fits the nature of the trial elections that we were about to conduct.

In just two months, Clarke completed a prototype of the DRE-i voting system. We were ready to put the prototype to a practical test.

13.5.2 Favorite Chocolate Election

As for the first trial, our goal was to have something fun and involve as many partic-ipants as possible. Hence, we decided to conduct a "favorite chocolate" election.

The trial was held in October 2011. We bought three boxes of chocolates of different brands: *Quality Street*, *Roses* and *Celebrations*. The boxes were put on a table in a common room, where staff and postgraduate students usually had tea breaks during the day. Next to the chocolates was a box of randomly mixed paper slips. Each slip printed a web voting address and a one-time passcode. A signboard was put on the table, inviting people to taste different chocolates, take a random paper slip and vote for their favorite chocolate.

With the paper slip, a voluntary participant could use any computer to vote. After entering the passcode onto the voting website, the voter was shown a set of choices: voting for *Quality Street*, *Roses* or *Celebrations* (Figure 13.3(a)). Following the DRE-i protocol, voters voted for their favorite candidate. In the end, 39 peo-ple participated and cast their votes. The winner was *Quality Street*, which received 18 out of 39 votes. Besides displaying the voting results, the bulletin board (Fig-ure 13.3(b)) also contained a link to download the audit data (an XML file) and an open-source Java program for verifying the audit data.

After voting, voters were asked to answer a questionnaire and also write free-text comment in the feedback. The questionnaire consisted of a set of six questions. For each question, voters were asked to indicate their agreement or disagreement on a Likert scale from 1 to 5 (i.e., "strongly agree," "agree," "neural," "disagree" and "strongly disagree"). The questionnaire answers and free-text comments are summa-rized in Figure 13.3(c).

The user feedback was generally positive and encouraging. With minimum in-struction (just a web address and a one-time passcode), voters generally understood how to vote and found voting easy.

However, this trial also exposed two main issues. The first was the low auditing rate. Only 4 out of 39 people (i.e., 10%) tried user auditing (by clicking the "cancel" option). The purpose of user-initiated auditing was not clear to many voters. The second issue concerns the difficulty of verifying the receipt. The receipt contained a long string of random-looking characters (in base-64 encoding). Comparing this random string with the one published on the bulletin board proved not that easy for a human.

You can choose to vote for the following candidates.

Candidate	Picture	Select
Quality Street		⦿
Roses		◯
Celebrations		◯

(Submit)

Election Results - Favorite Chocolate Election

Candidate	Votes
Quality Street	18
Celebrations	11
Roses	10

Ballot Type	Number
Confirmed	39
Cancelled	4
Unused	107

Download the GUI Election Checker - requires Java 5.0 or greater.

Download the GUI Election Checker Source Code

Right click to save the receipt XML file for verification

Ballot Number	Link
0	Click Here
1	Click Here
2	Click Here
3	Click Here

(a) Web voting interface   (b) Result on the web bulletin board

Feedback Page - Favorite Chocolate Election

The current feedback results are:

Statement	Average Score Given	Nearest Option to Average Score
I understood how to vote.	1.57	Agree
Voting was easy.	1.78	Agree
I understood how to check my ballot had been recorded correctly.	2.39	Agree
Checking that my ballot had been correctly recorded was easy.	3.13	Neutral
I understood why I was being asked to check ballots.	2.87	Neutral
I felt confident that my vote had been recorded correctly.	2.43	Agree

The comments received were:

A lot of these answers are biased - I have a good idea how the system works.

Checking the cryptograms was too long - I just looked at the first and last entry - might be easier ways of doing this? with an image perhaps?

Wrong https certificate gave an immediate bad impression. The cryptograms were so long as to be next to impossible to check by hand. The whole process would be completely opaque to someone without a Computing Science degree. The only electronic voting system I would trust is one which counts my vote electronically, and which I can see a ballot paper being retained for later hand scrutiny.

(c) Summary of questionnaire answers and free-text feedback

Figure 13.3: Favorite chocolate voting.

13.5.3   *Favorite Cheese Election*

Based on the user feedback, we improved the DRE-i prototype. Instead of using the 2048-bit multiplicative group in a finite field (DSA-like setting), we changed to implement DRE-i using the NIST-256 (ECDSA-like setting) additive group over an elliptic curve. This makes the representation of the cryptograms more compact. By reducing the size of the receipt, our hope was that voters would find it easier to verify the receipt. When the changes were done, we decided to have a second trial. This time, we chose to conduct a "favorite cheese" election.

The second trial was held in November 2011. We bought three different brands of cheeses: *Wensleydale*, *Camembert* and *Blue Stilton*. As before, we put the cheeses (along with crackers) in the common room, and also a box of randomly mixed passcode slips. Staff and postgraduate students were invited to taste different cheeses, take a random passcode slip, and vote for their favorite cheese. Voluntary participants cast their votes through a web interface, as shown in Figure 13.4(a). This time, 35 people cast their votes. The winner was *Wensleydale*, which received 14 votes. The tallying results are shown in Figure 13.4(b). The answers to the questionnaire and free-text comments are presented in Figure 13.4(c).

While the general feedback from participants was still positive, we observed that the same two issues remained.

First, this time the auditing rate was even lower. Only 1 out of 35 people chose auditing (i.e., 3%), which was lower than the previous 10%. This was likely because many of the voters participated in the previous trial. When they were more familiar with the system, they became less inclined to verify it. However, if the auditing rate is very low, this can invalidate the basic assurance of "individual verifiability" in an E2E voting system. This shows that if voters are entirely left to their own devices to audit votes, it is likely very few of them will actually do it.

Two solutions may help address this problem. The first one was originally suggested by my colleague, Brian Randell, and we named it the "Waitrose scheme" [290]. The solution was inspired by an existing practice in Waitrose (which is a chain of British supermarkets). When customers shop in a Waitrose supermarket, they are given a charity token at the cashier. At the exit of the supermarket, customers are free to denote the token to a preferred charity organization by dropping it in the designated box. The similar idea can be applied to encourage auditing in e-voting. If voters choose to audit their vote, they receive a charity token, which they can denote to a preferred charity organization near the exit of the polling station. Randell vividly described the essence of this solution as "ethical bribery" (which is a term I particularly like). Another practical solution is to employ dedicated auditors from different voting parties. A dedicated auditor is allowed to vote at any time during the election day, but is limited to cast dummy votes only. In a real election, we expect that the two solutions might be combined to improve the user auditing rate.

Second, though the data on the receipt became more compact, it remained difficult for a voter to compare the receipt against the bulletin board. The main limiting factor is the size of the digital signature. Using ECDSA at the 128-bit security level, the size of a digital signature is at least 64 bytes, i.e., 85 characters using the base-64 encoding. Comparing two strings of 85 random characters is trivial for a computer, but can prove rather difficult for a human.

It seemed unavoidable that we needed to limit the size of a receipt to a very short human-readable string. Through experiments, we determined that a string of 10 characters was acceptable to common users. This was adopted in the subsequent

You can choose to vote for the following candidates.

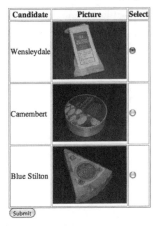

Candidate	Picture	Select
Wensleydale		⊙
Camembert		○
Blue Stilton		○

Submit

(a) Vote for favorite cheese

Election Results - Favorite Cheese Election

Candidate	Votes
Wensleydale	14
Camembert	13
Blue Stilton	8

Ballot Type	Number
Confirmed	35
Cancelled	1
Unused	114

Download the GUI Election Checker - requires Java 5.0 or greater.

Download the GUI Election Checker Source Code

Right click to save the receipt XML file for verification

Ballot Number	Link
0	Click Here
1	Click Here
2	Click Here
3	Click Here

(b) Vote for favorite cheese

Feedback Page - Favorite Cheese Election

The current feedback results are:

Statement	Average Score Given	Nearest Option to Average Score
I understood how to vote.	1.43	Strongly Agree
Voting was easy.	1.81	Agree
I understood how to check my ballot had been recorded correctly.	2.43	Agree
Checking that my ballot had been correctly recorded was easy.	3.10	Neutral
I understood why I was being asked to check ballots.	2.76	Neutral
I felt confident that my vote had been recorded correctly.	2.52	Neutral
I felt confident that my vote was anonymous.	2.43	Agree

The comments received were:

I had the problem with ""l"" vs ""1"" suggest use of different fount on passcodes

Passcode quite long & fiddly but I guess this is needed.

Next time bring beer to sample!

Pre-selecting your preferred candiate and "confirm" makes if far too easy to elect a dictatorial Tyke.

(c) Vote for favorite chocolate

Figure 13.4: Favorite cheese voting.

prototyping of a verifiable classroom voting system based on DRE-i. The shortening of the receipt presents a trade-off between security and usability. While it significantly improves usability in verifying the receipt, the fact that the string is too short to contain a digital signature makes it subject to false claims (digital signatures are still available on the bulletin board, but not printed on receipts). A dishonest user may modify the receipt and claim it mismatches the data published on the bulletin board. It will not be easy for a third party to distinguish if the system prints the wrong receipt or the user makes a false claim (in order to discredit the voting system). In practice when such a dispute arises, it needs to be dealt with on a case-by-case basis.

Besides the two issues, another important lesson we learned from this trial is that details really matter. The result that *Wensleydale* was the winner was most likely helped by the fact that it was a pre-selected choice in the voting interface. The same observation applies to explain why *Quality Street* won the previous trial (since it was also a pre-selected choice; see Figure 13.3(b)). So, this seemingly innocuous detail in the implementation may have inadvertently biased the voting outcome. We did not realize this issue until the result of the second trial was available and then the correlation between the winner and the pre-selected choice became evident. (This issue was also pointed out by an anonymous comment; see Figure 13.4). In another example, the passcode was initially generated as a random mixing of upper, lower letters, digits and symbols to get the maximum entropy. However, voters found it difficult to distinguish the digit "1" from the capital letter "I" in the printed passcode. They also found it difficult to enter capital letters and symbols on a small-screen mobile phone. This prompted us to change to use Crockford's Base32 encoding (`http://www.crockford.com/wrmg/base32.html`) in the subsequent developments. These practical issues could have been easily neglected if the system had not been implemented and trialled in practice.

13.5.4 ERC Starting Grant on Self-Enforcing E-Voting

Despite the identified issues, the two trial elections greatly increased our confidence about the practical feasibility of DRE-i. Because of the removal of TAs, managing an election became almost effortless. The setup was done in minutes. Once the setup was completed, the election could commence immediately. Voters did not need to perform any cryptographic operation in the client browser, hence they could just use a plain web browser (without enabling any Java plug-in or JavaScript) on a slow computer (say a mobile phone) without noticing any significant latency in voting. Finally, the voting results were instantly available once the election was ended, since there was no delay in waiting for TAs' inputs.

The success of the preliminary trials highlighted the potential of a new category of voting systems that are E2E verifiable and TA-free. We called this new category "self-enforcing e-voting" (SEEV). The "self-enforcing" property for security protocols is generally considered powerful, since it serves to minimize the dependence on trusted third parties. However, the concept of "self-enforcing e-voting" had not been actively explored by previous research. The work of DRE-i shows that a "self-enforcing e-voting" system is possible for simple approval type voting schemes, but the question remains if DRE-i can be extended to support more complex ranking-based voting schemes such as single transferable vote (STV) (see Chapter 4 for details on STV).

Towards the end of 2011, I submitted a research proposal to the European Research Council (ERC) to continue the investigation on SEEV. About six months later, I was informed that my application was successful – ERC agreed to provide a five-year Starting Grant of €1.5m (2013-2017). This grant allowed me to assemble an interdisciplinary research team to investigate SEEV further.

In 2013, two researchers, Siamak Shahandashti and Peter Lee, joined my ERC team, supported by the ERC Starting Grant. They soon proposed an improvement to the basic DRE-i scheme. In DRE-i, the verification of the tallying integrity involves multiplying *all* the encrypted votes published on the bulletin board. If one or more votes are missing (or corrupted), the verification process will fail. This is a potential weakness that worried some reviewers. To address this dependability issue, Shahandashti and Lee came up with an efficient fail-safe mechanism for DRE-i: i.e., in case one or more ballots are missing, the DRE system can gracefully recover from the effect of missing ballots by publishing additional audit data that allow the integrity of the remaining votes to be verified while preserving the secrecy of the missing ballots (details can be found in [288]). This fail-safe solution is a significant enhancement to the theory of the basic DRE-i protocol, and contributes to the final acceptance of the DRE-i paper by the *USENIX Journal of Election Technology and Systems* in 2014 [288]

13.5.5 A Verifiable Classroom Voting System

The two trial elections proved to be an invaluable experience to us. The desire to run more e-voting trials directed us to "classroom voting."

Classroom voting is a modern pedagogy, invented by Professor Eric Mazur in the 1990s during his teaching of physics at Harvard University, and later extended to teaching mathematics, chemistry and other subjects [385]. Newcastle University, among several other UK universities, has been trialling this pedagogy by using a commercial classroom voting product from the TurningPoint company.

As part of the training required for new academic staff in the UK, I attended a seminar on "changing how we teach with voting technology." An instructor from Newcastle University Teaching Unit showed us a demo of the TurningPoint voting system. After a short briefing, he handed out a set of hand-held devices, known as "clickers." Each clicker was able to communicate with a special receiver installed on the instructor's computer through a radio-frequency wireless signal. To synchronize each clicker with the receiver, we were instructed to enter a 2-digital channel code on the clicker. Once the sync was completed, voting was ready to start. The instructor showed a multiple-choice question over a PowerPoint slide. We were then asked to use the clicker to vote for the best answer. Each clicker had a small light indicator. A green light indicated that the vote had been recorded by the receiver, while an amber light indicated failure. Once everyone had voted for answers, the instructor closed the voting session by using TurningPoint software that was installed in PowerPoint as a plug-in. The tallying result of the answers was then displayed over the PowerPoint projector in a colorful bar chart. In a real class, the tallying result would give the

Figure 13.5: TurningPoint voting system. It comprises a receiver that is plugged into the USB port of a computer and a set of custom-built voting devices known as clickers.

teacher instant feedback about the students' learning outcome, so the teacher could adjust teaching accordingly.

I was impressed by the pedagogical value of classroom voting, but as a security researcher, I could not help wondering if security aspects of voting had been considered. So I asked the instructor how could voters verify if the tallying results were accurate. The instructor replied: "You need to trust the system." He went on to explain that one could gain the trust by testing the product before the class.

The instructor's reply echoed similar arguments in other e-voting applications. For example, many e-voting systems deployed in real-world national elections were unverifiable. Voters cast their votes using electronic means (e.g., through a DRE machine) but were not able to verify if the votes had been recorded and tallied correctly. When the security concern of such voting systems was raised, the typical response from the government was: "You need to trust the system." Usually, the "trust" is formalized by a process of certification: a panel of authorities examine the product and declare it "trustworthy" since nothing wrong is identified. However, without verifiability, if there is anything wrong with the tallying (e.g., due to software bugs, implementation error or malicious tampering), voters will not be able to notice.

In a classroom voting application, one might question if the integrity of the voting outcome is worth protecting. After all, if the tallying results turn out to be wrong, it seems to do no serious harm. However, I believed the "integrity" was still important in a classroom voting application. While questions in classroom voting are typically insensitive, sometimes they do carry stakes. For example, students may be asked to assess the module or rate the performance of the lecturer. In those cases, the integrity of the voting process should be guaranteed and the results be externally auditable (e.g., by university administrative units). Adding "verifiability" to the classroom voting process can significantly broaden the traditional scope of classroom voting, covering all types of voting questions from low to high stakes.

From a research perspective, classroom voting presents an ideal opportunity to put the theory of verifiable voting to practical test. If a verifiable e-voting scheme is really practical, one should be able to apply it to practical voting scenarios on a *routine* basis without incurring any significant cost in usability. It is important that students should find using a "verifiable" e-voting product as convenient as using an "unverifiable" e-voting counterpart. If the "verifiability" is obtained at the great expense of convenience, voters would most likely vote with their feet, refusing to use the product eventually.

Based on the above considerations, we decided that it was worthwhile to implement a verifiable classroom voting (VCV) system based on DRE-i and try it out. I submitted a proposal to Newcastle University Innovation Funds about developing such a VCV system for pedagogical use. My proposal was subsequently accepted by the university teaching unit with a £6,000 pump-priming fund to support the system development. This enabled me to recruit two students to work on the project: Carlton Shepherd who was a second year Computer Science undergraduate, and Dylan Clarke who was then a fresh PhD graduate.

After three months' hard work during the summer of 2012, Shepherd and Clarke completed a working prototype of the VCV system. The back-end is a web server hosted at the School of Computing Science, Newcastle University. All cryptographic operations are performed at the server side. On the front-end, the prototype supports three different voting interfaces: a web browser, an Android app and an iPhone app. Among the three, the web browser is generally recommended, as it does not require installing any app. However, some students prefer apps to a web browser, so the Android/iPhone apps are still provided. Figure 13.6 shows the web voting interface, which also contains links at the bottom to 1) help; 2) the Android app; 3) the iPhone app and 4) coordinator's login. Any user with a Newcastle University campus account is able to log in as a coordinator and create classroom voting sessions.

The VCV system supports two types of authentication: using group passcode and individual passcode. The former uses a single passcode for the whole voting session, which is the most common choice in the routine use of the system. A teacher creates a voting session with a set of questions and answers, and specifies a single passcode (which may be empty). During the class, all students are allowed to vote after entering the passcode. Of course, a student may reuse the passcode to vote more than once. In most scenarios, this is an acceptable trade-off, given the low-stake nature of the voting result. In other scenarios where voting results carry high stakes, the one-man-one-vote rule must be strictly enforced. In this case, the second authentication option should be used. The system generates a list of random passcodes that match

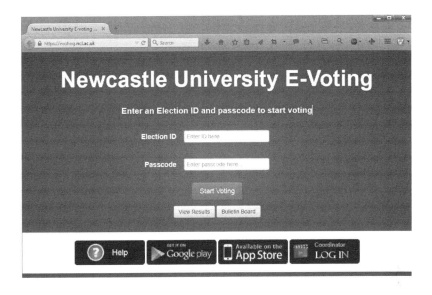

Figure 13.6: Web interface for classroom voting.

the estimated number of legitimate voters. The passcodes are printed on physical paper and cut into small paper slips with each slip containing one random passcode. All paper slips are physically mixed in a container before being manually distributed to voters. (This method was used in the 2015 "best paper" voting competition in our school in January 2015.)

13.5.6 Cryptography Meeting Pedagogy

Since the first semester in October 2012, I have been using the VCV system in real teaching in my own classes: i.e., a "System Security" module for MSc students and a "Cryptography" module for BSc students in the School of Computing Science. Normally I create a voting session on the day before the lecture. On the lecture day, I use the first ten minutes for voting, asking students to select best answers for a set of multi-choice questions that are drawn from the previous lecture. To make the voting process more interactive, I encourage students to discuss with peers who sit next to them before voting, to ensure they have seriously thought about answers before sending votes. Once students have answered all recap questions, I close the election by using a web interface (after logging on as coordinator using the Newcastle University campus account). The tallying results are instantly shown on the bulletin board (a web page). Based on the results, I can quickly assess the student learning outcome and adjust my teaching accordingly.

By practicing verifiable classroom voting in real teaching on a routine daily basis, I came to appreciate the powerful potential of this modern pedagogy. The use of

Table 13.4: Student survey.

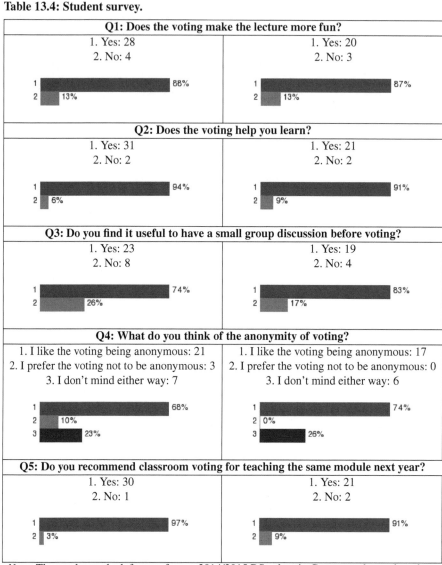

Note: The results on the left were from a 2014/2015 BSc class in Cryptography, and on the right from a 2014/2015 MSc class in System security.

classroom voting has evidently improved the student interactions in the class and made them more engaged. To gauge the effectiveness of using VCV for pedagogy, in January 2015, I conducted two student surveys in the "System Security" (MSc) and "Cryptography" (BSc) classes respectively. Students were asked to select answers to five questions. The answers are summarized in Table 13.4.

As shown in Table 13.4, the vast majority of students (around 90%) agreed that the classroom voting system made the lecture more fun and helped them learn. Between 74% and 83% students found the small group discussion useful. While only a few students did not mind whether voting was anonymous, the majority (68-74%) liked the current design that preserved anonymity. Finally, nearly all students (91-97%) supported the continued use of classroom voting in teaching in the following year. These results are largely consistent with the previous surveys conducted in [290] and [287].

Since the VCV system became first available for practical use in a live teaching environment in 2013, it has been used by students at both the undergraduate and postgraduate levels. Based on students' feedback, the system was improved and made freely available across the campus to anyone who has a valid Newcastle University account. Gradually, the system has been adopted by lecturers across the university, including computing science, electrical engineering, politics and business.

The public verifiability of the VCV system is a distinguishing advantage over all other classroom voting systems. Voters can vote anywhere, at any time with ability to independently verify the integrity of the tallying results. This makes it possible to extend the VCV system beyond the traditional classroom voting. For example, in 2015 the VCV system was used by members of the School of Computing Science at Newcastle University to vote for the "best paper" that had been published in the school during 2014. By comparison, this kind of election cannot be securely supported by existing commercial classroom voting systems due to a lack of verifiability.

In future, we plan to extend the VCV system for public use outside Newcastle University. Our aim is to make the system as freely available as possible over the Internet, so universities around the world can benefit from practicing the modern classroom voting pedagogy. Our business plan has recently been approved by the 2015 ERC Proof-of-Concept grant (which supports commercialization of ERC research results). Work is currently in progress in this regard.

13.6   Conclusion

This chapter describes a ten-year journey of exploring a practically useful e-voting system. The journey started from a seeming coincidence – the discovery of an efficient solution to the Dining Cryptographers problem. The essence of that solution, through the cancellation of random factors by juggling public keys, was subsequently applied to construct efficient e-voting protocols for both small-scale boardroom voting and large-scale voting. The end result of this journey is a new E2E verifiable voting system called DRE-i. As compared with other E2E voting systems, DRE-i does not require any tallying authorities, and hence the system is "self-enforcing." Trial elections based on the DRE-i protocol have been conducted with promising results. A verifiable classroom voting system, based on DRE-i, is currently being used at Newcastle University for pedagogical purposes, and will be publicly available in the near future.

In retrospect, one interesting observation of this journey is that it is fueled by uncertainty. At each stage of the journey, the goal towards the next challenge is clear, but its reachability has remained largely uncertain until a solution is finally worked out. The next challenge that we are working on is how to extend DRE-i to support more complex voting schemes, such as STV. I have no answer at this stage and I do not even know if this is achievable – that feelings of déjà vu remind me that the journey is still continuing.

Acknowledgment

The author would like to thank Brian Randell for his invaluable comments and feedback. This work is supported by the ERC Starting Grant, No. 306994.

Chapter 14

STAR-Vote: A Secure, Transparent, Auditable and Reliable Voting System

Susan Bell
Office of the Travis County Clerk

Josh Benaloh
Microsoft Research

Michael D. Byrne
Rice University

Dana DeBeauvoir
Office of the Travis County Clerk

Bryce Eakin
Independent Researcher

Gail Fisher
Office of the Travis County Clerk

Philip Kortum

Rice University

Neal McBurnett

ElectionAudits

Julian Montoya

Office of the Travis County Clerk

Michelle Parker

Office of the Travis County Clerk

Olivier Pereira

Université catholique de Louvain

Philip B. Stark

University of California, Berkeley

Dan S. Wallach

Rice University

Michael Winn

Office of the Travis County Clerk

CONTENTS

(An earlier version of this chapter, with the same authors and title, was published in the *USENIX Journal of Election Technologies and Systems (JETS)*, volume 1, number 1, August 2013.)

14.1   Introduction

A decade ago, DRE voting systems promised to improve many aspects of voting. By having a computer mediating the user's voting experience, they could ostensibly improve usability through summary screens and a variety of accessibility features including enlarged text, audio output, and specialized input devices. They also promised to improve the life of the election administrator, yielding quick, accurate tallies without any of the ambiguities that come along with hand-marked paper ballots. And, of course, they were promised to be secure and reliable, tested and certified. In practice, DRE systems had problems in all these areas.

Many current DRE voting systems experienced their biggest sales volume after the failures of punch card voting systems in Florida in the 2000 presidential election. The subsequent Help America Vote Act provided a one-time injection of funds that made these purchases possible. Now, more than a decade later, these machines are near the end of their service lifetimes.

In 2012, the Travis County election administration, having used Hart InterCivic's eSlate DRE system for over a decade, concluded that no system on the market—DRE or optical scan—met their future needs. They prefer to avoid hand-marked paper ballots because they open the door to ambiguous voter intent, a source of frustration in their previous centrally-tabulated optical scan system. They didn't want to go back.

Travis County's needs and preferences impose several significant constraints on the design of STAR-Vote:

DRE-style UI Hand-marked ballots are not to be used, for the reason above. DRE-style systems were also preferred for their ability to offer facilities for voters with disabilities.

Printed paper ballot summaries While the DRE-style UI was desired for entering selections, printed ballots were desired for their security benefits, verifiability by voters and redundancy against failures in the electronic system. In order to save on paper and paper management, the county wished to only print a list of each voter's selections, analogous to the summary screens on many current-generation DRE systems.

All-day battery life Power failures happen. Current-generation DRE systems have batteries that can last for hours. The new system must also be able to operate for hours without external power.

Early voting and election-day vote centers Travis County supports two weeks of early voting, where any voter may vote in any of more than 20 locations. Also, on election day, any voter may go to any local polling place. Our county's voters informally report their appreciation of these benefits.

COTS hardware Current DRE systems are surprisingly expensive. Travis County wants to use commercially available, off-the-shelf equipment, whenever possible, to reduce costs and shorten upgrade cycles. That is, "office equipment" rather than "election equipment" should be used where possible.

Long ballots While voters in many countries only select a candidate for member of parliament, in the U.S., voters regularly face 100 or more contests for federal, state and regional offices; judges; propositions; and constitutional amendments. STAR-Vote must support very long ballots as well as long lists of contestants in each race.

These constraints interact in surprising ways. Even if the county did not have a strong preference for a DRE-like UI, pre-printed paper ballots are inefficient for vote centers, which may need to support hundreds or thousands of distinct ballot styles. Likewise, the requirement to run all day on battery backup eliminates the possibility of using laser printers for ballot-on-demand printing, which consume far too much power.[1] We note that counties that face fewer constraints may choose to adopt quite different architectures. For example, a county without election-day vote centers might instead use pre-printed ballots and electronic ballot marking devices.

These constraints likewise eliminate prior-fielded E2E systems like Scantegrity [133, 144], and Prêt à Voter [502, 125], which rely on hand-marked paper, and Helios [46, 44], which is meant for use in web browsers, not traditional polling locations. Wombat [80] has a paper trail, but it's only designed for single-issue ballots. Vote-Box [510] has a DRE-like interface, but it's an entirely paperless system. Instead, to satisfy our constraints, we must build something new, or at least extend an existing system to satisfy our constraints.

We were charged with using the latest advances in human factors, end-to-end cryptography and statistical auditing techniques, while keeping costs down and satisfying many challenging constraints. We want to generate quick, verifiable tallies when the election is over, yet incorporate a variety of audit mechanisms (some voter-verifiable, others facilitated by auditors with additional privileges).

---

[1] A laser printer might consume 1000 watts or more while printing. A reasonably good UPS, weighing 26 kg, can provide that much power for only ten minutes. Since a printer must warm up for each page when printed one-off (perhaps 10 seconds per page), the battery might be exhausted by printing as few as 60 ballots.

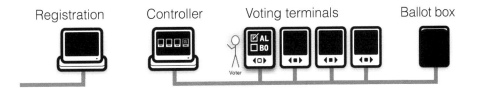

Registration   Controller   Voting terminals   Ballot box

Figure 14.1: The design of the STAR-Vote system. The voter registration system (left) is connected to the Internet but not to the internal LAN. Voters move left to right. First, the voter's registration is validated, and a thermal printout indicates the proper ballot style. This moves to the controller, which scans it and issues the voter a PIN, again printed on thermal paper. The voter proceeds to any open voting terminal, enters the PIN, and is given the proper ballot style. The ballot summary is printed, and deposited into the ballot box (right).

We notably have chosen to design STAR-Vote without explicitly worrying about the constraints of state or federal certification. Of course, for STAR-Vote to go into production, these challenges need to be addressed, but at least for now, our focus has been on designing the best possible voting system given our constraints.

14.2   Voter Flow

Figure 14.1 shows how STAR-Vote works from the perspective of a voter. The STAR-Vote voting system bears a resemblance to the Hart InterCivic eSlate system and to VoteBox [510], in that the voting machines are networked together, simplifying the movement of data. Like eSlate, our design contains a networked group of voting machines that share a common judge's station with a computer like Hart InterCivic's "Judge Booth Controller" (JBC) that manages everything.

1. *Registration (poll book).* The first step for the voter is to check in with a poll worker. This is where voter registration is verified and the voter's precinct and ballot style are determined. The registration system, via cellular modem, notifies a centralized database of the voter's change in status, to eliminate any risk of double-voting.

   The registration system will use a thermal label printer to generate a sticker with the voter's name, precinct and ballot style indicated. The precinct and ballot style are also indicated with a 1-D barcode. This sticker goes into a poll book which the voter signs, providing a backup to the online database. The barcode can also be read by an off-the-shelf scanner connected to the controller. This represents the only data flow from the outside world into the internal voting network, and helps avoid data entry errors that might come from human transcription. Nothing in the barcode is secret nor is it unique to the voter. Consequently, the flow of this information does not compromise the voter's privacy, so long as the voter is not the only voter with the same precinct and ballot style to vote at that polling location.

Provisional voters will be indicated with a suitable prefix to their precinct code, allowing the voting system to suitably distinguish their ballots from regular ones. (Provisional votes are cast by voters who, for whatever reason, do not appear in the voter registration database, and believe this to be in error. They are only tabulated after the voter's registration status is verified, typically not until at least a few days after the end of voting.)

2. *Controller.* The controller scans the barcode on the sticker to identify the voter's precinct and ballot style. The controller then prints a 5-digit code, unique for the remainder of the election in this polling place. Holding this printout, the voter can then approach any open voting terminal, enter the code, and be presented with the correct ballot style. (There will probably need to be a special alternative for ADA compliance as not all voters can see or handle paper. One possible solution is that a poll worker could enter the relevant code, then depart before the voter begins voting.)

   There are only ever a small number of 5-digit codes active at any one time, reducing the odds of a voter successfully guessing an active code and casting multiple ballots. We note that there will be no record binding the 5-digit code to the voter, helping ensure voter anonymity. We also note that these codes reduce the attack surface, relative to other voting systems that use smartcards or other active electronic devices to initialize a voting machine for each voter.

3. *Voting terminals.* The voter makes selections with the GUI (for sighted voters) or auditory UI (for non-sighted voters). There is a review screen (or the auditory equivalent) so that the voter can confirm all selections before producing a paper record.

4. *Print.* When the voter has finished making selections, the voting terminal prints two (possibly joined) items: (1) a paper ballot which includes a human-readable summary of the voter's selections and a random (non-sequential) serial number, and (2) a take-home receipt that identifies the voting terminal used, the time of the vote, and a short (16-20 character) hash code that serves as a commitment to the vote but does not reveal its contents.[2] The voting terminal also sends data about the vote and receipt to the judge's station. (See Section 14.6 for the exact cryptographic design.)

5. *Review printed record.* The voter may then review the printed record to confirm the indicated selections. There will be at least one offline station available that can scan the paper record and read it back to the voter for those who cannot visually read the paper record.

---

[2]A secondary hash code with as many as 16-20 additional characters may be included for additional assurance.

6. *Option: Cast or challenge/spoil.* After reviewing the ballot, the voter has a choice: Cast the ballot or spoil it. A voter might spoil the ballot because of an error (or change of heart) or because the voter wishes to challenge the voting terminal, demanding it to show that the voter's selections were correctly recorded and committed to. This process represents a novel variant on Benaloh challenges [84, 85]; rather than asking the voter a "cast or challenge" question, the voter either deposits the ballot in the box or not. This represents a potentially significant usability gain over prior variants of the Benaloh challenge.

The two procedures are described below. Note also that there is a special procedure for provisional ballots.

Regardless, the voter may keep the take-home paper receipt. We note that most thermal printers include a cutting device that leaves a small paper connection between the two sides of the cut. It is therefore a simple matter for the voting terminal to print a single sheet that the voter can easily separate into the ballot summary and the take-home receipt. We also note that "privacy sleeves" (i.e., simple paper folders) can protect the privacy of these printed ballots as voters carry them from the voting machine either to the ballot box to be cast, or to the judge's station to be spoiled.

   (a) *Ballot box: cast ballot.* A voter who wishes to cast the ballot takes the paper ballot summary to the ballot box. The ballot box has a simple scanner that can read the serial number from the ballot (the serial number might also be represented as a one-dimensional barcode for reliability) and communicate this to the controller, allowing the controller to keep a record of which ballots have found their way to the ballot box, and thus, which ballots should be tabulated. *An electronic ballot record is not considered complete and should not be included in the tally unless and until its corresponding paper ballot summary has been deposited in the ballot box.*

   (b) *Spoil ballot.* If the paper record is to be spoiled, the voter returns to a poll worker. The ballot serial number is scanned so that the controller can record that the ballot is to be spoiled. This informs the controller that the corresponding encrypted ballot record should not be included in contest results. Instead, it should be decrypted and published as such after the election is over. The original printed paper ballot thus corresponds to a *commitment* by the voting machine, before it ever "knew" it might be challenged. If the voting machine cannot produce a suitable proof that the ballot encryption matches the plaintext, then it has been caught cheating. Voters who don't care about verification can simply restart the process. For voters who may feel uncomfortable with this process, as it might reveal their intent to a poll worker, we note that voters could deliberately spoil ballots that misstate their true intent. We note that dedicated election monitors could be allowed to use voting machines, producing printed ballots that they would be forbidden from placing in the ballot box, but which would be spoiled and then the corresponding ciphertext would be decrypted. In effect, election monitors can conduct *parallel testing in the field* on any voting machine at any time during the live election.

(c) *Provisional ballot.* In the case of a provisional ballot, the voter must return the printed ballot to a poll worker. The voter can choose to spoil the ballot and re-vote or to cast the ballot provisionally by having it placed—under an identifying seal—into a distinct provisional ballot box. The voter may retain the receipt to see if the ballot ends up being counted. Because the ballot box is connected to the controller over the LAN, it can also query the controller as to whether the ballot is provisional. In the event that a voter accidentally puts a provisional ballot into the ballot box, the scanner can detect this and reject the printed ballot. (Provisional ballots need to go into dedicated envelopes that are processed after the voting has ended.)

7. *At home (optional): Voter checks crypto.* The encrypted votes will be posted on a public "bulletin board" (i.e., a website maintained by the county). The voter receipt corresponds to a cryptographic hash of the encrypted vote. A voter should be able to easily verify that this vote is present on the bulletin board. If a voter spoiled a ballot, that should also be visible on the bulletin board together with its decrypted selections. This allows independent observers to know which ballots to include in the tally and allows independent verifiers to check that all spoiled ballots are correctly decrypted. Individual voters can check, without any mathematics, that the decryptions of their own spoiled ballots match their expectations.

While this process is more cumbersome than a traditional DRE voting system, it has several advantages. By having the paper elements, this system not only benefits from sophisticated end-to-end cryptographic techniques (described in Section 14.6), it also can be audited post-election, by hand, using a risk-limiting audit (see Section 14.5). Voters also have the confidence that comes from holding, verifying and casting a tangible record of their votes, whether or not they trust the computers.

14.3 Design

From the perspective of voters, the process of registration and poll-station sign-in is unchanged from current practice. Once authorized, voters proceed to a voting terminal where they use a rich interface that prevents overvotes, warns of undervotes and supports alternative input/output media for disabled and impaired voters. The printed ballot summary and the corresponding electronic ballot record both include a variety of cryptographic features, which we now describe.

14.3.1   Crypto Overview

From the perspective of election officials, the first new element in the election regimen is to generate the cryptographic keys. A set of election trustees is designated as key holders and a threshold number is fixed. The functional effect is that if there are n election trustees and the threshold value is k, then any k of the n trustees can complete the election, even if the remaining $n - k$ are unavailable. This threshold mechanism provides robustness while preventing any fewer than k of the trustees from performing election functions that might compromise voter privacy. Threshold cryptosystems are straightforward extensions of traditional public-key cryptosystems [199].

The trustees each generate a key pair consisting of a private key and a public key; they publish their public keys. A standard public procedure is then used to compute a single public key from the n trustee public keys such that decryptions can be performed by any k of the trustees. This single election public key K is published and provided to all voting terminals together with all necessary ballot style information to be used in the election. A start value z_0, which is unpredictable and unique to the election, is also chosen and distributed to each voting terminal for reasons discussed below.

During the election, voters use voting terminals to make their selections. Once selections are completed, the voting terminal produces paper printouts of two items. The first is the paper ballot summary which consists of the selections made by the voter and also includes a random (non-sequential) serial number. The second is a receipt that consists of an identification number for the voting terminal, the date and time of the vote and a short hash of the encryption of the voter's selections together with the previous hash value. Specifically, if the voter's selections are denoted by v, the ith hash value produced by a particular voting terminal m in an election is computed as

$$z_i = H(E_K(v), m, z_{i-1})$$

where H denotes the hash function and E denotes encryption. This separation of the ballots into two parts makes sure that the ballot summary does not contain any voter-related information, while the take-home receipt does not leak any information about the voter choices. Furthermore, since we only store votes in an encrypted form, and since the decryption keys are kept out of the system, there is no problem with storing the votes with timestamps: they could only allow linking a voter to a ciphertext that will never be decrypted, which is harmless.

The voting terminal should retain both the encrypted ballots and the current hash value. At the conclusion of the election (if not sooner), the encrypted ballots should be posted on a publicly-accessible web page and digitally signed by the election office using a simple signature key (not the key generated by the trustees). The posting of each encrypted ballot should also include a non-interactive zero-knowledge (NIZK) proof that the ballot is well-formed. Once they receive their ballot summaries and take-home receipts, voters may either deposit their ballot summaries into a ballot box or take them to a poll worker and have them spoiled. Ballot summaries deposited in a ballot box have their serial numbers scanned and recorded. The electronically stored encrypted vote is not considered complete (and not included in the tally) unless and until its corresponding serial number has been recorded in the ballot box.

Any electronically stored encrypted ballots for which no corresponding serial number has been scanned and recorded are deemed spoiled. The published election record should include all spoiled ballots as well as all cast ballots, but for each spoiled ballot the published record should also include a verifiable decryption of the ballot's contents. Voters should be able to easily look up digitally-signed records for any receipts they hold and verify their presence and, for spoiled receipts, the ballot contents.

A voter who takes a completed paper ballot summary to a poll worker can request that the poll worker spoil the ballot and give the voter an opportunity to re-vote. The poll worker marks both the take-home receipt and the paper ballot summary as spoiled (including removing or marking the serial number so that it will not be recorded if subsequently placed in the ballot box) and returns the spoiled ballot summary to the voter.

Upon completion of the election, the election office homomorphically combines the cast ballots into an aggregate encryption of the election tally (this can be as simple as a multiplication of the public encrypted ballots). At least k of the election trustees then each perform their share of the decryption of the aggregate as well as individual decryptions of each of the spoiled ballots. The trustees also post data necessary to allow observers to verify the accuracy of the decryptions.

A privacy-preserving risk-limiting audit is then performed by randomly selecting paper ballot summaries and matching each selected ballot with a corresponding encrypted ballot to demonstrate the correct matching and provide software-independent evidence of the outcome [488, 367, 541].

14.3.2 Triple Assurance

Three lines of evidence are produced to support each election outcome [541]. The homomorphic tallying process proves that the announced tally corresponds to the posted encrypted ballot records. The ballot challenge and receipt checking processes allow voters to check that these encrypted ballot records correctly reflect their selections. The risk-limiting audit process serves to verify the correspondence between the paper records and the electronic records. In addition, the paper records remain available in case of systemic failure of the electronic records or if a manual count is ever desired. The paper and electronic records are conveyed to the local election office separately, providing additional physical security of the redundant audit trail.

The design of the election system ensures that all three of these checks should be perfectly consistent. There is sufficient information in the records so that if any discrepancies arise (for instance because of loss of some of the electronic or paper records), the discrepancies can be isolated to individual ballots that are mismatched or counted differently.

Why combine E2E with risk-limiting auditing? Each provides different guarantees and they support each other's strengths. E2E techniques, for example, provide cryptographically strong evidence that a voter's receipt corresponds to a ballot, on the bulletin board, which has been included correctly in the final tally—a guarantee that risk-limiting audits alone cannot accomplish. However, if there's a discrepancy, E2E techniques cannot necessarily identify where things went wrong. Risk-limiting audits provide a backstop to prevent cryptographic failures from ruining the election outcome. They also provide a secondary check against machines that might be producing paper and electronic records that disagree, even if voters aren't bothering to conduct E2E challenge audits.

14.3.3 Software and Hardware Engineering

An important criteria for STAR-Vote is that it should leverage commodity components whenever feasible. This reduces cost and simplifies the ability for an election administrator to replace aging hardware by sourcing it from multiple vendors. While this paper isn't intended to cover certification issues, the separation of hardware and software allows for the possibility of *commercial off-the-shelf* (COTS) hardware, which *could* be subject to a lower bar for certification than the software.

Ideally, the voting terminals and the judge station could use identical hardware. In particular, we believe that a reasonable target might be "point of sale" terminals. These are used in restaurants worldwide. They are used in relatively demanding environments and, on the inside, are ordinary PCs, sometimes built from low-power laptop-class parts. The only missing hardware from a COTS point of sale terminal, relative to our needs for STAR-Vote, are a printer and a battery.

If you want a reliable, low-power printer, without having to worry about consumable ink or toner, there's only one choice: thermal printers. They come in a variety of widths, up to US Letter size. Thermal paper, particularly higher cost thermal paper, can last for years in an air-conditioned warehouse, although some experimentation would be required to see whether it can survive an un-air-conditioned trip in a hot car in the summer. Every shipping label from major online vendors like Amazon is printed thermally, lending some credence to its survivability in tough conditions.

Specifying a battery is more complicated. We could require that the voting terminal have an internal (and removable) battery, but this eliminates COTS point of sale terminals. Tablet computers come with built-in batteries that, at least in some cases, can last all day. Tablet computers have smaller screens than we might prefer, but they don't have hardware Ethernet ports or enough USB ports to support accessibility devices and printers.[3] Also, we would prefer to use wired networks, rather than the wireless networks built into most tablets. We note that a number of vendors are now releasing touchscreen-enabled laptops and larger touchscreen desktop models to

---

[3]While a single USB port can connect to a USB hub, which would then have more expandability, a *powered* USB hub might be necessary to drive some devices like a USB Ethernet adapter, complicating our requirement to keep STAR running even when on battery power.

support Windows 8. This new hardware is likely to provide good options for running STAR.

For the software layer, we see no need for anything other than a commodity operating system, like Linux, which can be stripped of unessential features to reduce the attack surface. For example, we don't need a full-blown window system or 3D graphics pipeline. All we need are basic pre-rendered ballots, as in pVote [584, 583] or VoteBox [510]. We would specify that the voting system software be engineered in a type-safe language like Java or C# (eliminating buffer overflow vulnerabilities, among other problems) and we would also specify that the software be engineered with *privilege separation* [473], running separate parts of the voting software as distinct applications, with distinct Unix user-ids, and with suitably reduced privileges. For example, the storage subsystem can maintain append-only storage for ballots. The voter-facing UI would then have no direct access to ballot storage, or the network, and could be "rebooted" for every voter. Consequently, a software compromise that impacts the UI application could impact at most one voter. A tablet that includes a Trusted Platform Module (TPM) can provide additional assurance that the correct software — and only the correct software — is running on the device.

A separation architecture like this also provides some degree of protection over sensitive cryptographic key materials, e.g., if we want every voting terminal to have a unique private key to compute digital signatures over ballots, then we must restrict the ability for compromised software to extract the private keys. DStar [587], for example, used this technique to protect the key material in an SSL/TLS web server.

14.4 Usability

14.4.1 *Design Considerations*

In designing this reference voting system it was important to maximize the usability of the system within the framework of enhanced security and administrative expediency. The overall design of the system was strongly influenced by usability concerns. For example, a proposal was put forth to have all voters electronically review the paper record on a second station; this was rejected on usability grounds. ISO 9241 Part 11 [319] specifies the three metrics of usability as effectiveness, efficiency and satisfaction, and these are the parameters we attempt to maximize in this design. Effectiveness of the system means that users should be able to reliably accomplish their task, as they see it. In voting, this means completing a ballot that correctly records the candidate selections of their choice, whether that be through individual candidate selection by race, straight party voting, or candidate write-ins. Efficiency measures the ability of a voter to complete the task with a minimum of effort, as measured through time on task or number of discrete operations required to complete a task. Efficiency is important because users want to complete the voting task quickly and voting officials are concerned about voter throughput. Reduced efficiency means longer lines for waiting voters, more time in the polling booth, and higher equipment costs for election officials. Satisfaction describes a user's subjective assessment of the overall experience. While satisfaction does not directly impact a voter's ability to cast a vote in the current election, it can have direct impact on their willingness to engage in the process of voting at all, so low satisfaction might disenfranchise voters even if they can cast their ballots effectively and efficiently. How does this design seek to maximize these usability metrics? For voting systems, the system must generally be assumed to be walk-up-and-use. Voting is an infrequent activity for most, so the system must be intuitive enough that little to no instruction is required to use it. The system should minimize the cognitive load on voters, so that they can focus on making candidate selections and not on system navigation or operation. The system should also mitigate the kinds of error that humans are known to make, and support the easy identification and simple correction of those errors before the ballot is cast.

Why Not Paper?

Paper ballots (bubble ballots in particular) have many characteristics that make them highly usable [228, 127]. Users are familiar with paper, and most have had some experience with bubble-type item selection schemes. Voting for write-in candidates can be relatively simple and intuitive. Unlike electric voting machines, paper is nearly 100% reliable and is immune from issues of power interruption. Further, paper leaves an auditable trail, and wholesale tampering is extremely difficult. However, paper is not a perfect solution. Voters actually show higher satisfaction with electronic voting methods than they do with paper [226] and paper has significant weaknesses that computers can overcome more easily. First, the ambiguity that can be caused by partial marks leads to substantial problems in counting, recounting and re-interpreting paper ballots. Second, voting by individuals with disabilities can be more easily accommodated using electronic voting methods (e.g., screen readers, jelly switches). Third, electronic voting can significantly aid in the reduction of error (e.g., undervotes, overvotes, stray marks) by the user in the voting process. Fourth, electronic voting can more easily support users whose first language is not English, since additional ballots for every possible language request do not have to be printed, distributed and maintained at every polling location. This advantage is also evident in early voting and vote center administration; rather than having to print, transport, secure and administer every possible ballot for every precinct, the correct ballot can simply be displayed for each voter. Computers also facilitate sophisticated security and cryptography measures that are more difficult to implement in a pure paper format. Finally, administration of the ballots can be easier with electronic formats, since vote counting and transportation of the results are more efficient. We have taken a hybrid approach in this design, by using both paper and electronic voting methods in order to create a voting system that retains the benefits of each medium while minimizing their weaknesses.

Usability vs. Security

Usability and security are often at odds with each other. Password design is a perfect example of this tension. A system that requires a user have a 32-character password with upper and lower case letters, digits and symbols with no identifiable words embedded might be highly secure, but it would have significant usability issues. Further, security might actually be *compromised* since users are likely to write such a difficult password down and leave it in an insecure location (e.g., stuck to the computer monitor). For voting systems, we must strive for maximum usability while not sacrificing the security of the system (our security colleagues might argue that we need to maximize security while not sacrificing usability). In our implementation, many of the security mechanisms are invisible to the user. Those that are not invisible are designed in such a way that only those users who choose to exercise the enhanced security/verifiability of the voting process are required to navigate additional tasks (e.g., ballot challenge, post-voting verification).

Accessibility vs. Security

STAR-Vote makes strategic use of paper to enhance the overall security and auditability of the voting process. From an auditability standpoint, the presence of the paper ballot allows matching of the paper and electronic records and preserves a separate physical copy apart from the electronic tally. From a security standpoint, it allows a voter to verify that the choices selected on the electronic voting terminal (DRE) have been faithfully recorded on the paper ballot (although this voter verification is not as robust as one might hope [227]), and challenge their vote if they choose to do so. However, the added benefits provided by the inclusion of paper come at a cost to the accessibility of the system. Visually impaired voters must now be given a way to verify the contents of printed material and be guided in the handling of that paper into the scanners and ballot boxes. Voters with mobility impairments must now handle these paper ballots with moderate dexterity in order to feed them into the scanning ballot boxes as well. Solutions to this trade-off are still under evaluation. Many obvious solutions, such as giving voters with disabilities the option to simply cast an electronic ballot without a paper record, seriously compromise the overall security and auditability of the voting system, and also present significant privacy concerns, since voters who opt out of the main flow might be easily identified. Simple but non-optimal solutions are being considered (test-to-speech scanning stations, ballot privacy sleeves and increased poll worker involvement), but we continue to investigate more elegant solutions that involve automatic paper handling mechanisms. A final design has still not been identified.

Error Reduction

The use of computers in combination with paper is anticipated to reduce errors committed by voters. Because voters will fill out the ballot on electronic voting terminals, certain classes of errors are completely eliminated. For example, it will be impossible to over vote or make stray ballot marks, as the interface will preclude the selection of more than a single candidate per race. Under voting will be minimized by employing sequential race presentation, forcing the voter to make a conscious choice to skip a race [268]. Under votes will also be highlighted in color on the review screen, providing further opportunity for users to correct accidental under votes. This review screen will also employ a novel party identification marker (see below) that will allow a voter to easily discern the party for which they cast a vote in each race. The use of the paper ballot (printed when the voter signals completion) provides the voter with a final chance to review all choices before casting the final ballot.

14.4.2   User Interface Design Specification

The basic design for the UI is a standard touchscreen DRE with auditory interface for visually impaired voters and support for voter-supplied hardware controls for physical impairments (e.g., jelly switches).

The VVSG

The starting point for UI specifications is the 2012 draft version 1.1 of the Voluntary Voting System Guidelines (VVSG). These guidelines specify many of the critical properties required for a high-quality voting system user interface, from simple visual properties such as font size and display contrast to more subtle properties such as ballot layout. They also require that interfaces meet certain usability benchmarks in terms of error rates and ballot completion time. We believe that no extant commercial voting UI meets these requirements, and that any new system that could meet them would be a marked improvement in terms of usability. That said, there are some additional requirements that we believe should be met.

Accessibility

While the VVSG includes many guidelines regarding accessibility, more recent research aimed at meeting the needs of visually-impaired voters [462] has produced some additional recommendations that should be followed. These include:

- In order to capitalize on user preference, a synthesized male voice should be used.

- Navigation should allow users to skip through sections of speech that are not important to them as well as allowing them to replay any parts they may have missed or not comprehended the first time.

- At the end of the voting process, a review of the ballot must be included, but should not be required for the voter.

Review Screens

Another area where the VVSG can be augmented concerns review screens. Voter detection of errors (or possible malfeasance) on review screens is poor [227], but there is some evidence that UI manipulations can improve detection in some cases [132]. Thus, STAR-Vote requires the following in addition to the requirements listed in the VVSG:

■ Full names of contests and candidates should be displayed on the review screen; that is, names should be text-wrapped rather than truncated. Party affiliation should also be displayed.

■ Undervotes should be highlighted using an orange-colored background.

■ Activating (that is, touching on the visual screen or selecting the relevant option in the auditory interface) should return the voter to the full UI for the selected contest.

■ In addition to party affiliation in text form, graphic markings should be used to indicate the state of each race: voted Republican, voted Democratic, voted Green, etc.—with a distinctive graphic for "not voted" as well. These graphic markings should be highly distinguishable from each other so that a rapid visual scan quickly reveals the state of each race, while taking note of potential usability issues with graphics symbols [533]. Exact graphic symbols for STAR-Vote have not yet been determined.

Paper Record

The VVSG has few recommendations for the paper record. For usability, the paper record should meet VVSG guidelines for font size and should contain full names for office and candidate. To facilitate scanner-based retabulations, the font should be OCR-friendly. Contest names should be left-justified while candidate names should be right-justified to a margin that allows for printing of the same graphic symbols used in the review screen to facilitate rapid scanning of ballots for anomalies. Candidate names should not be placed on the same line of text as the contest name and a thin horizontal dividing line should appear between each office and the next in order to minimize possible visual confusion.

14.4.3 Issues That Still Need to Be Addressed

There are still several issues that need to be addressed in order to make the system have the highest usability. The first of these is straight party voting (SPV). SPV can be quite difficult for a voter to understand and accomplish without error, particularly if voters intend to cross-vote in one or more races [131]. Both paper and electronic methods suffer from these difficulties, and the optimum method of implementation will require additional research. Races in which voters are required to select more than one candidate (k of n races) also create some unique user difficulties, and solutions to those problems are not yet well understood.

14.5 Audit

The E2E feature of STAR-Vote enables individual voters to confirm that their votes were included in the tabulation, and that the encrypted votes were added correctly. The challenge feature, if used by enough voters, assures that the encryption was honest and that substantially all the votes are included in the tabulation. But there might not be many voters who challenge the system; the voters who do are hardly representative of the voting public; and some problems may go unnoticed. Moreover, the anonymized form of E2E used here does not allow a voter to confirm that *others'* ballots were included in the tabulation, only that those ballots that were included were included correctly.

The paper audit trail enables an entirely independent check that the votes were included and tabulated accurately, that the visible trace of voter intent as reflected in the ballot agrees with the encryption, and, importantly, that the winners reported by the voting system are the winners that a full hand count of the audit trail would reveal. The key is to perform a compliance audit to ensure that the audit trail of paper ballots is adequately intact to determine the outcomes, and then to perform a risk-limiting audit of the machine interpretation against a manual interpretation of the paper ballots. For the risk-limiting audit, STAR-Vote uses SOBA [87] with improvements given by [367].

A risk-limiting audit guarantees a large minimum chance of a full hand count of the audit trail if the reported outcome (i.e., the set of winners) disagrees with the outcome that the full hand count would reveal. The full hand count then sets the record straight, correcting the outcome before it becomes official. Risk-limiting audits are widely considered best practice for election audits [366, 114].

The most efficient risk-limiting audits, ballot-level comparison audits, rely on comparing the machine interpretation of individual ballots (cast vote records or CVRs) against a hand interpretation of the same ballots [540, 87, 367]. Current federally certified voting systems do not report cast vote records, so they cannot be audited using the most efficient techniques [367, 541]. This necessitates expensive work-arounds.[4] The preamble to conducting a ballot-level comparison audit using currently deployed voting systems can annihilate the efficiency advantage of ballot-level comparison audits [541].

A big advantage of STAR-Vote is that it records and stores individual cast vote records in a way that *can* be linked to the paper ballot each purports to represent,

---

[4]For instance, a *transitive audit* might require marking the ballots with unique identifiers or keeping them in a prescribed order, re-scanning all the ballots to make digital images, and processing those images with software that can construct CVRs from the images and associate the CVRs with the ballots. That software in turn needs to be programmed with all the ballot definitions in the contest, which itself entails a great deal of error-prone handwork.

through encrypted identifiers of the ballot corresponding to each voter's selections, separately for each contest. This makes ballot-level comparison audits extremely simple and efficient. It also reduces the vulnerability of the audit to human error, such as accidental changes to the order of the physical ballots.[5]

A comparison audit can be thought of as consisting of two parts: Checking the addition of the data,[6] and randomly spot-checking the accuracy of the data added, to confirm that they are accurate enough for their tabulation to give the correct electoral outcome. The data are the votes as reported by the voting system. For the audit to be meaningful, the election official must commit to the vote data before the spot-checking begins. Moreover, for the public to verify readily that the reported votes sum to the reported contest totals, it helps to publish the individual reported votes. However, if these votes were published ballot by ballot, pattern voting could be used to signal voter identity, opening a communication channel that might enable widespread wholesale coercion [482, 87].

The SOBA risk-limiting protocol [87] solves both of these problems: It allows the election official to commit cryptographically and publicly to the vote data; it publishes the vote data in plain text but "unbundled" into separate contests so that pattern voting cannot be used to signal. Moreover, the computations that SOBA requires are extremely simple (they are simplified even further by [367]). The simplicity increases transparency, because observers can confirm that the calculations were done correctly with a pencil and paper or a hand calculator.

The encrypted ballot/contest identifiers on the ballot that STAR-Vote produces allow the electronic cast vote records for each contest to be linked to the paper they purport to represent. This simplifies SOBA procedures because it eliminates the need to store ballots in a rigid order. Moreover, because the voting terminal generates both the electronic vote data and the paper ballot, the audit should find very few if any discrepancies between them.

But since voters and election workers will handle the ballots in transit from the voting terminal to the scanner to the audit, voters might make marks on their ballots. Depending on the rules in place for ascertaining voter intent from the ballot, those marks might be interpreted as expressing voter intent different from the machine-printed selections, in which case the SOBA audit might find discrepancies.

It could also happen that a ballot enters the ballot box but its serial number is not picked up, so the electronic vote data ends up in the "untallied but unspoiled" group. This should be detectable by a compliance audit [87, 367, 541] as a mismatch between the number of recorded votes and the number of pieces of paper, providing an opportunity to resolve the problem before the audit begins.

---

[5]For instance, we have seen groups of ballots dropped on the floor accidentally; even though none was lost, restoring them to their original order was impossible.

[6]This presupposes that the contest under audit is a plurality, majority, super-majority, or vote-for-k contest. The operation that must be checked to audit an instant-runoff contest is not addition, but the same principle applies.

If such cases remain and turn up in the audit sample, SOBA would count them as discrepancies and the sample might need to expand, either until there is strong evidence that the electoral outcomes are correct despite any errors the audit uncovers, or until there has been a complete hand count.

The random selection of ballots for the SOBA audit should involve public participation in generating many bits of entropy to seed a high-quality, public, pseudo-random number generator (PRNG), which is then used to select a sequence of ballots to inspect manually [367]. (For instance, audit observers might roll 10-sided dice repeatedly to generate a 20-digit number.) Publishing the PRNG algorithm adds transparency by allowing observers to verify that the selection of ballots was fair.

14.6   The Cryptographic Workflow

The Core Elements

At its core, the cryptographic workflow of STAR-Vote follows the approach of Cramer, Gennaro and Schoenmakers [178], also used in Helios [46] and Vote-Box[510], among others. Cryptographic analyses of this approach can be found in [99, 171]. We then augment this approach in various ways in order to ease the detection of and recovery from potential problems.

STAR-Vote keeps an electronic record of all the votes encrypted with a threshold cryptosystem (so that decryption capabilities are distributed to protect voter privacy) that has an additive homomorphic property (to allow individual encrypted ballots to be combined into an aggregate encryption of the tally). The common exponential version of the ElGamal cryptosystem [213] satisfies the required properties, and stronger security is obtained by using PPATS encryption [186], in particular against key manipulation errors by the trustees and long-term security. The encryption scheme comes with an extraction function *Ext* that, from a ciphertext, extracts a commitment on the encrypted value. In the case of ElGamal, this commitment is the ciphertext itself, while in the case of PPATS, it is a perfectly hiding homomorphic commitment.

Cryptographic key generation can be accomplished in one of two ways, depending on the availability of the election trustees and the desired amount of robustness. The preferred process offers general threshold key generation requiring multiple rounds (see [252] for ElGamal and PPATS), but can be simplified into a single-round solution if redundancy is eliminated (as in Helios for instance [46]). At the end of the key generation procedure, the trustees each hold a private key share that does not contain any information on the full private key, and the unique public key K corresponding to those shares is published.

During the polling phase, the ballot-marking devices encrypt the votes of each voter using the public key K. This encryption procedure is randomized in order to make sure that two votes for the same candidates result in ciphertexts that look independent to any observer.

Following Benaloh [84], a cryptographic hash value of the commitment extracted from each ciphertext (and of a few more data, as discussed below) is also computed, fingerprinting the ballot to a 256-bit string. An abridged form of this is provided to the voter in a human readable form as part of the take-home receipt. All the hashes and commitments are computed and posted on a publicly accessible web page, as soon as the polls are closed. This web page is digitally signed by the election office using a traditional signature key (as performed by [46]). This signature operation makes it infeasible to consistently modify the content of the web page without the help of the signer, and provides evidence against a malicious signer who would try to sign various versions of the bulletin board.

The posting of all the hashes gives all voters the ability to verify that their ballots have been recorded properly. The commitments can also be checked for consistency with the hashes and used to confirm the homomorphic aggregation of the individual ballots into a single encryption of the sum of the ballots, which constitutes an encryption of the election tallies.

At the end of the election, any set of trustees that achieve the pre-set quorum threshold use their respective private keys to decrypt the derived aggregate tally encryption. This procedure is simple and efficient and can be completed locally without interaction between the trustees. We note that the individual encrypted ballots, from which the aggregate encryption of the tallies is formed, are never individually decrypted. However, each spoiled ballot *is* individually decrypted using exactly the same process that is used to decrypt the aggregate tally encryption.

The elements we just described make the core of the workflow and are sufficient to compute an election tally while preserving the privacy of the votes. We now explain various ways in which this simple workflow is hardened in order to make sure that the tally is also correct. All the techniques that follow enable the verification of different aspects of the ballot preparation and casting.

Hardening Encryption

Since the tally does not involve the decryption of any individual ballot, and since the audit procedure relies on the fact that all counted ballots are properly formed, it is crucial to make sure that all the encrypted ballots that are added correspond to valid votes [161]. This is achieved by requiring the ballot-marking devices to compute, together with the encryption of the votes, a non-interactive zero-knowledge (NIZK) proof that each ballot is well-formed. Such a proof guarantees that each ciphertext encrypts a valid vote and does not leak any other information about the content of the vote. As a side benefit, this proof can be designed to make the ballots non-malleable, which provides an easy technique to prevent the replay of old ballots (i.e., reject duplicates). Traditional sigma proofs provide the required security properties and are described and analyzed in [99].

We note that, if malicious software were to get into the voting system, it could use the randomness inherent in the encryption process to encode a subliminal message to an external observer. This sort of threat, along with the threat of a malicious voting machine that simply records every vote cast, in plaintext, in internal memory, is something that cryptography cannot address. (More discussion on this appears in Section 14.3.3.)

Hardening Decryption

Making sure that the encrypted ballots are valid is not enough: we also need to make sure that the tally is correctly decrypted as a function of those encrypted ballots: otherwise, malicious trustees (or trustees using corrupted devices) could publish an outcome that does not correspond to these ballots. As a result, we require the trustees to provide evidence of the correctness of the decryption operations that they perform. This can also be accomplished with sigma proofs in the case of ElGamal or more simply by publishing commitment openings in the case of PPATS.

Hardening the Timeline

The procedures described above prevent malfunctioning or corrupted voting terminals or trustees to falsify individual ballots or decryption operations.

The detection of manipulation of encrypted ballots can be more effective by linking ballots with each other, using hash chaining [511, 88]. For this purpose, each ballot marking device is seeded, at the beginning of the election, with a public start value z_0 that includes a unique identifier for the election. This unique identifier is chosen at random shortly before the election, either in a central way or by the poll workers themselves at the beginning of election day.

From this seed, all election events are chain hashed, with z_{i+1} being computed as a hash of z_i concatenated to the id of the machine on which the event happens and to the event content. Two such chains are maintained and properly separated. One is internal and contains the full election data, including the encryption of the votes, the casting time of each paper ballot, and information on machines being added or removed. The second is public and chains the commitment extracted from all encrypted votes, together with time and identifiers for the election and voting machine. The public hash is the one actually printed on the take-home receipt. When the polls close, the final value of the hash chains are digitally signed, and the public chain is made public together with all the information needed for its reconstruction.

As a result of this procedure, any removed ballot will invalidate the hash chain which is committed to at the close of the election and whose constituents appear on the voter take-home receipts.

Hardening the Link between the Paper and Electronic Election Outcome

As described in Section 14.5, STAR-Vote includes a risk-limiting audit (RLA) based on the human-readable versions of each ballot summary printed by the voting terminals and inspected for correctness by voters. This RLA comes in addition to the cast or challenge procedure discussed above, and the production of the inputs for the RLA is an original contribution of STAR-Vote.

The requirement for running the RLA is to commit on a full electronic record including a 1-to-1 mapping and evidence that this electronic record leads to the announced outcome. This is achieved as follows.

1. For each ballot, the ballot marking device selects a random ballot id sequence number bid. This bid is printed on the ballots as a barcode. Furthermore, for each race r in which the voter participates, an encryption of $H(bid|0r)$ is also computed and appended to the encryption of the choices.

2. At the end of the day, and before decryption of the tallies, the trustees (or their delegates) shuffle and rerandomize all encrypted votes, race by race. This shuffle does not need to be verifiable, even though a verifiable shuffle would improve accountability by making it possible to verify that the shufflers did not cheat if it happens that a discrepancy is detected during the RLA. However, in the case of a non-verifiable shuffle, the shufflers must save their permutation and randomness until the end of the election audit. The non-verifiable solution is preferred for its simplicity (verifiable shuffles are particularly challenging to implement properly) and for its efficiency (permutations and reencryption factors can be precomputed, leaving only one multiplication to perform per ciphertext in the online phase, which is convenient when millions of ciphertexts have to be shuffled).

3. When the trustees decrypt the homomorphically added votes, they also decrypt the output of this shuffle. For each race, this provides a list of elements of the form $H(bid|0r)$ and the corresponding cleartext choices.

4. Now, auditors can sample the paper ballots, read the bid printed on them, recompute the value of $H(bid|0r)$ for all races present on the paper ballot, and compare to the electronic record (as well as check many other things, as prescribed for the risk-limiting audit).

The use of hashed bid's has the important benefit of making sure that someone who does not know a bid value cannot, by looking at the electronic record, link the selections made for the different races on a single ballot, which protects from pattern voting attacks. There is no need for such a protection from someone who can access the paper ballots, since that person can already link all races just by looking at the paper.

The Full Cryptographic Protocol

The resulting cryptographic workflow is as follows.

1. The trustees jointly generate a threshold public key/private key encryption pair. The encryption key K is published.

2. Each voting terminal is initialized with the ballot and election parameters, the public key K and seeds z_0^p and z_0^i that are computed by hashing all election parameters and a public random salt z_0.

3. When a voter completes the ballot marking process selection to produce a ballot v, the voting terminal performs the following operations:

   (a) It selects a unique and unpredictable ballot identifier bid, as well as a unique (but possibly predictable) ballot casting identifier $bcid$.

   (b) It computes an encryption $c_v = E_K(v)$ of the vote, as well as a NIZK proof p_v that c_v is an encryption of a valid ballot. This proof is written in such a way that it can be verified from $Ext(c_v)$ only.

   (c) For each race $r_1, \ldots, r_n$ in which the voter takes part, it computes an encryption $c_{bid} = E_K(bid|0r_1)|0 \cdots |0E_K(bid|0r_n)$.

   (d) It computes a public hash code $z_i^p = H(bcid|0Ext(c_v)|0p_v|0m|0z_{i-1}^p)$, where m is the voting terminal unique identifier, as well as an internal hash $z_i^i = H(bcid|0c_v|0p_v|0c_{bid}|0|0m|0z_{i-1}^i)$.

   (e) It prints a paper ballot in two parts. The first contains v in a human readable format as well as c_{bid} and $bcid$ in a robust machine readable format (e.g., as barcodes). The second is a voter take-home receipt that includes, the voting terminal identifier m, the date and time, and the hash code z_i^p (or a truncation thereof), all in a human-readable format.

   (f) It transmits $(bcid, c_v, p_v, c_{bid}, m, z_i^p, z_i^i)$ to the judge's station.

4. When a ballot is cast, the ballot casting id $bcid$ is scanned and sent to the judge's station. The judge's station then marks the associated ballot as cast and ready to be included in the tally. This information is also broadcast and added in the two hash chains.

5. When the polls are closed, the tally is computed: the product of all cast encrypted votes is computed and verifiably decrypted, providing an election result.

6. The data needed for the risk limiting audit is computed, as described above.

All the data included in the public hash chain are eventually digitally signed and published by the local authority. Those audit data are considered to be valid if the hash chain checks, if all cryptographic proofs check, that is, if the ballot validity proofs check, if the homomorphic aggregation of the committed votes is computed and opened correctly, and if all spoiled ballots are decrypted correctly.

Write-In Votes

So far, we have not described how our cryptographic construction can support write-in voting. Support for write-in votes is required in many states. To be general-purpose, STAR-Vote adopts the vector-ballot approach [346], wherein there is a separate homomorphic counter for the write-in slot plus an encryption of the string in the write-in. If there are enough write-in votes to influence the election outcome, then the write-in slots, across the whole election, will be mixed and tallied (together with the corresponding counters).

We note that, at least for elections in our state, write-in candidates must be registered in advance. It's conceivable that we could simply allocate a separate homomorphic counter for each registered candidate and have the STAR-Vote terminal help the voter select the desired "write-in" candidate. Such an approach could have significant usability benefits but is expected to require some update of regulations.

14.7 Threats

To evaluate the design and engineering of STAR-Vote, it's helpful to have a threat model in mind. The obvious place to start would be VoteBox [510], which is closely related to STAR-Vote. The original VoteBox authors did not state a concise threat model, but considered several kinds of threats and security design goals:

Software independence STAR-Vote, like VoteBox, should be able to produce a proof of the correctness of an election that does not require any statement about the correctness of the software used in STAR-Vote. VoteBox achieved this through end-to-end cryptographic means. STAR-Vote uses similar cryptography and adds a risk-limiting audit that can verify the correspondence between STAR-Vote printed ballot records and their electronic counterparts, adding a degree of flexibility if the cryptography cannot prove an exact correspondence to determine exactly what went wrong.

Reduced trusted computing base STAR-Vote, like VoteBox or any other software artifact, would benefit from having simpler code and less of it. This makes it easier to verify and less likely to have bugs. Software independence means that STAR-Vote's software is not required for *correctness* of the election outcome, but it does help defeat attacks which could disable the system, destroy records, or otherwise cause grief to election officials running STAR-Vote. VoteBox specifies that it uses pre-rendered user interfaces [583, 584]. STAR-Vote should probably use this technique as well.

Robustness against data loss STAR-Vote, like VoteBox, specifies that vote records be stored on every voting terminal in the local polling place, using tamper-evident logging techniques. STAR-Vote adds a printed ballot record, stored in a ballot box. VoteBox went a step further by considering the real-time one-way transfer of vote records out of the polling place, across the Internet, to a central election headquarters. While STAR-Vote could add this in the future, it's not part of the initial design.

Mega attacks In the VoteBox paper, the authors considered a variety of attacks with highly capable attackers. Such attackers might run a concurrent election on parallel equipment, in an attempt to substitute the results for genuine votes. Other attackers might mount a "booth capture" attack, wherein armed gunmen take over a polling place and cast votes as fast as possible until the police arrive. These attacks, needless to say, are well within the ability of STAR-Vote's cryptographic and risk-limiting infrastructure to detect. The best such attackers can hope to do is, in effect, mount a denial of service attack against the election. Attackers with that as their goal can arrive at much simpler approaches and STAR-Vote has relatively little it can offer beyond any other election system in this regard.

A full consideration of threats to STAR-Vote and their corresponding counter-measures or mitigations would be far too long to fit in this paper. Instead, we focus on several areas where STAR-Vote differs from other E2E voting systems in the literature.

14.7.1 Coercion

In designing STAR-Vote, we made several explicit decisions regarding how much to complicate the protocol and impede the voter experience in order to mitigate known coercion threats. Specifically, one known threat is that a voter is instructed to create a ballot in a particular way but to then execute a decision to cast or spoil the ballot according to some stimulus received after the ballot has been completed and the receipt has been generated. The stimulus could come, for example, from subtle motions by a coercer in the poll site, the vibration of a cell phone in silent mode, or some of the (unpredictable) data that is printed on the voter's receipt. Some prior protocols have required that the receipt, although committed to by the voting device, not be visible to the voter until after a cast or spoil decision has been made (perhaps by printing the receipt face down behind a glass barrier) and configuring poll sites so that voters cannot see or be seen by members of the public until after they have completed all steps. We could insist on similar measures here, but in an era where cell phones with video recording capabilities are ubiquitous and eyeglasses with embedded video cameras can easily be purchased, it seems unwise to *require* elaborate measures which mitigate some coercion threats but leave others unaddressed.

14.7.1.1 Chain Voting

A similar threat of "chain voting" is possible with this system wherein a voter early in the day is instructed to neither cast nor spoil a ballot but to instead leave the poll site with a printed ballot completed in a specified way. This completed ballot is delivered to a coercer who will then give this ballot to the next voter with instructions to cast the ballot and return with a new printed ballot—again completed as specified. Chain voting can be mitigated by instituting timeouts which automatically spoil ballots that have not been cast within a fixed period after having been printed. We also expect to have procedures in place to prevent voters from accidentally leaving poll sites with printed ballots. We note that the timeout period need only cover the time we expect will be required for a voter to cross the room with a printed ballot and place it in the box, allowing for a relatively tight time bound, probably less than 5 minutes, although we'd need to run this in practice to understand the distribution of times that might happen in the real world.

(We note that traditional paper ballots sometimes include a perforated header section which includes a serial number. A poll worker keeps one copy of this number and verifies that the ballot a voter wishes to cast matches the expected serial number. If so, the serial number is then detached from the ballot and deposited in the box. STAR-Vote could support this, but we believe it would damage STAR-Vote's usability. The timeout mechanism seems like an adequate mitigation.)

We do, however, take measures to prevent wholesale coercion attacks such as those that may be enabled by pattern voting. For instance, The SOBA audit process is explicitly designed to prevent pattern-voting attacks; and the high assurances in the accuracy of the tally are acheived without ever publishing the full set of raw ballots.

An interesting concern is that our paper ballots have data on them to connect them to electronic ballot records from the voting terminals and judge's console. The very data that links a paper ballot to an electronic, encrypted ballot creates a potential vulnerability. Since some individual paper ballot summaries will be selected for post-election audit and made public at that time, we are careful to not include any data on the voter's take-home receipt which can be associated with the corresponding paper ballot summary.

14.7.1.2 Absentee and Provisional Ballots

There are several methods available for incorporating ballots which are not cast within the STAR-Vote system, such as absentee and provisional ballots. The simplest approach is to completely segregate votes and tallies, but this has several disadvantages, including a reduction in voter privacy and much lower assurance of the accuracy of the combined tally.

It may be possible to eliminate all "external" votes by providing electronic means for capturing provisional and remote ballots. However, for the initial design of the STAR-Vote system, we have chosen to avoid this complexity. Instead, we ask that voting officials receive external votes and enter them into the STAR-Vote system as a proxy for voters. While this still does not allow remote voters to audit their own ballots, the privacy-preserving risk-limiting audit step is still able to detect any substantive deviations between the paper records of external voters and their electronically recorded ballots. This provides more supporting evidence of the veracity of the outcome without reducing voter privacy.

14.7.2 Further Analysis

If we wished to conduct a more in-depth threat modeling exercise, one place to begin would be the threat model developed by the California Top To Bottom Review's source code audit teams (see, e.g., [318]). They considered different levels of attacker access, ranging from voters to election officials. They also considered different attacker motives (disrupt elections, steal votes, coerce voters) and different attack outcomes (detectable vs. undetectable, recoverable vs. unrecoverable, prevention vs. detection, wholesale vs. retail, and casual vs. sophisticated). A complete consideration of STAR-Vote against all these criteria would take far more space than is available in this venue. Instead, we now focus on where STAR-Vote advances the state of the art in these areas.

Most notably, STAR-Vote's combination of end-to-end cryptography with risk-limiting audits of paper ballots is a game changer, in terms of thwarting attackers who might want to disrupt elections. Unlike paperless systems, STAR-Vote has the ability to fall back to the paper records, with efficient processes to detect when inconsistencies exist that would require this. This radically improves STAR-Vote's recoverability from extreme failures.

Similarly, while STAR-Vote is "software independent," we must concern ourselves with software tampering that does not change any of the cryptographic computations, but instead causes the STAR-Vote machines to silently record everything the voter does. This threat cannot be mitigated by better cryptography or ballot auditing. The only likely solution is some sort of trusted platform management (TPM), where the hardware will refuse to run third-party code (more discussion on this appears in Section 14.3.3).

Lastly, we consider a threat that only arises in E2E systems: presentation of a fraudulent voting receipt. Consider the case where a voter may spoil her ballot and take it home to verify against the public bulletin board. A malicious voter with access to similar printers could produce a seemingly legitimate ballot for which there is no correspondence on the public bulletin board, thus "proving" that the election system lost a record. Similar defaming attacks could be made by forging the receipt that a voter can take home after casting a ballot. For STAR-Vote, we have considered a number of mitigations against these attacks, ranging from cryptographic (having the voting terminals compute a digital signature, with protected key material) to procedural (e.g., watermarking the paper or having poll workers physically sign spoiled ballots). Real STAR-Vote deployments will inevitably use one or more of these mitigations.

14.8   Conclusions and Future Work

In many ways, STAR-Vote is a straightforward evolution from existing commercial voting systems, like the Hart InterCivic eSlate, mixing in advanced cryptography, software engineering, usability and auditing techniques from the research literature in a way that will go largely unnoticed by most voters, but that has huge impact on the reliability, accuracy, fraud-resistance and transparency of elections. Of course, we can also take this opportunity to improve more pragmatic features, such as offering better support for the election administration's desired workflow. Clearly, we're long overdue for election systems engineered with all the knowledge we now have available.

STAR-Vote also opens the door to a variety of interesting future directions. For example, while STAR-Vote is intended to service any given county as an island unto itself, there's no reason why it cannot also support *remote voting*, where ballot definitions could be transmitted to a remote supervised kiosk, which securely returns the electronic and paper records. By virtue of STAR-Vote's cryptographic mechanisms, such a remote vote is really no different than a local provisional vote and can be resolved in a similar fashion, preserving the anonymity of the voter. (A variation on this idea was earlier proposed as the RemoteBox extension [512] to VoteBox [510].) This could have important ramifications for overseas and military voters with access to a suitable impromptu polling place, e.g., on a military base or in a consular office.

(We do not want to suggest that STAR-Vote would be suitable for *Internet* voting. Using computers of unknown provenance, with inevitable malware infections, and without any systematic way to prevent voter bribery or coercion, would be a foolhardy way to cast ballots. A STAR-Vote variant, running in a web browser and printing a paper ballot returned through the postal mail, might well be feasible as a replacement for current vote-by-mail practices. A full consideration of this is left for future work.)

STAR-Vote anticipates the possibility that voting machine hardware might be nothing more than commodity computers running custom software. It remains unclear whether off-the-shelf computers can be procured to satisfy all the requirements of voting systems (e.g., long-term storage without necessarily having any climate control, or having enough battery life to last for a full day of usage), but perhaps such configurations might be possible, saving money and improving the voting experience.

For additional details on STAR-Vote, Travis County has recently published a detailed "request for information" (RFI)[7] which refines the specification here with additional details on every aspect of the system. They're soliciting feedback as part of the RFI process,[8] which will hopefully then lead to a subsequent "request for proposals" (RFP, also called a "tender").

---

[7]http://traviscountyclerk.org/eclerk/content/images/pdf_STARVote_2015.06.03_RFI.pdf

[8]http://traviscountyclerk.org/eclerk/Content.do?code=News.StarVote

Acknowledgments

Pereira's work was supported by the Belgian French Community through the SCOOP ARC project and by the European Commission through the HOME/2010/ISEC/AG/INT-011 B-CCENTRE project. Wallach and Kortum are supported, in part, by the National Science Foundation (CNS-1409401).

References

[1] ACCURATE: A Center for Correct, Usable, Reliable, Auditable, and Transparent Elections. http://accurate-voting.org/.

[2] The American Statistical Association, by-laws, article III.2. http://www.amstat.org/about/bylaws.cfm.

[3] Chapter 2, rule 13: election of president - opening address. http://www.europarl.europa.eu/.

[4] Comment on the article published in the Guardian. http://vvk.ee/valimiste-korraldamine/vvk-uudised/vabariigi-valimiskomisjoni-vastulause-the-guardianis-ilmunud-artiklile/.

[5] Communities in America currently using proportional voting. The FairVote website archives. http://archive.fairvote.org/?page=2101.

[6] The constitution of FSFE, section 6, article 3. http://fsfe.org/about/legal/Constitution.en.pdf.

[7] Cumulative voting in Texas. The Texas Politics Project website, University of Texas at Austin. http://texaspolitics.utexas.edu/.

[8] Debian voting information. http://www.debian.org/vote/.

[9] Derwent Valley Council results in the 2014 Tasmanian local government elections, Tasmanian electoral commission. http://www.tec.tas.gov.au/LocalGovernmentElections2014/2014LGResults/DerwentValley.html.

[10] e-Estonia: Electronic ID card. https://e-estonia.com/component/electronic-id-card/.

[11] E-voting concept security: analysis and measures. `http://www.vvk.ee/public/dok/E-voting_concept_security_analysis_and_measures_2010.pdf`.

[12] E-voting system general overview. `http://www.vvk.ee/public/dok/General_Description_E-Voting_2010.pdf`.

[13] Election of the speaker of the house. `http://www.parl.gc.ca/About/House/compendium/web-content/c_d_electionspeakerhouse-e.htm`.

[14] Frequently asked questions: speaker's election. `http://www.parliament.uk/about/faqs/house-of-commons-faqs/speakers-election/`.

[15] Gauteng provincial legislature results in the 2014 national and provincial elections, electoral commission of South Africa. `http://www.elections.org.za/resultsNPE2014`.

[16] IMDb votes/ratings top frequently asked questions. `http://www.imdb.com/help/show_leaf?votestopfaq`.

[17] The institute for operations research and the management sciences, by-law 3. `http://www.informs.org/About-INFORMS/Constitution-and-Bylaws`.

[18] International Association for Voting Systems Sciences. `http://www.iavoss.org/`.

[19] Internet voting in Estonia. `http://www.vvk.ee/voting-methods-in-estonia/engindex/`.

[20] The ISU judging system general rules. `http://www.isu.org/en/single-and-pair-skating-and-ice-dance/isu-judging-system`.

[21] The Mathematical Association of America, by-laws, article IX.9. `http://www.maa.org/about-maa/governance-documents/bylaws`.

[22] Our response to the national election committee's statement. `https://estoniaevoting.org/press-release/response-national-election-committees-statement/`.

[23] Riigikogu election act. `https://www.riigiteataja.ee/en/eli/ee/514112013015/consolide/current`.

[24] Rules of procedures for online voting, section 3.4.1. `https://ev.kde.org/rules/online_voting.php`.

[25] Sejm constituency no. 28 (częstochowa) results in the 2011 parliamentary elections, the polish national electoral commission, IOS Press. http://www.wybory2011.pkw.gov.pl/wsw/en/sjm-28.html.

[26] Should the IACR use e-voting for its elections? http://www.iacr.org/elections/eVoting/.

[27] The south region results in the 2009 aboriginal land council of Tasmania, Tasmanian electoral commission. http://www.tec.tas.gov.au/OtherElections/ALCT.

[28] Statistics about internet voting in Estonia. http://www.vvk.ee/voting-methods-in-estonia/engindex/statistics.

[29] Ubuntu IRC council position. http://fridge.ubuntu.com/2012/05/17/ubuntu-irc-council-position/.

[30] Voting at home. http://www.vvk.ee/voting-methods-in-estonia/voting-on-election-day/voting-at-home/.

[31] Voting systems in the UK. http://www.parliament.uk/about/how/elections-and-voting/voting-systems/.

[32] What is Digi-ID, how can I get it and what can I do with it? http://www.id.ee/index.php?id=34410.

[33] Wombat voting system. http://www.wombat-voting.com/.

[34] e-voting security study, July 2002. CESG Report Issue 1.2.

[35] ECRYPT II yearly report on algorithms and keysizes, 2012. http://www.ecrypt.eu.org/ecrypt2/documents/D.SPA.20.pdf.

[36] Public rules of the 60th Eurovision song contest. European Broadcasting Union, 2015. http://www.eurovision.tv.

[37] The Federal Constitutional Court Press Release No. 19/2009. Use of voting computers in 2005 bundestag election unconstitutional, March 3 2009. http://www.bundesverfassungsgericht.de/SharedDocs/Pressemitteilungen/EN/2009/bvg09-019.html.

[38] Jussi Aaltonen. Electronic voting case law in Finland. In Ardita Driza / Jordi Barrat, editor, *E-Voting Case Law. A Comparative Analysis*, pages 173–181. Farnham: Ashgate, 2015.

[39] ABC News. Computer voting may feature in March NSW election, February 4, 2015. http://www.abc.net.au/news/2015-02-04/computer-voting-may-feature-in-march-nsw-election/6068290.

[40] Claudia Z Acemyan, Philip Kortum, Michael D Byrne, and Dan S Wallach. Usability of voter verifiable, end-to-end voting systems: Baseline data for Helios, Prêt à Voter, and Scantegrity II. *The USENIX Journal of Election Technology and Systems*, page 26, 2014.

[41] ACM. *ACM Statement on Voting Systems*. Association of Computer Machinery, 2004. `usacm.acm.org/images/documents/acm_evoting_reccomendations_press_release.pdf`.

[42] ACM Council Election. `http://www.acm.org/acmelections`.

[43] Ben Adida. *Advances in cryptographic voting systems*. PhD thesis, Massachusetts Institute of Technology, 2006.

[44] Ben Adida. Helios: Web-based open-audit voting. In *USENIX Security Symposium*, volume 17, pages 335–348, 2008.

[45] Ben Adida. Encrypting your vote in JavaScript. In *Rump Session for EVT/WOTE*, 2011.

[46] Ben Adida, Olivier De Marneffe, Olivier Pereira, and Jean-Jacques Quisquater. Electing a university president using open-audit voting: analysis of real-world use of Helios. In *International Conference on Electronic Voting Technology/Workshop on Trustworthy Elections*, 2009.

[47] Ben Adida and C Andrew Neff. Ballot casting assurance. In *USENIX/Accurate Electronic Voting Technology Workshop*, 2006.

[48] Ben Adida and Olivier Pereira. State of Helios 2010: features and deployments. In *EVT/WOTE'10 – Rump Session Talk*, 8 2010.

[49] Ben Adida and Ronald L Rivest. Scratch & vote: self-contained paper-based cryptographic voting. In *The 5th ACM Workshop on Privacy in Electronic Society*, pages 29–40. ACM, 2006.

[50] David Adrian, Karthikeyan Bhargavan, Zakir Durumeric, Pierrick Gaudry, Matthew Green, J Alex Halderman, Nadia Heninger, Drew Springall, Emmanuel Thomé, Luke Valenta, Benjamin VanderSloot, Eric Wustrow, Santiago Zanella–Béguelin, and Paul Zimmermann. Imperfect forward secrecy: How Diffie–Hellman fails in practice. In *ACM Conference on Computer and Communications Security (CCS'15)*, October 2015.

[51] Anziani Alain and Antoine Lefèvre. *Information Report on Behalf the Commission on Constitutional Laws, Legislation, Universal Suffrage, on the e-Voting Regulations and General Management*. 2014. `http://www.senat.fr/rap/r13-445/r13-4451.pdf`. Title translated from French.

[52] Joel Albarrán Bugié and Jesús Sancho. Hereu admits that the system did not work. *La Vanguardia*, May 12th 2010, 2010. `http://ves.cat/mfkr`. Translated from Catalan.

[53] Jordi Puiggalí Allepuz and Sandra Guasch Castelló. Universally verifiable efficient re-encryption mixnet. *Electronic Voting*, 167:241–254, 2010.

[54] Jordi Puiggalí Allepuz and Sandra Guasch Castelló. Internet voting system with cast as intended verification. In *E-Voting and Identity*, pages 36–52. Springer, 2012.

[55] R Michael Alvarez and Thad E Hall. *Electronic Elections: The Perils and Promises of Digital Democracy*. Princeton University Press, 2010.

[56] Francisco Amato, Iván A Barrera Oro, Enrique Chaparro, Sergio Demian Lerner, Alfredo Ortega, Juliano Rizzo, Fernando Russ, Javier Smaldone, and Nicolas Waisman. Vot.Ar: Una mala elección, July 2015. `http://ivan.barreraoro.com.ar/vot-ar-una-mala-eleccion/`. In Spanish.

[57] Ross Anderson, Serge Vaudenay, Bart Preneel, and Kaisa Nyberg. The newton channel. In *Information Hiding*, pages 151–156. Springer, 1996.

[58] Rudy B Andeweg. The Netherlands: the sanctity of proportionality. In Michael Gallagher and Paul Mitchell, editors, *The Politics of Electoral Systems*, pages 491–510. Oxford University Press, 2005.

[59] Andrew W Appel. How to defeat Rivest's ThreeBallot voting system. *Manuskrypt, pazdziernik*, 2006.

[60] Andrew W Appel, Maia Ginsburg, Harri Hursti, Brian W Kernighan, Christopher D Richards, and Gang Tan. Insecurities and inaccuracies of the Sequoia AVC Advantage 9.00H DRE voting machine, October 17, 2008. `https://www.cs.princeton.edu/~appel/papers/advantage-insecurities-redacted.pdf`.

[61] Marlos Ápyus. Na Câmara, o PT foi o único partido a votar contra a impressão do voto na urna eletrônica, November 18, 2015. `http://www.implicante.org/blog/na-camara-o-pt-foi-o-unico-partido-a-votar-contra-a-impressao-do-voto-na-urna-eletronica/`. In Portuguese.

[62] Diego F Aranha, Marcelo Monte Karam, André de Miranda, and Felipe Scarel. Software vulnerabilities in the Brazilian voting machine. In *Design, Development, and Use of Secure Electronic Voting Systems*, pages 149–175. IGI Global, 2014.

[63] Roberto Araujo, Sébastien Foulle, and Jacques Traoré. A practical and secure coercion-resistant scheme for internet voting. In *Towards Trustworthy Elections*, pages 330–342. Springer, 2010.

[64] Kenneth J Arrow. A difficulty in the concept of social welfare. *Journal of Political Economy*, 58(4):328–346, 1950.

[65] Kenneth J Arrow. *Social Choice and Individual Values*. Yale University Press, 1951.

[66] Javed A Aslam, Raluca A Popa, and Ronald L Rivest. On auditing elections when precincts have different sizes. In *EVT*, 2008.

[67] UN General Assembly. Universal declaration of human rights. *Resolution adopted by the General Assembly*, 10(12), 1948.

[68] Rishab Bailey and Rohit Sharma. E-voting case law in India. In Ardita Driza / Jordi Barrat, editor, *E-Voting Case Law. A Comparative Analysis*, pages 89–104. Farnham: Ashgate, 2015.

[69] Melle Bakker. The Netherlands. In *5th Review Meeting of Recommendation CM Rec(2004)11 on legal, operation and technical standards for e-voting*, 2014. http://www.coe.int/t/DEMOCRACY/ELECTORAL-ASSISTANCE/themes/evoting/5thmeeting/Netherlands.pdf.

[70] Michael Bär, Christian Henrich, Jörn Müller-Quade, Stefan Röhrich, and Carmen Stüber. Real world experiences with Bingo Voting and a comparison of usability. In *Workshop on Trustworthy Elections (WOTE)*, volume 2008, 2008.

[71] Jordi Barrat. The certification of e-voting mechanisms. fighting against opacity. In Robert Krimmer / Rüdiger Grimm, editor, *Electronic Voting*, volume P-131 of *(Col. "Lecture Notes in Informatics-LNI")*, pages 197–206. Bonn: Gesellschaft für Informatik, 2008.

[72] Jordi Barrat. E-voting certification procedures. In Paloma Biglino, editor, *New Democratic and Electoral Expectations*, pages pp. 157–192. Title translated from Spanish. Madrid: Iustel, 2008.

[73] Jordi Barrat. Electoral observation and evoting. *Revista Catalana de Dret Públic*, 39, 2009. http://ves.cat/fEUH. Title translated from Catalan.

[74] Jordi Barrat. E-voting vis-à-vis contradictory interests: Profit motivations against democracy. with an special emphasis on non disclosure agreements (NDA). In *Digital Democracy, Participation and Electronic Voting*, pages 57–69. Title translated from Spanish. Valencia: CEPS, 2010.

[75] Jordi Barrat, Ben Goldsmith, Rakesh Sharma, Michel Chevallier, and John Turner. Internet voting and individual verifiability: The Norwegian return codes. In *Electronic Voting*, volume P-205 of *(Col. "Lecture Notes in Informatics-LNI")*. Bonn: Gesellschaft für Informatik, 2012.

[76] Olivier Baudron, Pierre-Alain Fouque, David Pointcheval, Jacques Stern, and Guillaume Poupard. Practical multi-candidate election system. In *Annual ACM Symposium on Principles of Distributed Computing*, pages 274–283. ACM, 2001.

[77] Susan Bell, Josh Benaloh, Michael D Byrne, Dana DeBeauvoir, Bryce Eakin, Gail Fisher, Philip Kortum, Neal McBurnett, Julian Montoya, Michelle Parker, Olivier Pereira, Philip B Stark, Dan S Wallach, and Michael Winn. Star-vote: A secure, transparent, auditable, and reliable voting system. *The USENIX Journal of Election Technology Systems, 1 (1)*, pages 18–37, 2013.

[78] Giampaolo Bella, Peter Y A Ryan, and Vanessa Teague. Virtually perfect democracy. In *Security Protocols XVIII*, pages 161–166. Springer, 2014.

[79] Mihir Bellare and Phillip Rogaway. Random oracles are practical: A paradigm for designing efficient protocols. In *ACM Conference on Computer and Communications Security*, pages 62–73. ACM, 1993.

[80] Jonathan Ben-Nun, Niko Fahri, Morgan Llewellyn, Ben Riva, Alon Rosen, Amnon Ta-Shma, and Douglas Wikström. A new implementation of a dual (paper and cryptographic) voting system. In *Electronic Voting*, pages 315–329, 2012.

[81] Eli Ben-Sasson, Alessandro Chiesa, Daniel Genkin, Eran Tromer, and Madars Virza. Snarks for c: Verifying program executions succinctly and in zero knowledge. In *Advances in Cryptology–CRYPTO 2013*, pages 90–108. Springer, 2013.

[82] Eli Ben-Sasson, Alessandro Chiesa, Eran Tromer, and Madars Virza. Scalable zero knowledge via cycles of elliptic curves. In *Advances in Cryptology–CRYPTO 2014*, pages 276–294. Springer, 2014.

[83] Josh Benaloh. *Verifiable Secret-Ballot Elections*. PhD thesis. Yale University, Department of Computer Science Department, 1987.

[84] Josh Benaloh. Simple verifiable elections. In *USENIX/Accurate Electronic Voting Technology Workshop*, pages 5–5. USENIX Association, 2006.

[85] Josh Benaloh. Ballot casting assurance via voter-initiated poll station auditing. In *USENIX Workshop on Accurate Electronic Voting Technology*, 2007.

[86] Josh Benaloh. Administrative and public verifiability: can we have both? *EVT*, 8:1–10, 2008.

[87] Josh Benaloh, Douglas Jones, Eric Lazarus, Mark Lindeman, and Philip B Stark. Soba: Secrecy-preserving observable ballot-level audits. *EVT/WOTE*, 2011.

[88] Josh Benaloh and Eric Lazarus. The trash attack: An attack on verifiable voting systems and a simple mitigation. Technical report, Technical Report MSR-TR-2011-115, Microsoft, 2011.

[89] Josh Benaloh and Dwight Tuinstra. Receipt-free secret-ballot elections. In *ACM Symposium on Theory of Computing*, pages 544–553. ACM, 1994.

[90] Josh Benaloh, Serge Vaudenay, and Jean-Jacques Quisquater. Iacr 2010 election results, 2010. http://www.iacr.org/elections/2010.

[91] Josh C Benaloh and Moti Yung. Distributing the power of a government to enhance the privacy of voters. In *ACM Symposium on Principles of Distributed Computing*, pages 52–62. ACM, 1986.

[92] Cory Bennett. States ditch electronic voting machines, November 2, 2014. http://thehill.com/policy/cybersecurity/222470-states-ditch-electronic-voting-machines.

[93] Scott Bennett and Rob Lundie. Australian electoral systems, 2007. Parliamentary Library Research Paper Series, No. 5, Parliament of Australia, Department of Parliamentary Services.

[94] Lynn Bennie. Transition to STV: Scottish local government elections 2007. *Representation*, 42(4):273–287, 2006.

[95] Kenneth Benoit. Hungary: Holding back the tiers. In Michael Gallagher and Paul Mitchell, editors, *The Politics of Electoral Systems*, pages 231–252. Oxford University Press, 2005.

[96] David Bernhard, Veronique Cortier, David Galindo, Olivier Pereira, and Bogdan Warinschi. SoK: A comprehensive analysis of game-based ballot privacy definitions. In *IEEE Symposium on Security and Privacy*. IEEE Computer Society, 5 2015.

[97] David Bernhard, Véronique Cortier, Olivier Pereira, Ben Smyth, and Bogdan Warinschi. Adapting Helios for provable ballot privacy. In *Computer Security–ESORICS 2011*, pages 335–354. Springer, 2011.

[98] David Bernhard, Véronique Cortier, Olivier Pereira, and Bogdan Warinschi. Measuring vote privacy, revisited. In *ACM Conference on Computer and Communications Security*, pages 941–952. ACM, 2012.

[99] David Bernhard, Olivier Pereira, and Bogdan Warinschi. How not to prove yourself: Pitfalls of the Fiat–Shamir heuristic and applications to Helios. In *Advances in Cryptology–ASIACRYPT 2012*, pages 626–643. Springer, 2012.

[100] David Bernhard and Bogdan Warinschi. Cryptographic voting – a gentle introduction. In *Foundations of Security Analysis and Design VII*, pages 167–211. Springer, 2014.

[101] John Bethencourt, Dan Boneh, and Brent Waters. Cryptographic methods for storing ballots on a voting machine. In *NDSS*, 2007.

[102] Benjamin Beurdouche, Karthikeyan Bhargavan, Antoine Delignat-Lavaud, Cédric Fournet, Markulf Kohlweiss, Alfredo Pironti, Pierre-Yves Strub, and Jean Karim Zinzindohoue. A messy state of the union: Taming the composite state machines of TLS. In *IEEE Symposium on Security and Privacy*, 2015.

[103] David Bismark, James Heather, Roger Peel, Steve Schneider, Zhe Xia, and Peter Y A Ryan. Experiences gained from the first pret a voter implementation. In *International Workshop on Requirements Engineering for e-Voting Systems (RE-VOTE)*, pages 19–28. IEEE, 2010.

[104] André Blais. The classification of electoral systems. *European Journal of Political Research*, 16(1):99–110, 1988.

[105] Matt Blaze, Arel Cordero, Sophie Engle, Chris Karlof, Naveen Sastry, Micah Sherr, Till Stegers, and Ka-Ping Yee. Source code review of the Sequoia voting system, July 2007. http://votingsystems.cdn.sos.ca.gov/oversight/ttbr/sequoia-source-public-jul26.pdf.

[106] David Bogado and Danny O'Brien. Buenos Aires censors and raids the technologists fixing its flawed e-voting system. EFF Deeplinks Blog, July 15, 2015. https://www.eff.org/deeplinks/2015/07/buenos-aires-censors-and-raids-technologists-fixing-its-flawed-e-voting-system.

[107] J-M Bohli, Christian Henrich, Carmen Kempka, J Muller-Quade, and S Rohrich. Enhancing electronic voting machines on the example of Bingo voting. *IEEE Transactions on Information Forensics and Security*, 4(4):745–750, 2009.

[108] Jens-Matthias Bohli, Jörn Müller-Quade, and Stefan Röhrich. Bingo voting: Secure and coercion-free voting using a trusted random number generator. In *E-Voting and Identity*, pages 111–124. Springer, 2007.

[109] Ingo Boltz. evoting system certification in the USA. federal vs. state. In *eVoting Certification Seminar*, 2009. http://www.coe.int/t/dgap/goodgovernance/Source/EVoting/Workshops/Certification/26-27Nov_2009/Certification_USA.ppt.

[110] Dan Boneh. The decision Diffie–Hellman problem. In *Algorithmic Number Theory Symposium*, pages 48–63. Springer, 1998.

[111] Shaun Bowler, Todd Donovan, and Jennifer Van Heerde. The United States of America: Perpetual campaigning in the absence of competition. *The Politics of Electoral Systems*, pages 185–207, 2005.

[112] Udo C Braendle. Shareholder protection in the USA and Germany - "law and finance" revisited. *German Law Journal*, 7(3):257–278, 2006.

[113] Felix Brandt. Efficient cryptographic protocol design based on distributed el gamal encryption. In *Information Security and Cryptology-ICISC 2005*, pages 32–47. Springer, 2006.

[114] Jennie Bretschneider, Sean Flaherty, Susannah Goodman, Mark Halvorson, Roger Johnston, Mark Lindeman, Ronald L Rivest, Pam Smith, and Philip B Stark. Risk-limiting post-election audits: Why and how, 2012. http://statistics.berkeley.edu/~stark/Preprints/RLAwhitepaper12.pdf.

[115] Ian Brightwell, Jordi Cucurull, David Galindo, and Sandra Guasch. An overview of the iVote 2015 voting system, August 2015. https://www.elections.nsw.gov.au/__data/assets/pdf_file/0019/204058/An_overview_of_the_iVote_2015_voting_system_v4.pdf.

[116] Jonathan Brossard. Hardware backdooring is practical. *BlackHat, Las Vegas, USA*, 2012.

[117] Shuki Bruck, David Jefferson, and Ronald L Rivest. A modular voting architecture ("frog voting"). In *Towards Trustworthy Elections*, pages 97–106. Springer, 2010.

[118] Amilcar Brunazo Filho and Augusto Tavares Rosa Marcacini. Legal aspects of e-voting in Brazil. In Ardita Driza / Jordi Barrat, editor, *E-Voting Case Law. A Comparative Analysis*, pages 65–87. Farnham: Ashgate, 2015.

[119] Johannes Buchmann, Denise Demirel, and Jeroen van de Graaf. Towards a publicly-verifiable mix-net providing everlasting privacy. In *Financial Cryptography and Data Security*, pages 197–204. Springer, 2013.

[120] Jurlind Budurushi, Stephan Neumann, Maina M Olembo, and Melanie Volkamer. Pretty understandable democracy: A secure and understandable Internet voting scheme. In *International Conference on Availability, Reliability and Security (ARES)*, pages 198–207. IEEE, 2013.

[121] Philippe Bulens, Damien Giry, Olivier Pereira, et al. Running mixnet-based elections with Helios. In *Electronic Voting Technology Workshop/Workshop on Trustworthy Elections. Usenix*, 2011.

[122] Bundesverfassungsgericht Press release no. 19/2009. Use of voting computers in 2005 Bundestag election unconstitutional, 2009. https://www.bundesverfassungsgericht.de/SharedDocs/Pressemitteilungen/EN/2009/bvg09-019.html.

[123] Sergiu Bursuc, Gurchetan S Grewal, and Mark Ryan. Trivitas: Voters directly verifying votes. In *E-Voting and Identity*, pages 190–207. Springer, 2012.

[124] Craig Burton, Chris Culnane, James Heather, Thea Peacock, Peter Y A Ryan, Steve Schneider, Sriramkrishnan Srinivasan, Vanessa Teague, Roland Wen, and Zhe Xia. A supervised verifiable voting protocol for the Victorian Electoral Commission. In *International Conference on Electronic Voting*, 2012.

[125] Craig Burton, Chris Culnane, James Heather, Thea Peacock, Peter Y A Ryan, Steve Schneider, Sriramkrishnan Srinivasan, Vanessa Teague, Roland Wen, and Zhe Xia. Using prêt á Voter in the Victorian state elections. In *Electronic Voting Technology Workshop/Workshop on Trustworthy Elections (EVT/WOTE'12)*, 2012.

[126] Craig Burton, Chris Culnane, and Steve Schneider. Verifiable electronic voting in practice: the use of vvote in the victorian state election. *IEEE Security & Privacy*, 2016.

[127] Michael D Byrne, Kristen K Greene, and Sarah P Everett. Usability of voting systems: Baseline data for paper, punch cards, and lever machines. In *PSIGCHI Conference on Human Factors in Computing Systems*, pages 171–180. ACM, 2007.

[128] Susanne Caarls. *E-voting Handbook: Key Steps in the Implementation of e-Enabled Elections*. Council of Europe, 2010.

[129] Joseph A Calandrino, Ariel J Feldman, J Alex Halderman, David Wagner, Harlan Yu, and William P Zeller. Source code review of the Diebold voting system, July 2007. `http://votingsystems.cdn.sos.ca.gov/oversight/ttbr/diebold-source-public-jul29.pdf`.

[130] California Secretary of State's Office. "Top-to-Bottom" Review of voting systems, main website, 2007. `http://www.sos.ca.gov/elections/voting-systems/oversight/top-bottom-review/`.

[131] Bryan Campbell, Michael D Byrne, et al. Straight-party voting: what do voters think? *IEEE Transactions on Information Forensics and Security*, 4(4):718–728, 2009.

[132] Bryan A Campbell and Michael D Byrne. Now do voters notice review screen anomalies? A look at voting system usability. In *Proceedings of the 2009 Electronic Voting Technology Workshop/Workshop on Trustworthy Elections*, 2009.

[133] Richard Carback, David Chaum, Jeremy Clark, John Conway, Aleksander Essex, Paul S Herrnson, Travis Mayberry, Stefan Popoveniuc, Ronald L Rivest, Emily Shen, et al. Scantegrity ii municipal election at takoma park: the first e2e binding governmental election with ballot privacy. In *USENIX Security*, pages 19–19. USENIX Association, 2010.

[134] Richard Carback, Alan Sherman, and Lynn Baumeister. Data analysis report from Takoma Park 2011 municipal election. Technical report, Scantegrity, 2012.

[135] Richard Carback, Alan Sherman, Travis Mayberry, Paul Herrnson, Bimal Sinha, Aleks Essex, Jeremy Clark, Ron Rivest, Emily Shen, Poorvi Vora, Stefan Popoveniuc, John Conway, and David Chaum. Exploring reactions to Scantegrity: Analysis of surveys of Takoma Park voters and election judges. Technical report, Scantegrity, 2009.

[136] Richard T Carback III, Jeremy Clark, Aleks Essex, and Stefan Popoveniuc. On the independent verification of a Punchscan election. *Proceedings of the 2007 University Voting Systems Competition (VoComp)*, 42, 2007.

[137] Carter Center. Developing a methodology for observing electronic voting. *Atlanta*, 2007.

[138] Carter Center. Observing the 2006 presidential elections in venezuela. *Final Report of the Technical Mission*, 2007.

[139] David Chaum. The dining cryptographers problem: Unconditional sender and recipient untraceability. *Journal of cryptology*, 1(1):65–75, 1988.

[140] David Chaum. Elections with unconditionally-secret ballots and disruption equivalent to breaking RSA. In *Advances in Cryptology–EUROCRYPT'88*, pages 177–182. Springer, 1988.

[141] David Chaum. SureVote, 2000. http://www.surevote.com.

[142] David Chaum. Surevote: technical overview. In *Workshop on Trustworthy Elections (WOTE'01)*, 2001.

[143] David Chaum. Secret-ballot receipts: True voter-verifiable elections. *IEEE Security & Privacy*, 2(1):38–47, 2004.

[144] David Chaum, Richard Carback, Jeremy Clark, Aleksander Essex, Stefan Popoveniuc, Ronald L Rivest, Peter Y A Ryan, Emily Shen, and Alan T Sherman. Scantegrity ii: end-to-end verifiability for optical scan election systems using invisible ink confirmation codes. In *Conference on Electronic Voting Technology (EVT'08)*, page 14. USENIX Association, 2008.

[145] David Chaum, Richard T Carback, Jeremy Clark, Aleksander Essex, Stefan Popoveniuc, Ronald L Rivest, Peter Y A Ryan, Emily Shen, Alan T Sherman, and Poorvi L Vora. Scantegrity ii: End-to-end verifiability by voters of optical scan elections through confirmation codes. *IEEE Transactions on Information Forensics and Security*, 4(4):611–627, 2009.

[146] David Chaum, Aleks Essex, Richard Carback, Jeremy Clark, Stefan Popoveniuc, Alan Sherman, and Poorvi Vora. Scantegrity: End-to-end voter-verifiable optical-scan voting. *Security & Privacy, IEEE*, 6(3):40–46, 2008.

[147] David Chaum, Jan-Hendrik Evertse, Jeroen van de Graaf, and René Peralta. Demonstrating possession of a discrete logarithm without revealing it. In *Advances in Cryptology—CRYPTO'86*, pages 200–212. Springer, 1987.

[148] David Chaum, Ben Hosp, Stefan Popoveniuc, and Poorvi L Vora. Accessible voter-verifiability. *Cryptologia*, 33(3):283–291, 2009.

[149] David Chaum and Torben Pryds Pedersen. Wallet databases with observers. In *Advances in Cryptology–CRYPTO'92*, pages 89–105. Springer, 1993.

[150] David Chaum, Peter Y A Ryan, and Steve Schneider. A practical, voter-verifiable election scheme. Technical Report CS-TR-880, University of Newcastle upon Tyne School of Computing Science, December 2004. `http://www.cs.ncl.ac.uk/research/pubs/trs/papers/880.pdf`.

[151] David Chaum, Peter Y A Ryan, and Steve Schneider. A practical voter-verifiable election scheme. In *Computer Security – ESORICS 2005*, volume 3679 of *Lecture Notes in Computer Science*, pages 118–139. Springer Berlin Heidelberg, 2005.

[152] David Chaum, Jeroen Van De Graaf, Peter Y A Ryan, and Poorvi L Vora. *Secret Ballot Elections with Unconditional Integrity*. University of Newcastle upon Tyne, Computing Science, 2007.

[153] David L Chaum. Untraceable electronic mail, return addresses, and digital pseudonyms. *Communications of the ACM*, 24(2):84–90, 1981.

[154] Stephen Checkoway, Ariel J Feldman, Brian Kantor, J Alex Halderman, Edward W Felten, and Hovav Shacham. Can DREs provide long-lasting security? the case of return-oriented programming and the avc advantage. *EVT/WOTE*, 2009, 2009.

[155] Jacek Cichoń, Mirosław Kutyłowski, and Bogdan Weglorz. Short ballot assumption and threeballot voting protocol. In *SOFSEM 2008: Theory and Practice of Computer Science*, pages 585–598. Springer, 2008.

[156] J Clark, A Essex, and C Adams. Secure and observable auditing of electronic voting systems using stock indices. In *Proceedings, IEEE CCECE*, 2007.

[157] Jeremy Clark and Urs Hengartner. On the use of financial data as a random beacon. In *Proceedings of the 2010 International Conference on Electronic Voting Technology/Workshop on Trustworthy Elections*, EVT/WOTE'10, 2010.

[158] Jeremy Clark and Urs Hengartner. Selections: Internet voting with over-the-shoulder coercion-resistance. In *Financial Cryptography and Data Security*, pages 47–61. Springer, 2012.

[159] Michael R Clarkson, Stephen Chong, and Andrew C Myers. Civitas: Toward a secure voting system. In *IEEE Symposium on Security and Privacy*, pages 354–368. IEEE Computer Society, 2008.

[160] Mark Clayton. Ukraine election narrowly avoided "wanton destruction" from hackers, June 2014. http://www.csmonitor.com/World/Security-Watch/Cyber-Conflict-Monitor/2014/0617/Ukraine-election-narrowly-avoided-wanton-destruction-from-hackers-video.

[161] Josh D Cohen and Michael J Fischer. A robust and verifiable cryptographically secure election scheme. In *26th Annual Symposium on Foundations of Computer Science*, pages 372–382. IEEE, 1985.

[162] Kevin J Coleman and Eric A Fischer. The Help America Vote Act and elections reform: Overview and issues, CRS Report RS20898, 2011. https://www.fas.org/sgp/crs/misc/RS20898.pdf

[163] MacCárthaigh Colm. *Electronic Voting in Ireland*. Irish Citizens for Trustworthy E-voting, 2004. http://www.stdlib.net/~colmmacc/e-voting-ireland.pdf.

[164] Commission. *Report and Recommendations of the Presidential Commission on Election Administration*. 2014. http://www.supportthevoter.gov.

[165] European Commission. *Code of Good Practice in Electoral Matters: Guidelines and Explanatory Report*. 2002.

[166] European Commission. *Methodological Guide to Electoral Assistance, European Commission: Brussels*. 2006.

[167] European Commission. *Compendium of International Electoral Standards: Second Edition*. 2007.

[168] Compuware. Direct recording electronic (DRE) technical security assessment report, 2003. http://www.sos.state.oh.us/sos/hava/compuware112103.pdf.

[169] Clyde H. Coombs. *A theory of data*. John Wiley & Sons, 1964.

[170] Véronique Cortier, David Galindo, Stéphane Glondu, and Malika Izabachène. Distributed ElGamal á la pedersen: application to Helios. In *ACM Workshop on Workshop on Privacy in the Electronic Society*, pages 131–142. ACM, 2013.

[171] Véronique Cortier, David Galindo, Stephane Glondu, and Malika Izabachene. A generic construction for voting correctness at minimum cost-application to Helios. *IACR Cryptology ePrint Archive*, 2013:177, 2013.

[172] Véronique Cortier, David Galindo, Stephane Glondu, and Malika Izabachene. Election verifiability for Helios under weaker trust assumptions. In *Computer Security-ESORICS*, pages 327–344. Springer, 2014.

[173] Véronique Cortier and Ben Smyth. Attacking and fixing Helios: An analysis of ballot secrecy. *Journal of Computer Security*, 21(1):89–148, 2013.

[174] Olivier Costa, André Freire, and Jean-Benoit Pilet. Political representation in Belgium, France and Portugal: MPs and their constituents in very different political systems. *Representation*, 48(4):351–358, 2012.

[175] Gary W Cox, Frances M Rosenbluth, and Michael F Thies. Electoral rules, career ambitions, and party structure: comparing factions in Japan's upper and lower houses. *American Journal of Political Science*, 44(1):115–122, 2000.

[176] Ronald Cramer, Ivan Damgård, and Berry Schoenmakers. Proofs of partial knowledge and simplified design of witness hiding protocols. In *Advances in Cryptology—CRYPTO'94*, pages 174–187. Springer, 1994.

[177] Ronald Cramer, Matthew Franklin, Berry Schoenmakers, and Moti Yung. Multi-authority secret-ballot elections with linear work. In *Advances in Cryptology—EUROCRYPT'96*, pages 72–83. Springer, 1996.

[178] Ronald Cramer, Rosario Gennaro, and Berry Schoenmakers. A secure and optimally efficient multi-authority election scheme. In *Advances in Cryptology–EUROCRYPT'97*, pages 103–118. Springer, 1997.

[179] Lorrie Faith Cranor and Ron K Cytron. Sensus: A security-conscious electronic polling system for the internet. In *Thirtieth Hawaii International Conference on System Sciences*, volume 3, pages 561–570. IEEE, 1997.

[180] Mariano Cucho and Mariano Augusto. Electronic voting: Lessons learned before and after its implementation on ERM 2014. *Elecciones*, 14:11–29, 2014. titled translated from Spanish.

[181] Chris Culnane, David Bismark, James Heather, Steve Schneider, Sriramkrishnan Srinivasan, and Zhe Xia. Authentication codes. In *USENIX/ACCURATE Electronic Voting Technology Workshop (EVT'11)*, 2011.

[182] Chris Culnane, James Heather, Rui Joaquim, Peter Y A Ryan, Steve Schneider, and Vanessa Teague. Faster print on demand for prêt à voter. *USENIX Journal of Election Technology and Systems*, 2(1), 2013.

[183] Chris Culnane, Peter Y A Ryan, Steve Schneider, and Vanessa Teague. vVote: a verifiable voting system. *arXiv preprint arXiv:1404.6822*, 2014.

[184] Chris Culnane, Peter Y A Ryan, Steve Schneider, and Vanessa Teague. vVote: A verifiable voting system. *ACM Transactions on Information and System Security*, 18(1):3:1–3:30, 2015.

[185] Chris Culnane and Steve Schneider. A peered bulletin board for robust use in verifiable voting systems. In *IEEE 27th Computer Security Foundations Symposium (CSF)*, pages 169–183. IEEE, 2014.

[186] Edouard Cuvelier, Olivier Pereira, and Thomas Peters. Election verifiability or ballot privacy: Do we need to choose? In *Computer Security–ESORICS 2013*, pages 481–498. Springer, 2013.

[187] Ivan Damgård. On Σ-protocols, 2004. `http://www.daimi.au.dk/~ivan/Sigma.ps`.

[188] Ivan Damgård and Mads Jurik. A generalisation, a simplification and some applications of paillier's probabilistic public-key system. In *Public Key Cryptography*, volume 1992 of *LNCS*, pages 119–136. Springer, 2001.

[189] George Danezis. *Better Anonymous Communications*. PhD thesis, University of Cambridge, 2004.

[190] DCBOEE press release. Board announces public test of Digital Vote by Mail service, September 2010. `http://www.dcboee.org/popup.asp?url=/pdf_files/nr_588.pdf`.

[191] Ajuntament de Barcelona. *Report on the Popular Consultation of Diagonal Avenue*. Barcelona: Ajuntament de Barcelona, 2010. `http://www.vilaweb.cat/media/attach/vwedts/docs/informediagonal.pdf`. Title translated from Catalan.

[192] Nicolas de Condorcet. *Essai sur l'application de l'analyse à la probabilité des décisions rendues à la pluralité des voix*. Paris: l'Imprimerie Royale, 1785.

[193] Fédération Internationale de Gymnastique. FIG code of points 2013–2016, trampoline gymnastics. `http://www.fig-gymnastics.com/site/`.

[194] Stephanie Delaune, Steve Kremer, and Mark Ryan. Coercion-resistance and receipt-freeness in electronic voting. In *Computer Security Foundations Workshop, 2006. 19th IEEE*, pages 12–pp. IEEE, 2006.

[195] Alex Delis, Konstantina Gavatha, Aggelos Kiayias, Charalampos Koutalakis, Elias Nikolakopoulos, Lampros Paschos, Mema Rousopoulou, Georgios Sotirellis, Panos Stathopoulos, Pavlos Vasilopoulos, Thomas Zacharias, and Bingsheng Zhang. Pressing the button for European elections: verifiable e-voting and public attitudes toward internet voting in Greece. In *International Conference on Electronic Voting: Verifying the Vote (EVOTE)*, pages 1–8. IEEE, 2014.

[196] Denise Demirel, Jeroen Van De Graaf, and Roberto Araújo. Improving Helios with everlasting privacy towards the public. In J Alex Halderman and Olivier Pereira, editors, *Electronic Voting Technology Workshop / Workshop on Trustworthy Elections, EVT/WOTE'12*. USENIX Association, 2012.

[197] Community Department of the Environment and The Government of the Republic of Ireland Local Government. How the president is elected. `http://www.environ.ie/en/LocalGovernment/Voting/`.

[198] Yvo Desmedt and Pyrros Chaidos. Applying divertibility to blind ballot copying in the Helios internet voting system. In *Computer Security–ESORICS 2012*, pages 433–450. Springer, 2012.

[199] Yvo Desmedt and Yair Frankel. Threshold cryptosystems. In *Advances in Cryptology–CRYPTO'89 Proceedings*, pages 307–315. Springer, 1990.

[200] Collège d'Experts. *Report on Elections June 13th 1999*. 1999. http://www.poureva.be/IMG/pdf/19990701.pdf. Title translated from French.

[201] Collège d'Experts. *Report on Elections May 18th 2003*. 2003. http://www.poureva.be/IMG/pdf/RapportExpert20030605.pdf. Title translated from French.

[202] Collège d'Experts. *The Simultaneous Elections on May 25th 2014*. 2014. http://www.poureva.be/IMG/pdf/54K0014001.pdf. Title translated from French.

[203] Roberto Di Cosmo. On privacy and anonymity in electronic and non electronic voting: the ballot-as-signature attack. *Hyper Articles en Ligne hal-00142440 (2)*, 2007.

[204] Alberto Díaz-Cayeros and Beatriz Magaloni. Mexico: Designing electoral rules by a dominant party. In Josep M. Colomer, editor, *Handbook of Electoral System Choice*, pages 145–154. Palgrave Macmillan, 2004.

[205] Diebold Election Systems. Press release: State of Maryland awards Diebold electronic voting equipment order valued at up to $55.6 million, 2003. http://www.diebold.com/news/newsdisp.asp?id=2979.

[206] Diebold Election Systems. Technical response to the Johns Hopkins study on voting systems, 2003. http://www-personal.umich.edu/~wmebane/gov317/diebold/technical.25jul2003.htm.

[207] Jérôme Dossogne and Frédéric Lafitte. Blinded additively homomorphic encryption schemes for self-tallying voting. *Journal of Information Security and Applications*, 2014.

[208] John Duggan and Thomas Schwartz. Strategic manipulability without resoluteness or shared beliefs: Gibbard-satterthwaite generalized. *Social Choice and Welfare*, 17(1):85–93, 2000.

[209] Zakir Durumeric, David Adrian, Ariana Mirian, Michael Bailey, and J Alex Halderman. Tracking the FREAK attack, March 2015. https://freakattack.com/.

[210] Maurice Duverger. *Political Parties: Their Organisation and Activity in the Modern State*. London: Methuen, Wiley, 1963.

[211] Election Science Institute. 2006 voting equipment study. `http://www.edssurvey.com/images/File/ve2006_nrpt.pdf`.

[212] Princeton Undergraduate Elections. `https://princeton.heliosvoting.org/`.

[213] Taher ElGamal. A public key cryptosystem and a signature scheme based on discrete logarithms. In *Advances in Cryptology*, pages 10–18. Springer, 1985.

[214] Robert Elgie. France: Stacking the deck. In Michael Gallagher and Paul Mitchell, editors, *The Politics of Electoral Systems*, pages 119–136. Oxford University Press, 2005.

[215] Aleks Essex, Jeremy Clark, and Carlisle Adams. Aperio: High integrity elections for developing countries. In *Towards Trustworthy Elections*, pages 388–401. Springer, 2010.

[216] Aleks Essex, Jeremy Clark, Richard Carback, and Stefan Popoveniuc. Punchscan in practice: an e2e election case study. In *Workshop on Trustworthy Elections*, 2007.

[217] Aleks Essex, Jeremy Clark, Urs Hengartner, and Carlisle Adams. How to print a secret. In *Proceedings of the 4th USENIX Conference on Hot Topics in Security, Hot-Sec*, volume 9, pages 3–3, 2009.

[218] Aleksander Essex, Jeremy Clark, Urs Hengartner, and Carlisle Adams. Eperio: Mitigating technical complexity in cryptographic election verification. *IACR Cryptology ePrint Archive*, 2012:178, 2012.

[219] Aleksander Essex and Urs Hengartner. Hover: Trustworthy elections with hash-only verification. *IEEE Security & Privacy*, 10(5):18–24, 2012.

[220] Aleksander Essex and Urs Hengartner. Oblivious printing of secret messages in a multi-party setting. In *Financial Cryptography and Data Security*, pages 359–373. Springer, 2012.

[221] Aleksander Essex, Christian Henrich, and Urs Hengartner. Single layer optical-scan voting with fully distributed trust. In *E-Voting and Identity*, pages 122–139. Springer, 2012.

[222] Saghar Estehghari and Yvo Desmedt. Exploiting the client vulnerabilities in internet e-voting systems: Hacking Helios 2.0 as an example. In *Electronic Voting Technology Workshop/Workshop on Trustworthy Elections (EVT/WOTE)*, 2010.

[223] Estonian Internet Voting Committee. Statistics about Internet voting in Estonia, May 2014. `http://www.vvk.ee/voting-methods-in-estonia/engindex/statistics`.

[224] Estonian Internet Voting Committee. Using ID-card and mobil-ID, May 2014. `https://www.valimised.ee/eng/kkk`.

[225] Estonian Public Broadcasting. Center Party petitions European human rights court over e-voting, 2013. `http://news.err.ee/v/politics/4ee0c8a2-b9c2-4d28-8ae4-061e7d9386a4`.

[226] Sarah Everett, Kristen Greene, Michael Byrne, Dan Wallach, Kyle Derr, Daniel Sandler, and Ted Torous. Is newer always better? The usability of electronic voting machines versus traditional methods. *CHI*, 2008.

[227] Sarah P Everett. *The Usability of Electronic Voting Machines and How Votes Can Be Changed without Detection.* PhD thesis, RICE UNIVERSITY, 2007.

[228] Sarah P Everett, Michael D Byrne, and Kristen K Greene. Measuring the usability of paper ballots: Efficiency, effectiveness, and satisfaction. In *Proceedings of the Human Factors and Ergonomics Society Annual Meeting*, volume 50, pages 2547–2551. SAGE Publications, 2006.

[229] David Farrell and Ian McAllister. Australia: the alternative vote in a compliant political culture. In Michael Gallagher and Paul Mitchell, editors, *The Politics of Electoral Systems*, pages 79–98. Oxford University Press, 2005.

[230] David M Farrell. *Electoral Systems: A Comparative Introduction.* Palgrave Macmillan, 2nd edition, 2011.

[231] David M Farrell, Malcolm Mackerras, and Ian McAllister. Designing electoral institutions: STV systems and their consequences. *Political Studies*, 44(1):24–43, 1996.

[232] Ariel J Feldman, J Alex Halderman, and Edward W Felten. Security analysis of the Diebold AccuVote-TS voting machine. 2006.

[233] Ariel J Feldman, J Alex Halderman, and Edward W Felten. Security analysis of the Diebold AccuVote-TS voting machine. In *USENIX/ACCURATE Electronic Voting Technology Workshop (EVT'07)*, 2007.

[234] Edward W Felten. "Hotel minibar" keys open Diebold voting machines. Freedom to Tinker blog, 2006. `https://freedom-to-tinker.com/blog/felten/hotel-minibar-keys-open-diebold-voting-machines/`.

[235] Niels Ferguson and Bruce Schneier. *Practical Cryptography.* Wiley New York, 2003.

[236] Amos Fiat and Adi Shamir. How to prove yourself: Practical solutions to identification and signature problems. In *Advances in Cryptology—CRYPTO'86*, pages 186–194. Springer, 1987.

[237] Russell A Fink, Alan T Sherman, and Richard Carback. TPM meets DRE: reducing the trust base for electronic voting using trusted platform modules. *Information Forensics and Security, IEEE Transactions on*, 4(4):628–637, 2009.

[238] Kevin Fisher, Richard Carback, and Alan T Sherman. Punchscan: Introduction and system definition of a high-integrity election system. In *Workshop on Trustworthy Elections (WOTE)*, 2006.

[239] Catherine Fisk and Erwin Chemerinsky. The filibuster. *Stanford Law Review*, 49(2):181–254, 1997.

[240] Office for Democratic Institutions and Human Rights. *Estonia Parliamentary Elections 6 March 2011 OCSE/ODIHR Election Assessment Mission Final Report.*

[241] Centre for Human Rights. Professional training series no.2: Human rights and elections – a handbook on the legal technical and human rights aspects of elections. 1994.

[242] Organization for Security and Cooperation in Europe. *Supplementary Human Dimension Meeting on Challenges of Election Technologies and Procedures, 21-22 April 2005: Final Report.* Organization for Security and Cooperation in Europe, 2005. http://www.osce.org/odihr/elections/15996.

[243] Organization for Security and Cooperation in Europe. *Election Observation Handbook: Fifth Edition.* The OSCE Office for Democratic Institutions and Human Rights, 2007. http://www.osce.org/odihr/elections/14355?download=true.

[244] Organization for Security and Cooperation in Europe. *Discussion Paper in Preparation of Guidelines for the Observation of Electronic Elections.* Organization for Security and Cooperation in Europe, 2008. http://www.osce.org/odihr/elections/34725.

[245] Organization for Security and Cooperation in Europe. *Handbook for the Observation of New Voting Technologies.* Organization for Security and Cooperation in Europe, 2013. http://www.osce.org/odihr/elections/104939.

[246] Organization for Security and Cooperation in Europe (OSCE). Netherlands. Parliamentary Elections, 22 November 2006. Election Assessment Mission Report, 2006. http://www.osce.org/odihr/elections/netherlands/24322.

[247] Michael Gallagher. Comparing proportional representation electoral systems: Quotas, thresholds, paradoxes and majorities. *British Journal of Political Science*, 22(04):469–496, 1992.

[248] Michael Gallagher. Ireland: the discreet charm of PR-STV. In Michael Gallagher and Paul Mitchell, editors, *The Politics of Electoral Systems*, pages 511–532. Oxford University Press, 2005.

[249] Michael Gallagher and Paul Mitchell, editors. *The Politics of Electoral Systems*. Oxford University Press, 2005.

[250] David Geer. Technical maturity, reliability, implicit taxes, and wealth creation. *login: The Magazine of Usenix & Sage*, 26(8), 2001.

[251] Rosario Gennaro, Craig Gentry, Bryan Parno, and Mariana Raykova. Quadratic span programs and succinct nizks without pcps. In *EUROCRYPT*, volume 7881, pages 626–645. Springer, 2013.

[252] Rosario Gennaro, Stanislaw Jarecki, Hugo Krawczyk, and Tal Rabin. Secure distributed key generation for discrete-log based cryptosystems. *Journal of Cryptology*, 20(1):51–83, 2007.

[253] Allan Gibbard. Manipulation of voting schemes: A general result. *Econometrica: Journal of the Econometric Society*, pages 587–601, 1973.

[254] Kristian Gjøsteen. A latency-free election scheme. In *Topics in Cryptology– CT-RSA 2008*, pages 425–436. Springer, 2008.

[255] Kristian Gjøsteen. Analysis of an internet voting protocol. *IACR Cryptology ePrint Archive*, 380, 2010.

[256] Kristian Gjøsteen. The Norwegian internet voting protocol. *IACR Cryptology ePrint Archive*, 473, 2013.

[257] Marcin Gogolewski, Marek Klonowski, Przemysław Kubiak, Mirosław Kutyłowski, Anna Lauks, and Filip Zagórski. Kleptographic attacks on e-voting schemes. In *Emerging Trends in Information and Communication Security*, pages 494–508. Springer, 2006.

[258] Oded Goldreich. A short tutorial of zero-knowledge. In *Secure Multi-Party Computation*, Secure Multi-Party Computation 10, pages 28–60, 2013.

[259] Ben Goldsmith. *Electronic Voting & Counting Technologies: A Guide to Conducting Feasibility Studies*. International Foundation for Electoral Systems, 2011. http://www.ifes.org/~/media/Files/Publications/ Books/2011/Electronic_Voting_and_Counting_Tech_ Goldsmith.pdf.

[260] Shafi Goldwasser and Silvio Micali. Probabilistic encryption. *Journal of Computer and System Sciences*, 28(2):270–299, 1984.

[261] Shafi Goldwasser, Silvio Micali, and Charles Rackoff. The knowledge complexity of interactive proof systems. *SIAM Journal on Computing*, 18(1):186– 208, 1989.

[262] Rop Gonggrijp and Willem-Jan Hengeveld. *Nedap/Groenendaal ES3B voting computer security analysis*. Amsterdam: Foundation "Wij vertrouwen stemcomputers niet", 2006. `wijvertrouwenstemcomputersniet.nl/images/9/91/Es3b-en.pdf`.

[263] Rop Gonggrijp and Willem-Jan Hengeveld. Studying the nedap/groenendaal es3b voting computer: A computer security perspective. In *USENIX Workshop on Accurate Electronic Voting Technology (EVT'07)*, pages 1–1. USENIX Association, 2007.

[264] Rop Gonggrijp, Willem-Jan Hengeveld, Eelco Hotting, Sebastian Schmidt, and Frederik Weidemann. RIES—Rijnland internet election system: A cursory study of published source code. In *VOTE-ID*, 2009.

[265] Ezequiel Gonzalez-Ocantos, Chad Kiewiet De Jonge, Carlos Meléndez, Javier Osorio, and David W Nickerson. Vote buying and social desirability bias: Experimental evidence from Nicaragua. *American Journal of Political Science*, 56(1):202–217, 2012.

[266] Guy S Goodwin-Gill. *Free and Fair Elections*. Inter-Parliamentary Union, 2006.

[267] Amanda Gouws and Paul Mitchell. South Africa: one party dominance despite perfect proportionality. In Michael Gallagher and Paul Mitchell, editors, *The Politics of Electoral Systems*, pages 353–374. Oxford University Press, 2005.

[268] Kristen K Greene. *Usability of New Electronic Voting Systems and Traditional Methods: Comparisons Between Sequential and Direct Access Electronic Voting Interfaces, Paper Ballots, Punch Cards, and Lever Machines*. PhD thesis, RICE UNIVERSITY, 2008.

[269] Gurchetan S Grewal, Mark Ryan, Sergiu Bursuc, and Peter Y A Ryan. Caveat coercitor: Coercion-evidence in electronic voting. In *IEEE Symposium on Security and Privacy (SP)*, pages 367–381. IEEE, 2013.

[270] Jens Groth. Efficient maximal privacy in boardroom voting and anonymous broadcast. In *Financial Cryptography*, pages 90–104. Springer, 2004.

[271] Jens Groth. Evaluating security of voting schemes in the universal composability framework. In *Applied Cryptography and Network Security*, pages 46–60. Springer, 2004.

[272] Jens Groth. Review of RIES. Technical report, Cryptomathic, 2004.

[273] Eitan Grundland. An analysis of the wombat voting system model, 2012. `http://www.grundland.org/An\%20Analysis\%20of\%20the\%20Wombat\%20Voting\%20System\%20Model.pdf`.

[274] Rolf Haenni and Reto E Koenig. A generic approach to prevent board flooding attacks in coercion-resistant electronic voting schemes. *Computers & Security*, 33:59–69, 2013.

[275] Alireza Toroghi Haghighat, Mohammad Sadeq Dousti, and Rasool Jalili. An efficient and provably-secure coercion-resistant e-voting protocol. In *Annual International Conference on Privacy, Security and Trust (PST)*, pages 161–168. IEEE, 2013.

[276] Lim Hong Hai. Electoral politics in Malaysia: 'managing' elections in a plural society. *Electoral Politics in Southeast and East Asia*, pages 101–148, 2002.

[277] J Alex Halderman. Diebold shows how to make your own voting machine key. Freedom to Tinker blog, 2007. `https://freedom-to-tinker.com/blog/jhalderm/diebold-shows-how-make-your-own-voting-machine-key/`.

[278] J Alex Halderman. Electronic voting researcher arrested over anonymous source. Freedom to Tinker blog, August 2010. `https://freedom-to-tinker.com/blog/jhalderm/electronic-voting-researcher-arrested-over-anonymous-source/`.

[279] J Alex Halderman. Are DREs toxic waste? EVT/WOTE rump session talk, August 2011.

[280] J Alex Halderman. Hacking the D.C. Internet voting pilot. Freedom to Tinker blog, 2011. `http://www.freedom-to-tinker.com/blog/jhalderm/hacking-dc-internet-voting-pilot`.

[281] J Alex Halderman and Ariel J Feldman. PAC-MAN on the Sequoia AVC-Edge DRE voting machine, August 2010. `https://jhalderm.com/pacman/`.

[282] J Alex Halderman and Vanessa Teague. The New South Wales iVote system: Security failures and verification flaws in a live online election. In *International Conference on E-Voting and Identity (VoteID'15)*, August 2015.

[283] Joseph Lorenzo Hall. *Design and the Support of Transparency in VVPAT Systems in the US Voting Systems Market*. National Institute of Standards and Technology (NIST), 2006. `http://www.nist.gov/itl/vote/upload/jlh-vvpat-design-transparency.pdf`.

[284] Joseph Lorenzo Hall. Transparency and access to source code in electronic voting. In *EVT'06*. Vancouver: Usenix / Accurate, 2006. `josephhall.org/papers/jhall_evt06.pdf`.

[285] Joseph Lorenzo Hall. Post-election manual auditing of paper records: Bibliography, 2007. `http://www.josephhall.org/papers/auditing_biblio.pdf`.

[286] Ursula Hall. Greeks and Romans and the secret ballot. *Owls to Athens: Essays on Classical Subjects Presented to Sir Kenneth Dover*, ed. EM Craik, Oxford, 191:199, 1990.

[287] Feng Hao, Dylan Clarke, and Carlton Shepherd. Verifiable classroom voting: Where cryptography meets pedagogy. In *Security Protocols Workshop*. Springer, 2013.

[288] Feng Hao, Matthew Kreeger, Brian Randell, Dylan Clarke, Siamak F Shahandashti, and Peter Hyun-Jeen Lee. Every vote counts: ensuring integrity in large-scale electronic voting. *The USENIX Journal of Election Technology and Systems*, pages 1–25, 2014.

[289] Feng Hao and Matthew Nicolas Kreeger. Every vote counts: Ensuring integrity in large-scale dre-based electronic voting, 2010. https://eprint.iacr.org/2010/452.pdf.

[290] Feng Hao, Brian Randell, and Dylan Clarke. Self-enforcing electronic voting. In *Security Protocols Workshop*. Springer, 2012.

[291] Feng Hao, Peter Y A Ryan, and Piotr Zieliński. Anonymous voting by two-round public discussion. *IET Information Security*, 4(2):62–67, 2010.

[292] Feng Hao and Piotr Zieliński. A 2-round anonymous veto protocol. In *Security Protocols Workshop 2006*, pages 202–211. Springer, 2009.

[293] Feng Hao and Piotr Zieliński. A 2-round anonymous veto protocol (transcript). In *Security Protocols Workshop 2006*, pages 212–214. Springer, 2009.

[294] Feng Hao and Piotr Zieliński. The power of anonymous veto in public discussion. In *Transactions on Computational Science IV*, pages 41–52. Springer, 2009.

[295] Thomas Hare. *The Machinery of Representation*. W. Maxwell, 1857.

[296] Joseph Pratt Harris. *Election Administration in the United States*. Number 27. Brookings Institution, 1934. http://www.nist.gov/itl/vote/josephharrisrpt.cfm.

[297] Ricardo Hausmann and Roberto Rigobón. *Looking for the Black Swan: Statistical Evidence Analysis on Electoral Fraud in Venezuela*. Boston: Harvard University / MIT, 2004. http://www.proveo.org/hausmann.pdf. Title translated from Spanish.

[298] Anthony Heath, Siana Glouharova, and Oliver Heath. India: Two-party contests within a multiparty system. In Michael Gallagher and Paul Mitchell, editors, *The Politics of Electoral Systems*, pages 137–156. Oxford University Press, 2005.

[299] James Heather. Implementing stv securely in prêt à voter. In *Computer Security Foundations Symposium (CSF'07)*, pages 157–169. IEEE, 2007.

[300] James Heather and David Lundin. The append-only web bulletin board. In *Formal Aspects in Security and Trust*, pages 242–256. Springer, 2009.

[301] James Heather, Peter Y A Ryan, and Vanessa Teague. Pretty good democracy for more expressive voting schemes. In *Computer Security–ESORICS 2010*, pages 405–423. Springer, 2010.

[302] Mario Heiderich, Tilman Frosch, Marcus Niemietz, and Jörg Schwenk. The bug that made me president a browser-and web-security case study on Helios voting. In *E-voting and Identity*, pages 89–103. Springer, 2012.

[303] Christian Henrich. *Improving and Analysing Bingo Voting*. PhD thesis, Karlsruhe, Karlsruher Institut für Technologie (KIT), Diss., 2012, 2012.

[304] Kevin Henry, Douglas R Stinson, and Jiayuan Sui. The effectiveness of receipt-based attacks on threeballot. *Information Forensics and Security, IEEE Transactions on*, 4(4):699–707, 2009.

[305] Paul S Herrnson, Richard G Niemi, Michael J Hanmer, Benjamin B Bederson, Frederick G Conrad, and Michael Traugott. The importance of usability testing of voting systems. In *USENIX/ACCURATE Electronic Voting Technology Workshop*, 2006.

[306] Mark A Herschberg. *Secure Electronic Voting Over the World Wide Web*. PhD thesis, Massachusetts Institute of Technology, 1997.

[307] Allen Hicken. Thailand: Combating corruption through electoral reform. In Andrew Reynolds, Ben Reilly, and Andrew Ellis, editors, *Electoral System Design: The New International IDEA Handbook*, pages 105–107. International Institute for Democracy and Electoral Assistance, 2005.

[308] Richard Hill. Challenging the Geneva e-voting system in court. In *E-Voting Seminar*. Biel: Evoting.ch, 2013. `http://e-voting.bfh.ch/seminar/fall-2013/`.

[309] Martin Hirt and Kazue Sako. Efficient receipt-free voting based on homomorphic encryption. In *Advances in Cryptology–EUROCRYPT 2000*, pages 539–556. Springer, 2000.

[310] Jonathan K Hodge and Richard E Klima. *The Mathematics of Voting and Elections: A Hands-on Approach*, volume 22 of *Mathematical World*. American Mathematical Society, 2005.

[311] Kjell Hole and Lars-Helge Netland. Toward risk assessment of large-impact and rare events. *IEEE Security & Privacy*, (3):21–27, 2010.

[312] Jonathan Hopkin. Spain: Proportional representation with majoritarian outcomes. In Michael Gallagher and Paul Mitchell, editors, *The Politics of Electoral Systems*, pages 375–396. Oxford University Press, 2005.

[313] HT Correspondent. Enhance confidence in EVMs. Hindustan Times, New Delhi, October 4, 2015.

[314] Engelbert Hubbers, Bart Jacobs, Berry Schoenmakers, Henk van Tilborg, and Benne de Weger. Description and analysis of the RIES internet voting system. Technical report, Eindhoven Institute for the Protection of Systems and Information (EiPSI), 2008.

[315] Harri Hursti. Critical security issues with Diebold TSx (unredacted), May 2006. http://www.bbvdocs.org/reports/BBVreportIIunredacted.pdf.

[316] ICTE. *The Accuracy, Secrecy and Testing of the Nedap/Powervote Electronic Voting System*. Irish Citizens for Trustworthy Evoting, 2004. http://www.stdlib.net/~colmmacc/CEV/icte-cev.pdf.

[317] Srinivas Inguva, Eric Rescorla, Hovav Shacham, and Dan S Wallach. Source code review of the Hart InterCivic voting system, July 2007. http://votingsystems.cdn.sos.ca.gov/oversight/ttbr/Hart-source-public.pdf.

[318] Srinivas Inguva, Eric Rescorla, Hovav Shacham, and Dan S Wallach. *Source Code Review of the Hart InterCivic Voting System*. California Sec. of State's "Top to Bottom" Review, July 2007. http://www.sos.ca.gov/elections/voting_systems/ttbr/Hart-source-public.pdf.

[319] ISO, Geneva, Switzerland. *Ergonomic requirements for office work with visual display terminal (VDT's) – Part 11: Guidance on usability*. ISO 9241-11(E).

[320] Bart Jacobs and Wolter Pieters. Electronic voting in the Netherlands: from early adoption to early abolishment. In *Foundations of Security Analysis and Design V: FOSAD 2007/2008/2009 Tutorial Lectures*, volume 5705 of *LNCS*, pages 121–144. Springer, 2009.

[321] Markus Jakobsson, Ari Juels, and Ronald L Rivest. Making mix nets robust for electronic voting by randomized partial checking. In *USENIX Security Symposium*, pages 339–353, 2002.

[322] David R Jefferson, Aviel D Rubin, Barbara Simons, and David A Wagner. A security analysis of the secure electronic registration and voting experiment (SERVE), 2004. http://servesecurityreport.org/paper.pdf.

[323] Peter Sandholt Jensen and Mogens K Justesen. Poverty and vote buying: Survey-based evidence from africa. *Electoral Studies*, 33:220–232, 2014.

[324] Rui Joaquim, Paulo Ferreira, and Carlos Ribeiro. Eviv: An end-to-end verifiable internet voting system. *Computers & Security*, 32:170–191, 2013.

[325] Rui Joaquim and Carlos Ribeiro. An efficient and highly sound voter verification technique and its implementation. In *E-voting and Identity*, pages 104–121. Springer, 2012.

[326] Rui Joaquim, Carlos Ribeiro, and Paulo Ferreira. Veryvote: A voter verifiable code voting system. In *E-voting and Identity*, pages 106–121. Springer, 2009.

[327] Douglas Jones. *A Brief Illustrated History of Voting*. Iowa: The University of Iowa, 2001.

[328] Douglas Jones. Some problems with end-to-end voting. In *End-to-End Voting Systems Workshop*. Washington DC: NIST, 2009. `homepage.cs.uiowa.edu/~jones/voting/E2E2009.pdf`.

[329] Douglas Jones and Barbara Simons. *Broken Ballots. Will Your Vote Count?* Chicago: The University of Chicago Press, 2012.

[330] Douglas W Jones. The case of the Diebold FTP site, 2003. `http://homepage.cs.uiowa.edu/~jones/voting/dieboldftp.html`.

[331] Douglas W Jones. Kazakhstan: The sailau e-voting system. In Michael Yard, editor, *Direct Democracy: Progress and Pitfalls of Election Technology*. Washington: IFES, 2010. `http://homepage.cs.uiowa.edu/~jones/voting/IFESkazakhstan.pdf`.

[332] Douglas W Jones and Tom C Bowersox. Secure data export and auditing using data diodes. *Technology*, 6:7, 2006.

[333] Harvey Jones, Jason Juang, and Greg Belote. Threeballot in the field. Term paper for MIT course, 6, 2006.

[334] Hugo Jonker, Sjouke Mauw, and Jun Pang. Privacy and verifiability in voting systems: Methods, developments and trends. *Computer Science Review*, 10:1–30, 2013.

[335] Ari Juels, Dario Catalano, and Markus Jakobsson. Coercion-resistant electronic elections. In *ACM Workshop on Privacy in the Electronic Society*, pages 61–70. ACM, 2005.

[336] Ralf Küsters, Tomasz Truderung, and Andreas Vogt. Accountability: definition and relationship to verifiability. In *Proceedings of the 17th ACM Conference on Computer and Communications Security*, pages 526–535. ACM, 2010.

[337] Erik Kain. Report: NSA intercepting laptops ordered online, installing spyware, December 29, 2013. `http://www.forbes.com/sites/erikkain/2013/12/29/report-nsa-intercepting-laptops-ordered-online-installing-spyware/`.

[338] Fatih Karayumak, Michaela Kauer, Maina M Olembo, Tobias Volk, and Melanie Volkamer. User study of the improved Helios voting system interfaces. In *Workshop on Socio-Technical Aspects in Security and Trust (STAST)*, pages 37–44. IEEE, 2011.

[339] Fatih Karayumak, Maina M Olembo, Michaela Kauer, and Melanie Volkamer. Usability analysis of Helios – an open source verifiable remote electronic voting system. In *USENIX Electronic Voting Technology Workshop/Workshop on Trustworthy Elections*, 2011.

[340] Chris Karlof, Naveen Sastry, and David Wagner. Cryptographic voting protocols: A systems perspective. In *USENIX Security*, volume 5, pages 33–50, 2005.

[341] John Kelsey, Andrew Regenscheid, Tal Moran, and David Chaum. Attacking paper-based e2e voting systems. In *Towards Trustworthy Elections*, pages 370–387. Springer, 2010.

[342] S Khazaei and D Wikström. Randomized partial checking revisited. In *Topics in Cryptology - CT-RSA 2013*, volume 7779 of *Lecture Notes in Computer Science*, pages 115–128. Springer Berlin Heidelberg, 2013.

[343] Aggelos Kiayias, Michael Korman, and David Walluck. An internet voting system supporting user privacy. In *Annual Computer Security Applications Conference (ACSAC'06), 2006*, pages 165–174. IEEE, 2006.

[344] Aggelos Kiayias and Moti Yung. Self-tallying elections and perfect ballot secrecy. In *Public Key Cryptography*, pages 141–158. Springer, 2002.

[345] Aggelos Kiayias and Moti Yung. Non-interactive zero-sharing with applications to private distributed decision making. In *Financial Cryptography*, pages 303–320. Springer, 2003.

[346] Aggelos Kiayias and Moti Yung. The vector-ballot e-voting approach. In *Financial Cryptography*, pages 72–89. Springer, 2004.

[347] Joe Kilian. A note on efficient zero-knowledge proofs and arguments. In *Annual ACM Symposium on Theory of Computing*, STOC '92, pages 723–732, 1992.

[348] Melanie Kiser. Internet voting 2.0 and other advances in election technology in Takoma Park, 2011. `http://www.fairvote.org/internet-voting-2-0-and-other-advances-in-election-technology-in-takoma-park`.

[349] Marek Klonowski, Mirosław Kutyłowski, Anna Lauks, and Filip Zagórski. A practical voting scheme with receipts. In *Information Security*, pages 490–497. Springer, 2005.

[350] Reto Koenig, Rolf Haenni, and Stephan Fischli. Preventing board flooding attacks in coercion-resistant electronic voting schemes. In *Future Challenges in Security and Privacy for Academia and Industry*, pages 116–127. Springer, 2011.

[351] Tadayoshi Kohno, Adam Stubblefield, Aviel D Rubin, and Dan S Wallach. Analysis of an electronic voting system. In *IEEE Symposium on Security and Privacy, 2004. Proceedings*, pages 27–40. IEEE, 2004.

[352] Petr Kopecký. The Czech Republic: Entrenching proportional representation. In Josep M Colomer, editor, *Handbook of Electoral System Choice*, pages 347–358. Palgrave Macmillan, 2004.

[353] Steve Kremer, Mark Ryan, and Ben Smyth. Election verifiability in electronic voting protocols. *Computer Security–ESORICS*, pages 389–404, 2010.

[354] Robert Krimmer. Electronic voting. *GI Lecture Notes in Informatics, P-86, Bonn*, 2006.

[355] Taisya Krivoruchko. Robust coercion-resistant registration for remote e-voting. In *Workshop on Trustworthy Elections (WOTE'07)*, 2007.

[356] R Kusters, T Truderung, and A Vogt. Clash attacks on the verifiability of e-voting systems. In *2012 IEEE Symposium on Security and Privacy*, pages 395–409, 2012.

[357] Ralf Kusters, Tomasz Truderung, and Andreas Vogt. Clash attacks on the verifiability of e-voting systems. In *IEEE Symposium on Security and Privacy (SP)*, pages 395–409. IEEE, 2012.

[358] Mirosław Kutyłowski and Filip Zagórski. Scratch, click & vote: E2e voting over the internet. In *Towards Trustworthy Elections*, pages 343–356. Springer, 2010.

[359] Lucie Langer, Axel Schmidt, Johannes Buchmann, and Melanie Volkamer. A taxonomy refining the security requirements for electronic voting: analyzing Helios as a proof of concept. In *International Conference on Availability, Reliability, and Security (ARES'10)*, pages 475–480. IEEE, 2010.

[360] Sharon J Laskowski, Marguerite Autry, John Cugini, William Killam, and James Yen. Improving the usability and accessibility of voting systems and products. *NIST Special Publication*, 2004.

[361] Arjen K Lenstra and Hendrik W Lenstra Jr. Algorithms in number theory. Technical report, Elsevier, 1990.

[362] Rafi Letzter. A new voting machine could make sure every vote really counts, 2014. http://www.popsci.com/article/technology/new-voting-machine-could-make-sure-every-vote-really-counts.

[363] Samantha Levine. Hanging Chads: As the Florida Recount Implodes, the Supreme Court Decides Bush v. Gore, Jan. 17 2008. `http://www.usnews.com/news/articles/2008/01/17/the-legacy-of-hanging-chads`.

[364] LexisNexis. 2014 LexisNexis true cost of fraud study, August 2014. `http://www.lexisnexis.com/risk/downloads/assets/true-cost-fraud-2014.pdf`.

[365] Andra Lim. Travis county, tx developing electronic voting system with a paper trail, July 15 2014. `http://www.govtech.com/products/Travis-County-TX-Developing-Electronic-Voting-System-With-a-Paper-Trail.html`.

[366] Mark Lindeman, Mark Halvorson, Pamela Smith, Lynn Garland, and Vittorio Addona. Principles and best practices for post-election audits. 2008. `http://www.electionaudits.org/files/best%20practices%20final_0.pdf`.

[367] Mark Lindeman and Philip B Stark. A gentle introduction to risk-limiting audits. *IEEE Security & Privacy*, (5):42–49, 2012.

[368] Helger Lipmaa. Paper-voted (and why I did so), 2011. `http://helger.wordpress.com/2011/03/05/paper-voted-and-why-i-did-so/`.

[369] Yining Liu, Peiyong Sun, Jihong Yan, Yajun Li, and Jianyu Cao. An improved electronic voting scheme without a trusted random number generator. In *Information Security and Cryptology*, pages 93–101. Springer, 2012.

[370] Mieke Loncke and Jos Dumortier. Online voting: a legal perspective. *International Review of Law, Computers & Technology*, 18(1):59–79, 2004.

[371] Panos Louridas, Georgios Tsoukalas, Kostas Papadimitriou, and Panayiotis Tsanakas. Zeus: Bringing internet voting to greece. In *E-Democracy, Security, Privacy and Trust in a Digital World*, pages 213–223. Springer, 2014.

[372] Simon Luechinger, Myra Rosinger, and Alois Stutzer. The impact of postal voting on participation: Evidence for switzerland. *Swiss Political Science Review*, 13(2):167–202, 2007.

[373] Anders Smedstuen Lund. Refining the internet voting protocol. Master's thesis, Norwegian University of Science and Technology, June 2011.

[374] David Lundin and Peter Y A Ryan. Human readable paper verification of Prêt à Voter. In *European Symposium on Research in Computer Security (ESORICS'08)*, pages 379–395. Springer-Verlag, 2008.

[375] Georg Lutz. First come, first served: the effect of ballot position on electoral success in open ballot PR elections. *Representation*, 46(2):167–181, 2010.

[376] Epp Maaten. Towards remote e-voting: Estonian case. *Electronic Voting in Europe*, 47:83–100, 2004.

[377] Ülle Madise and Tarvi Martens. E-voting in Estonia 2005. the first practice of country-wide binding internet voting in the world. *Electronic Voting*, 86, 2006.

[378] Pieter Maene. Helios election system. `https://github.com/Pmaene/Helios`.

[379] Mandiant. APT1: Exposing one of China's cyber espionage units, February 2013. `http://intelreport.mandiant.com/Mandiant_APT1_Report.pdf`.

[380] Tarvi Martens. Electronic identity management in Estonia between market and state governance. *Identity in the Information Society*, 3(1):213–233, 2010.

[381] Rubén Martínez Dalmau. Venezuela: Finding the relationship between e-voting and democracy. In Ardita Driza / Jordi Barrat, editor, *E-Voting Case Law. A Comparative Analysis*, pages 261–275. Farnham: Ashgate, 2015.

[382] Louis Massicotte. Canada: Sticking to first-past-the-post, for the time being. In Michael Gallagher and Paul Mitchell, editors, *The Politics of Electoral Systems*, pages 99–118. Oxford University Press, 2005.

[383] Richard E Matland. Enhancing women's political participation: Legislative recruitment and electoral systems. *Women in Parliament: Beyond Numbers. International IDEA Handbook*. Stockholm, pages 93–111, 2005.

[384] Kenneth O May. A set of independent necessary and sufficient conditions for simple majority decision. *Econometrica: Journal of the Econometric Society*, 20(4):680–684, 1952.

[385] Eric Mazur. *Peer Instruction*. Upper Saddle River, NJ: Prentice Hall, 1997.

[386] Neal McBurnett, Richard T Carback, David Chaum, Jeremy Clark, John Conway, Aleksander Essex, Paul S Herrnson, Travis Mayberry, Stefan Popoveniuc, Ronald L Rivest, Emily Shen, Alan T Sherman, and Poorvi L Vora. Scantegrity Responds to Rice Study on Usability of the Scantegrity II Voting System, December 2014. In review, *Journal of Election Technology and Systems (JETS)*.

[387] Patrick McDaniel, Kevin Butler, William Enck, Harri Hursti, Steve McLaughlin, Patrick Traynor, Matt Blaze, Adam Aviv, Pavol Černý, Sandy Clark, Eric Cronin, Gaurav Shah, Micah Sherr, Giovanni Vigna, Richard Kemmerer, Davide Balzarotti, Greg Banks, Marco Cova, Viktoria Felmetsger, William Robertson, Fredrik Valeur, Joseph Lorenzo Hall, and Laura Quilter. EVEREST: Evaluation and Validation of Election-Related Equipment, Standards and Testing, final report, December 2007. `http://www.patrickmcdaniel.org/pubs/everest.pdf`.

[388] Ronan McDermott. *Electronic Voting in Ireland. A Case Study.* Brussels: EC-UNDP Partnership on Electoral Assistance, 2012. Thematic Workshop / Mombassa (Kenia).

[389] Margaret McGalley and J Paul Gibson. *Electronic Voting: A Safety Critical System.* Maynooth: National University of Ireland, 2003. http://www.umic.pt/images/stories/publicacoes1/nuim-cs-tr-2003-02.pdf.

[390] Iain McLean. Forms of representation and systems of voting. *Political Theory Today*, pages 172–196, 1991.

[391] Juan Manuel Mecinas Montiel. *Constitutional Analysis of the Internet Voting.* PhD thesis, Universidad Complutense de Madrid, 2013. Doctoral dissertation. Title translated from Spanish.

[392] Paul Melia and Luke Byrne. €54m voting machines scrapped for €9 each. *Independent*, June 29th, 2012. http://www.independent.ie/irish-news/54m-voting-machines-scrapped-for-9-each-26870212.html.

[393] Silvio Micali. Computationally sound proofs. *SIAM Journal on Computing*, 30(4):1253–1298, 2000.

[394] Paul Mitchell. The United Kingdom: plurality rule under siege. In Michael Gallagher and Paul Mitchell, editors, *The Politics of Electoral Systems*, pages 157–184. Oxford University Press, 2005.

[395] Ester Moher, Jeremy Clark, and Aleksander Essex. Diffusion of voter responsibility: Potential failings in E2E voter receipt checking. *USENIX Journal of Election Technology and Systems (JETS)*, 1, 2014.

[396] David Molnar, Tadayoshi Kohno, Naveen Sastry, and David Wagner. Tamper-evident, history-independent, subliminal-free data structures on prom storage-or-how to store ballots on a voting machine. In *IEEE Symposium on Security and Privacy*, pages 6–pp. IEEE, 2006.

[397] Tal Moran and Moni Naor. Receipt-free universally-verifiable voting with everlasting privacy. In *Advances in Cryptology-CRYPTO 2006*, pages 373–392. Springer, 2006.

[398] Tal Moran and Moni Naor. Split-ballot voting: everlasting privacy with distributed trust. *ACM Transactions on Information and System Security (TISSEC)*, 13(2):16, 2010.

[399] Dan Morrell. Secret Ballots, Verifiable Votes, May-June 2010. http://harvardmagazine.com/2010/05/secret-ballots-verifiable-votes.

[400] Robert G Moser. Electoral systems and the number of parties in postcommunist states. *World Politics*, 51:359–384, 1999.

[401] Mozilla wiki. Security/server side TLS configuration guide. `https://wiki.mozilla.org/Security/Server_Side_TLS`.

[402] Judith Murray. Usability testing for end-to-end verifiable internet voting project feasibility study. *Publication Pending*, 2015.

[403] Satoshi Nakamoto. Bitcoin: A peer-to-peer electronic cash system, May 24 2009. (Posted on Cryptography Mailing List at metzdowd.com).

[404] Mridul Nandi, Stefan Popoveniuc, and Poorvi L Vora. Stamp-it: a method for enhancing the universal verifiability of e2e voting systems. In *Information Systems Security*, pages 81–95. Springer, 2010.

[405] Moni Naor and Adi Shamir. Visual cryptography. In *Advances in Cryptology–EUROCRYPT'94*, pages 1–12. Springer, 1995.

[406] C Andrew Neff. A verifiable secret shuffle and its application to e-voting. In *ACM Conference on Computer and Communications Security*, pages 116–125. ACM, 2001.

[407] Stephan Neumann, Jurlind Budurushi, and Melanie Volkamer. Analysis of security and cryptographic approaches to provide secret and verifiable electronic voting. In *Design, Development, and Use of Secure Electronic Voting Systems*. IGI Global, 2014.

[408] Stephan Neumann, Christian Feier, Melanie Volkamer, and Reto E Koenig. Towards a practical jcj/civitas implementation. *IACR Cryptology ePrint Archive*, 2013:464, 2013.

[409] Stephan Neumann, Oksana Kulyk, and Melanie Volkamer. A usable android application implementing distributed cryptography for election authorities. In *International Conference on Availability, Reliability and Security (ARES)*, pages 207–216. IEEE, 2014.

[410] Stephan Neumann, M Maina Olembo, Karen Renaud, and Melanie Volkamer. Helios verification: To alleviate, or to nominate: Is that the question, or shall we have both? In *Electronic Government and the Information Systems Perspective (EGOVIS)*, pages 246–260. Springer, 2014.

[411] Stephan Neumann and Melanie Volkamer. Civitas and the real world: Problems and solutions from a practical point of view. In *International Conference on Availability, Reliability and Security (ARES)*, pages 180–185. IEEE, 2012.

[412] Glenn M Newkirk. Trends in American trust in voting technology. Technical report, whitepaper for InfoSENTRY Services, 2008.

[413] NewsGram. EVM controversy: VVPAT to be used as Delhi votes tomorrow, February 6, 2015. `http://www.newsgram.com/evm-controversy-and-vvpat-in-delhi/`.

[414] Jairo M Nicolau. Brazil: Democratizing with majority runoff. In Josep M Colomer, editor, *Handbook of Electoral System Choice*, pages 121–132. Palgrave Macmillan, 2004.

[415] Valtteri Niemi and Ari Renvall. How to prevent buying of votes in computer elections. In *Advances in Cryptology–ASIACRYPT'94*, pages 164–170. Springer, 1995.

[416] Kees Niemoller. Experiences with voting machines in the Netherlands and in Germany. In Commission on Electronic Voting, editor, *Secrecy, Accuracy and Testing of the Chosen Electronic Voting System. Interim report. Appendix 2K*, pages 327–348. Commission on Electronic Voting, 2004. `wijvertrouwenstemcomputersniet.nl/images/a/a2/Bijlage_over_Nederland_bij_rapport_Ierse_commissie.pdf`.

[417] NIST. *Accessibility and Usability Considerations for UOCAVA Remote Electronic Voting Systems*. Gaithersburg: National Institute of Standards and Technology (NIST), 2011. `http://www.eac.gov/assets/1/Documents/Usability\%20Accessibility\%20for\%20Remote\%20Voting\%20Systems\%202011-02-14\%20v3-final.pdf`.

[418] C Andrew Neff. Practical high certainty intent verification for encrypted votes. vote-here (2004), 2004. `http://www.votehere.net/vhti/documentation`.

[419] Lawrence Norden, David Kimball, Whitney Quesenbery, and Margaret Chen. *Better Ballots*. New York: Brennan Center for Justice, 2008. `http://www.brennancenter.org/sites/default/files/legacy/Democracy/Better\%20Ballots.pdf`.

[420] Donald F Norris. Maryland registered voters' opinions about voting and voting technologies. Technical report, National Center for the Study of Elections of the Maryland Institute for Policy Analysis & Research University of Maryland, Baltimore County, 2006.

[421] Notimerica. Mexico to use electronic voting in presidential elections. 2015. `http://www.notimerica.com/politica/noticia-mexico-probara-voto-electronico-elecciones-presidenciales-20150601213118.html`. Title translated from Spanish.

[422] NSW Electoral Commission. 2015 legislative council—final distribution of preferences. `http://vtr.elections.nsw.gov.au/lc-home.htm#lc/state/dop/dop_index`.

[423] NSW Electoral Commission. Index of iVote reports. `http://www.elections.nsw.gov.au/about_us/plans_and_reports/ivote_reports`.

[424] NSW Electoral Commission. iVote threat analysis and risk assessment, January 2014. `http://www.elections.nsw.gov.au/__data/assets/pdf_file/0008/175760/NSW_Election_-_iVote_Threat_Analysis_and_Risk_Assessment_v3.0.pdf`.

[425] NSW Electoral Commission. iVote system security implementation statement, March 2015. `http://www.elections.nsw.gov.au/__data/assets/pdf_file/0007/193219/iVote-Security_Implementation_Statement-Mar2015.pdf`.

[426] Marianne Wiik Øberg. Improving the Norwegian internet voting protocol. Master's thesis, Norwegian University of Science and Technology, June 2011.

[427] OSCE / ODIHR. *The Netherlands. Parliamentary Elections 22 November 2006. OSCE/ODIHR Election Assessment Mission Report.* Warsaw: OSCE/ODIHR, 2007. `http://www.osce.org/odihr/elections/netherlands/24322`.

[428] Council of Europe. *Legal, Operational and Technical Standards for E-Voting, Recommendation Rec(2004)11 adopted by the Committee of Ministers of the Council of Europe on 30 September 2004 and Explanatory Memorandum.* 2004.

[429] Council of Europe. *E-Voting Handbook: Key steps in the implementation of e-enabled elections.* 2010.

[430] Council of Europe. *Certification of e-voting systems: Guidelines for developing processes that confirm compliance with prescribed requirements and standards.* 2011.

[431] Council of Europe. *Guidelines on transparency of e-enabled elections.* 2011.

[432] General Secretariat of the Organization of American States. *Observing the Use of Electoral Technologies: A Manual for OAS Electoral Observation Missions.* Organization of America States, 2010. `https://www.oas.org/es/sap/docs/Technology\%20English-FINAL-4-27-10.pdf`.

[433] Title 29 of the United States Code. Vocational rehabilitation act, 1973. § 794d, Section 508.

[434] Ohio Secretary of State's Office. Evaluation and Validation of Election-Related Equipment, Standards and Testing (EVEREST), 2007. `http://siis.cse.psu.edu/everest.html`.

[435] Stephen C Pohlig and Martin E Hellman. An improved algorithm for computing logarithms over gf(p) and its cryptographic significance (corresp.). *Information Theory, IEEE Transactions on*, 24(1):106–110, Jan 1978.

[436] Urmas Oja. Paavo Pihelgas: Elektroonilise hääletamise vaatlemine on lihtsalt võimatu, 2011. `http://forte.delfi.ee/news/digi/paavo-pihelgas-elektroonilise-haaletamise-vaatlemine-on-lihtsalt-voimatu.d?id=41933409`. In Estonian.

[437] Tatsuaki Okamoto. An electronic voting scheme. In *Advanced IT Tools*, pages 21–30. Springer, 1996.

[438] Tatsuaki Okamoto. Receipt-free electronic voting schemes for large scale elections. In *Security Protocols Workshop*, pages 25–35. Springer, 1998.

[439] Ersin Öksüzoglu and Dan S Wallach. Votebox nano: A smaller, stronger fpga-based voting machine (short paper). In *USENIX/Accurate Electronic Voting Technology Workshop/Workshop on Trustworthy Elections*, 2009.

[440] M Maina Olembo, Karen Renaud, Steffen Bartsch, and Melanie Volkamer. Voter, what message will motivate you to verify your vote. In *Workshop on Usable Security, USEC*, 2014.

[441] Maina M Olembo, Steffen Bartsch, and Melanie Volkamer. Mental models of verifiability in voting. In *E-Voting and Identify*, pages 142–155. Springer, 2013.

[442] Commission on Electronic Voting. *Secrecy, Accuracy and Testing of the Chosen Electronic Voting System*. 2006. `http://www.stdlib.net/~colmmacc/www.cev.ie/htm/report/download_second.htm`. Second Report.

[443] ONPE. *Electronic Voting History 1996-2004*. Lima: Oficina Nacional de Procesos Electorales (ONPE), 2011. `http://www.web.onpe.gob.pe/modEducacion/Publicaciones/dt-28.pdf`. Title translated from Spanish.

[444] ONPE. *Electronic Voting in Practice: Perspectives and Dynamics From the Experience of Local and Regional Elections 2014*. Lima: Oficina Nacional de Procesos Electorales (ONPE), 2014. `http://www.web.onpe.gob.pe/modEducacion/Publicaciones/L-0102.pdf`. Title translated from Spanish.

[445] Anne-Marie Oostveen and Peter Van den Besselaar. Internet voting technologies and civic participation: the users' perspective. *Javnost-the public*, 11(1):61–78, 2004.

[446] Anne-Marie Oostveen and Peter Van den Besselaar. Security as belief. user's perceptions on the security of electronic voting systems. In A Prosser

/ Robert Krimmer, editor, *Electronic Voting in Europe: Technology, Law, Politics and Society*, volume P47 of *(Col. Lecture Notes in Informatics)*, pages 73–82. Bonn: Gesellschaft für Informatik, 2004. http://www.social-informatics.net/ESF2004.pdf.

[447] Open Source Digital Voting Foundation. District of Columbia's Board of Elections and Ethics adopts open source digital voting foundation technology to support ballot delivery, June 2010. http://www.businesswire.com/news/home/20100622006238/en/District-Columbia%E2%80%99s-Board-Elections-Ethics-Adopts-Open.

[448] OSCE/ODIHR. *Norway Parliamentary Elections 9 September 2013, OSCE/ODIHR Election Assessment Mission Final Report.* Warsaw: OSCE/ODIHR, 2013. http://www.osce.org/odihr/elections/109517?download=true.

[449] OSCE/ODIHR. *Estonia. Parliamentary Elections 1 March 2015. OSCE / ODIHR Election Expert Team, Final Report.* Warsaw: OSCE /ODIHR, 2015. http://www.osce.org/odihr/elections/estonia/160131?download=true.

[450] OSCE/ODIHR. *Swiss Confederation. Federal Assembly Elections 18 October 2015. OSCE / ODIHR Needs Assessment Mission Report.* Warsaw: OSCE/ODIHR, 2015. http://www.osce.org/odihr/elections/switzerland/172056?download=true.

[451] Eric Pacuit. Voting methods. In Edward N Zalta, editor, *The Stanford Encyclopedia of Philosophy*. Winter 2012 edition, 2012. http://plato.stanford.edu/archives/win2012/entries/voting-methods.

[452] Pascal Paillier. Public-key cryptosystems based on composite degree residuosity classes. In *Advances in Cryptology–EUROCRYPT'99*, pages 223–238. Springer, 1999.

[453] Choonsik Park, Kazutomo Itoh, and Kaoru Kurosawa. Efficient anonymous channel and all/nothing election scheme. In Tor Helleseth, editor, *Advances in Cryptology — EUROCRYPT '93*, volume 765 of *Lecture Notes in Computer Science*, pages 248–259. Springer Berlin Heidelberg, 1994.

[454] Brian Parno, Craig Gentry, Jon Howell, and Mariana Raykova. Pinocchio: Nearly practical verifiable computation. In *IEEE Symposium on Security and Privacy*, S&P '13, pages 238–252, 2013.

[455] Nathanael Paul, David Evans, Avi Rubin, and Dan Wallach. Authentication for remote voting. In *Workshop on Human-Computer Interaction and Security Systems, Fort Lauderdale*, 2003.

[456] Nathanael Paul and Andrew S Tanenbaum. Trustworthy voting: From machine to system. *IEEE Computer*, 42(5):23–29, 2009.

[457] Torben Pryds Pedersen. A threshold cryptosystem without a trusted party. In *Advances in Cryptology–EUROCRYPT'91*, pages 522–526. Springer, 1991.

[458] Torben Pryds Pedersen. Non-interactive and information-theoretic secure verifiable secret sharing. In *Advances in Cryptology–CRYPTO'91*, pages 129–140. Springer, 1992.

[459] Gonçalo David Martins Tourais Pereira. Scroll, match & vote: An e2e coercion resistant mobile voting system. In *EVOTE*, pages 149–152. IEEE, 2014.

[460] Birgit Pfitzmann and Andreas Pfitzmann. How to break the direct rsa-implementation of mixes. In *Advances in Cryptology–EUROCRYPT'89*, pages 373–381. Springer, 1990.

[461] W Pieters and MJ Becker. Ethics of e-voting: An essay on requirements and values in internet elections. *Ethics of New Information Technology: Proceedings of the Sixth International Conference of Computer Ethics: Philosophical Inquiry*, pages 307–318, 2005.

[462] Gillian E Piner and Michael D Byrne. The experience of accessible voting results of a survey among legally-blind users. In *Proceedings of the Human Factors and Ergonomics Society Annual Meeting*, volume 55, pages 1686–1690. SAGE Publications, 2011.

[463] John M Pollard. Monte Carlo methods for index computation (mod p). *Mathematics of Computation*, 32(143):918–924, Jul 1978.

[464] Stefan Popoveniuc. Speakup: remote unsupervised voting. *Industrial Track ACNS*, 2010.

[465] Stefan Popoveniuc and Ben Hosp. An introduction to Punchscan. In *Workshop on Trustworthy Elections (WOTE)*, 2006.

[466] Stefan Popoveniuc, John Kelsey, Andrew Regenscheid, and Poorvi Vora. Performance requirements for end-to-end verifiable elections. In *International Conference on Electronic Voting Technology/Workshop on Trustworthy Elections*, pages 1–16. USENIX Association, 2010.

[467] Stefan Popoveniuc and David Lundin. A simple technique for safely using Punchscan and prêt à voter in mail-in elections. In *E-Voting and Identity*, pages 150–155. Springer, 2007.

[468] Stefan Popoveniuc and Poorvi L Vora. Remote ballot casting with captchas. In *Workshop on Information and System Security*, 2008.

[469] Nicolas Pouillard. Helios pull request #46, 2013. `https://github.com/benadida/helios-server/pull/46`.

[470] Vladimir Pran and Patrick Merloe. Monitoring electronic technologies in electoral processes. *National Democratic Institute*, 2007.

[471] prometheus. Monitoring electronic technologies in electoral processes. Github repository, June 2015. `https://github.com/prometheus-ar/vot.ar`.

[472] Estat Propi. Declared innocent the journalist who impersonated Alberto Fernández Díaz during the popular consultation on diagonal avenue ... *Racó Català*, February 23rd, 2013. `http://ves.cat/mfkl`. Title translated from Catalan.

[473] Niels Provos, Markus Friedl, and Peter Honeyman. Preventing privilege escalation. In *USENIX Security*, volume 3, 2003.

[474] PSDB. Auditoria do PSDB nas urnas eletrônicas mostra que sistema eleitoral brasileiro é vulnerável, November 4, 2015. `http://www.psdb.org.br/auditoria-do-psdb-nas-urnas-eletronicas-mostra-que-sistema-eleitoral-brasileiro-e-vulneravel/`. In Portuguese.

[475] RABA Technologies. Trusted agent report: Diebold AccuVote-TS voting system, 2004. `http://www.raba.com/press/TAReportAccuVote.pdf`.

[476] Douglas W Rae. *The Political Consequences of Electoral Laws*. Yale University Press, New Haven, 1967.

[477] Kim Ramchen and Vanessa Teague. Parallel shuffling and its application to prêt à voter. In *USENIX Accurate Electronic Voting Technology Workshop*, 2010.

[478] Brian Randell and Peter Y A Ryan. Voting technologies and trust. *IEEE Security & Privacy*, 4(5):0050–56, 2006.

[479] Steven R Reed. Japan: haltingly toward a two-party system. In Michael Gallagher and Paul Mitchell, editors, *The Politics of Electoral Systems*, pages 277–294. Oxford University Press, 2005.

[480] Ben Reilly, Andrew Ellis, and Andrew Reynolds. *Electoral System Design: The New International IDEA Handbook*. International Institute for Democracy and Electoral Assistance, 2005.

[481] Benjamin Reilly. Social choice in the south seas: Electoral innovation and the Borda count in the Pacific island countries. *International Political Science Review*, 23(4):355–372, 2002.

[482] Eric Rescorla. Understanding the security properties of ballot-based verification techniques. In *Electronic Voting Technology Workshop/Workshop on Trustworthy Elections*, volume 1, 2009.

[483] Pedro A D Rezende. Electronic elections: a balancing act. In *Towards Trust-worthy Elections*, pages 124–140. Springer, 2010.

[484] Timothy S Rich. Evaluating South Korea's mixed legislative system: A cross-national analysis of district competition. *Korea Observer*, 44(3):365, 2013.

[485] Ronald L Rivest. Electronic voting. In *Financial Cryptography*, volume 1, pages 243–268, 2001.

[486] Ronald L Rivest. On the notion of 'software independence' in voting systems. *Philosophical Transactions of The Royal Society A*, 366(1881):3759–3767, August 6, 2008.

[487] Ronald L Rivest and Warren D Smith. Three voting protocols: Threeballot, vav, and twin. In *USENIX Workshop on Accurate Electronic Voting Technology*, volume 16. USENIX Association, 2007.

[488] Ronald L Rivest and John P Wack. On the notion of "software independence" in voting systems, July 28, 2006. http://vote.nist.gov/SI-in-voting.pdf.

[489] E Arthur Robinson Jr and Daniel H Ullman. *A Mathematical Look at Politics*. CRC Press, Taylor & Francis, 2010.

[490] Tom Roeder. Pyrios library, 2014. `https://github.com/google/pyrios/`.

[491] Jörg Rothe and Irene Rothe. *Economics and Computation: An Introduction to Algorithmic Game Theory, Computational Social Choice, and Fair Division*. Springer, 2015.

[492] Avi Rubin. Security considerations for remote electronic voting over the Internet. `http://avirubin.com/e-voting.security.html`.

[493] Avi Rubin. *Brave New Ballot*. New York: Morgan Road Books, 2006. `http://www.bravenewballot.org`.

[494] Peter Y A Ryan. A variant of the Chaum voter-verifiable scheme. Technical Report CS-TR-864, University of Newcastle upon Tyne School of Computing Science, October 2004. `http://www.cs.newcastle.ac.uk/publications/trs/papers/864.pdf`.

[495] Peter Y A Ryan. Human readable paper verification of Prêt à Voter. Technical Report CS-TR-966, Newcastle University, 2006.

[496] Peter Y A Ryan. Human readable paper verification of Prêt à Voter. Technical Report CS-TR-1038, Newcastle University, 2007.

[497] Peter Y A Ryan. Putting the human back in voting protocols. In *Security Protocols Workshop*, pages 20–25. Springer, 2009.

[498] Peter Y A Ryan. Prêt à voter with confirmation codes. In *USENIX Electronic Voting Technology Workshop*, 2011.

[499] Peter Y A Ryan, David Bismark, James Heather, Steve Schneider, and Zhe Xia. Prêt à voter: a voter-verifiable voting system. *IEEE Transactions on Information Forensics and Security*, 4(4):662–673, 2009.

[500] Peter Y A Ryan and Jeremy Bryans. A simplified version of the chaum voting scheme. Technical Report CS-TR-843, Newcastle University, 2004.

[501] Peter Y A Ryan and Thea Peacock. Prêt à Voter: A system perspective. Technical Report CS-TR-929, University of Newcastle upon Tyne School of Computing Science, September 2005. http://www.cs.ncl.ac.uk/research/pubs/trs/papers/929.pdf.

[502] Peter Y A Ryan and Thea Peacock. A threat analysis of prêt à voter. In *Towards Trustworthy Elections*, pages 200–215. Springer, 2010.

[503] Peter Y A Ryan and Steve Schneider. Prêt à Voter with re-encryption mixes. Technical Report CS-TR-956, University of Newcastle upon Tyne School of Computing Science, April 2006. http://www.cs.ncl.ac.uk/research/pubs/trs/papers/956.pdf.

[504] Peter Y A Ryan and Steve Schneider. Prêt à voter with re-encryption mixes. In *ESORICS*, number 4189 in LNCS. Springer-Verlag, 2006.

[505] Peter Y A Ryan and Vanessa Teague. Ballot permutations in prêt à voter. In *USENIX/ACCURATE Electronic Voting Technology Workshop*, 2009.

[506] Peter Y A Ryan and Vanessa Teague. Pretty good democracy. In *Security Protocols Workshop XVII*, pages 111–130. Springer, 2013.

[507] Thomas Saalfeld. Germany: stability and strategy in a mixed-member proportional system. In Michael Gallagher and Paul Mitchell, editors, *The Politics of Electoral Systems*, pages 209–229. Oxford University Press, 2005.

[508] Kazue Sako and Joe Kilian. Receipt-free mix-type voting scheme. In *Advances in Cryptology–EUROCRYPT'95*, pages 393–403. Springer, 1995.

[509] Bassel F Salloukh. The limits of electoral engineering in divided societies: elections in postwar Lebanon. *Canadian Journal of Political Science*, 39(03):635–655, 2006.

[510] Daniel Sandler, Kyle Derr, and Dan S Wallach. Votebox: A tamper-evident, verifiable electronic voting system. In *USENIX Security Symposium*, volume 4, page 87, 2008.

[511] Daniel Sandler and Dan S Wallach. Casting votes in the auditorium. In *USENIX/ACCURATE Electronic Voting Technology Workshop (EVT'07)*, 2007.

[512] Daniel Sandler and Dan S Wallach. The case for networked remote voting precincts. *EVT*, 8:1–7, 2008.

[513] David E Sanger. Obama order sped up wave of cyberattacks against Iran. The New York Times, June 1, 2012. http://www.nytimes.com/2012/06/01/world/middleeast/obama-ordered-wave-of-cyberattacks-against-iran.html.

[514] Bo Särlvik. Party and electoral system in Sweden. In Bernard Grofman and Arend Lijphart, editors, *The Evolution of Electoral and Party Systems in the Nordic Countries*, page 225. Algora Publishing, 2007.

[515] Mark Allen Satterthwaite. Strategy-proofness and Arrow's conditions: Existence and correspondence theorems for voting procedures and social welfare functions. *Journal of Economic Theory*, 10(2):187–217, 1975.

[516] Steve Schneider, Morgan Llewellyn, Chris Culnane, James Heather, Sriramkrishnan Srinivasan, and Zhe Xia. Focus group views on prêt à voter 1.0. In *Workshop on Requirements Engineering for Electronic Voting Systems*, pages 56–65, 2011.

[517] Claus-Peter Schnorr. Efficient signature generation by smart cards. *Journal of cryptology*, 4(3):161–174, 1991.

[518] Guido Schryen and Eliot Rich. Security in large-scale internet elections: A retrospective analysis of elections in Estonia, the Netherlands, and Switzerland. *IEEE Transactions on Information Forensics and Security*, 4(4):729–744, Dec 2009.

[519] Markus Schulze. A new monotonic, clone-independent, reversal symmetric, and condorcet-consistent single-winner election method. *Social Choice and Welfare*, 36(2):267–303, 2011.

[520] Bryan P Schwartz and Dan Grice. Establishing a legal framework for e-voting in Canada. *Man. LJ*, 36:301, 2012.

[521] Science Applications International Corporation. Risk assessment report: Diebold AccuVote-TS voting system and processes (unredacted), 2003. http://www.bradblog.com/?p=3731.

[522] Bock Segaard, Dag Arne Christensen, Bjarte Folkestad, and Jo Saglie. Internettvalg: Hva gjør og mener velgerne?, 2014. https://www.regjeringen.no/globalassets/upload/kmd/komm/rapporter/isf_internettvalg.pdf. In Norwegian.

[523] Hovav Shacham. The geometry of innocent flesh on the bone: Return-into-libc without function calls (on the x86). In *ACM Conference on Computer and Communications Security (CCS'07)*, pages 552–561. ACM, 2007.

[524] Daniel Shanks. Class number, a theory of factorization, and genera. In *Symposium on Pure Math*, volume 20, pages 415–440, 1971.

[525] Alan T Sherman, Richard Carback, David Chaum, Jeremy Clark, John Conway, Aleksander Essex, Paul S Herrnson, Travis Mayberry, Stefan Popoveniuc, Ronald L Rivest, Anne Sergeant, Emily Shen, Bimal Sinha, and Poorvi Vora. Scantegrity mock election at Takoma Park (summary), October 2009. NIST End-to-End Voting Systems Workshop.

[526] Alan T Sherman, Richard T Carback, David Chaum, Jeremy Clark, Aleksander Essex, Paul S Hernson, Travis Mayberry, Stefan Popoveniuc, Ronald L Rivest, Emily Shen, Bimal Sinha, and Poorvi L Vora. Scantegrity mock election at Takoma Park. In *EVOTE*, 2010.

[527] Alan T Sherman, Russell A Fink, Richard Carback, and David Chaum. Scantegrity iii: automatic trustworthy receipts, highlighting over/under votes, and full voter verifiability. In *Conference on Electronic Voting Technology/Workshop on Trustworthy Elections*, pages 7–7. USENIX Association, 2011.

[528] Victor Shoup and Rosario Gennaro. Securing threshold cryptosystems against chosen ciphertext attack. *Journal of Cryptology*, 15(2):75–96, 2002.

[529] Matthew Shugart and Martin P Wattenberg. *Mixed-Member Electoral Systems: The Best of Both Worlds?* Oxford University Press, 2001.

[530] Gustavus J Simmons. The prisoners' problem and the subliminal channel. In *Advances in Cryptology*, pages 51–67. Springer, 1984.

[531] Barbara Simons. Report on the Estonian Internet voting system. Verified Voting Blog, September 3, 2011. https://www.verifiedvoting.org/report-on-the-estonian-internet-voting-system-2/.

[532] Matt Smart and Eike Ritter. True trustworthy elections: remote electronic voting using trusted computing. In *Autonomic and Trusted Computing*, pages 187–202. Springer, 2011.

[533] Benjamin Smith, Sharon Laskowski, and Svetlana Lowry. Implications of graphics on usability and accessibility for the voter. In *E-Voting and Identity*, pages 54–74. Springer, 2009.

[534] Eivind Smith. Secret electronic vote? *Lov og rett: Norsk Juridisk Tidsskrift*, 49(6):307–323, 2010. title translated from Norwegian.

[535] Drew Springall, Travis Finkenauer, Zakir Durumeric, Jason Kitcat, Harri Hursti, Margaret MacAlpine, and J Alex Halderman. Security analysis of the Estonian Internet voting system. In *ACM Conference on Computer and Communications Security*, CCS'14, pages 703–715. ACM, 2014.

[536] Oliver Spycher, Reto Koenig, Rolf Haenni, and Michael Schläpfer. A new approach towards coercion-resistant remote e-voting in linear time. In *Financial Cryptography and Data Security*, volume 7035, page 182. Springer Science & Business Media, 2012.

[537] Sriramkrishnan Srinivasan, Chris Culnane, James Heather, Steve Schneider, and Zhe Xia. Countering ballot stuffing and incorporating eligibility verifiability in Helios. In *Network and System Security (NDSS)*, pages 335–348. Springer, 2014.

[538] Richard P Stanley. Enumerative combinatorics. vol. 2, volume 62 of *Cambridge Studies in Advanced Mathematics*, 1999.

[539] Emily Stark, Mike Hamburg, and Dan Boneh. Stanford JavaScript crypto library. http://bitwiseshiftleft.github.io/sjcl/.

[540] Philip B Stark. Super-simple simultaneous single-ballot risk-limiting audits. In *Electronic Voting Technology Workshop/Workshop on Trustworthy Elections (EVT/WOTE'10)*, 2010.

[541] Philip B Stark and David Wagner. Evidence-based elections. *Security & Privacy, IEEE*, 10(5):33–41, 2012.

[542] Paul Stenbjorn. An overview and design rationale memo, September 2010. http://www.dcboee.us/dvm/DCdVBM-DesignRationale-v3.pdf.

[543] Ida Sofie Gebhardt Stenerud and Christian Bull. When reality comes knocking Norwegian experiences with verifiable electronic voting. In *Electronic Voting*, volume P-205 of *(Col. "Lecture Notes in Informatics-LNI")*. Bonn: Gesellschaft für Informatik, 2012.

[544] John Stewart. A Banana Republic? The investigation into electoral fraud by the Birmingham election court. *Parliamentary Affairs*, 59(4):654–667, 2006.

[545] Stichting Wij Vertrouwen Stemcomputers Niet. The Netherlands return to paper ballots and red pencils, October 2009. http://wijvertrouwenstemcomputersniet.nl/English.

[546] Douglas R Stinson. *Cryptography: Theory and Practice*. CRC Press, 2005.

[547] Susan Stokes, Thad Dunning, Marcelo Nazareno, and Valeria Brusco. What killed vote-buying in britain and the united states? 2012. http://www.princeton.edu/csdp/online-community/historical-theoretical-pe/What-Killed-Vote-Buying-in-Britain-and-the-US.pdf.

[548] Nicolas Strauch and Robertas Pogorelis. Electoral systems: The link between governance, elected members and voters. An OPPD publication on topical parliamentary affairs, European Parliament – Office for Promotion of Parliamentary Democracy, 2011.

[549] Supreme Court of India. Dr. Subramanian Swamy v. Election Commission of India, civil appeal no. 9093 of 2013. Judgment, October 8, 2013. `http://supremecourtofindia.nic.in/outtoday/9093.pdf`.

[550] Vanessa Teague and J Alex Halderman. Security flaw in New South Wales puts thousands of online votes at risk. Freedom to Tinker blog, March 22, 2015. `https://freedom-to-tinker.com/blog/teaguehalderman/ivote-vulnerability/`.

[551] Vanessa Teague and J Alex Halderman. Thousands of NSW election online votes open to tampering, March 23, 2015. `https://theconversation.com/thousands-of-nsw-election-online-votes-open-to-tampering-39164`.

[552] Björn Terelius and Douglas Wikström. Proofs of restricted shuffles. In *Progress in Cryptology–AFRICACRYPT*, pages 100–113. Springer, 2010.

[553] The portal of the Swiss government The Federal Council. Federal council elections since 1848. `https://www.admin.ch/gov/en/start/federal-council.html`.

[554] The Standards, Procedures and Public Appointment Committee, Scottish Parliament Website, Election of Parliamentary Posts. `http://www.scottish.parliament.uk`.

[555] TNN. New EVMs to have paper trail. Times of India, January 20, 2012. `http://timesofindia.indiatimes.com/india/New-EVMs-to-have-paper-trail/articleshow/11561762.cms`.

[556] Ian Traynor. Russia accused of unleashing cyberwar to disable Estonia, May 17, 2007. `http://www.theguardian.com/world/2007/may/17/topstories3.russia`.

[557] Ian Traynor. GCHQ: EU surveillance hearing is told of huge cyber-attack on Belgian firm, October 3, 2013. `http://www.theguardian.com/uk-news/2013/oct/03/gchq-eu-surveillance-cyber-attack-belgian`.

[558] Georgios Tsoukalas, Kostas Papadimitriou, Panos Louridas, and Panayiotis Tsanakas. From Helios to Zeus. *The USENIX Journal of Election Technology and Systems*, 1(1):1–17, 2013.

[559] Jim Tyre. 2010 Pioneer Award winner Hari Prasad defends India's democracy. EFF Deeplinks Blog, November 1, 2010. `https://www.eff.org/deeplinks/2010/11/2010-pioneer-award-winner-hari-prasad-defends`.

[560] European Union. *Final Report. Presidential Election Venezuela 2006*. Caracas: European Union Election Observation Mission, 2006.

http://eeas.europa.eu/eueom/pdf/missions/moe_ue_
venezuela_2006_final_eng.pdf.

[561] United Nations Office on Drugs and Crime. United nations convention against corruption. 2005.

[562] Antti Vähä-Sipilä. *A Report on the Finnish E-Voting Pilot.* Helsinki: Electronic Frontier Finland, 2009. http://www.effi.org/
system/files?file=FinnishEVotingCoEComparison_Effi_
20080801.pdf.

[563] Vabariigi Valimiskomisjon. Internet voting in Estonia, 2007. http://www.
vvk.ee/public/dok/Internet_Voting_in_Estonia.pdf.

[564] Jeroen Van De Graaf. Voting with unconditional privacy by merging prêt à voter and Punchscan. *IEEE Transactions on Information Forensics and Security*, 4(4):674–684, 2009.

[565] Henk van der Kolk. Local electoral systems in Western Europe. *Local Government Studies*, 33(2):159–180, 2007.

[566] Carlos Vegas González. The new Belgian e-voting system. In *Electronic Voting*, volume P-205 of *(Col. Lecture Notes in Informatics-LNI)*, pages 199–211. Bonn: Gesellschaft für Informatik, 2012.

[567] Victorian Electoral Commission. Report to Parliament on the 2006 Victorian State election, July 2007.

[568] Melanie Volkamer. Electronic voting in Germany. In Serge Gurwirth / Yves Poullet / Paul de Hert, editor, *Data Protection in a Profiled World*, pages 177–191. Dordrecht: Springer, 2010.

[569] Melanie Volkamer and Rüdiger Grimm. Determine the resilience of evaluated internet voting systems. In *International Workshop on Requirements Engineering for e-Voting Systems (RE-VOTE'09)*, pages 47–54. IEEE, 2010.

[570] Vot.ar: Sistema de boleta unica electrónica. http://www.vot-ar.com.
ar/. In Spanish.

[571] Jack Vowles. New Zealand: the consolidation of reform. In Michael Gallagher and Paul Mitchell, editors, *The Politics of Electoral Systems*, pages 295–313. Oxford University Press, 2005.

[572] Janna-Lynn Weber and Urs Hengartner. Usability study of the open audit voting system Helios. INCLUDE, 2009.

[573] Michael Wei, Laura M Grupp, Frederick E Spada, and Steven Swanson. Reliably erasing data from flash-based solid state drives. In *Proceedings of the 9th USENIX Conference on File and Storage Technologies*, FAST'11, 2011.

[574] Wikipedia. Booth capturing. `https://en.wikipedia.org/w/index.php?title=Booth_capturing&oldid=689575624`.

[575] Wikipedia. Results of the Indian general election, 2014. `https://en.wikipedia.org/w/index.php?title=Results_of_the_Indian_general_election,_2014&oldid=691240029`.

[576] Douglas Wikström. A commitment-consistent proof of a shuffle. In *Australasian Conference on Information Security and Privacy (ACISP'09)*, pages 407–421. Springer, 2009.

[577] Douglas Wikström. User manual for the verificatum mix-net version 1.4. 0. *Verificatum AB, Stockholm, Sweden*, 2013.

[578] Scott Wolchok, Eric Wustrow, J Alex Halderman, Hari K Prasad, Arun Kankipati, Sai Krishna Sakhamuri, Vasavya Yagati, and Rop Gonggrijp. Security analysis of India's electronic voting machines. In *ACM Conference on Computer and Communications Security*, CCS'10, pages 1–14. ACM, 2010.

[579] Scott Wolchok, Eric Wustrow, Dawn Isabel, and J Alex Halderman. Attacking the washington, dc internet voting system. In *Financial Cryptography and Data Security*, pages 114–128. Springer, 2012.

[580] Peter Wolf and Nadia Handal Zander. *The Use of Open Source Technology in Elections*. Stockholm: IDEA, 2014.

[581] Zhe Xia, Chris Culnane, James Heather, Hugo Jonker, Peter Y A Ryan, Steve Schneider, and Sriramkrishnan Srinivasan. Versatile prêt à voter: Handling multiple election methods with a unified interface. In *Progress in Cryptology-INDOCRYPT 2010*, pages 98–114. Springer, 2010.

[582] Alec Yasinsac. Independent computations for safe remote electronic voting. In *Security Protocols Workshop XXI*, pages 71–83. Springer, 2013.

[583] Ka-Ping Yee. Extending prerendered-interface voting software to support accessibility and other ballot features. In *USENIX Workshop on Accurate Electronic Voting Technology*, pages 5–5. USENIX Association, 2007.

[584] Ka-Ping Yee, David Wagner, Marti Hearst, and Steven M Bellovin. Prerendered user interfaces for higher-assurance electronic voting. In *USENIX/ACCURATE Electronic Voting Technology Workshop*, 2006.

[585] Adam Young and Moti Yung. Bandwidth-optimal kleptographic attacks. In *Cryptographic Hardware and Embedded Systems — CHES 2001*, volume 2162 of *Lecture Notes in Computer Science*, pages 235–250. Springer Berlin Heidelberg, 2001.

[586] Filip Zagórski, Richard T Carback, David Chaum, Jeremy Clark, Aleksander Essex, and Poorvi L Vora. Remotegrity: Design and use of an end-to-end verifiable remote voting system. In *Applied Cryptography and Network Security*, pages 441–457. Springer, 2013.

[587] Nickolai Zeldovich, Silas Boyd-Wickizer, and David Mazieres. Securing distributed systems with information flow control. In *NSDI*, volume 8, pages 293–308, 2008.

Index

Printed and bound by CPI Group (UK) Ltd, Croydon, CR0 4YY

28/10/2024

01780263-0001